Oxford

The world's most trusted dictionaries

School
Spanish
Dictionary

Editors
Valerie Grundy

Nicholas Rollin
with the assistance of Carmen Fernández-Marsden

OXFORD
UNIVERSITY PRESS

OXFORD
UNIVERSITY PRESS

Great Clarendon Street, Oxford OX2 6DP

Oxford University Press is a department of the University of Oxford.
It furthers the University's objective of excellence in research,
scholarship, and education by publishing worldwide in

Oxford   New York

Auckland   Cape Town   Dar es Salaam   Hong Kong   Karachi
Kuala Lumpur   Madrid   Melbourne   Mexico City   Nairobi
New Delhi   Shanghai   Taipei   Toronto

With offices in

Argentina   Austria   Brazil   Chile   Czech Republic   France   Greece
Guatemala   Hungary   Italy   Japan   Poland   Portugal   Singapore
South Korea   Switzerland   Thailand   Turkey   Ukraine   Vietnam

Oxford is a registered trade mark of Oxford University Press
in the UK and in certain other countries

British Library Cataloguing in Publication Data
Data available

ISBN: 978-0-19-840799-7

10 9 8 7 6

Printed in China by Golden Cup

Introduction

This dictionary has been specially written for students who are in their first years of learning Spanish all the way through to preparing for exams. We have paid particular attention to making the dictionary user-friendly. With the help of colour headwords, alphabet tabs, easy-to-follow signposts, and examples, the right translation can quickly be found. Spanish verbs on both sides of the dictionary are numbered to direct the student to the appropriate table in the centre pages.

Throughout the writing of this dictionary we have worked in close consultation with students, teachers, inspectors, and examining boards. We gratefully acknowledge the examining boards AQA, OCR, and EDEXCEL, who have read and commented on the dictionary text.

Since the first edition of this dictionary there have been many changes in Spanish life. This new edition takes full account of these changes and many new words and examples have been included in order to provide the best possible learner's dictionary of Spanish at this level.

How a bilingual dictionary works

A bilingual dictionary contains two languages. When you look up a word in one of the languages, it gives the translation for that word in the other language. This dictionary is divided into two halves separated by a section of verb tables. In the first half you look up Spanish words, which are in alphabetical order, to find out what they mean in English and in the second half you look up English words, also in alphabetical order, to find out how to say them in Spanish. How to use the verb tables is explained further on in this section.

At each entry you will find not only translations but also other information that will help you get the right translation and use the word correctly. Here is a guide to the different things you will find printed in an entry:

headword	a word you look up in the dictionary
translation	In this dictionary all the Spanish words are in blue and all the English words are in black
NOUN	word class (part of speech): tells you whether the word you are looking up is a noun, a verb, an adjective, or another word class. One headword can be more than one word class. For instance, **book** can be a noun **she was reading a book** or a verb **I've booked the seats**
(informal)	helpful information: to guide you to the right translation, to show you how to use the translation, or to give you extra information about either the headword or the translation
example	a phrase or sentence using the word you have looked up. You should read through them carefully to see if they are close to what you want to understand or say
MASC	gender: after a Spanish noun, to tell you that it is masculine
FEM	or feminine
•	indicates a phrasal verb such as • **to carry on** or an idiomatic expression such as • **to be over the moon**
[27]	verb number – tells you which verb pattern to look up in the central pages of the dictionary

You can think of a dictionary entry as being made out of different sorts of building bricks. In the entries below you can see how they fit together to help you find what you need. The more you use your dictionary, the more confident you will feel about finding your way around it.

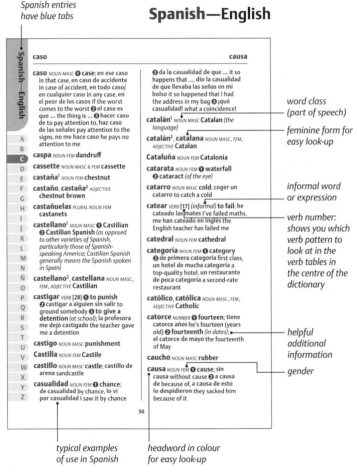

Spanish entries have blue tabs

Spanish—English

caso NOUN MASC ❶ **case**; en ese caso in that case, en caso de accidente in case of accident, en todo caso/ en cualquier caso in any case, en el peor de los casos if the worst comes to the worst ❷ el caso es que ... the thing is ... ❸ hacer caso de to pay attention to, haz caso de las señales pay attention to the signs, no me hace caso he pays no attention to me

caspa NOUN FEM **dandruff**

cassette NOUN MASC & FEM **cassette**

castaña[1] NOUN FEM **chestnut**

castaño, castaña[2] ADJECTIVE **chestnut brown**

castañuelas PLURAL NOUN FEM **castanets**

castellano[1] NOUN MASC ❶ **Castilian** ❷ **Castilian Spanish** (as opposed to other varieties of Spanish, particularly those of Spanish-speaking America; Castilian Spanish generally means the Spanish spoken in Spain)

castellano[2], **castellana** NOUN MASC, FEM, ADJECTIVE **Castilian**

castigar VERB [28] ❶ **to punish** ❷ castigar a alguien sin salir to ground somebody ❸ **to give a detention** (at school); la profesora me dejó castigado the teacher gave me a detention

castigo NOUN MASC **punishment**

Castilla NOUN FEM **Castile**

castillo NOUN MASC **castle**; castillo de arena sandcastle

casualidad NOUN FEM ❶ **chance**; de casualidad by chance, lo vi por casualidad I saw it by chance ❷ da la casualidad de que ... it so happens that ..., dio la casualidad de que llevaba las señas en mi bolso it so happened that I had the address in my bag ❸ ¡qué casualidad! what a coincidence!

catalán[1] NOUN MASC **Catalan** (the language)

catalán[2], **catalana** NOUN MASC, FEM, ADJECTIVE **Catalan**

Cataluña NOUN FEM **Catalonia**

catarata NOUN FEM ❶ **waterfall** ❷ **cataract** (of the eye)

catarro NOUN MASC **cold**; coger un catarro to catch a cold

catear VERB [17] (informal) **to fail**; he cateado las mates I've failed maths, me han cateado en inglés the English teacher has failed me

catedral NOUN FEM **cathedral**

categoría NOUN FEM ❶ **category** ❷ de primera categoría first class, un hotel de mucha categoría a top-quality hotel, un restaurante de poca categoría a second-rate restaurant

católico, católica NOUN MASC, FEM, ADJECTIVE **Catholic**

catorce NUMBER ❶ **fourteen**; tiene catorce años he's fourteen (years old) ❷ **fourteenth** (in dates): el catorce de mayo the fourteenth of May

caucho NOUN MASC **rubber**

causa NOUN FEM ❶ **cause**; sin causa without cause ❷ a causa de because of, a causa de esto lo despidieron they sacked him because of it

50

word class (part of speech)

feminine form for easy look-up

informal word or expression

verb number: shows you which verb pattern to look at in the verb tables in the centre of the dictionary

helpful additional information

gender

typical examples of use in Spanish

headword in colour for easy look-up

v

Using the dictionary

To find out what a Spanish word means

Suppose you want to find out what the Spanish word **comida** means. You need to use the first half of the dictionary to find the Spanish word that you are looking for. To help you do this, the guide words at the top of each page show the alphabetical range of words on the pages you have open. Notice that hyphens and spaces between words in Spanish headwords make no difference to their alphabetical order.

When you find the entry for **comida** you will find the translation. But you will also see that **comida** is a noun and because all nouns are either masculine or feminine in Spanish, you are given the gender *MASC* or *FEM* (*MASC* = masculine gender, *FEM* = feminine gender).

However, it often happens that a Spanish word has more than one translation in English. If you look at the entry for **comida** you can see that there are three different translations, each of which is numbered:

comida *NOUN FEM* ❶ **food**; tenemos
  suficiente comida we have enough
  food, la comida rápida fast food
  ❷ **lunch**; a la hora de la comida at
  lunch time ❸ **meal**; cuatro comidas
  al día four meals a day, mi comida
  fuerte es a mediodía I have my
  main meal at midday

So **comida** can mean **food**, **lunch**, or **meal**. You will need to look at all the translations and decide which one fits best in the sentence you are trying to understand.

Most adjectives in Spanish have a masculine form and a feminine form. Both of these are given as headwords, so if you are trying to find out what **complicada** means, you will be able to find it easily:

complicado, **complicada** *ADJECTIVE*
complicated

To find an English word and how to say it in Spanish

You can see that it is quite easy once you know how the dictionary works, to look up a Spanish word and find out what it means. Students usually find it harder to use the dictionary to find out how to say something in Spanish. This dictionary is written specially to help you do this and to make it easy to find the right way of saying things in Spanish.

Suppose you want to know how to say **garden** in Spanish. Look up the word in the second part of the dictionary. If you follow the same method of going through the alphabetical order of the headwords as you did when you were looking up a Spanish word, you will find **garden** on page 428.

garden NOUN jardín MASC

Now you can see that the Spanish word for **garden** is jardín. But if you want to make a sentence using a noun such as jardín you need to know whether it is masculine or feminine. The MASC after jardín tells you that it is masculine so **in the garden** is en el jardín.

It is not always easy to work out which Spanish word you need. When the dictionary gives you more than one translation, it is very important to take the time to read through the whole entry. If you look up **hall** the entry looks like this:

hall NOUN ❶ (in a house) **entrada** FEM
❷ (public) **salón** (MASC); **the village
hall** el salón de actos del pueblo ❸ **a
concert hall** una sala de conciertos

You can see that ❶ tells you that the Spanish word for a **hall** in your house is entrada, ❷ that the word for a public place like a **village hall** or a **school hall** is salón, and ❸ and that the phrase for a **concert hall** is sala de conciertos.

Remember that the information which is in brackets and italics, or both, is there to guide you to the right translation but *will never* be the translation itself. Often it is not enough to find the translation of one single word. In the case of frequently used words, the dictionary also gives you a selection of common phrases you will want to use. In the entry **hair** you can see how the translation works in different expressions:

hair NOUN ❶ **pelo** MASC; **to have short
hair** tener [9] el pelo corto, **to brush
your hair** cepillarse [17] el pelo, **to
wash your hair** lavarse [17] el pelo,
to have your hair cut cortarse [17]
el pelo, **she's had her hair cut** se
ha cortado el pelo ❷ **a hair** (from
the head) un pelo (from the body)
un vello

How to use the verb tables

On the Spanish side of the dictionary all the headwords which are verbs look like this:

cerrar *VERB* [29]

On the English side of the dictionary all the verbs given as translations of English verbs look like this:

frighten *VERB* asustar [17]

If you look at the pages in the centre of the dictionary, you will find tables showing you how to use the different types of Spanish verbs.

The verb **cerrar** above has the number [29]. If you look up number [29] in the verb tables, you will find the tense patterns for this verb. The same is true for verb numbers after Spanish verbs in the **English – Spanish** side of the dictionary.

With practice you will soon be able to find your way easily around the dictionary and identify what you are looking for in each entry. Some entries may seem long and complicated at first glance. Reading carefully through the signposts and examples will lead you to the translation you need.

Aa

a PREPOSITION **❶** (note that 'a + el' becomes 'al') **to**; iremos a Italia we'll go to Italy, tuerce a la derecha turn right, voy a casa I'm going home **❷** está a la izquierda it's on the left, sentados a la mesa sitting at the table, siéntate al sol sit in the sun, estaban a mi lado they were by my side **❸** **at**; a las diez at ten o'clock, a medianoche at midnight, se casó a los treinta años she married at thirty, ¿a qué hora termina? what time does it finish? **❹** hoy estamos a dos de enero it's the second of January today **❺** está a diez kilómetros de aquí it's ten kilometres from here, la vi a lo lejos I saw her in the distance **❻** dos veces al día twice a day, están a tres euros el kilo they're three euros a kilo, a ochenta kilómetros por hora at eighty kilometres an hour **❼** ir a pie to go on foot, hecho a mano handmade, escrito a mano handwritten, a lápiz in pencil **❽** **to**; se lo di a Laura I gave it to Laura, le mandé un regalo a mi madre I sent a present to my mother, le da clases de piano a mi hermana he gives my sister piano lessons **❾** (not translated after certain verbs when followed by a person) no se lo dije a Mar I didn't tell Mar, vi a tu madre I saw your mother **❿** voy a hacer los deberes I'm going to do my homework, nos fuimos a dormir we went to sleep, se han ido a nadar they've gone swimming, salimos a pasear we went out for a walk **⓫** (in commands) ¡a dormir! go to sleep!, ¡a callar! shut up!, ¡a comer! food's ready!

abadía NOUN FEM **abbey**

abajo ADVERB **❶** aquí abajo down here, allí abajo down there **❷** **downstairs**; hay otro piso abajo there's another flat downstairs, los vecinos de abajo the downstairs neighbours **❸** el piso de abajo the flat below, the bottom flat

abalanzarse REFLEXIVE VERB [22] abalanzarse sobre alguien/algo to leap on somebody/something, se abalanzaron hacia la ventana they rushed towards the window

abandonado, abandonada ADJECTIVE **❶** **deserted** **❷** **abandoned**; sentirse abandonado to feel abandoned **❸** **neglected**

abandonar VERB [17] **❶** **to leave**; abandonó a su familia he left his family **❷** **to abandon**; abandonar el barco to abandon ship

abanico NOUN MASC **fan**

abarrotado, abarrotada ADJECTIVE **packed**; un bar abarrotado de gente a bar packed with people

abecedario NOUN MASC **alphabet**

abedul NOUN MASC **birch**

abeja NOUN FEM **bee**

abejón, abejorro NOUN MASC **bumble-bee**

abertura NOUN FEM **opening**

abeto NOUN MASC **fir**

abierto, abierta ADJECTIVE **❶** **open**; la puerta está abierta the door's

a
b
c
d
e
f
g
h
i
j
k
l
m
n
ñ
o
p
q
r
s
t
u
v
w
x
y
z

open, abierto al público open to the public, abierto de par en par wide open, siempre dejas el grifo abierto you always leave the tap running ❷ **open-minded**; mis padres son muy abiertos my parents are very open-minded

abochornado, abochornada ADJECTIVE **embarrassed**

abogado, abogada NOUN MASC, FEM ❶ **lawyer** ❷ **solicitor**

abolir VERB [19] **to abolish**

abolladura NOUN FEM **dent**

abollar VERB [17] **to dent**

abollarse REFLEXIVE VERB [17] **to get dented**

abonar VERB [17] ❶ **to pay** (a bill) ❷ **to fertilize** (a field or plant)

abonarse REFLEXIVE VERB [17] ❶ **to subscribe**; abonarse a una revista to subscribe to a magazine ❷ **to buy a season ticket**

abono NOUN MASC ❶ **fertilizer** ❷ **a season ticket**

abordar VERB [17] ❶ **to tackle** (a problem) ❷ **to raise** (a subject)

aborrecer VERB [35] **to detest**

aborto NOUN MASC ❶ **abortion** ❷ **miscarriage**

abotonarse REFLEXIVE VERB [17] **to do your buttons up**; me abotoné la chaqueta I buttoned my jacket up

abrasado, abrasada ADJECTIVE ❶ **burnt**; murieron abrasados they burned to death ❷ estoy abrasada I'm boiling

abrasador, abrasadora ADJECTIVE **burning**

abrasar VERB [17] **to burn**

abrazar VERB [22] **to hug**

abrazarse REFLEXIVE VERB [22] **to hug each other**

abrazo NOUN MASC **hug**

abrebotellas NOUN MASC (does not change in the plural) **bottle opener**

abrelatas NOUN MASC (does not change in the plural) **tin opener**

abreviatura NOUN FEM **abbreviation**

abridor NOUN MASC ❶ **bottle opener** ❷ **tin opener**

abrigar VERB [28] **to be warm** (a jumper or coat)

abrigarse REFLEXIVE VERB [28] **to wrap up warmly**

abrigo NOUN MASC ❶ **coat** ❷ ropa de abrigo warm clothes

abril NOUN MASC **April**

abrir VERB [46] ❶ **to open**; abre la ventana open the window, abrió la boca para hablar he opened his mouth to speak, no abrió la boca en toda la tarde she didn't say a word all afternoon, abrir algo de par en par to open something wide ❷ **to turn on** (a tap); abrir el agua to turn the water on ❸ ¡abran paso! make way!

abrirse REFLEXIVE VERB [46] **to open**; la puerta se abrió the door opened

abrocharse REFLEXIVE VERB [17] ❶ **to do up your buttons**; abróchate la chaqueta do your jacket up ❷ **to fasten** (a seat belt); abróchense los cinturones fasten your seat belts

absoluto, absoluta ADJECTIVE ❶ **absolute** ❷ en absoluto not at all, '¿te importa?' – 'en absoluto' 'do you mind?' – 'not at all'

absorbente ADJECTIVE **absorbent**

absorber VERB [18] **to absorb**

abstracto, **abstracta** ADJECTIVE **abstract**

absurdo, **absurda** ADJECTIVE **absurd**

abuchear VERB [17] **to boo**; the crowd booed the referee el público abucheó al árbitro

abuelo, **abuela** NOUN MASC, FEM ❶ **grandfather/grandmother** ❷ mis abuelos my grandparents

aburrido, **aburrida** ADJECTIVE ❶ **boring**; ser aburrido/aburrida to be boring ❷ **bored**; estar aburrido/ aburrida to be bored

aburrimiento NOUN MASC **boredom**; ¡qué aburrimiento! how boring!

aburrirse REFLEXIVE VERB [19] **to get bored**

abusar VERB [17] ❶ abusar (de) to take too much/many (alcohol or pills, for example) ❷ abusar de to take advantage of, están abusando de tu amabilidad they are taking advantage of your kindness

abusivo, **abusiva** ADJECTIVE ❶ **excessive** (price) ❷ **unfair** (a law or rule, for example)

abuso NOUN MASC ❶ **abuse**; el abuso del alcohol alcohol abuse ❷ **outrage**; ¡esto es un verdadero abuso! this is really outrageous!

aC ABBREVIATION (short for antes de Cristo) **BC**, before Christ

acá ADVERB **here**; ¡ven acá! come here!

acabado, **acabada** ADJECTIVE **finished**

acabar VERB [17] ❶ **to finish**; aún no he acabado de leer el libro I haven't finished reading the book yet, ¿has acabado con el lápiz? have you finished with the pencil? ❷ **to be over**; cuando acabó la fiesta when the party was over ❸ **to end**; la palabra acaba en 'r' the word ends in 'r', la historia acaba bien the story has a happy ending ❹ acabar de hacer to have just done, acabo de hablar con él I've just spoken to him, acaban de llegar they've just arrived, acabábamos we had just finished

acabarse REFLEXIVE VERB [17] ❶ **to be over** (a party or film, for example); cuando se acabó la clase when the class was over ❷ **to run out** (money or food, for example); se ha acabado el pan we've run out of bread, se me acabó el dinero I ran out of money

academia NOUN FEM **school**; academia de idiomas language school

académico, **académica** ADJECTIVE **academic**

acampada NOUN FEM **camping**; ir de acampada to go camping

acampar VERB [17] **to camp**

acantilado NOUN MASC **cliff**

acariciar VERB [17] ❶ **to caress** (a person) ❷ **to stroke** (a cat or dog)

acaso ADVERB por si acaso just in case

acatarrado, **acatarrada** ADJECTIVE estar acatarrado/acatarrada to have a cold

a
b
c
d
e
f
g
h
i
j
k
l
m
n
ñ
o
p
q
r
s
t
u
v
w
x
y
z

acatarrarse *REFLEXIVE VERB* [17] **to catch a cold**

acceder *VERB* [18] ❶ acceder a algo to agree to something ❷ **to access** *(information or a file)*

accesible *ADJECTIVE* ❶ **accessible** *(a place, for example)* ❷ **affordable**

accesorios *PLURAL NOUN MASC* **accessories**

accidental *ADJECTIVE* **accidental**

accidente *NOUN MASC* **accident**; tener un accidente/sufrir un accidente to have an accident, un accidente de circulación a road accident

acción *NOUN FEM* ❶ **act**; una buena acción a good deed ❷ **share** *(in a company)*

acebo *NOUN MASC* **holly**

aceite *NOUN MASC* **oil**; aceite de oliva olive oil

aceitoso, aceitosa *ADJECTIVE* **oily**

aceituna *NOUN FEM* **olive**

acelerador *NOUN MASC* **accelerator**; pisar el acelerador to put your foot down *(accelerate)*

acelerar *VERB* [17] **to accelerate**

acento *NOUN MASC* ❶ **accent**; tener acento andaluz to have an Andalusian accent, casi no tienes acento you have hardly any accent ❷ **accent** *(on a letter in written Spanish)*; un acento agudo an acute accent

acentuarse *REFLEXIVE VERB* [20] **to have an accent**; se acentúa en la última sílaba it has an accent on the last syllable

aceptable *ADJECTIVE* **acceptable**

aceptar *VERB* [17] ❶ **to accept** *(an invitation or apology, for example)* ❷ aceptar hacer to agree to do, aceptaron dejármelo they agreed to lend it to me

acera *NOUN FEM* **pavement**

acerca de *PREPOSITION* **about**

acercar *VERB* [31] ❶ acerqué la silla a la ventana I moved the chair nearer the window, acércame un poco la lámpara bring the lamp closer to me ❷ **to pass**; acércame ese libro pass me that book ❸ acercar a alguien a to give somebody a lift to, me acercó a la oficina she gave me a lift to the office

acercarse *REFLEXIVE VERB* [31] **to come/go near**; acércate más come/get closer, se acercó a la ventana she went over to the window

acero *NOUN MASC* **steel**

acertado, acertada *ADJECTIVE* **right** *(decision or answer)*

acertar *VERB* [29] ❶ **to be right**; ¡has acertado! you've got it right! ❷ acertar algo to get something right ❸ acertar en el blanco to hit the target

ácido *NOUN MASC* **acid**

acierto *NOUN MASC* ❶ **correct answer** ❷ **good decision**; ese regalo ha sido un acierto that present was a good idea

aclaración *NOUN FEM* **explanation**

aclarar *VERB* [17] **to make clear**

aclararse *REFLEXIVE VERB* [17] *(informal)* **to understand**; aún no me aclaro I still don't understand

acné *NOUN MASC* **acne**

acoger *VERB* [3] **❶ to receive** *(news or a proposal)* **❷ to take in** *(refuge)*

acompañar *VERB* [17] **❶ to go with**; la acompañé al dentista I went with her to the dentist's, te acompaño a tu casa I'll see you home **❷ to keep company**; el perro me acompaña mucho the dog keeps me company

aconsejar *VERB* [17] **to advise**

acordarse *REFLEXIVE VERB* [24] **to remember**; no me acuerdo I don't remember, acordarse de algo to remember something

acorde *NOUN MASC* **chord**

acordeón *NOUN MASC* **accordion**

acortar *VERB* [17] **to shorten**

acoso *NOUN MASC* **❶ harassment ❷ bullying**

acostarse *REFLEXIVE VERB* [24] **❶ to go to bed**; ¿a qué hora te acuestas? what time do you go to bed? **❷** acostarse con alguien **to sleep with somebody**

acostumbrado, acostumbrada *ADJECTIVE* estar acostumbrado/ acostumbrada a algo **to be used to something**, está acostumbrada a tener muchos deberes she's used to having lots of homework

acostumbrarse *REFLEXIVE VERB* [17] acostumbrarse a algo **to get used to something**

acróbata *NOUN MASC & FEM* **acrobat**

actitud *NOUN FEM* **attitude**

actividad *NOUN FEM* **activity**

activo, activa *ADJECTIVE* **active**

acto *NOUN MASC* **❶ act ❷** en el acto **immediately**

actor *NOUN MASC* **actor**

actriz *NOUN FEM* **actress**; quiere ser actriz she wants to be an actress

actuación *NOUN FEM* **performance** *(in a play or film)*

actual *ADJECTIVE* **present, current**; la situación actual the present situation, el actual presidente the current president

actualidad *NOUN FEM* **❶** en la actualidad **at present, at the moment**, en la actualidad viven en Madrid at present they're living in Madrid **❷ nowadays**; en la actualidad es más fácil viajar nowadays it's easier to travel

actualmente *ADVERB* **❶ at present**; actualmente trabaja en un banco at present he's working in a bank **❷ nowadays**; actualmente se fabrica con máquinas nowadays it's made by machine

actuar *VERB* [20] **to act**

acuarela *NOUN FEM* **watercolour**

acuario[1] *NOUN MASC* **aquarium**

acuario[2] *NOUN MASC & FEM* **Aquarius**; soy acuario I'm an Aquarius

Acuario *NOUN MASC* **Aquarius**

acudir *VERB* [19] acudir a **to attend**

acuerdo *NOUN MASC* **❶ agreement**; llegaron a un acuerdo they reached an agreement **❷** estar de acuerdo (en algo) **to agree (on something)**, están de acuerdo en la fecha they agree on the date, no estoy de acuerdo I don't agree, ponerse de

acuerdo to come to an agreement ❸ ¡de acuerdo! okay!

acusación NOUN FEM accusation

acusar VERB [17] to accuse; acusar a alguien de algo to accuse somebody of something, me acusó de mentir he accused me of lying

acústica NOUN FEM acoustics

adaptador NOUN MASC adaptor (electrical)

adaptar VERB [17] to adapt

adaptarse REFLEXIVE VERB [17] adaptarse a to adapt to

a. de C. ABBREVIATION (short for antes de Cristo) BC, before Christ

adecuado, adecuada ADJECTIVE ❶ adecuado/adecuada para suitable for ❷ el momento adecuado the right moment

adelantado, adelantada ADJECTIVE ❶ advanced ❷ fast (a clock or watch); tu reloj va adelantado your watch is fast ❸ pagar por adelantado to pay in advance

adelantamiento NOUN MASC overtaking

adelantar VERB [17] ❶ to bring forward (a date or trip) ❷ to overtake (when driving) ❸ adelantar el reloj to put the clock forward

adelante ADVERB ❶ forward; ir hacia adelante to go forward ❷ seguir adelante to go on ❸ más adelante further on ❹ later ❺ ¡adelante! come in!

adelgazar VERB [22] to lose weight; he adelgazado tres kilos I've lost three kilos

además ADVERB ❶ besides; además, no es mi problema besides, it's not my problem, no ayuda y además se queja he doesn't help and on top of that he complains ❷ además de apart from, además de eso, no sabes conducir apart from that, you can't drive, además de estos tres, tengo cinco más besides these three, I've got five more, son tres, además de la madre there are three, not counting the mother

adentro ADVERB inside, in; vete adentro go inside

adicto, adicta ADJECTIVE adicto/ adicta a addicted to

adiós EXCLAMATION ❶ bye! ❷ hello! (when passing somebody in the street)

aditivo NOUN MASC additive

adivinanza NOUN FEM riddle

adivinar VERB [17] to guess

adivino, adivina NOUN MASC, FEM fortune-teller

adjetivo NOUN MASC adjective

adjuntar VERB [17] ❶ to enclose ❷ to attach

adjunto, adjunta ADJECTIVE enclosed

administración NOUN FEM administration; la administración pública the civil service

admirable ADJECTIVE admirable

admiración NOUN FEM ❶ admiration; sentir admiración por alguien to admire someone ❷ signo de admiración exclamation mark

admirador, admiradora NOUN MASC, FEM **admirer**

admirar VERB [17] **to admire**

admitir VERB [19] ❶ **to admit**; admitió su responsabilidad she admitted her responsibility ❷ 'no se admiten perros' 'no dogs', 'no se admiten devoluciones' 'goods cannot be returned'

adolescente NOUN MASC & FEM **adolescent**

adonde ADVERB **where**; la ciudad adonde iban the city where they were going

adónde ADVERB **where**; ¿adónde vas? where are you going?

adoptar VERB [17] **to adopt**

adoptivo, adoptiva ADJECTIVE ❶ **adoptive** (parents) ❷ **adopted** (child)

adorar VERB [17] **to adore**

adorno NOUN MASC **ornament**; los adornos de Navidad Christmas decorations

adquirir VERB [47] **to acquire**

adrede ADVERB **on purpose**

aduana NOUN FEM **customs**; libre de derechos de aduana duty-free

adulto, adulta NOUN MASC, FEM

adulto ADJECTIVE **adult**

adverbio NOUN MASC **adverb**

advertencia NOUN FEM **warning**

advertir VERB [14] **to warn**; quedas/ estás advertido you've been warned, le advertí que no llegase tarde otra vez I warned him not to be late again

aéreo, aérea ADJECTIVE **air** (traffic); el puente aéreo the shuttle

aerobic NOUN MASC (PLURAL die aerobics) **aerobics**

aeropuerto NOUN MASC **airport**

aerosol NOUN MASC **aerosol**

afán NOUN MASC **eagerness**; tienen afán de aprender they are eager to learn

afectar VERB [17] **to affect**

afecto NOUN MASC **affection**; tenerle afecto a alguien/sentir afecto por alguien to be fond of somebody

afectuoso, afectuosa ADJECTIVE **affectionate** (person); recibe un afectuoso saludo kind regards (in a letter)

afeitarse REFLEXIVE VERB [17] ❶ **to shave**; hoy no me he afeitado I haven't shaved today ❷ **to shave off** (a beard or moustache)

afición NOUN FEM **interest, hobby**; ¿qué aficiones tienes? what are your interests?, por afición as a hobby

aficionado aficionada ADJECTIVE ser aficionado/aficionada a algo to be fond of something

aficionado, aficionada NOUN MASC, FEM ❶ **fan**; un aficionado al jazz a jazz fan, un aficionado al rugby a rugby fan, para los aficionados a la cocina for those who like cooking ❷ **amateur**; un grupo de aficionados a group of amateurs

aficionarse REFLEXIVE VERB [17] aficionarse a algo to become fond of something

afilar VERB [17] **to sharpen**

afinar *VERB* [17] **to tune** *(an instrument)*

afirmación *NOUN FEM* ❶ **statement** ❷ **yes answer**

afirmar *VERB* [17] ❶ **to state**; afirmó que era de su familia he stated that it belonged to his family ❷ afirmar con la cabeza to nod

afirmativo, afirmativa *ADJECTIVE* **affirmative**

aflojar *VERB* [17] ❶ **to loosen** ❷ aflojar la marcha to slow down

afónico, afónica *ADJECTIVE* estar afónico/afónica to have lost your voice

afortunadamente *ADVERB* **fortunately**

afortunado, afortunada *ADJECTIVE* **fortunate**

África *NOUN FEM* **Africa**

africano, africana *NOUN MASC, FEM, ADJECTIVE* **African**

afuera *ADVERB* **outside, out**; salimos afuera we went outside

afueras *PLURAL NOUN FEM* las afueras the outskirts

agachar *VERB* [17] agachar la cabeza to lower your head

agacharse *REFLEXIVE VERB* [17] ❶ **to bend down** ❷ **to duck**

agarrar *VERB* [17] **to grab**

agarrarse *REFLEXIVE VERB* [17] **to hold on**; se agarró a la barandilla she held on to the handrail

agencia *NOUN FEM* **agency**; agencia inmobiliaria estate agent's office, agencia de viajes travel agency

agenda *NOUN FEM* **diary**

agente *NOUN MASC & FEM* ❶ **agent**; agente inmobiliario estate agent ❷ agente de policía police officer

agitar *VERB* [17] **to shake**

agosto *NOUN MASC* **August**

agotado, agotada *ADJECTIVE* ❶ **worn out**; estoy agotado I'm worn out ❷ **sold out** ❸ **flat** *(a battery)*

agotador, agotadora *ADJECTIVE* **exhausting**

agotarse *REFLEXIVE VERB* [17] ❶ **to wear yourself out** ❷ **to sell out** *(goods)* ❸ **to go flat** *(a battery)* ❹ **to run out** *(reserves or supplies)* ❺ se me está agotando la paciencia my patience is running out

agradable *ADJECTIVE* **pleasant**

agradecer *VERB* [35] ❶ agradecerle algo a alguien to be grateful to somebody for something, te agradezco tu ayuda I'm grateful for your help ❷ **to thank**; te lo agradezco thank you, ¡y así nos lo agradeces! and that's all the thanks we get from you!

agradecido, agradecida *ADJECTIVE* **grateful**; le estoy muy agradecido I'm very grateful to you

agradecimiento *NOUN MASC* **gratitude**

agresión *NOUN FEM* **aggression**

agresivo, agresiva *ADJECTIVE* **aggressive**

agricultor, agricultora *NOUN MASC, FEM* **farmer**

agricultura *NOUN FEM* ❶ **agriculture** ❷ **farming**; agricultura biológica organic farming

agrio, **agria** ADJECTIVE **sour**

agua NOUN FEM **water** (even though 'agua' is feminine, it is takes 'el' or 'un' in the singular); el agua está fría the water is cold, agua mineral con gas sparkling mineral water, agua mineral sin gas still mineral water, agua potable drinking water, agua corriente running water, agua de colonia eau de cologne
• estar más claro que el agua to be crystal clear (literally: to be clearer than water)

aguacate NOUN MASC **avocado**

aguacero NOUN MASC **downpour**

aguafiestas NOUN MASC & FEM (does not change in the plural) **spoilsport**

aguanieve NOUN FEM **sleet**

aguantar VERB [17] ❶ **to bear** (pain or heat); no aguanto este calor I can't bear this heat ❷ **to take**; no aguanto más I can't take any more ❸ aguantar la respiración to hold your breath, aguantar la risa to stop yourself laughing ❹ **to hold** (an object); aguanta esta caja un momento hold this box for a minute

aguantarse REFLEXIVE VERB [17] tendrás que aguantarte you'll have to put up with it

agudo, **aguda** ADJECTIVE ❶ **acute** (pain) ❷ **acute** (an accent) ❸ **high-pitched** (a voice or sound) ❹ **stressed on the last syllable** (a word)

aguijón NOUN MASC **sting**

águila NOUN FEM **eagle** (even though 'águila' is feminine, it takes 'el' or 'un' in the singular); vimos un águila we saw an eagle

aguja NOUN FEM ❶ **needle** (for sewing or knitting) ❷ **hand** (of a watch or clock)

agujero NOUN MASC **hole**

agujetas PLURAL NOUN FEM **stiffness**; tengo muchas agujetas I'm really stiff

ahí ADVERB ❶ **there**; ahí están there they are, ponlo ahí put it there ❷ tenemos que ir por ahí we have to go that way, dejó las llaves por ahí she left the keys somewhere

ahijado, **ahijada** NOUN MASC, FEM ❶ **godson/goddaughter** ❷ mis ahijados my godchildren

ahogado, **ahogada** ADJECTIVE ❶ morir ahogado to drown ❷ morir ahogado to suffocate

ahogarse REFLEXIVE VERB [28] ❶ **to drown**; se ahogó en el río he drowned in the river ❷ **to suffocate**

ahora ADVERB ❶ **now**; ¿qué vas a hacer ahora? what are you going to do now?, de ahora en adelante from now on, ahora mismo right now ❷ **nowadays** ❸ **in a moment**; ahora vuelvo I'll be back in a moment, ahora lo hago I'll do it in a moment, ahora viene he's coming ❹ por ahora for the time being

ahorcar VERB [31] **to hang** (execute)

ahorcarse REFLEXIVE VERB [31] **to hang yourself**

ahorrar VERB [17] **to save**

ahorros PLURAL NOUN MASC **savings**; todos mis ahorros all my savings

ahumado, **ahumada** ADJECTIVE **smoked**

aire NOUN MASC ❶ **air**; al aire libre in the open air, teatro al aire libre open-air theatre, mis hijos disfrutan jugando al aire libre my children enjoy playing outdoors, aire acondicionado air conditioning, salir a tomar el aire to go out for some fresh air ❷ **wind**; hace mucho aire it's very windy ❸ tiene un aire interesante he looks interesting, llegó con aire preocupado she arrived looking worried

aislado, aislada ADJECTIVE **isolated**

ajedrez NOUN MASC **chess**; jugar al ajedrez to play chess

ajillo NOUN MASC al ajillo with garlic, gambas al ajillo garlic prawns

ajo NOUN MASC **garlic**; un diente de ajo a clove of garlic, una cabeza de ajo a head of garlic

ajustar VERB [17] ❶ **to adjust** (a seat or safety belt) ❷ **to fit**

al (formed by 'a + el'; look under 'a' for more examples) ❶ fuimos al colegio we went to school, se lo di al camarero I gave it to the waiter ❷ (with infinitive) **when**; al salir nos encontramos con Marta when we were leaving we met Marta, tengan cuidado al bajar del autobús be careful when leaving the bus

ala¹ NOUN FEM ❶ (even though 'ala' is feminine, it takes 'el' or 'un' in the singular) **wing**; el ala del avión the wing of the plane, el pájaro batió las alas the bird beat its wings, el hospital tiene dos alas the hospital has two wings ❷ **brim** (of a hat)

ala² NOUN MASC & FEM **winger**

alabanza NOUN FEM **praise**

alabar VERB [17] **to praise**

alambre NOUN MASC **wire**; alambre de púas barbed wire

alargador NOUN MASC **extension lead**

alargar VERB [28] ❶ **to lengthen**; voy a alargar esta falda un poco I'm going to lengthen this skirt a bit ❷ **to extend** (a visit or holiday, for example); el presidente ha alargado su visita the president has extended his visit ❸ **to stretch out** (an arm); alargué el brazo para alcanzarlo I stretched out my arm to reach it

alargarse REFLEXIVE VERB [28] ❶ **to get longer**; los días se van alargando the days are getting longer ❷ **to go on**; la conferencia se alargó mucho the conference went on for a long time

alarma NOUN FEM **alarm**; alarma contra incendios fire alarm

alarmante ADJECTIVE **alarming**

albañil NOUN MASC ❶ **builder** ❷ **bricklayer**

albaricoque NOUN MASC **apricot**

albergue NOUN MASC ❶ **hostel**; albergue juvenil youth hostel ❷ **refuge** (in the mountains)

albóndiga NOUN FEM **meatball**

albornoz NOUN MASC **bathrobe**

alborotar VERB [17] alborotar a los niños to get the children excited

alborotarse REFLEXIVE VERB [17] **to get excited**

alboroto NOUN MASC **racket**; ¡qué alboroto! what a racket!

álbum NOUN MASC **album**; un álbum de fotografías a photograph album, el mejor álbum del grupo the group's best album

alcachofa NOUN FEM **artichoke**

alcalde NOUN MASC **mayor**

alcaldesa NOUN FEM **mayoress, mayor** (woman)

alcanzar VERB [22] **❶ to reach**; la temperatura alcanzó los cuarenta grados the temperature reached forty, no alcanzo a la ventana I can't reach the window **❷ to catch up with**; no pude alcanzar al resto del grupo I couldn't catch up with the rest of the group **❸** alcanzarle algo a alguien to pass somebody something, ¿me alcanzas las tijeras? can you pass me the scissors?

alcohol NOUN MASC **alcohol**

alcohólico, alcohólica NOUN MASC, FEM, ADJECTIVE **alcoholic**

alcoholismo NOUN MASC **alcoholism**

aldaba NOUN FEM **knocker**

aldea NOUN FEM **village**

aldeano, aldeana NOUN MASC, FEM **villager**

alegrar VERB [17] **to cheer up**; verla les alegró un poco seeing her cheered them up a bit, me alegra saberlo I'm glad to hear it

alegrarse REFLEXIVE VERB [17] **to be happy**; me alegro mucho por ellos I'm very happy for them, ¡cuánto me alegro! I'm so happy!, se alegró de venir he was glad to come, me alegro de haberte llamado I'm glad I phoned you, me alegro de verte it's nice to see you

alegre ADJECTIVE **❶ happy**; una cara alegre a happy face **❷ cheerful**; soy una persona muy alegre I'm a cheerful kind of person **❸ bright** (a colour)

alegría NOUN FEM **happiness**; ¡qué alegría veros! it's great to see you!, ¡qué alegría me das! that makes me really happy!, saltar de alegría to jump for joy

alejar VERB [17] alejar algo de alguien to move something away from somebody

alejarse REFLEXIVE VERB [17] **to move away**; ¡aléjate del fuego! move away from the fire!

alemán[1] NOUN MASC **German** (the language)

alemán[2], **alemana** NOUN MASC, FEM, ADJECTIVE **German**

Alemania NOUN FEM **Germany**

alergia NOUN FEM **allergy**; tener alergia a algo to be allergic to something, alergia al polen hayfever

alerta ADJECTIVE **alert**

alerta NOUN FEM estar al alerta por algo to be on the alert for something, hay que estar al alerta por los carteristas be on the alert for pickpockets

alfabético/alfabética ADJECTIVE **alphabetical**; por orden alfabético in alphabetical order

alfabeto NOUN MASC **alphabet**

alfarería NOUN FEM **pottery**

alféizar NOUN MASC **sill**; el alféizar de la ventana the windowsill

alfiler NOUN MASC **pin**

alfombra NOUN FEM ❶ rug ❷ carpet

alfombrilla NOUN FEM mat; alfombrilla de baño bath mat

alga NOUN FEM seaweed

algo PRONOUN ❶ something; algo así something like that, ¿te pasa algo? is there something wrong? ❷ anything; ¿has cogido algo de aquí? have you taken anything from here? ❸ some; algo de leche some milk ❹ any; ¿tienes algo de leche? do you have any milk?

algo ADVERB a bit; estoy algo cansado I'm a bit tired

algodón NOUN MASC cotton; una camisa de algodón a cotton shirt

alguien PRONOUN ❶ somebody, someone; vino alguien preguntando por ti somebody came asking for you ❷ anybody, anyone; ¿has hablado con alguien? have you talked to anybody?

algún ▸ SEE alguno/alguna

alguno, alguna PRONOUN ❶ alguno/ alguna one, alguno de vosotros one of you, tiene que haber alguno aquí there must be one here, para alguna de sus hijas for one of her daughters ❷ algunos/algunas some, faltan algunos there are some missing ❸ (in questions) any; tengo demasiadas plantas, ¿quieres alguna? I've got too many plants, do you want any?

alguno ADJECTIVE ❶ ('alguno' becomes 'algún' before a masculine singular noun) some; compré algunos libros I bought some books, algún día iré I'll go some day ❷ (in questions) any; ¿tienes alguna razón para no ir? do you have any reason for not going?, ¿tienes algún problema?

do you have any problems? ❸ en algún lugar somewhere, en algún momento sometime ❹ alguna vez lo he pensado I've thought about it sometimes, ¿has estado alguna vez en España? have you ever been to Spain?

aliado, aliada NOUN MASC, FEM ally

aliado ADJECTIVE allied

alianza NOUN FEM alliance

aliarse REFLEXIVE VERB [32] aliarse con alguien to form an alliance with somebody

alicates PLURAL NOUN MASC ❶ pliers; unos alicates a pair of pliers ❷ nail clippers

aliento NOUN MASC breath; mal aliento bad breath, estar sin aliento to be breathless, recuperar el aliento to get your breath back

alimentación NOUN FEM diet; una alimentación equilibrada a balanced diet

alimentar VERB [17] ❶ to feed ❷ to be nutritious; las lentejas alimentan mucho lentils are very nutritious

alimentarse REFLEXIVE VERB [17] to feed; se alimentan de insectos they feed on insects

alimenticio, alimenticia ADJECTIVE productos alimenticios foodstuffs, valor alimenticio nutritional value

alimento NOUN MASC ❶ food; el arroz es su alimento básico rice is their staple food, buenos alimentos good food ❷ tiene mucho alimento it's very nutritious

aliñar VERB [17] ❶ to dress (salad) ❷ to season

aliño NOUN MASC ❶ salad dressing ❷ seasoning

alioli NOUN MASC garlic mayonnaise

alistarse REFLEXIVE VERB [17] to join up; alistarse en el ejército to join the army

aliviar VERB [17] to relieve (pain)

allá ADVERB ❶ there; allá abajo down there, ¡allá voy! here I come/go!, ahora vamos para allá we're on our way ❷ más allá further away, no lo pongas muy allá don't put it too far away ❸ allá tú that's your lookout

allí ADVERB there; allí arriba up there, lo puso por allí she put it somewhere around there, se fueron por allí they went that way

alma NOUN FEM (even though 'alma' is feminine, it takes 'el' or 'un' in the singular) soul

almacén NOUN MASC warehouse

almacenar VERB [17] to store (goods)

almacenes PLURAL NOUN MASC unos (grandes) almacenes a department store

almeja NOUN FEM clam (shellfish)

almendra NOUN FEM almond

almíbar NOUN MASC syrup; peras en almíbar pears in syrup

almidón NOUN MASC starch

almohada NOUN FEM pillow; una almohada de plumas a feather pillow, una funda de almohada a pillowcase
- consultarlo con la almohada to sleep on it (a decision)
- **almohadón** NOUN MASC cushion

almorzar VERB [26] ❶ to have a mid-morning snack ❷ to have lunch (in some areas of Spain)

almuerzo NOUN MASC ❶ mid-morning snack ❷ lunch (in some areas of Spain)

alojamiento NOUN MASC accommodation, lodgings

alojarse REFLEXIVE VERB [17] to stay; se alojaron en un hotel they stayed in a hotel

alondra NOUN FEM lark (bird)

Alpes PLURAL NOUN MASC los Alpes the Alps

alpinismo NOUN MASC mountaineering

alpinista NOUN MASC & FEM mountaineer

alquilar VERB [17] ❶ to rent; hemos alquilado un apartamento en la playa we've rented an apartment at the seaside ❷ to hire (a car or equipment, for example); alquilar una bicicleta to hire a bike ❸ to let (a house, flat, or room); se aquila esa casa that house is to let ❹ to hire out (equipment); allí alquilan botas de esquiar they hire out ski boots there

alquilarse REFLEXIVE VERB [17] se alquila local premises to let, se alquilan coches cars for hire

alquiler NOUN MASC ❶ rent (for a flat or premises) ❷ hire charge (for cars or equipment) ❸ una casa de alquiler a rented house, una casa en alquiler a house to let, coches de alquiler hire cars

alquitrán NOUN MASC tar

alrededor ADVERB ❶ **around**; a nuestro alrededor around us, mirar alrededor to look around ❷ alrededor de algo around something, se sentaron alrededor de la mesa they sat around the table ❸ de alrededor surrounding, los campos de alrededor the surrounding fields

alrededores PLURAL NOUN MASC ❶ **outskirts** (of a town or city) ❷ **surrounding area** (of an airport or building)

alta NOUN FEM ❶ darse de alta to sign on, to join ❷ dar de alta a alguien to discharge someone (from hospital)

altavoz NOUN MASC ❶ **loudspeaker** ❷ **megaphone**

alternar VERB [17] **to alternate**

alternarse REFLEXIVE VERB [17] **to take turns**; nos alternábamos para hacer la comida we took turns to cook

alternativa¹ NOUN FEM **alternative**; no tenemos otra alternativa we have no alternative

alternativo, alternativa² ADJECTIVE **alternative**

altitud NOUN FEM **altitude**

altivo, altiva ADJECTIVE **arrogant**

alto¹, **alta** ADJECTIVE ❶ **high**; la montaña más alta de España the highest mountain in Spain, habitaciones de techo alto rooms with high ceilings, los precios están muy altos prices are very high, en lo alto de la torre at the top of the tower, tiene la tensión alta he has high blood pressure ❷ **tall**; todos sus hijos son muy altos all their children are very tall, ¡qué alta está!

hasn't she grown! ❸ **loud**; en voz alta in a loud voice, no pongas la radio tan alta don't have the radio on so loud

alto² NOUN MASC de alto high, un muro de dos metros de alto a two-metre high wall

alto ADVERB ❶ **loud**; habla un poco más alto, por favor speak a little louder, please ❷ **high**; volar alto to fly high

altura NOUN FEM ❶ **height**; a la misma altura at the same height, ¿qué altura tiene? how high is it? ❷ **altitude**; volar a una altura de 10.000m to fly at an altitude of 10,000 metres ❸ a estas alturas at this stage, a estas alturas no importa it doesn't matter at this stage

alubia NOUN FEM **haricot bean**

alucinación NOUN FEM **hallucination**

alucinado, alucinada ADJECTIVE (informal) estar alucinado/alucinada to be stunned, nos quedamos alucinados we were stunned

alucinante ADJECTIVE (informal) **amazing**; es un espectáculo alucinante it's an amazing spectacle

alucinar VERB [17] (informal) ❶ **to amaze**; me alucina it amazes me ❷ **to be amazed**; con este disco es que alucinas this record's amazing

alud NOUN MASC ❶ **avalanche** ❷ **landslide**

aluminio NOUN MASC **aluminium**

alumno, alumna NOUN MASC & FEM **pupil, student**

alusión NOUN FEM **allusion**

amabilidad NOUN FEM **kindness**; tuvieron la amabilidad de ayudarme they were kind enough to help me

amable ADJECTIVE **kind**; ¿sería tan amable de sujetar esto? would you be so kind as to hold this?

ama de casa NOUN FEM *(even though 'ama de casa' is feminine, it takes 'el' or 'un' in the singular)* **housewife**; un ama de casa a housewife

amado, **amada** ADJECTIVE **beloved**; mi amado my beloved

amaestrar VERB [17] **to train** *(an animal)*

amanecer NOUN MASC **dawn**; al amanecer at dawn

amanecer VERB [35] **to get light**; ¿a qué hora amanece? what time does it get light?

amante NOUN MASC & FEM **lover**

amante ADJECTIVE ser amante de algo to be fond of something, son grandes amantes del cine they're great film-lovers

amapola NOUN FEM **poppy**

amar VERB [17] **to love**

amargo, **amarga** ADJECTIVE **bitter**

amarillo¹ NOUN MASC **yellow**

amarillo², **amarilla** ADJECTIVE **yellow**

amasar VERB [17] **to knead** *(dough)*

Amazonas NOUN MASC el Amazonas the Amazon

ambición NOUN FEM **ambition**

ambicioso, **ambiciosa** ADJECTIVE **ambitious**

ambientador NOUN MASC **air freshener**

ambiental ADJECTIVE **environmental**

ambiente NOUN MASC
❶ **environment**; la contaminación del ambiente the pollution of the environment ❷ **atmosphere** *(at a party, for example)*; había muy buen ambiente there was a good atmosphere

ambiguo, **ambigua** ADJECTIVE **ambiguous**

ambos, **ambas** PLURAL PRONOUN, PLURAL ADJECTIVE **both**; se lo dije a ambos I told both of them, ambas ciudades both cities

ambulancia NOUN FEM **ambulance**

ambulante ADJECTIVE **travelling**; un grupo de teatro ambulante a travelling theatre group, una biblioteca ambulante a mobile library

ambulatorio NOUN MASC **outpatients department**

amén NOUN MASC **amen**

amenaza NOUN FEM **threat**

amenazador, **amenazadora** ADJECTIVE **threatening**

amenazar VERB [22] **to threaten**; amenazó con despedirme he threatened to fire me, amenazar de muerte a alguien to threaten to kill somebody

América NOUN FEM **America**; América Central Central America, América del Sur South America, América Latina Latin America

americana NOUN FEM **jacket**

americano, **americana** NOUN MASC, FEM, ADJECTIVE **American**

A
B
C
D
E
F
G
H
I
J
K
L
M
N
Ñ
O
P
Q
R
S
T
U
V
W
X
Y
Z

ametralladora NOUN FEM **machine gun**

amigo, **amiga** NOUN MASC, FEM **friend**; amigo/amiga por correspondencia penfriend, un amigo nuestro a friend of ours, un amigo de Carmen a friend of Carmen's, son amigos íntimos they are very close friends, mi amigo del alma my best friend

amigo ADJECTIVE son muy amigos they are very good friends, hacerse amigos to become friends

amistad NOUN FEM **friendship**

amistades PLURAL NOUN FEM **friends**; mis amistades my friends

amistoso, **amistosa** ADJECTIVE **friendly**

amo, **ama** NOUN FEM (even though 'ama' is feminine, it takes 'el' or 'un' in the singular) **owner** (of an animal); el ama del perro the owner of the dog

amontonar VERB [17] **to pile up**

amontonarse REFLEXIVE VERB [17] **to pile up**

amor NOUN MASC **❶ love**; amor mío my love, amor a primera vista love at first sight **❷** amor propio self esteem
• por amor al arte for the sake of it

amoroso, **amorosa** ADJECTIVE las relaciones amorosas love relationships

ampliar VERB [32] **❶ to enlarge** (a photograph) **❷ to extend** (a road or building) **❸ to increase** (vocabulary or knowledge)

amplificador NOUN MASC **amplifier**

amplio, **amplia** ADJECTIVE **❶ wide** (a road) **❷ spacious** (a room) **❸ loose-fitting** (a garment)

amplitud NOUN FEM **❶ width** (of a road) **❷ spaciousness** (of a room)

ampolla NOUN FEM **blister**; me han salido ampollas en las manos I've got blisters on my hands

amueblar VERB [17] **to furnish** (a house or room)

analfabeto, **analfabeta** ADJECTIVE **illiterate**

analgésico NOUN MASC **painkiller**

análisis NOUN MASC **analysis**

analizar VERB [22] **to analyse**

anatomía NOUN FEM **anatomy**

ancho¹ NOUN MASC **width**; ¿cuánto tiene de ancho?/¿qué ancho tiene? how wide is it?, mide/tiene dos metros de ancho it's two metres wide

ancho², **ancha** ADJECTIVE **❶ wide**; una carretera muy ancha a very wide road **❷ broad**; ser ancho de espaldas to have broad shoulders **❸ loose-fitting** (a garment); te está muy ancho it's too loose for you

anchoa NOUN FEM **anchovy**

anchura NOUN FEM **width**; tiene una anchura de cinco metros it's five metres wide, ¿qué anchura tiene? how wide is it?

anciano, **anciana** NOUN **old man, old woman**

anciano ADJECTIVE **elderly**; un hombre muy anciano a very elderly man

ancla NOUN FEM (even though 'ancla' is feminine noun, it takes 'el' or 'un' in the singular) **anchor**; el ancla the anchor, echar (las) anclas to drop anchor

Andalucía NOUN FEM **Andalusia**

andaluz, andaluza NOUN MASC, FEM, ADJECTIVE **Andalusian**

andamio NOUN MASC **scaffolding**

andar VERB [21] ❶ **to walk**; ¿has venido andando? did you walk here?, casi no podía andar I could hardly walk ❷ ¿cómo andas? how are you?, ¿cómo andas de dinero? how are you doing for money? ❸ **to work**; mi coche no anda my car's not working ❹ (expressing surprise) ¡anda! si es Pedro well, if it isn't Pedro! ❺ (urging somebody to do something) anda, date prisa come on, hurry up

andén NOUN MASC **platform**

Andes PLURAL NOUN MASC los Andes the Andes

Andorra NOUN FEM **Andorra**

andrajo NOUN MASC **rag**; iba vestido de andrajos he was dressed in rags

anécdota NOUN FEM **anecdote**

anestesia NOUN FEM ❶ **anaesthesia** ❷ **anaesthetic**

anfitrión NOUN MASC **host**

anfitriona NOUN FEM **hostess**

ángel NOUN MASC **angel**; no es ningún angelito he's no angel
• que sueñes con los angelitos sweet dreams (literally: dream with the angels)

angelical ADJECTIVE **angelic**

anginas PLURAL NOUN FEM **throat infection**; tener anginas to have a throat infection

anglicano, anglicana NOUN MASC, FEM **Anglican**

anguila NOUN FEM **eel**

angustiado, angustiada ADJECTIVE **worried**; sus padres están angustiados porque no saben nada de él his parents are really worried because they haven't heard from him

angustiarse REFLEXIVE VERB [17] **to get worried**; no hay por qué angustiarse there's no reason to get worried

angustioso, angustiosa ADJECTIVE **worrying**

anillo NOUN MASC **ring**; anillo de boda wedding ring

animado, animada ADJECTIVE ❶ **lively** (a bar or party, for example) ❷ **in good spirits**; muy animada she was in high spirits

animal[1] NOUN MASC **animal**; animal doméstico pet, domestic animal

animal[2] NOUN MASC & FEM **brute**; es un animal he's a brute

animal ADJECTIVE **stupid**; ¡qué animal eres! you're so stupid!

animar VERB [17] ❶ **to liven up** (a party, for example) ❷ **to cheer up** (a person) ❸ **to cheer on**

animarse REFLEXIVE VERB [17] **to cheer up**; ¡anímate! cheer up!

ánimo NOUN MASC ❶ no tengo ánimo para nada I don't feel in the mood for anything, se la ve con mucho ánimo she's in high spirits, con el ánimo por los suelos feeling really low **②** ¡ánimo! cheer up!

anís NOUN MASC **anisette**

aniversario NOUN MASC **anniversary**

anoche ADVERB **last night**; anoche no dormí bien I didn't sleep well last night, antes de anoche the night before last

anochecer NOUN MASC **nightfall**; al anochecer at nightfall

anochecer VERB [35] **to get dark**; está anocheciendo it's getting dark

anónimo¹, anónima ADJECTIVE **anonymous**

anónimo² NOUN MASC **anonymous letter**

anormal ADJECTIVE **abnormal**

anotar VERB [17] **to write down**

ansiedad NOUN FEM **anxiety**

ante¹ NOUN MASC **suede**

ante² PREPOSITION **before**; ante el juez before the judge

anteanoche ADVERB **the night before last**

anteayer ADVERB **the day before yesterday**

antemano ADVERB de antemano in advance

antena NOUN FEM **①** **aerial** **②** **antenna**

antepasados PLURAL NOUN MASC **ancestors**

anterior ADJECTIVE **previous**; la noche anterior the previous night, anterior a algo prior to something

antes ADVERB **①** **before**; la noche antes the night before, deberías haberlo dicho antes you should have said it before **②** antes de before, antes del viernes before Friday, piénsalo antes de comprarlo think about it before you buy it **③** **earlier**; este año la primavera ha llegado antes this year spring has come earlier, a las cinco está bien, no hace falta que vengas antes five is fine, you don't need to come any earlier **④** **first**; esta va antes this goes first **⑤** lo antes posible as soon as possible

antibiótico NOUN MASC **antibiotic**

anticipación NOUN FEM con mucha anticipación well in advance, con dos días de anticipación two days in advance

anticipo NOUN MASC **advance**

anticoncepción NOUN **contraception**

anticonceptivo NOUN MASC **contraceptive**

anticuado, anticuada ADJECTIVE **old-fashioned**

antídoto NOUN MASC **antidote**

antiguamente ADVERB **in the old days**

antigüedad NOUN FEM **①** **antique**; tienda de antigüedades antique shop **②** **seniority** (at work) **③** en la antigüedad in the old days

antiguo, antigua ADJECTIVE **①** **old**; una costumbre muy antigua a very old tradition **②** **former**; el antiguo presidente the former president **③** **ancient**; una civilización antigua an ancient civilization

Antillas PLURAL NOUN FEM las Antillas the West Indies

antipático, antipática *ADJECTIVE*
unpleasant; es muy antipático he's
very unpleasant, ¡qué mujer más
antipática! what a horrible woman!

antojarse *REFLEXIVE VERB* [17] se le
antojó un helado he fancied an ice
cream, se me antojó comprar el
jarrón I felt like buying the vase

antropología *NOUN FEM*
anthropology

anual *ADJECTIVE* annual

anualmente *ADVERB* yearly

anunciar *VERB* [17] ❶ to announce
(news or a decision) ❷ to advertise
(a product, for example)

anuncio *NOUN MASC*
❶ announcement
❷ advertisement

anzuelo *NOUN MASC* hook

añadidura *ADVERB* por añadidura in
addition

añadir *VERB* [19] to add

año *NOUN MASC* ❶ year; el año pasado
last year, los años cincuenta the
50s, el Año Nuevo the New Year,
año bisiesto leap year ❷ *(talking
about age)* mi madre tiene
cincuenta años my mother is fifty,
¿cuántos años tienes? how old are
you?

apagado, apagada *ADJECTIVE* ❶ off;
con la luz apagada with the light
off, ¿está la televisión apagada? is
the television off? ❷ out; el fuego
estaba casi apagado the fire was
almost out

apagar *VERB* [28] ❶ to switch off *(the
television or a light)* ❷ to put out
(a fire or cigarette)

apagón *NOUN MASC* power cut

aparato *NOUN MASC* ❶ appliance;
aparatos eléctricos electrical
appliances ❷ los aparatos de
laboratorio laboratory equipment
❸ piece of apparatus *(in the gym)*

aparcamiento *NOUN MASC* car park

aparcar *VERB* [31] to park

aparecer *VERB* [35] ❶ to appear
(a person or symptom) ❷ to turn up
(a lost object)

aparente *ADJECTIVE* apparent

apariencia *NOUN FEM* ❶ appearance;
a juzgar por las apariencias judging
by appearances, en apariencia no
estaba roto it appeared not to be
broken ❷ un niño de apariencia
delicada a delicate-looking child

apartado, apartada *ADJECTIVE*
isolated

apartamento *NOUN MASC* flat,
apartment

apartar *VERB* [17] ❶ to move away;
aparta la manta del fuego move
the blanket away from the fire ❷ to
move out of the way; aparta la
planta para que pueda ver move
the plant out of the way so that I
can see

apartarse *REFLEXIVE VERB* [17] to move
away; se apartó de la ventana she
moved away from the window

aparte *ADVERB* ❶ aside; poner algo
aparte to put something aside,
llamar a alguien aparte to call
somebody aside ❷ separately;
esto lo pago aparte I'll pay for this
separately ❸ aparte de eso apart
from that

apasionado, **apasionada** ADJECTIVE
passionate

apasionar VERB [17] el deporte me apasiona I have a passion for sports, la ópera no me apasiona I'm not wild about opera

apearse REFLEXIVE VERB [17] apearse de to get off (a bus or train), to get out of (a car), to dismount from (a horse)

apellidarse REFLEXIVE VERB [17] me apellido Alejos my surname is Alejos

apellido NOUN MASC **surname**; ¿qué apellido tienes?/¿cuál es tu apellido? what's your surname?, apellido de soltera maiden name

apenas ADVERB ❶ hardly; apenas hay suficiente there's hardly enough ❷ hardly ever; ahora apenas nos vemos we hardly ever see each other now ❸ scarcely; hace apenas tres horas que se fueron it's scarcely three hours since they went, apenas lo veo I can scarcely see it ❹ apenas me había sentado, cuando sonó el teléfono no sooner had I sat down than the telephone rang

apéndice NOUN MASC **appendix**

apendicitis NOUN FEM **appendicitis**

aperitivo NOUN MASC ❶ aperitif (before a meal) ❷ nibbles (food)

apetecer VERB [35] no me apetece I don't feel like it, ¿te apetece ir a cenar fuera? do you fancy going out for dinner?, haz lo que te apetezca do whatever you feel like

apetito NOUN MASC **appetite**; no tengo apetito I don't feel hungry, para abrir el apetito to give you an appetite

apio NOUN MASC **celery**

aplastar VERB [17] to squash

aplaudir VERB [19] to applaud

aplauso NOUN MASC **round of applause**; los aplausos del público the applause of the audience

aplazamiento NOUN MASC **postponement**

aplazar VERB [22] to postpone

aplicado, **aplicada** ADJECTIVE **hard-working**

aplicar VERB [31] to apply

apodo NOUN MASC **nickname**

apostar VERB [24] to bet; te apuesto cincuenta euros I bet you fifty euros, te apuesto a que no viene I bet she won't come, apostar a las carreras to bet on horses, apostaron por el favorito they bet on the favourite

apóstrofo NOUN MASC **apostrophe**

apoyar VERB [17] ❶ to support (a candidate or plan, for instance) ❷ to lean; apoyé la bicicleta en la pared I leaned the bicycle against the wall ❸ to rest; apoya la cabeza en este cojín rest your head on this cushion

apoyarse REFLEXIVE VERB [17] apoyarse en to lean on, me apoyé en la puerta I leaned against the door

apoyo NOUN MASC **support**

apreciar VERB [17] ❶ to appreciate ❷ apreciar a alguien to be fond of somebody, la aprecio mucho I'm very fond of her

aprecio NOUN MASC sentir aprecio por alguien to be fond of somebody

aprender VERB [18] **to learn**;
aprender español to learn Spanish,
aprender a conducir to learn to
drive, aprender algo de memoria to
learn something by heart

aprendiz, **aprendiza** NOUN MASC,
FEM **apprentice**

aprendizaje NOUN MASC
apprenticeship

apretado, **apretada** ADJECTIVE **tight**

apretar VERB [29] ❶ **to press** (a
button) ❷ **to tighten** (a bolt or knot)
❸ apretar el acelerador to put your
foot on the accelerator ❹ **to be
too tight** (shoes) ❺ **to squeeze**;
me apretó el brazo she squeezed
my arm

apretón NOUN MASC un apretón de
manos a handshake

aprieto NOUN MASC **predicament**;
meterse en un aprieto to get into
a predicament, poner a alguien en
un aprieto to put somebody in an
awkward situation

aprisa ADVERB **quickly**

aprobar VERB [24] ❶ **to approve** (a
plan or decision, for example) ❷ **to
approve of** (behaviour or an idea)
❸ **to pass**; aprobar un examen to
pass an exam

apropiado, **apropiada** ADJECTIVE
appropriate

aprovechado, **aprovechada**
ADJECTIVE es un aprovechado he
takes advantage of people

aprovechar VERB [17] ❶ **to use**;
podemos aprovechar estos
trozos de madera we can use
these pieces of wood ❷ **to make
the most of** (time or resources)

❸ **to take advantage of** (an
opportunity or offer) ❹ aproveché
para decírselo I took the chance
to tell him, quiero aprovechar
esta oportunidad para ... I want to
take this opportunity to ... ❺ ¡que
aproveche! enjoy your meal!

aproximadamente ADVERB
approximately, **roughly**

aproximado, **aproximada**
ADJECTIVE **approximate**, **rough**

aproximar VERB [17] **to bring
nearer**

aproximarse REFLEXIVE VERB [17]
❶ **to go/come up to**; se aproximó
a la ventana she went/came up
to the window ❷ **to approach**;
se aproximaba el momento the
moment was approaching, se
me aproximó un hombre a man
approached me

apto, **apta** ADJECTIVE apto para algo
suitable for something

apuesta NOUN FEM **bet**; hacerle una
apuesta a alguien to make a bet
with somebody, me hicieron una
apuesta they made a bet with me

apuntar VERB [17] ❶ **to write down**
(telephone number or address, for
example) ❷ **to point out**; apuntó
con el dedo hacia la torre she
pointed out to the tower ❸ **to aim**;
me apuntó con la pistola he aimed
the gun at me ❹ me apuntaron
las respuestas they whispered the
answers to me

apuntarse REFLEXIVE VERB [17]
apuntarse a algo to enrol on
something, to put your name down
for something

apuntes PLURAL NOUN MASC **notes**;
tomar apuntes to take notes

apuro NOUN MASC estar en un apuro to be in a tight spot, pasar apuros to go through a lot

aquel, aquella ADJECTIVE ❶ that; en aquel momento at that moment ❷ aquellos/aquellas those

aquel, aquella PRONOUN ❶ that one; quiero aquel I want that one ❷ aquellos/aquellas those, estas no, dame aquellas not these, give me those

aquél, aquélla PRONOUN (old forms) ▸ SEE **aquel, aquella**

aquello PRONOUN that; ¿qué es aquello? what's that?, aquello que vimos what we saw

aquí ADVERB here; lo puse aquí abajo I put it down here, aquí llegan here they are, debe estar por aquí it must be around here, el vino es de aquí the wine is from here

árabe¹ NOUN MASC Arabic (the language)

árabe² NOUN MASC & FEM, ADJECTIVE Arab

Aragón NOUN MASC Aragon

aragonés, aragonesa NOUN MASC, FEM, ADJECTIVE Aragonese

araña NOUN FEM spider

arañar VERB [17] to scratch

arañazo NOUN MASC scratch

árbitro, árbitra NOUN MASC, FEM ❶ referee ❷ umpire

árbol NOUN MASC tree; un árbol de Navidad a Christmas tree

arbusto NOUN MASC shrub

arcén NOUN MASC hard shoulder (on the motorway)

archivador NOUN MASC ❶ filing cabinet ❷ ring binder

archivar VERB [17] to file

archivo NOUN MASC ❶ archive ❷ file (on a computer)

arcilla NOUN FEM clay

arco NOUN MASC ❶ arch ❷ bow (for firing arrows or playing the violin) ❸ arco iris rainbow

arder VERB [18] to burn; el bosque estaba ardiendo the forest was burning

ardiente ADJECTIVE burning

ardilla NOUN FEM squirrel

área NOUN FEM area (even though 'área' is feminine, it takes 'el' or 'un' in the singular); el área de penalty the penalty area, las áreas más peligrosas the most dangerous areas

arena NOUN FEM sand

Argentina NOUN FEM Argentina

argentino, argentina NOUN MASC, FEM, ADJECTIVE Argentinian

argot NOUN MASC slang; el argot juvenil youth slang

argumento NOUN MASC ❶ argument ❷ plot (of a film, for example)

aries NOUN MASC & FEM Aries; soy aries I'm Aries

Aries NOUN MASC Aries

aritmética NOUN FEM arithmetic

arma NOUN FEM weapon (even though 'arma' is a feminine noun, it takes 'el' or 'un' in the singular); un arma de fuego a fire arm, armas nucleares nuclear weapons, un arma blanca a knife (as a weapon)

armado, **armada** ADJECTIVE **armed**

armar VERB [17] ❶ **to arm** ❷ **to assemble** *(a piece of furniture)* ❸ **to pitch** *(a tent)* ❹ *(informal)* armar ruido to make a noise, armar jaleo to make a racket, armar un escándalo to cause a scene

armarse REFLEXIVE VERB [17] ❶ armarse un lío to get confused, me armé un lío con las fechas I got confused with the dates ❷ armarse de paciencia to be patient

armario NOUN MASC **wardrobe**

armonía NOUN FEM **harmony**

armónica NOUN FEM **harmonica**

armonioso, **armoniosa** ADJECTIVE **harmonious**

aro NOUN MASC ❶ **hoop** ❷ **hoop earring**

aroma NOUN MASC ❶ **scent** ❷ **aroma**

aromático, **aromática** ADJECTIVE **aromatic**

arpa NOUN FEM **harp** *(even though 'arpa' is feminine, it takes 'el' or 'un' in the singular)*

arqueología NOUN FEM **archaeology**

arqueólogo, **arqueóloga** NOUN MASC, FEM **archaeologist**

arquitecto, **arquitecta** NOUN MASC, FEM **architect**

arquitectura NOUN FEM **architecture**

arrancar VERB [31] ❶ **to tear out**; arrancar una hoja del cuaderno to tear out a sheet from the notebook ❷ **to tear off**; arrancar una etiqueta to tear off a label ❸ **to pull up** *(a plant)* ❹ **to pull off** *(a button)* ❺ **to snatch**; me arrancó el libro de las manos she snached the book from my hands ❻ **to start** *(a car or engine)*

arrastrar VERB [17] **to drag** *(an object)*

arrastrarse REFLEXIVE VERB [17] **to crawl**

arrebatar VERB [17] **to snatch**

arreglado, **arreglada** ADJECTIVE ❶ **tidy**; deja tu habitación arreglada leave your room tidy ❷ **well dressed**; siempre va muy arreglado he's always very well dressed

arreglar VERB [17] ❶ **to fix** ❷ **to mend** ❸ **to tidy** *(a room or house)* ❹ **to sort out** *(a problem, for example)*; no te preocupes, yo lo arreglaré don't worry, I'll sort it out

arreglarse REFLEXIVE VERB [17] ❶ **to get ready**; me arreglo enseguida y salimos I'll get ready straight away and we can go out ❷ **to dress up**; mi hermana siempre se arregla mucho my sister always dresses up a lot ❸ arreglárselas to manage, se las arregla muy bien sola she manages very well on her own

arrepentirse REFLEXIVE VERB [14] arrepentirse de algo to regret something, no me arrepiento I don't regret it

arrestar VERB [17] **to arrest**; queda usted arrestado you're under arrest

arresto NOUN MASC **arrest**

arriba ADVERB ❶ **up**; aquí arriba up here, lo puse más arriba I put it a bit higher up ❷ de arriba *(next up)* above, *(highest)* top, el cajón de arriba *(the next up)* the drawer above, *(highest)* the top drawer

a
b
c
d
e
f
g
h
i
j
k
l
m
n
ñ
o
p
q
r
s
t
u
v
w
x
y
z

❸ **upstairs**; ha ido arriba he's gone upstairs, viven en el piso de arriba they live upstairs ❹ arriba de todo at the very top, de arriba abajo from top to bottom

arriesgado, **arriesgada** ADJECTIVE risky

arriesgar VERB [28] **to risk**

arriesgarse REFLEXIVE VERB [28] **to take a risk**

arroba NOUN FEM ❶ **@, at** (in email addresses; punto = dot); juanrobledoARROBAeasycomPUNTOcom juanrobledo@easycomDOTcom ❷ (former measurement of weight)

arrodillarse REFLEXIVE VERB [17] **to kneel down**; estaba arrodillado he was on his knees

arrogante ADJECTIVE **arrogant**

arrojar VERB [17] **to throw**

arropar VERB [17] ❶ **to wrap up** (a child or sick person) ❷ **to tuck in** (in bed)

arroparse REFLEXIVE VERB [17] **to wrap up**; arrópate bien wrap up well

arroyo NOUN MASC **stream**

arroz NOUN MASC **rice**

arruga NOUN FEM **wrinkle**

arrugar VERB [28] ❶ **to wrinkle** ❷ **to crease** ❸ **to crumple up**

arruinar VERB [17] **to ruin**

arruinarse REFLEXIVE VERB [17] **to go bankrupt**

arte NOUN MASC **art** ('arte' is masculine in the singular and feminine in the plural); el arte moderno modern

art, las artes gráficas graphic arts
• por arte de magia as if by magic

artesanía NOUN FEM **crafts**; objetos de artesanía handicrafts

artesanía NOUN MASC ❶ **craftsmanship** ❷ **craftwork**

artesano, **artesana** NOUN MASC, FEM **craftsman/craftswoman**

ártico, **ártica** ADJECTIVE **Arctic**

Ártico NOUN MASC el Ártico the Arctic

articulación NOUN FEM **joint** (in arm, etc.)

artículo NOUN MASC **article**; el artículo definido the definite article, artículos de papelería stationery

artificial ADJECTIVE **artificial**

artista NOUN MASC & FEM **artist**

artístico, **artística** ADJECTIVE **artistic**

arzobispo NOUN MASC **archbishop**

asa NOUN FEM **handle** (even though 'asa' is feminine, it takes 'el' or 'un' in the singular); cógelo por el asa take it by the handle

asado NOUN MASC **roast**

asamblea NOUN FEM **meeting**

asar VERB [17] ❶ **to roast** (meat) ❷ **to bake** (vegetables)

ascender VERB [36] ❶ **to be promoted**; ha ascendido he's been promoted ❷ **to promote** ❸ **to rise** (temperature, prices or a balloon); ascender a to amount to, la cuenta asciende a quinientos euros the bill amounts to five hundred euros

ascenso NOUN MASC **promotion**

ascensor NOUN MASC **lift**

asco NOUN MASC **le dio asco** it made him feel sick, **¡qué asco!** how disgusting!

asegurar VERB [17] ❶ to **insure** ❷ to **secure** ❸ to **assure**; **te aseguro que ...** I can assure you that ...

asegurarse REFLEXIVE VERB [17] to **make sure**; **asegúrate de que cierras el grifo** make sure you turn the tap off

asentir VERB [14] **asentir con la cabeza** to nod (in agreement)

aseo NOUN MASC **toilet**; **los aseos de señoras** the Ladies

asesinar VERB [17] to **murder**

asesinato NOUN MASC **murder**

asesino, asesina NOUN MASC, FEM **murderer**

asesor, asesora NOUN MASC, FEM **adviser**

asfixia NOUN FEM ❶ **asphyxia** ❷ **suffocation**; **tenía sensación de asfixia** I felt I was suffocating

asfixiante ADJECTIVE ❶ **asphyxiating** (air or fumes) ❷ **suffocating** (heat)

asfixiarse REFLEXIVE VERB [17] ❶ to **suffocate** ❷ to **choke to death**

así ADVERB ❶ **like this**; **hazlo así** do it like this ❷ **like that**; **el pueblo se llama Robellón, o algo así** the village is called Robellón, or something like that ❸ **that way**; **me llevaré el coche, así podremos volver pronto** I'll take the car, that way we can come back early ❹ **así que** so, **así que te vas de vacaciones** so you're going on holiday ❺ **así**

es that's right ❻ **así, así** so, **'¿te gusta?' – 'así, así'** 'do you like it?' – 'so-so' ❼ **¡así me gusta!** that's what I like to see!, **¡así se hace!** well done!

Asia NOUN FEM **Asia**

asiático, asiática NOUN MASC, FEM, ADJECTIVE **Asian**

asiento NOUN MASC **seat**; **asiento delantero** front seat, **asiento trasero** back seat

asignatura NOUN FEM **subject**

asilo NOUN MASC **home** (for old people)

asilo político NOUN MASC **political asylum**

asistenta NOUN FEM **cleaning lady**; **¿hay servicio de asistenta?** is there a maid service?

asistente NOUN MASC & FEM **assistant**

asistente social NOUN MASC & FEM **social worker**

asistir VERB [19] **aisitir a algo** to attend something; **asistió a la reunión** he attended the meeting

asma NOUN FEM **asthma** (even though 'asma' is feminine, it takes 'el' or 'un' in the singular)

asmático, asmática ADJECTIVE **asthmatic**

asociación NOUN FEM **association**

asociar VERB [17] to **associate** (two ideas or words, for example)

asociarse REFLEXIVE VERB [17] to **go into partnership** (in business)

asomar VERB [17] **asomar la cabeza** to stick your head out/in, **'no asomar la cabeza por la ventana'** 'do not lean out of the window'

a
b
c
d
e
f
g
h
i
j
k
l
m
n
ñ
o
p
q
r
s
t
u
v
w
x
y
z

asomarse *REFLEXIVE VERB* [17] se asomó a la ventana he had a look out of the window, 'prohibido asomarse por la ventana' 'do not lean out of the window'

asombrar *VERB* [17] to amaze; me asombra su actitud I'm amazed by her attitude

asombrarse *REFLEXIVE VERB* [17] to be amazed; ya no me asombro con/de nada nothing amazes me any more

asombro *NOUN MASC* surprise; con cara de asombro with a look of surprise on her face

asombroso, **asombrosa** *ADJECTIVE* amazing

aspecto *NOUN MASC* look; tiene aspecto de policía he looks like an policeman, una mujer de aspecto elegante an elegant-looking woman, ¿qué aspecto tenían? what did they look like?, tienes muy buen aspecto you look very well

áspero, **áspera** *ADJECTIVE* rough

aspirador *NOUN MASC*
►SEE **aspiradora**

aspiradora *NOUN FEM* vacuum cleaner; pasar la aspiradora por el salón to vacuum the living room

aspirina *NOUN FEM* aspirin

asqueroso, **asquerosa** *ADJECTIVE* disgusting

asterísco *NOUN MASC* asterisk

astilla *NOUN FEM* splinter

astrología *NOUN FEM* astrology

astrólogo, **astróloga** *NOUN MASC, FEM* astrologer

astronauta *NOUN MASC & FEM* astronaut

astronomía *NOUN FEM* astronomy

astrónomo, **astrónoma** *NOUN* astronomer

astuto, **astuta** *ADJECTIVE* ❶ shrewd ❷ crafty; eso fue muy astuto por su parte that was very crafty of her

asunto *NOUN MASC* ❶ matter; asuntos de negocios business matters, un asunto complicado a complicated matter ❷ business; no quiero saber nada de este asunto I don't want to know anything about this business, no es asunto tuyo mind your own business

asustar *VERB* [17] to frighten

asustarse *REFLEXIVE VERB* [17] to get frightened; me asusté al oír un ruido I got frightened when I heard a noise

atacar *VERB* [31] to attack

atajo *NOUN MASC* shortcut

ataque *NOUN MASC* ❶ attack; un ataque cardíaco/, un ataque al corazón a heart attack ❷ fit; un ataque de celos a fit of jealousy, me dio un ataque de risa I got a fit of the giggles

atar *VERB* [17] to tie (up)

atardecer *NOUN MASC* dusk; al atardecer at dusk

atardecer *VERB* [35] to get dark; estaba atardeciendo it was getting dark

atascar *VERB* [31] to block (a pipe)

atascarse *REFLEXIVE VERB* [31] to get blocked

atasco *NOUN MASC* ❶ traffic jam ❷ blockage

ataúd *NOUN MASC* **coffin**

atención *NOUN FEM* **attention**; presta atención pay attention, no pones atención en lo que haces you don't concentrate on what you are doing, ¡atención, por favor! your attention, please!

atender *VERB* [36] ❶ **to pay attention**; atiende a la profesora pay attention to your teacher ❷ ¿la atiende alguien? are you being served?

atentado *NOUN MASC* un atentado terrorista a terrorist attack

atentado *NOUN MASC* **attack**; un atentado terrorista a terrorist attack, un atentado contra el presidente an attempted assasination of the president

atentamente *ADVERB* ❶ **attentively** ❷ le saluda atentamente yours faithfully, yours sincerely

atento, **atenta** *ADJECTIVE* **attentive**

ateo, **atea** *NOUN MASC, FEM* **atheist**

aterrizaje *NOUN MASC* **landing** (of a plane)

aterrizar *VERB* [22] **to land** (a plane)

aterrorizar *VERB* [22] **to terrify**

ático *NOUN MASC* ❶ **top-floor apartment** ❷ **loft**

atizador *NOUN MASC* **poker** (for fire)

atlántico, **atlántica** *ADJECTIVE* **Atlantic**

Atlántico *NOUN MASC* el Atlántico the Atlantic

atlas *NOUN MASC* **atlas**

atleta *NOUN MASC & FEM* **athlete**

atlético, **atlética** *ADJECTIVE* ❶ **athletic** (person) ❷ competición atlética athletics competition

atletismo *NOUN MASC* **athletics**

atómico, **atómica** *ADJECTIVE* **atomic**

átomo *NOUN MASC* **atom**

atracador, **atracadora** *NOUN MASC, FEM* ❶ **robber** ❷ **mugger**

atracar *VERB* [31] ❶ **to hold up** (a bank or shop) ❷ **to mug** (a person)

atracción *NOUN FEM* **attraction**

atraco *NOUN MASC* ❶ **hold-up** (of a bank or shop) ❷ **mugging**

atractivo, **atractiva** *ADJECTIVE* **attractive**

atraer *VERB* [42] **to attract**

atragantarse *REFLEXIVE VERB* [17] atragantarse con algo to choke on something

atrapar *VERB* [17] **to catch**

atrás *ADVERB* ❶ **back**; nos sentamos demasiado atrás we sat too far back, hacia atrás backwards, la parte de atrás the back ❷ **at the back**; esto va atrás this goes at the back ❸ quedarse atrás to be left behind

atrasado, **atrasada** *ADJECTIVE* ❶ **slow** (a watch or clock); llevo el reloj atrasado my watch is slow ❷ **backward** (a country) ❸ **old-fashioned** (ideas or a person) ❹ **behind**; voy atrasado en los estudios I'm behind at school, van muy atrasados con los ensayos they're very behind with the rehearsals ❺ pagos atrasados **outstanding payments**

atrasar VERB [17] ❶ **to put back** (a watch or clock); hay que atrasar los relojes una hora we have to put the clocks back an hour ❷ **to lose time** (a watch or clock); este reloj atrasa this watch loses time ❸ **to postpone**

atrasarse REFLEXIVE VERB [17] **to lose time** (a watch or clock)

atravesar VERB [29] **to cross**

atrayente ADJECTIVE **appealing**

atreverse REFLEXIVE VERB [18] **to dare**; no me atrevo a preguntarle I don't dare ask him

atrevido, atrevida ADJECTIVE ❶ **daring** ❷ **cheeky**; ¡qué niño más atrevido! what a cheeky child!

atropellar VERB [17] **to run over, to knock down**; lo atropelló un coche he was run over by a car

atún NOUN MASC **tuna**

audiencia NOUN FEM **audience**

audífono NOUN MASC **hearing aid**

aula NOUN FEM ❶ (even though 'aula' is feminine, it takes 'el' or 'un' in the singular) **classroom** ❷ **lecture theatre**

aullido NOUN MASC **howl**

aumentar VERB [17] ❶ **to increase**; aumentarel suelo to give/get a rise ❷ **to rise** (temperature or pressure)

aumento NOUN MASC ❶ **increase** ❷ **rise**

aun ADVERB **even**; aun así even so, ni aun con tu ayuda not even with your help

aún ADVERB ❶ **still**; aún estoy esperando I'm still waiting ❷ **yet**;

aún no se lo he dicho a ellos I haven't told them yet ❸ **even**; este es aún mejor this one is even better

aunque CONJUNCTION ❶ **although**; aunque estaba cansada, la ayudé although I was tired, I helped her ❷ **even though** ❸ **even if**; aunque llegues tarde, llámame even if you arrive late, give me a ring, aunque no lo parezca even if it doesn't look like it

au pair NOUN MASC & FEM (PLURAL **au pairs**) **au pair**

auricular NOUN MASC ❶ **receiver** (of a phone) ❷ auriculares **headphones**

ausente ADJECTIVE estar ausente to be absent, to be away

Australia NOUN FEM **Australia**

australiano, australiana NOUN MASC, FEM, ADJECTIVE **Australian**

Austria NOUN FEM **Austria**

austriaco, austriaca NOUN MASC, FEM, ADJECTIVE **Austrian**

auténtico, auténtica ADJECTIVE **authentic**

auto NOUN MASC **car**

autoadhesivo ADJECTIVE **self-adhesive**

autobiografía NOUN FEM **autobiography**

autobús NOUN **bus**; coger el autobús to take the bus, perder el autobús to miss the bus

autocar NOUN MASC **coach**

autoescuela NOUN FEM **driving school**

autógrafo NOUN MASC **autograph**

automático, automática *ADJECTIVE* **automatic**

automóvil *NOUN MASC* **car**

automovilismo *NOUN MASC* **motor racing**

automovilista *NOUN MASC & FEM* **motorist**

autonomía *NOUN FEM* ❶ **autonomy** ❷ **autonomous region** *(of Spain)*

autonómico, autonómica *ADJECTIVE* **regional** *(elections or a candidate)*

autopista *NOUN FEM* **motorway**

autor, autora *NOUN MASC & FEM* **author**

autoridad *NOUN FEM* **authority**

autoritario, autoritaria *ADJECTIVE* **authoritarian**

autorización *NOUN FEM* **authorization**

autorizar *VERB* [22] **to authorize**

autoservicio *NOUN MASC* ❶ **self-service restaurant** ❷ **supermarket**

autostop *NOUN MASC* **hitch-hiking**; hacer autostop **to hitch-hike**

autostop *NOUN MASC* **hitchhiking**; hacer autostop **to hitchhike**

autostopista *NOUN MASC & FEM* **hitch-hiker**

autovía *NOUN FEM* **dual carriageway**

auxiliar *NOUN MASC & FEM* **assistant**; auxiliar de vuelo **flight attendant**

auxilio *NOUN MASC* **aid**; acudir en auxilio de alguien **to go to the aid** of somebody, primeros auxilios **first aid**

avalancha *NOUN FEM* **avalanche**

avanzar *VERB* [22] ❶ **to move forward** *(traffic or a person)* ❷ **to make progress** *(a student or researcher)* ❸ **to wind on** *(a tape)*

avaricia *NOUN FEM* **greed**

avaricioso, avariciosa *ADJECTIVE* **greedy**

avaro, avara *ADJECTIVE* **miserly**

Avda. *ABBREVIATION (short for avenida)* **Ave., Avenue**

ave *NOUN FEM* **bird** *(even though 'ave' is feminine, it takes 'el' or 'un' in the singular)*; un ave **a bird**, las aves **the birds**

avellana *NOUN FEM* **hazelnut**

avenida *NOUN FEM* **avenue**

aventura *NOUN FEM* **adventure**

aventurero, aventurera *ADJECTIVE* **adventurous**

avergonzado, avergonzada *ADJECTIVE* ❶ **ashamed** ❷ **embarrassed**

avería *NOUN FEM* **breakdown** *(of a car, for example)*; sufrir una avería **to break down**

averiado, averiada *ADJECTIVE* ❶ **broken down** ❷ **out of order**

averiguar *VERB* [17] **to find out**

avestruz *NOUN MASC* **ostrich**

avión *NOUN MASC* **aeroplane**; avión a reacción **jet** *(plane)*

avisar *VERB* [17] ❶ avisar a alguien de algo **to let somebody know about**

something, le avisé del problema
I let him know about the problem,
me avisaron que llegarían tarde
they told me they would be late
❷ to warn; avisar a alguien del
peligro to warn somebody about
the danger ❸ avisar al médico to
call the doctor

aviso NOUN MASC ❶ warning; el
profesor ya le ha dado tres avisos
the teacher has already given him
three warnings, sin previo aviso
without prior warning ❷ notice;
hasta nuevo aviso until further
notice ❸ último aviso para los
pasajeros del vuelo ... last call for
passengers on flight ...

avispa NOUN FEM wasp

axila NOUN FEM armpit

ayer ADVERB yesterday; antes de ayer
the day before yesterday

ayuda NOUN FEM ❶ help; ir en ayuda
de alguien to go to somebody's
assistance ❷ aid

ayudante NOUN MASC & FEM helper,
assistant

ayudar VERB [17] to help; ¿en qué
puedo ayudarle? how can I help
you?

ayuntamiento NOUN MASC ❶ town
council, city council ❷ town hall

azafata NOUN FEM ❶ flight attendant
❷ trade fair attendant

azar NOUN MASC ❶ chance; por azar
by chance ❷ al azar at random

azote NOUN MASC smack

azotea NOUN FEM (flat) roof

azúcar NOUN MASC & FEM sugar
('azúcar' always takes 'el', but it can

take an adjective in the feminine
form); el azúcar blanca/blanco
white sugar, el azúcar de caña cane
sugar, azúcar glas/glaseado icing,
el azúcar morena/moreno brown
sugar, un terrón de azúcar a sugar
lump

azucarero NOUN MASC sugar bowl

azul NOUN MASC blue; azul claro light
blue, azul marino navy blue, azul
celeste sky blue

azul ADJECTIVE blue; ojos azules blue
eyes

azulejo NOUN MASC tile

Bb

baca NOUN FEM **luggage-rack**

bacalao NOUN MASC **cod**

bachillerato NOUN MASC
❶ **secondary education**
❷ Bachillerato *(the two-year course leading to university entrance in Spain)*

bádminton NOUN MASC **badminton**

baguette NOUN FEM **baguette, French stick**

Bahamas NOUN FEM & PLURAL las Bahamas the Bahamas, las islas Bahamas the Bahama Islands

bahameño, bahameña ADJECTIVE, NOUN **Bahamian**

bahía NOUN FEM **bay**

bailar VERB [17] **to dance**

bailarín, bailarina NOUN MASC, FEM **dancer**

baile NOUN MASC ❶ **dance** ❷ **dancing**; una clase de baile a dancing class

bajar VERB [17] ❶ **to bring down**; ¿puedes bajarme el abrigo? could you bring down my coat? ❷ **to take down**; baja las maletas a recepción take the suitcases down to reception ❸ **to go down**; el ascensor está bajando the lift's going down, bajamos por las escaleras we went down the stairs, bajar la calle to go down the street

❹ **to come down**; ¡ya bajo! I'm coming down!, creo que ya bajan I think they're coming down now ❺ **to fall** *(the temperature or prices)* ❻ **to turn down** *(volume)*; baja un poco la tele turn the television down a bit ❼ **to lower** *(a blind or prices)*

bajarse REFLEXIVE VERB [17] bajarse de un coche to get out of a car, se bajó de la bicicleta he got off the bike

bajo¹ NOUN MASC **ground floor**

bajo PREPOSITION ❶ **under**; bajo los árboles under the trees ❷ bajo cero below zero

bajo ADVERB ❶ **low**; volar bajo to fly low ❷ **quietly**; hablar bajo to speak quietly

bajo², baja ADJECTIVE ❶ **short** *(a person)*; soy bastante baja I'm quite short ❷ **low**; pon la música baja put the music on low, los precios están bajos prices are low

bala NOUN FEM **bullet**

balancín NOUN MASC ❶ **swing seat** ❷ **seesaw** ❸ **rocking chair**

balanza NOUN FEM **scales**

balbucear, balbucir VERB [17] **to stammer**

balcón NOUN MASC **balcony**

baldosa NOUN FEM **tile**

Baleares PLURAL NOUN FEM las islas Baleares the Balearic Islands

ballena NOUN FEM **whale**

ballet NOUN MASC **ballet**

balón NOUN MASC **ball**; un balón de fútbol a football

baloncesto NOUN MASC **basketball**

a
b
c
d
e
f
g
h
i
j
k
l
m
n
ñ
o
p
q
r
s
t
u
v
w
x
y
z

balonmano NOUN MASC **handball**

balonvolea NOUN MASC **volleyball**

balsa NOUN FEM **❶ raft ❷ pond**

banca NOUN FEM **banking**

banco NOUN MASC **❶ bench** (in a park) **❷ pew** (in church) **❸ bank**; trabaja en un banco she works in a bank

banda NOUN FEM **❶ band** (of musicians) **❷ gang** (of criminals) **❸** banda sonora soundtrack

bandeja NOUN FEM **tray**

bandera NOUN FEM **flag**

banderilla NOUN FEM **banderilla** (a decorated dart used in bullfighting)

bandido, bandida NOUN MASC, FEM **bandit**

banquero, banquera NOUN MASC, FEM **banker**

banqueta NOUN FEM **stool**

banquete NOUN MASC **banquet**; un banquete de bodas a wedding banquet

bañador NOUN MASC **❶ swimming trunks ❷ swimming costume**

bañar VERB [17] bañar a to bath (a baby)

bañarse REFLEXIVE VERB [17] **❶ to have a bath**; voy a bañarme esta noche I'm going to have a bath tonight **❷ to have a swim**; ¿te apetece bañarte? do you fancy going for a swim?

bañera NOUN FEM **bath** (bathtub)

baño NOUN MASC **❶ bath**; darse un baño to have a bath, voy a darme un baño I'm going to have a bath **❷ swim**; darse un baño to go for a swim, ¿te apetece darte un baño? do you fancy going for a swim? **❸ bathroom**; ¿dónde está el baño? where's the bathroom?

bar NOUN MASC **bar**

baraja NOUN FEM **pack of cards**

barajar VERB [17] **to shuffle** (cards)

barandilla NOUN FEM **rail**

baratija NOUN FEM **knick-knack**

barato, barata ADJECTIVE **cheap**

barba NOUN FEM **beard**; afeitarse la barba to shave off your beard, dejarse barba to grow a beard, voy a dejarme barba I'm going to grow a beard

barbacoa NOUN FEM **barbecue**

barbadense ADJECTIVE, NOUN **Barbadian**

Barbados NOUN MASC **Barbados**

barbaridad NOUN FEM **❶ fortune**; nos cobraron una barbaridad they charged us a fortune **❷** eso es una barbaridad that's far too much **❸** deja de decir barbaridades stop talking nonsense **❹** ¡qué barbaridad! my God!

barbero NOUN MASC **barber**

barbilla NOUN FEM **chin**

barca NOUN FEM **boat**; una barca de pesca a fishing boat, una barca de remos a rowing boat

Barcelona NOUN FEM **Barcelona**

barco NOUN MASC **❶ boat**; viajar en barco to travel by boat, un barco de pesca a fishing boat **❷ ship**; un barco de guerra a warship

barniz *NOUN MASC* ❶ **varnish** ❷ barniz de uñas nail varnish

barómetro *NOUN MASC* **barometer**

barra *NOUN FEM* ❶ **rail** *(for clothes)* ❷ **bar**; una barra de jabón a bar of soap, nos sirvieron en la barra they served us at the bar ❸ una barra de pan a baguette ❹ una barra de labios a lipstick

barrer *VERB* [18] **to sweep**

barrera *NOUN FEM* **barrier**

barriga *NOUN FEM* **stomach**, **tummy**; tener dolor de barriga to have a stomachache

barril *NOUN MASC* **barrel**

barrio *NOUN MASC* **area** *(of a town)*; los barrios bajos the slums

barro *NOUN MASC* ❶ **mud**; lleno de barro covered in mud ❷ **clay** *(for making pots)*

bártulos *PLURAL NOUN MASC (informal)* **stuff**, **things**; coge todos tus bártulos take all your stuff

basar *VERB* [17] **to base**; basar algo en algo to base something on something

basarse *REFLEXIVE VERB* [17] ¿en qué te basas para decir eso? what basis do you have for saying that?

base *NOUN FEM* ❶ **base** ❷ base de datos database ❸ base de maquillaje foundation *(make-up)* ❹ a base de by, lo aprendió a base de repetirlo he learnt it by repeating it
• a base de bien *(informal)* a lot; nos divertimos a base de bien we enjoyed ourselves a lot

básico, **básica** *ADJECTIVE* **basic**

bastante *ADJECTIVE* ❶ **enough**; no tenemos bastante pan we don't have enough bread, ya tenemos bastantes sillas we've got enough chairs now ❷ **quite a lot of**; bastante gente quite a lot of people, bebimos bastante café we drank quite a lot of coffee

bastante *PRONOUN* **enough**; con esto ya hay bastante there's enough with this

bastante *ADVERB* ❶ **enough**; ¿has comido bastante? have you eaten enough? ❷ *(before an adjective or adverb)* **quite**; se puso bastante contenta she was quite happy ❸ **quite a lot**; ha mejorado bastante he's improved quite a lot

bastar *VERB* [17] ❶ **to be enough**; con esto basta this is enough, ¡ya basta! that's enough! ❷ basta con preguntarle you just need to ask him

bastón *NOUN MASC* **walking stick**

bastoncillo *NOUN MASC* **cotton bud**

basura *NOUN FEM* ❶ **rubbish**; hay que sacar la basura we have to put the rubbish out ❷ **dustbin**, **bin**; tirar algo a la basura to throw something in the bin

basurero¹ *NOUN MASC* **rubbish tip**

basurero², **basurera** *NOUN MASC, FEM* **refuse collector**

bata *NOUN FEM* ❶ **dressing gown** ❷ una bata de médico a white coat *(doctor's)*

batalla *NOUN FEM* **battle**

bate *NOUN MASC* **bat**

batería¹ *NOUN FEM* ❶ **battery** *(for a car)* ❷ **drum kit**; tocar la batería to play the drums

batería[2] *NOUN MASC & FEM* **drummer**

batido *NOUN MASC* **milkshake**; un batido de fresa a strawberry milkshake

batidora *NOUN FEM* **food mixer**

batir *VERB* [19] **❶ to beat**; batir las claras a punto de nieve beat the egg whites until stiff **❷ to whip** *(cream)* **❸** batir un récord to break a record

baúl *NOUN MASC* **trunk** *(for clothes)*

bautismo *NOUN MASC* **christening**

bautizar *VERB* [22] **to christen**

bautizo *NOUN MASC* **christening**

baya *NOUN FEM* **berry**

bayeta *NOUN FEM* **cloth** *(for wiping)*

bebé *NOUN MASC* **baby**

beber *VERB* [18] **to drink**; ¿quieres beber algo? do you want something to drink?

bebida *NOUN FEM* **drink**; una bebida caliente a hot drink

beca *NOUN FEM* **❶ grant ❷ scholarship**

béisbol *NOUN MASC* **baseball**

belén *NOUN MASC* **nativity scene, crib**

belga *NOUN MASC & FEM, ADJECTIVE* **Belgian**

Bélgica *NOUN FEM* **Belgium**

belleza *NOUN FEM* **beauty**

bello, bella *ADJECTIVE* **beautiful**

bendito, bendita *ADJECTIVE* **❶ blessed ❷ holy** *(water or bread)*

beneficiar *VERB* [17] **to benefit**

beneficio *NOUN MASC* **benefit**

benéfico, benéfica *ADJECTIVE* **charity**; una organización benéfica a charity

berenjena *NOUN FEM* **aubergine**

berro *NOUN MASC* **watercress**

besamel *NOUN FEM* **white sauce**

besar *VERB* [17] **to kiss**

beso *NOUN MASC* **kiss**; dame un beso give me a kiss, me dio un beso en la mejilla he gave me a kiss on the cheek

bestia *NOUN FEM* **❶ beast** *(animal)* **❷ ignorant person**; es un bestia, no sabe nada he's so ignorant, he doesn't know a thing **❸ brute**

bestia *ADJECTIVE* **❶ ignorant ❷** no seas bestia y habla bien don't be so rude, mind your language

betún *NOUN MASC* **shoe polish**

Biblia *NOUN FEM* **Bible**

biblioteca *NOUN FEM* **library**

bibliotecario, bibliotecaria *NOUN MASC, FEM* **librarian**

bicho *NOUN MASC* **creepy-crawly**

bici *NOUN FEM (informal)* **bike**; montar en bici to ride a bike

bicicleta *NOUN FEM* **bicycle**; montar en bicicleta to ride a bicycle, ¿sabes montar en bicicleta? can you ride a bicycle?

bien *NOUN MASC* **good**; la diferencia entre el bien y el mal the difference between good and evil

bien *ADVERB, ADJECTIVE* **❶ well**; lo has hecho muy bien you've done it very well, no me siento bien I don't feel

well, '¿cómo están tus padres?'
– 'muy bien, gracias' 'how are your
parents?' – 'very well, thank you',
¡bien hecho! well done! ¡muy bien!
(expressing approval) well done!
❷ all right; ¿estás bien en esa
silla? are you all right in that chair?,
así está bien it's all right like this,
¡está bien! *(expressing agreement)*
all right!, okay! **❸** huele bien it
smells nice, sabe bien it tastes
nice **❹** hablas muy bien español
you speak very good Spanish
❺ properly; no funciona bien it
doesn't work properly **❻** ¡bien!
hoorray!

bienestar NOUN MASC **welfare**

bienvenida[1] NOUN FEM **welcome**; dar
la bienvenida a alguien to welcome
somebody

bienvenido, bienvenida[2] ADJECTIVE
welcome; ¡bienvenido! welcome!,
aquí siempre sois bienvenidos
you're always welcome here

bigote NOUN MASC **moustache**

bikini NOUN MASC **bikini**

bilingüe ADJECTIVE **bilingual**

billar NOUN MASC **❶ billiards ❷ pool
❸ snooker**

billares PLURAL NOUN MASC
amusement arcade

billete NOUN MASC **❶ note** *(money)*;
un billete de cincuenta euros a
fifty euro note **❷ ticket**; un billete
de tren a train ticket, un billete
sencillo/un billete de ida a single
ticket, un billete de ida y vuelta a
return ticket

billetera NOUN MASC & FEM **wallet**

billetero NOUN ▸ SEE **billetera**

biografía NOUN FEM **biography**

biología NOUN FEM **biology**

biólogo, bióloga NOUN MASC, FEM
biologist

biquini NOUN MASC **bikini**

bisabuela NOUN FEM **great-
grandmother**

bisabuelo NOUN MASC **❶ great-
grandfather ❷** mis bisabuelos my
great-grandparents

bisnieta NOUN FEM
great-granddaughter

bisnieto NOUN MASC **❶
great-grandson ❷** mis bisnietos
my great-grandchildren

bistec NOUN MASC **steak**

bizcocho NOUN MASC **sponge cake**

blanco[1] NOUN MASC **❶ white
❷ target**; dar en el blanco to hit
the target

blanco[2]**, blanca** ADJECTIVE **white**

blando, blanda ADJECTIVE **❶ soft**; un
colchón blando a soft mattress, la
mantequilla se ha puesto blanda
the butter's gone soft **❷ tender**
(meat) **❸ soft** *(person)*

bloc NOUN MASC **writing pad**

blog NOUN MASC *(PLURAL* los blogs*)*
blog

bloque NOUN MASC **block**; un bloque
de pisos a block of flats

bloquear VERB [17] **to block**; una
muchedumbre nos bloqueaba el
camino a crowd was blocking our
way

blusa NOUN FEM **blouse**

bobo, boba ADJECTIVE (informal) **silly**; eres bobo you are silly

boca NOUN FEM ❶ **mouth**; no abrió la boca en toda la tarde he didn't say a word all afternoon ❷ una boca de metro an entrance to the underground, una boca de incendios a fire hydrant, una boca de riego an irrigation hydrant ❸ boca arriba face up (card or photograph), pon el vaso boca arriba put the glass the right way up, túmbate boca arriba lie on your back ❹ boca abajo (card or photograph) face down, upside down, estaba tumbado boca abajo he was lying face down
• quedarse con la boca abierta to be flabbergasted

bocacalle NOUN FEM **side street**; es la segunda bocacalle a la derecha it's the second turning on the right

bocadillo NOUN MASC ❶ **baguette sandwich**; un bocadillo de queso a cheese baguette ❷ **speech bubble**

bocado NOUN MASC ❶ **mouthful (of food)** ❷ **bite to eat**

bocata NOUN FEM **sandwich**

bocatería NOUN FEM **sandwich bar**

bochorno NOUN MASC ❶ hoy hace bochorno it's really muggy today ❷ **embarrassment**; ¡qué bochorno pasamos! we were so embarrassed!, fue un bochorno it really was embarrassing

bocina NOUN FEM **horn** (of a car)

boda NOUN FEM **wedding**; bodas de plata silver wedding, bodas de oro golden wedding

bodega NOUN FEM ❶ **wine merchant's** ❷ **cellar** ❸ **wine bar**

bofetada NOUN FEM **slap**

bofetón NOUN MASC **slap**

boina NOUN FEM **beret**

bola NOUN FEM ❶ **ball**; una bola de nieve a snowball, una bola de billar a billiard ball ❷ **scoop** (of ice cream) ❸ (informal) **fib**; contar bolas to tell fibs

bolera NOUN FEM **bowling alley**

boletín NOUN MASC ❶ **bulletin**; boletín informativo news bulletin, boletín meteorológico weather report ❷ **school report**

boleto NOUN MASC ❶ **ticket** (for a raffle or lottery) ❷ **coupon** (football pools)

boli NOUN MASC (informal) **(ballpoint) pen**

bolígrafo NOUN MASC **ballpoint pen**

Bolivia NOUN FEM **Bolivia**

boliviano, boliviana NOUN MASC, FEM, ADJECTIVE **Bolivian**

bollo NOUN MASC **bun**

bolsa NOUN FEM ❶ **bag**; una bolsa de palomitas a bag of popcorn, una bolsa de plástico a plastic bag, una bolsa de viaje a travel bag, una bolsa de la basura a bin liner, mi bolsa de la compra my shopping bag ❷ la bolsa (de valores) the stock exchange

bolsillo NOUN MASC **pocket**; un diccionario de bolsillo a pocket dictionary, libro de bolsillo paperback book

bolso NOUN MASC **handbag**; me robaron el bolso they stole my handbag, bolso de mano/bolso de viaje overnight bag

bomba NOUN FEM ❶ **bomb**; pusieron una bomba en un restaurante they planted a bomb in a restaurant, lanzar una bomba to drop a bomb, la bomba atómica the atomic bomb
• pasarlo bomba **to have a terrific time** ❷ **pump**; una bomba de bicicleta a bicycle pump, una bomba de agua a water pump

bombero, bombera NOUN MASC, FEM **firefighter**

bombilla NOUN FEM **light bulb**; se ha fundido la bombilla the bulb's gone

bombón NOUN MASC **chocolate**; una caja de bombones a box of chocolates

bonachón, bonachona ADJECTIVE (informal) **kind**

bondad NOUN FEM **kindness**

bonito, bonita ADJECTIVE ❶ **pretty**; es una chica muy bonita she's a very pretty girl, un pueblo muy bonito a very pretty village ❷ **nice**; ropa bonita nice clothes

bono NOUN MASC **voucher**

bonobús NOUN MASC (PLURAL die bonobuses) **bus pass**

boquiabierto, boquiabierta ADJECTIVE **astonished**; me quedé boquiabierto I was astonished

bordado NOUN MASC **embroidery**

bordar VERB [17] **to embroider**

borde NOUN MASC ❶ **edge**; me di con el borde de la mesa I bumped myself on the edge of the table, se acercó al borde del andén he went up to the edge of the platform ❷ **rim** (of a glass or cup) ❸ llenar algo hasta el borde to fill something to the brim ❹ el borde

del río the river bank ❺ al borde de la guerra on the brink of war, al borde de las lágrimas on the verge of tears

borde ADJECTIVE (informal) **stroppy**; se puso muy borde conmigo he got very stroppy with me

bordear VERB [17] **to go round** (the edge of something); bordeamos el lago we went round the lake

bordillo NOUN MASC **kerb**

bordo NOUN MASC a bordo on board, subimos a bordo we went on board

borrachera NOUN FEM cogerse una borrachera to get drunk

borracho, borracha NOUN MASC, FEM **drunk**

borracho ADJECTIVE **drunk**; estaban borrachos they were drunk

borrador NOUN MASC ❶ **rough draft**; hacedlo primero en borrador do it in rough first, papel de borrador rough paper ❷ **board rubber** (eraser)

borrar VERB [17] ❶ **to rub out** (a pencil mark or word) ❷ **to erase** (a track or tape) ❸ **to clean** (the blackboard)

borrarse REFLEXIVE VERB [17] **to fade**; se ha borrado el nombre the name has faded

borrasca NOUN FEM ❶ **area of low pressure** ❷ **storm**

borrón NOUN **blot**

borroso, borrosa ADJECTIVE ❶ **blurred** (image or photograph) ❷ **vague** (memory)

bosque NOUN MASC ❶ **wood** ❷ **forest**; el bosque ecuatorial the tropical rainforest

A
B
C
D
E
F
G
H
I
J
K
L
M
N
Ñ
O
P
Q
R
S
T
U
V
W
X
Y
Z

bostezar VERB [22] **to yawn**

bota NOUN FEM **boot**; botas de esquiar ski boots, botas de agua wellingtons

botadura NOUN FEM **launch** (of ship)

botánica[1] NOUN FEM **botany**

botánico, botánica[2] ADJECTIVE **botanical**

botar VERB [17] **to launch** (a ship)

botavara NOUN FEM (of boat) **boom**

bote NOUN MASC ❶ **boat**; un bote de pesca a fishing boat, un bote de remos a rowing boat, un bote salvavidas a lifeboat ❷ **jar**; un bote de aceitunas a jar of olives ❸ **can**; un bote de barniz a can of varnish ❹ **jump**; pegar un bote to jump, pegué un bote de alegría I jumped for joy

botella NOUN FEM **bottle**

botellón NOUN MASC **outdoor drinking session**

botijo NOUN MASC **drinking jug** (with a long spout: with practice you can drink the water as it spurts out in an arc)

botiquín NOUN MASC **medicine cabinet**; botiquín de primeros auxilios first aid kit

botón NOUN MASC **button** (on a garment or a machine); se me ha caído un botón I've lost a button, coser un botón to sew on a button, para encender la tele tienes que apretar este botón to switch on the television you have to press this button, el botón de grabar the record button

boxeador, boxeadora NOUN MASC, FEM **boxer**

boxear VERB [17] **to box**

boxeo NOUN MASC **boxing**; un combate de boxeo a boxing match

bragas PLURAL NOUN FEM **knickers, panties**; un par de bragas a pair of knickers

bragueta NOUN FEM **flies** (in trousers)

Brasil NOUN MASC **Brazil**

brasileño, brasileña NOUN MASC, FEM, ADJECTIVE **Brazilian**

bravo, brava ADJECTIVE **fierce** (animal)

bravo EXCLAMATION ¡bravo! well done!, bravo!

brazo NOUN MASC **arm**; me cogió del brazo he took me by the arm, iban del brazo they were arm in arm, cruzar los brazos to cross your arms, cogió al niño en brazos he picked the child up in his arms, yo llevaba al bebé en brazos I was carrying the baby in my arms, el brazo del sofá the arm of the sofa
• con los brazos abiertos with open arms
• ser el brazo derecho de alguien to be somebody's right-hand man/woman

brecol NOUN MASC **broccoli**

breve ADJECTIVE **short**; una pausa breve a short pause

brevemente ADECTIVE **briefly**

brezo NOUN MASC **heather**

bribón, bribona NOUN MASC, FEM **rascal**

bricolaje NOUN MASC **DIY**

brillante NOUN MASC **diamond**

brillante ADJECTIVE ❶ shiny ❷ bright *(light or colour)*

brillar VERB [17] ❶ to shine ❷ to sparkle

brindar VERB [17] to toast

brindis NOUN MASC toast; hacer un brindis por alguien to drink a toast to somebody

brisa NOUN FEM breeze

británico, británica NOUN MASC, FEM British man/woman; los británicos the British

británico ADJECTIVE British

brocha NOUN FEM ❶ paintbrush ❷ brocha de afeitar shaving brush

broche NOUN MASC brooch

brocheta NOUN FEM ❶ skewer ❷ kebab

broma NOUN FEM joke; hacerle/ gastarle una broma a alguien to play a joke on somebody, lo he dicho en broma I was joking, bromas aparte joking apart, ¡ni en broma! no way!

bromear VERB [17] to joke

bromista NOUN MASC & FEM, ADJECTIVE es un bromista/es muy bromista he's always joking

bronca NOUN FEM (informal) ❶ armar una bronca to kick up a fuss, si no me devuelven el dinero, voy a armar una bronca if they don't give me the money back I'm going to kick up a fuss ❷ telling-off; echar una bronca a alguien to tell somebody off, tu madre te va a echar una buena bronca your mum's going to give you a good telling-off

bronceado, bronceada ADJECTIVE suntanned

bronceador NOUN MASC suntan lotion

broncearse REFLEXIVE VERB [17] to get a suntan

bronquitis NOUN FEM bronchitis

brote NOUN MASC bud

bruja NOUN FEM witch

brujo NOUN MASC wizard

brújula NOUN FEM compass

bruma NOUN FEM mist

bruto, bruta ADJECTIVE ❶ ignorant ❷ rude; es muy bruto, ¡dice unas cosas! he's very rude, he says such things! ❸ ¡qué bruto! ¡cómo trata a su hijo! what a brute! what a way to treat his child!

buceador, buceadora NOUN MASC, FEM diver

bucear VERB [17] to dive

budista NOUN MASC & FEM, ADJECTIVE Buddhist

buen ADJECTIVE ▸ SEE **bueno, buena**

bueno¹ ADVERB ❶ okay; ¿quieres venir?' – 'bueno' 'do you want to come?' – 'okay' ❷ bueno, no importa well, it doesn't matter, bueno, no estoy segura well, I'm not sure, bueno, ya basta right, that's enough

bueno², buena ADJECTIVE ('bueno' becomes 'buen' before a masculine singular noun) ❶ good; es muy buena persona she's a very good person, de buena calidad good quality, ser bueno para algo to be good at something, es muy buena para las matemáticas she's very good at maths, es muy buen amigo mío he's a very good friend of mine, ¡buen viaje! have a good journey! ❷ buenos días good morning, buenas tardes good afternoon, good evening, buenas noches good evening, goodnight ❸ nice; hace buen tiempo the weather is nice, el pastel estaba muy bueno the cake was very nice, ¡está buenísimo! it's delicious!

bufanda NOUN FEM **scarf**

bufar VERB [17] **to snort**

bufet NOUN MASC **buffet**

bufón NOUN MASC **clown** (silly person)

buhardilla NOUN FEM **attic**

búho NOUN MASC **owl**

bujía NOUN FEM **spark plug**

bulto NOUN MASC ❶ **shape**; vi un bulto en la oscuridad I saw a shape in the darkness ❷ **piece of luggage**; ¿cuántos bultos llevas? how many pieces of luggage do you have? ❸ **bag**; yo te llevos los bultos I'll carry your bags for you, iba cargada de bultos she was carrying lots of bags ❹ **bulk** ❺ **lump, swelling** (on the body)

bungalow NOUN MASC **cabin, chalet** (in holiday resorts)

buñuelo NOUN MASC **fritter**

buque NOUN MASC **ship**; buque de guerra warship

burbuja NOUN FEM ❶ **bubble** ❷ una bebida sin burbujas a still drink, una bebida con burbujas a fizzy drink

burdo, **burda** ADJECTIVE **coarse**

burlarse REFLEXIVE VERB [17] burlarse de alguien to make fun of somebody, ¡deja de burlarte de mí! stop making fun of me!

burocracia NOUN FEM **bureaucracy**

burrada NOUN FEM ¡vaya burrada has dicho! what a stupid thing to say, ¡no hagas esa burrada! don't do such a stupid thing, solo dijo burradas he just talked rubbish

burro[1] NOUN MASC ❶ **donkey** ❷ es un burro he's really stupid

burro[2], **burra** NOUN MASC, FEM es un burro he's really stupid

burro ADJECTIVE **stupid**

bus NOUN MASC (informal) **bus**

busca NOUN FEM **search**; ir en busca de algo to go in search of something

buscador NOUN MASC **search engine** (in computers)

buscar VERB [31] ❶ **to look for**; ¿qué buscas? what are you looking for?, mi hermana está buscando trabajo my sister's looking for a job, estoy buscando un ayudante I'm looking for an assistant ❷ **to look**; si no lo encuentras aquí busca en la oficina if you don't find it here look in the office ❸ ir a buscar algo to go to pick up something, mañana iré a buscar mis cosas I'll go and pick up my things tomorrow ❹ ir a buscar a alguien to pick somebody up, yo te iré a buscar al aeropuerto I'll pick you up at the airport ❺ ir a buscar a alguien to go to get someone (the police or a doctor, for example), fueron a buscar a un médico enseguida they went to get a doctor straight away

búsqueda *NOUN FEM* **search**

butaca *NOUN FEM* **❶ armchair ❷ seat** *(in a cinema or theatre)*; **una butaca de patio** a seat in the stalls

butano *NOUN MASC* **butane gas**; **una bombona de butano** a bottle of butane gas

buzo *NOUN MASC* **diver**

buzón *NOUN MASC* **❶ letterbox ❷ postbox**

caballa *NOUN FEM* **mackerel**

caballero *NOUN MASC* **❶ gentleman**; **es un verdadero caballero** he's a real gentleman **❷ sir**; **caballero, ¿me deja pasar?** could you let me through, sir? **❸ caballeros** Gents *(toilets)*, men's department *(in a store)*

caballo *NOUN MASC* **❶ horse**; **montar a caballo** to ride a horse, **un caballo de carreras** a racehorse **❷ knight** *(in chess)* **❸ horse** *(in Spanish cards: equivalent to the queen)*

cabaña *NOUN FEM* **cabin**

cabecear *VERB* [17] **to head** *(a ball)*

cabecera *NOUN FEM* **❶ headboard ❷ head** *(of table)*; **se sentó a la cabecera de la mesa** he sat at the head of the table

cabello *NOUN MASC* **hair**; **tener el cabello rubio** to have blond hair, **cabello rizado** curly hair, **cabello liso** straight hair

caber *VERB* [33] **❶ caber en** to fit into, **es demasiado grande, no cabe en la caja** it's too big, it doesn't fit into the box, **no vamos a caber en el coche** we won't all fit in the car **❷ aquí ya no cabe nada más** there's no room for anything else in here, **¿caben estos libros en la maleta?** is there room for these books in the suitcase? **❸ caber por algo** to fit

a
b
c
d
e
f
g
h
i
j
k
l
m
n
ñ
o
p
q
r
s
t
u
v
w
x
y
z

through something, no cabía por la puerta it wouldn't fit through the door

cabeza NOUN FEM ❶ **head**; me duele la cabeza I've got a headache, asentir con la cabeza to nod ❷ lavarse la cabeza to wash your hair, tengo que lavarme la cabeza I've got to wash my hair ❸ una cabeza de ajo a bulb of garlic ❹ tirarse al agua de cabeza to dive ❺ cabeza abajo upside down, el cuadro está cabeza abajo the picture's upside down ❻ a la cabeza de at the head of, iban a la cabeza de la manifestación they were at the head of the demonstration

• está mal de la cabeza he's not right in the head

cabeza rapada NOUN MASC, FEM **skinhead**

cabina NOUN FEM ❶ **cab** (of a lorry) ❷ **cockpit** (of a plane) ❸ **cabin** (on a plane or boat) ❹ **booth** (in a language lab) ❺ cabina de teléfonos telephone box

cabo NOUN MASC ❶ **corporal** ❷ **cape**; cabo de Buena Esperanza Cape of Good Hope ❸ al cabo de after, al cabo de tres semanas after three weeks ❹ **end** (of a length of rope or piece of string)

• atar cabos to put two and two together

cabra NOUN FEM **goat**

cabré, cabría, etc VERB ▶ SEE **caber**

cacahuete NOUN MASC **peanut**

cacao NOUN MASC ❶ **cocoa** (drink) ❷ **lipsalve**

cacerola NOUN FEM **saucepan**

cachete NOUN MASC **slap**

cachorro, cachorra NOUN MASC, FEM **puppy**

cada ADJECTIVE ❶ **each**; un alumno de cada clase a pupil from each class, hay diez para cada uno there are ten each ❷ **every**; me llaman cada día they phone me every day, cada tres días every three days ❸ cada vez más more and more, se parecen cada vez más they look more and more alike, cada vez menos less and less, cada vez mejor better and better, lo hace cada vez mejor she's getting better and better all the time, cada vez peor worse and worse

cadena NOUN FEM ❶ **chain**; una cadena de hierro an iron chain, una cadena antirrobo a bicycle lock, una cadena de supermercados a supermarket chain ❷ **channel** (on the TV); lo ponen en la segunda cadena they're showing it on Channel Two ❸ **station** (on the radio) ❹ cadena musical hi-fi system ❺ cadenas snow chains ❻ tirar de la cadena to flush the toilet ❼ condenar a alguien a cadena perpetua to sentence somebody to life imprisonment

cadera NOUN FEM **hip**

caducar VERB [17] **to expire** (credit cards, cheques, etc); caduca a los tres años it expires in three years

caer VERB [34] ❶ **to fall**; el jarrón cayó al suelo the vase fell to the ground ❷ dejar caer algo to drop something (on purpose), dejé caer la bandeja I dropped the tray ❸ se dejó caer en el sofá he flopped into the sofa ❹ (informal) tu hermano me cae bien I like your brother, Ana me cae fatal I can't stand Ana

caerse *REFLEXIVE VERB* [34] ❶ **to fall over**; tropecé y me caí I tripped and fell over ❷ **to fall**; casi se cayó del tejado he almost fell from the roof, me caí por las escaleras I fell down the stairs, se cayó de la bici he fell off his bike ❸ se me cayó el plato I dropped the plate *(accidentally)* ❹ se le ha caído un diente he's lost a tooth, se me está cayendo el pelo I'm losing my hair

café *NOUN MASC* ❶ **coffee**; ¿quieres un café? do you want a cup of coffee?, un café solo a black coffee, un café con leche a white coffee, un café cortado a coffee with a dash of milk, café descafeinado decaffeinated coffee ❷ *(place)* **cafe**

cafetera *NOUN FEM* **coffee maker**

cafetería *NOUN FEM* **cafe**

caído, caída *ADJECTIVE* **fallen**

caiga, caigo, *etc VERB* ▸ SEE **caer**

caimán *NOUN MASC* **alligator**

caja *NOUN FEM* ❶ **box**; una caja de cartón a cardboard box, caja de las herramientas toolbox, caja de cambios gearbox ❷ **crate**; una caja de naranjas a crate of oranges ❸ **checkout** *(in a supermarket)*; pague en caja pay at the checkout ❹ **till** *(in a shop)* ❺ una caja fuerte a safe ❻ caja de ahorros savings bank

cajero, cajera *NOUN MASC, FEM* ❶ **cashier** ❷ **checkout operator** ❸ cajero automático cash dispenser

cajón *NOUN MASC* **drawer**

calabacín *NOUN MASC* **courgette**

calamar *NOUN MASC* **squid**; calamares a la romana squid rings in batter

calambre *NOUN MASC* ❶ **cramp**; me dio un calambre I got cramp ❷ **electric shock**; la lámpara me ha dado calambre the lamp gave me an electric shock

calamidad *NOUN FEM* **disaster**

calavera *NOUN FEM* **skull**

calcetín *NOUN MASC* **sock**; unos calcetines a pair of socks

calcomanía *NOUN FEM* **transfer** *(sticker)*

calculadora *NOUN FEM* **calculator**

calcular *VERB* [17] **to calculate, to work out**

caldo *NOUN MASC* ❶ **stock**; caldo de verdura vegetable stock ❷ **broth**

calefacción *NOUN FEM* **heating**; calefacción central central heating, calefacción de gas gas heating

calendario *NOUN MASC* **calendar**

calentador *NOUN MASC* ❶ **boiler** ❷ **water heater**

calentamiento global *NOUN MASC* **global warming**

calentar *VERB* [29] ❶ **to heat (up)**; voy a calentar la sopa I'm going to heat up the soup ❷ **to give off heat**; esta estufa calienta mucho this heater gives off a lot of heat ❸ calentar los músculos to warm up *(before sport or dancing)*

calentarse *REFLEXIVE VERB* [29] **to heat up**

calidad *NOUN FEM* **quality**; materiales de calidad high quality materials, productos de mala calidad poor quality products

calienta, **caliento**, *etc VERB*
▶ SEE **calentar**

caliente *ADJECTIVE* ❶ hot; los platos están muy calientes the plates are very hot ❷ warm; un baño caliente a hot bath, en el salón se está más caliente it's warmer in the living-room

calificación *NOUN FEM* mark; obtuvo buenas calificaciones he got good marks

callado, **callada** *ADJECTIVE* quiet; ¡estate callado! be quiet!

callar *VERB* [17] to be quiet; calla, no oigo be quiet, I can't hear, ¡calla ya! shut up!

callarse *REFLEXIVE VERB* [17] to go quiet; al verla todos se callaron everybody went quiet when they saw her, ¡cállate! shut up!

calle *NOUN FEM* street; una calle cortada a cul-de-sac, una calle de sentido único a one way street *(when writing an address, the word 'calle' is abbreviated to 'C/')*

callejón *NOUN MASC* alley; un callejón sin salida a blind alley

calma *NOUN FEM* calm; hazlo con calma do it calmly, mantener la calma to keep calm, la ciudad está en calma the city is calm

calmar *VERB* [17] to calm down

calmarse *REFLEXIVE VERB* [17] to calm down; después de un rato me calmé I calmed down after a while

calor *NOUN MASC* ❶ heat; el calor de la estufa the heat of the stove ❷ hoy hace mucho calor it's very hot today, ¡qué calor hace! it's so hot! ❸ tener calor to be hot, tengo mucho calor I'm very hot

caluroso, **calurosa** *ADJECTIVE* hot *(a day or place)*

calvo, **calva** *ADJECTIVE* bald; quedarse calvo to go bald

calzado *NOUN MASC* footwear

calzar *VERB* [22] ¿qué número calzas? what shoe size do you take?

calzoncillos *PLURAL NOUN MASC* underpants; unos calzoncillos a pair of underpants

cama *NOUN FEM* bed; una cama individual a single bed, una cama doble/una cama de matrimonio a double bed, camas gemelas twin beds, una cama elástica a trampoline, hacer la cama to make the bed, ¡a la cama! off to bed!

cámara *NOUN FEM* camera; una cámara de fotos a camera, una cámara de vídeo a video camera

camarera *NOUN FEM* ❶ waitress ❷ camarera de habitación chambermaid

camarero *NOUN MASC* waiter

camarón *NOUN MASC* shrimp

cambiar *VERB* [17] ❶ to change; no has cambiado you haven't changed, cambiar libras a euros to change pounds into euros ❷ cambiar de to change, ha cambiado de trabajo he's changed his job, cambiar de idea to change your mind, cambiar de canal to change channels ❸ to exchange; quiero cambiar estos zapatos I want to exchange these shoes ❹ cambiar de casa to move house ❺ to swap; te cambio mi pluma por esa cinta I'll swap my pen for that tape

cambiarse *REFLEXIVE VERB* [17] ❶ to get changed; voy a cambiarme y ahora vuelvo I'm going to get changed, I'll be back in a minute, voy a cambiarme de ropa I'm going to change my clothes ❷ cambiarse de sitio to change places

cambio NOUN MASC ❶ change; un cambio a mejor a change for the better, ha habido un cambio de planes there's been a change of plan ❷ exchange; no se admiten cambios goods will not be exchanged ❸ change; ¿tienes cambio? do you have any change?, me dieron mal el cambio they gave me the wrong change, 'cambio' 'bureau de change' ❹ a cambio de in return for, a cambio de información in return for information

camello NOUN MASC camel

camilla NOUN FEM ❶ stretcher ❷ trolley (in hospital)

caminar VERB [17] to walk; me gusta caminar I like walking

caminata NOUN FEM long walk

camino NOUN MASC ❶ road; todos los caminos están cortados all the roads are closed, el camino al éxito the road to success ❷ path; un camino por el bosque a path through the forest ❸ way; ¿puede indicarme el camino a la estación? could you tell me the way to the station?, yo sé el camino I know the way

camión NOUN MASC lorry; el camión de la mudanza the removal van, un camión cisterna a petrol tanker

camionero, **camionera** NOUN MASC, FEM lorry driver

camioneta NOUN FEM van

camisa NOUN FEM shirt

camiseta NOUN FEM ❶ T-shirt ❷ vest

camisón NOUN MASC nightdress

campamento NOUN MASC camp; se han ido de campamento they've gone camping

campana NOUN FEM bell; tocar la campana to ring the bell

campaña NOUN FEM campaign; campaña electoral electoral campaign

campeón, **campeona** NOUN MASC, FEM champion

campeonato NOUN MASC championship

campesino, **campesina** NOUN MASC, FEM ❶ country person ❷ peasant

camping NOUN MASC campsite; ir de camping to go camping

campista NOUN MASC & FEM camper

campo NOUN MASC ❶ country; una casa en el campo a house in the country ❷ countryside; el campo está muy bonito the countryside looks very beautiful ❸ field; un campo de trigo a field of wheat ❹ un campo de fútbol a football pitch

cana NOUN FEM white hair; le están saliendo canas he's going grey

Canadá NOUN MASC Canada

canadiense NOUN MASC & FEM, ADJECTIVE Canadian

canal NOUN MASC ❶ channel (on the TV); no cambies de canal don't change channels ❷ channel (water); el canal de la Mancha the English Channel ❸ canal; el canal de Panamá the Panama Canal

canario[1] NOUN MASC **canary**

canario[2], **canaria** ADJECTIVE **of/from the Canary Islands**

canario NOUN MASC & FEM **Canary Islander**

canasta NOUN FEM **basket**

canasto NOUN MASC **basket** *(usually with a lid)*

cancelar VERB [17] **to cancel**

cáncer[1] NOUN MASC **cancer**; tiene cáncer he's got cancer, cáncer de mama breast cancer, cáncer de piel skin cancer

cáncer[2] NOUN MASC & FEM **Cancer**; soy Cáncer I'm Cancer

Cáncer NOUN MASC **Cancer**

cancha NOUN FEM **court**; una cancha de baloncesto a basketball court

canción NOUN FEM **song**; canción de cuna lullaby

candelabro NOUN MASC **candlestick**; un candelabro dorado a brass candlestick

candidato, **candidata** NOUN MASC, FEM **candidate**

canela NOUN FEM **cinnamon**; canela en rama stick cinnamon, canela en polvo ground cinnamon

cangrejo NOUN MASC ❶ **crab** ❷ **crayfish**

canguro[1] NOUN MASC **kangaroo**

canguro[2] NOUN MASC & FEM **babysitter**

canica NOUN FEM **marble**; jugar a las canicas to play marbles

canoa NOUN FEM **canoe**

cansado, **cansada** ADJECTIVE ❶ **tired**; estoy muy cansado I'm very tired ❷ **tiring**; esperar es muy cansado waiting's very tiring

cansar VERB [17] ❶ **to make tired**; le cansa andar walking makes him tired ❷ **to be tiring**; es un trabajo que cansa mucho it's a very tiring job ❸ **to be boring**; esta música cansa un poco this music's a bit boring

cansarse REFLEXIVE VERB [17] ❶ **to get tired**; se cansa muy fácilmente he gets tired very easily, se me cansa la vista my eyes get tired ❷ **to get bored**; me canso de repetir siempre lo mismo I get bored always repeating the same thing

Cantábrico NOUN MASC el mar Cantábrico the Bay of Biscay

cantante NOUN MASC & FEM **singer**

cantar VERB [17] **to sing**

cantera NOUN FEM **quarry**

cantidad NOUN FEM ❶ **amount**; una enorme cantidad de nieve a huge amount of snow ❷ ¿qué cantidad de vasos necesitamos? how many glasses do we need?, es increíble la cantidad de aceite gastas it's incredible how much oil you use ❸ tanta cantidad so much, no pongas tanta cantidad de leche don't put so much milk in ❹ cantidad de/cantidades de lots of, había cantidad de gente there were lots of people, con grandes cantidades de flores with lots of flowers ❺ **sum**; una cantidad importante de dinero a considerable sum of money

cantina NOUN FEM ❶ **cafeteria** ❷ **canteen**

canto NOUN MASC **singing**

caña NOUN FEM ❶ **cane**; caña de azúcar sugar cane ❷ caña de pescar fishing rod

cañería *NOUN FEM* **pipe**

cañón *NOUN* **cannon**

capa *NOUN FEM* ❶ **layer**; la capa de ozono the ozone layer ❷ **cape**, **cloak**

capacidad *NOUN FEM* **capacity**

capacitación *NOUN FEM* **training**

capaz *ADJECTIVE* ❶ **capable**; es capaz de cualquier cosa he's capable of anything, soy capaz de no ir I'm quite capable of not going ❷ **able**; no fueron capaces de darme una respuesta they weren't able to give me an answer

capital *NOUN FEM* ❶ **capital**; la capital de España the capital of Spain ❷ Valencia **capital** the city of Valencia *(as opposed to the province)*

capitán, **capitana** *NOUN MASC, FEM* **captain** *(in sports)*

capítulo *NOUN MASC* ❶ **chapter** ❷ **episode** *(of a TV series)*

capó *NOUN MASC* **bonnet** *(of a car)*

capricho *NOUN MASC* **whim**

capricornio *NOUN MASC & FEM* **Capricorn**; es capricornio he's Capricorn

Capricornio *NOUN MASC* **Capricorn**

capucha *NOUN FEM* **hood** *(of an anorak, etc)*

cara *NOUN FEM* ❶ **face**; tiene una cara bonita she has a pretty face, tienes cara de cansada you look tired, al oírlo puso cara de sorpresa he looked surprised when he heard it, tu hermana tenía mala cara your sister looked ill
• ¡qué cara más dura tienes! *(informal)* **you've got some nerve!**

(literally: what a hard face you have!) ❷ **side**; la otra cara del disco the other side of the record ❸ ¿cara o cruz? **heads or tails?**

caracol *NOUN MASC* ❶ **snail** ❷ **winkle**

carácter *NOUN MASC* ❶ **character**; el carácter Latino the Latin character ❷ tiene muy mal carácter he's got a very bad temper, es una persona de buen carácter she's a good-natured person ❸ no tiene mucho carácter he doesn't have much personality

caramba *EXCLAMATION* ❶ **good heavens!** ❷ **damn it!**

caramelo *NOUN MASC* ❶ **sweet**; un caramelo de menta a mint ❷ **caramel**

caravana *NOUN FEM* ❶ **tailback**; hay caravana para entrar en Sevilla there's a tailback into Seville, una caravana de diez kilómetros a ten-kilometre tailback ❷ **caravan**

carbón *NOUN MASC* **coal**; carbón vegetal charcoal

cárcel *NOUN FEM* **jail**; meter a alguien en la cárcel to put somebody in jail

cardenal *NOUN MASC* ❶ **bruise** ❷ **cardinal**

cardíaco, **cardíaca** *ADJECTIVE* **heart**; un ataque cardíaco a heart attack

careta *NOUN FEM* **mask**

carga *NOUN FEM* ❶ **burden**; no quiero ser una carga para nadie I don't want to be a burden on anybody ❷ **freight**, **cargo** ❸ **load**; carga máxima maximum load ❹ **refill** *(for a pen)* ❺ ¡a la carga! **charge!**

cargado, **cargada** *ADJECTIVE* ❶ **loaded**; la pistola estaba cargada the gun was loaded, vas muy cargada you're loaded down, iba cargado de paquetes he was loaded down with parcels ❷ un café cargado a strong coffee

cargar VERB [28] ❶ to load (a lorry or weapon) ❷ to fill (a pen)

cargo NOUN MASC ❶ position; un cargo de responsabilidad a position of responsibility ❷ a cargo de in charge of, estoy a cargo del departamento I'm in charge of the department, dejó los niños a mi cargo she left the children in my care

Caribe NOUN MASC el Caribe the Caribbean, el mar Caribe the Caribbean Sea

caribeño, caribeña NOUN MASC, FEM, ADJECTIVE **Caribbean**

caridad NOUN FEM **charity**

cariño NOUN MASC ❶ affection; tenerle cariño a to be fond of, les tengo cariño I'm fond of them, tomarle cariño a to become fond of, les tomó cariño he became fond of them ❷ con cariño, Maya love, Maya (in letters) ❸ dear; ven, cariño come here, dear

cariñoso, cariñosa ADJECTIVE ❶ affectionate, loving (a person) ❷ warm; un cariñoso saludo warm regards (in a letter)

carmín NOUN MASC **lipstick**

carnaval NOUN MASC **carnival**

carne NOUN FEM ❶ meat; carne de vaca beef, carne de cerdo pork, carne de cordero lamb, carne de ternera veal ❷ flesh

carné, carnet NOUN MASC **card**; carné de identidad identity card, carné de

estudiante student card, carné de conducir driving licence

carnicería NOUN FEM **butcher's**

carnicero, carnicera NOUN MASC, FEM **butcher**

carnívoro, carnívora ADJECTIVE **carnivorous**

caro, cara ADJECTIVE **expensive**; cuesta muy caro it's very expensive, eso ya lo vas a pagar caro you're going to pay dearly for this

carpa NOUN FEM **tent**

carpeta NOUN FEM **folder**; carpeta de anillas ring binder

carpintero, carpintera NOUN MASC, FEM **carpenter**

carrera NOUN FEM ❶ race; una carrera automovilística a car race, las carreras de caballos the races, una carrera de obstáculos a steeplechase, una carrera de relevos a relay race ❷ echar una carrera to have a race (against somebody), echamos una carrera let's have a race, te echo una carrera I'll race you ❸ echar una carrera to run, eché una carrera y alcancé el autobús I ran and got the bus ❹ degree course; hacer una carrera to study for a degree, no quiero hacer una carrera I don't want to go to university, está haciendo la carrera de medicina she's studying medicine

carreta NOUN FEM **cart**

carretera NOUN FEM **road**; carretera nacional A-road, carretera comarcal B-road, carretera de circunvalación ringroad

carretilla NOUN FEM **wheelbarrow**

carril *NOUN MASC* **lane**; carril bus bus lane

carrito *NOUN MASC* **trolley**

carro *NOUN MASC* **cart**

carta *NOUN FEM* ❶ **letter**; mandar una carta to send a letter, echar una carta al correo to post a letter, una carta certificada a registered letter ❷ **menu**; ¿nos puede traer la carta, por favor? could you bring us the menu, please? ❸ **card** *(in a pack)*; jugar a las cartas to play cards

cartel *NOUN MASC* ❶ **poster** *(for publicity)* ❷ **sign**; ¿qué dice el cartel? what does the sign say?

cartelera *NOUN FEM* la cartelera de cine 'what's on' at the cinema, la obra lleva tres años en cartelera the play has been running for three years, la película sigue en cartelera the film is still showing

cartera *NOUN FEM* ❶ **wallet** ❷ **briefcase** ❸ **satchel**

carterista *NOUN MASC & FEM* **pickpocket**

cartero, **cartera** *NOUN MASC, FEM* **postman/postwoman**

cartón *NOUN MASC* **cardboard**

cartucho *NOUN MASC* **cartridge**

casa *NOUN FEM* ❶ **house**; una casa adosada a semi-detached house, una casa de campo a country house, una casa de huéspedes guesthouse ❷ **flat**; su casa está en la quinta planta her flat's on the fifth floor ❸ **home**; no están en casa they're not at home, estoy pasando unos días en casa de Juan I'm staying at Juan's for a few days

casado, **casada** *ADJECTIVE* **married**; estar casado/ser casado to be married

casamiento *NOUN MASC* ❶ **wedding** ❷ **marriage**

casarse *REFLEXIVE VERB* [17] **to get married**; se casó con mi primo she married my cousin

cascar *VERB* [31] **to crack**

cáscara *NOUN FEM* ❶ **peel** ❷ **shell**

casco *NOUN MASC* ❶ **helmet**; un casco protector a safety helmet, crash helmet ❷ **hoof** *(of a horse)* ❸ **empty bottle**; guardo los cascos para reciclarlos I keep the empty bottles for recycling ❹ cascos **headphones**

caserío *NOUN MASC* ❶ **farmhouse** ❷ **hamlet**

casero, **casera** *NOUN MASC, FEM* **landlord/landlady**

casero *ADJECTIVE* **homemade**

caseta *NOUN FEM* ❶ **hut** *(for a watchman or guard)* ❷ **stand** *(in an exhibition)* ❸ **kennel**

casete *NOUN MASC OR FEM* **cassette**

casi *ADVERB* ❶ **almost**; casi me pierdo I almost got lost, ¡casi, casi! almost! ❷ **hardly**; casi no había gente there was hardly anybody there, casi nunca hardly ever

casilla *NOUN FEM* ❶ **square** *(in a crossword)* ❷ **box** *(on a form)*

caso *NOUN MASC* ❶ **case**; en ese caso in that case, en caso de accidente in case of accident, en todo caso/ en cualquier caso in any case, en el peor de los casos if the worst comes to the worst ❷ el caso es que ... the thing is ... ❸ hacer caso de to pay attention to, haz caso de las señales pay attention to the signs, no me hace caso he pays no attention to me

caspa NOUN FEM **dandruff**

cassette NOUN MASC & FEM **cassette**

castaña[1] NOUN FEM **chestnut**

castaño, castaña[2] ADJECTIVE **chestnut brown**

castañuelas PLURAL NOUN FEM **castanets**

castellano[1] NOUN MASC ❶ **Castilian** ❷ **Castilian Spanish** *(as opposed to other varieties of Spanish, particularly those of Spanish-speaking America; Castilian Spanish generally means the Spanish spoken in Spain)*

castellano[2], **castellana** NOUN MASC, FEM, ADJECTIVE **Castilian**

castigar VERB [28] ❶ **to punish** ❷ castigar a alguien sin salir to ground somebody ❸ **to give a detention** *(at school)*; la profesora me dejó castigado the teacher gave me a detention

castigo NOUN MASC **punishment**

Castilla NOUN FEM **Castile**

castillo NOUN MASC **castle**; castillo de arena sandcastle

casualidad NOUN FEM ❶ **chance**; de casualidad by chance, lo vi por casualidad I saw it by chance ❷ da la casualidad de que ... it so happens that ..., dio la casualidad de que llevaba las señas en mi bolso it so happened that I had the address in my bag ❸ ¡qué casualidad! what a coincidence!

catalán[1] NOUN MASC **Catalan** *(the language)*

catalán[2], **catalana** NOUN MASC, FEM, ADJECTIVE **Catalan**

Cataluña NOUN FEM **Catalonia**

catarata NOUN FEM ❶ **waterfall** ❷ **cataract** *(of the eye)*

catarro NOUN MASC **cold**; coger un catarro to catch a cold

catear VERB [17] *(informal)* **to fail**; he cateado las mates I've failed maths, me han cateado en inglés the English teacher has failed me

catedral NOUN FEM **cathedral**

categoría NOUN FEM ❶ **category** ❷ de primera categoría first class, un hotel de mucha categoría a top-quality hotel, un restaurante de poca categoría a second-rate restaurant

católico, católica NOUN MASC, FEM, ADJECTIVE **Catholic**

catorce NUMBER ❶ **fourteen**; tiene catorce años he's fourteen (years old) ❷ **fourteenth** *(in dates)*; el catorce de mayo the fourteenth of May

caucho NOUN MASC **rubber**

causa NOUN FEM ❶ **cause**; sin causa without cause ❷ a causa de because of, a causa de esto lo despidieron they sacked him because of it

causar VERB [17] **to cause**

cautiverio NOUN MASC **captivity**; mantener a alguien en cautiverio to keep someone in captivity

cautivo, cautiva NOUN MASC, FEM **prisoner**

cava NOUN MASC **cava** *(sparkling wine)*

cavar VERB [17] **to dig**

caverna NOUN FEM **cave**

cayendo ▸ SEE **caer**

caza NOUN FEM **hunting**; **ir de caza** to go hunting

cazadora NOUN FEM **jacket**

cazar VERB [22] **to hunt**

cazuela NOUN FEM **casserole**

CD NOUN MASC **CDs**

cebada NOUN FEM **barley**

cebolla NOUN FEM **onion**

cebolleta NOUN FEM **spring onion**

cebollino NOUN MASC **chives**

ceder VERB [18] ❶ **to give in**; finalmente cedí I finally gave in ❷ **ceder el paso** to give way ❸ le cedí mi asiento a un anciano I gave up my seat to an elderly man

ceguera NOUN FEM **blindness**

ceja NOUN FEM **eyebrow**

celda NOUN FEM **cell** *(in a prison)*

celebración NOUN FEM **celebration**

celebrar VERB [17] ❶ **to celebrate** ❷ **to hold** *(a meeting)*

celebrarse REFLEXIVE VERB [17] **to take place**; la boda se celebró el sábado pasado the wedding took place last Saturday

célebre ADJECTIVE **famous**

celo NOUN MASC **Sellotape**

celos PLURAL NOUN MASC ❶ **jealousy** ❷ **tener celos de alguien** to be jealous of somebody, tiene celos de su hermana pequeña she's jealous of her little sister ❸ **darle celos a alguien** to make somebody feel jealous, lo hace para darte celos he does it to make you feel jealous

celoso, celosa ADJECTIVE **jealous**

cementerio NOUN MASC **cemetery**

cemento NOUN MASC **cement**

cena NOUN FEM ❶ **dinner** *(evening meal)* ❷ **supper**; ¿qué hay de cena? what's for supper?

cenar VERB [17] **to have dinner**; normalmente cenamos a las nueve we normally have dinner at nine, salimos a cenar fuera we went out for dinner

cenicero NOUN MASC **ashtray**

ceniza NOUN FEM **ash**

centavo NOUN MASC ❶ **one hundredth** ❷ **cent** *(in the dollar system)*

centenar NOUN MASC **hundred**; un centenar de libros (about) a hundred books, centenares de cartas hundreds of letters

centenario NOUN MASC **centenary**

centeno NOUN MASC **rye**

centésima NOUN FEM **hundredth**; una centésima de segundo a hundredth of a second

centésimo, centésima² ADJECTIVE **hundredth**

centígrado ADJECTIVE **centigrade**

centímetro NOUN MASC **centimetre**

céntimo NOUN ❶ **cent** *(in the euro system)*; el euro se divide en cien céntimos the euro is divided into a

a
b
c
d
e
f
g
h
i
j
k
l
m
n
ñ
o
p
q
r
s
t
u
v
w
x
y
z

hundred cents ❷ **penny**; no tengo ni un céntimo I am penniless

central NOUN FEM ❶ **head office** ❷ central telefónica **telephone exchange**, central de correos **general post office** ❸ **power station**; central nuclear **nuclear power station**

central ADJECTIVE **central**

céntrico, céntrica ADJECTIVE **central**; un barrio céntrico an area in the centre of town

centrifugar VERB [28] **to spin-dry**

centro NOUN MASC ❶ **centre**; el centro de la ciudad the town/city centre, un centro cultural a cultural centre, estaba justo en el centro it was right in the middle ❷ un centro comercial a **shopping mall**

ceñido, ceñida ADJECTIVE **tight**; una camiseta muy ceñida a very tight T-shirt

ceño NOUN MASC fruncir el ceño to frown

cepillar VERB [17] **to brush**

cepillarse REFLEXIVE VERB [17] **to brush**; cepillarse los dientes to brush your teeth, cepillarse el pelo to brush your hair

cepillo NOUN MASC **brush**; un cepillo de dientes a toothbrush, un cepillo del pelo a hairbrush

cera NOUN FEM **wax**

cerámica NOUN FEM **pottery**

cerca ADVERB ❶ **near**, **close**; viven aquí cerca they live near here, ponlos cerca el uno del otro put them close to each other ❷ **nearby**; mi casa está cerca my house is

nearby ❸ cerca de **near**, se sentó cerca de mí he sat near me, está cerca de la estación it's near the station, vive muy cerca de mí she lives very near me ❹ cerca de **almost**, cerca de diez mil personas almost ten thousand people

cercanía NOUN FEM **proximity**

cercanías PLURAL NOUN FEM ❶ **surrounding area**; Barcelona y sus cercanías Barcelona and the surrounding area, en las cercanías del aeropuerto in the area around the airport ❷ **vicinity**; en las cercanías del bar in the vicinity of the bar

cercano, cercana ADJECTIVE ❶ **nearby**; las casas cercanas the nearby houses ❷ cercano a algo **near something**, los pueblos cercanos al aeropuerto the villages near the airport ❸ **near**; en un futuro cercano in the near future

cerdo¹ NOUN MASC **pork**; no como cerdo I don't eat pork

cerdo², cerda NOUN MASC, FEM **pig**

cereales PLURAL NOUN MASC **cereals**

cerebro NOUN MASC **brain**

ceremonia NOUN FEM **ceremony**

cereza NOUN FEM **cherry**

cerilla NOUN FEM **match**

cero NOUN MASC ❶ **zero**; tres grados bajo cero three degrees below zero, mi prefijo en Londres es cero, dos, cero my dialling code in London is 020 ❷ **love** (in tennis) ❸ **nil** (in football)

cerrado, cerrada ADJECTIVE ❶ **closed**; la ventana está cerrada the window's closed ❷ cerrado con llave locked, cerrado con cerrojo bolted ❸ el grifo está cerrado the tap's turned off

cerradura NOUN FEM ❶ lock ❷ el ojo de la cerradura the keyhole

cerrar VERB [29] ❶ to close; cierrra la puerta close the door, cerramos a las ocho we close at eight, han cerrado la fábrica the factory has been closed ❷ cerrar algo de un portazo to slam something, cerró la puerta de un portazo he slammed the door shut ❸ cerrar con llave to lock, no te olvides de cerrar con llave don't forget to lock up ❹ cerrar con cerrojo to bolt ❺ cerrar el grifo to turn off the tap ❻ cierra la botella put the top on the bottle, ¿has cerrado el frasco? have you put the lid on the jar? ❼ cerrar una carta to seal a letter

cerrarse REFLEXIVE VERB [29] to close; la puerta se cerró the door closed, cerrarse de un portazo to slam shut

certificado¹ NOUN MASC certificate

certificado², **certificada** ADJECTIVE registered (a letter or parcel)

certificar VERB [31] to certify

cervecería NOUN FEM ❶ brewery ❷ bar (selling lots of different beers)

cerveza NOUN FEM beer; ¿quieres una cerveza? do you want a beer?, cerveza de barril draught beer, cerveza negra stout, cerveza rubia lager

césped NOUN MASC lawn; 'prohibido pisar el césped' 'keep off the grass'

cesta NOUN FEM ❶ basket; una cesta de mimbre a wicker basket ❷ una cesta de Navidad a Christmas hamper

cesto NOUN MASC basket

chalado, **chalada** ADJECTIVE (informal) crazy

chalé, **chalet** NOUN MASC ❶ villa ❷ detached house (on estate) ❸ semi-detached house (on estate)

chaleco NOUN MASC waistcoast; un chaleco de punto a sleeveless sweater

champán NOUN MASC champagne

champaña NOUN MASC OR FEM champagne

champiñón NOUN MASC mushroom

champú NOUN MASC shampoo

chanclas NOUN FEM & PLURAL flip-flops

chándal NOUN MASC tracksuit

chapa NOUN FEM ❶ top (of a bottle) ❷ badge; una chapa de policía a police badge

chapapote NOUN MASC oil (washed up on a beach)

chaparrón NOUN MASC downpour

chaqueta NOUN FEM jacket; chaqueta de punto cardigan

charca NOUN FEM pond

charco NOUN MASC puddle; no pises los charcos don't walk in the puddles

charcutería NOUN FEM delicatessen (specializing in pork products)

charlar VERB [17] to chat

chasco NOUN MASC disappointment; me llevé un chasco I felt really disappointed

chat NOUN MASC chatroom

a
b
c
d
e
f
g
h
i
j
k
l
m
n
ñ
o
p
q
r
s
t
u
v
w
x
y
z

chatear VERB [17] **to chat** (online)

cheque NOUN MASC **cheque**; extender un cheque to write out a cheque, me puedes extender un cheque a mi nombre you can make out a cheque to me, un cheque a nombre de Alberto López a cheque payable to Alberto López, cobrar un cheque to cash a cheque, un cheque de viaje/un cheque de viajero a traveller's cheque

chequeo NOUN MASC **checkup**; hacerse un chequeo to have a checkup

chica NOUN FEM **girl**

chichón NOUN MASC **bump**; me di un golpe en la frente y me ha salido un chichón I banged my forehead and now I've got a bump

chicle NOUN MASC **chewing gum**; ¿quieres un chicle? do you want some chewing gum?

chico NOUN MASC ❶ **boy** ❷ unos chicos some children, había unos chicos jugando en la calle there were some children playing in the street ❸ **guy**; sale con un chico she's going out with a guy

chiflado, chiflada ADJECTIVE (informal) **crazy**

chile NOUN MASC **chilli**

Chile NOUN MASC **Chile**

chileno, chilena NOUN MASC, FEM, ADJECTIVE **Chilean**

chillar VERB [17] **to shout**

chimenea NOUN FEM ❶ **chimney** ❷ **fireplace**

China NOUN FEM (la) China **China**

chincheta NOUN FEM **drawing pin**

chino¹ NOUN MASC **Chinese** (the language)

chino², china NOUN MASC, FEM **Chinese man/Chinese woman**

chino ADJECTIVE **Chinese**

Chipre NOUN FEM **Cyprus**

chirriar VERB [32] **to squeak** (a door)

chis EXCLAMATION ❶ **shush!** ❷ ¡chis, chis! hey! (calling somebody in the street, for example)

chisme NOUN MASC ❶ **piece of gossip**; siempre está contando chismes he's always gossiping ❷ **thing**; ¿para qué sirve este chisme? what's this thing for?, tiene un montón de chismes que no sirven para nada he's got all sorts of useless stuff

chispa NOUN FEM ❶ **spark**; saltaron chispas del fuego sparks flew out of the fire ❷ una chispa de (informal) **a drop of**, una chispa de ginebra a drop of gin, pon una chispa de sal add a tiny bit of salt

chispa ADJECTIVE (informal) **tipsy**; estaba un poco chispa she was a bit tipsy

chiste NOUN MASC **joke**; contar un chiste to tell a joke, un chiste verde a dirty joke

chocar VERB [31] ❶ **to crash**; dos coches chocaron en la autopista two cars crashed on the motorway ❷ chocar con to run into, chocaron con una farola they ran into a lamp-post, me choqué con ella I bumped into her

chocolate NOUN MASC **chocolate**; chocolate con leche milk chocolate, chocolate negro dark chocolate, una barra de chocolate a bar of chocolate

chocolatina NOUN FEM **chocolate bar**

chollo NOUN MASC (informal) ❶ **cushy job** ❷ este chico es un chollo, sabe hacer de todo this guy's a real find, he can do anything

choque NOUN MASC ❶ **crash**; un choque frontal a head-on collision ❷ **clash**; choques entre los manifestantes y la policía clashes between demonstrators and police

chorizo NOUN MASC **chorizo** (spicy salami-shaped sausage)

chorrada NOUN FEM (informal) eso es una chorrada that's nonsense, decir chorradas to talk nonsense, se enfada por cualquier chorrada he gets upset over the smallest thing

choza NOUN FEM **hut**

chubasco NOUN MASC ❶ **shower** ❷ **downpour**

chuchería NOUN FEM **trinket**

chuleta NOUN FEM **chop**; una chuleta de cerdo a pork chop

chupar VERB [17] ❶ **to suck** ❷ **to absorb**; este papel chupa la tinta this paper absorbs ink

chuparse REFLEXIVE VERB [17] **to suck**; chuparse el dedo to suck your thumb

churro NOUN MASC ❶ **fritter** ❷ (informal) **botched job**; ¡vaya churro ha salido! it's turned out a real mess!

chutar VERB [17] **to shoot** (at goal)

cibercafé NOUN MASC **Internet cafe**; ¿dónde hay un cibercafé? where is there an Internet cafe?

cibernauta NOUN MASC & FEM **surfer**

cicatriz NOUN FEM **scar**

ciclismo NOUN MASC **cycling**

ciclista NOUN MASC & FEM **cyclist**

ciclomotor NOUN MASC **moped**

ciego, ciega NOUN MASC, FEM **blind person**; los ciegos the blind

ciego ADJECTIVE **blind**; quedarse ciego to go blind

cielo NOUN MASC ❶ **sky** ❷ **heaven**; ir al cielo to go to heaven, ¡cielos! good heavens!

cien NUMBER **hundred** (see also 'ciento'); cien personas a hundred people, el cien por cien a hundred per cent, cien mil euros a hundred thousand euros

ciencia NOUN FEM ❶ **science**; ciencia ficción science fiction ❷ **ciencias science** (subject at school), ciencias naturales natural science, Ciencias Económicas Economic Sciences, Ciencias Empresariales Business Studies, Ciencias de la Información Media Studies

cieno NOUN MASC **silt**

científico, científica NOUN MASC, FEM **scientist**

científico ADJECTIVE **scientific**

ciento NUMBER ❶ **hundred**; ciento cinco one hundred and five, dos cientos diez two hundred and ten, cientos de cartas hundreds of letters ❷ por ciento per cent, cinco por ciento five per cent, tanto por ciento percentage

cierra, cierro, etc VERB ▸ SEE **cerrar**

cierto, cierta ADJECTIVE ❶ **true**; eso no es cierto that's not true ❷ **certain**; cierta clase de negocios certain types of business, en cierta ocasión on a certain occasion ❸ en cierto modo in a way, en cierto modo, lo entiendo in a way, I understand ❹ hasta cierto punto up to a point ❺ por cierto by the way, por cierto, ¿se lo has preguntado? by the way, did you ask him?

ciervo *NOUN MASC* ❶ deer ❷ stag

cifra *NOUN FEM* figure; una cifra muy alta a very high figure

cigarrillo *NOUN MASC* cigarrette

cigüeña *NOUN FEM* stork

cilindro *NOUN MASC* cylinder

cima *NOUN FEM* top *(of a mountain)*

cinco *NUMBER* ❶ five; Julia tiene cinco años Julia's five (years old) ❷ fifth *(in dates)*; hoy es día cinco today is the fifth ❸ five *(in clock time)*; son las cinco it's five o'clock, a las dos y cinco at five past two

cincuenta *NUMBER* fifty; mi madre tiene cincuenta años my mum's fifty (years old), cincuenta y ocho fifty-eight, los años cincuenta the fifties

cine *NOUN MASC* cinema; ir al cine to go to the cinema, ¿qué ponen en el cine? what's on at the cinema?, cine de barrio local cinema, la cartelera de cine 'what's on' at the cinemas

cineasta *NOUN MASC, FEM* film-maker

cinta *NOUN FEM* ❶ ribbon; una cinta para el pelo a hair ribbon ❷ tape; una cinta de vídeo a video tape, grabar una cinta to record a tape, una cinta virgen a blank tape, cinta magnetofónica magnetic tape, cinta adhesiva adhesive tape, cinta métrica tape measure

cintura *NOUN FEM* waist; ¿cuánto tienes de cintura? what's your waist measurement?

cinturón *NOUN MASC* belt; cinturón de seguridad seatbelt, es cinturón negro de karate he's a karate black belt
• apretarse el cinturón to tighten one's belt

circo *NOUN MASC* circus

circulación *NOUN FEM* ❶ circulation ❷ traffic

circular *NOUN FEM*

circular *ADJECTIVE* circular

circular *VERB* [17] ❶ to flow *(blood or water)* ❷ to drive; circulen por la derecha drive on the right, el coche circulaba a mucha velocidad the car was travelling very fast

círculo *NOUN MASC* circle

circunferencia *NOUN FEM* circumference

circunstancia *NOUN FEM* ❶ reason; por alguna circunstancia no pudo hacerlo he couldn't do it for some reason ❷ circumstances; bajo ninguna circunstancia under no circumstances, en estas circunstancias in these circumstances, dadas las circunstancias given the circumstances

cirio *NOUN MASC* candle

ciruela *NOUN FEM* plum; ciruela pasa prune

cirugía *NOUN FEM* surgery; cirugía estética plastic surgery; cirugía láser laser surgery

cirujano, cirujana *NOUN MASC, FEM* surgeon

cisne NOUN MASC **swan**

cita NOUN FEM ❶ **appointment**; tengo cita con el médico I've got an appointment to see the doctor, el dentista me ha dado cita para el jueves the dentist has given me an appointment for Thursday, pedir cita to make an appointment, llamé al abogado para pedir cita I phoned the lawyer to make an appointment ❷ **date**; esta noche tengo una cita I've got a date tonight, I'm meeting somebody tonight ❸ **quotation**

citar VERB [17] ❶ **to quote** *(a writer or book)* ❷ **to mention**; citó algunos casos he mentioned a few cases ❸ **to give an appointment**; el médico me ha citado para esta tarde the doctor's given me an appointment for this afternoon

citarse REFLEXIVE VERB [17] **to arrange to meet**; se citaron para las cinco they arranged to meet at five

ciudad NOUN FEM ❶ **town**; ciudad dormitorio dormitory town ❷ **city** ❸ ciudad universitaria university campus

ciudadano, ciudadana NOUN MASC, FEM **citizen**

civil ADJECTIVE ❶ **civil**; un matrimonio civil a civil marriage ❷ **civilian**; la población civil the civilian population

civil NOUN MASC & FEM **civilian**

clarinete NOUN MASC **clarinet**

claro ADJECTIVE ❶ **light**; un verde claro a light green, un chico de ojos claros a guy with light-coloured eyes *(blue, green, or grey: opposite of 'dark eyes')* ❷ **bright**; un día claro a bright, sunny day ❸ **clear**; está muy claro it's very clear, no lo

tengo muy claro I'm not very clear about it

claro ADVERB ❶ **clearly**; no habla claro he doesn't speak clearly, lo veo claro I can see it clearly ❷ ¡claro! of course!, claro que sí of course, claro que no of course not

clase NOUN FEM ❶ **kind, type**; ¿qué clase de material? what kind of material? ❷ de primera clase top-quality ❸ **class**; la clase de matemáticas the maths class, entro en clase a las nueve I start my classes at nine, toda la clase ha ido al museo the whole class has gone to the museum ❹ dar clase de algo to teach something, da clase de física en un colegio he teaches physics in a school, dar clase a alguien to give somebody lessons, me da clases de inglés he gives me English lessons ❺ dar clase de algo to have lessons in something, da clases de música por las tardes she has music lessons in the evenings ❻ **classroom**; ¿en qué clase están? what classroom are they in? ❼ clase social social class, un familia de clase media a middle-class family ❽ **class** *(of travel)*; viajar en primera clase to travel first class, clase turista economy class, clase ejecutiva/clase preferente business class ❾ **class** *(elegance)*; tener clase to have class

clásico, clásica ADJECTIVE ❶ **classical** *(decoration)* ❷ **traditional** *(method)* ❸ **classic**; la clásica broma the classic joke

clasificación NOUN FEM ❶ **classification** ❷ **qualifying** *(in sports)*; sin posibilidades de clasificación with no chance of qualifying ❸ **placings** *(in sports)*; la clasificación es la siguiente ... the placings are as follows ...

a
b
c
d
e
f
g
h
i
j
k
l
m
n
ñ
o
p
q
r
s
t
u
v
w
x
y
z

clasificar VERB [31] **to sort into order** *(papers, for example)*

clasificarse REFLEXIVE VERB [17] **to qualify**; clasificarse para la final to qualify for the final

clavar VERB [17] **to hammer**; clavar un clavo en la pared to hammer a nail into the wall

clave NOUN FEM **❶ key** *(to a mystery or problem)*; la clave es ... the key to it is ... **❷ code**; mensaje en clave coded message **❸ clef** *(in music)*; clave de sol treble clef

clave ADJECTIVE **key**; un factor clave a key factor

clavija NOUN FEM **❶ peg ❷ plug** *(for an electrical appliance)*

clavo NOUN MASC **❶ nail ❷ clove** *(spice)*

claxon NOUN MASC **horn**

clic NOUN MASC **click**; un doble clic a double click, hacer doble clic to double-click, haz clic dos veces en el icono click the icon twice

cliente, **clienta** NOUN MASC, FEM **❶ customer ❷ client** *(of a company or a lawyer)* **❸ guest** *(in a hotel)*

clima NOUN MASC **climate**

climático, **climática** ADJECTIVE **climactic**

climatizado, **climatizada** ADJECTIVE **air-conditioned**

clínica NOUN FEM **private hospital**

clip NOUN MASC **❶ paper clip ❷ un clip para el pelo a hairgrip ❸ de clip clip-on**

cliquear VERB [17] **to click**

club NOUN MASC **club**; club de jóvenes youth club

coartada NOUN FEM **alibi**

cobarde NOUN MASC & FEM **coward**

cobarde ADJECTIVE **cowardly**

cobaya NOUN FEM **guinea pig**

cobrador, **cobradora** NOUN MASC, FEM **conductor**

cobrar VERB [17] **❶ to get paid**; cobro mil cuatro cientos euros al mes I get paid one thousand four hundred euros a month, cobramos a fin de mes we get paid at the end of the month, cobra el paro he's on unemployment benefit, cobra bastante de pensión he gets a good pension **❷ to charge**; me cobraron sesenta euros por todo they charged me sixty euros for everything, cobrar de más to overcharge, cobrar de menos to undercharge **❸ to collect**; han venido a cobrar la deuda they've come to collect the money owing **❹ to draw**; cobrar un cheque to draw a cheque, cuando vengas a cobrar tu pensión when you come to draw your pension

cobre NOUN MASC **copper**

cocaína NOUN FEM **cocaine**

cocer VERB [41] **❶ to boil** *(in water)*; cocer algo a fuego lento to simmer something over a low heat **❷ to bake**

coche NOUN MASC **❶ car**; he venido en coche I came by car, coche bomba car bomb, coche de alquiler hire car, coche de carreras racing car, coche patrulla patrol car **❷ carriage**, **coach** *(on a train)*; ¿qué número de coche es? what coach number is it?, coche cama sleeping car, coche restaurante restaurant car ❸ coche de bomberos fire engine

cochecito de bebé NOUN MASC **pram**

cochera NOUN FEM **bus depot**

cocido NOUN MASC **stew** *(made with chickpeas)*

cocina NOUN FEM ❶ **kitchen**; ¿dónde está la cocina? where's the kitchen? ❷ **cooker**; cocina de gas gas cooker, cocina eléctrica electric cooker ❸ **cooking**; la cocina española Spanish cooking, un libro de cocina a cookery book

cocinar VERB [17] **to cook**; cocinar algo a fuego lento to cook something on a low heat

cocinero, cocinera NOUN MASC, FEM **cook**

coco NOUN MASC ❶ **coconut** ❷ *(informal)* **head**; me duele el coco I've got a headache
· darle al coco *(informal)* to think
· comerse el coco *(informal)* to worry your head off; no te comas el coco don't worry your head about it
· comerle el coco a alguien *(informal)* to try to convince somebody

cocodrilo NOUN MASC **crocodile**

cóctel NOUN MASC ❶ **cocktail** ❷ **cocktail party**

código NOUN MASC **code**; código de barras bar code, código postal postcode

codo NOUN MASC **elbow**

codorniz NOUN FEM **quail**

coger VERB [3] ❶ **to take**; voy a coger el autobús I'm going to take the bus, ¿has cogido los paquetes que había aquí? have you taken the parcels that were here?, la cogí del brazo I took her by the arm ❷ **to get**; cogió un resfriado he got a cold, coger una insolación to get sunstroke, voy a coger entradas para el teatro I'll get tickets for the theatre ❸ coger el teléfono to answer the phone ❹ **to catch**; no pudo coger la pelota he couldn't catch the ball, ¡a que no me coges! I bet you can't catch me!, cogieron al asesino they caught the murderer, no me dio tiempo a coger el tren I didn't have time to catch the train ❺ **to pick**; coger fresas to pick strawberries, coger algo del suelo to pick something up from the floor

cogerse REFLEXIVE VERB [3] ❶ cogerse de algo to hold on to something, cógete de la barra hold on to the rail ❷ se cogieron de la mano they held hands

cogido, cogida ADJECTIVE ❶ **taken**; esta silla ya está cogida this chair is already taken ❷ ir cogidos de la mano to walk hand in hand, ir cogidos del brazo to walk arm in arm

cohibido, cohibida ADJECTIVE ❶ **self-conscious** ❷ **shy**

coincidencia NOUN FEM **coincidence**; ¡qué coincidencia! what a coincidence!, dio la coincidencia de que ... it so happened that ...

coincidir VERB [19] **to coincide**

coja, cojo, etc VERB ▸ SEE **coger**

cojín NOUN MASC **cushion**

cojo, coja ADJECTIVE ❶ **lame**; es cojo he's lame ❷ está cojo he has a limp ❸ andar a la pata coja to hop

col NOUN FEM **cabbage**; coles de Bruselas Brussels sprouts

cola NOUN FEM ❶ **tail** ❷ **queue**; hacer cola to queue up, saltarse la cola to jump the queue, me puse a la cola I joined the queue ❸ **glue**; cola de carpintero wood glue, lo pegué con cola I glued it

colada NOUN FEM **laundry**; hacer la colada to do the washing

colador NOUN MASC **strainer**

colar VERB [24] **to strain** (vegetables)

colarse REFLEXIVE VERB [24] ❶ **to jump the queue**; esa señora se ha colado that lady has jumped the queue ❷ colarse en un sitio to get in somewhere without paying, se coló en el cine he got into the cinema without paying

colcha NOUN FEM **bedspread**

colchón NOUN MASC **mattress**

cole NOUN MASC (informal) **school**

colección NOUN FEM **collection**

coleccionar VERB [17] **to collect**

coleccionista NOUN **collector**

colega NOUN MASC & FEM **colleague**

colegial, colegiala NOUN MASC, FEM **schoolboy/schoolgirl**

colegio NOUN MASC **school**; colegio público state school, colegio privado private school, un colegio de curas a catholic boys' school

coleta NOUN FEM **ponytail**

colgado, colgada ADJECTIVE ❶ colgado de algo hanging from something ❷ el teléfono está mal colgado the phone's off the hook,

¿tienes el teléfono bien colgado? have you put the phone down properly?

colgar VERB [23] ❶ **to hang** ❷ colgar la ropa to hang out the washing ❸ colgar un cuadro to put up a picture ❹ **to put down** (telephone); cuelga el teléfono put the phone down, me ha colgado she's hung up on me, no cuelgue, por favor hold the line, please

colgarse REFLEXIVE VERB [23] colgarse de algo to hang from something

coliflor NOUN FEM **cauliflower**

colilla NOUN FEM **cigarette end**

colina NOUN FEM **hill**

collar NOUN MASC ❶ **necklace**; un collar de perlas a string of pearls ❷ **collar**; el collar del perro the dog's collar

colmo NOUN MASC ❶ el colmo de la incompetencia the height of incompetence ❷ ¡esto es el colmo! this is the limit!, ¡y para colmo ...! and to cap it all ...!, sería el colmo que no viniesen it would be the limit if they didn't come

colocación NOUN FEM **job**; está buscando colocación he's looking for a job

colocar VERB [31] ❶ **to put**; colócalo ahí put it there, ¿dónde coloco esta silla? where should I put this chair? ❷ aún tenemos que colocar los muebles we still have to arrange the furniture ❸ colocar a alguien to get somebody a job, su tío lo ha colocado his uncle's got him a job

colocarse REFLEXIVE VERB [31] **to find a job**; se ha colocado muy bien she's found a very good job

Colombia NOUN FEM **Colombia**

colombiano, colombiana NOUN MASC, FEM, ADJECTIVE **Colombian**

colonia NOUN FEM ❶ **(eau de) cologne** ❷ **colony** ❸ **una colonia de vacaciones a summer camp**

coloquial ADJECTIVE **colloquial**

coloquio NOUN MASC **discussion**

color NOUN MASC **colour**; ¿de qué color es? what colour is it?, colores claros light colours, es de color azul it's blue, telas de colores coloured fabrics, televisión en color colour television

colorado, colorada ADJECTIVE **red**; ponerse colorado to go red, ¡te has puesto colorado! you've gone red!

colorante NOUN MASC **colouring**

colorear VERB [17] **to colour**; colorear algo de rojo to colour something red

colorete NOUN MASC **blusher**

columna NOUN FEM ❶ **column** ❷ **spine**; la columna vertebral the spine

columpiar VERB [17] **to push** (on a swing)

columpiarse REFLEXIVE VERB [17] **to swing**

columpio NOUN MASC **swing**

coma NOUN FEM ❶ **comma** ❷ **decimal point**; dos coma cinco two point five

coma NOUN MASC **coma**; entrar en coma to go into a coma

comadrona NOUN FEM **midwife**

comandante NOUN MASC & FEM **major**

comba NOUN FEM **skipping rope**; saltar a la comba to skip, jugar a la comba to skip

combate NOUN MASC ❶ **combat** ❷ **fight**

combatir VERB [17] **to combat**

combinación NOUN FEM **combination**

combinar VERB [17] **to combine**

combustible NOUN MASC **fuel**

comedia NOUN FEM **comedy**; una comedia musical a musical

comedor NOUN MASC ❶ **dining-room** ❷ **dining hall** ❸ **canteen**

comentar VERB [17] ❶ **to talk about**; comentamos un poco la noticia we talked a bit about the news ❷ **to mention**; me lo comentó de pasada he mentioned it to me in passing ❸ **to remark**; comentó que ... he remarked that ...

comentario NOUN MASC **comment**; sin comentarios no comment

comenzar VERB [25] **to begin**

comer VERB [18] ❶ **to eat** ❷ **to have lunch**; normalmente comemos a las dos we normally have lunch at two, ¿qué había de comer? what was for lunch? ❸ **to take** (a piece in chess or draughts); te como el caballo I take your knight

comercial ADJECTIVE **commercial**; el centro comercial de la ciudad the commercial centre of the town, un centro comercial a shopping centre

comerciante NOUN MASC & FEM ❶ **shopkeeper** ❷ **trader**

comercio NOUN MASC ❶ **trade**; el comercio de animales exóticos the

a b c d e f g h i j k l m n ñ o p q r s t u v w x y z

trade in exotic animals ❷ **shop**; un comercio pequeño a small shop

comestibles PLURAL NOUN MASC **foodstuffs**

cometa NOUN FEM ❶ **kite**; hacer volar una cometa to fly a kite ❷ **comet**

cometer VERB [18] ❶ **to commit** (a crime) ❷ **to make** (a mistake); he cometido un error I've made a mistake

cómic NOUN MASC **comic**

cómico, cómica ADJECTIVE ❶ **funny** (a situation or face) ❷ **comedy** (actor)

cómico NOUN MASC, FEM ❶ **comedian** ❷ **comedy actor/comedy actress**

comida NOUN FEM ❶ **food**; tenemos suficiente comida we have enough food, la comida rápida fast food ❷ **lunch**; a la hora de la comida at lunch time ❸ **meal**; cuatro comidas al día four meals a day, mi comida fuerte es a mediodía I have my main meal at midday

comienza, comienzo¹, etc VERB ▸ SEE **comenzar**

comienzo² NOUN MASC **beginning**; al comienzo in the beginning

comillas PLURAL NOUN FEM **inverted commas**; poner algo entre comillas to put something in inverted commas

comino NOUN MASC **cumin**
• me importa un comino (informal) I couldn't care less

comisaría NOUN FEM **police station**

comisión NOUN FEM **commission**

como ADVERB ❶ **like**; uno como este one like this, ser como to be like,

eres como tu padre you're like your father, pienso como tú I agree with you ❷ **as**; negro como el carbón as black as coal ❸ **such as**; metales como el hierro metals such as iron ❹ **around**; eran como cincuenta personas there were around fifty people, como a las dos y media around half past two ❺ como mucho at the most, como poco at least, serán como poco quince niños there will be at least fifteen children

como CONJUNCTION ❶ **since**; como estaba cerca de su casa, me pasé a verla since I was near her house, I went to see her ❷ **if**; como no tengas cuidado te vas a caer if you're not careful you'll fall ❸ como si as if, como si no me importase as if I didn't care ❹ **the way**; así es como lo hizo that's the way he did it ❺ como quieras whatever you want, however you want, hazlo como quieras do it however you want

cómo ADVERB ❶ **how**; ¿cómo estás? how are you?, ¿cómo se dice 'mesa' en francés? how do you say 'table' in French?, ¿cómo se escribe tu nombre? how do you write your name?, no sé cómo se enteraron I don't know how they found out ❷ ¿cómo es? what's it like?, ¿cómo es tu casa? what's your house like? ❸ ¿cómo? pardon? (when you haven't heard properly) ❹ (in exclamations) ¡cómo quema! it's so hot!, ¡cómo se parecen! they are so like each other!, ¡cómo no! of course!, ¡cómo! ¿no la has visto aún? what, you haven't seen her yet?

cómoda¹ NOUN FEM **chest of drawers**

comodín NOUN MASC **joker** (in cards)

cómodo, cómoda² *ADJECTIVE*
comfortable; ¿estás cómodo? are you comfortable?, un sillón muy cómodo a very comfortable armchair, ponerse cómodo to make yourself comfortable

compact disc, compacto *NOUN MASC* ❶ CD ❷ CD player

compañero, compañera *NOUN MASC, FEM* ❶ colleague; mis compañeros de trabajo my colleagues at work ❷ un compañero de clase a school mate, su compañera de piso her flatmate ❸ partner *(in a relationship)*

compañía *NOUN FEM* company; hacerle compañía a alguien to keep somebody company, el director de la compañía the company director

comparación *NOUN FEM* comparison; hacer una comparación to make a comparison, en comparación con in comparison with

comparar *VERB* [17] to compare

compartimento *NOUN MASC* compartment

compartir *VERB* [19] to share; compartir algo con alguien to share something with somebody, compartieron su comida conmigo they shared their food with me

compás *NOUN MASC* ❶ time, rhythm; llevar el compás to keep time ❷ pair of compasses

compensar *VERB* [29] to compensate

competencia *NOUN FEM* competition; nos hacen la competencia they're in competition with us

competición *NOUN FEM* competition *(in a magazine, for example)*

competir *VERB* [57] to compete

compita, compito, *etc VERB* ▸ SEE **competir**

completar *VERB* [17] to complete

completo, completa *ADJECTIVE* ❶ complete ❷ full; el hotel está completo the hotel is full, 'completo' 'no vacancies'

complicado, complicada *ADJECTIVE* complicated

complicar *VERB* [31] to complicate

complicarse *REFLEXIVE VERB* [31] to become complicated; la situación se ha complicado the situation has become complicated

componer *VERB* [11] ❶ to make up; el equipo está compuesto de once jugadores the team is made up of eleven players ❷ to compose *(music or a poem)*

componerse *REFLEXIVE VERB* [11] componerse de to be made up of

comportamiento *NOUN MASC* behaviour; mal comportamiento bad behaviour

comportarse *REFLEXIVE VERB* [17] to behave; comportarse mal to misbehave

composición *NOUN FEM* composition

compositor, compositora *NOUN MASC, FEM* composer

compra *NOUN FEM* purchase; fue una buena compra it was a good buy, ir de compras to go shopping, hacer la compra to do the shopping

comprador, **compradora** NOUN
MASC, FEM **buyer**

comprar VERB [17] ❶ **to buy**
❷ comprar algo a alguien to buy
something for somebody (as a
present), le he comprado un jersey
por su cumpleaños I've bought
him a jumper for his birthday
❸ comprar algo a alguien to buy
something from somebody, voy a
comprarle su bicicleta I'm going to
buy his bike from him

comprender VERB [18] **to
understand**; no me comprenden
they don't understand me, no
comprendo su actitud I don't
understand his attitude

comprensión NOUN FEM
comprehension; un ejercicio de
comprensión a comprehension test

comprensivo, **comprensiva**
ADJECTIVE **understanding**

compresa NOUN FEM **sanitary towel**

comprimido NOUN MASC **pill**

comprobar VERB [24] **to check**; creo
que sí, pero voy a comprobarlo
I think so, but I'm going to check it

comprometerse REFLEXIVE VERB
[17] **to promise**; se comprometió
a terminarlo para el lunes she
promised to finish it by Monday

compromiso NOUN MASC
❶ **commitment**; compromiso
político political commitment
❷ **obligation**; sin compromiso
without obligation ❸ poner a
alguien en un compromiso to put
somebody in an awkward situation,
ahora me has puesto en un
compromiso now you've put me in
an awkward situation

computador, **computadora**
NOUN MASC, FEM **computer** (large,
mainframe machine)

común ADJECTIVE **common**; en
común in common, no tenemos
nada en común we have nothing
in common, trabajar en común to
work together

comunicación NOUN FEM
❶ **communication** ❷ ponerse en
comunicación con alguien to get
in touch with someone ❸ cortarse
la comunicación to be cut off
(on the phone), se ha cortado la
comunicación I've been cut off
❹ (in transport) las comunicaciones
son buenas the communications
are good, un barrio con buena
comunicación an area with good
public transport services

comunicar VERB [31] ❶ **to inform**;
debo comunicarles que ...
I must inform you that ... ❷ **to be
engaged** (a telephone); estaba
comunicando it was engaged

comunicarse REFLEXIVE VERB [31] ❶ **to
communicate**; comunicarse por
carta to communicate by letter
❷ **to be connected**

comunidad NOUN FEM **community**;
la Comunidad Europea the
European Community

comunión NOUN FEM **communion**;
hacer la primera comunión to take
communion for the first time

con PREPOSITION ❶ **with**; lo hice con
un cuchillo I did it with a knife
❷ **to**; hablar con alguien to speak
to somebody, estar casado con
alguien to be married to somebody
❸ **and**; bistec con patatas steak
and chips, pan con mantequilla
bread and butter ❹ con tal de que

as long as, te lo dejo, con tal de que lo cuides I'll lend it to you as long as you look after it

concejal, **concejala** NOUN MASC, FEM **councillor**; su tío es concejal her uncle is a councillor

concentración NOUN FEM **concentration**

concentrar VERB [17] **to concentrate**

concentrarse REFLEXIVE VERB [17] **to concentrate**; me concentré en mi trabajo I concentrated on my work

concha NOUN FEM **shell**

concienzudo, **concienzuda** ADJECTIVE **conscientious**

concierto NOUN MASC **concert**

conclusión NOUN FEM **conclusion**; llegar a una conclusión to reach a conclusion

concurrido, **concurrida** ADJECTIVE **❶ busy** (bar or street) **❷ well-attended** (concert or exhibition)

concurso NOUN MASC **competition**; concurso hípico show-jumping competition; programa concurso quiz show

conde NOUN MASC **count**

condesa NOUN FEM **countess**

condición NOUN FEM **condition**; a condición de que/con la condición de que on condition that

condón NOUN MASC **condom**

conducir VERB [60] **❶ to drive**; yo conduzco I'll drive **❷ to lead**; el camino que conduce al pueblo the road that leads to the village

conducta NOUN FEM **behaviour**

conductor, **conductora** NOUN MASC, FEM **driver**

conduje, **condujo** VERB
▸ SEE **conducir**

conduzca, **conduzco**, etc VERB
▸ SEE **conducir**

conectar VERB [17] **to connect**; el teléfono aún no está conectado the telephone's not connected yet

conejillo de Indias NOUN MASC **guinea pig**

conejo, **coneja** NOUN MASC, FEM **rabbit**

conexión NOUN FEM **connection**

conferencia NOUN FEM **❶ lecture**; una conferencia de prensa a press conference **❷ long-distance call**; poner una conferencia a alguien to make a long distance call to somebody

confesar VERB [29] **to confess**

confianza NOUN FEM **❶ trust**; una persona de confianza a trustworthy person **❷ tener confianza en alguien** to have confidence in somebody, tiene mucha confianza en sí mismo he's very self-confident **❸ tener confianza con alguien** to know somebody very well, tenemos mucha confianza we know each other very well

confiar VERB [32] **to trust**; confío en ti I trust you

confidencia NOUN FEM **confidence**; hacerle una confidencia a alguien to tell somebody something in confidence

confirmar VERB [17] **to confirm**

confitería NOUN FEM **patisserie**

a b c d e f g h i j k l m n ñ o p q r s t u v w x y z

confitura NOUN FEM **fruit preserve**

conforme ADJECTIVE ❶ estar conforme to agree, no estoy conforme I don't agree, ¿conforme? do you agree? ❷ ¡conforme! ok!, estar conforme con algo to be happy with something

confortable ADJECTIVE **comfortable**

confortar VERB [17] **to comfort**

confundir VERB [19] ❶ **to confuse**; no me confundas don't confuse me ❷ **to get mixed up**; he confundido las fechas I've got the dates mixed up ❸ confundir a alguien con alguien to mistake somebody for somebody, la confundí con Cristina I mistook her for Cristina

confundirse REFLEXIVE VERB [19] ❶ **to make a mistake**; creo que te has confundido con la cuenta I think you've made a mistake with the bill ❷ se confundió de carpeta he got the wrong folder

confusión NOUN FEM **confusion**

confuso, confusa ADJECTIVE ❶ **confused**; estaba confuso he was confused ❷ **confusing**; esto es muy confuso this is very confusing

congelado, congelada ADJECTIVE ❶ **frozen**; ¡estoy congelada! I'm freezing!, alimentos congelados frozen food ❷ murió congelado he died from exposure ❸ tenía un dedo congelado he had frostbite in one finger

congelador NOUN MASC ❶ **freezer compartment** ❷ **deep freezer**

congelar VERB [17] **to freeze**

congelarse REFLEXIVE VERB [17] **to freeze**; ¡me estoy congelando! I'm freezing!

conjugar VERB [28] **to conjugate**

conjunto¹, conjunta ADJECTIVE **joint**; un esfuerzo conjunto a joint effort

conjunto² NOUN MASC ❶ **group**; un conjunto de personas a group of people, un conjunto de música a pop group ❷ **collection**; un conjunto de cosas a collection of things ❸ **outfit**; ¡qué conjunto más bonito! what a nice outfit!, un conjunto de falda y chaleco a matching skirt and waistcoat, hacer conjunto con algo to match something ❹ en conjunto as a whole

conmigo PRONOUN ❶ **with me**; ven conmigo come with me ❷ **to me**; no habló conmigo he didn't talk to me ❸ conmigo mismo/misma with myself, no estoy contento conmigo mismo I'm not happy with myself

conocer VERB [35] ❶ **to know**; conozco la historia I know that story, los conozco de vista I know them by sight, se conocen bien they know each other well ❷ **to meet**; ¿conoces a su hermana? have you met her sister?, aún no conozco al nuevo profesor I haven't met the new teacher yet ❸ ¿conoces España? have you been to Spain? ❹ **to recognize**; te conocí por la forma de andar I recognized you by the way you walk

conocido, conocida NOUN MASC, FEM **acquaintance**

conocido ADJECTIVE ❶ **well-known** (actor or song) ❷ **familiar**; una cara conocida a familiar face

conocimiento NOUN MASC **knowledge**

conozca, **conozco**, *etc VERB*
▸ SEE **conocer**

conque *CONJUNCTION* so; conque esta es tu novia so, this is your girlfriend

consecuencia *NOUN FEM* consequence

conseguir *VERB* [64] ❶ to achieve; han conseguido su objetivo they've achieved their objective ❷ to get; he conseguido un trabajo I've got a job

consejero, **consejera** *NOUN MASC, FEM* ❶ adviser ❷ minister *(in certain autonomous Spanish regions)* ❸ board member *(of a company)*; consejero/consejera delegado/ delegada managing director

consejo *NOUN MASC* ❶ piece of advice; te voy a dar un consejo I'm going to give you a piece of advice ❷ consejos advice no hacen caso de mis consejos, they aren't following my advice ❸ board; el consejo de administración the board of directors, consejo escolar board of governors *(of a school)* ❹ meeting; un consejo de ministros a cabinet meeting ❺ council; el Consejo de Europa the Council of Europe

conserje *NOUN MASC & FEM* ❶ caretaker *(in a school or a public building)* ❷ receptionist *(in a hotel)*

conservador, **conservadora** *NOUN MASC, FEM*

conservador *ADJECTIVE* conservative

conservar *VERB* [17] ❶ to preserve *(food)* ❷ to keep up *(traditions)* ❸ to keep; conservo todas tus cartas I keep all your letters, intenta conservar la calma try to keep calm

conservarse *REFLEXIVE VERB* [17] to keep *(food)*; las manzanas se conservan bien apples keep well

conservas *PLURAL NOUN FEM* tinned food

considerable *ADJECTIVE* considerable; un número considerable de estudiantes a considerable number of students

consideración *NOUN FEM* consideration; tomar algo en consideración to take something into consideration

considerar *VERB* [17] to consider

consiga, **consigo**[1], **consiguiendo**, *etc VERB* ▸ SEE **conseguir**

consigna *NOUN FEM* left-luggage office

consigo[2] *PRONOUN* ❶ with him/ her; lo trae consigo he's bringing it with him/she's bringing it with her ❷ consigo mismo with himself, consigo misma with herself, no está contento consigo mismo he is not happy with himself ❸ consigo mismo to himself, consigo misma to herself, estaba hablando consigo misma she was talking to herself ❹ with them; el dinero que tenían consigo the money they had with them ❺ with you *(talking politely to somebody)*; si usted quiere lo puede traer consigo if you wish, you can bring it with you

consistir *VERB* [19] consistir en algo to consist of something, consiste en tres piezas de madera it consists of three pieces of wood, el trabajo consiste en … the job involves …

consola *NOUN FEM* console; una consola de juegos a games console

consonante NOUN FEM **consonant**

constante ADJECTIVE **constant**

constipado¹, **constipada** ADJECTIVE estar constipado to have a cold

constipado² NOUN MASC **cold**; coger un constipado to catch a cold

constiparse REFLEXIVE VERB [17] to **catch cold**

constructor, **constructora** NOUN MASC, FEM **builder**

construir VERB [54] to **build**

construya, **construyendo**, **construyo**, etc VERB ▸ SEE **construir**

cónsul NOUN MASC **consul**

consulado NOUN MASC **consulate**

consulta NOUN FEM ❶ hacer una consulta to ask something ❷ de consulta reference, libro de consulta reference book ❸ **surgery**; tiene su consulta en esta calle his surgery is in this street, horas de consulta surgery hours

consultar VERB [17] ❶ to **consult**; consultarle algo a alguien to consult somebody about something ❷ tengo que consultarlo en diccionario I have to look it up in the dictionary

consultorio NOUN MASC **surgery**

consumición NOUN FEM **drink** (in bar, café); consumición mínima cuatro euros minimum charge four euros

consumo NOUN **consumption**

contable NOUN MASC & FEM **accountant**

contactar VERB [17] to **contact**; contactar con alguien to contact somebody

contacto NOUN MASC ❶ **contact**; estar en contacto to be in contact ❷ **ignition** (in a car)

contado NOUN MASC al contado cash, pagar al contado to pay cash, lo compré al contado I paid for it in cash

contador NOUN MASC **meter**

contagiar VERB [17] to **pass on** (an illness); no me beses, no quiero contagiarte el resfriado don't kiss me, I don't want to give you my cold

contagiarse REFLEXIVE VERB [17] to **become infected**; se ha contagiado de su hermana she's got it from her sister

contaminación NOUN FEM ❶ **pollution** ❷ **contamination** (by radioactivity)

contaminar VERB [17] ❶ to **pollute** (air or water, for example) ❷ to **contaminate** (with radioactivity)

contar VERB [24] ❶ to **count**; cuenta el dinero count the money ❷ contar con alguien to count on somebody, nunca puedo contar contigo I can never count on you ❸ to **tell**; cuéntamelo tell me about it, le conté el secreto I told him the secret ❹ to **count**; eso no cuenta that doesn't count, el trabajo cuenta para mi nota final the essay counts towards my final mark

contenedor NOUN MASC ❶ **container** ❷ **skip** ❸ un contenedor de vidrio a bottle bank

contener VERB [9] ❶ to **contain**; no contiene conservantes it does not contain preservatives ❷ **contener las lágrimas** to hold back the tears, **contener la risa** to stop yourself laughing, **contener la respiración** to hold your breath

contenido NOUN MASC ❶ **contents**; **el contenido de la botella** the contents of the bottle ❷ **content**; **el contenido del libro** the content of the book

contento, contenta ADJECTIVE ❶ **happy**; **los niños estaban muy contentos** the children were very happy ❷ **pleased**; **estoy contento de verte** I'm pleased to see you

contestación NOUN FEM ❶ **answer**; **no nos dio una contestación** he didn't give us an answer ❷ **reply**; **quedo a la espera de su contestación** looking forward to your reply

contestador (automático) NOUN MASC **answering machine**

contestar VERB [17] ❶ **answer**; **contestar el teléfono** to answer the phone, **no contestó** he didn't answer ❷ **reply**; **no ha contestado a mi carta** he hasn't replied to my letter

contexto NOUN MASC **context**

contigo PRONOUN ❶ **with you**; **yo voy contigo** I'll go with you ❷ **to you**; **no estoy hablando contigo** I'm not talking to you ❸ **contigo mismo/misma** with yourself, **¿estás contento contigo mismo?** are you pleased with yourself?

continente NOUN MASC **continent**

continuación NOUN FEM **continuation**; **a continuación** ... next ...

continuar VERB [20] **to continue**; **continuaron hablando** they went on talking, **continuará** to be continued

continuo, continua ADJECTIVE **constant**

contra PREPOSITION ❶ **against**; **se apoyó contra la pared** he leant against the wall, **son dos contra uno** it's two against one, **estar en contra de algo** to be against something ❷ **chocar contra algo** to run into something

contrabandista NOUN MASC & FEM **smuggler**

contrabando NOUN MASC ❶ **smuggling**; **pasar algo de contrabando** to smuggle something ❷ **smuggled goods**

contrario¹, contraria ADJECTIVE ❶ **opposite**; **la dirección contraria** the opposite direction, **soy contrario a las reformas** I'm opposed to the reforms, **pasarse al bando contrario** to change sides, **todo lo contrario** quite the opposite ❷ **de lo contrario** otherwise

contrario² NOUN MASC ❶ **opposite**; **al contrario** on the contrary, **al contrario, me gusta mucho** on the contrary, I like it a lot **es al contrario** it's the opposite way round ❷ **por el contrario** on the other hand

contrarreloj ADJECTIVE **a contrarreloj** against the clock

contraseña NOUN FEM **password**

contrato NOUN MASC **contract**

contribución NOUN FEM ❶ **contribution** ❷ **tax**

contribuir *VERB* [17] to contribute

control *NOUN MASC* ❶ control; bajo control under control, control de pasaportes passport control, control remoto remote control ❷ llevar el control de algo to keep a check on something ❸ test

control *NOUN MASC* control de la natalidad birth control

controlar *VERB* [17] ❶ to control ❷ to keep a check on ❸ controlar la línea to watch your weight

controvertido, controvertida *ADJECTIVE* controversial; una decisión controvertida a controversial decision

convencer *VERB* [44] ❶ to convince ❷ to persuade; le convencimos para que fuera we persuaded him to go ❸ no me convence mucho la idea I'm not sure about the idea

conveniente *ADJECTIVE* ❶ convenient ❷ advisable

convenir *VERB* [15] ❶ te conviene preguntar you should ask, te conviene descansar you should rest, conviene informarse antes it's advisable to find out in advance ❷ *(in negative sentences)* no te conviene cansarte you should avoid tiring yourself out, por ese sueldo no te conviene for that salary it's not worth your while ❸ convenir en algo to agree on something ❹ sueldo a convenir salary negotiable

convento *NOUN MASC* convent

convenza, convenzo, *etc VERB* ▸ SEE **convencer**

conversación *NOUN FEM* conversation

convertir *VERB* [14] ❶ convertir algo en algo to turn something into something, convertir agua en vino to turn water into wine, convertir libras en euros to convert pounds into euros ❷ to convert *(to a religion)*

convertirse *REFLEXIVE VERB* [14] ❶ convertirse en algo to turn into something ❷ to convert; convertirse al budismo to convert to Buddhism

convierta, convierto, *etc VERB* ▸ SEE **convertir**

coñac *NOUN MASC* brandy

cooperar *VERB* [17] to cooperate

copa *NOUN FEM* ❶ wine glass; una copa de vino a glass of wine ❷ drink; te invito a una copa I'll buy you a drink, tomar una copa to have a drink

copia *NOUN FEM* copy; copia de seguridad back-up copy

copiar *VERB* [17] ❶ to copy ❷ to make a copy of ❸ to copy down

coraje *NOUN MASC* courage

corazón *NOUN MASC* heart; un ataque al corazón a heart attack, una persona de buen corazón a kind-hearted person
• partirle el corazón a alguien to break someone's heart

corbata *NOUN FEM* tie

corcho *NOUN MASC* cork

cordero *NOUN MASC* lamb; una pierna de cordero a leg of lamb, una chuleta de cordero a lamb chop

cordón *NOUN MASC* string; un cordón de zapato a shoelace

coro NOUN MASC **choir**; a coro in chorus

corona NOUN FEM ❶ **crown** ❷ **wreath**; una corona de flores a wreath of flowers

coronel NOUN MASC **colonel**

corral NOUN MASC **farmyard**

correa NOUN FEM ❶ **strap**; correa de reloj watchstrap ❷ **lead** (for a dog)

correctamente ADVERB ❶ **politely** ❷ **correctly**; ¿has rellenado el formulario correctamente? have you filled in the form correctly?

correcto, correcta ADJECTIVE ❶ **correct**; la respuesta correcta the correct answer ❷ **polite**; siempre es muy correcto he's always very correct

corrector ortográfico NOUN MASC **spelling checker**

corredor, corredora NOUN MASC, FEM ❶ **runner**; corredor de fondo long-distance runner ❷ corredor de coches racing driver

corregir VERB [48] **to correct**

correo NOUN MASC **post**; mandar algo por correo to send something by post, echar algo al correo to post something, correo aéreo airmail, correo electrónico electronic mail, (la oficina de) correos the post office, correo urgente special delivery

correr VERB [18] ❶ **to run**; crucé la calle corriendo I ran across the street, salió corriendo de la habitación she ran out of the room, bajar las escaleras corriendo to run down the stairs, echar a correr to start running, correr mucho to run very fast (a person), to drive very fast (a driver), to go very fast (a car or bike) ❷ ¡corre, vístete! hurry up and get dressed!, hice la comida corriendo I made dinner quickly, vino corriendo a verme she rushed to see me, se tiene que marchar corriendo he has to rush off ❸ correr las cortinas to draw the curtains ❹ no debemos correr riesgos we shouldn't take any risks ❺ correr peligro to be in danger

correspondencia NOUN FEM **correspondence**

correspondiente ADJECTIVE **corresponding**

corresponsal NOUN MASC & FEM **correspondent** (in journalism)

corrida NOUN FEM **bullfight**

corrido, corrida ADJECTIVE **embarrassed**

corriente NOUN FEM ❶ **current** (water or electricity); me ha dado la corriente I got an electric shock, no hay corriente there's no electricity ❷ **draught**; hace corriente there's a draught

corriente ADJECTIVE ❶ **common**; un error muy corriente a very common mistake, una chica normal y corriente an ordinary kind of girl, lo más corriente es ... the most usual thing is ... ❷ agua corriente running water ❸ estar al corriente de algo to be aware of something, mantener a alguien al corriente de algo to keep somebody up to date about something

corrija, corrijo, etc VERB ►SEE **corregir**

corrompido, corrompida ADJECTIVE **corrupt**

corrupto, **corrupta** ADJECTIVE
corrupt

cortacésped NOUN MASC
lawnmower

cortado[1] NOUN MASC **small coffee**
(with a dash of milk)

cortado[2], **cortada** ADJECTIVE
❶ **closed** (a road or street) ❷ la
leche está cortada the milk is sour,
la mayonesa está cortada the
mayonnaise has separated ❸ ser
muy cortado (informal) to be very
shy, ser un poco cortado (informal)
to be a bit shy ❹ estar cortado
(informal) to be embarrassed

cortar VERB [17] ❶ **to cut**; cortar un
pastel to cut a cake, cortar algo
por la mitad to cut something in
two, cortar algo a rodajas to slice
something ❷ cortar el césped to
mow the lawn ❸ **to chop**; cortar
leña to chop wood, cortar un
árbol to chop down a tree ❹ **to
cut off**; nos han cortado la luz our
electricity has been cut off, corta
esa punta cut this end off

cortarse REFLEXIVE VERB [17] ❶ **to cut
oneself**; me he cortado la mano
I've cut my hand ❷ cortarse el pelo
to have your hair cut, mañana me
voy a cortar el pelo I'm going to
have my hair cut tomorrow ❸ se ha
cortado el agua the water's been
cut off ❹ **to curdle** ❺ (informal) **to
get embarrassed**; ¡no te cortes!
don't get embarrassed

cortaúñas NOUN MASC **nail clippers**

corte[1] NOUN MASC ❶ **cut**; hacerse
un corte to cut yourself, se hizo
un corte en el dedo he cut his
finger, un corte de pelo a haircut,
ha habido un corte de agua the
water's been cut off ❷ corte

y confección dressmaking
❸ (informal) **embarrassment**;
me da corte preguntar I'm
embarrassed to ask, ¡qué corte!
how embarrassing!

corte[2] NOUN FEM ❶ **court** ❷ las Cortes
the Spanish Parliament

cortés ADJECTIVE **polite**

corteza NOUN FEM ❶ **bark** (of a tree)
❷ **rind** (of cheese) ❸ **crust** (of bread)
❹ **peel** (of an orange or a lemon)

cortina NOUN FEM **curtain**

corto, **corta** ADJECTIVE **short**

cosa NOUN FEM ❶ **thing**; te he
comprado una cosa I've bought
something for you, ¿qué tal van
las cosas? how are things going?,
se llevó todas sus cosas he took all
his things, ¡qué cosa más rara! how
strange! ❷ cualquier cosa anything
❸ alguna cosa something, por si
pasa alguna cosa in case something
happens ❹ alguna cosa anything
(in questions), ¿buscas alguna cosa
en especial? are you looking for
anything in particular?, ¿quiere
alguna otra cosa? do you want
anything else?

cosecha NOUN FEM ❶ **harvest** ❷ **crop**
❸ **vintage**

cosechar VERB [17] **to harvest**

coser VERB [18] **to sew**

cosmético[1] NOUN MASC **cosmetic**

cosmético[2], **cosmética** ADJECTIVE
cosmetic

cosquillas PLURAL NOUN FEM hacerle
cosquillas a alguien to tickle
somebody, tener cosquillas to be
ticklish

costa NOUN FEM **coast**

costado NOUN MASC **side**

costar VERB [24] ❶ **to cost**; ¿cuánto cuesta? how much is it?, cuesta muy caro it's very expensive, la comida cuesta poco food is cheap, me costó barato it didn't cost me very much ❷ **to be hard**; cuesta mucho entenderlo it's very hard to understand, cuesta un poco acostumbrarse it takes a bit of getting used to, me costó hacerlo I found it difficult to do

Costa Rica NOUN FEM **Costa Rica**

costarricense NOUN MASC, FEM, ADJECTIVE **Costa Rican**

coste NOUN MASC **cost**

costilla NOUN FEM **rib**

costoso, **costosa** ADJECTIVE **expensive**

costra NOUN FEM **scab**

costumbre NOUN FEM ❶ **habit**; coger la costumbre de hacer algo to get into the habit of doing something, tengo la costumbre de leer un poco antes de dormir I normally read for a bit before I go to sleep, por costumbre out of habit ❷ de costumbre usual, el lugar de costumbre the usual place ❸ **custom** (in a country or place)

costura NOUN FEM ❶ **needlework** ❷ **seam**

cotidiano, **cotidiana** ADJECTIVE **daily**

cotilla NOUN MASC & FEM, ADJECTIVE **gossip**; es muy cotilla he's such a gossip

cotillear VERB [17] **to gossip**

cráneo NOUN FEM **skull**

creación NOUN FEM **creation**

creador, **creadora** NOUN MASC, FEM **creator**

creador ADJECTIVE **creative**

crear VERB [17] **to create**

crecer VERB [35] ❶ **to grow**; ¡cuánto has crecido! you've really grown! ❷ **to grow up**; creció en Escocia she grew up in Scotland

crédito NOUN MASC ❶ **credit** (in a shop, for example); tengo crédito aquí they give me credit here ❷ **loan**; me han concedido el crédito they've granted me the loan, crédito hipotecario mortgage

creer VERB [37] ❶ **to think**; creo que se llama Nekane I think she's called Nekane, ¿crees que me llamará? do you think he'll phone me?, creo que sí I think so, no creo I don't think so ❷ **to believe**; no creo en el destino I don't believe in fate, ¡no lo puedo creer! I don't believe it!

creíble ADJECTIVE **believable**

crema NOUN FEM **cream**; crema hidratante moisturizer, crema bronceadora suntan lotion

cremallera NOUN FEM **zip**; subirse la cremallera to do up your zip

crepúsculo NOUN MASC **twilight**

creyendo, **creyó**, etc VERB ►SEE **creer**

crezca, **crezco**, etc VERB ►SEE **crecer**

cría NOUN FEM **baby animal**; una cría de leopardo a baby leopard

criada NOUN FEM **maid**

criado NOUN MASC **servant**

criar *VERB* [17] **❶ to bring up**; lo crió su tía he was brought up by his aunt **❷ to raise**; criar ganado to raise cattle

criarse *REFLEXIVE VERB* [17] **to grow up**; se crió en un pueblo he grew up in a village

crimen *NOUN MASC* **❶ crime**; cometer un crimen to commit a crime **❷ murder**

criminal *NOUN MASC & FEM* **criminal**

crío, cría *NOUN MASC, FEM* **child**

crisis *NOUN FEM* **crisis**; estar en crisis to be in crisis, sufrir una crisis nerviosa to have a nervous breakdown

cristal *NOUN MASC* **❶ glass**; viene en botella de cristal it comes in a glass bottle **❷ cristal**; cristal tallado cut glass **❸ window pane**; tengo que limpiar los cristales del salón I've got to clean the sitting-room windows, la pelota rompió un cristal the ball broke a window **❹ piece of broken glass**; el suelo estaba lleno de cristales the floor was covered with broken glass

cristianismo *NOUN MASC* **Christianity**

cristiano, cristiana *NOUN MASC, FEM, ADJECTIVE* **Christian**

Cristo *NOUN MASC* **Christ**

criterio *NOUN MASC* **❶ criterion ❷ judgement**

crítica *NOUN FEM* **❶ criticism**; recibió duras críticas he's come in for a lot of harsh criticism **❷ review**; la película ha recibido muy buenas críticas the film has had very good reviews

criticar *VERB* [31] **❶ to criticize ❷ to review**

cromo *NOUN MASC* **sticker**

cruce *NOUN MASC (PLURAL* die **cruces) ❶ crossroads ❷** 'cruce peligroso' 'dangerous junction' **❸ crossing**; cruce de peatones pedestrian crossing

crucero *NOUN MASC* **cruise**

crucigrama *NOUN MASC* **crossword**

crudo, cruda *ADJECTIVE* **❶ raw**; una zanahoria cruda a raw carrot **❷** la verdura aún está cruda the vegetables aren't cooked yet **❸ harsh**; la cruda realidad the harsh reality

cruel *ADJECTIVE* **cruel**

crueldad *NOUN FEM* **cruelty**; los trataron con gran crueldad they were treated with great cruelty

cruz *NOUN FEM* **❶ cross ❷** ¿cara o cruz? heads or tails?

cruzar *VERB* [22] **to cross**; ten cuidado al cruzar be careful when you cross the road, crucé la calle corriendo I ran across the road, cruzar los brazos to cross your arms

cruzarse *REFLEXIVE VERB* [22] **❶ to intersect** *(roads, for example)* **❷ to pass each other**; los dos coches se cruzaron the two cars passed each other **❸** me crucé con ella en la calle I met her in the street

Cruz Roja *NOUN FEM* **Red Cross**

cuaderno *NOUN MASC* **❶ exercise book ❷ notebook**

cuadra *NOUN FEM* **stable**

cuadrado¹, cuadrada *ADJECTIVE* **square**; de forma cuadrada square-shaped

cuadrado² NOUN MASC **square**

cuadro NOUN MASC ❶ **painting**
❷ **picture** ❸ a cuadros/de cuadros
checked, una tela a cuadros a piece
of checked material

cual PRONOUN ❶ el cual/la cual/los
cuales/las cuales who, pregunté
a mi hermano, el cual me dio las
señas I asked my brother, who gave
me the address ❷ el cual/la cual/
los cuales/las cuales whom, los
familiares a los cuales invité the
relatives whom he invited ❸ el cual/
la cual/los cuales/las cuales which,
los instrumentos con los cuales se
hace la operación the instruments
with which the operation is carried
out ❹ lo cual which, no ha llamado,
lo cual es extraño he hasn't rung,
which is strange ❺ cada cual
everybody ❻ por lo cual therefore

cuál PRONOUN ❶ **which**; ¿cuál te
gusta? which do you like? ❷ **what**;
¿cuál es el problema? what's the
problem?

cualesquiera ADJECTIVE, PRONOUN
▸ SEE **cualquiera**

cualidad NOUN FEM **quality**

cualquier ADJECTIVE ▸ SEE **cualquiera**

cualquiera ADJECTIVE (PLURAL die
cualesquiera) ('cualquiera' becomes
'cualquier' before a singular noun)
any; en un país cualquiera in any
country, cualquier cosa anything,
cualquier persona anybody, si por
cualquier motivo if for any reason

cualquiera PRONOUN ❶ **anybody**,
anyone; cualquiera sabe algo así
anybody knows that sort of thing
❷ **either**, **both**; '¿cuál de los dos
quieres?' – 'cualquiera' 'which of
the two do you want?' – 'either'

❸ **whichever** (when referring to
more than two people or things); coge
cualquiera de los que hay ahí pick
whichever you want from the ones
that are there

cuando CONJUNCTION **when**; cuando
estuve en Barcelona when I was
in Barcelona, cuando la vea the
próxima semana when I see her
next week

cuándo ADVERB **when?**; ¿cuándo la
conociste? when did you meet her?,
¿desde cuándo? since when?

cuanto¹, **cuanta** ADJECTIVE ❶ **as
much as**; cuanta tela necesites as
much fabric as you need ❷ cuantos/
cuantas as many as, compra
cuantos libros necesites buy as
many books as you need ❸ unos
cuantos a few, unos cuantos
empleados a few employees

cuanto PRONOUN ❶ tengo cuanto
necesito I've got everything I need
❷ cuantos/cuantas as many as,
coge cuantas quieras take as many
as you want ❸ unos cuantos a few

cuanto² ADVERB ❶ **as much as**; llama
cuanto quieras phone as much as
you want ❷ cuanto más the more,
cuanto más insiste, menos quiero
to, the more he insists, the less I want
to, cuanto menos ruido hagas
mejor the less noise you make, the
better ❸ cuanto antes as soon as
possible ❹ en cuanto pueda as soon
as I can

cuánto¹, **cuánta** ADJECTIVE ❶ cuánto,
cuánta how much, ¿cuánto café
quieres? how much coffee do you
want? ❷ cuántos/cuántas how
many, ¿cuántas tazas saco? how
many cups should I put out? ❸ (in
exclamations) ¡cuántas personas

hay! there are so many people!, ¡cuánta comida has hecho! you've made so much food! ❹ (in time) ¿cuanto tiempo has tardado en hacerlo? how long did you take to do it?, ¿cada cuánto tiempo la ves? how often do you see her?

cuánto PRONOUN ❶ cuánto, cuánta how much, 'pon agua' – '¿cuánta?' 'add some water – 'how much?' ❷ cuántos, cuántas how many, dime cuántos necesitas tell me how many you need ❸ **how long** (in time); ¿cuánto se tarda en llegar? how long does it take to get there?, ¿cada cuánto la llamas? how often do you call her? ❹ (in exclamations) ¡cuántas hay! there are so many!, ¡cuánto ha quedado! there's so much left!, ¡cuánto has tardado! you've taken so long!

cuánto² ADVERB ❶ **how much**; ¿cuánto cuesta? how much is it?, no sabes cuánto te he echado de menos you don't know how much I've missed you ❷ ¿cuánto mide la mesa? what's the size of the table?, ¿cuánto mide de ancho? how wide is it? ❸ (in exclamations) ¡cuánto te quiero! I love you so much!

cuarenta NUMBER **forty**; mi madre tiene cuarenta años my mum's forty, cuarenta y siete forty-seven

cuaresma NOUN FEM **Lent**

cuarta NOUN FEM **fourth gear**; meter la cuarta to change into fourth

cuartel NOUN **barracks**; el cuartel general the headquarters

cuarto¹ NOUN MASC ❶ **room**; el cuarto de estar the living room, el cuarto de baño the bathroom, el cuarto de los niños the children's bedroom ❷ **quarter** (in clock time); son las

dos y cuarto it's quarter past two, a las doce menos cuarto at quarter to twelve ❸ **quarter**; corté la tarta en cuatro cuartos I cut the cake into four quarters, un cuarto de kilo a quarter of a kilo ❹ los cuartos de final **the quarter finals**

cuarto², cuarta² ADJECTIVE **fourth**; en el cuarto piso on the fourth floor, llegar en cuarto lugar to finish in fourth position

cuatro NUMBER ❶ **four**; Juan tiene cuatro años Juan's four (years old) ❷ **fourth** (in dates); el cuatro de mayo the fourth of May ❸ **four** (in clock time); son las cuatro it's four o'clock

cuatrocientos, cuatrocientas NUMBER **four hundred**; cuatrocientos quince four hundred and fifteen

Cuba NOUN FEM **Cuba**

cubano, cubana NOUN MASC, FEM, ADJECTIVE **Cuban**

cubierto¹, cubierta ADJECTIVE **covered**

cubierto² NOUN MASC ❶ los cubiertos the cutlery, pon los cubiertos en la mesa put the knives and forks on the table, cubiertos de plata silver cutlery ❷ poner otro cubierto en la mesa to lay another place at the table

cubo NOUN MASC ❶ **cube** ❷ **bucket**; un cubo de agua a bucket of water ❸ el cubo de la basura the bin

cubrecama NOUN MASC **bedspread**

cubrir VERB [46] **to cover**

cubrirse REFLEXIVE VERB [46] ❶ **to cover yourself**; me cubrí las rodillas I covered my legs **2 to cloud over**; esta mañana hacía sol, pero ahora se ha cubierto this morning it was sunny, but now it's clouded over

cucaracha NOUN FEM **cockroach**

cuchara NOUN FEM **spoon**; cuchara de postre dessert spoon, cuchara sopera soup spoon

cucharada NOUN FEM **spoonful**

cucharadita NOUN FEM **teaspoonful**

cucharilla, cucharita NOUN FEM **teaspoon**; una cucharilla de café/ una cucharita de café a coffee spoon

cuchichear VERB [17] **to whisper**

cuchilla NOUN FEM **blade**; una cuchilla de afeitar a razor blade

cuchillo NOUN MASC **knife**

cuelga, cuelgo, etc VERB
► SEE **colgar**

cuello NOUN MASC **1 neck 2 collar**; el cuello de la camisa the shirt collar, un jersey de cuello redondo a round-neck jumper, un jersey de cuello alto a polo-neck jumper

cuenco NOUN MASC **bowl**

cuenta¹, cuento¹, etc VERB
► SEE **contar**

cuenta² NOUN FEM **1 bill**; ¿nos puede traer la cuenta, por favor? could you bring us the bill, please? **2 sum**; hacer una cuenta to do a sum, hacer cuentas to work something out, haz las cuentas de lo que te debo work out how much I owe you **3 llevar la cuenta de algo** to keep count of something, perder la cuenta de algo to lose count

of something **4 account**; cuenta corriente current account, cuenta de ahorros savings account, abrir una cuenta to open an account **5 tener algo en cuenta** to bear something in mind **6 darse cuenta de algo** to realize something, me di cuenta de que había perdido la cartera I realized I'd lost my wallet **7 trabajar por su cuenta** to be self-employed, trabajo por mi cuenta I'm self-employed, montar una tienda por su cuenta to set up your own shop **8 más de la cuenta** too much, bebieron más de la cuenta they drank too much **9 cuenta atrás** countdown **10 bead** (of necklace)

cuento² NOUN MASC **1 short story 2 tale**; un cuento de hadas a fairy tale **3 eso no viene a cuento** that has nothing to do with it
• ¡eso es un cuento chino! (informal) that's a load of rubbish!

cuerda NOUN FEM **1 rope 2 saltar a la cuerda** to skip **3 dar cuerda a un juguete** to wind up a toy, dar cuerda a un reloj to wind a watch

cuerno NOUN MASC **1 horn 2 antler**

cuero NOUN MASC **leather**; un bolso de cuero a leather bag, el cuero cabelludo the scalp

cuerpo NOUN MASC **body**

cuervo NOUN MASC **crow**

cuesta¹, cueste, etc VERB
► SEE **costar**

cuesta² NOUN FEM **1 slope**; subir una cuesta to go up a slope, ir cuesta arriba to go uphill, ir cuesta abajo to go downhill **2 llevar algo a cuestas** to carry something on your back

cuestión NOUN FEM ❶ **matter**; en la reunión se hablará de esta cuestión this matter will be discussed in the meeting ❷ la cuestión es ... the thing is ...

cueva NOUN FEM **cave**

cueza, cuezo, etc VERB ▸ SEE **cocer**

cuidado NOUN MASC ❶ tener cuidado con to be careful with, ten cuidado con los vasos be careful with the glasses, ¡cuidado con el escalón! mind the step!, ¡cuidado con el perro! beware of the dog! ❷ hacer algo con cuidado to do something carefully, lo cogí con cuidado I picked it up carefully ❸ **care**; el cuidado de las manos es muy importante hand care is very important ❹ cuidados intensivos intensive care

cuidado EXCLAMATION ¡cuidado! watch out!

cuidadoso, cuidadosa ADJECTIVE **careful**

cuidar VERB [17] ❶ **to look after**; yo me quedo cuidando a los niños I'll stay and look after the children, cuidan de su padre enfermo they look after their sick father ❷ **to take care of**; sé cuidar de mí misma I can take care of myself

culebra NOUN FEM **snake**

culebrón NOUN MASC (informal) **soap opera**

culo NOUN MASC (informal) ❶ **bum** ❷ el culo del vaso the bottom of the glass

culpa NOUN FEM ❶ **fault**; no es mi culpa it's not my fault, es su culpa si se queda sin ir it's his fault if he ends up not going, no lo

terminamos a tiempo por tu culpa it's your fault we didn't finish it on time, ¿y qué culpa tengo yo? and why is it my fault? ❷ echarle la culpa a alguien to blame someone, me echan la culpa de lo sucedido they blame me for what happened ❸ **guilt**; sentimiento de culpa guilty feelings

culpable NOUN MASC & FEM él es el único culpable de todo esto he's the only one to blame for all this

culpable ADJECTIVE ❶ **guilty**; sentirse culpable de algo to feel guilty about something ❷ ser culpable de algo to be to blame for something, yo no soy culpable de la situación I'm not to blame for the situation ❸ ser culpable de algo to be guilty of something (a crime)

culpar VERB [17] **to blame**; culpar a alguien de algo to blame somebody for something

cultivar VERB [17] ❶ **to grow** (fruit or vegetables) ❷ **to cultivate** (land)

cultivo NOUN MASC **crop**

culto NOUN MASC ❶ **cult** ❷ **worship**; la libertad de culto the freedom of worship

cultura NOUN FEM ❶ **culture** ❷ **knowledge**; preguntas de cultura general general knowledge questions

culturismo NOUN MASC **bodybuilding**

cumpleaños NOUN MASC **birthday**; fiesta de cumpleaños birthday party, ¿cuándo es tu cumpleaños? when's your birthday?, ¡feliz cumpleaños! Happy Birthday!

cumplir _VERB_ [19] ❶ ¿cuándo cumples años? when's your birthday?, mañana cumplo quince años I'll be fifteen tomorrow, ¡que cumplas muchos más! many happy returns! ❷ cumplir una promesa to keep a promise, no has cumplido con tu palabra you haven't kept your word ❸ to fulfil (_conditions_) ❹ to carry out (_a task or an order_) ❺ cumplir una condena to serve a sentence

cuna _NOUN FEM_ ❶ cradle ❷ cot

cuñada _NOUN FEM_ sister-in-law

cuñado _NOUN MASC_ brother-in-law

cupe, **cupiera**, **cupo**, _etc VERB_
▸ SEE **caber**

cura[1] _NOUN MASC_ priest

cura[2] _NOUN FEM_ cure

curar _VERB_ [17] ❶ to cure (_an illness or sick person_) ❷ to dress (_a wound_)

curarse _REFLEXIVE VERB_ [17] to get better

curioso, **curiosa** _NOUN MASC & FEM_ busybody

curioso _ADJECTIVE_ ❶ nosy; ¡qué curiosa eres! you're so nosy! ❷ lo curioso es que ... the funny thing is ..., es curioso que ... it's strange that ...

curriculum _NOUN MASC_ CV, curriculum vitae

cursillo _NOUN MASC_ (short) course

cursiva _NOUN FEM_ italics; en cursiva in italics

curso _NOUN MASC_ ❶ year; ¿en qué curso estás? what year are you in?, mi hermana está en el primer curso my sister's in first year, el curso escolar the academic year ❷ course; un curso intensivo an intensive course

cursor _NOUN MASC_ cursor

curva[1] _NOUN FEM_ bend; curva peligrosa sharp bend, tomar una curva to take a bend

curvo, **curva**[2] _ADJECTIVE_ curved

cuyo, **cuya** _ADJECTIVE_ whose; el amigo cuyo ordenador utilicé the friend whose computer I used

a
b
c
d
e
f
g
h
i
j
k
l
m
n
ñ
o
p
q
r
s
t
u
v
w
x
y
z

Dd

dabuten ADJECTIVE (informal)
fantastic, cool; unos pantalones
dabuten a fantastic pair of trousers

dabuten ADVERB lo pasé dabuten
I had a fantastic time

dabuti ADJECTIVE (informal)
▸ SEE **dabuten**

dado NOUN MASC **dice**; tirar los dados
to throw the dice

dama NOUN FEM **lady**; damas y
caballeros ladies and gentlemen,
una dama de honor a bridesmaid

danés¹ NOUN MASC **Danish** (the
language)

danés², **danesa** NOUN MASC, FEM
Dane

danés, **danesa** ADJECTIVE **Danish**

danza NOUN FEM

danza NOUN FEM **dance**; estudiar
danza to study dance

dañar VERB [17] **to damage**

dañino, **dañina** ADJECTIVE **harmful**

daño NOUN MASC ❶ hacerse daño to
hurt yourself, te vas a hacer daño
you are going to hurt yourself, ¿se
hizo daño al caer? did she hurt
herself when she fell?, me hice daño
en la pierna I hurt my leg ❷ hacerle
daño a alguien to hurt someone, no
quiero hacerte daño I don't want
to hurt you ❸ daños y perjuicios
damages

dar VERB [4] ❶ **to give**; me dio su
número de teléfono he gave me
his telephone number, dale esta
carta a María give this letter to
María, dale recuerdos give him my
regards, dame un beso give me a
kiss ❷ ¿me da un kilo de tomates?
can I have a kilo of tomatoes? ❸ me
dieron un premio I got a prize ❹ **to
turn on**; dar la luz to turn on the
light ❺ darle a un botón to press
a button, darle a un interruptor
to flick a switch ❻ el reloj dio las
doce the clock struck twelve ❼ dar
una fiesta to have a party ❽ **to say**;
dar las gracias to say thank you,
dar los buenos días to say good
morning, darle la bienvenida a
alguien to welcome someone ❾ dar
un grito to shout ❿ darle la mano
a alguien to shake somebody's
hand ⓫ dar un paseo to go for a
walk, fuimos a dar una vuelta we
went for a walk ⓬ dar de comer a
alguien to feed somebody, darle de
beber a alguien to give somebody
something to drink ⓭ me dio
miedo it scared me, las patatas
fritas le dieron sed the crisps made
him feel thirsty, este jersey da
mucho calor this jumper is very
warm ⓮ da lo mismo it doesn't
matter, da lo mismo si lo hacemos
luego it doesn't matter if we do
it later ⓯ me da lo mismo I don't
mind, si te da lo mismo, te hago un
cheque if you don't mind, I'll write
you a cheque ⓰ el hotel da al mar
the hotel faces the sea, la puerta
da al salón the door opens onto the
living room

darse REFLEXIVE VERB [4] ❶ **to have**;
darse un baño to have a bath,
darse una ducha to have a shower
❷ darse un golpe to bump yourself,
me di con el pie en el bordillo I hit

my foot on the kerb ❸ **darse prisa** to hurry up ❹ **darse cuenta de algo** to realize something, **me di cuenta de que se me habían olvidado las llaves** I realized I'd forgotten my keys ❺ **se le dan bien las matemáticas** she's good at maths, **no se me da bien pintar** I'm not good at painting

dardo NOUN MASC **dart**

dársena NOUN FEM ❶ **bay** (in bus station) ❷ (for ships) **dry dock**

datos PLURAL NOUN MASC ❶ **data** ❷ **details**; **datos personales** personal details

dC ABBREVIATION (short for después de Cristo) **AD**

d. de J.C. ABBREVIATION (short for después de Jesucristo) **AD**

de PREPOSITION (note that 'de' + 'el' becomes 'del') ❶ **el coche de mis padres** my parent's car, **esto es de Juan** this is Juan's, **fuimos a casa de Isa** we went to Isa's ❷ **of**; **el nombre del libro** the name of the book, **el respaldo del asiento** the back of the chair ❸ **from**; **soy de Sevilla** I'm from Sevilla, **de Madrid a Bilbao** from Madrid to Bilbao, **de la cabeza a los pies** from head to toe, **no hemos tenido noticias de María** we haven't heard from María ❹ **una silla de madera** a wooden chair, **flores de plástico** plastic flowers ❺ **of** (in quantities); **un vaso de leche** a glass of milk, **una caja de naranjas** a box of oranges ❻ **una clase de conducir** a driving lesson, **los vasos del vino** the wine glasses, **una moneda de dos euros** a two-euro coin, **el cubo de la basura** the rubbish bin, **una película de miedo** a scary film ❼ **la estación**

de Victoria Victoria Station, **la ciudad de Barcelona** Barcelona, **el mes de marzo** the month of March ❽ (describing people) **un hombre de cincuenta años** a fifty-year-old man, **una niña de pelo corto** a girl with short hair, ('de' + 'el' becomes 'del') **with short hair**, **es la chica del jersey a rayas** it's the girl with a striped jumper, **yo iba vestida de rojo** I was dressed in red ❾ **el mejor de todos** the best of all, **el más bonito de los tres** the nicest of the three, **más de quince** more than fifteen, **el más inteligente de la clase** the cleverest in the class ❿ **un tercio del total** a third of the total, **el doble de lo que yo gano** twice what I earn, **poco a poco** little by little, **de tres en tres** three at a time ⓫ **a las dos de la tarde** at two in the afternoon, **de noche** by night, **trabajan de noche** they work at night, **viajaron de día** they travelled by day ⓬ **trabajar de algo** to work as something, **trabajo de enfermera** I work as a nurse

dé VERB ▸ SEE **dar**

debajo ADJECTIVE ❶ (note that) **underneath**; **pon un plato debajo** put a plate underneath ❷ **el que está debajo** the one underneath, **el de debajo del todo** the one right at the bottom ❸ **debajo de** under, **está debajo de la caja** it's under the box ❹ **por debajo de** under, **pasé por debajo de la valla** I went under the fence, **por debajo de los diez grados** below ten degrees

deber¹ NOUN MASC ❶ **duty**; **cumplir con tu deber** to do your duty ❷ **deberes** homework, **hacer los deberes** to do your homework, **aún no he hecho los deberes** I haven't done my homework yet

deber² VERB [18] **❶ to owe**; te debo veinte euros I owe you twenty euros **❷ must**; debes intentarlo you must try, deberás estudiar mucho you will have to study hard **❸** deberías descansar you should have a rest, deberías haber seguido mis consejos you should have followed my advice

debido, debida ADJECTIVE **❶ due**; a su debido tiempo in due course, con el debido respeto with due respect, con el debido cuidado with the necessary care **❷** como es debido properly, pórtate como es debido behave properly **❸** debido a due to, debido al accidente due to the accident

débil ADJECTIVE **weak**

década NOUN FEM **decade**; la década de los sesenta the sixties

decena NOUN FEM una decena de libros about ten books, divídelos por decenas divide them into tens

decente ADJECTIVE **decent**

decepción NOUN FEM **disappointment**

decepcionante ADJECTIVE **disappointing**

decepcionar VERB [17] **to disappoint**; la película nos decepcionó the film disappointed us

decidir VERB [19] **to decide**; decidí quedarme I decided to stay

decidirse REFLEXIVE VERB [19] **to make up your mind**; aún no se ha decidido del todo she hasn't completely made up her mind

décimo, décima ADJECTIVE **tenth**; el décimo piso the tenth floor

decir VERB [5] **❶ to say**; ¿qué has dicho? what did you say?, aquí dice que ... here it says that ... **❷ to tell**; me ha dicho que no viene he's told me he's not coming, dime lo que quieres tell me what you want **❸ to mean**; ¿qué quieres decir? what do you mean?, ¿qué quiere decir 'paloma'? what does 'paloma' mean? **❹** no digas tonterías don't talk nonsense **❺** ¿diga? hello? (on the phone) **❻** dime yes? (when somebody says your name), '¡mamá!' – '¿dime?' 'Mum!' – 'yes?'

decisión NOUN FEM **decision**; tomar una decisión to make a decision

declarar VERB [17] **❶ to declare**; declarar la guerra to declare war, ¿algo que declarar? anything to declare? (at customs) **❷ to give evidence**; se ha negado a declarar he's refused to give evidence

declararse REFLEXIVE VERB [17] declararse culpable to plead guilty, declararse inocente to plead not guilty

decorador, decoradora NOUN MASC, FEM **interior designer**

decorar VERB [17] **to decorate**

dedicar VERB [17] **to dedicate**

dedicarse REFLEXIVE VERB [17] **to promise**; ¿a qué te dedicas? what do you do?, se dedica a pintar en sus ratos libres she spends her free time painting

dedo NOUN MASC **❶ finger**; dedo índice index finger, dedo anular ring finger, dedo meñique little finger, dedo pulgar thumb, dedo corazón middle finger **❷** dedo del pie toe, el dedo gordo del pie the big toe **❸** hacer dedo to hitchhike

defecto NOUN MASC **flaw, defect**

defectuoso, **defectuosa** ADJECTIVE **faulty**

defender VERB [36] **to defend**

defenderse REFLEXIVE VERB [36] ❶ **to defend yourself** ❷ me defiendo en ingles I get by in English

defensa NOUN FEM ❶ **defence**; defensa personal self-defence ❷ **defender** (in sport)

defensor, **defensora** NOUN MASC, FEM **defender**; el defensor del pueblo the ombudsman

deficiente ADJECTIVE ❶ **deficient** ❷ **inadequate**

definición NOUN FEM **definition**

definitivo, **definitiva** ADJECTIVE **definitive**

dejar VERB [17] ❶ **to leave**; quiere dejar el colegio she wants to leave school, ha dejado a su novia he's left his girlfriend, ¡déjala en paz! leave her alone! ❷ **to let**; no la dejan salir los domingos they don't let her go out on Sundays, ¡déjame entrar! let me in! ❸ **to lend**; le he dejado mis apuntes I've lent him my notes, ¿me dejas un boli? can you lend me a pen? ❹ dejar caer algo to drop something ❺ dejar paso to give way ❻ dejar de hacer algo to stop doing something, ¡deja de molestar! stop being a nuisance!, dejar de fumar to give up smoking ❼ no dejes de llamarme cuando llegues make sure you phone me when you get there

dejarse REFLEXIVE VERB [17] ❶ **to leave**; me he dejado las gafas en el coche I left my glasses in the car ❷ dejarse el pelo largo to grow your hair long, dejarse barba to grow a beard

del (formed by 'de + el'; look under 'de' for more examples) el dedo gordo del pie the big toe

delantal NOUN MASC **apron**

delante ADVERB ❶ delante de in front of, delante de la iglesia in front of the church, delante de mí in front of me ❷ el asiento de delante the front seat, la parte de delante the front ❸ ir delante to go ahead ❹ lleva un bolsillo por delante it has a pocket at the front, entraron por delante they came in through the front

delantero, **delantera** NOUN MASC, FEM **forward** (in sport)

delantero ADJECTIVE **front**; la rueda delantera the front wheel

deletrear VERB [17] **to spell**

delfín NOUN MASC **dolphin**

delgado, **delgada** ADJECTIVE **thin**

delicado, **delicada** ADJECTIVE ❶ **delicate**; una situación delicada a delicate situation ❷ **fragile** (a piece of china, etc.) ❸ **sensitive** (skin)

delicioso, **deliciosa** ADJECTIVE **delicious**

delincuente NOUN MASC & FEM **criminal**

delito NOUN MASC **crime**; cometer un delito to commit a crime

demás ADJECTIVE los demás alumnos the rest of the pupils, las demás cartas the rest of the letters

demás PRONOUN ❶ lo demás the rest, lo demás lo traigo mañana I'll bring the rest tomorrow, aquí está todo lo demás here's everything else ❷ los/las demás the rest, the others, los demás pueden venir conmigo the rest can come with me, los problemas de los demás other people's problems

demasiado[1], **demasiada** ADJECTIVE, PRONOUN ❶ too much; gasta demasiado dinero he spends too much money ❷ too many; hay demasiadas personas aquí there are too many people here ❸ demasiadas veces too often ❹ hacía demasiado calor it was too hot

demasiado[2] ADVERB ❶ too much; gasta demasiado he spends too much, no trabajes demasiado don't work too hard ❷ too; los billetes eran demasiado caro the tickets were too expensive

democracia NOUN FEM democracy

demoler VERB [38] to demolish

demolición NOUN FEM demolition

demonio NOUN MASC devil

demora NOUN FEM delay; sin demora without delay

demos, dan, den, etc VERB ▸ SEE **dar**

densidad NOUN FEM ❶ density ❷ denseness

dentado, dentada ADJECTIVE jagged

dentífrico NOUN MASC toothpaste

dentista NOUN MASC & FEM dentist

dentro ADVERB ❶ inside; pasar dentro to go inside, desde dentro from inside ❷ aquí dentro in here, allí dentro in there, ponlo aquí dentro put it in here ❸ dentro de inside, in, dentro del edificio inside the building, dentro de la caja in

the box ❹ por dentro on the inside, por dentro es verde it's green on the inside, lo limpié por dentro I've cleaned the inside

denunciar VERB [17] to report (a person or crime)

departamento NOUN MASC department

depender VERB [18] to depend; depender de algo to depend on something, depende del resultado it depends on the result, '¿se lo vas a decir?' – 'depende' 'are you going to tell him?' – 'it depends'

dependiente, dependienta NOUN MASC, FEM shop assistant

deporte NOUN MASC sport; hacer deporte to play sports, me gusta hacer deporte I like playing sports, los deportes acuáticos water sports, los deportes de invierno winter sports

deportista NOUN MASC & FEM sportsman/sportswoman

deportista ADJECTIVE sporty; soy muy deportista I do a lot of sport, Jack es muy buen deportista Jack's very good at games

deportivo[1] NOUN MASC sports car

deportivo[2], **deportiva** ADJECTIVE sports; club deportivo sports club, ropa deportiva sports clothes, casual clothes

depositar VERB [17] ❶ to place; deposite su solicitud en esta caja place your application in this box ❷ to deposit (money in an account)

depósito NOUN MASC deposit

deprimido, deprimida ADJECTIVE depressed

deprimirse REFLEXIVE VERB [19] **to get depressed**

deprisa ADVERB **fast**, **quickly**; no lo hagas tan deprisa don't do it so quickly, andaba muy deprisa he was walking very fast, ¡deprisa, vístete! hurry up and get dressed!

derecha¹ NOUN FEM ❶ **right**; gira a la derecha turn right, conducir por la derecha to drive on the right, la segunda calle a la derecha the second road on the right ❷ **right hand**; escribo con la derecha I write with my right hand ❸ la derecha the right (in politics), ser de derechas to be right-wing

derecho¹ NOUN MASC ❶ **right**; tener derecho a to have a right to, tienes derecho a reclamar you've got the right to claim, los derechos humanos human rights ❷ **law**; estudiar derecho to study law, derecho penal criminal law ❸ derechos de autor royalties

derecho² ADVERB **straight**; ponlo derecho put it straight, siga todo derecho go straight on, siéntate derecho sit up straight

derecho³, **derecha**² ADJECTIVE ❶ **right**; el guante derecho the right glove, en la esquina superior derecha in the top right-hand corner ❷ **straight**; no está derecho it's not straight

derramar VERB [17] **to spill**; he derramado el café en la alfombra I've spilt the coffee on the carpet

derramarse REFLEXIVE VERB [7] **to spill**; se derramó la leche the milk has spilt

derribar VERB [17] ❶ **to demolish** (a building or wall, for example) ❷ **to**

break down (a door) ❸ **to shoot down** (a plane)

derrotar VERB [17] **to defeat**

des VERB ▸ SEE **dar**

desabrochar VERB [17] **to undo** (a jacket or shirt)

desabrocharse REFLEXIVE VERB [17] **to undo**; se desabrochó la chaqueta he undid his jacket

desactivar VERB [17] ❶ **to deactivate** ❷ **to defuse** (a bomb)

desafilado, **desafilada** ADJECTIVE **blunt**

desafortunadamente ADVERB **unfortunately**

desafortunado, **desafortunada** ADJECTIVE ❶ **unlucky** (a person) ❷ **unfortunate** (an event)

desagradable ADJECTIVE **unpleasant**

desanimado, **desanimada** ADJECTIVE **discouraged**

desaparecer VERB [35] ❶ **to disappear**; la tradición está desapareciendo the tradition is dying out ❷ **to go missing**

desaparición NOUN FEM **disappearance**

desaprovechar VERB [17] **to waste**; han desaprovechado mucho papel they've wasted a lot of paper

desarrollo NOUN MASC **development**

desastre NOUN MASC **disaster**

desatar VERB [17] **to untie**

desatarse REFLEXIVE VERB [17] **to come undone**

desatornillar VERB [17] **to unscrew**

desayunar *VERB* [17] ❶ **to have breakfast**; desayuné muy temprano I had breakfast very early ❷ **to have for breakfast**; desayuno café y tostadas I have coffee and toast for breakfast

desayuno *NOUN MASC* **breakfast**; tomar el desayuno to have breakfast

desbordar *VERB* [17] **to exceed**

desbordarse *REFLEXIVE VERB* [17] **to overflow**; el río se desbordó the river overflowed its banks

descafeinado, descafeinada *ADJECTIVE* **decaffeinated**

descalificar *VERB* [31] **to disqualify**

descalzarse *REFLEXIVE VERB* [22] **to take your shoes off**

descalzo, descalza *ADJECTIVE* **barefoot**

descansado, descansada *ADJECTIVE* **rested**

descansar *VERB* [17] ❶ **to rest**; necesitas descansar you need to rest, descansar la vista to give your eyes a rest ❷ que descanses sleep well ❸ ¡descansen! at ease! *(in the army)*

descansillo *NOUN MASC* **landing** *(on stairs)*

descanso *NOUN MASC* ❶ **rest** ❷ **half-time**

descapotable *NOUN MASC*

descapotable *ADJECTIVE* **convertible**

descargar *VERB* [28] **to unload**

descender *VERB* [36] ❶ **to go down** *(a mountaineer)* ❷ **to descend** *(a plane)* ❸ **to fall** *(prices or temperature, for example)*

descenso *NOUN MASC* ❶ **fall** *(in temperature, etc)* ❷ **descent**

descolgar *VERB* [23] ❶ **to pick up** *(the phone)* ❷ han dejado el teléfono descolgado they've left the phone off the hook ❸ **to take down** *(a picture, for example)*

desconectar *VERB* [17] **to disconnect**; ¿has desconectado el ordenador? have you disconnected the computer?

desconfiar *VERB* [32] **to mistrust**; desconfiar de alguien to mistrust someone

descongelar *VERB* [17] **to defrost** *(the fridge or food)*

decongelarse *REFLEXIVE VERB* [17] **to defrost** *(the fridge or food)*

desconocido, desconocida *NOUN MASC, FEM* **stranger**

desconocido *ADJECTIVE* **unknown**

descontento¹ *NOUN MASC* **dissatisfaction**

descontento², descontenta *ADJECTIVE* **dissatisfied**; quedar descontento con algo to be dissatisfied with something

describir *VERB* [52] **to describe**

descripción *NOUN FEM* **description**

descrito *VERB* ▸ *SEE* **describir**

descubrir *VERB* [53] ❶ **to discover** ❷ **to unveil** *(a statue)*

descuento *NOUN MASC* **discount**

descuidado, descuidada *ADJECTIVE* ❶ **careless** *(a person)* ❷ **neglected**; el jardín está muy descuidado the garden is very neglected

desde *PREPOSITION* **❶** since; desde la semana pasada since last week, desde que nos conocimos since we met **❷** from; mídelo desde este extremo hasta el otro measure it from this end to the other, puedo mandarlo desde Madrid I can send it from Madrid, desde el principio from the beginning, desde el primer momento right from the start **❸** desde hace for, no les veo desde hace años I haven't seen them for years, trabajo allí desde hace tres meses I've been working there for three months **❹** desde luego of course

desear *VERB* [17] **❶** to wish; te deseo lo mejor I wish you all the best, te deseo un feliz cumpleaños wishing you a happy birthday *(in a card)* **❷** ¿qué desea? can I help you? *(in a shop, for example)* **❸** estoy deseando verte I'm looking forward to seeing you, están deseando que llegue el verano they can't wait for the summer to come

desembarcar *VERB* [31] **❶** to unload **❷** to disembark

desempleado, desempleada *NOUN MASC & FEM* **unemployed person**

desempleado *ADJECTIVE* **unemployed**

desempleo *NOUN MASC* **unemployment**; cobrar subsidio de desempleo to get unemployment benefit

desenchufar *VERB* [17] **to unplug**

desenvolver *VERB* [45] **to unwrap**

deseo *NOUN MASC* **❶** wish; pedir un deseo to make a wish, se cumplió mi deseo my wish came true **❷** con

mis mejores deseos best wishes **❸** desire

desfavorable *ADJECTIVE* **unfavourable**

desfile *NOUN MASC* **❶** parade **❷** un desfile de modelos a fashion show

desgracia *NOUN FEM* **misfortune**; por desgracia unfortunately
• las desgracias nunca vienen solas it never rains but pours

desgraciado, desgraciada *ADJECTIVE* **❶** unhappy; soy muy desgraciado I'm very unhappy **❷** ill-fated; aquel desgraciado día that ill-fated day

deshacer *VERB* [7] **❶** to undo *(a knot)* **❷** to unwrap *(a parcel)* **❸** to take apart *(a mechanism)* **❹** to crumble *(a biscuit or stock cube, for example)* **❺** deshacer las maletas to unpack

deshacerse *REFLEXIVE VERB* [7] **❶** to come undone *(a knot or seam)* **❷** to melt *(ice)* **❸** to come apart, se deshizo en mis manos it came apart in my hands **❹** deshacerse de algo to get rid of something, voy a deshacerme de este sofá I'm going to get rid of this sofa

deshielo *NOUN MASC* **thaw**

desierto¹ *NOUN MASC* **desert**

desierto², desierta *ADJECTIVE* **deserted**

designar *VERB* [17] **to appoint**

desigual *ADJECTIVE* **❶** uneven *(a surface or road)* **❷** unequal *(a fight)*

desigualdad *NOUN FEM* **inequality**

desmaquillarse *REFLEXIVE VERB* [17] **to remove your make-up**

desmayarse *REFLEXIVE VERB* [17] **to faint**

a
b
c
d
e
f
g
h
i
j
k
l
m
n
ñ
o
p
q
r
s
t
u
v
w
x
y
z

desmontar VERB [17] ❶ to take apart ❷ to take down *(a tent)*

desnudar VERB [17] to undress

desnudarse REFLEXIVE VERB [17] to take your clothes off, to undress

desnudo, **desnuda** ADJECTIVE ❶ naked ❷ bare; con los hombros desnudos with bare shoulders

desobedecer VERB [35] to disobey; desobedeció el reglamento she disobeyed the rules

desobedezca, **desobedezco**, *etc* VERB ▸ SEE **desobedecer**

desobediente NOUN MASC, FEM eres un desobediente you are very disobedient

desobediente ADJECTIVE disobedient

desodorante NOUN MASC deodorant; desodorante en barra stick deodorant

desorden NOUN MASC mess

desordenado, **desordenada** ADJECTIVE untidy

desorganizado, **desorganizada** ADJECTIVE disorganized

despacho NOUN MASC ❶ office ❷ study *(at home)* ❸ despacho de billetes ticket office, despacho de lotería lottery agency

despacio ADVERB slowly; hazlo despacio do it slowly, ¡más despacio! slower!

despedida NOUN FEM farewell; una cena de despedida a farewell dinner

despedir VERB [57] ❶ to dismiss; lo han despedido del trabajo they've sacked him ❷ to lay off; han tenido que despedir a algunos empleados they've had to lay off some employees ❸ to say goodbye; fuimos todos a despedirla we all went to say goodbye to her, ¿vendrás a despedirme a la estación? will you come to see me off at the station?

despedirse REFLEXIVE VERB [57] to say goodbye; despedirse de alguien to say goodbye to someone

despegar VERB [28] ❶ to take off *(a plane)* ❷ to peel off *(a label or a sticker)*

despegarse REFLEXIVE VERB [28] to come unstuck

despegue NOUN MASC takeoff *(of a plane)*

despejado, **despejada** ADJECTIVE clear *(sky or a day, for example)*

despejar VERB [17] to clear

desperdiciar VERB [17] to waste

desperdicio NOUN MASC ❶ waste; no tiene desperdicio it's excellent ❷ desperdicios scraps

despertador NOUN MASC alarm (clock); poner el despertador to set the alarm

despertar VERB [29] to wake up; ¿puedes despertarme a las siete? can you wake me up at seven?

despertarse REFLEXIVE VERB [29] to wake up; me desperté a las diez I woke up at ten

despida, **despido**, *etc* VERB ▸ SEE **despedir**

despierta¹, **despierto¹**, *etc* VERB ▸ SEE **despertar**

despierto², **despierta²** ADJECTIVE awake

despistado, **despistada** NOUN MASC, FEM **scatterbrain**

despistado ADJECTIVE **absent-minded**

desplegar VERB [30] to **unfold**

despliega, **despliego**, etc VERB ► SEE **desplegar**

después ADVERB ❶ **afterwards**; después me arrepentí I regretted it afterwards, poco después shortly afterwards ❷ **later**; lo haré después I'll do it later, se vieron mucho después they saw each other much later ❸ después de **after**, después de las clases after school ❹ después de todo **after all**

destino NOUN MASC ❶ **destination**; ¿qué destino tiene? what's its destination?, el vuelo con destino a Milán the plane to Milan ❷ **fate**

destornillador NOUN MASC **screwdriver**

destrucción NOUN FEM **destruction**

destruir VERB [54] to **destroy**

desván NOUN MASC **attic**

desventaja NOUN FEM **disadvantage**; estar en desventaja to be at a disadvantage

desvestirse REFLEXIVE VERB [57] to **undress**

desviar VERB [32] to **divert** (a plane or traffic)

desvío NOUN MASC **diversion**; tomar un desvío to make a detour

detalle NOUN MASC **detail**; describir algo con todo detalle to describe something in great detail

detective NOUN MASC & FEM **detective**; detective privado private detective

detener VERB [9] ❶ to **stop** (traffic) ❷ to **arrest**; ¡queda detenido! you're under arrest!

detenerse REFLEXIVE VERB [9] to **stop**; detenerse a hacer to stop to do, me detuve a descansar I stopped to rest

detergente NOUN MASC ❶ **washing powder** ❷ **washing-up liquid**

detestar VERB [17] to **detest**

detrás ADVERB ❶ **behind**; creo que están detrás I think they're behind ❷ detrás de **behind**, ponte detrás de mí go behind me, detrás de la estación behind the station ❸ se abrocha por detrás it buttons up at the back, entraron por detrás they got in through the back

deuda NOUN FEM **debt**; tiene muchas deudas he has a lot of debts

devolver VERB [45] ❶ to **bring back**; te devolveré el libro mañana I'll bring you the book back tomorrow ❷ to **take back**; he devuelto la camisa I've taken the shirt back ❸ to **return**; lo devolví a su dueño I returned it to its owner ❹ to **refund** (money) ❺ to **be sick** (vomit); creo que voy a devolver I think I'm going to be sick

devuelto, **devuelvo**, etc VERB ► SEE **devolver**

di VERB ► SEE **dar**

día NOUN MASC ❶ **day**; el día siguiente the following day, el día anterior the previous day, el día tres de mayo the third of May, ¿qué día es hoy? what day is it today?, todos los días every day, cada día every day, un día festivo a public holiday, se ha tomado el día libre she's taken the day off, día de Reyes Twelfth

Night *(the 6th of January, which is when people get Christmas presents in Spain)*, el día de los Inocentes the 28th of December *(equivalent to April Fool's Day in Spain)*, el día de los enamorados St Valentine's Day, día del padre Father's Day ❷ buenos días good morning ❸ hacerse de día to get light *(in the morning)*, aún no se ha hecho de día it's not light yet, en pleno día in broad daylight ❹ estar al día to be up to date, poner a alguien al día to bring someone up to date

diabético, diabética NOUN MASC, FEM, ADJECTIVE **diabetic**

diablo NOUN MASC **devil**

diagnóstico NOUN MASC **diagnosis**; emitir un diagnóstico to make a diagnosis

diagonal NOUN FEM, ADJECTIVE **diagonal**

diagrama NOUN MASC **diagram**

dial NOUN MASC **dial**

diálogo NOUN MASC ❶ **conversation** ❷ **dialogue**

diamante NOUN MASC **diamond**

diámetro NOUN MASC **diameter**

diapositiva NOUN FEM **slide**

diario¹ NOUN MASC ❶ **diary**; llevar un diario to keep a diary ❷ **newspaper**

diario², diaria ADJECTIVE ❶ **daily**; la rutina diaria the daily routine, a diario every day, se escriben a diario they write to each other every day ❷ **a day**; ensayan dos horas diarias they practise two hours a day ❸ de diario everyday, ropa de diario everyday clothes

diarrea NOUN FEM **diarrhoea**

dibujar VERB [17] **to draw**

dibujo NOUN MASC ❶ **drawing**; hacer un dibujo to do a drawing, dibujo técnico technical drawing ❷ dibujos animados cartoons, una película de dibujos animados an animated cartoon film

diccionario NOUN MASC **dictionary**

dice, dicho, *etc* VERB ▸ SEE **decir**

diciembre NOUN MASC **December**

dictado NOUN MASC **dictation**

diecinueve NUMBER ❶ **nineteen**; tiene diecinueve años she's nineteen (years old) ❷ **nineteenth** *(in dates)*; el diecinueve de agosto the nineteenth of August

dieciocho NUMBER ❶ **eighteen**; tiene dieciocho años she's eighteen (years old) ❷ **eighteenth** *(in dates)*; el dieciocho de agosto the eighteenth of August

dieciséis NUMBER ❶ **sixteen**; tiene dieciséis años she's sixteen (years old) ❷ **sixteenth** *(in dates)*; el dieciséis de agosto the sixteenth of August

diecisiete NUMBER ❶ **seventeen**; tiene diecisiete años she's seventeen (years old) ❷ **seventeenth** *(in dates)*; el diecisiete de agosto the seventeenth of August

diente NOUN MASC ❶ **tooth**; se le ha caído un diente she's lost a tooth, ya le están saliendo los dientes he's already teething ❷ un diente de ajo a clove of garlic

diera, dieras, *etc* VERB ▸ SEE **dar**

diesel NOUN MASC

diesel ADJECTIVE diesel

dieta NOUN FEM diet; estar a dieta to be on a diet, ponerse a dieta to go on a diet

diez NUMBER ❶ ten; tiene diez años she's ten (years old) ❷ tenth (in dates); el diez de agosto the tenth of August ❸ ten (in clock time); son las diez it's ten o'clock, a las diez y cinco at five past ten

diferencia NOUN FEM ❶ difference; hay poca diferencia de precio there's not much difference in price ❷ a diferencia de unlike, a diferencia de su padre unlike his father

diferente ADJECTIVE different; ser diferente a/de to be different from

difícil ADJECTIVE difficult

dificultad NOUN FEM difficulty; con muchas dificultades with great difficulty

diga, **digo**, etc VERB ▸ SEE decir

digital ADJECTIVE digital

diluir VERB [54] ❶ to dilute ❷ to thin (paint)

dimensión NOUN FEM dimension

dimisión NOUN FEM resignation; presentar la dimisión to hand in your resignation

dimitir VERB [19] to resign

dimos VERB ▸ SEE dar

Dinamarca NOUN FEM Denmark

dinámico, **dinámica** ADJECTIVE dynamic

dinero NOUN MASC money; dinero de bolsillo pocket money, dinero en efectivo cash, dinero suelto change, no tengo dinero suelto I haven't got any change

dinosaurio NOUN MASC dinosaur

dio VERB ▸ SEE dar

dios NOUN MASC god

Dios NOUN MASC God; gracias a Dios thank heavens, ¡por Dios! for heaven's sake!, ¡Dios mío! oh, my God!, ¡sabe Dios! God knows!

diploma NOUN MASC diploma

diplomático, **diplomática** NOUN MASC, FEM diplomat

diplomático ADJECTIVE diplomatic

diputado, **diputada** NOUN MASC, FEM member of parliament

dirá, **diré**, etc VERB ▸ SEE decir

dirección NOUN FEM ❶ address; mi dirección es ... my address is ... ❷ direction; ¿en qué dirección se fueron? what direction did they go in?, venían en dirección contraria they were coming the other way ❸ 'dirección prohibida' 'no entry', 'dirección obligatoria' 'one way' ❹ management (of a company)

directo¹, **directa** ADJECTIVE ❶ direct; ¿hay un vuelo directo a Santiago? is there a direct flight to Santiago? ❷ un tren directo a through train ❸ en directo live, retransmisión en directo live broadcast

directo² ADVERB direct; el autobús va directo al aeropuerto the bus goes direct to the airport

director, **directora** NOUN MASC, FEM ❶ headmaster/headmistress

a
b
c
d
e
f
g
h
i
j
k
l
m
n
ñ
o
p
q
r
s
t
u
v
w
x
y
z

❷ **manager** (of a company)
❸ **director** (of a film or play)
❹ **conductor** (of an orchestra)
❺ **editor** (of a newspaper)

dirigir VERB [49] ❶ **to manage** (a company) ❷ **to direct** (a film or play) ❸ **to conduct** (an orchestra) ❹ no me dirigió la palabra en toda la tarde he didn't say a word to me all afternoon

dirigirse REFLEXIVE VERB [49] dirigirse a hacia algo to head towards something, se dirigió hacia la puerta he headed towards the door

discapacidad NOUN FEM **disability**; ¿tiene alguna discapacidad? does she have a disability?

disciplina NOUN FEM **discipline**

disco NOUN MASC ❶ **record**; grabar un disco to make a record, disco sencillo single, disco compacto compact disc disco compacto interactivo interactive compact disc ❷ **disk**; disco duro hard disk ❸ **traffic light**; el disco se ha puesto rojo the lights are red

discoteca NOUN FEM **disco**

discriminación NOUN FEM **discrimination**

disculpa NOUN FEM **apology**; pedir disculpas a alguien por algo to apologize to someone for something

disculparse REFLEXIVE VERB [17] **to apologize**

discusión NOUN FEM ❶ **argument** ❷ **discussion**

discutir VERB [19] ❶ **to argue**; ha discutido con su novio she's had an argument with her boyfriend ❷ **to discuss**

diseñador, **diseñadora** NOUN MASC, FEM **designer**; diseñador/ diseñadora gráfico/gráfica graphic designer

diseñar VERB [17] **to design**

diseño NOUN MASC **design**

disfraz NOUN MASC ❶ **disguise** ❷ **costume**, **fancy dress outfit**; un disfraz de pirata a pirate outfit, una fiesta de disfraces a fancy dress party

disfrazarse REFLEXIVE VERB [22] **to dress up**; me disfracé de bruja I dressed up as a witch

disfrutar VERB [17] **to enjoy yourself**; disfrutar de algo to enjoy something, he disfrutado mucho de las vacaciones I really enjoyed my holiday

disgustar VERB [17] **to upset**

disgustarse REFLEXIVE VERB [17] **to get upset**

disgusto NOUN MASC tengo un disgusto enorme I'm very upset

disminución NOUN FEM **decrease**

disminuir VERB [54] ❶ **to decrease**; el número de visitantes ha diminuido the number of visitors has decreased ❷ **to reduce** (speed, costs)

disolvente NOUN MASC **solvent**

disolver VERB [45] **to dissolve**

disolverse REFLEXIVE VERB [45] **to dissolve**

disparar VERB [17] ❶ **to fire** ❷ **to shoot**

disparo NOUN MASC **shot**

disposición NOUN FEM
❶ **arrangement** ❷ **aptitude**
❸ estoy a tu disposición I'm at your disposal

dispuesto, dispuesta ADJECTIVE
❶ **arranged** ❷ **ready**; ya está todo dispuesto everything's ready ❸ estar dispuesto a hacer to be prepared to do, no estoy dispuesto a esperar I'm not prepared to wait

disputa NOUN MASC ❶ **dispute** ❷ **argument**

disputarse REFLEXIVE VERB [17] ❶ **to compete for** (title, cup) ❷ **to fight over** (inheritance)

disquete NOUN MASC **diskette**

disquetera NOUN FEM **disk drive**

distancia NOUN FEM **distance**; ¿a qué distancia está el colegio de tu casa? how far is the school from your house?, los dos postes están a una distancia de dos metros the two posts are two metres apart, está a poca distancia it's quite near

diste VERB ▸ SEE **dar**

distinguir VERB [50] **to distinguish**

distinguirse REFLEXIVE VERB [50]
❶ distinguirse por algo to distinguish yourself by something ❷ distinguirse de algo to be different from something

distintivo, distintiva ADJECTIVE **distinctive**

distinto ADJECTIVE **different**; ser distinto a to be different from, es distinto al resto it's different from the rest

distracción NOUN FEM
❶ **entertainment**; es su distracción favorita it's his favourite entertainment, la tele le sirve de distracción television is a way of passing the time for him ❷ se lo quitaron en un momento de distracción they stole it from her when she wasn't paying attention

distraer VERB [42] ❶ **to distract**; distraer a alguien de algo to distract somebody from something ❷ la costura me distrae sewing gives me somthing to do

distraerse REFLEXIVE VERB [42] ❶ **to get distracted** ❷ se distrae con la jardinería gardening gives him something to do

distribuidor, distribuidora NOUN MASC, FEM **distributor**

distribuir VERB [54] **to distribute**

distrito NOUN MASC **district**; distrito postal postal area

diversión NOUN FEM ❶ **fun**; por diversión for fun ❷ un lugar lleno de diversiones a place with plenty of things to do

divertido, divertida ADJECTIVE
❶ **funny**; es un chico muy divertido he's really funny ❷ la fiesta fue muy divertida the party was real fun

divertir VERB [14] **to amuse**

divertirse REFLEXIVE VERB [14] ❶ **to amuse yourself** ❷ **to have fun**; ¡que te diviertas! have fun!

dividir VERB [19] **to divide**

divisa NOUN FEM **currency**; divisas extranjeras foreign currency

división NOUN FEM **division**

divorciado, **divorciada** NOUN MASC & FEM **divorcee**

divorciado ADJECTIVE **divorced**; mis padres están divorciados my parents are divorced

divorciarse REFLEXIVE VERB [17] **to get divorced**; se divociaron en México they got divorced in Mexico

divorcio NOUN MASC **divorce**

DNI ABBREVIATION MASC (short for Documento Nacional de Identidad) **identity card**

doblar VERB [17] ❶ **to fold** (a piece of paper or clothes) ❷ **to bend** (a piece of metal or your leg) ❸ **to double** (an offer or amount) ❹ doblar la esquina **to turn the corner**

doble NOUN MASC ❶ el doble de personas twice as many people, el doble de harina que de azúcar twice as much flour as sugar, el doble de peso twice the weight, el doble de largo twice the length ❷ dobles **doubles** (in tennis)

doble ADJECTIVE **double**

doce NUMBER ❶ **twelve**; tiene doce años she's twelve (years old) ❷ **twelfth** (in dates); el doce de enero the twelfth of January ❸ **twelve** (in clock time); a las doce at twelve o'clock, son las doce del mediodía it's twelve noon, a las doce de la noche at midnight

doceavo, **doceava** ADJECTIVE **twelfth**

docena NOUN FEM **dozen**; una docena de huevos a dozen eggs

docencia NOUN FEM **teaching**

doctor, **doctora** NOUN MASC, FEM **doctor**

documentación NOUN FEM ❶ **papers**; no llevaba mi documentación I didn't have my papers on me ❷ **documents** (for a car)

documental NOUN MASC **documentary**

documental ADJECTIVE un programa documental a documentary

documento NOUN MASC **document**; mi documento de identidad my identity card

dólar NOUN MASC **dollar**

doler VERB [38] ❶ **to hurt** ❷ me duele el tobillo my ankle hurts, ¿te duele mucho? does it hurt a lot?, me duele la cabeza I've got a headache, le dolía el estómago he had stomachache

dolor NOUN MASC **pain**; tengo dolor de garganta I have a sore throat, tengo dolor de muelas I have toothache, con dolor de estómago with a stomachache

doméstico, **doméstica** ADJECTIVE **domestic**

domicilio NOUN MASC ¿cuál es su domicilio? what's your address?, en su domicilio particular in his own home

domingo NOUN MASC **Sunday**; domingo de Resurrección Easter Sunday, vienen el domingo they're coming on Sunday, el domingo pasado last Sunday, el domingo por la mañana on Sunday morning, un domingo sí y otro no every other Sunday, cierran los domingos they close on Sundays

dominical NOUN MASC ❶ **Sunday newspaper** ❷ **Sunday supplement**

dominó NOUN MASC **dominoes**; jugar al dominó to play dominoes

don NOUN MASC **Mr**; Don Juan Pozo Mr Juan Pozo

donación NOUN FEM **donation**

donde ADVERB **where**; el sitio donde nací the place where I was born, el lugar a donde nos dirigimos the place we're going to, iré a donde quiera I'll go wherever I want, ponlo donde sea put it down anywhere

dónde ADVERB **where**; ¿dónde está mi abrigo? where's my coat?, ¿de dónde eres? where are you from?, no sé dónde lo guarda I don't know where he keeps it, ¿por dónde se va a la oficina de correos? what's the way to the post office?

donut NOUN MASC **doughnut**

doña NOUN FEM **Mrs, Ms**; Doña María del Valle Mrs María del Valle

dorado, dorada ADJECTIVE **gold, golden**

dormido, dormida ADJECTIVE **asleep**; estar dormido to be asleep, quedarse dormido to fall asleep

dormir VERB [51] **❶ to sleep**; ¿has dormido bien? did you sleep well?, no he dormido nada I couldn't sleep at all **❷** ¡a dormir! time for bed!, ya es hora de irse a dormir it's time to go to bed **❸ to get to sleep**; no puedo dormir I can't get to sleep **❹** estar durmiendo to be asleep, Juan está todavía durmiendo Juan is still asleep **❺** dormir la siesta to have a nap

dormirse REFLEXIVE VERB [51] **❶ to fall asleep**; no puedo dormirme I can't get to sleep **❷ to oversleep**; me dormí y llegué tarde al trabajo I overslept and was late for work

dormitorio NOUN MASC **❶ bedroom ❷ dormitory**

dorso NOUN MASC **back**; el dorso de la mano the back of the hand

dos NUMBER **❶ two**; tiene dos años she's two (years old) **❷ second** (in dates); el dos de enero the second of January **❸ two** (in clock time); son las dos it's two o'clock

doscientos, doscientas NUMBER **two hundred**; doscientos veinte two hundred and twenty

dotado, dotada ADJECTIVE **adviser**; estar dotadopara algo to have a talent for something

doy VERB ▸ SEE **dar**

dragón NOUN MASC **dragon**

drama NOUN MASC **drama**

dramático, dramática ADJECTIVE **dramatic**

droga NOUN FEM **drug**

drogadicto, drogadicta NOUN MASC, FEM **drug addict**

drogarse REFLEXIVE VERB [17] **to take drugs**

droguería NOUN FEM **❶ hardware shop** (specializing in household items) **❷ chemist's**

ducha NOUN FEM **shower**; pegarse una ducha to have a shower

ducharse REFLEXIVE VERB [17] **to have a shower**

duda NOUN FEM **❶ doubt**; sin duda es el mejor it's undoubtedly the best, no me queda la menor duda I have no doubts whatsoever **❷ query**; ¿tienes alguna duda? do you have any queries?, tengo algunas dudas I have a few queries

dudar *VERB* [17] **to doubt**; no lo dudo I don't doubt it, dudo que sepa hacerlo I doubt he knows how to do it

duela, **duelo**, *etc VERB* ▸ SEE **doler**

dueño, **dueña** *NOUN MASC* ❶ **owner**; ¿quién es el dueño de este coche? who's the owner of this car?, se lo devolví a la dueña I returned it to its owner ❷ **landlord/landlady** *(of a pub or a guesthouse)*

duerma, **duermo**, *etc VERB* ▸ SEE **dormir**

dulce *NOUN MASC* no me gustan los dulces I don't like sweet things

dulce *ADJECTIVE* **sweet**

duna *NOUN FEM* **dune**

duodécimo, **duodécima** *ADJECTIVE* **twelfth**

duque *NOUN MASC* **duke**

duquesa *NOUN FEM* **duchess**

duración *NOUN FEM* ❶ **length**; la duración de la película the length of the film ❷ disco de larga duración LP

durante *PREPOSITION* ❶ **during**; durante aquel tiempo during that time, lo haré durante las vacaciones I'll do it during the holidays ❷ **for**; no se vieron durante tres semanas they didn't see each other for three weeks ❸ **throughout**; durante todo el partido throughout the match

durar *VERB* [17] **to last**; la guerra duró tres años the war lasted three years, ¿cuánto dura? how long is it?, no dura mucho it's not very long

dureza *NOUN FEM* **hardness**

duro¹, **dura** *ADJECTIVE* ❶ **hard**; al secarse se pone duro it goes hard when it dries, fue un golpe muy duro para todos it was a hard blow for all of us, un profesor muy duro a very strict teacher ❷ **tough** *(meat)* ❸ **stale** *(bread)* ❹ un huevo duro a hard-boiled egg ❺ ser duro de oído to be hard of hearing

duro *ADVERB* **hard**; estudiar duro to study hard

duro², **dura** *NOUN MASC* **five-peseta coin**

DVD *NOUN MASC* **DVD**

Ee

e CONJUNCTION **and** (*'y' becomes 'e' before words beginning with 'i-' or 'hi-'*); padres e hijos parents and children

echar VERB [17] **❶ to put**; echa más sal a la sopa put more salt in the soup, eché el monedero en la bolsa I put my purse in my bag, tengo que echar gasolina al coche I have to put some petrol in the car **❷ to give**; ¿te echo un poco de salsa? shall I give you some sauce? **❸ to throw**; eché agua al fuego I threw water on the fire **❹** echar a alguien to throw someone out, los eché de mi casa I threw them out of my house **❺** echar a alguien del trabajo to sack someone, lo han echado del trabajo he's been sacked **❻ to show**; echan una película en la tele they're showing a film on the television, ¿qué echan en el cine? what's on at the cinema? **❼** echar una carta (al correo) to post a letter **❽** echar de menos a alguien to miss somebody, echo de menos a mi hermana I miss my sister, te echo mucho de menos I miss you a lot

echarse VERB REFLEXIVE [17] **❶** echarse al suelo to throw yourself on the ground **❷** echarse a la derecha to move to the right, echarse para atrás to move backwards, me eché a un lado I moved to one side **❸** echarse una siesta to have a nap

eclipse NOUN MASC **eclipse**

eco NOUN MASC **echo**

ecológico, **ecológica** ADJECTIVE **ecological**

ecologista NOUN MASC & FEM **ecologist**

economía NOUN FEM **economics**

económico, **económica** ADJECTIVE **❶ economic**; una crisis económica an economic crisis **❷ financial**; los problemas económicos financial problems **❸ cheap**; un hotel muy económico a very cheap hotel **❹ thrifty** (*person*)

ecuación NOUN FEM **equation**

ecuador NOUN MASC **equator**

Ecuador NOUN MASC **Equador**

ecuatoriano, **ecuatoriana** NOUN MASC, FEM, ADJECTIVE **Ecuadorian**

edad NOUN FEM **age**; ¿qué edad tienes? how old are you?, Carmen y yo tenemos la misma edad Carmen and I are the same age, tendrá tu edad más o menos he must be around the same age as you, una mujer de unos treinta años de edad a woman of about thirty, la edad de piedra the Stone Age, la edad media the Middle Ages, está en la edad del pavo he's at that awkward age

edición NOUN FEM **❶ publication** **❷ edition**; edición de bolsillo pocket edition

edificio NOUN MASC **building**

editar VERB [17] **❶ to publish** **❷ to edit** (*a text*)

editorial NOUN FEM **publishing company**

edredón NOUN MASC **quilt**; un edredón nórdico a duvet

a b c d e f g h i j k l m n ñ o p q r s t u v w x y z

Spanish—English

A
B
C
D
E
F
G
H
I
J
K
L
M
N
Ñ
O
P
Q
R
S
T
U
V
W
X
Y
Z

educación NOUN FEM ❶ **education**; educación física physical education, educación secundaria secondary education, educación a distancia distance learning ❷ **upbringing** ❸ **manners**; tiene mucha educación she's very polite, eso es de mala educación that's bad manners

educado, educada ADJECTIVE **polite**; una persona mal educada a rude person

educar VERB [31] ❶ **to educate** ❷ **to bring up**

educativo, educativa ADJECTIVE **educational**

EE.UU. ABBREVIATION (short for Estados Unidos) **USA**

efectivo¹ NOUN MASC **cash**; un millón de euros en efectivo a million euros in cash, pagar en efectivo to pay cash

efectivo², efectiva ADJECTIVE **effective** (remedy or method)

efecto NOUN MASC **effect**; la pastilla no me hizo efecto the pill didn't have any effect on me, efectos secundarios side effects, efectos especiales special effects, el efecto invernadero the greenhouse effect

efectuar VERB [20] ❶ **to carry out**; efectuar un registro to carry out a search ❷ efectuar un viaje to go on a trip ❸ el tren efectuará su salida a las nueve treinta the train will depart at 9:30 ❹ efectuar un disparo to fire a shot

eficaz ADJECTIVE **effective**

egoísta NOUN MASC & FEM eres un egoísta you're really selfish

egoísta ADJECTIVE **selfish**

ejecutar VERB [17] **to execute**

ejecutivo, ejecutiva NOUN MASC, FEM, ADJECTIVE **executive**

ejemplar NOUN MASC ❶ **copy** (of a book) ❷ **issue** (of a magazine) ❸ **specimen** (of an animal or a plant)

ejemplo NOUN MASC **example**; por ejemplo for example, no puedes poner ese caso como ejemplo you can't take that case as an example, dar buen ejemplo to set a good example

ejercer VERB [17] ❶ **to practise**; es abogada pero no ejerce she's a lawyer but she doesn't practise ❷ **to exercise** (a right)

ejercicio NOUN MASC **exercise**; hacer ejercicio to do exercise

ejército NOUN MASC **army**; el ejército de tierra the army, el ejército de aire the air force, alistarse en el ejército to join the army

el DEFINITE ARTICLE ❶ ('el' is used before masculine singular nouns; see also 'la', 'los' and 'las') **the**; el libro blanco the white book, el sol the sun ❷ ('el' is also used before feminine nouns that start with stressed 'a') el águila the eagle, el hada the fairy ❸ ('a' followed by 'el' becomes 'al') le llevaron al hospital they took him to hospital ❹ (sometimes 'el' is not translated) el caviar es muy caro caviar is very dear, este es el señor Martínez this is Mr Martínez, el coche de Juan Juan's car ❺ (with parts of the body or personal belongings) se rompió el brazo she broke her arm, se afeitó el bigote he shaved off his

moustache, me quité el abrigo I
took my coat off ❻ *(talking about
dates and days of the week)* el dos
de mayo the second of May, iré el
próximo lunes I'll go next Monday,
el miércoles abren a las diez they
open at ten on Wednesdays ❼ me
gustó el rojo I liked the red one ❽ el
mío es mejor mine is better, el suyo
es más caro his is more expensive
❾ el mío y el de usted mine and
yours, este es el de María this one
is María's, me gusta más el de Toni
I like Toni's better ❿ el que the one
(that),
el que yo compré the one I bought,
el que quieras whichever you want

él *PRONOUN* ❶ **he**; él no lo sabe he
doesn't know ❷ **him**; estaba
hablando con él I was talking to
him, pregúntale a él ask him, iba
detrás de él I was behind him ❸ es
de él it's his ❹ él mismo he himself

elástico, elástica *ADJECTIVE* **elastic**

elección *NOUN FEM* ❶ **choice**; no
tener elección to have no choice
❷ las elecciones the election,
convocar elecciones to call an
election

electorado *NOUN MASC* **electorate**

electoral *ADJECTIVE* campaña
electoral election campaign

electricidad *NOUN FEM* **electricity**

electricista *NOUN MASC & FEM*
electrician

eléctrico, eléctrica *ADJECTIVE*
❶ **electric** ❷ **electrical**

electrocutar *VERB* [17] **to
electrocute**

electrodoméstico *NOUN MASC*
electrical appliance

electrónico, electrónica *ADJECTIVE*
electronic

elefante *NOUN MASC* **elephant**

elegante *ADJECTIVE* ❶ **elegant**
❷ **smart**; siempre va muy elegante
he's always very smartly dressed

elegir *VERB* [48] **to choose**

elemento *NOUN MASC* **element**

elepé *NOUN MASC* **LP**

elija, elijo *VERB* ▸ SEE **elegir**

eliminar *VERB* [17] ❶ **to eliminate**
❷ **to remove**

eliminatorio, eliminatoria
ADJECTIVE **qualifying** *(round or
match)*

ella *PRONOUN* ❶ **she**; ella no lo sabe
she doesn't know ❷ **her**; estaba
hablando con ella I was talking to
her, pregúntale a ella ask her, yo
iba detrás de ella I was behind her
❸ es de ella it's hers ❹ ella misma
she herself

ellas *PRONOUN* ❶ *('ellas' is the feminine
plural form of the pronoun; it is used
to refer to two or more females)*
they; ellas no lo saben they don't
know ❷ **them**; estaba hablando
con ellas I was talking to them,
pregúntales a ellas ask them, iba
detrás de ellas I was behind them
❸ es de ellas it's theirs ❹ ellas
mismas they themselves

ello *PRONOUN* ❶ **it**; se beneficiaron de
ello they benefited from it ❷ **this**;
para ello es necesario ... for this, it
is necessary ...

ellos *PRONOUN* ❶ *('ellos' is the
masculine plural form of the
pronoun; it is used to refer to two or
more males or a group of mixed sex)*

a
b
c
d
e
f
g
h
i
j
k
l
m
n
ñ
o
p
q
r
s
t
u
v
w
x
y
z

they; ellos no lo saben they don't know **❷ them**; estaba hablando con ellos I was talking to them, pregúntales a ellos ask them, iba detrás de ellos I was behind them **❸ es de ellos** it's theirs **❹ ellos mismos** they themselves

embajada *NOUN FEM* **embassy**

embajador, embajadora *NOUN MASC, FEM* **ambassador**

embalse *NOUN MASC* **reservoir**

embarazada *NOUN FEM* **pregnant woman**

embarazada *ADJECTIVE* **pregnant**; quedarse embarazada to get pregnant, estoy embarazada de tres meses I'm three months pregnant

embarazo *NOUN MASC* **❶ pregnancy ❷ embarrassment**

embarcación *NOUN FEM* **vessel** *(boat)*

embarcadero *NOUN MASC* **wharf**

embarcar *VERB* [31] **❶ to board** *(a plane)* **❷ to embark** *(on a boat)* **❸ to load** *(goods or luggage)*

embarcarse *REFLEXIVE VERB* [31] **❶ to board** *(a plane)* **❷ to embark** *(on a boat)* **❸ embarcarse en algo** to get involved in something

embargo *NOUN MASC* **❶ embargo ❷ sin embargo** nevertheless

emborracharse *REFLEXIVE VERB* [17] **to get drunk**

emboscada *NOUN FEM* **ambush**

embotellamiento *NOUN MASC* **traffic jam**

embrague *NOUN MASC* **clutch**

embrujado, embrujada *ADJECTIVE* **❶ haunted ❷ bewitched**

emergencia *NOUN FEM* **emergency**

emigrante *NOUN MASC & FEM* **emigrant**

emigrar *VERB* [17] **to emigrate**

emisión *NOUN FEM* **emission**

emisora *NOUN FEM* **radio station**

emoción *NOUN FEM* **❶ emotion ❷ excitement**; ¡qué emoción! how exciting!, un espectáculo lleno de emoción a really exciting show

emocionado, emocionada *ADJECTIVE* **❶ moved ❷ excited**

emocional *ADJECTIVE* **emotional**

emocionante *ADJECTIVE* **❶ moving ❷ exciting**; ¡qué emocionante! how exciting!

emoticón *NOUN MASC* **smiley, emoticon**

empacho *NOUN MASC (informal)* tener empacho to have a stomach-ache *(from eating too much)*, se cogió un empacho de pasteles he ate so many cakes he had a stomachache

empalme *NOUN MASC* **junction** *(on railway)*

empanada *NOUN FEM* **pie**; empanada de atún tuna pie

empapado, empapada *ADJECTIVE* **soaking wet**; venían empapados they were soaking wet

empaparse *VERB* [17] **to get soaking wet**

empastar *VERB* [17] **to fill** *(a tooth)*

empaste *NOUN MASC* **filling** *(in a tooth)*

empatar *VERB* [17] **to draw**; empataron a dos they drew two all

empate NOUN MASC **draw** *(in sports)*

empecé VERB ▸ SEE **empezar**

empeorar VERB [17] ❶ to get worse; la situación ha empeorado things have got worse ❷ to make worse; va a empeorar las cosas it's going to make things worse

emperador NOUN MASC **emperor**

emperatriz NOUN FEM **empress**

empezar VERB [25] ❶ to begin; el colegio empieza el quince de septiembre school begins on the fifteenth of September ❷ to start; tendré que empezar otra vez I'll have to start again, empezó a llover it started raining

empiece, empieza, empiezo, *etc* VERB ▸ SEE **empezar**

empinado, empinada ADJECTIVE **steep** *(a road or street)*

empleado, empleada NOUN MASC, FEM ❶ **employee** ❷ **clerk** *(in a bank or office)* ❸ **shop assistant** ❹ los empleados the staff *(in a company)*, todos los empleados se beneficiarán all the staff will benefit

emplear VERB [17] ❶ to employ ❷ to use; emplearon materiales viejos they used old materials

empleo NOUN MASC ❶ **employment** ❷ **job**; buscar empleo to look for a job ❸ estar sin empleo to be unemployed

empollar VERB [17] ❶ *(informal)* to lock up *(a person)* ❷ to incubate *(eggs)*

emprendedor, emprendedora ADJECTIVE **enterprising**

empresa NOUN FEM **company**

empresario, empresaria NOUN MASC, FEM **businessman, businesswoman**

empujar VERB [17] to push

en PREPOSITION ❶ **in**; ponlo en el cajón put it in the drawer, vivo en Londres I live in London, en español in Spanish, en invierno in winter ❷ **into**; entró en la casa he went into the house ❸ **on**; está en la mesa it's on the table, en el segundo piso on the second floor ❹ **at**; estaré en casa toda la tarde I'll be at home all afternoon, es muy buena en inglés she's very good at English ❺ nunca he estado en París I've never been to Paris ❻ **by**; ir en coche to go by car

enagua NOUN FEM **petticoat**

enaguas NOUN FEM & PLURAL **petticoat**

enamorado, enamorada ADJECTIVE **in love**; estar enamorado de alguien to be in love with someone

enamorarse REFLEXIVE VERB [17] to fall in love; enamorarse de alguien to fall in love with someone

encantado, encantada ADJECTIVE ❶ **delighted**; están encantados con la casa they're delighted with the house ❷ ¡encantado de conocerte! pleased to meet you! ❸ **enchanted**

encantador, encantadora NOUN MASC, FEM **magician**; encantador de serpientes snake-charmer

encantador ADJECTIVE ❶ **lovely** *(thing)* ❷ **charming** *(person)*

encantar VERB [17] me encantó el libro I loved the book, nos encantó el hotel we loved the hotel, le encantaría venir a verte he'd love to come and see you

encargado, **encargada** NOUN MASC, FEM **manager**

encargado ADJECTIVE encargado de algo responsible for something, la persona encargada del reparto the person responsible for the delivery

encargarse REFLEXIVE VERB [17] encargarse de algo to take care of something

encendedor NOUN MASC **lighter**

encender VERB [36] ❶ to light ❷ to turn on

encendido, **encendida** ADJECTIVE ❶ on ❷ alight

encerado NOUN MASC **blackboard**

encerrar VERB [17] ❶ to lock up (a person) ❷ to lock away (papers, money)

enchufar VERB [17] ❶ to plug in ❷ to turn on

enchufe NOUN MASC **plug**

enciclopedia NOUN FEM **encyclopedia**

encienda, **enciendo**, etc VERB ▸ SEE **encender**

encima ADVERB ❶ on; pon un plástico encima put a piece of plastic on it, ponlo ahí encima put it on there, el piso de encima the flat above, no llevaba el carnet de identidad encima he didn't have his identity card on him ❷ encima de on, on top of, está encima de la cama it's on the bed, encima del armario on top of the wardrobe, llevaba una gabardina encima de la chaqueta I was wearing a raincoat over my jacket, el niño estaba sentado encima de su madre the baby was sitting on his mother's lap ❸ el/la

de encima the top one ❹ por encima de over ❺ encima de llegar tarde se queja he arrives late and on top of that he complains, ¡y encima no me lo devolvió! and on top of that he didn't give it back to me!

encontrar VERB [24] to find; no he encontrado cerillas en ninguna parte I couldn't find any matches anywhere

encontrarse REFLEXIVE VERB [24] ❶ to meet; me encontré con Carmen en la calle I met Carmen in the street ❷ to find; me encontré un billete de diez euros I found a ten-euro note ❸ to be; el pueblo se encuentra situado en la montaña the village is situated in the mountains

encuentra, **encuentro**, etc VERB ▸ SEE **encontrar**

encuesta NOUN FEM **survey**; encuesta de opinión opinion poll

enemigo, **enemiga** NOUN MASC, FEM **enemy**

energía NOUN FEM **energy**

enérgico, **enérgica** ADJECTIVE **energetic**

enero NOUN MASC **January**

enfadado, **enfadada** ADJECTIVE ❶ angry ❷ annoyed

enfadar VERB [17] ❶ to make angry ❷ to annoy

enfadarse REFLEXIVE VERB [17] ❶ to get angry; se enfadó muchísimo he got really angry ❷ to get annoyed; se enfadó conmigo he got annoyed with me ❸ to get cross; mamá se va a enfadar Mum's going to get cross

énfasis NOUN MASC **emphasis**

enfermar VERB [17] **to get ill**

enfermedad NOUN FEM **illness**

enfermería NOUN FEM ❶ **nursing** ❷ **infirmary**

enfermero, **enfermera** NOUN MASC, FEM **nurse**

enfermo, **enferma** NOUN MASC, FEM **sick person**; los enfermos sick people

enfermo ADJECTIVE **ill**; está gravemente enferma she's seriously ill, caer enfermo to fall ill

enfrente ADVERB **opposite**; la tienda está justo enfrente de la casa the shop is just opposite the house

engañar VERB [17] ❶ **to deceive** ❷ **to cheat, swindle** ❸ **to be unfaithful to**

engañarse REFLEXIVE VERB [17] **to fool yourself**

engaño NOUN MASC ❶ **deception** ❷ **swindle**

engordar VERB [17] ❶ **to put on weight** ❷ **to be fattening**

engreído, **engreída** ADJECTIVE **conceited**

enhorabuena NOUN FEM ¡enhorabuena por tu trabajo nuevo! congratulations on your new job!, darle la enhorabuena a alguien to congratulate someone

enjuagar VERB [28] **to rinse**

enjuagarse REFLEXIVE VERB [28] enjuagarse el pelo to rinse your hair

enlace NOUN MASC **link**

enmohecerse REFLEXIVE VERB [35] **to go mouldy**

enojado, **enojada** ADJECTIVE ❶ **angry** ❷ **annoyed**

enorme ADJECTIVE **huge**

enormemente ADVERB **extremely, a lot**; enormemente preocupado extremely worried

enrollar VERB [17] **to roll up**

enroscar VERB [31] ❶ **to wind** ❷ **to screw on**

ensaimada NOUN FEM **light round cake covered in icing sugar**

ensalada NOUN FEM **salad**; ensalada mixta mixed salad, ensalada de frutas fruit salad

ensaladera NOUN FEM **salad bowl**

ensaladilla, **ensaladilla rusa** NOUN FEM **potato salad**

ensanchar VERB [17] **to widen**

ensayo NOUN MASC **rehearsal**; ensayo general dress rehearsal

enseguida ADVERB **right away**; enseguida lo hago I'll do it right away

enseñanza NOUN FEM ❶ **teaching**; me gusta la enseñanza I like teaching ❷ **education**; enseñanza primaria primary education, enseñanza secundaria secondary education, enseñanza superior higher education

enseñar VERB [17] ❶ **to teach**; le enseñé a montar en bicicleta I taught him to ride a bike ❷ **to show**; nos enseñó la casa he showed us the house

ensuciar VERB [17] **to make dirty**; no ensucies la mesa don't make the table dirty, ensucié el mantel de salsa de tomate I got tomato sauce on the tablecloth

a
b
c
d
e
f
g
h
i
j
k
l
m
n
ñ
o
p
q
r
s
t
u
v
w
x
y
z

ensuciarse REFLEXIVE VERB [17] **to get dirty**; te vas a ensuciar las manos you'll get your hands dirty, me he ensuciado las botas de barro I've got mud on my boots

entender VERB [36] **❶ to understand**; entiendo un poco de español I can understand a little bit of Spanish, entiendo lo que dices I understand what you are saying, no te entiendo I can't understand you **❷** entender algo mal to misunderstand something, la entendí mal I misunderstood her **❸** dar a entender algo to imply something **❹** entender de algo to know about something, entiendo un poco de fontanería I know a bit about plumbing

entenderse REFLEXIVE VERB [36] **❶** entenderse con alguien to communicate with someone, nos entendimos por señas we communicated with each other by signs **❷** entenderse con alguien to get along with someone, se entiende muy bien con su hermana she gets along very well with her sister

entendido, entendida ADJECTIVE **❶ understood**; queda bien entendido it's clearly understood, ¿entendido? is that clear? **❷** ser entendido en algo to know about something

entero, entera ADJECTIVE **❶ whole**; un día entero a whole day **❷** leche entera full-cream milk

enterrar VERB [29] **to bury**

entienda, entiendo, etc VERB ▸ SEE **entender**

entonces ADVERB **❶ then**; desde entonces since then, entonces llegó Carlos then Carlos arrived **❷ so**; entonces nos vemos mañana so we'll see each other tomorrow

entrada NOUN FEM **❶ entrance**; ¿dónde está la entrada? where is the entrance? **❷ ticket** (for the cinema or theatre); ya he comprado las entradas para el teatro I've already bought the tickets for the theatre, ¿cuánto cuesta la entrada? how much is a ticket?, los niños pagan media entrada it's half-price for children **❸** 'entrada libre' 'admission free' **❹ deposit**; pagué la entrada para el coche I put down a deposit on the car **❺ tackle** (in football)

entrar VERB [17] **❶ to get in**; no puedo entrar I can't get in, entraron por una ventana they got in through a window **❷ to go in**; han entrado en esa tienda they've gone into that shop, entraron en la clase corriendo they ran into the classroom **❸ to come in**; ¡entra! come in! **❹** dejar entrar a alguien to let someone in **❺** hacer entrar a alguien to show someone in **❻ to fit**; no entra por la puerta it doesn't fit through the door **❼ to join**; entrar en la ONU to join UN **❽** me entró hambre I got hungry, te va a entrar frío si te sientas ahí you'll get cold if you sit there **❾ to be included**; el desayuno no entra en el precio breakfast is not included in the price **❿** no me entra (informal) I don't get it, no le entran las matemáticas (informal) he just can't get to grips with maths

entre PREPOSITION **❶ between**; estaba sentado entre Jaime y Margarita I was sitting between Jaime and Margarita **❷ among**; lo encontré entre mis papeles I found it among my papers ❸ lo hicimos entre todos we did it all together ❹ by; nueve dividido entre tres nine divided by three ❺ entre paréntesis in brackets ❻ cerrado entre semana closed during the week

entreabierto, **entreabierta** *ADJECTIVE* half-open

entreacto *NOUN MASC* interval

entrega *NOUN FEM* ❶ delivery *(of goods)* ❷ presentation *(of a prize or award)* ❸ la fecha límite para la entrega de formularios the deadline for handing in the forms

entregar *VERB* [28] ❶ to deliver; vino a entregar una carta he came to deliver a letter ❷ to give, to hand; me entregó los documentos he handed me the documents, tenemos que entregar el trabajo el próximo lunes we have to hand in the essay next Monday ❸ to present *(a prize or award)* ❹ to surrender *(a town or weapons)* ❺ to turn in *(a criminal)*

entregarse *REFLEXIVE VERB* [28] to give yourself up; se entregó a la policía he gave himself up to the police

entremés *NOUN MASC* starter *(in a meal)*

entrenador, **entrenadora** *NOUN MASC, FEM* trainer

entrenamiento *NOUN MASC* training

entrenar *VERB* [17] to train

entrenarse *REFLEXIVE VERB* [17] to train

entretanto *ADVERB* in the meantime

entretenido, **entretenida** *ADJECTIVE* entertaining

entretenimiento *NOUN MASC* entertainment

entrevista *NOUN FEM* interview; una entrevista de trabajo a job interview

entrevistar *VERB* [17] to interview

entumecido, **entumecida** *ADJECTIVE* numb

entusiasmado, **entusiasmada** *ADJECTIVE* excited

entusiasmar *VERB* [17] me entusiasmó la idea I loved the idea, le entusiasma el deporte she's really keen on sports, no me entusiasma viajar I'm not very keen on travelling

entusiasmarse *REFLEXIVE VERB* [17] entusiasmarse con algo/por algo to get excited about something

entusiasmo *NOUN MASC* enthusiasm

envase *NOUN MASC* container; un envase de cartón a carton, envases de plástico plastic packaging

enviar *VERB* [32] to send

envidia *NOUN FEM* ❶ envy; se muere de envidia he's green with envy ❷ jealousy; tenerle envidia a alguien to be jealous of someone, me tienen envidia they're jealous of me, le da envidia que yo tenga una bici mejor she's jealous because I've got a better bike

envidia *NOUN FEM* envy; tiene envidia de su hermana she's envious of her sister

envidiar *VERB* [17] to be envious of; me envidia el resultado de los exámenes she's envious of my exam results

a b c d e f g h i j k l m n ñ o p q r s t u v w x y z

envidioso, **envidiosa** ADJECTIVE
envious

envolver VERB [45] to wrap up

envuelto[1], **envuelta** ADJECTIVE
❶ wrapped; envuelto para regalo
gift-wrapped ❷ envuelto en algo
involved in something

envuelto[2] VERB ▸ SEE **envolver**

epidemia NOUN FEM epidemic

Epifanía NOUN FEM Epiphany (the 6th
January)

episodio NOUN MASC episode

época NOUN FEM ❶ age; era otra
época it was a different age
❷ time; en aquella época at that
time ❸ times; en la época de los
romanos in Roman times

equilibrado, **equilibrada** ADJECTIVE
balanced

equilibrio NOUN MASC balance; estar
en equilibrio to be balanced, perder
el equilibrio to lose your balance

equipaje NOUN MASC luggage;
equipaje de mano hand luggage

equipo NOUN MASC ❶ team; formar
un buen equipo to make a good
team, el equipo visitante the away
team, trabajo en equipo team work
❷ equipment ❸ equipo de música
sound system, equipo de alta
fidelidad hi-fi system

equis NOUN FEM the Spanish name
for the letter 'x'

equitación NOUN FEM horse riding

equivaler VERB [43] equivaler a algo
to be equivalent to something

equivocado, **equivocada** ADJECTIVE
wrong

equivocarse REFLEXIVE VERB [31] ❶ to
make a mistake; creo que me
he equivocado I think I've made
a mistake ❷ to be wrong; te
equivocas si piensas eso you're
wrong if you think like that ❸ me
equivoqué de carpeta I picked up
the wrong folder, se equivocó de
calle he took the wrong street

era, **érais**, **eras**, **eres**, etc VERB
▸ SEE **ser**

error NOUN MASC mistake; cometer
un error to make a mistake, un
error tipográfico a typing error, un
error de cálculo a miscalculation

eructar VERB [17] to burp

eructo NOUN MASC burp

es VERB ▸ SEE **ser**

esa[1] DETERMINER that ▸ SEE **ese**[1],
esa

esa[2] PRONOUN that one ▸ SEE **ese**[2],
esa

esas[1] DETERMINER those ▸ SEE **esos**[1],
esas

esas[2] PRONOUN those ones
▸ SEE **esos**[2], esas

escala NOUN FEM ❶ stopover; hacer
escala en París to stop over in Paris
❷ scale (of a map or measurements);
hacer algo a escala to do something
to scale, a gran escala on a large
scale ❸ scale (in music)

escalada NOUN FEM ❶ (rock)
climbing ❷ climb

escalador, **escaladora** NOUN MASC,
FEM climber

escalar VERB [17] to climb

escalera NOUN FEM staircase; subir
las escaleras to go up the stairs,
una escalera de caracol a spiral

staircase, **una escalera mecánica** an escalator, **una escalera de incendios** a fire escape, **una escalera de mano** a ladder

escalofrío NOUN MASC **shiver**; **tener escalofríos** to be shivering

escalón NOUN MASC **step**

escalope NOUN MASC **escalope**

escándalo NOUN MASC ❶ **scandal**; **un escándalo político** a political scandal, **¡su comportamiento fue un escándalo!** his behaviour was really outrageous! ❷ **racket**; **armar un escándalo** to make a racket, **¡qué escándalo están armando!** what a racket they are making!

escandaloso, escandalosa ADJECTIVE ❶ **shocking** (behaviour or clothes) ❷ **noisy** (people)

Escandinavia NOUN FEM **Scandinavia**

escandinavo, escandinava NOUN MASC, FEM **Scandinavian**; **los escandinavos** Scandinavians

escandinavo ADJECTIVE **Scandinavian**

escáner NOUN MASC ❶ **scanner** ❷ **scan**

escapar VERB [17] **to escape**; **escapar de algo** to escape from something

escaparse REFLEXIVE VERB [17] ❶ **to escape**; **se ha escapado de la cárcel** he's escaped from prison ❷ **to run away**; **escaparse de casa** to run away from home ❸ **to leak** (gas or water)

escaparate NOUN MASC **shop window**

escarabajo NOUN MASC **beetle**

escarcha NOUN FEM **frost**

escasez NOUN FEM **shortage**; **hay escasez de agua** there's a water shortage

escaso, escasa ADJECTIVE ❶ **limited**; **un país de escasos recursos** a country with limited resources ❷ **andar escaso de algo** to be short of something

escena NOUN FEM **scene**

escenario NOUN MASC **stage**

esclavo, esclava NOUN MASC, FEM **slave**

esclusa NOUN FEM **lock** (on a canal)

escoba NOUN FEM **broom**

escocés, escocesa NOUN MASC, FEM **Scot**

escocés, escocesa ADJECTIVE **Scottish**

Escocia NOUN FEM **Scotland**

escoger VERB [3] **to choose**

escoja, escojo, etc VERB ▸ SEE **escoger**

escolar NOUN MASC & FEM **schoolboy, schoolgirl**

escolar ADJECTIVE **school**; **la vida escolar** school life

esconder VERB [18] **to hide**

esconderse REFLEXIVE VERB [18] **to hide**; **esconderse de algo** to hide from something

escondido, escondida ADJECTIVE **hidden**

escorpión¹, escorpio NOUN MASC, FEM **Scorpio**; **soy escorpión** I'm Scorpio

escorpión² *NOUN MASC* **scorpion**

Escorpión, **Escorpio** *NOUN MASC* **Scorpio**

escribir *VERB* [52] ❶ **to write**; escribir una novela to write a novel, le escribí una carta I wrote a letter to him ❷ escribir a máquina to type ❸ **to spell**; ¿cómo se escribe tu nombre? how do you spell your name?

escrito *VERB* ▶ SEE **escribir**

escritor, **escritora** *NOUN MASC, FEM* **writer**

escritorio *NOUN MASC* **desk**

escuchar *VERB* [17] ❶ **to listen**; escuchamos atentamente we listen carefully ❷ **to listen to**; escucha bien lo que digo listen carefully to what I say, escúchame listen to me

escuela *NOUN FEM* **school**; escuela primaria primary school, escuela nocturna night school

escultor, **escultora** *NOUN MASC, FEM* **sculptor**

escultura *NOUN FEM* **sculpture**

escupir *VERB* [19] ❶ **to spit**; escupir a alguien to spit at someone ❷ **to spit out**; escupió la comida he spat out the food

ese¹, **esa** *DETERMINER* **that**; ese libro that book, esa chica that girl

ese², **esa** *PRONOUN* **that one**; ese es más bonito that one is nicer, esa es tu bolsa that one is your bag

esforzarse *REFLEXIVE VERB* [17] **to try hard**; tienes que esforzarte más you have to try harder, esforzarse por hacer algo to try hard to do something

esfuerzo *NOUN MASC* **effort**; hacer un esfuerzo to make an effort

esgrima *NOUN FEM* **fencing**

esguince *NOUN MASC* **sprain**

eslogan *NOUN MASC* **slogan**

eslovaco, **eslovaca** *NOUN MASC, FEM, ADJECTIVE* **Slovak**

Eslovaquia *NOUN FEM* **Slovakia**

Eslovenia *NOUN FEM* **Slovenia**

esloveno, **eslovena** *NOUN MASC, FEM, ADJECTIVE* **Slovene**

eso *PRONOUN* **that**; eso no importa that doesn't matter, por eso that's why

ESO *ABBREVIATION FEM (short for Educación Secundaria Obligatoria)* **compulsory secondary education programme in Spain for the 12-16 age group**

esos¹, **esas** *DETERMINER* **those**; esos libros those books, esas chicas those girls

esos², **esas** *PRONOUN* **those ones**; esos son más bonitos those ones are nicer

espabilado, **espabilada** *ADJECTIVE* **alert**

espacio *NOUN MASC* ❶ **space**; la conquista del espacio the conquest of space, dejar un espacio leave a space ❷ **room**; no tengo mucho espacio para ponerlo I haven't got much room for it

espada *NOUN FEM* **sword**

espaguetis *PLURAL NOUN MASC* **spaghetti**

espalda *NOUN FEM* **back**; ser ancho de espaldas to be broad-shouldered, darle la espalda a alguien to have your back to somebody, to turn your back on somebody, nos daba la espalda he had his back to us, nadar de espaldas to swim backstroke, tumbarse de espaldas to lie on your back

espantapájaros NOUN MASC **scarecrow**

espantoso, **espantosa** ADJECTIVE ❶ **horrific** *(crime)* ❷ **horrible**; un vestido espantoso a horrible dress, tiene un gusto espantoso he has a horrible sense of taste ❸ hacía un frío espantoso it was terribly cold, tengo un sueño espantoso I'm terribly sleepy

España NOUN FEM **Spain**

español[1] NOUN MASC **Spanish** *(the language)*

español[2], **española** NOUN MASC, FEM **Spaniard**; los españoles the Spanish

español ADJECTIVE **Spanish**

esparadrapo NOUN MASC **sticking plaster**

esparcimiento NOUN MASC & MASC **relaxation**

espárrago NOUN MASC **asparagus**

especia NOUN FEM **spice**

especial ADJECTIVE **special**

especialidad NOUN FEM **speciality**

especialmente ADVERB ❶ **especially**; fue muy duro, especialmente para él It was very hard, especially for him ❷ **specially**; está especialmente diseñado para nosotros It is specially designed for us

especie NOUN FEM ❶ **species**; una especie en vías de extinción an endangered species ❷ **kind**; era

una especie de sopa it was a kind of soup

espectáculo NOUN MASC ❶ **sight**; era un espectáculo espantoso it was a terrible sight ❷ **show**; el mundo del espectáculo show business

espectador, **espectadora** NOUN MASC & FEM **spectator**

espejo NOUN MASC **mirror**; espejo retrovisor rear-view mirror

espera NOUN FEM **wait**; una corta espera a short wait, estar a la espera de algo to be waiting for something

esperanza NOUN FEM **hope**; darle esperanzas a alguien to build up somebody's hopes, hay pocas esperanzas de encontrarlos there's little hope of finding them

esperar VERB [17] ❶ **to wait**; espera aquí wait here ❷ **to wait for**; te he estado esperando más de una hora I've been waiting for you for more than an hour ❸ **to hope**; espero que vengas I hope you'll come, espero que sí/espero I hope so ❹ **to expect**; no esperaba esa respuesta I didn't expect that answer

espeso, **espesa** ADJECTIVE **thick**

espesor NOUN MASC **thickness**

espesura NOUN FEM **thickness**; tiene diez centímetros de espesura it's ten centimetres thick

espía NOUN MASC & FEM **spy**

espiar VERB [32] **to spy on**

espina NOUN FEM **thorn**

espinacas NOUN FEM **spinach**

espionaje NOUN MASC **spying**, **espionage**

A
B
C
D
E
F
G
H
I
J
K
L
M
N
Ñ
O
P
Q
R
S
T
U
V
W
X
Y
Z

espléndido, **espléndida** *ADJECTIVE*
❶ **splendid** *(a party, day, or house)*
❷ **generous** *(a person)*

espliego *NOUN MASC* **lavender**

esponja *NOUN FEM* **sponge**

esposa *NOUN FEM* ❶ **wife**; la esposa
de Juan Juan's wife ❷ **esposas**
handcuffs

esposo *NOUN MASC* **husband**; el
esposo de mi hermana my sister's
husband

espuma *NOUN FEM* ❶ **foam**;
espuma de afeitar shaving foam
❷ **lather** *(of soap)* ❸ **froth** *(of beer)*
❹ espuma para el pelo styling
mousse

espumoso, **espumosa** *ADJECTIVE*
❶ **foaming** ❷ **frothy** *(beer)* ❸ vino
espumoso sparkling wine

esqueleto *NOUN MASC* **skeleton**
• estar hecho un esqueleto to be all
skin and bones

esquí *NOUN MASC* ❶ **ski** ❷ **skiing**;
practicar el esquí to go skiing,
esquí acuático waterskiing, esquí
nórdico/esquí de fondo cross-
country skiing

esquiador, **esquiadora** *NOUN MASC*,
FEM **skier**

esquiar *VERB* [32] **to ski**

esquimal *NOUN MASC & FEM*, *ADJECTIVE*
Eskimo

esquina *NOUN FEM* **corner**; doblar la
esquina to turn the corner, vivo en
la esquina de la calle León con la
calle Viriato I live on the corner of
León Street and Viriato Street

esta¹ *DETERMINER* **this** ▸ SEE **este**, **esta**

esta² *PRONOUN* **this one** ▸ SEE **este**³,
esta

está *VERB* ▸ SEE **estar**

estable *ADJECTIVE* **stable**; una relación
estable a stable relationship

estación *NOUN FEM* ❶ **station**; la
estación de autobuses the bus
station, una estación de servicio
a petrol station ❷ **season**; el otoño
es mi estación preferida autumn is
my favourite season, la estación de
las lluvias the rainy season ❸ una
estación de esquí a ski resort

estacionar *VERB* [17] **to park**;
estacionar en doble fila to double
park

estacionario, **estacionaria**
ADJECTIVE **stationary**

estadio *NOUN MASC* **stadium**; el
estadio de fútbol the football
stadium

estado *NOUN MASC* ❶ **state**; estado
de guerra state of war ❷ en buen
estado in good condition *(a picture,
table, etc.)* ❸ estado civil marital
status ❹ estar en estado to be
pregnant ❺ un estado de cuenta
a bank statement

Estados Unidos *PLURAL NOUN MASC*
United States

estadounidense *ADJECTIVE*
American, US

estafa *NOUN FEM* **swindle**; ¡qué
estafa! what rip-off!

estáis *VERB* ▸ SEE **estar**

estallar *VERB* [17] ❶ **to explode** *(a
bomb)* ❷ **to burst** *(a balloon)* ❸ **to
blow out** *(a tyre)*

estancia *NOUN FEM* **stay**; su estancia
en Madrid durará tres días his stay
in Madrid will last three days

estanco *NOUN MASC* **tobacconist's**

estanque *NOUN MASC* **pond**

estante *NOUN MASC* **shelf**

estantería *NOUN FEM* ❶ **shelves** ❷ **bookcase**

estar *VERB* [2] ❶ *(location)* **to be**; ¿dónde está mi abrigo? where's my coat?, ¿has estado en Buenos Aires? have you been to Buenos Aires?, estaré en Leeds un mes I'll be in Leeds for a month ❷ *(state)* **to be**; estoy contento I'm happy, está casado he's married, ¿cómo estás? how are you?, desde que hablé con él está más simpático he's nicer since I had a chat with him ❸ *(appearance, taste)* esta paella está muy buena this paella is very nice, con ese vestido estás muy guapa you look very nice in that dress ❹ *(with dates)* estamos a tres de julio it's the third of July today ❺ estar de to be, estar de viaje to be away on a trip, están de vacaciones they're on holiday ❻ *(with a gerund or past participle)* **to be**; están trabajando en Soria they're working in Soria, está nevando it's snowing, estaban sentados allí they were sitting over there, aún no está terminado it's not finished yet ❼ *(talking about how clothes fit)* la chaqueta no me está bien the jacket doesn't fit me, esa falda te está corta this skirt is too short for you, me está grande it's too big for me ❽ lo firmas y ya está you sign it and that's that, ¿están ya las fotocopias? are the photocopies ready?, las patatas ya están the potatoes are done

estarse *REFLEXIVE VERB* [2] ❶ **to be**; se estuvo sentado toda la tarde he was sitting down all afternoon ❷ **to stay**; se está horas mirando la tele he stays in front of the TV for hours, ¡estate quieto! keep still!

estatua *NOUN FEM* **statue**

estatus *NOUN MASC* **status**

este¹ *NOUN MASC* **east**

este², **esta** *ADJECTIVE* **this**; este libro this book, esta chica this girl

este³, **esta** *PRONOUN* **this one**; este es más bonito this one is nicer, esta es tu bolsa this one is your bag

esté, **estén** *VERB* ▸ SEE **estar**

estera *NOUN FEM* ❶ **rush matting** ❷ **rush mat** ❸ **beach mat**

estéreo *NOUN MASC* **stereo**

estés *VERB* ▸ SEE **estar**

esteticista *NOUN MASC & FEM* **beautician**

estilo *NOUN MASC* ❶ **style** ❷ ni nada por el estilo or anything like that, o algo por el estilo or something of the kind

estilográfica *NOUN FEM* **fountain pen**

estirar *VERB* [17] **to stretch**

esto *PRONOUN* **this**; ¿qué es esto? what is this?, esto es lo más importante this is the most important thing

estofado *NOUN MASC* **stew**

estómago *NOUN MASC* **stomach**; me duele el estómago I've got stomachache

Estonia *NOUN FEM* **Estonia**

estonio, **estonia** *NOUN MASC, FEM, ADJECTIVE* **Estonian**

estornudar *VERB* [17] **to sneeze**

estornudo NOUN MASC **sneeze**

estoy VERB ▸ SEE **estar**

estrecho, estrecha ADJECTIVE
❶ **narrow**; una calle estrecha a
narrow street ❷ **tight**; me queda
muy estrecho it's too tight for me

estrella NOUN FEM **star**; estrella fugaz
shooting star, estrella de cine film
star

estrellarse REFLEXIVE VERB [17] **to
crash**; estrellarse contra algo to
crash into something

estrenar VERB [17] ❶ la película
se estrena el próximo lunes the
film comes out next Monday ❷ el
domingo estrenaré los zapatos I'll
wear my new shoes on Sunday, aún
no he estrenado la bici I haven't
used the new bike yet

estreno NOUN MASC **première, first
showing** (of a film)

estreñido, estreñida ADJECTIVE
constipated

estrés NOUN MASC **stress**

estresado, estresada ADJECTIVE
stressed

estresante ADJECTIVE **stressful**

estricto, estricta ADJECTIVE **strict**

estropear VERB [17] ❶ **to break**;
vas a estropear la tele si sigues
haciendo eso you'll wreck the TV
if you carry on doing that ❷ **to
spoil**; el tiempo nos estropeó las
vacaciones the weather spoiled
our holidays ❸ **to damage**; me
estropeó el coche he damaged my
car ❹ **to ruin** (a carpet or dress, for
example)

estropearse REFLEXIVE VERB [17] ❶ **to
break down**; se ha estropeado
el coche otra vez the car's broken
down again ❷ **to go off** (fruit)
❸ **to go bad** (milk or fish) ❹ **to
get ruined** (a carpet or dress, for
example)

estructura NOUN FEM **structure**

estuche NOUN MASC **case** (for glasses,
pencils etc)

estudiante NOUN MASC & FEM **student**

estudiar VERB [17] ❶ **to study**;
estudiar medicina to study
medicine ❷ **to learn**; tenemos que
estudiar dos tomas para mañana
we have to study two topics for
tomorrow

estudio NOUN MASC ❶ **studio** (in a
house) ❷ **studio flat** ❸ **study**; el
estudio de la naturaleza the study
of nature

estudios PLURAL NOUN MASC **studies**;
estudios de medicina medical
studies, estudios de mercado
market research

estufa NOUN FEM **heater, fire**

estupendo, estupenda ADJECTIVE
great; ¿ganaste? ¡estupendo! did
you win? great!

estúpido, estúpida NOUN MASC, FEM
stupid person; es un estúpido he's
really stupid

estúpido ADJECTIVE **stupid**

estuve, estuvo, etc VERB ▸ SEE **estar**

etapa NOUN FEM **stage**; por etapas
in stages

etcétera NOUN MASC **etcetera**

eternidad NOUN FEM **eternity**

ética NOUN FEM **ethics**

etiqueta NOUN MASC ❶ **label** ❷ **price tag**

euro NOUN MASC **euro**; el euro se divide en cien céntimos the euro is divided into a hundred cents

Europa NOUN FEM **Europe**

europeo, europea NOUN MASC, FEM, ADJECTIVE **European**

eurozona NOUN FEM **eurozone**

Euskadi NOUN FEM **the Basque Country**

euskera NOUN MASC **Basque** (the language)

euskera ADJECTIVE **Basque**

evaluación NOUN FEM **assessment**

evaporarse REFLEXIVE VERB [17] **to evaporate**

evidencia NOUN FEM **evidence**

evidente ADJECTIVE **obvious**

evidentemente ADVERB **obviously**

evitar VERB [17] ❶ **to avoid**; evitan tomar la responsabilidad they avoid taking responsibility ❷ **to prevent**; evitar un accidente to prevent an accident

evolución NOUN FEM **evolution**

exactamente ADVERB **exactly**

exacto, exacta ADJECTIVE ❶ **exact** ❷ **accurate**

exagerar VERB [17] **to exaggerate**

examen NOUN MASC **exam**; hacer un examen to take an exam, presentarse a un examen to sit an exam, aprobar un examen to pass an exam, un examen oral an oral exam

examinar VERB [17] **to examine**

examinarse REFLEXIVE VERB [17] **to take an exam**

excelente ADJECTIVE **excellent**

excepción NOUN FEM **exception**; hacer una excepción to make an exception, a excepción de with the exception of

excepcional ADJECTIVE **exceptional**

excepcionalmente ADVERB **exceptionally**

excepto PREPOSITION **except for**

exclusivo, exclusiva ADJECTIVE **exclusive**

excursión NOUN FEM **trip**; ir de excursión al campo to go on a trip to the countryside

excursionismo NOUN MASC **hiking**; hacer excursionismo to go hiking

excusa NOUN FEM **excuse**; poner excusas to make excuses

exigente ADJECTIVE **demanding**

exigir VERB [49] **to demand**

existir VERB [19] ❶ **to exist** ❷ existen motivos para pensarlo there are reasons to think that

éxito NOUN MASC **success**; tener éxito to be successful

exitoso, exitosa ADJECTIVE **successful**

expectativa NOUN FEM **expectation**

expediente NOUN MASC **file**

experiencia *NOUN FEM* **experience**

experimentado, experimentada *ADJECTIVE* **experienced**

experimentar *VERB* [17] **to experiment**

experimento *NOUN MASC* **experiment**

experto, experta *NOUN MASC, FEM* **expert**

explicación *NOUN FEM* **explanation**

explicar *VERB* [31] **to explain**

explorar *VERB* [17] **to explore**

explotar *VERB* [17] **explode**

exportación *NOUN FEM* **export**; la lana es la exportación más importante wool is the most important export

exportar *VERB* [17] **to export**; Rusia exporta mucha madera y petróleo Russia exports a lot of oil and timber

exposición *NOUN FEM* **exhibition**

expresar *VERB* [17] **to express**

expresión *NOUN FEM* **expression**

expreso[1] *NOUN MASC* ❶ **express train** ❷ **espresso** *(coffee)*

expreso[2]**, expresa** *ADJECTIVE* **express**; correo expreso express mail

extenderse *REFLEXIVE VERB* [17] **to stretch out**; se extiende hasta Tierra del Fuego it stretches as far as Tierra del Fuego

exterior *NOUN MASC* ❶ **exterior, outside**; el exterior de la casa the outside of the house ❷ **outward**

appearance; en su exterior estaba tranquilo his outward appearance was calm

exterior *ADJECTIVE* ❶ **outer** *(layer)* ❷ **outside** *(temperature)* ❸ la parte exterior de la casa the outside of the house ❹ **foreign**; política exterior foreign policy

externo, externa *ADJECTIVE* ❶ **outward** *(appearance or signs)* ❷ **external**

extinción *NOUN FEM* **extinction**; una especie en en vías de extinción an endangered species

extincto *ADJECTIVE* **extinct**

extintor *NOUN MASC* extintor (de incendios) **fire extinguisher**

extraescolar *ADJECTIVE* **out-of-school**; actividades extraescolares out-of-school activities

extranjero[1] *NOUN MASC* vivir en el extranjero to live abroad, viaja mucho al extranjero he travels abroad a lot

extranjero[2]**, extranjera** *NOUN MASC, FEM* **foreigner**

extranjero *ADJECTIVE* **foreign**

extrañar *VERB* [17] me extraña que no hayan llamado I'm surprised they haven't phoned, le extrañó verla allí he was surprised to see her there

extraño, extraña *NOUN MASC, FEM* **stranger**

extraño *ADJECTIVE* **strange**

extraordinario, extraordinaria *ADJECTIVE* **extraordinary**

extraterrestre *NOUN MASC & FEM* **alien** *(from outer space)*

extremo¹ *NOUN MASC* ❶ extreme
❷ end

extremo², extrema *NOUN MASC, FEM*
winger *(in sports)*

extremo *ADJECTIVE* extreme

extrovertido, extrovertida
ADJECTIVE extrovert

fábrica *NOUN FEM* factory

fabricar *VERB* [31] to manufacture

fácil *ADJECTIVE* easy; es un trabajo fácil
it's an easy job, fácil de hacer easy
to do, es fácil de entender it's easy
to understand

facilidad *NOUN FEM* ❶ ease; lo hice
con facilidad I did it with ease
❷ tener facilidad de palabra to
have a way with words

fácilmente *ADVERB* easily

factura *NOUN FEM* ❶ invoice ❷ bill

facultad *NOUN FEM* ❶ faculty; perder
facultades to lose your faculties
❷ ir a la facultad to go to college,
la Facultad de Medicina the Faculty
of Medicine

facultativo, facultativa *ADJECTIVE*
❶ optional ❷ medical

faena *NOUN FEM* task; las faenas de la
casa/domésticas the housework

faisán *NOUN MASC* pheasant

falda *NOUN FEM* skirt; una falda
escocesa a tartan skirt, a kilt, una
falda de tubo a straight skirt

falla *NOUN FEM* flaw

fallar *VERB* [17] ❶ to fail *(equipment or
brakes, for example)* ❷ to go wrong
(a plan); algo ha fallado something's
gone wrong ❸ me falló la puntería I
missed *(the target)*

fallo NOUN MASC **❶ fault**; el motor tiene un fallo there's something wrong with the engine **❷ failure**; un fallo en el sistema a failure in the system **❸** fallo humano human error **❹ verdict** (in court or competition)

falsificación NOUN FEM **forgery**; el cuadro es una falsificación the picture is a forgery

falso, falsa ADJECTIVE **❶ false ❷ fake** (a diamond or picture, for example)

falta NOUN FEM **❶ lack**; falta de algo lack of something, por falta de dinero due to lack of money, falta de personal staff shortage **❷** falta de educación bad manners, eso es una falta de educación that's bad manners, fue una falta de educación por su parte it was really rude of him **❸ misdemeamour**; una falta grave a serious misdemeanour **❹** falta de asistencia absence (from school), poner una falta a alguien to mark someone absent, ya tiene tres faltas he's been absent three times already **❺** una falta de ortografía a spelling mistake **❻ foul** (in sport) sacar la falta to take the free kick **❼** hace falta lavarlo it needs to be washed, hace falta comprar pan we need to buy bread, no hace falta cambiarlo it doesn't need to be changed, no hace falta que me esperes you don't need to wait for me **❽** me hace falta un bolígrafo I need a pen, no me hace falta nada más, gracias I don't need any more, thank you

faltar VERB [17] **❶ to be missing**; ¿quién falta? who's missing? **❷** faltar al colegio to be absent from school **❸** nos falta práctica we need practice, nos faltan mil euros para poder comprarlo we need a thousand euros to buy it, le falta interés he lacks interest **❹** solo faltan tres días there are only three more days to go, faltan diez días para mi cumpleaños it's ten days to my birthday, falta poco para el verano it's almost summertime, aún falta mucho para las doce there's still a long way to go till twelve o'clock, ¿te falta mucho? are you going to be long?, no les falta mucho para terminar they've almost finished, nos faltó tiempo we didn't have enough time

fama NOUN FEM **❶ fame ❷ reputation**; tener buena fama to have a good reputation, tener fama de mentiroso to have a reputation for being a liar

familia NOUN FEM **family**; ser de familia numerosa to be from a large family

familiar NOUN MASC & FEM **relative**

familiar ADJECTIVE **❶ family**; tuve problemas familiares I had family problems **❷ familiar**

famoso, famosa ADJECTIVE **famous**

fan NOUN MASC & FEM (PLURAL die fan) **fan**

fantasía NOUN FEM **❶ fantasy**; un mundo de fantasía a fantasy world **❷ imagination**; tener mucha fantasía to have a lot of imagination **❸** joyas de fantasía costume jewellery

fantasma NOUN MASC **ghost**

fantástico, fantástica ADJECTIVE **fantastic**

farmacéutico, farmacéutica NOUN MASC, FEM **chemist, pharmacist**

farmacéutico *ADJECTIVE*
pharmaceutical

farmacia *NOUN FEM* **chemist's, pharmacy**; farmacia de guardia/de turno duty chemist

farmacia *NOUN FEM* **chemist's**; farmacia de guardia/de turno duty chemist

faro *NOUN MASC* ❶ **lighthouse** ❷ **headlamp**

farola *NOUN FEM* ❶ **streetlight** ❷ **lamp post**

fascinar *VERB* [17] **to fascinate**

fastidiar *VERB* [17] **to annoy**; solo lo hacen para fastidiar they only do it to annoy, ¡deja de fastidiar! stop being a pain!

fastidiarse *REFLEXIVE VERB* [17] ¡que se fastidie! he'll have to put up with it!, ¡te fastidias! tough!

fastidio *NOUN MASC* **annoyance**; ¡qué fastidio! how annoying!

fatal *ADJECTIVE* ❶ (informal) **awful**; sentirse fatal to feel awful, estar fatal to be really ill, to be really badly done ❷ **fatal** (an accident or illness)

fatal *ADVERB* canto fatal I am hopeless at singing

favor *NOUN MASC* ❶ **favour**; hacerle un favor a alguien to do someone a favour, pedir un favor to ask for a favour, estar a favor de algo to be in favour of something ❷ **por favor** please

favorito, favorita *ADJECTIVE* **favourite**

fe *NOUN FEM* **faith**

febrero *NOUN MASC* **February**

fecha *NOUN FEM* **date**; fecha de nacimiento date of birth, ¿a qué fecha estamos hoy? what's the date today?, fecha de caducidad expiry date (for medicines), use-by date (for food)

felicidad *NOUN FEM* ❶ **happiness** ❷ ¡felicidades! happy birthday!, congratulations!

felicitaciones *PLURAL NOUN FEM* **congratulations**

felicitar *VERB* [17] felicitar a alguien to wish someone happy birthday, to congratulate someone

feliz *ADJECTIVE* (PLURAL die **felices**) **happy**; ¡feliz Año Nuevo! Happy New Year!, ¡feliz Navidad! Merry Christmas!, feliz cumpleaños happy birthday, felices Pascuas Happy Easter

felpudo *NOUN MASC* **doormat**

femenino¹ *NOUN MASC* **feminine**

femenino², femenina *ADJECTIVE* ❶ **woman's**; el equipo femenino the women's team ❷ **feminine** (style, manners, or noun) ❸ **female**; el sexo femenino the female sex

fenomenal *ADJECTIVE* (informal) **great**

fenomenal *ADVERB* **great**; pasarlo fenomenal to have a great time

feo, fea *ADJECTIVE* **ugly**

feria *NOUN FEM* **fair**

feroz *ADJECTIVE* **fierce**

ferretería *NOUN FEM* **ironmonger's**

ferrocarril *NOUN MASC* **railway**

ferry *NOUN MASC* **ferry**

festejar *VERB* [17] **celebrate**

festival *NOUN MASC* **festival**

festivo, festiva *ADJECTIVE* ❶ **festive** *(atmosphere)* ❷ un día festivo a public holiday

fiable *ADJECTIVE* **reliable**

fiambre *NOUN MASC* **cold meats**

fiarse *REFLEXIVE VERB* [32] ❶ fiarse de to believe, no te fíes de los periódicos don't believe what the newspapers say ❷ fiarse de alguien to trust someone

fibra *NOUN FEM* **fibre**

ficción *NOUN FEM* **fiction**

ficha *NOUN FEM* ❶ **card** ❷ ficha médica medical card, ficha policial police records ❸ **token** *(for the telephone)* ❹ **counter** *(in games)*

fideo *NOUN MASC* **noodle**

fiebre *NOUN FEM* ❶ **temperature**; tener fiebre to have a temperature, le ha subido la fiebre his temperature has gone up ❷ **fever**; fiebre del heno hay fever

fiel *ADJECTIVE* ❶ **faithful**; no le es fiel a su mujer he's not faithful to his wife ❷ **loyal** ❸ **accurate** *(a translation or copy, for example)*

fiesta *NOUN FEM* ❶ **party** ❷ **public holiday**; mañana es fiesta tomorrow's a holiday

figura *NOUN FEM* **figure**

figurar *VERB* [17] **to appear**

figurarse *REFLEXIVE VERB* [17] **to imagine**; me figuro que sí I imagine so

fijar *VERB* [17] **to fix**; fijar una fecha to fix a date

fijarse *REFLEXIVE VERB* [17] ❶ fijarse en algo to look at something ❷ to **notice**; se fija en todo she notices everything

fijo, fija *ADJECTIVE* ❶ **fixed**; precios fijos fixed prices, está fijo a la pared it's fixed to the wall ❷ **permanent** *(a job)* ❸ ¿está la escalera bien fija? is the ladder steady?

fila *NOUN FEM* ❶ **line**; hacer fila to form a line, en fila india in single line ❷ **row** *(of seats in the theatre or cinema)*

filete *NOUN MASC* ❶ **steak** ❷ **fillet** *(of fish)*

filmar *VERB* [17] ❶ **to shoot** *(a film)* ❷ **to film**

filosofía *NOUN FEM* **philosophy**

fin *NOUN MASC* ❶ **end**; llegar al fin to get to the end, el fin de semana the weekend, a fin de mes at the end of the month, fin de año New Year's Eve ❷ al fin/por fin at last ❸ en fin, ya te llamaré anyway, I'll give you a ring

final *NOUN MASC* ❶ **end**; el final de las vacaciones the end of the holidays ❷ **ending**; una película con final feliz a film with a happy ending ❸ al final at the end, al final del libro at the end of the book ❹ al final in the end, al final lo conseguí hacer I managed to do it in the end

final *NOUN FEM, ADJECTIVE* **final**

finca *NOUN FEM* ❶ **plot of land** ❷ **farm**

finlandés[1] *NOUN MASC* **Finnish** *(the language)*

finlandés[2]**, finlandesa** *NOUN MASC, FEM* **Finn**

finlandés, finlandesa *ADJECTIVE* **Finnish**

Finlandia *NOUN FEM* **Finland**

fino¹ *NOUN MASC* **dry sherry**

fino², fina *ADJECTIVE* ❶ **fine** *(a line, for example)* ❷ **thin** *(a layer or slice)* ❸ **slender** *(waist or finger)* ❹ **refined** *(a person)* ❺ **subtle** *(sense of humour)* ❻ tener el oído muy fino to have a very acute sense of hearing, tener el olfato muy fino to have a very acute sense of smell

firma *NOUN FEM* ❶ **signature** ❷ **company**

firmar *VERB* [17] **to sign**

firme *ADJECTIVE* ❶ **steady** *(a ladder or chair, for example)*; con pulso firme with a steady hand ❷ **firm** ❸ estudiar de firme to study hard

física¹ *NOUN FEM* **physics**

físico¹ *NOUN MASC* ❶ **physique** ❷ **appearance**

físico², física² *NOUN MASC, FEM* **physicist**

físico *ADJECTIVE* **physical**

fisiculturismo *NOUN MASC* **bodybuilding**

fisioterapia *NOUN FEM* **physiotherapy**

fitness *NOUN MASC* **fitness training**

flaco, flaca *ADJECTIVE* **thin**

flamenco¹ *NOUN MASC* **flamenco**

flamenco², flamenca *ADJECTIVE* **flamenco**; baile flamenco flamenco dancing

flan *NOUN MASC* **caramel custard**

flauta *NOUN FEM* **flute**; flauta dulce recorder

flecha *NOUN FEM* **arrow**

flequillo *NOUN MASC* **fringe**

flexible *ADJECTIVE* **flexible**

flojo, floja *ADJECTIVE* ❶ **loose** *(a knot or screw)* ❷ **slack** *(rope)* ❸ **weak** *(coffee or tea)* ❹ **poor** *(piece of work)*

flor *NOUN FEM* **flower**; de flores flower-patterned, una falda de flores a flower-patterned skirt, estar en flor to be in flower

florero *NOUN MASC* **flowerpot**

florista *NOUN MASC & FEM* **florist**

floristería *NOUN FEM* **florist's**

flota *NOUN FEM* **fleet**

flotar *VERB* [17] **to float**

fluido¹, fluida *ADJECTIVE* **fluid, freeflowing**; la circulación está fluida the traffic is flowing freely

fluido² *NOUN MASC* **fluid**

fluir *VERB* [54] **to flow**

flujo *NOUN MASC* **flow**

foca *NOUN FEM* **seal** *(animal)*

foco *NOUN MASC* ❶ **focus**; el foco de atención the focus of attention ❷ **spotlight**

folclórico, folclórica *ADJECTIVE* **folk**; musica folclórica folk music

folleto *NOUN MASC* ❶ **leaflet** ❷ **brochure**

fondo *NOUN MASC* ❶ **bottom**; el fondo del lago the bottom of the lake, al fondo del baúl at the bottom of the trunk, llegar al fondo de la cuestión to get to the bottom of the matter, **sin fondo** bottomless ❷ **back**; **está al fondo de la sala** it's at the back of the room ❸ **end**; **al fondo del pasillo** at the end of the corridor ❹ **kitty**; **hacer un fondo común** to make a kitty ❺ **fondos** funds *(money)* ❻ **estudiar algo a fondo** to study something in depth, **prepararse a fondo** to prepare thoroughly ❼ **ruido de fondo** background noise, **música de fondo** background music

fontanero, fontanera *NOUN MASC, FEM* **plumber**

footing *NOUN MASC* **jogging**; **hacer footing** to go jogging

forastero, forastera *NOUN MASC, FEM* **stranger**

forma *NOUN FEM* ❶ **shape**; **con la forma de una hoja** leaf-shaped, **tiene forma cuadrada** it's square ❷ **way**; **es mi forma de ser** it's the way I am ❸ **en forma** fit, **mantenerse en forma** to keep fit ❹ **de todas formas** anyway

formación *NOUN FEM* ❶ **education**; **un chico con una buena formación** a well-educated boy ❷ **training**; **formación profesional** vocational training

formal *ADJECTIVE* ❶ **reliable** *(person)* ❷ **formal** *(dinner or invitation)* ❸ **firm** *(offer)*

formar *VERB* [17] ❶ **to form**; **formar un grupo de música** to form a band ❷ **to make up**; **el equipo está formado por doce miembros** the team's made up of twelve members ❸ **formar parejas** to get into pairs *(in class or games)* ❹ **to educate** *(a person)*

formarse *REFLEXIVE VERB* [17] ❶ **to be educated** ❷ **to form**; **formarse una opinión** to form an opinion, **se formó un atasco** a traffic jam formed

formidable *ADJECTIVE* **formidable**

fórmula *NOUN FEM* **formula**

formulario *NOUN MASC* **form**

fortaleza *NOUN FEM* **fortress**

fortuna *NOUN FEM* ❶ **fortune**; **ganar una fortuna** to earn a fortune ❷ **por fortuna** fortunately ❸ **tener la buena fortuna de hacer** to have the good fortune of doing, **tuve la buena fortuna de conocerlos** I had the good fortune of meeting them ❹ **probar fortuna** to try your luck

forzar *VERB* [26] ❶ **to force**; **me forzaron a aceptar** they forced me to accept ❷ **forzar la vista** to strain your eyes

forzarse *REFLEXIVE VERB* [26] **forzarse a hacer** to force yourself to do

fosa *NOUN FEM* **pit**; **las fosas nasales** the nostrils

fósforo *NOUN MASC* **match** *(that you strike)*

foto *NOUN FEM* **photo**; **sacar/hacer una foto** to take a photo

fotocopia *NOUN FEM* **photocopy**

fotocopiadora *NOUN FEM* **photocopier**

fotocopiar *VERB* [17] **to photocopy**

fotografía *NOUN FEM* ❶ **photography** ❷ **photograph**; **sacar una fotografía** to take a photograph

fotógrafo, fotógrafa *NOUN MASC, FEM* **photographer**

fracasar *VERB* [17] **to fail**

fracaso *NOUN MASC* **failure**

fractura *NOUN FEM* **fracture**

frágil *ADJECTIVE* **fragile**

frambuesa *NOUN FEM* **raspberry**; mermelada de frambuesas raspberry jam

francés¹ *NOUN MASC* **French** *(the language)*

francés², francesa *NOUN MASC, FEM* **Frenchman/Frenchwoman**

francés, francesa *ADJECTIVE* **French**

Francia *NOUN FEM* **France**

frasco *NOUN MASC* ❶ **bottle** ❷ **jar**; un frasco de mermelada a jar of jam

frase *NOUN FEM* ❶ **sentence** ❷ **phrase**; frase hecha set phrase

fraude *NOUN MASC* **fraud**

frecuencia *NOUN FEM* **frequency**; con frecuencia often

frecuente *ADJECTIVE* **frequent**

frecuentemente *ADVERB* **often**, **frequently**

fregadero *NOUN MASC* **sink**

fregar *VERB* [30] ❶ **to wash**; fregar los platos to wash the dishes ❷ fregar el suelo to mop the floor ❸ **to scrub**

freír *VERB* [53] **to fry**

frenar *VERB* [17] ❶ **to brake** ❷ **to slow down** *(a process)* ❸ **to curb** *(inflation)*

freno *NOUN MASC* **brake**

frente *NOUN MASC* ❶ **front** ❷ al frente de la manifestación at the head

of the demostration, al frente de la patrulla leading the patrol ❸ al frente del equipo in charge of the team ❹ dar un paso al frente to step forward ❺ hacer frente a to face *(a problem or attacker)*

frente *NOUN FEM* **forehead**

fresa *NOUN FEM* **strawberry**; mermelada de fresas strawberry jam

fresco¹ *NOUN MASC* ❶ **fresh air**; tomar el fresco to get some fresh air, estar al fresco to be out in the fresh air ❷ hace fresco it's chilly ❸ **fresco** *(painting)*

fresco², fresca *ADJECTIVE* ❶ **cool**; una bebida fresca a cool drink, una brisa fresca a cool breeze ❷ hoy hace fresco it's chilly today ❸ **fresh**; pescado fresco fresh fish ❹ pintura fresca wet paint ❺ ¡qué fresco! what a nerve!, ser muy fresco to have a nerve

fría, frío, *etc VERB* ▶ SEE **freír**

friega, friego, friegue, *etc VERB* ▶ SEE **fregar**

frigorífico *NOUN MASC* **fridge**

frijol *NOUN MASC* **bean**; frijoles volteados fried beans

frío¹ *NOUN MASC* **cold**; hace frío it's cold, tengo frío I'm cold, un día frío a cold day

frío², fría *ADJECTIVE* **cold**

frito, frita *ADJECTIVE* ❶ **fried** ❷ quedarse frito *(informal)* to fall asleep

frontera *NOUN FEM* **border** cruzamos la frontera en Irún we crossed the border at Irún

frotar _VERB_ [17] **to rub**

frotarse _REFLEXIVE VERB_ [17] **to rub**

fruncir _VERB_ [66] fruncir el ceño to frown

frustrante _ADJECTIVE_ **frustrating**

frustrar _VERB_ [17] ❶ **to frustrate** _(person)_; me frustra que … I find it frustrating that … ❷ **to thwart** _(plans)_

fruta _NOUN FEM_ **fruit**

frutería _NOUN FEM_ **fruit shop**

frutero _NOUN MASC_ **fruit bowl**

fruto _NOUN MASC_ **fruit**; frutos secos nuts and dried fruits

fue _VERB_ ▸ SEE **ser**, **ir**

fuego _NOUN MASC_ ❶ **fire**; encender el fuego to light the fire, prender fuego a algo to set fire to something ❷ ¿tienes fuego? have you got a light? ❸ a fuego lento on a low heat

fuegos artificiales _NOUN MASC & PLURAL_ **fireworks**

fuente _NOUN FEM_ ❶ **spring** ❷ **fountain** ❸ **large dish**; una fuente de servir a serving dish, una fuente de horno an ovenproof dish

fuera, fuéramos, etc _VERB_ ▸ SEE **ser**, **ir**

fuera _ADVERB_ ❶ **out**; ¡sal fuera! go out!, ahí fuera out there, salimos a cenar fuera we went out for dinner ❷ **outside**; están esperando fuera they're waiting outside, la parte de fuera de la maleta the outside of the suitcase, deja las cajas fuera leave the boxes outside, por fuera es plateado it's silver on the outside ❸ **away**; el jefe está fuera the boss

is away ❹ **abroad**; están fuera del país they're abroad ❺ fuera de peligro out of danger, fuera de lugar out of place, fuera de serie exceptional ❻ fuera de juego offside

fueron _VERB_ ▸ SEE **ser**, **ir**

fuerte _ADJECTIVE_ ❶ **strong**; ser fuerte to be strong, un olor fuerte a strong smell ❷ **loud**; no pongas la música tan fuerte don't play the music so loud ❸ **hard** _(blow)_ ❹ **big**; un beso fuerte a big kiss ❺ **substantial**; tomamos una comida fuerte al mediodía we have a big meal at lunchtime ❻ un dolor fuerte an intense pain

fuerte _ADVERB_ ❶ **hard**; pegar fuerte hit it hard ❷ **tight**; agárralo fuerte hold it tight

fuerza _NOUN FEM_ ❶ **strength**; tener fuerza to be strong, no tuvo fuerza para levantarlo he wasn't strong enough to lift it ❷ hice fuerza y conseguí abrirlo I used all my strength and I managed to open it ❸ empujar con fuerza to push hard ❹ por la fuerza by force, lo obligaron a entrar en el coche por la fuerza they forced him to get into the car ❺ a fuerza de by, a fuerza de empujar by pushing ❻ **force**; fuerza aérea air force, fuerzas armadas armed forces ❼ fuerza de voluntad willpower

fuga _NOUN FEM_ ❶ **leak**; una fuga de gas a gas leak ❷ una fuga de prisioneros a jailbreak ❸ darse a la fuga to flee

fui, fuimos, fuiste, etc _VERB_ ▸ SEE **ser**, **ir**

fumador, fumadora _NOUN MASC, FEM_ **smoker**

fumar *VERB* [17] to smoke

función *NOUN FEM* ❶ function ❷ performance; función de noche late-night performance, función benéfica charity performance

funcionar *VERB* [17] ❶ to work; ¿cómo funciona? how does it work?, 'no funciona' 'out of order' ❷ to run; funciona con electricidad it runs on electricity

funcionario, funcionaria *NOUN MASC & FEM* government employee

funda *NOUN FEM* ❶ cover *(for a cushion, pillow, etc.)* ❷ sleeve *(of a record)* ❸ pillow case

fundamental *ADJECTIVE* fundamental

fundir *VERB* [19] to melt

fundirse *REFLEXIVE VERB* [19] to melt

funeral *NOUN MASC* funeral

funeraria *NOUN FEM* funeral director's

furgoneta *NOUN FEM* van

furia *NOUN FEM* fury; estar hecho una furia *(informal)* to be furious

furioso, furiosa *ADJECTIVE* furious; ponerse furioso to get furious

fusible *NOUN MASC* fuse; saltaron los fusibles the fuses blew

fusil *NOUN MASC* rifle

fusionar *VERB* to merge

futbito *NOUN MASC* five-a-side football

fútbol *NOUN MASC* football; jugar al fútbol to play football

futbolín *NOUN MASC* ❶ table football ❷ los futbolines the amusement arcade

futbolista *NOUN MASC & FEM* footballer

fútbol sala *NOUN MASC* indoor-football

futuro[1] *NOUN MASC* future

futuro[2]**, futura** *ADJECTIVE* future

Gg

gafas PLURAL NOUN FEM **glasses**; gafas de sol sunglasses, llevar gafas to wear glasses

galápago NOUN MASC **❶ giant turtle ❷ terrapin**

galaxia NOUN FEM **galaxy**

galería NOUN FEM **❶ gallery**; galería de arte art gallery **❷** galería comercial shopping arcade

Gales NOUN MASC el país de Gales **Wales**

galés[1] NOUN MASC **Welsh** (the language)

galés[2], **galesa** NOUN MASC, FEM **Welshman, Welshwoman**

galés, galesa ADJECTIVE **Welsh**

gallego[1] NOUN MASC **Galician** (the language)

gallego[2], **gallega** NOUN MASC, FEM **Galician**

gallego ADJECTIVE **Galician**

galleta NOUN FEM **biscuit**

gallina NOUN FEM **hen**

gallo NOUN MASC **cockerel**

galopar VERB [17] **to gallop**

gamba NOUN FEM **prawn**

gamberro, gamberra NOUN MASC, FEM **❶ rowdy ❷ hooligan**

gamberro ADJECTIVE es muy gamberro he's a real rowdy, he's a real hooligan

gana NOUN FEM **❶** tener ganas de hacer algo to feel like doing something, no tengo ganas de ir al cine I don't feel like going to the cinema **❷** tengo ganas de verlos I'm looking forward to seeing them **❸** (informal) no lo hace porque no le da la gana hacerlo he doesn't do it because he doesn't want to, voy porque me da la gana I'm going because I feel like it, hace siempre lo que le da la gana she always does as she pleases **❹** hacer algo sin ganas to do something half-heartedly, hacer algo de buena gana to do something willingly, hacer algo de mala gana to do something reluctantly

ganado NOUN MASC **cattle**; ganado vacuno cattle (cows)

ganador, ganadora NOUN MASC, FEM **winner**

ganador ADJECTIVE **winning** (number)

ganancia NOUN FEM **profit**

ganar VERB [17] **❶ to win**; ganar una carrera to win a race, ganaron el primer premio they won first prize **❷ to earn**; gano un buen sueldo I earn a good salary

ganarse REFLEXIVE VERB [17] **❶ to earn**; ganarse la vida to earn your living, se gana la vida pintando he earns his living painting **❷ to win**; ganarse la confianza de alguien to win someone's trust

gancho NOUN MASC **hook**

ganga NOUN FEM **bargain**

ganso, gansa NOUN MASC, FEM
❶ **goose** ❷ (informal) ser un ganso
to be a clown, hacer el ganso to
clown around

garaje NOUN MASC **garage**

garantía NOUN FEM **guarantee**; bajo
garantía under guarantee

garantizar VERB [22] to **guarantee**

garbanzo NOUN MASC **chickpea**

garganta NOUN FEM **throat**; me duele
la garganta I have a sore throat

gas NOUN MASC ❶ **gas**; una cocina a
gas a gas cooker ❷ gases tóxicos
toxic fumes

gaseosa NOUN FEM **lemonade**

gasoil, gasóleo NOUN MASC
❶ **heating oil** ❷ **diesel**

gasolina NOUN FEM **petrol**; voy a
echar gasolina al coche I'm going to
put some petrol in the car, gasolina
sin plomo unleaded petrol

gasolinera NOUN FEM **petrol station**

gastar VERB [17] ❶ to **spend**; gastan
mucho en comida they spend a
lot of money on food ❷ to **use**; mi
coche gasta mucha gasolina my
car uses a lot of petrol, me gastó
todo el champú she used up all my
shampoo ❸ ¿qué número de pie
gastas? what shoe size do you take?

gastarse REFLEXIVE VERB [17] to **run
out**; se han gastado las pilas the
batteries have run out

gasto NOUN MASC **expense**;
tenemos muchos gastos we
have a lot of expenses, gastos de
desplazamiento travel expenses,
gastos de envío postage and
packing

gastronomía NOUN FEM
gastronomy

gatear VERB [17] to **crawl**

gato, gata NOUN MASC, FEM **cat**

gaviota NOUN FEM **seagull**

gazpacho NOUN MASC **gazpacho**
(a chilled soup made with tomatoes,
cucumber, and other vegetables)

gel NOUN MASC **gel**

gelatina NOUN FEM **jelly**

gemelo, gemela NOUN MASC, FEM,
ADJECTIVE **twin**

gemelos PLURAL NOUN MASC
binoculars

géminis NOUN MASC & FEM **Gemini**; soy
géminis I'm Gemini

Géminis NOUN MASC **Gemini**

gemir VERB [57] to **groan**; gemir de
dolor to groan with pain

generación NOUN FEM **generation**

general NOUN MASC & FEM **general**; el
general Serrano General Serrano

general ADJECTIVE **general**; en
general in general, por lo general
generally, en líneas generales
broadly speaking

generalmente ADVERB **generally**

género NOUN MASC **gender**

generoso, generosa ADJECTIVE
generous

genética NOUN FEM **genetics**

genial ADJECTIVE ❶ **brilliant**; una idea
genial a brilliant idea ❷ (informal)
great, brilliant; ¡es genial! it's
great!

genio *NOUN MASC* ❶ **genius**; Ana es un genio Ana is a genius ❷ **temper**; tener mal genio to be bad-tempered, ¡vaya genio! what a temper!

gente *NOUN FEM* **people**; vino mucha gente a lot of people came, la gente dice que … people say that …

geografía *NOUN FEM* **geography**

geología *NOUN FEM* **geology**

geometría *NOUN FEM* **geometry**

gerente *NOUN MASC & FEM* **manager**

gestión *NOUN FEM* ❶ **management**; la gestión de la empresa the management of the company ❷ tengo que hacer una gestión en el consulado I have to sort things out at the consulate

gesto *NOUN MASC* **gesture**; me hizo un gesto para que me acercara he gestured to me to come over, hice un gesto de asentimiento I nodded

Gibraltar *NOUN MASC* **Gibraltar**

gigabyte *NOUN MASC* **gigabyte**; un disco duro de veinte gigabytes a twenty gigabyte hard disk

gigante, giganta *NOUN MASC, FEM* **giant**

gimnasia *NOUN FEM* ❶ **gymnastics** ❷ **exercise**; es bueno hacer gimnasia it's good to get exercise, gimnasia de mantenimiento keep-fit, clase de gimnasia PE class

gimnasio *NOUN MASC* **gym**

ginebra *NOUN FEM* **gin**

gin tonic *NOUN MASC* **gin and tonic**

girar *VERB* [17] ❶ **to turn**; gira a la derecha en el semáforo turn right at the traffic lights, girar la cabeza to turn your head ❷ **to go round**; la tierra gira alrededor del sol the earth goes round the sun ❸ **to spin** ❹ girar un cheque to draw a cheque ❺ girar dinero to send money

girasol *NOUN MASC* **sunflower**

gitano, gitana *NOUN MASC, FEM* **gypsy**

glaciar *NOUN MASC* **glacier**

globo *NOUN MASC* ❶ **balloon** ❷ **lob** *(in tennis)*

gloria *NOUN FEM* **glory**

glorieta *NOUN FEM* ❶ **square** *(in a town)* ❷ **roundabout** *(on the road)*

glotón, glotona *ADJECTIVE* **greedy**

gobernar *VERB* [17] ❶ **to rule** ❷ **to govern**

gobierno *NOUN MASC* **government**

gol *NOUN MASC* **goal**; marcar/meter un gol to score a goal, ganar/perder por tres goles a dos to win/lose by three goals to two

golf *NOUN MASC* **golf**; jugar al golf to play golf

golfista *NOUN MASC & FEM* **golfer**

golfo *NOUN MASC* ❶ **gulf** *(in geography)* ❷ **scoundrel**; eres un golfo you're a scoundrel ❸ **little rascal** *(to a child)*

golondrina *NOUN FEM* **swallow**

golosina *NOUN FEM* **sweet**; no comas tantas golosinas don't eat so many sweets

golpe *NOUN MASC* ❶ **knock**; darse un golpe to knock yourself, se dió un golpe en la pierna he knocked his leg ❷ **blow**; fue un duro golpe it was a hard blow ❸ darle un golpe a alguien to hit someone ❹ tap; dar unos golpes en la mesa to tap the table ❺ la ventana se cerró de golpe the window slammed shut, cerré el baúl de golpe I slammed the trunk shut

golpear VERB [17] ❶ to hit; le golpeé el brazo con una revista I hit him on the arm with a magazine ❷ to bang; la ventana golpeaba por el viento the window was banging in the wind ❸ to beat; golpear un tambor to beat a drum ❹ to tap

golpearse REFLEXIVE VERB [17] to bang; se golpeó el brazo con la mesa he banged his arm on the table

goma NOUN FEM ❶ rubber; botas de goma rubber boots, goma espuma foam rubber ❷ una goma (de borrar) a rubber ❸ una goma (elástica) a rubber band

gorda¹ NOUN FEM fat woman

gordo¹ NOUN MASC ❶ fat man ❷ jackpot (in the state lottery)

gordo², **gorda²** ADJECTIVE ❶ fat; ponerse gordo to get fat ❷ thick (book or jumper) ❸ serious (problem or mistake)
- me cae gordo (informal) I can't stand him

gorila NOUN MASC gorilla

gorra NOUN FEM cap

gorro NOUN MASC cap

gota NOUN FEM drop

gotear VERB [17] ❶ to drip ❷ una gota de (informal) a drop of, tomaré una gota de café I'll have a drop of coffee, no tiene ni una gota de paciencia he hasn't got the slightest bit of patience

goucho NOUN MASC goucho (South American cowboy)

gozar VERB [22] to enjoy; gozo mucho oyendo música I enjoy listening to music a lot, todos gozamos del espectáculo we all enjoyed the show

grabación NOUN FEM recording

grabador NOUN MASC tape recorder

grabadora NOUN FEM tape recorder

grabar VERB [17] to record

gracia NOUN FEM ❶ joke; hacer una gracia to make a joke ❷ tener gracia to be funny, esa broma no tiene gracia that joke isn't funny, tiene mucha gracia contando cosas she's very good at telling funny stories ❸ me hace gracia verlo seeing it makes me laugh ❹ no me hace ninguna gracia ir I don't like the idea of going at all

gracias PLURAL NOUN FEM thank you; muchas gracias thank you very much, darle las gracias a alguien to thank someone, gracias a ellos thanks to them

gracioso, **graciosa** ADJECTIVE funny

grado NOUN MASC degree; veinte grados centígrados twenty degrees centigrade, cinco grados bajo cero five degrees below zero

gradual ADJECTIVE gradual

graduarse REFLEXIVE VERB [20] to graduate

gráfico NOUN MASC graph; gráficos graphics (in computing)

gramática NOUN FEM grammar

gramo NOUN MASC gram

gran ADJECTIVE ▸ SEE **grande**

Gran Bretaña NOUN FEM
Great Britain

grande, gran ADJECTIVE ❶ ('grande' becomes 'gran' before a singular noun) big; tienen una casa muy grande they have a very big house, la chaqueta me queda grande the jacket's too big for me, un gran número de personas a great number of people ❷ great; soy un gran admirador suyo I'm a great admirer of hers, es un gran actor he's a great actor, una gran oportunidad a great opportunity ❸ grown-up; cuando sea grande when I grow up, ya eres muy grande para hacer eso you're too grown-up to do that ❹ grandes almacenes department store

granizado NOUN MASC crushed ice drink; granizado de limón iced lemon drink

granizar VERB [22] to hail

granizo NOUN MASC hail

granja NOUN FEM farm

granjero, granjera NOUN MASC, FEM farmer; es granjero he's a farmer

grano NOUN MASC ❶ grain; un grano de arena a grain of sand ❷ (coffee) bean ❸ spot, pimple; me ha salido un grano I've got a spot

grapa NOUN FEM staple

grapadora NOUN FEM stapler

grapar VERB [17] to staple

grasa NOUN FEM ❶ fat; el contenido de grasa the fat content ❷ grease; el horno estaba llena de grasa the oven was covered in grease

grasiento, grasienta ADJECTIVE greasy

gratis ADJECTIVE free; entrada gratis free entry

gratis ADVERB free; los niños viajan gratis children travel free

gratuito, gratuita ADJECTIVE free; entrada gratuita free entry

grava NOUN FEM gravel

grave ADJECTIVE serious; está muy grave he's seriously ill

gravedad NOUN FEM ❶ gravity (in physics) ❷ seriousness (of problem)

Grecia NOUN FEM Greece

griego[1] NOUN MASC Greek (the language)

griego[2], **griega** NOUN MASC, FEM, ADJECTIVE Greek

grifo NOUN MASC tap; abrir el grifo to turn the tap on, cerrar el grifo to turn the tap off

grillo NOUN MASC cricket

gripe NOUN FEM flu; tener (la) gripe/ estar con gripe to have flu

gris NOUN MASC ADJECTIVE grey

gritar VERB [17] to shout; gritar de alegría to shout for joy, gritar de dolor to scream with pain

grito NOUN MASC ❶ shout; dar un grito to shout ❷ cry; un grito de protesta a cry of protest ❸ un grito de dolor a cry of pain, un grito de horror a scream of horror

grosella NOUN FEM redcurrant

grosería NOUN FEM no digas groserías don't be so rude, ¡qué grosería! how rude!

grosero, grosera ADJECTIVE **rude**

grúa NOUN FEM **crane**

grueso, gruesa ADJECTIVE ❶ **thick** ❷ **fat** *(person)*

gruñón, gruñona ADJECTIVE **grumpy**

grupo NOUN MASC **group**; salir en grupo to go out in a group, un grupo musical a group *(playing music)*

guante NOUN MASC **glove**

guapo, guapa ADJECTIVE **good-looking**

guarda NOUN MASC & FEM ❶ **guard** ❷ **keeper** *(in museum)*

guardabarros NOUN MASC **mudguard**

guardaespaldas NOUN MASC, FEM **bodyguard**

guardar VERB [17] ❶ **to keep**; guardo todas sus cartas I keep all his letters ❷ **to put away**; guarda tus juguetes put your toys away ❸ guardar cama to stay in bed

guardería infantil NOUN FEM **nursery**

guardia[1] NOUN MASC & FEM ❶ **policeman/policewoman** ❷ la Guardia Civil the Civil Guard ❸ guardia jurado security guard ❹ guardia urbano police officer *(in local force)*

guardián, guardiana NOUN MASC, FEM ❶ **guard** ❷ **guardian**

guarnición NOUN FEM ❶ **side dish** ❷ **topping**

guarro, guarra ADJECTIVE *(informal)* ❶ **filthy** ❷ **disgusting** *(a person)*

guarro/guarra NOUN MASC, FEM *(informal)* **filthy pig**

guatemalteco, guatemalteca NOUN MASC, FEM, ADJECTIVE **Guatemalan**

guau EXCLAMATION **wow!**

guay ADJECTIVE *(informal)* **fantastic, cool**; ¡qué música más guay! what cool music!

guay ADVERB lo pasé guay I had a fantastic time

guerra NOUN FEM **war**

guerrilla NOUN FEM **guerrilla unit**

guerrillero, guerrillera NOUN MASC, FEM **guerrilla, guerrilla fighter**

guía NOUN FEM ❶ **guide**; guía de restaurantes restaurant guide ❷ **map** *(of a city or town)* ❸ guía telefónica telephone directory

guía NOUN MASC & FEM **guide** *(person)*; es guía turístico he's a tourist guide

guiar VERB [32] **to guide**

guiarse REFLEXIVE VERB [32] guiarse por un mapa to follow a map

guijarro NOUN MASC **pebble**

guiñar VERB [17] **to wink**

guiño NOUN MASC **wink**

guión NOUN MASC ❶ **dash** ❷ **hyphen**; una palabra con guión a hyphenated word ❸ **script** *(of a film)*

guisante NOUN MASC **pea**

guisar VERB [17] **to cook**; guisa muy bien he's a very good cook

guitarra[1] NOUN FEM **guitar**; guitarra española Spanish guitar

a
b
c
d
e
f
g
h
i
j
k
l
m
n
ñ
o
p
q
r
s
t
u
v
w
x
y
z

guitarra² *NOUN MASC & FEM* **guitarist**

guitarrista *NOUN MASC & FEM* **guitarist**

gusano *NOUN MASC* **worm**

gustar *VERB* [17] me gusta mucho
I like it a lot, me gustan los animales
I like animals, no le gustó el libro
he didn't like the book, a mi padre
le gustan las fresas my dad likes
strawberries, el que más me gusta
the one I like the best, les gusta
mirar la tele they like watching
telly, ¡así me gusta! that's what I
like to hear/see!

gusto *NOUN MASC* ❶ **taste**; tiene
gusto a menta it tastes of mint,
tiene buen gusto it tastes nice,
tengo mal gusto en la boca I have
a nasty taste in my mouth ❷ tiene
muy buen gusto she has very good
taste ❸ mucho gusto en conocerle
pleased to meet you

Hh

ha *VERB* ▸ SEE **haber**

haba *NOUN FEM* ❶ **bean** ❷ **broad
bean**

habéis *VERB* ▸ SEE **haber**

haber *VERB* [6] ❶ *(used with another
verb in the same way as 'have' in
English to form past tenses)*; he
escrito a mi hermano I have written
to my brother, él no lo ha cogido
he hasn't taken it, aún no había
comido I hadn't eaten yet, después
de haberlo pensado bien after
having thought about it properly
❷ **there is**; aquí no hay suficiente
there's not enough here, había
un paquete en recepción there
was a parcel in reception ❸ **there
are**; hay varios errores there are
various mistakes, había más de
treinta personas en la sala there
were more than thirty people in
the room ❹ ¿qué hay que hacer?
what needs to be done?, hay que
limpiar la cocina the kitchen needs
to be cleaned, hay que sacar dinero
we need to take some money out,
ahora hay que pintarlo it needs
painting now ❺ hola, ¿qué hay? hi,
how are things? ❻ 'muchas gracias'
– 'no hay de qué' 'thank you very
much' – 'don't mention it'

hábil *ADJECTIVE* ❶ **skilful**; un jugador
hábil a skilful player ❷ **clever**; es
muy hábil para conseguir lo que
quiere he's very clever when it
comes to getting what he wants

habilidad NOUN FEM **skill**

habitación NOUN FEM **room**; una habitación sencilla/individual a single room, una habitación doble a double room

habitante NOUN MASC & FEM **inhabitant**

habla NOUN FEM ❶ **speech**; se quedó sin habla he was speechless ❷ un país de habla hispana a Spanish-speaking country ❸ al habla speaking (on the phone), '¿el Señor López?' – 'al habla' 'Mr López?' – 'speaking'

hablador, habladora NOUN MASC, FEM ❶ **chatterbox** ❷ **gossip**

hablador ADJECTIVE ❶ **talkative** ❷ **gossipy**

hablar VERB [17] ❶ **to speak**; sabe hablar inglés he speaks English, ¿hablas algún idioma? do you speak any foreign languages? ❷ **to talk**; no habla mucho she doesn't talk very much, hablar de to talk about, siempre habla mucho de ti she's always talking about you, me habló de sus proyectos he talked to me about his plans

habrán, habré, etc VERB ▸ SEE **haber**

hacer VERB [7] ❶ **to make**; hacer un pastel to make a cake, hacer la cama to make the bed ❷ **to do**; no sé qué hacer I don't know what to do, hacer los deberes to do your homework, ¿qué haces? what are you doing?, estoy haciendo derecho I'm doing law ❸ hacer la comida to cook lunch, hacer la cena to cook dinner ❹ **to build** (a house or road, for example) ❺ hacer una visita to pay a visit ❻ hacer un regalo a

alguien to give somebody a present ❼ hace (el papel) de Otelo he plays Othello ❽ (talking about the weather) hace frío it's cold, hacía mucho viento it was very windy, este verano ha hecho muy mal tiempo the weather's been very bad this summer ❾ (talking about time) hace tres días three days ago, hace tres días que se fueron they left three days ago, eso pasó hace mucho tiempo that happened a long time ago, ¿cuánto tiempo hace que vives aquí? how long have you been living here?, hacía dos meses que no iba a verlos I hadn't been to see them for two months, trabaja aquí desde hace tres meses she's been working here for three months now ❿ hacer a alguien hacer algo to make someone do something, le hice repetirlo I made him do it again, eso me hizo pensar that made me think

hacerse REFLEXIVE VERB [7] ❶ **to become**; hacerse famoso to become famous, se hicieron amigos they became friends ❷ se están haciendo viejos they're getting old ❸ hacerse daño to hurt yourself, me he hecho un corte en el dedo I've cut my finger ❹ me he hecho un vestido I've made myself a dress, se ha hecho una mesa para la cocina she's made a table for her kitchen ❺ ¿cómo se hace? how do you do it?

hacha NOUN FEM **axe** (even though 'hacha' is feminine, it takes 'el' or 'un' in the singular)

hacia PREPOSITION ❶ **towards**; vinieron hacia mí they came towards me, hacia el norte northwards, muévelo hacia abajo move it down ❷ (with time) **about**;

llamaré hacia las dos de la tarde I'll call at about two o'clock, te pagaré hacia final de mes I'll pay you towards the end of the month

hacienda NOUN FEM **estate, ranch**

hada NOUN FEM **fairy** *(even though 'hada' is feminine, it takes 'el' or 'un' in the singular)*

haga, hago, *etc* VERB ▸ SEE **hacer**

Haití NOUN MASC **Haiti**

haitiano, haitiana NOUN MASC, FEM, ADJECTIVE **Haitian**

halagar VERB [28] **to flatter**

halcón NOUN MASC **falcon**

hallar VERB [17] **to find**; no pudieron hallar una solución they couldn't find a solution

hallarse REFLEXIVE VERB [17] **❶ to be**; el pueblo se halla (situado) cerca del mar the village is (situated) near the sea **❷ to feel**; me hallaba tranquilo I was feeling calm

hamaca NOUN FEM **hammock**

hambre NOUN FEM **hunger** *(even though 'hambre' is feminine, it takes 'el' or 'un')*; tener hambre to be hungry, me muero de hambre *(informal)* I'm starving, el aire del mar me da hambre the sea air makes me feel hungry

hamburguesa NOUN FEM **hamburger**

hamburguesería NOUN FEM **hamburger bar**

hámster NOUN MASC **hamster**

han VERB ▸ SEE **haber**

harán, haré, *etc* VERB ▸ SEE **hacer**

harina NOUN FEM **flour**; harina integral wholemeal flour

hartarse REFLEXIVE VERB [17] **to get fed up**; me estoy hartando de este color I'm getting fed up with this colour, se hartó de esperar he got fed up of waiting

harto, harta ADJECTIVE estar harto de to be fed up of/with, están hartos de comer siempre lo mismo they're fed up of always eating the same thing, estoy harta de tus excusas I'm fed up with your excuses

has VERB ▸ SEE **haber**

hasta PREPOSITION **❶ until**; me quedaré hasta la semana que viene I'll stay until next week, hasta que until, no lo mandes hasta que yo lo diga don't send it until I tell you **❷** ¡hasta mañana! see you tomorrow!, ¡hasta luego! see you later!, ¡hasta pronto! see you soon! **❸ up to**; hasta ahora up to now, hasta hace tres meses up to three months ago **❹** la falda me llega hasta los tobillos the skirt goes down to my ankles **❺ as far as**; llegamos hasta Bilbao we went as far as Bilbao

hay VERB ▸ SEE **haber**

haz VERB ▸ SEE **hacer**

he VERB ▸ SEE **haber**

hechizo NOUN MASC **spell**

hecho¹ NOUN MASC **❶ fact**; el hecho es que ... the fact is ..., ¿cuáles son los hechos? what are the facts? **❷** tenemos que pasar de las palabras a los hechos we must stop talking and do something **❸** de hecho in fact

hecho², **hecha** ADJECTIVE ❶ made; hecho a mano hand-made, un trabajo bien hecho a job well done ❷ ¡bien hecho! well done!

helada¹ NOUN FEM frost

heladería NOUN FEM ice-cream parlour

heladero, **heladera** NOUN MASC, FEM ice cream seller

helado¹ NOUN MASC ice cream; un helado de fresa a strawberry ice cream

helado², **helada²** ADJECTIVE ❶ frozen; el río estaba helado the river was frozen, la pobre chica estaba helada the poor girl was frozen ❷ freezing; tienes las manos heladas your hands are freezing, estoy helado I'm freezing, la casa está helada the house is freezing

helar VERB [29] esta noche va a helar there's going to be a frost tonight

helarse REFLEXIVE VERB [29] to freeze; el río se ha helado the river has frozen over

hélice NOUN FEM propeller

helicóptero NOUN MASC helicopter

hemos VERB ▸ SEE haber

heno NOUN MASC hay; fiebre del heno hay fever

heredar VERB [17] ❶ to inherit ❷ heredar el trono to succeed to the throne

heredero, **heredera** NOUN MASC, FEM heir

herida¹ NOUN FEM injury

herido, **herida²** ADJECTIVE ❶ injured; estar seriamente herido to be seriously injured ❷ wounded; resultó herido en la pelea he was wounded in the fight

herir VERB [14] ❶ to wound ❷ to hurt; hirieron mis sentimientos they hurt my feelings

hermana NOUN FEM sister; hermana gemela twin sister, hermana política sister-in-law

hermanastro, **hermanastra** NOUN MASC, FEM ❶ stepbrother/ stepsister ❷ half-brother/ half-sister

hermano NOUN MASC ❶ brother; hermano gemelo twin brother, hermano político brother-in-law ❷ hermanos brothers, brothers and sisters, ¿tienes hermanos? do you have any brothers and sisters?

hermoso, **hermosa** ADJECTIVE beautiful

héroe NOUN MASC hero

heroína NOUN FEM ❶ heroine ❷ heroin

herramienta NOUN FEM tool

hervir VERB [14] to boil; hervir unas patatas to boil some potatoes

hice VERB ▸ SEE hacer

hidratante ADJECTIVE moisturizing

hiedra NOUN FEM ivy

hielo NOUN MASC ice; cubito de hielo ice cube

hierba NOUN FEM ❶ grass; 'no pisar la hierba' 'do not walk on the grass' ❷ herb; hierbas de cocina (cooking) herbs ❸ una hierba mala a weed

a
b
c
d
e
f
g
h
i
j
k
l
m
n
ñ
o
p
q
r
s
t
u
v
w
x
y
z

hierro *NOUN MASC* **iron**

hígado *NOUN MASC* **liver**

higiénico, higiénica *ADJECTIVE* **hygienic**

higo *NOUN MASC* **fig**

hija *NOUN FEM* **daughter**; hija política daughter-in-law

hijo *NOUN MASC* ❶ **son**; su hijo se llama Carlos his son is called Carlos, hijo político son-in-law ❷ hijos children, tienen tres hijos they've got three children

hilo *NOUN MASC* **thread**

himno *NOUN MASC* **hymn**

hincha *NOUN MASC & FEM* **supporter**; es hincha del Sevilla he's a Seville supporter

hinchado, hinchada *ADJECTIVE* **swollen**

hinchar *VERB* [17] ❶ **to blow up** *(a balloon)* ❷ **to pump up** *(a tyre)*

hincharse *REFLEXIVE VERB* [17] **to swell up**; se me ha hinchado el tobillo my ankle has swollen up

hinchazón *NOUN FEM* **swelling**

hindú *NOUN MASC & FEM, ADJECTIVE* **Hindu**

hipermercado *NOUN MASC* **hypermarket**

hipnotizar *VERB* [25] **hypnotize**

hipo *NOUN MASC* **hiccups**; tener hipo to have hiccups

hipoteca *NOUN FEM* **mortgage**

hispano, hispana *NOUN MASC, FEM* **Hispanic**

hispano *ADJECTIVE* ❶ **Hispanic, Spanish**; países de habla hispana Spanish-speaking countries ❷ **Spanish American**

Hispanoamérica *NOUN FEM* **Spanish America**

hispanoamericano, hispanoamericana *NOUN MASC, FEM, ADJECTIVE* **Spanish American**

hispanohablante *NOUN MASC & FEM* **Spanish-speaker**

hispanohablante *ADJECTIVE* **Spanish-speaking**

historia *NOUN FEM* ❶ **history**; la historia de Chile the history of Chile ❷ **story**; una historia de miedo a horror story

histórico, histórica *ADJECTIVE* ❶ **historical** ❷ **historic**

historieta *NOUN FEM* **cartoon**

hizo *VERB* ▸ SEE **hacer**

hogar *NOUN MASC* **home**; este es mi hogar this is my home, labores del hogar housework

hoguera *NOUN FEM* **bonfire**

hoja *NOUN FEM* ❶ **leaf** *(of a tree or plant)* ❷ **sheet** *(of paper or metal)* ❸ **page** *(of a book)*

hola *EXCLAMATION* **hello**

Holanda *NOUN FEM* **Holland**

holandés¹ *NOUN MASC* **Dutch** *(the language)*

holandés², holandesa *NOUN MASC, FEM* **Dutchman, Dutchwoman**

holandés, holandesa *ADJECTIVE* **Dutch**

holgado, holgada *ADJECTIVE* **loose-fitting**

hombre NOUN MASC ❶ man; un hombre de negocios a businessman, el hombre del tiempo the weatherman, un hombre rana a frogman, el hombre moderno es más alto que sus antepasados **modern man is taller than his ancestors** ❷ ¡hombre! ¡tú por aquí! hey! look who's here!, ¡no, hombre! of course not!

hombro NOUN MASC shoulder

homenaje NOUN MASC tribute; un homenaje al autor a ceremony to honour the author

homosexual NOUN MASC & FEM, ADJECTIVE homosexual

hondo¹ ADVERB respirar hondo to breathe deeply

hondo², **honda** ADJECTIVE ❶ deep; un pozo hondo a deep well ❷ en lo más hondo de mi corazón deep in my heart

hondureño, **hondureña** NOUN MASC, FEM, ADJECTIVE Honduran

honesto, **honesta** ADJECTIVE honest

hongo NOUN MASC ❶ fungus ❷ tener hongos to have athlete's foot

honor NOUN MASC honour; tener el honor de to have the honour of, en honor de in honour of

honra NOUN FEM honour

honradez NOUN FEM honesty

honrado, **honrada** ADJECTIVE honest

hora NOUN FEM ❶ hour; la película dura dos horas the film lasts two hours, media hora half an hour, hora y media an hour and a half, a las quince horas at fifteen hours, la hora punta the rush hour, durante las horas de trabajo during working hours, horas de visita visiting hours (at the hospital), hay un bus que sale cada hora there is an hourly bus ❷ time; ¿qué hora es? what's the time?, ¿a qué hora empieza? what time does it start?, ¿tiene hora? have you got the time?, ¿me puede dar la hora? could you tell me what time it is?, a la hora de comer at lunchtime, es hora de ir a la cama it's bedtime, ya es hora de entrar it's time to go in, en mis horas libres in my free time, hacer horas extra to do overtime, llegar a la hora to arrive on time ❸ pedir hora to make an appointment, he pedido hora con el dentista I made an appointment to see the dentist ❹ a primera hora de la mañana first thing in the morning, una noticia de última hora a news flash

horario NOUN MASC ❶ timetable; el horario de clase the school timetable ❷ horario de visitas visiting hours (at the hospital)

horchata NOUN FEM a cold drink made from tiger nuts

horchatería NOUN FEM refreshments stall (selling horchata)

horizontal ADJECTIVE horizontal

horizonte NOUN MASC horizon

hormiga NOUN FEM ant

hormigón NOUN MASC concrete

horno NOUN MASC ❶ oven; verduras al horno roast vegetables, un horno microondas a microwave oven ❷ kiln

horóscopo NOUN MASC horoscope

horquilla NOUN FEM hairpin

a
b
c
d
e
f
g
h
i
j
k
l
m
n
ñ
o
p
q
r
s
t
u
v
w
x
y
z

horrible ADJECTIVE **horrible**

horror NOUN MASC ❶ **horror** ❷ *(informal)* ¡qué horror! how awful!

horrorizar VERB [22] **to horrify**

horroroso, horrorosa ADJECTIVE ❶ **horrific** *(crime)* ❷ *(informal)* **awful** *(a dress, book or picture, for example)*

hortaliza NOUN FEM **vegetable**

hospedar VERB [17] **to provide accommodation for**

hospedarse REFLEXIVE VERB [17] **to stay**; nos hospedamos en una pensión we stayed in a guesthouse

hospital NOUN MASC **hospital**

hospitalidad NOUN FEM **hospitality**

hostal NOUN MASC **hotel** *(small and not expensive)*

hostelería NOUN FEM **hotel industry**

hotel NOUN MASC **hotel**

hotelero, hotelera NOUN MASC, FEM **hotel manager**

hotelero ADJECTIVE **hotel**

hoy ADVERB ❶ **today**; hoy es mi cumpleaños it's my birthday today, ¿a qué estamos hoy? what day is it today? ❷ hoy en día nowadays, hoy en día son bastante comunes nowadays they are quite common

hoyo NOUN MASC **hole**

hube, hubo, *etc* VERB ▸ SEE **haber**

hucha NOUN FEM **moneybox**

hueco¹ NOUN MASC ❶ **hollow**; suena a hueco it sounds hollow ❷ **space**; hazme un hueco make some room

for me, un hueco para aparcar a parking space ❸ el hueco de la escalera the stairwell, el hueco del ascensor the lift shaft ❹ **gap** *(in timetable)*

hueco², hueca ADJECTIVE **hollow**

huela, huelo, *etc* VERB ▸ SEE **oler**

huelga NOUN FEM **strike**; hacer huelga to strike, estar en huelga to be on strike, huelga de celo work-to-rule

huella NOUN FEM ❶ **footprint** ❷ **track** *(of an animal or tyre, for example)* ❸ huellas dactilares fingerprints

huérfano, huérfana NOUN MASC, FEM **orphan**

huerto, huerta NOUN MASC, FEM ❶ **vegetable garden** ❷ **orchard**

hueso NOUN MASC ❶ **bone**; romperse un hueso to break a bone ❷ **stone** *(in fruit)*

huésped NOUN MASC & FEM **guest**

huesudo ADJECTIVE **bony**

huevo NOUN MASC **egg**; huevo duro hard-boiled egg, huevo pasado por agua soft-boiled egg, huevo escalfado poached egg, huevo frito fried egg, huevos revueltos scrambled eggs, huevo de Pascua Easter egg

huir VERB [54] **to flee**; huir de la cárcel to escape from prison

humanidades PLURAL NOUN FEM **humanities**

humano, humana NOUN MASC, FEM **human being**

humano ADJECTIVE ❶ **human**; la naturaleza humana human nature ❷ **humane**

humedad *NOUN FEM* ❶ **dampness**; la casa tiene humedad the house is damp ❷ **humidity**

húmedo, húmeda *ADJECTIVE* ❶ **damp** ❷ **wet** ❸ **moist**

humillar *VERB* [17] **to humiliate**

humo *NOUN MASC* **smoke**

humor *NOUN MASC* ❶ **humour**; tener sentido del humor to have a sense of humour ❷ **mood**; estar de buen humor to be in a good mood, estar de mal humor to be in a bad mood, no estoy de humor para verlos I'm not in the mood to see them

hundir *VERB* [19] **to sink**

hundirse *REFLEXIVE VERB* [19] **to sink**

húngaro¹ *NOUN MASC* **Hungarian** *(the language)*

húngaro², húngara *NOUN MASC, FEM*

húngaro *ADJECTIVE* **Hungarian**

Hungría *NOUN FEM* **Hungary**

huracán *NOUN MASC* **hurricane**

hurra *EXCLAMATION* **hurrah!**

huyas, huyo, *etc VERB* ▸ SEE **huir**

iba, iban, *etc VERB* ▸ SEE **ir**

iceberg *NOUN MASC* **iceberg**

icono *NOUN MASC* **icon**

ida¹ *NOUN FEM* **departure**; un billete de ida a single ticket, un billete de ida y vuelta a return ticket

ida² *VERB* ▸ SEE **ir**

idea *NOUN FEM* **idea**; '¿a qué hora llegan?' – 'no tengo ni idea' 'what time will they arrive?' – 'I haven't a clue', no tienen ni idea de cómo ir they have no idea how to get there, tengo una idea I've got an idea

ideal *ADJECTIVE* **ideal**

idéntico, idéntica *ADJECTIVE* **identical**; es idéntico a su padre he's just like his father

identidad *NOUN FEM* **identity**; un carné de identidad an identity card

identificación *NOUN FEM* **identification**

identificar *VERB* [31] **to identify**

identificarse *REFLEXIVE VERB* [31] ❶ **to identify yourself** ❷ identificarse con to identify with, me identifico mucho con la protagonista del libro I identify a lot with the heroine of the book

idioma *NOUN MASC* **language**; hablar idiomas varios to speak several foreign languages

idiota NOUN MASC & FEM **idiot**

idiota ADJECTIVE **stupid**

ido VERB ▸ SEE **ir**

iglesia NOUN FEM **church**

ignorante ADJECTIVE **ignorant**

ignorar VERB [17] ❶ to ignore; no me gusta que me ignoren I don't like being ignored ❷ not to know; ignoro las razones I don't know the reasons

igual ADJECTIVE ❶ same; uno de igual tamaño one of the same size, parecen todos iguales they all look the same ❷ igual a, igual que the same as, era igual a este it was the same as this one, no es igual que los demás it's not the same as the others ❸ todo le da igual he doesn't care about anything, '¿quieres ir al cine o al teatro?' – 'me da igual' 'do you want to go to the cinema or to the theatre?' – 'I don't mind', les da igual lo uno que lo otro either way it makes no difference to them

igual ADVERB ❶ the same; suenan igual they sound the same ❷ equally; los quiero a todos igual I love them all equally, los dos sistemas son igual de eficientes both systems are equally efficient ❸ (in comparisons) es igual de alto que su padre he's as tall as his father, es igual de ancho que la mesa it's as wide as the table, es Géminis, igual que yo she's a Gemini, just like me ❹ maybe; igual la vemos en la fiesta maybe we'll see her at the party ❺ al igual que just like

igualdad NOUN FEM **equality**; igualdad de oportunidades equal opportunities, en igualdad de condiciones on equal terms

igualmente ADVERB ❶ equally; igualmente aburrido equally boring ❷ 'que pases una feliz Navidad' – 'igualmente' 'have a good Christmas' – 'you too'

ilegal ADJECTIVE **illegal**

ilegalmente ADVERB **illegally**

ileso, ilesa ADJECTIVE **unhurt, uninjured**

ilimitado, ilimitada ADJECTIVE **unlimited**

iluminación NOUN FEM ❶ lighting (in a room or theatre) ❷ illumination (of a building or statue)

iluminar VERB [17] ❶ to light (a room or theatre) ❷ to illuminate (a building or statue)

ilusión NOUN FEM ❶ hope ❷ me hace ilusión ir I'm excited about going ❸ illusion

ilustración NOUN FEM **illustration**

ilustrar VERB [17] to illustrate

imagen NOUN FEM ❶ image; es la viva imagen de su madre she's the image of her mother ❷ picture (on a TV screen) ❸ reflection (in a mirror)

imaginación NOUN FEM **imagination**; son imaginaciones suyas he's just imagining things

imaginar VERB [17] to imagine

imaginarse REFLEXIVE VERB [17] ❶ to imagine; me imaginaba que sería más grande I imagined it would be bigger ❷ me imagino que no I suppose not, me imagino que sí I imagine so

imán NOUN MASC **magnet**

imbécil NOUN MASC & FEM **idiot**

imbécil ADJECTIVE **stupid**

imitar VERB [17] **to imitate**

impacientar VERB [17] **to make impatient**

impacientarse REFLEXIVE VERB [17] **to get impatient**

impaciente ADJECTIVE **impatient**

impacto NOUN MASC **impact**

impar ADJECTIVE **odd**

impecable ADJECTIVE **impeccable**

impedir VERB [57] ❶ **to prevent**; impedirle a alguien hacer algo to prevent someone from doing something ❷ impedir el paso to block the way

imperativo NOUN MASC **imperative**

imperdible NOUN MASC **safety pin**

imperfecto[1] NOUN MASC **imperfect**

imperfecto[2], **imperfecta** ADJECTIVE **imperfect**

impermeable NOUN MASC **raincoat**

impersonal ADJECTIVE **impersonal**

implicar VERB [31] **to involve**

imponer VERB [11] **to impose** (a condition or punishment)

importación NOUN FEM **import**; artículos de importación imports

importado, **importada** ADJECTIVE **imported**

importancia NOUN FEM **importance**; darle importancia a algo to attach importance to something

importante ADJECTIVE ❶ **important**; lo importante es … the important thing is … ❷ **considerable**; una importante suma de dinero a considerable sum of money

importar VERB [17] ❶ **to matter**; no importa, déjalo así it doesn't matter, leave it like this, no importa mucho el color the colour doesn't matter very much ❷ no me importa ayudarles I don't mind helping them, ¿te importa que use el teléfono? do you mind if I use your phone?, ¿le importaría comprobarlo? would you mind checking it? ❸ ¿y a ti que te importa? it's none of your business, no me importa lo que diga I don't care what he says ❹ **to import** (goods)
• me importa un comino/un rábano (informal) I couldn't care less

imposible ADJECTIVE **impossible**

impresión NOUN FEM ❶ **impression**; causar una buena impresión to make a good impression ❷ me da la impresión de que … I've got the feeling that …

impresionante ADJECTIVE **impressive**

impresionar VERB [17] ❶ **to impress**; quiere impresionarte she wants to impress you ❷ **to affect**; me impresionó mucho verlos discutir seeing them argue really affected me, la violencia de la escena me impresionó mucho the violence of the scene shocked me

impreso[1] NOUN MASC **form**; impreso de solicitud application form

impreso[2], **impresa** ADJECTIVE **printed**

a
b
c
d
e
f
g
h
i
j
k
l
m
n
ñ
o
p
q
r
s
t
u
v
w
x
y
z

impresora *NOUN FEM* **printer**; una impresora láser a laser printer

imprevisible *ADJECTIVE*
❶ **unpredictable**
❷ **unforeseeable**

imprevisto[1] *NOUN MASC* **unforeseen event**

imprevisto[2], **imprevista** *ADJECTIVE* **unforeseen, unexpected**

imprimir *VERB* [17] **to print**

improvisado, improvisada *ADJECTIVE* **improvised**

improvisar *VERB* [17] **to improvise**

improviso *IN PHRASE* de improviso **unexpectedly, out of the blue**

imprudente *NOUN MASC & FEM*
❶ **careless person** ❷ **reckless person**; es un imprudente conduciendo he's a reckless driver

imprudente *ADJECTIVE* ❶ **careless** ❷ **reckless**

impuesto *NOUN MASC* **tax**

impulsivo, impulsiva *ADJECTIVE* **impulsive**

inaccesible *ADJECTIVE* **inaccessible**

inaceptable *ADJECTIVE* **unacceptable**

inadecuado, inadecuada *ADJECTIVE* ❶ **inappropriate** ❷ **inadequate**

inadmisible *ADJECTIVE* **unacceptable**

inadvertido, inadvertida *ADJECTIVE* pasar inadvertido **to go unnoticed**

inaguantable *ADJECTIVE* **unbearable**

inalámbrico, inalámbrica *ADJECTIVE* **cordless**

incapaz *ADJECTIVE* es incapaz de hacer daño a nadie he's incapable

of harming anyone, fui incapaz de entenderlo I was unable to understand it

incendio *NOUN MASC* **fire**

incertidumbre *NOUN FEM* **uncertainty**

incierto, incierta *ADJECTIVE* **uncertain**

incitar *VERB* [17] incitar a alguien a hacer **to incite someone to do**

incluido, incluida *ADJECTIVE* **included**; dos mil euros, todo incluido two thousand euros, everything included, seremos diez personas, nosotros incluidos there will be ten people including us

incluir *VERB* [54] **to include**

inclusive *ADJECTIVE* **inclusive**; los viernes inclusive including Fridays

incluso *ADVERB* **even**; es incluso mejor it's even better

incluya, incluyo, *etc VERB* ▸ *SEE* **incluir**

incoloro, incolora *ADJECTIVE* **colourless**

incómodo, incómoda *ADJECTIVE* **uncomfortable**

incompetente *ADJECTIVE* **incompetent**

incompleto, incompleta *ADJECTIVE* **incomplete**

incomprensible *ADJECTIVE* **incomprehensible**

incondicional *ADJECTIVE* **unconditional**

inconsciente *ADJECTIVE* **unconscious**

inconveniente NOUN MASC
drawback, disadvantage

inconveniente ADJECTIVE
inconvenient

incorporar VERB [17] to incorporate

incorporarse REFLEXIVE VERB [17]
to sit up

incorrecto, incorrecta ADJECTIVE
incorrect

increíble ADJECTIVE unbelievable,
incredible

indecente ADJECTIVE indecent

indeciso, indecisa ADJECTIVE
❶ indecisive ❷ undecided; están
indecisos sobre la cantidad they're
undecided about the quantity

indefenso, indefensa ADJECTIVE
defenceless

indefinidamente ADVERB
indefinitely, for good

indefinido, indefinida ADJECTIVE
❶ indefinite ❷ vague (outline, for
example)

indemnizar VERB [22] to
compensate; los indemnizaron
con veinte mil euros they received
twenty thousand euros in
compensation

indemnización NOUN FEM
compensation; le pagaron una
indemnización they paid her
compensation

independencia NOUN FEM
independence

independiente ADJECTIVE
independent

India NOUN FEM (la) India India

indicación NOUN FEM ❶ indication
❷ sign; me hizo una indicación
para que lo siguiese he signalled
to me to follow him, hay una
indicación en el camino there's a
sign on the road

indicar VERB [31] ❶ to indicate ❷ to
point to

índice NOUN MASC index

indiferente ADJECTIVE ❶ indifferent
❷ me es indiferente it makes no
difference to me

indígena ADJECTIVE native

indigestión NOUN FEM indigestion

indigesto, indigesta ADJECTIVE
indigestible

indignación NOUN FEM
❶ indignation ❷ outrage

indignar VERB [17] ❶ to make angry
❷ to outrage

indignarse REFLEXIVE VERB [17] ❶ to
get angry ❷ to be outraged

indio, india NOUN MASC, FEM, ADJECTIVE
Indian

indirecta¹ NOUN FEM hint

indirecto, indirecta² ADJECTIVE
indirect

indiscreto, indiscreta ADJECTIVE
indiscreet

indispensable ADJECTIVE essential

indispuesto, indispuesta ADJECTIVE
estar indispuesto to be unwell

individual ADJECTIVE individual

individuo NOUN MASC ❶ person;
un individuo con pelo largo a
person with long hair ❷ (pejorative)
character; un individuo con

a
b
c
d
e
f
g
h
i
j
k
l
m
n
ñ
o
p
q
r
s
t
u
v
w
x
y
z

muy mal aspecto a nasty looking character

industria NOUN FEM **industry**

industrial ADJECTIVE **industrial**

ineficaz ADJECTIVE ❶ **ineffective** (remedy, measure) ❷ **inefficient** (person)

inepto, **inepta** NOUN MASC, FEM

inepto ADJECTIVE **incompetent**

inesperado, **inesperada** ADJECTIVE **unexpected**

inevitable ADJECTIVE **unavoidable**; era inevitable que pase it was bound to happen

inexperto, **inexperta** ADJECTIVE **inexperienced**

infancia NOUN FEM **childhood**

infantil ADJECTIVE ❶ **childish**; eres muy infantil you're so childish ❷ **childlike** ❸ literatura infantil children's books

infarto NOUN MASC **heart attack**; le dio un infarto he had a heart attack

infección NOUN FEM **infection**

infectado, **infectada** ADJECTIVE **infected**

infectar VERB [17] **to infect**

infectarse REFLEXIVE VERB [17] **to become infected**

infeliz ADJECTIVE **unhappy**

infiel ADJECTIVE **unfaithful**; serle infiel a alguien to be unfaithful to someone

infierno NOUN MASC **hell**

infinitivo NOUN MASC **infinitive**

infinito[1] NOUN MASC **infinity**

infinito[2], **infinita** ADJECTIVE **infinite**

inflable ADJECTIVE **inflatable**

inflación NOUN FEM **inflation**

inflamable ADJECTIVE **flammable**

inflar VERB [17] ❶ **to inflate** (a tyre, for example) ❷ **to blow up** (a balloon, for example)

influencia NOUN FEM **influence**

influir VERB [54] **to influence**

información NOUN FEM ❶ **information**; 'Información' 'Information Desk' (on a sign) ❷ **news** (in newspaper or TV news); la información internacional the foreign news ❸ **directory enquiries** (on the telephone); llamar a información to call directory enquiries

informal ADJECTIVE ❶ **informal** (a chat or meal, for example) ❷ **casual** (clothes) ❸ **unreliable** (person)

informar VERB [17] **to inform**; me informaron mal I was misinformed, ¿podría informarme sobre ...? could you give me information about ...?

informarse REFLEXIVE VERB [17] **to find out information**; me informaré sobre el horario I'll find out about the timetable

informática NOUN FEM **computer science**, **IT**

informático, **informática** NOUN MASC, FEM **computer technician**

informe NOUN MASC **report**

infracción NOUN FEM **offence**; cometer una infracción to commit an offence, una infracción de tráfico a traffic offence

infusión *NOUN FEM* **herbal tea**; una infusión de menta a peppermint tea

ingeniero, **ingeniera** *NOUN MASC, FEM* **engineer**

ingenuo, **ingenua** *NOUN MASC & FEM* eres un ingenuo you're so naive

ingenuo *ADJECTIVE* **naive**

Inglaterra *NOUN FEM* **England**

inglés¹ *NOUN MASC* **English** *(the language)*

inglés², **inglesa** *NOUN MASC, FEM* **Englishman**, **Englishwoman**; los ingleses the English, English people

inglés, **inglesa** *ADJECTIVE* **English**

ingrato, **ingrata** *ADJECTIVE* **ungrateful**

ingrediente *NOUN MASC* **ingredient**

ingreso *NOUN MASC* ❶ **admission** *(to hospital, university)* ❷ **deposit** *(in a bank account)* ❸ ingresos income

inicial *NOUN FEM* **initial**

inicial *ADJECTIVE* **initial**

iniciativa *NOUN FEM* **initiative**; por iniciativa propia on her own initiative

injusto, **injusta** *ADJECTIVE* **unfair**

inmaduro, **inmadura** *ADJECTIVE* **immature**

inmediatamente *ADVERB* **immediately**

inmediato, **inmediata** *ADJECTIVE* **immediate**; de inmediato immediately

inmenso, **inmensa** *ADJECTIVE* ❶ **immense** ❷ **huge**; un salón inmenso a huge living room

inmigración *NOUN FEM* **immigration**

inmigrante *NOUN MASC & FEM* **immigrant**

inmobiliaria *NOUN FEM* **estate agent's**

inmoral *ADJECTIVE* **immoral**

inmueble *NOUN MASC* **property**

inmunizar *VERB* [22] **to immunize**

innecesario, **innecesaria** *ADJECTIVE* **unnecessary**

innovación *NOUN FEM* **innovation**

innovar *VERB* [17] **to innovate**

innumerable *ADJECTIVE* **innumerable**

inocentada *NOUN FEM* **practical joke** *(this is also used for a joke played on someone on 28 December, which is the Spanish equivalent of April Fool's Day)*; gastarle una inocentada a alguien to play a practical joke on someone

inocente *ADJECTIVE* ❶ **innocent** ❷ **naive** ► SEE **día**

inofensivo, **inofensiva** *ADJECTIVE* **harmless**

inolvidable *ADJECTIVE* **unforgettable**

inoxidable *ADJECTIVE* acero inoxidable stainless steel

inquietante *ADJECTIVE* **disturbing**

inquietar *VERB* [17] **to worry**

inquieto, **inquieta** *ADJECTIVE* ❶ **worried** ❷ **restless**

a
b
c
d
e
f
g
h
i
j
k
l
m
n
ñ
o
p
q
r
s
t
u
v
w
x
y
z

inquietud NOUN FEM ❶ uneasiness ❷ interest

inquilino, **inquilina** NOUN MASC, FEM tenant

inscribir VERB [52] ❶ to register (on a course, for example) ❷ to engrave

inscribirse REFLEXIVE VERB [52] to register

inscripción NOUN FEM ❶ registration (on a course, for example) ❷ inscription

insecto NOUN MASC insect

inseguro, **insegura** ADJECTIVE insecure

insertar VERB [17] to insert

insignificante ADJECTIVE insignificant

insistir VERB [19] to insist; insistir en algo to insist on something

insolación NOUN FEM sunstroke; coger una insolación to get sunstroke

insolente ADJECTIVE rude

insólito, **insólita** ADJECTIVE unheard of

insonorizado, **insonorizada** ADJECTIVE soundproofed

insoportable ADJECTIVE unbearable

inspección NOUN FEM inspection

inspeccionar VERB [17] to inspect

inspector, **inspectora** NOUN MASC, FEM inspector

inspiración NOUN FEM inspiration

inspirar VERB [17] to inspire

inspirarse REFLEXIVE VERB [17] inspirarse en algo to be inspired by something

instalación NOUN FEM installation

instalar VERB [17] to install (a washing machine or a computer, for example)

instalarse REFLEXIVE VERB [17] to install yourself

instantáneo, **instantánea** ADJECTIVE ❶ instant ❷ immediate

instante NOUN MASC moment; un instante, por favor one moment, please

instinto NOUN MASC instinct; instinto de conservación survival instinct, por instinto instinctively

instituto NOUN MASC institute; instituto de bachillerato secondary school

instrucción NOUN FEM ❶ education ❷ training; instrucción militar military training ❸ instrucciones instructions (for a computer, for example)

instructor, **instructora** NOUN MASC, FEM instructor; instructor de autoescuela driving instructor, instructor de esquí ski instructor

instruir VERB [54] ❶ to instruct ❷ to educate

instrumento NOUN MASC instrument; tocar un instrumento to play an instrument

insuficiente NOUN MASC fail (at school)

insuficiente ADJECTIVE inadequate

insultar VERB [17] to insult

insulto *NOUN MASC* **insult**

intacto, **intacta** *ADJECTIVE* **intact**

integral *ADJECTIVE* ❶ **comprehensive** ❷ pan integral wholemeal bread

íntegro, **íntegra** *ADJECTIVE* la versión íntegra de la película the full-length version of the film, el texto íntegro the unabridged text

intelectual *NOUN MASC & FEM*

intelectual *ADJECTIVE* **intellectual**

inteligencia *NOUN FEM* **intelligence**

inteligente *ADJECTIVE* **intelligent**

intención *NOUN FEM* **intention**; no fue mi intención it wasn't my intention, no era mi intención ofenderla I didn't mean to offend her, tiene buenas intenciones she means well, lo preguntó con mala intención he asked the question to cause trouble

intensivo, **intensiva** *ADJECTIVE* **intensive**

intenso, **intensa** *ADJECTIVE* ❶ **intense** ❷ **deep** *(feeling)*

intentar *VERB* [17] **to try**; ¡inténtalo otra vez! try again!, intentar hacer to try to do, intenté cerrarlo I tried to shut it, intenta llegar temprano try to arrive early

intento *NOUN MASC* **attempt**; lo consiguió al tercer intento she succeeded at the third attempt

intercambiar *VERB* [17] ❶ **to exchange** ❷ **to swap**

intercambiarse *REFLEXIVE VERB* [17] **to swap**; se intercambiaron las revistas they swapped their magazines

intercambio *NOUN MASC* ❶ **exchange** ❷ **swap**

interés *NOUN MASC* **interest**; es de gran interés para mí it's of great interest to me, su interés por la historia her interest in history

interesante *ADJECTIVE* **interesting**; un película interestante an interesting film, resulta interesante que ... it's interesting that ...

interesar *VERB* [17] no me interesa el deporte I'm not interested in sport, ¿te interesa la historia? are you interested in history?

interesarse *REFLEXIVE VERB* [17] interesarse en algo/interesarse por algo to take an interest in something

interfono *NOUN MASC* ❶ **entryphone** ❷ **intercom**

interior *NOUN MASC* ❶ **inside**; el interior de la caja the inside of the box ❷ en mi interior, tenía miedo deep down inside, I was afraid

interior *ADJECTIVE* ❶ **interior**; escalera interior interior staircase ❷ un piso interior a flat with windows facing into an inner courtyard ❸ **inside**; en la parte interior on the inside

intermediario, **intermediaria** *NOUN MASC, FEM* **intermediary**

intermedio¹ *NOUN MASC* **interval**

intermedio², **intermedia** *ADJECTIVE* ❶ **intermediate** *(level or stage, for example)* ❷ **medium**; de tamaño intermedio medium-sized

intermitente *ADJECTIVE* ❶ **flashing** *(a light)* ❷ **intermittent**

internacional ADJECTIVE
international

internado[1] NOUN MASC **boarding school**

internado[2], **internada** ADJECTIVE
está internado he's been taken into hospital

internauta NOUN MASC & FEM **surfer**
(on the Internet)

Internet NOUN MASC **Internet** (Spanish omits 'el' with Internet); en Internet on the Internet

interno, **interna** NOUN MASC, FEM
boarder (in a school)

interno ADJECTIVE **internal**

interpretar VERB [17] ❶ to interpret
❷ interpretar un papel to play a part (in a play or film), interpretar una pieza de música to perform a piece of music, interpretar una canción to sing a song

intérprete NOUN MASC & FEM
❶ interpreter ❷ performer (of a piece of music) ❸ singer (of a song)

interrogación NOUN FEM
interrogation

interrogante NOUN MASC OR FEM
❶ question; quedan muchos interrogantes sin responder there are many questions left unanswered ❷ question mark; pon un interrogante write a question mark

interrogar VERB [28] to question
(a suspect)

interrumpir VERB [19] to interrupt

interrupción NOUN FEM interruption

interruptor NOUN MASC **switch**

interurbano, **interurbana**
ADJECTIVE ❶ long-distance; una llamada interurbana a long-distance call ❷ un tren interurbano an intercity train

intervalo NOUN MASC **interval**

intervención NOUN FEM
intervention

intervenir VERB [15] ❶ to take part;
intervenir en las negociaciones to take part in the negotiations
❷ to intervene; no quiero intervenir I don't want to intervene
❸ intervenir a alguien to operate on somebody

interviú NOUN FEM **interview**

intimidación NOUN FEM
❶ intimidation ❷ bullying

intimidar VERB [17] to intimidate

íntimo, **íntima** ADJECTIVE ❶ private;
mi vida íntima my private life
❷ intimate; un ambiente íntimo an intimate atmosphere ❸ mis amigos íntimos my close friends ❹ una cena íntima a candlelit dinner

intolerante ADJECTIVE **intolerant**

intoxicación NOUN FEM **poisoning**;
intoxicación alimenticia food poisoning

intransitivo, **intransitiva** ADJECTIVE
intransitive

intriga NOUN FEM **intrigue**

introducir VERB [60] ❶ to introduce;
introducir cambios to introduce changes ❷ to insert; introducir la moneda en la ranura insert the coin in the slot

introducirse REFLEXIVE VERB [60] ❶ to be introduced ❷ to get in; el ladrón se introdujo por la ventana the burglar got in through the window

intruso, **intrusa** *NOUN MASC, FEM* intruder

intuitivo, **intuitiva** *ADJECTIVE* intuitive

inundación *NOUN FEM* **flooding**; ha habido inundaciones en Cataluña there's been flooding in Catalonia

inútil *NOUN MASC & FEM* es una inútil she's useless

inútil *ADJECTIVE* ❶ **useless** ❷ es inútil intentarlo it's useless trying

invadir *VERB* [19] to invade

inválido, **inválida** *NOUN MASC, FEM* disabled person

invasión *NOUN FEM* invasion

inventar *VERB* [17] ❶ to invent ❷ to make up *(a story or game)*

inventarse *REFLEXIVE VERB* [17] to invent, to make up; se inventó una excusa he made up an excuse

invento *NOUN MASC* invention

invernadero *NOUN MASC* greenhouse

inversión *NOUN FEM* investment

inverso, **inversa** *ADJECTIVE* reverse

investigación *NOUN FEM* ❶ investigation *(of a crime or accident, for example)* ❷ research; investigación de mercado market research

investigar *VERB* [17] ❶ to investigate ❷ to research

invierno *NOUN MASC* winter; en invierno in winter, el invierno pasado last winter

invisible *ADJECTIVE* invisible

invitación *NOUN FEM* invitation

invitado, **invitada** *NOUN MASC, FEM* guest

invitar *VERB* [17] ❶ to invite; invitar a alguien a una fiesta to invite someone to a party, me han invitado a su casa they've invited me to their house ❷ te invito a cenar I'll take you out for dinner, nos invitó a una copa he bought us a drink, ¡yo invito! it's on me!

involuntario, **involuntaria** *ADJECTIVE* involuntary

inyección *NOUN FEM* injection

ir *VERB* [8] ❶ to go; van a casa de Alicia they're going to Alicia's, iremos al museo we'll go to the museum, ¿adónde vas? where are you going?, ¿dónde van los platos? where do the plates go?, aún no va al colegio she doesn't go to school yet ❷ to come; ¡ya voy! I'm coming! ❸ *(talking about how things are progressing)*; ¿cómo van las cosas? how are things?, ¿cómo te va? how are you doing?, ¿cómo va el enfermo? how is the patient doing?, le va muy bien en el trabajo he's doing very well at work, me fue muy mal en la entrevista I did very badly at the interview, el proyecto va bien the project is going well ❹ *(talking about how something works)* la lavadora no va bien the washing machine is not working properly ❺ to be; iba solo he was alone, ellos iban en la parte de delante they were at the front, yo iba de pie I was standing up ❻ *(referring to the way you dress)* iba con un abrigo marrón he was wearing a brown coat, iban bien vestidos they were well dressed ❼ *(talking about whether something suits you)* el negro te va bien black suits you ❽ *(talking about an activity)* ir de vacaciones to go on holiday, voy a ir a España de vacaciones I'm going to Spain for my holidays, ir de compras to go shopping, ir a la compra to do the shopping, siempre tengo yo que ir a la compra I'm always the one who does the shopping ❾ *(talking about transport)* ir en coche to go by car, fueron en coche they drove here, ir en avión to go by plane, ir en bicicleta to go by bike, va en bicicleta a todas partes she goes everywhere by bike, ir a pie to go on foot, ir a caballo to go on horseback ❿ ir a por algo/ alguien to go to get something/ someone, voy a por pan I'm going to buy some bread, fuimos a por ella we went to fetch her, vete a por el médico go and get the doctor ⓫ ir a hacer to go to do, fuimos a ver su casa nueva we went to see their new house, ve a recoger tu habitación go and tidy up your room ⓬ *(expressing the future)* voy a comprar leche I'm going to buy some milk, voy a ser médico I'm going to be a doctor, iré a recogerla I'll go to pick her up, iba a mandártelo hoy I was going to send it to you today ⓭ su salud va mejorando her health is getting better, iban acercándose they were getting closer ⓮ ¡vamos! come on! ⓯ *(expressing surprise or annoyance)* ¡vaya hombre, un billete de cincuenta euros! hey look, a fifty-euro note!, ¡vaya, si es Carlos! what a surprise, it's Carlos!, ¡vaya, se ha fundido la luz! oh dear, the light has gone!, ¡vaya, no lo encuentro! bother, I can't find

it! ⓰ '¿lo ha hecho él solo?' – '¡qué va!' 'did he do it on his own?' – 'not likely!', '¿te molesta?' – '¡qué va!' 'do you mind?' – 'not at all!'

irse *REFLEXIVE VERB* [8] ❶ to leave; nos fuimos pronto we left early, bueno, me voy well, I'm off ❷ to go; se fueron a casa they went home ❸ ¿cómo se va a la estación? which is the way to the station

ira *NOUN FEM* rage; en un arrebato de ira in a fit of rage
• ciego de ira in a blind rage

Irlanda *NOUN FEM* Ireland

irlandés[1] *NOUN MASC* Irish *(the language)*

irlandés[2], **irlandesa** *NOUN MASC, FEM* Irishman/Irishwoman

irlandés, **irlandesa** *ADJECTIVE* Irish

ironía *NOUN FEM* irony

irónico, **irónica** *ADJECTIVE* ironic

irreal *ADJECTIVE* unreal

irresponsable *ADJECTIVE* irresponsible

irritación *NOUN FEM* irritation

irritante *ADJECTIVE* irritating

irritar *VERB* [17] to irritate

irritarse *REFLEXIVE VERB* [17] ❶ to get irritated *(a person)* ❷ to become irritated

isla *NOUN FEM* island

islam *NOUN MASC* Islam

islámico, **islámica** *ADJECTIVE* Islamic

islandés, **islandesa** *NOUN MASC, FEM* Icelander

Islandia *NOUN FEM* Iceland

Israel *NOUN MASC* Israel

israelí *NOUN MASC & FEM, ADJECTIVE* Israeli

Italia *NOUN FEM* **Italy**

italiano¹ *NOUN MASC* **Italian**
(the language)

italiano², **italiana** *NOUN MASC, FEM,*
ADJECTIVE **Italian**

itinerario *NOUN MASC* **itinerary,**
route

IVA *ABBREVIATION MASC (short for*
Impuesto al Valor Agregado) **VAT**

izquierda¹ *NOUN FEM* ❶ **left**; tuerce
a la izquierda turn left, se sentaron
a mi izquierda they sat on my left
❷ está a la izquierda it's on the left-
hand side ❸ ser de izquierdas to be
left-wing *(in politics)*

izquierdo, **izquierda²** *ADJECTIVE* **left**

jabalí *NOUN MASC* **wild boar**

jabón *NOUN MASC* **soap**; una pastilla
de jabón a cake of soap

jabonera *NOUN FEM* **soapdish**

Jamaica *NOUN FEM* **Jamaica**

jamaicano, **jamaicana** *NOUN MASC,*
FEM, ADJECTIVE **Jamaican**

jamás *ADVERB* **never**; no lo he visto
jamás I've never seen it, nunca
jamás volveré I'll never ever go
back again

jamón *NOUN MASC* **ham**; jamón de
York cooked ham, jamón serrano
cured raw ham

Japón *NOUN MASC* (el) Japón Japan

japonés, **japonesa** *NOUN MASC, FEM,*
ADJECTIVE **Japanese**

jarabe *NOUN MASC* **syrup**; jarabe para
la tos cough mixture

jardín *NOUN MASC* ❶ **garden**; está
en el jardín she's in the garden
❷ jardín de infancia nursery
(school)

jardinero, **jardinera** *NOUN MASC,*
FEM **gardener**

jarra *NOUN FEM* ▸ SEE **jarro**

jarro *NOUN MASC* **jug**

jarrón *NOUN MASC* **vase**

a
b
c
d
e
f
g
h
i
j
k
l
m
n
ñ
o
p
q
r
s
t
u
v
w
x
y
z

jaula *NOUN FEM* **cage**

jefe, **jefa** *NOUN MASC, FEM* ❶ **boss** *(at work)* ❷ **manager** *(of a company)* ❸ **chief**; el jefe de policía the chief of police, el jefe de bomberos the chief fire officer ❹ **leader** *(of a group)*

jengibre *NOUN MASC* **ginger**

jerez *NOUN MASC* **sherry**

jersey *NOUN MASC* **sweater**

Jesucristo *NOUN MASC* **Jesus Christ**

jinete *NOUN MASC* ❶ **rider** ❷ **jockey**

JJ.OO. *ABBREVIATION MASC PLURAL (short for Juegos Olímpicos)* **Olympic Games**

jornada *NOUN FEM* **day**; una jornada de trabajo a working day, trabajar media jornada to work part time, trabajar la jornada completa to work full time

joven *NOUN MASC & FEM* un joven a young man, una joven a young woman

joven *ADJECTIVE* **young**; moda joven young fashion

jovencito, **jovencita** *NOUN MASC, FEM* **young man/young woman**

joya *NOUN FEM* ❶ **piece of jewellery**; no me gustan las joyas I don't like jewellery ❷ esa chica es una joya that girl's a real gem

joyería *NOUN FEM* **jeweller's**

jubilación *NOUN FEM* **retirement**

jubilado, **jubilada** *NOUN MASC, FEM* **pensioner**; los jubilados retired people

jubilado *ADJECTIVE* **retired**

jubilarse *REFLEXIVE VERB* [17] **to retire**

judaísmo *NOUN MASC* **Judaism**

judía[1] *NOUN FEM* **bean**; judías blancas haricot beans, judías pintas kidney beans, judías verdes green beans

judío, **judía**[2] *NOUN MASC, FEM* **Jew**

judío *ADJECTIVE* **Jewish**

judo *NOUN MASC* **judo**

juega, **juego**[1], *etc VERB ▸ SEE* **jugar**

juego[2] *NOUN MASC* ❶ **game**; juegos de mesa board games, un juego de azar a game of chance, los Juegos Olímpicos the Olympic Games, los Juegos Paralímpicos **the Paralympic Games**; a los diez minutos de juego ten minutes into the game ❷ un juego de manos a conjuring trick ❸ **gambling**; es aficionado al juego he likes gambling ❹ **play**; un juego de palabras a play on words, juego limpio fair play ❺ **set**; un juego de cacerolas a set of pans, un juego de llaves a set of keys ❻ hacer juego con algo to match something, no hace juego con los pantalones it doesn't match the trousers ❼ fuera de juego offside
• es un juego de niños it's child's play

juegue *VERB ▸ SEE* **jugar**

juerga *NOUN FEM* ir de juerga *(informal)* to go out on the town

juerguista *NOUN MASC & FEM (informal)* **raver**

jueves *NOUN MASC* **Thursday**; el jueves on Thursday, el jueves por la mañana on Thursday morning, los jueves on Thursdays

juez NOUN MASC & FEM **❶** judge **❷** referee

jugador, jugadora NOUN MASC, FEM **❶** player **❷** gambler

jugar VERB [27] **❶** to play; jugar al fútbol to play football, jugar a la pelota to play ball, ¿a qué quieres jugar? what do you want to play? **❷** to gamble **❸** to move (in board games); te toca jugar a ti it's your turn (to move)

jugo NOUN MASC juice

jugoso, jugosa ADJECTIVE juicy

juguete NOUN MASC toy; un coche de juguete a toy car

juguetería NOUN FEM toyshop

juicio NOUN MASC **❶** trial; llevar a alguien a juicio to take someone to court **❷** sense; no tiene ningún juicio he's not very sensible **❸** no estar en su sano juicio to be out of one's mind, perder el juicio to lose one's mind

julio NOUN MASC July; en julio, en el mes de julio in July

jungla NOUN FEM jungle

junio NOUN MASC June; en junio, en el mes de junio in June

júnior ADJECTIVE junior

junta¹ NOUN FEM **❶** board, committee **❷** meeting

juntar VERB [17] **❶** to put together **❷** to join

juntarse REFLEXIVE VERB [17] **❶** to join **❷** to meet; me junté con unos amigos I met some friends **❸** to get closer; juntaos más come closer

junto, junta² ADJECTIVE **❶** together; ahora todos juntos all together now, no los pongas tan juntos don't put them so close together **❷** junto a next to, junto a la ventana next to the window **❸** junto con with, together with

jurado NOUN MASC jury

jurar VERB [17] to swear; te lo juro I swear

jurídico, jurídica ADJECTIVE legal

justamente ADVERB **❶** fairly; tratar a alguien justamente to treat someone fairly **❷** exactly; justamente eso es lo que yo quería decir that's exactly what I meant, ¡justamente! exactly!

justicia NOUN FEM justice

justificar VERB [31] to justify

justo¹, justa ADJECTIVE **❶** fair; no has sido justo con él you haven't been fair with him, una sociedad justa a fair society **❷** exact; la cantidad justa the exact amount, son ciento cincuenta euros justos it's exactly one hundred and fifty euros **❸** just enough; tengo lo justo para el autobús I have just enough for my bus fare, viven con lo justo they have just enough to live on **❹** tight; te está un poco justo it's a bit tight on you, los zapatos me quedan muy justos the shoes are too tight on me

justo² ADVERB **❶** just; justo a tiempo just in time **❷** justo en el centro right in the middle

juvenil ADJECTIVE **❶** youthful (appearance) **❷** young (fashion) **❸** junior (team or competition)

A
B
C
D
E
F
G
H
I
J
K
L
M
N
Ñ
O
P
Q
R
S
T
U
V
W
X
Y
Z

juventud NOUN FEM **youth**; la
juventud de hoy today's youth

juzgado NOUN MASC **court**

juzgar VERB [28] ❶ **to judge** (people
or behaviour); te he juzgado mal
I've misjudged you ❷ **to try** (a case
or person)

kaki ADJECTIVE **khaki**

kárate NOUN MASC **karate**

karting NOUN MASC **karting**

ketchup NOUN MASC **ketchup**

Kg. ABBREVIATION (short for kilogramo)
kg

kilo NOUN MASC **kilo**

kilogramo NOUN MASC **kilogram**

kilómetro NOUN MASC **kilometre**

kiosco NOUN MASC ❶ **kiosk**
(selling sweets, cigarrettes, etc)
❷ **newspaper kiosk** ❸ **stand**; un
kiosko de helados an ice cream
stand ❹ el kiosko de la orquesta
the bandstand

kiwi NOUN MASC ❶ **kiwifruit** ❷ **kiwi**

km. ABBREVIATION (short for kilómetro)
km

koala NOUN MASC **koala bear**

la[1] *DETERMINER* ❶ *('la' is used before feminine singular nouns; see also 'el', 'los' and 'las')* **the**; la casa es grande the house is big ❷ *(sometimes 'la' is not translated)* no me gusta la sandía I don't like watermelon, irse a la cama to go to bed, la maleta de Isabel Isabel's suitcase, esta es la señora Martínez this is Mrs Martínez ❸ *(with parts of the body or personal belongings)* se rompió la pierna she broke her leg, se afeitó la barba he shaved his beard off, me quité la chaqueta I took my jacket off ❹ *(talking about time)* iré la próxima semana I'll go next week ❺ me gustó la verde I liked the green one, la mía es roja mine is red, esa es la tuya that one is yours ❻ esta es la de Ana this one is Ana's, la mía y la de usted mine and yours, me gusta más la de Toni I like Toni's better ❼ la que yo compré the one I bought, la que quieras whichever you want

la[2] *PRONOUN* ❶ **her**; la acompañé a casa I took her home ❷ **it** *(referring to a Spanish feminine noun)*; compré una camiseta, pero la voy a cambiar I bought a T-shirt, but I'm going to change it

labio *NOUN MASC* **lip**

laborable *ADJECTIVE* día laborable working day

laboral *ADJECTIVE* accidentes laborales work-related accidents, la jornada laboral the working day, el mercado laboral the job market, normas laborales workplace regulations

laboratorio *NOUN MASC* **laboratory**

laca *NOUN FEM* ❶ **lacquer** ❷ **hairspray** ❸ laca de uñas nail varnish

lacio, lacia *ADJECTIVE* **straight** *(hair)*

ladera *NOUN FEM* **slope**

lado *NOUN MASC* ❶ **side**; el otro lado the other side, hacerse a un lado to move to the side, al otro lado de la carretera on the other side of the road ❷ al lado de next to, al lado de Miguel next to Miguel, se sentó a mi lado he sat next to me, viven en la casa de al lado they live next door ❸ de lado sideways, ponlo de lado put it sideways, tumbarse de lado to lie on your side ❹ en todos lados, por todos lados everywhere, he buscado por todos lados I've looked everywhere ❺ en otro lado somewhere else, deben estar en otro lado they must be somewhere else ❻ en cualquier lado anywhere, deja siempre sus cosas en cualquier lado he always leaves his things all over the place ❼ en algún lado somewhere, debe estar en algún lado it must be somewhere ❽ en ningún lado, por ningún lado nowhere, not anywhere, no está por ningún lado it's nowhere, no lo encuentro en ningún lado I can't find it anywhere ❾ por un lado ... por otro ... on the one hand ... on the other hand ...

ladrar *VERB* [17] **to bark**

ladrillo *NOUN MASC* **brick**

ladrón, ladrona *NOUN MASC, FEM* ❶ **thief, burglar** ❷ **robber**

lagarto *NOUN MASC* **lizard**

lago NOUN MASC **lake**

lágrima NOUN FEM **tear**

laguna NOUN FEM ❶ **lake** ❷ **lagoon**

lamentar VERB [17] ❶ **to regret**; lamento tener que informarle de ... I regret to have to inform you that ... ❷ lo lamento mucho I'm very sorry, lamento no poder ayudarle I'm sorry I can't help you

lamer VERB [18] **to lick**

lámpara NOUN FEM **lamp**; lámpara de pie standard lamp

lana NOUN FEM **wool**; una chaqueta de lana a wool jacket, pura lana virgen pure new wool

langosta NOUN FEM **lobster**

langostino NOUN MASC **king prawn**

lanza NOUN FEM **spear**

lanzamiento NOUN MASC **launch** (of rocket, product)

lanzar VERB [22] ❶ **to throw** (a ball or stone) ❷ **to launch** (a product or an attack)

lanzarse REFLEXIVE VERB [22] ❶ **to throw yourself**; se lanzó al agua he leapt into the water, lanzarse en paracaídas to parachute ❷ lanzarse sobre alguien to pounce on someone

lápiz NOUN MASC ❶ **pencil** ❷ un lápiz de color a crayon ❸ lápiz de ojos eyeliner, lápiz de labios lipstick

largo¹ NOUN MASC **length**; ¿cuánto mide de largo? how long is it?, cinco metros de largo five metres long

largo², larga ADJECTIVE ❶ **long**; una falda larga a long skirt, te está muy largo it's too long for you ❷ a lo largo de along, a lo largo de la costa along the coast ❸ a lo largo de throughout, a lo largo del día throughout the day

las¹ DEFINITE ARTICLE ❶ ('las' is used before feminine plural nouns; see also 'el', 'la' and 'los') **the**; deja las cajas ahí leave the boxes there ❷ (sometimes 'las' is not translated) no me gustan las naranjas I don't like oranges, las maletas de Isabel Isabel's suitcases ❸ (with parts of the body or personal belongings) se lavó las manos she washed her hands, me quité las botas I took my boots off ❹ las mías son rojas mine are red, esas son las tuyas those are yours, me gustaron las verdes I liked the green ones ❺ estas son las de Ana these ones are Ana's, las mías y las de usted mine and yours, me gustan más las de Toni I like Toni's better ❻ las que yo compré the ones I bought, las que quieras whichever you want

las² PRONOUN **them** (referring to a plural Spanish feminine noun); las vi ayer I saw them yesterday, te las puedes llevar you can take them with you

láser NOUN MASC **laser**; un rayo láser a laser beam

lástima NOUN FEM ❶ **shame**; es una lástima que no puedas venir it's a shame you can't come, ¡qué lástima! what a shame! ❷ sentir lástima de alguien to feel sorry for someone, su madre me da lástima I feel sorry for her mother ❸ estar hecho una lástima to be in a pitiful state

lata NOUN FEM ❶ **tin**; una lata de tomates a tin of tomatoes, en lata tinned, sardinas en lata tinned sardines ❷ *(informal)* **nuisance**; ¡qué lata! what a nuisance!, es una lata tener que esperar it's a nuisance having to wait ❸ dar la lata *(informal)* to be a nuisance, ¡deja de dar la lata! stop being a nuisance!, siempre están dando la lata they're always such a nuisance

latín NOUN MASC **Latin**

Latinoamérica NOUN FEM **Latin America**

latinoamericano, latinoamericana NOUN MASC, FEM, ADJECTIVE **Latin American**

latón NOUN MASC **brass**

laurel NOUN MASC ❶ **laurel** ❷ una hoja de laurel a bayleaf

lavabo NOUN MASC ❶ **washbasin** ❷ **toilet**; ¿dónde están los lavabos? where are the toilets?

lavado NOUN MASC **wash**; lavado en seco dry cleaning, lavado a mano handwashing

lavadora NOUN FEM **washing machine**

lavanda NOUN FEM **lavender**

lavandería NOUN FEM ❶ **laundry** ❷ **laundrette**

lavaplatos NOUN MASC *(does not change in the plural),* **dishwasher**

lavar VERB [17] ❶ **to wash**; lavar la ropa to wash the clothes, lavar los platos to wash the dishes ❷ lavar algo en seco to dry-clean something ❸ lavar y marcar wash and blow-dry

lavarse REFLEXIVE VERB [17] **to wash**; lavarse las manos to wash your hands, lavarse la cabeza to wash

your hair, me lavo la cabeza todos los días I wash my hair everyday, lavarse los dientes to clean your teeth

lavavajillas NOUN MASC *(does not change in the plural),* **dishwasher**

lazo NOUN MASC **ribbon**

le PRONOUN ❶ **him** *(as indirect object)*; quedé con Carlos y le di las llaves I met Carlos and gave him the keys, le mandé el paquete el lunes I sent him the parcel on Monday, ¿qué le quitaron? what did they take from him? ❷ **her** *(as indirect object)*; quedé con Inés y le di las llaves I met Inés and gave her the keys, le mandé el paquete el lunes I sent her the parcel on Monday, ¿qué le quitaron? what did they take from her? ❸ **you** *(polite form: as indirect object)*; ¿le llevo las maletas a su habitación? shall I carry your suitcases to your room?, le mandé el paquete el lunes I sent you the parcel on Monday ❹ **it** *(as indirect object)*; le puse la tapa I put the lid on it, le puse otra estantería I added another shelf to it

leal ADJECTIVE **loyal**

lección NOUN FEM **lesson**

leche NOUN FEM **milk**; leche desnatada, leche descremada skimmed milk, leche en polvo powdered milk

lechuga NOUN FEM **lettuce**

lector, lectora NOUN MASC, FEM **reader**

lector de DVD NOUN MASC **DVD player**

lectura NOUN FEM **reading**

leer VERB [37] **to read**; estoy leyendo una novela I'm reading a novel, ¿has leído a Lorca? have you read Lorca?

legal ADJECTIVE **legal**

legendario, legendaria ADJECTIVE **legendary**

legumbres PLURAL NOUN FEM **pulses** (beans, lentils, etc)

lejano, lejana ADJECTIVE **distant**; son parientes lejanos they are distant relatives, el Lejano Oriente the Far East

lejía NOUN FEM **bleach**

lejos ADVERB ❶ **far**; no está muy lejos it's not very far, está demasiado lejos para ir andando it's too far to walk ❷ **a long way**; está lejos del centro it's a long way from the centre, viven lejos de aquí they live a long way from here, está muy lejos it's a long way (away) ❸ desde lejos from a distance

lengua NOUN FEM ❶ **tongue**; morderse la lengua to bite your tongue ❷ **language**; una lengua muy difícil a very difficult language, mi lengua materna my mother tongue

lenguado NOUN MASC **sole**

lenguaje NOUN MASC **language**; lenguaje corporal body language

lente NOUN FEM **lens**; lentes de contacto contact lenses

lenteja NOUN FEM **lentil**

lentilla NOUN FEM **contact lens**

lento¹, lenta ADJECTIVE **slow**; son muy lentos they're very slow, cocinar algo a fuego lento to cook something over a low heat

lento² ADVERB **slowly**; caminan muy lento they're walking very slowly

leña NOUN FEM **firewood**

leño NOUN MASC **log**

leo NOUN MASC & FEM **Leo**; es leo she's Leo

Leo NOUN MASC **Leo**

león NOUN MASC **lion**

leopardo NOUN MASC **leopard**

leotardos PLURAL NOUN MASC **woollen tights**

les PRONOUN ❶ **them** (as indirect object); les di las llaves I gave them the keys, les mandé el paquete el lunes I sent them the parcel on Monday, ¿qué les quitaron? what did they take from them?, les puse la tapa I put the lids on them ❷ **you** (polite form, talking to more than one person: as indirect object); les mandé el paquete el lunes I sent you the parcel on Monday

lesión NOUN FEM **injury**

letón, letona NOUN MASC, FEM, ADJECTIVE **Latvian**

Letonia NOUN FEM **Latvia**

letra NOUN FEM ❶ **letter**; letras mayúsculas capital letters, letras minúsculas lower case letters ❷ **handwriting**; tiene muy buena letra she has very nice handwriting, casi no se le entiende la letra you can hardly read his handwriting ❸ **lyrics** (of a song) ❹ **instalment**; me quedan dos letras por pagar I still have two instalments to pay

letrero NOUN MASC **notice**, **sign**

levadura NOUN FEM **yeast**

levantar *VERB* [17] ❶ to lift; levantar un peso to lift a weight, levantar la tapadera to lift the lid ❷ to raise; levantar la mano to raise your hand ❸ to pick up; levantamos a la niña del suelo we picked the girl up from the floor ❹ ¡levanta ese ánimo! cheer up!

levantarse *REFLEXIVE VERB* [17] ❶ to get up; levantarse de la cama to get out of bed ❷ levántate del suelo get up off the floor ❸ levantarse de la mesa to leave the table

ley *NOUN FEM* law

leyenda *NOUN FEM* legend

leyó *VERB* ▸ SEE **leer**

libanés, **libanesa** *NOUN MASC, FEM, ADJECTIVE* Lebanese

Líbano *NOUN MASC* (el) Líbano Lebanon

liberar *VERB* [17] ❶ to free ❷ to liberate

libertad *NOUN FEM* freedom; libertad de expresión freedom of speech, libertad condicional parole

libra¹ *NOUN FEM* pound; diez libras esterlinas ten pounds sterling

libra² *NOUN MASC & FEM* Libra; Susana es libra Susana's Libra

Libra *NOUN MASC* Libra

librar *VERB* [17] librar a alguien de morir ahogado to save someone from drowning

librarse *REFLEXIVE VERB* [17] ❶ librarse de morir ahogado to save yourself from drowning, me libré del castigo I escaped punishment ❷ librarse de una obligación to get out of an obligation, se libró de lavar los platos he got out of doing the dishes

libre *ADJECTIVE* ❶ free; dejar libre a alguien to set someone free, ¿está libre este asiento? is this seat free?, quinientos metros libres five hundred metres freestyle ❷ trabajar por libre to work freelance ❸ al aire libre in the open air

librería *NOUN FEM* ❶ bookshop ❷ bookcase

libreta *NOUN FEM* notebook

libro *NOUN MASC* book; libro de texto textbook, libro de bolsillo paperback, libro de consulta reference book

licencia *NOUN FEM* licence, permit

licenciado, **licenciada** *NOUN MASC, FEM* graduate

licor *NOUN MASC* liqueur

licuadora *NOUN FEM* liquidizer

líder *NOUN MASC & FEM* leader

liebre *NOUN FEM* hare

liga *NOUN FEM* league; la liga de fútbol the football league

ligeramente *ADVERB* slightly

ligero, **ligera** *ADJECTIVE* ❶ light; un paquete ligero a light parcel, tener el sueño ligero to be a light sleeper ❷ slight; hay un ligero problema there's a slight problem, un ligero sabor a almendras a slight taste of almonds ❸ thin *(fabric)* ❹ fast; un caballo muy ligero a very fast horse ❺ agile

lima *NOUN FEM* ❶ file; una lima de uñas a nailfile ❷ lime

limitar *VERB* [17] **❶ to limit ❷** limitar con algo to border on something, España limita con Francia Spain has a border with France

limitarse *REFLEXIVE VERB* [17] **❶** el problema no se limita a eso the problem is not just that **❷** me limité a ayudarlos con el ordenador I just helped them with the computer

límite *NOUN MASC* **❶ limit**; el límite de velocidad the speed limit, hay un tiempo límite there's a time limit **❷** la fecha límite the deadline **❸** ¡todo tiene un límite! enough is enough! **❹ border** *(of a country)*

limón *NOUN MASC* **lemon**

limonada *NOUN FEM* **lemonade**

limonero *NOUN MASC* **lemon tree**

limosna *NOUN FEM* pedir limosna to beg, dar limosna to give money to beggars

limpiaparabrisas *NOUN MASC (does not change in the plural)* **windscreen wiper**

limpiar *VERB* [17] **❶ to clean**; limpiar la casa to clean the house **❷ to clean off**; limpiar una mancha de la mesa to clean a dirty mark off the table **❸** limpiar algo con un trapo to wipe something clean **❹** limpiar los zapatos to polish the shoes **❺** limpiar algo en seco to dry-clean something

limpieza *NOUN FEM* **❶** hacer la limpieza to do the cleaning, hacer una limpieza general to do a spring-clean **❷** limpieza en seco dry-cleaning **❸** una limpieza de cutis a facial

limpio, limpia *ADJECTIVE* **❶ clean** *(clothes, a house, or person, for*

example) **❷ fair** *(a game or business deal, for example)*

lince *NOUN MASC* **lynx**

lindo, linda *ADJECTIVE* **lovely**

línea *NOUN FEM* **❶ line**; línea de llegada finishing line, línea de meta goal line **❷** línea aérea airline, línea regular airline operating scheduled flights **❸** línea telefónica telephone line, no me da línea the line is dead **❹** escribirle unas líneas a alguien to drop someone a line, leer entre líneas to read between the lines **❺** un jugador de primera línea a top player, productos de primera línea top-quality products **❻ figure**; mantener la línea to watch your figure

lino *NOUN MASC* **linen**

linterna *NOUN FEM* **torch**

lío *NOUN MASC (informal)* **❶ mess**; ¡vaya lío! what a mess! **❷** hacerse un lío to get muddled up, me hice un lío con las fechas I got the dates all muddled up **❸** armar un lío to kick up a fuss **❹ trouble**; ¡no te metas en líos! keep out of trouble!

liquidación *NOUN FEM* **❶ sale**; liquidación por cierre closing-down sale, liquidación total clearance sale **❷ liquidation** *(of a business)* **❸ settlement** *(of a debt or an account)*

líquido¹ *NOUN MASC* **liquid**

líquido², líquida *ADJECTIVE* **liquid**

liso, lisa *ADJECTIVE* **❶ smooth**; piel lisa smooth skin **❷ straight**; tiene el pelo liso she's got straight hair **❸ flat** *(ground)*

lista¹ *NOUN FEM* **❶ list**; una lista de espera a waiting list, una lista de bodas a wedding list, una lista de precios a price list, la lista de vinos the wine list ❷ *(at school)* **register**; pasar lista to take the register

listín *NOUN MASC* listín telefónico, listín de teléfonos telephone directory

listo, lista² *ADJECTIVE* ❶ **clever** ❷ estar listo to be ready, ya estamos listos para salir we're ready to go now

litera *NOUN FEM* ❶ **bunk bed** ❷ **berth**

literatura *NOUN FEM* **literature**

litro *NOUN MASC* **litre**

Lituania *NOUN FEM* **Lithuania**

lituano, lituana *NOUN MASC, FEM, ADJECTIVE* **Lithuanian**

llama *NOUN FEM* ❶ **flame** ❷ **llama**

llamada *NOUN FEM* **call**; una llamada telefónica a telephone call, una llamada interurbana a long-distance call, una llamada urbana a local call, una llamada a cobro revertido a reverse-charge call

llamar *VERB* [17] ❶ **to call**; te llama tu madre your mother is calling you, llamar al médico to call the doctor, llamamos a un taxi we called a taxi, la llamamos Tintina we call her Tintina ❷ **to phone**; ¿cuándo llamarás? when will you phone?, le llamé por teléfono I phoned him

llamarse *REFLEXIVE VERB* [17] **to be called**; se llama Ángeles she's called Ángeles, ¿cómo te llamas? what's your name?

llano, llana *ADJECTIVE* **flat, level** *(ground)*

llave *NOUN FEM* ❶ **key**; una llave maestra a master key, la llave de

contacto the ignition key, cerrar algo con llave to lock something ❷ la llave del gas the gas tap, la llave del agua the mains water tap ❸ **switch** *(for a light)* ❹ **spanner**; una llave inglesa an adjustable spanner ❺ **hold**; una llave de judo a judo hold

llavero *NOUN MASC* **keyring**

llegada *NOUN FEM* **arrival**; a su llegada al hotel when he arrived at the hotel

llegar *VERB* [28] ❶ **to arrive**; llegan a las siete they arrive at seven, cuando lleguemos a casa when we get home ❷ **to come**; ya llega el invierno winter is coming ❸ llegar pronto a un sitio to get somewhere early, siempre llegas tarde you're always late, llegó justo a tiempo he was just in time ❹ **to reach**; no llego a la lámpara I can't reach the lamp ❺ la hierba me llega hasta las rodillas the grass comes up to my knees, las cortinas llegan hasta el suelo the curtains go down to the floor, mi parte del jardín llega hasta la valla my part of the garden goes up to the fence ❻ **to be enough**; con tres litros de leche llega para todos three litres of milk will be enough for everybody ❼ llegar a hacer to get to do, llegué a conocerlo I got to meet him, no llegué a verlo I didn't get to see it ❽ llegar a ser to become, llegó a ser famoso he became famous

llenar *VERB* [17] ❶ **to fill**; llenar la bañera to fill the bath ❷ **to fill up**; llene el depósito, por favor fill up the tank, please ❸ **fill in** *(a form, for example)*

lleno, llena *ADJECTIVE* ❶ **full**; la botella está llena de agua the bottle is full of water ❷ **covered**; el suelo estaba lleno de papeles the floor was covered with papers

llevar *VERB* [17] ❶ **to take**; te lo puedes llevar you can take it with you, llevaré una botella de vino a la fiesta I'll take a bottle of wine to the party, yo te puedo llevar a la estación I can take you to the station, la llevé a comer a un restaurante I took her for lunch to a restaurant ❷ **to carry**; yo llevaba al niño en brazos I was carrying the baby in my arms ❸ la llevé en coche a su casa I drove her home ❹ **to have**; ¿qué llevas en el bolso? what have you got in your bag?, no llevo las llaves encima I don't have the keys on me ❺ **to wear**; llevaba un vestido verde she was wearing a green dress ❻ lleva tiempo it takes time, me llevó dos semanas terminarlo it took me two weeks to finish it, le llevó mucho hacerlo it took her a lot of time to do it, lleva media hora hablando por teléfono he's been on the phone for half an hour, ¿cuánto tiempo llevas trabajando aquí? how long have you been working here?, llevamos dos semanas en Londres we've been in London for two weeks ❼ le llevo cuatro años I'm four years older than him ❽ **to lead**; el camino que lleva al río the road that leads to the river

llevarse *REFLEXIVE VERB* [17] ❶ **to take (away)**; se llevó los discos he took the records, ya puedes llevarte esto you can take this away now ❷ llevarse bien con alguien to get on with someone, no se llevan bien they don't get on

llorar *VERB* [17] **to cry**

llover *VERB* [38] **to rain**; está lloviendo it's raining

• está lloviendo a cántaros it's pouring down *(literally: it's raining in jugfuls)*

llovizna *NOUN FEM* **drizzle**

llueva, llueve, *etc VERB* ▶ SEE **llover**

lluvia *NOUN FEM* **rain**

lluvioso, lluviosa *ADJECTIVE* **rainy**

lo¹ *DEFINITE ARTICLE* ❶ **the**; lo mejor es … the best thing is …, lo curioso es … the funny thing is …, prefiero lo salado a lo dulce I prefer savoury things to sweet things ❷ lo mío mine, esto es lo tuyo that's yours, lo vuestro está en la habitación your things are in the bedroom ❸ esto es lo de mi madre this is my mother's, lo de Marta lo he puesto en la mesa I've put Marta's things on the table ❹ ¿sabes lo de Eva? have you heard about Eva?, lo de Pablo es muy raro it's really strange this thing with Pablo, lo del accidente fue horrible that thing about the accident was horrible, le conté lo tuyo I told her about you ❺ lo que what, eso es lo que yo compré that's what I bought, coge lo que quieras take whatever you want, dime todo lo que sepas tell me everything you know

lo² *PRONOUN* ❶ **him**; lo vi ayer I saw him yesterday ❷ **it**; lo metí en tu bolso I put it in your bag ❸ ya lo sé I know

lobo *NOUN MASC* **wolf**

local *NOUN MASC* **premises**

localidad *NOUN FEM* ❶ **town**; una pequeña localidad a small town ❷ **ticket**; 'no hay localidades' 'sold out'

loción *NOUN FEM* **lotion**; loción para después del afeitado aftershave

lotion, loción bronceadora suntan
lotion

loco, loca NOUN MASC, FEM **madman,
madwoman**

loco ADJECTIVE ❶ **mad**; ¡tú estás
loco! you're mad! ❷ estar loco
por alguien to be crazy about
somebody ❸ ¡este niño me va a
volver loco! that child's going to
drive me mad!, las fresas la vuelven
loca she loves strawberries
• estar loco de remate (informal)
to be completely bonkers
• hacer algo a lo loco to do
something any old how

locomotora NOUN FEM **engine**
(of a train)

locura NOUN FEM ❶ **madness** ❷ eso
es una locura that's crazy, otra de
sus locuras another one of his crazy
ideas

locutor, locutora NOUN MASC, FEM
❶ **announcer** ❷ **newsreader**
❸ locutor deportivo sports
commentator

lógico, lógica ADJECTIVE **logical**

lograr VERB [17] ❶ **to achieve**;
lograr la victoria to achieve victory
❷ lograr hacer to manage to do,
lograr que alguien haga to get
someone to do

lombriz NOUN FEM **worm**

lomo NOUN MASC ❶ **back** (of an
animal) ❷ **spine** (of a book) ❸ lomo
de cerdo loin of pork ❹ filete de
lomo sirloin steak

loncha NOUN FEM **slice**; una loncha de
jamón a slice of ham, una loncha de
bacon a rasher of bacon

londinense NOUN MASC & FEM
Londoner

londinense ADJECTIVE **London**

Londres NOUN MASC **London**

longaniza NOUN FEM **spicy pork
sausage**

longitud NOUN FEM ❶ **length**; tiene
doce metros de longitud it's
twelve metres long ❷ **longitude**
❸ longitud de onda wavelength

loro, lora NOUN MASC, FEM **parrot**
• hablar como un loro (informal) to
be a chatterbox
• repetir algo como un loro to repeat
something parrot-fashion

los¹ DEFINITE ARTICLE ❶ ('los' is used
before masculine plural nouns; see
also 'el', 'la' and 'las') **the**; deja los
libros ahí leave the books there
❷ (sometimes 'los' is not translated)
no me gustan los tomates I don't
like tomatoes, los discos de Isabel
Isabel's records ❸ (with parts of the
body or personal belongings) se frotó
los ojos she rubbed her eyes, me
quité los zapatos I took my shoes
off ❹ los míos son rojos mine are
red, esos son los tuyos those are
yours, me gustaron los verdes
I liked the green ones ❺ estos son
los de Ana these ones are Ana's, los
míos y los de usted mine and yours,
me gustan más los de Toni I like
Toni's better ❻ los que yo compré
the ones I bought, los que quieras
whichever you want

los² PRONOUN **them**; los vi ayer I saw
them yesterday, te los puedes llevar
you can take them with you

lote NOUN MASC **batch** a batch of
letters un lote de cartas

lotería NOUN FEM **lottery**; tocarle a
alguien la lotería to win the lottery

luces PLURAL NOUN ▶ SEE **luz**

lucha NOUN FEM **fight**

luchar *VERB* [17] ❶ **to fight**; luchar cuerpo a cuerpo to fight hand to hand ❷ **to struggle**

luego *ADVERB* ❶ **then**; luego vino su madre then her mother came ❷ **later**; luego te veo I'll see you later, ¡hasta luego! see you later! ❸ **afterwards**; luego te arrepentirás you'll be sorry afterwards, luego podemos cenar we can have dinner afterwards ❹ **then**; primero está su casa y luego la mía first comes her house and then mine, primero iré al banco y luego a tu casa I'll go to the bank first and then to your house ❺ desde luego of course

lugar *NOUN MASC* ❶ **place**; un lugar precioso a beautiful place, lugar de nacimiento place of birth, me siento fuera de lugar I feel out of place ❷ en cualquier lugar anywhere, por cualquier otro lugar anywhere else ❸ en otro lugar somewhere else ❹ yo en su lugar ... if I were him ... ❺ **position** *(in a race or competition)*; en primer lugar in first position, llegó en último lugar he finished in last place ❻ en primer lugar first of all, en segundo lugar ... second ..., en último lugar last of all ❼ en lugar de instead of

lúgubre *ADJECTIVE* **gloomy**

lujo *NOUN MASC* **luxury**; apartamentos de lujo luxury apartments

lujoso, lujosa *ADJECTIVE* **luxurious**

luminoso, luminosa *ADJECTIVE* ❶ **bright** ❷ **luminous**

luna *NOUN FEM* ❶ **moon**; esta noche hay luna the moon is out tonight, luna llena full moon, luna creciente waxing moon, luna menguante waning moon, la luna de miel the honeymoon ❷ una luna de espejo a mirror, la luna del escaparate the shop window

lunar *NOUN MASC* ❶ **mole** *(on your skin)* ❷ **polka-dot**; una camisa de lunares a polka-dot shirt

lunes *NOUN MASC* **Monday** ▸ SEE **domingo**

lupa *NOUN FEM* **magnifying glass**

luto *NOUN MASC* **mourning**; ir de luto to be in mourning, ponerse de luto to go into mourning

Luxemburgo *NOUN MASC* **Luxembourg**

luz *NOUN FEM (PLURAL* die **luces)** ❶ **light**; dar la luz to switch on the light, apagar la luz to switch off the light, la luz del sol the sunlight ❷ **electricity**; se ha ido la luz the electricity's gone off ❸ luces de cruce, luces cortas dipped headlights, luces largas full beam, luces de freno brake lights ❹ dar a luz to give birth
• tener pocas luces to be a bit dim

Mm

macarrones *PLURAL NOUN MASC*
macaroni

macedonia *NOUN FEM* **fruit salad**

maceta *NOUN FEM* **flowerpot**

machista *NOUN MASC & FEM* **male chauvinist**

machista *ADJECTIVE* **sexist**

macho *ADJECTIVE* **male**

madera *NOUN FEM* ❶ **wood** ❷ **timber**

madrastra *NOUN FEM* **stepmother**

madre *NOUN FEM* ❶ **mother**; ser madre soltera to be a single mother, madre política mother-in-law ❷ ¡madre mía! my goodness!

Madrid *NOUN FEM* **Madrid**

madrileño, madrileña *NOUN MASC, FEM* **person from Madrid**

madrileño *ADJECTIVE* **of/from Madrid**; las iglesias madrileñas the churches of Madrid

madrina *NOUN FEM* ❶ **godmother** ❷ **in Spanish weddings, the woman who accompanies the groom, usually his mother**

madrugada *NOUN FEM* **dawn**; de madrugada at dawn, nos levantamos de madrugada we got up at dawn, llegamos de madrugada we arrived in the early

hours of the morning, a las cuatro de la madrugada at four in the morning

madrugar *VERB* [17] **to get up early**

madurar *VERB* [17] ❶ **to ripen** ❷ **to mature**

maduro, madura *ADJECTIVE* ❶ **ripe** ❷ **mature**; es muy poco maduro he's quite immature

maestro, maestra *NOUN MASC, FEM* ❶ **teacher** *(primary school)* ❷ **master** *(of a trade)*

magdalena *NOUN FEM* **fairycake**

magia *NOUN FEM* **magic**

mágico, mágica *ADJECTIVE* **magical**

magnético, magnética *ADJECTIVE* **magnetic**

magnífico, magnífica *ADJECTIVE* ❶ **wonderful** ❷ **magnificent**

mago, maga *NOUN MASC, FEM* ❶ **magician** ❷ **wizard**

mahonesa *NOUN FEM* **mayonnaise**

maíz *NOUN MASC* ❶ **sweetcorn**; una mazorca de maíz a corn on the cob ❷ **maize**

mal *NOUN MASC* **evil**; el bien y el mal good and evil

mal *ADJECTIVE* ❶ **bad**; es un mal amigo he's a bad friend, vinieron en mal momento they came at a bad time ❷ **wrong**; la respuesta está mal the answer's wrong, está mal criticar it's wrong to criticize ❸ **ill**; ¿te sientes mal? do you feel ill?, su padre está muy mal his father's very ill

mal *ADVERB* ❶ **badly**; está muy mal pintado it's really badly painted, lo leyó muy mal she read it very badly, le va muy mal en el trabajo he's doing very badly at work, el país marcha mal the country's not doing well ❷ **wrong**; lo hizo mal he did it wrong, hace mal en no pedir perdón he's wrong not to apologize ❸ contestar mal a alguien to answer someone back ❹ te oigo mal I can't hear you very well ❺ la comida sabe mal the food tastes horrible, olía muy mal there was a nasty smell ❻ portarse mal to misbehave, entender mal algo to misunderstand something ❼ ¡menos mal! thank goodness!

malabarismos NOUN MASC & PLURAL hacer malabarismos to juggle

malabarista NOUN MASC & FEM **juggler**

malcriado, malcriada NOUN MASC, FEM es un malcriado he's really spoilt

malcriado ADJECTIVE ❶ **spoilt** ❷ **naughty**

maldición NOUN FEM ❶ **curse** ❷ soltar una maldición to swear ❸ ¡maldición! damn!

maleducado, maleducada NOUN MASC, FEM es una maleducada she's really rude

maleducado ADJECTIVE **rude**

malentendido NOUN MASC **misunderstanding**

maleta NOUN FEM **suitcase**

maletero NOUN MASC **boot** (of a car)

maletín NOUN MASC ❶ **briefcase** ❷ **overnight case** ❸ el maletín del médico the doctor's bag

malgastar VERB [17] **to waste**

malhumor NOUN MASC **bad temper**

malla NOUN FEM ❶ **mesh**; malla de alambre wire mesh ❷ **leotard** ❸ mallas leggings

Mallorca NOUN FEM **Majorca**

mallorquín, mallorquina NOUN MASC, FEM, ADJECTIVE **Majorcan**

malo, mala ADJECTIVE ❶ **bad**; una mala costumbre a bad habit, es malo para la salud it's bad for your health ❷ **naughty**; ¡qué niño más malo! what a naughty child! ❸ **nasty**; no seas mala y devuélveselo don't be nasty and give it back to her ❹ **poor**; de mala calidad poor quality ❺ ayer hizo malo the weather was bad yesterday, nos hizo muy malo durante las vacaciones we had horrible weather during the holidays ❻ estar malo to be ill, no puede venir porque está mala she can't come because she's ill, el pobre está muy malo the poor thing is in a really bad way ❼ estar malo to be off (food), la leche está mala the milk's gone off ❽ estar malo to taste horrible, la sopa estaba muy mala the soup was horrible ❾ ser malo para (a person) to be bad at, soy malo para las matemáticas I'm bad at maths ▸ SEE **mal**

malsano, malsana ADJECTIVE **unhealthy**

maltratar VERB [17] ❶ **to abuse** ❷ **to mistreat**

mamá NOUN FEM (informal) **Mum**

mamífero NOUN MASC **mammal**

manada NOUN FEM ❶ **herd** (of cattle) ❷ **pack** (of dogs) ❸ **gang** (of young people)

mancha NOUN FEM ❶ stain; una mancha de chocolate a chocolate stain, quitar una mancha to remove a stain ❷ mark ❸ mancha de petróleo oil slick

manchar VERB [17] ❶ to get (something) dirty; mancharon la alfombra de barro they got mud all over the carpet ❷ to stain

mancharse REFLEXIVE VERB [17] to get yourself dirty; cuidado, no te manches careful, don't get yourself dirty, se manchó los pantalones de barro he got mud all over his trousers

manchón NOUN FEM stain

mandar VERB [17] ❶ to order ❷ le gusta mandar she likes to give the orders ❸ mandar a alguien hacer to tell somebody to do, me mandó recoger la habitación she told me to tidy my bedroom, haz lo que te mandan do as you're told ❹ to send; mandar una carta a alguien to send somebody a letter, los mandé a comprar fruta I sent them to buy some fruit ❺ mandar llamar a alguien to send for someone

mandarina NOUN FEM mandarin, tangerine

mando NOUN MASC ❶ command; estar al mando de to be in charge of ❷ control (of a machine or a television, for example); mando a distancia remote control

mandón, mandona ADJECTIVE bossy

manejar VERB [17] ❶ to use (a computer, dictionary) ❷ to operate (a machine) ❸ to manage (a business)

manera NOUN FEM ❶ way; lo hice a mi manera I did it my way, no hubo manera de arreglarlo there was no way of fixing it, es su manera de ser it's the way he is ❷ de alguna manera somehow, me las arreglaré de alguna manera I'll do it somehow ❸ de cualquier manera, any old how, puedes decorarlo de cualquier manera you can decorate it any way you want ❹ de una manera u otra one way or another ❺ ¡de ninguna manera! no way!, '¿me dejas el coche?' – '¡de ninguna manera!' 'can I borrow your car?' – 'no way' ❻ de todas maneras anyway, de todas maneras no pensaba comprarlo I wasn't thinking of buying it anyway ❼ de manera que so, de manera que al final no la vi so I didn't see her in the end

manga NOUN FEM ❶ sleeve; una camisa de manga corta a short-sleeved shirt, sin mangas sleeveless ❷ hose (for watering)

mango NOUN MASC ❶ handle (of a knife or tool) ❷ mango

manguera NOUN FEM hosepipe

manía NOUN FEM ❶ tiene la manía del orden he's obsessed with tidiness, es maja pero tiene sus manías she's nice but she has her funny little ways ❷ tenerle manía a alguien to have it in for somebody

maniático, maniática NOUN MASC, FEM es una maniática de la limpieza she's obsessed with cleanliness

maniático ADJECTIVE fussy

manifestación NOUN FEM ❶ demonstration ❷ sign (of disapproval, for instance) ❸ manifestaciones statements

A
B
C
D
E
F
G
H
I
J
K
L
M
N
Ñ
O
P
Q
R
S
T
U
V
W
X
Y
Z

manifestar VERB [29] ❶ **to express** (disapproval or an opinion) ❷ **to show** (emotions)

manifestarse REFLEXIVE VERB [29] ❶ **to demonstrate** ❷ **to become evident** ❸ manifestarse en contra de algo **to come out against something**

manillar NOUN MASC **handlebars**

manipular VERB [17] ❶ **to operate** (a machine) ❷ **to manipulate** (data or information)

maniquí NOUN MASC **mannequin**

manivela NOUN FEM **handle**

mano NOUN FEM ❶ **hand**; levantar la mano **to raise your hand**, ir de la mano **to go hand in hand**, coger a alguien de la mano **to take somebody's hand** ❷ darle la mano a alguien **to give somebody your hand**, **to shake somebody's hand** ❸ decir adiós con la mano **to wave goodbye** ❹ **coat**; una mano de pintura **a coat of paint**

manómetro NOUN MASC **pressure gauge**

mansión NOUN FEM **mansion**

manso, mansa ADJECTIVE ❶ **tame** (an animal) ❷ **gentle** (a person)

manta NOUN FEM **blanket**

manteca NOUN FEM **lard**

mantecado NOUN MASC **almond delicacy** (eaten at Christmas)

mantel NOUN MASC **tablecloth**

mantendrá, mantendría, etc VERB ▸ SEE **mantener**

mantener VERB [9] ❶ **to keep**; mantener la calma **to keep calm,** mantener el equilibrio **to keep your balance** ❷ **to support** (a family, for example)

mantenerse REFLEXIVE VERB [9] **to keep**; mantenerse en equilibrio **to keep your balance,** mantenerse en contacto con alguien **to keep in touch with somebody**

mantengo, mantenga, etc VERB ▸ SEE **mantener**

mantenimiento NOUN MASC ❶ **maintenance** ❷ ejercicios de mantenimiento **keep-fit exercises**

mantequilla NOUN FEM **butter**

mantilla NOUN FEM **mantilla** (a lace headscarf)

mantuve, mantuvo, etc VERB ▸ SEE **mantener**

manual ADJECTIVE **manual**

manzana NOUN FEM ❶ **apple** ❷ **block** (in a town); dar una vuelta a la manzana **to go round the block**

manzanilla NOUN FEM ❶ **camomile tea** ❷ **dry sherry**

manzano NOUN MASC **apple tree**

mañana NOUN FEM **morning**; a la mañana siguiente **the next morning,** por la mañana **in the morning,** a las once de la mañana **at eleven o'clock in the morning**

mañana ADVERB **tomorrow**; pasado mañana **the day after tomorrow,** hasta mañana **see you tomorrow,** mañana por la tarde **tomorrow afternoon**

mapa NOUN MASC **map**; un mapa de carreteras **a road map**

maquillaje *NOUN MASC* **make-up**

maquillar *VERB* [17] **to make up**

maquillarse *REFLEXIVE VERB* [17] **to put your make-up on**; apenas se maquilla she hardly wears any make-up

máquina *NOUN FEM* **❶ machine**; una máquina de escribir a typewriter, escribir a máquina to type, una máquina de coser a sewing machine **❷** una máquina de fotos a camera **❸** una máquina de afeitar an electric shaver

maquinaria *NOUN FEM* **machinery**

maquinilla *NOUN FEM* **safety razor**

mar *NOUN MASC* **sea**; viajar por mar to travel by sea, el mar Cantábrico the Bay of Biscay

maratón *NOUN MASC OR FEM* **marathon**

maravilla *NOUN FEM* **wonder**; es una maravilla de casa it's a wonderful house
• a las mil maravillas (*informal*) wonderfully

maravilloso, maravillosa *ADJECTIVE* **wonderful**

marca *NOUN FEM* **❶ mark**; el cuadro ha dejado una marca en la pared the picture has left a mark on the wall **❷ brand**; artículos de marca brand products, ropa de marca designer clothes **❸** marca registrada registered trademark **❹ record** (*in sports*); establecer una nueva marca to establish a new record, batir una marca to break a record

marcador *NOUN MASC* **scoreboard**

marcar *VERB* [31] **❶ to mark**; la experiencia me marcó mucho the experience really marked me **❷** mi reloj marca las nueve my watch says nine o'clock, el termómetro marcaba cinco grados the thermometer was registering five degrees **❸** marcar un número to dial a number, marca 00 44 para Gran Bretaña dial 00 44 for Britain **❹** marcar un gol to score a goal **❺** marcar el ritmo, marcar el compás to beat time

marcha *NOUN FEM* **❶ hike**; ir de marcha to go hiking, fuimos de marcha a la montaña we went hiking in the mountains **❷ march** (*a demonstration*) **❸ gear** (*in a car*); marcha atrás reverse, meter la marcha atrás to put the car into reverse **❹ speed**; disminuir la marcha to reduce speed **❺** estar en marcha to be running (*a car engine, for example*) **❻** poner en marcha to start (*a car, for example*) **❼** ¡en marcha! let's go! **❽** (*informal*) una discoteca con mucha marcha a really fun disco, ¡qué marcha tiene ese grupo! this group's really wild! **❾** (*informal*) ir de marcha to go out partying

marchar *VERB* [17] **❶ to work** (*a machine or a company*); esto no marcha this isn't working **❷ to march ❸** ¡marchando dos cafés! two coffees coming up!

marcharse *REFLEXIVE VERB* [17] **to leave**; nos marchamos mañana we're leaving tomorrow

marco *NOUN MASC* **❶ frame ❷ framework ❸ goal** (*in football*)

marea NOUN FEM **tide**; está subiendo la marea the tide's coming in, cuando baje la marea when the tide goes out, marea negra oil slick

mareado, mareada ADJECTIVE
❶ estar mareado to feel dizzy, to feel queasy, me siento mareado/mareada I'm feeling dizzy/queasy ❷ estar mareado (informal) to be muddled up, estoy mareado con tantos números I'm all muddled up with all these numbers

marear VERB [17] ❶ to make (somebody) feel dizzy, to make (somebody) feel queasy ❷ (informal) to confuse; me marearon a preguntas they asked me so many questions my head was spinning

mareo NOUN MASC ❶ sick feeling; me dan mareos si viajo en coche I get carsick ❷ seasickness ❸ dizziness

marfil NOUN MASC **ivory**

margarina NOUN FEM **margarine**

margarita NOUN FEM ❶ daisy ❷ marguerite

margen NOUN MASC **margin**; escribir algo en el margen to write something in the margin

mariachi NOUN MASC **mariachi** (type of traditional Mexican folk music)

marido NOUN MASC **husband**

marina NOUN FEM **navy**

marinero NOUN MASC **sailor**

marioneta NOUN FEM **puppet**

mariposa NOUN FEM **butterfly**

mariquita NOUN FEM **ladybird**

marisco NOUN MASC **shellfish**; me gusta el marisco I like shellfish

mármol NOUN MASC **marble**

marrón NOUN MASC **brown**

marrón ADJECTIVE **brown**; zapatos marrones brown shoes, unos pantalones marrón claro a pair of light brown trousers (note that 'marrón' does not change in the plural when used with another adjective)

martes NOUN MASC **Tuesday** ▸ SEE **domingo**

martillo NOUN MASC **hammer**

marzo NOUN MASC **March**; en marzo, en el mes de marzo in March

más ADVERB, ADJECTIVE, PRONOUN
❶ more; este me gusta más I like this one more, pon más azúcar add more sugar, tres más three more, más o menos more or less, ¿necesitas más? do you need any more?, no comas más don't eat any more, no lo hagas más don't do it again ❷ es un poco más grande it's a bit bigger, tenemos que hacerlo más rápido we have to do it faster ❸ es más interesante que su primer libro it's more interesting than his first book, más que nunca more than ever, me gusta más el de cuero que el de tela I prefer the leather one to the cloth one, más blanco que la nieve as white as snow ❹ el de más peso the heaviest one, los de más prestigio the most prestigious ones, el libro con más páginas the book with the most pages ❺ el que más me gusta the one I like the most, los que son más altos the tallest ones ❻ más de more than, más de

veinte kilos more than twenty kilos, vinieron más de veinte personas more than twenty people came ❼ hay tres sillas de más there are three chairs too many, hay tres pasteles de más there are three cakes left over, si quieres venir, tengo un billete de más I've got a spare ticket if you want to come
• estar de más to feel out of place ❽ *(referring to time)* no les he visto más I've never seen them again, no me quedo más I won't stay any longer ❾ else; ¿esperas a alguien más? are you expecting anybody else?, nadie más nobody else, no quiero nada más I don't want anything else, ¿querías algo más? did you want anything else? ❿ no ... más only, no tardo más de diez minutos I'll only take ten minutes, no es más que un resfriado it's only a cold ⓫ *(in exclamations)* ¡es más bonito! it's so beautiful!, ¡había más gente! there were so many people!, ¡le gustó más! he liked it a lot!

más *PREPOSITION* plus; cinco más siete five plus seven

masa *NOUN FEM* ❶ dough; masa de pan bread dough ❷ pastry; masa de hojaldre puff pastry

masaje *NOUN MASC* massage

máscara *NOUN FEM* mask

mascarilla *NOUN FEM* mask

mascota *NOUN FEM* ❶ pet *(animal)* ❷ mascot

masculino[1] *NOUN MASC* masculine *(in grammar)*

masculino[2], **masculina** *ADJECTIVE* masculine

masticar *VERB* [31] to chew

mástil *NOUN MASC* ❶ mast ❷ flagpole

matador *NOUN MASC* matador

matanza *NOUN FEM* ❶ massacre *(of people)* ❷ slaughter *(of animals)*

matar *VERB* [17] to kill

matarse *REFLEXIVE VERB* [17] ❶ to kill yourself ❷ to get killed; si sigues conduciendo así, te vas a matar if you carry on driving like that you're going to get killed

mate *NOUN MASC* jaque mate checkmate

mate *ADJECTIVE* matt

matemáticas *PLURAL NOUN FEM* maths

materia *NOUN FEM* ❶ material; materia prima raw material ❷ materia grasa fat ❸ subject *(of study or of a book)*

material *NOUN MASC ADJECTIVE* material

maternal *ADJECTIVE* maternal

materno, materna *ADJECTIVE* ❶ motherly ❷ mother; lengua materna mother tongue ❸ abuelos maternos grandparents on the mother's side

matiz *NOUN MASC* shade *(of a colour)*

matrícula *NOUN FEM* ❶ registration; hacer la matrícula to register ❷ registration number *(of a car)*; un coche con matrícula de Sevilla a car with a Seville number plate ❸ matrícula de honor distinction, sacar matrícula en física to get a distinction in physics

a
b
c
d
e
f
g
h
i
j
k
l
m
n
ñ
o
p
q
r
s
t
u
v
w
x
y
z

matrimonio NOUN MASC
❶ **marriage**; matrimonio civil civil wedding ❷ **married couple**; son un matrimonio muy unido they're a very close couple

máximo, máxima ADJECTIVE
❶ **maximum** ❷ **top** (speed)
❸ **highest**; el punto máximo the highest point

mayo NOUN MASC **May**; en mayo, en el mes de mayo in May

mayonesa NOUN FEM **mayonnaise**

mayor NOUN MASC & FEM **adult**

mayor ADJECTIVE ❶ **greater**
❷ **greatest** ❸ **higher**; un número mayor que cien a number higher than one hundred, a la mayor altura at the maximum height ❹ **bigger**; ¿tienes una talla mayor? do you have a bigger size? ❺ **biggest**; el de mayor tamaño the biggest one ❻ **older**; es cinco años mayor que su mujer he's five years older than his wife ❼ **oldest**; mi hermana mayor my oldest sister, soy el mayor de todos mis hermanos I'm the oldest of my brothers and sisters ❽ cuando seas mayor when you grow up, las personas mayores the grown-ups, ya son muy mayores they're quite old now ❾ la mayor parte de most of, la mayor parte de los estudiantes most of the students ❿ ser mayor de edad to be of age

mayores PLURAL NOUN MASC los mayores the grown-ups, the elderly

mayoría NOUN FEM **majority**; la mayoría de most of

mayúscula[1] NOUN FEM **capital letter**

mayúsculo, mayúscula[2] ADJECTIVE
❶ **capital** (letter) ❷ (informal) **terrible** (mistake or fright)

mazapán NOUN MASC **marzipan**

me PRONOUN ❶ **me**; me invitaron a su fiesta they invited me to their party, no me han visto they haven't seen me ❷ **to me**; me lo dieron ellos they gave it to me, me mintió he lied to me, me lo ha comprado mi madre my mother bought it for me ❸ **myself**; me corté I cut myself ❹ (with reflexive verbs) me reí mucho I laughed a lot, voy a bañarme I'm going for a swim, me senté a la mesa I sat at the table ❺ (with parts of the body or clothes) me quité el abrigo I took my coat off, me limpié los pies al entrar I wiped my feet at the door ❻ (having things done) el sábado iré a cortarme el pelo I'll go and have my hair cut on Saturday

mecánico, mecánica[2] NOUN MASC, FEM **mechanic**

mecánico ADJECTIVE **mechanical**

mecanografía NOUN FEM **typing**

mecedora NOUN FEM **rocking chair**

mechero NOUN MASC **lighter**

medalla NOUN FEM **medal**

media[1] NOUN FEM **average**; la media de altura the average height, la media eúropea the European average

media[2] NOUN FEM ❶ **stocking**
❷ medias **tights** ❸ (telling the time) las dos y media half past two, dos horas y media two hours and a half ❹ hacer algo a medias to half-do something, lo dejó a medias he didn't finish it ❺ lo hicimos a medias we did it between the two

of us, pagar a medias to pay half each

mediados *PLURAL NOUN MASC* a mediados de semana midweek, a mediados de año halfway through the year

mediano, mediana *ADJECTIVE* ❶ **medium**; de peso mediano medium weight ❷ **average** ❸ de mediana calidad mediocre

medianoche *NOUN FEM* **midnight**; a media noche at midnight

medicamento *NOUN MASC* **medicine**

medicina *NOUN FEM* **medicine**; estudiar medicina to study medicine, tomarse la medicina to take your medicine

médico, médica *NOUN MASC, FEM* **doctor**; médico de cabecera family doctor

médico *ADJECTIVE* **medical**

medida *NOUN FEM* ❶ **measure**; tomar medidas a algo to measure something ❷ **measurement**; ¿qué medidas tiene la mesa? what are the measurements of the table? ❸ traje a medida a made-to-measure suit ❹ a medida que as, a medida que pase el tiempo as time goes by ❺ en gran medida to a large extent, en cierta medida to a certain extent, en la medida de lo posible as far as possible

medieval *ADJECTIVE* **medieval**

medio¹ *NOUN MASC* ❶ **middle**; ponlo en el medio put it in the middle, la casa de en medio the house in the middle ❷ quitarse de en medio to get out of the way ❸ **way**; es el mejor medio it's the best way, no hubo medio de localizarlo there was no way of finding him, lo

intenté por todos los medios I tried every possible way ❹ **means**; por cualquier medio by any means, por todos los medios by any possible means, medios de transporte means of transport ❺ por medio de through, por medio de un amigo through a friend ❻ en medio de todo aquel jaleo amidst all that racket ❼ los medios de comunicación the media

medio² *ADVERB* **half**; ya está medio convencido he's half convinced now

medio³, media *ADJECTIVE* ❶ **half**; medio kilo half a kilo, media docena half a dozen, media pensión half board ❷ **average**; de estatura media of average height ❸ *(in time expressions)* **half**; media hora half an hour

medioambiental *ADJECTIVE* **environmental**

medio ambiente *NOUN MASC* **environment**

mediodía *NOUN MASC* **midday**; al mediodía at midday

medir *VERB* [57] ❶ **to measure**; ¿cuánto mide de ancho? how wide is it?, mide sesenta centímetros de largo it's sixty centimetres long ❷ ¿cuánto mides? how tall are you?

mediterráneo, mediterránea *ADJECTIVE* **Mediterranean**

Mediterráneo *NOUN MASC* **Mediterranean**

mejicano, mejicana *NOUN MASC, FEM, ADJECTIVE* **Mexican**

Méjico *NOUN MASC* ▸ SEE **México**

mejilla *NOUN FEM* **cheek**

mejillón *NOUN MASC* **mussel**

mejor *NOUN MASC & FEM* **el/la mejor** the best one

mejor *ADJECTIVE* ❶ **better**; este es de mejor calidad this one is better quality, cuanto antes mejor the earlier the better, es mejor que no vayamos it's better if we don't go ❷ **best**; la mejor forma es ... the best way is ...

mejor *ADVERB* ❶ **better**; Isabel toca la guitarra mejor Isabel plays the guitar better, mejor que better than, mejor que el otro better than the other one, cada vez mejor better and better ❷ **best**; es la que mejor dibuja she's the one that draws the best, hazlo lo mejor que puedas do your best ❸ a lo mejor maybe, a lo mejor es de Sara maybe it's Sara's, a lo mejor no voy I might not go ❹ mejor no preguntes it's better if you don't ask, mejor déjalo así it's better if you leave it like this, mejor venid en tren you'd be better coming by train

mejora *NOUN FEM* **improvement**

mejorar *VERB* [17] ❶ **to improve** ❷ **to get better**; ha mejorado del estómago he's got over his stomach problems

mejorarse *REFLEXIVE VERB* [17] **to get better**; ¡que te mejores! get well soon!

mellizo, melliza *NOUN MASC, FEM*

mellizo *ADJECTIVE* **twin**

melocotón *NOUN MASC* **peach**

melodía *NOUN FEM* **melody**

melón *NOUN MASC* **melon**

memoria *NOUN FEM* ❶ **memory**; aprenderse algo de memoria

to learn something by heart ❷ **memorias memoirs**

mencionar *VERB* [17] **to mention**

mendigar *VERB* [17] **to beg**

mendigo, mendiga *NOUN MASC & FEM* **beggar**

menestra *NOUN FEM* **menestra de verduras vegetable stew**

menor *NOUN MASC & FEM* ❶ **el/la menor** the younger ❷ **un/una menor a minor**

menor *ADJECTIVE* ❶ **younger**; mi hermana menor my younger sister, soy menor que tú I'm younger than you ❷ **youngest**; el menor de la familia the youngest of the family ❸ **little**; con el menor esfuerzo posible with as little effort as possible ❹ **less**; su importancia es cada vez menor it gets less and less important all the time, en menor grado to a lesser extent ❺ **minor**; de menor importancia of minor importance ❻ **smaller**; un número menor de alumnos a smaller number of pupils ❼ **smallest**; hasta el menor detalle even the smallest detail ❽ no tengo la menor idea I haven't got the slightest idea

menos *ADJECTIVE* ❶ *(does not change in the plural)* **less**; de menos peso of less weight ❷ **few**; había menos de cien personas there were fewer than a hundred people

menos *ADVERB* ❶ **less**; ahora sale menos he goes out less now, cada vez menos less and less ❷ **least**; los menos informados the least well-informed, es lo menos que esperaba it's the least I expected ❸ el menos alto the shortest one, el que corre menos the slowest of all

❹ menos que less than, fewer than, habla menos que yo he speaks less than I do, cuesta menos que el otro it costs less than the other one, había menos que ayer there were fewer than yesterday ❺ menos de less than, cuesta menos de cien libras it costs less than a hundred pounds, adultos de menos de treinta años adults under thirty ❻ ahora los veo menos I don't see them as often now ❼ ahora sale menos she doesn't go out as much now

menos PRONOUN ❶ ahora compramos menos now we don't buy as much ❷ cobrar de menos to undercharge, hay diez tarjetas de menos there are ten cards too few ❸ al menos, por lo menos at least ❹ ¡menos mal! thank goodness!

menos PREPOSITION **except**; todos menos su madre everybody except her mother

mensaje NOUN MASC **message**; un mensaje de texto a text message; te mandaré un mensaje de texto mañana I'll send you a text message tomorrow

mensajero, mensajera NOUN MASC, FEM ❶ **messenger** ❷ **courier**; servicio de mensajeros courier service

mensual ADJECTIVE **monthly**; dos cientos euros mensuales two hundred euros a month

mensualmente ADVERB **monthly**

menta NOUN FEM **mint**; un caramelo de menta a mint

mental ADJECTIVE **mental**

mente NOUN FEM **mind**; se me quedó la mente en blanco my mind went blank

mentir VERB [14] **to lie**

mentira NOUN FEM **lie**

mentiroso, mentirosa NOUN MASC, FEM **liar**

mentón NOUN MASC **chin**

menú NOUN MASC **menu**; menú del día set menu

menudo, menuda ADJECTIVE ❶ **small**; es muy menuda she's quite small ❷ a menudo often, nos vemos a menudo we see each other often ❸ ¡menudo problema! what a problem!, ¡menuda moto! what an incredible motorbike!

meñique NOUN MASC **little finger**

mercado NOUN MASC **market**; ir al mercado to go to the market, el Mercado Común the Common Market

mercadotecnia NOUN FEM **marketing**

mercancías PLURAL NOUN FEM **goods**

mercería NOUN FEM **haberdashery**

merecer VERB [35] ❶ **to deserve**; mereces un castigo you deserve to be punished ❷ merecer la pena to be worthwhile, la película merece la pena the film is worth seeing

merecerse REFLEXIVE VERB [35] **to deserve**; no me merezco que me traten así I don't deserve to be treated like this

merendar VERB [29] **to have a teatime snack**; siempre merienda pan y chocolate he always has bread and chocolate in the afternoon, ¿quieres merendar algo? do you want something to eat?, ¡a merendar! teatime!

merezca, **merezco**, *etc VERB*
▶ SEE **merecer**

meridional *ADJECTIVE* **southern**

merienda¹ *NOUN FEM* ❶ **afternoon snack** ❷ merienda campestre picnic, ir de merienda to go for a picnic

merienda², **meriendo**, *etc VERB*
▶ SEE **merendar**

mérito *NOUN MASC* **merit**

merluza *NOUN FEM* **hake**

mermelada *NOUN FEM* **jam**

mes *NOUN MASC* **month**; el mes que viene next month, mil euros al mes a thousand euros a month, un bebé de siete meses a seven-month-old baby

mesa *NOUN FEM* **table**; sentarse a la mesa to sit at the table, poner la mesa to set the table, quitar la mesa, recoger la mesa to clear the table, ¡a la mesa! food's ready!

mesita *NOUN FEM* mesita de noche bedside table

meta *NOUN FEM* ❶ **finishing line** ❷ **aim**; tiene como meta ser actriz her aim is to become an actress

metal *NOUN MASC* **metal**

metálico, **metálica** *ADJECTIVE* **metallic**

meteorológico, **meteorológica** *ADJECTIVE* **meteorological**; parte meteorológico weather forecast

meter *VERB* [18] ❶ **to put (something) in**; metió la mano he put his hand in, métalo en la carpeta put it in the folder ❷ **to fit**; ¿puedes meter algo más en la maleta? can you fit anything else in

the suitcase? ❸ meter la primera to put the car in first gear, meter la marcha atrás to put the car into reverse ❹ meter un gol to score a goal

meterse *REFLEXIVE VERB* [18] ❶ meterse en to get in(to), meterse en la cama to get into bed ❷ meterse en algo to get involved in something, no te metas en mis asuntos mind your own business

método *NOUN MASC* **method**

métrico *ADJECTIVE* **metric**

metro *NOUN MASC* ❶ **underground** ❷ **metre**; los cien metros libres the hundred metres freestyle

mexicano, **mexicana** *NOUN MASC, FEM, ADJECTIVE* **Mexican**

México *NOUN MASC* **Mexico**

mezcla *NOUN FEM* ❶ **mixture** ❷ **mix**; una mezcla de culturas a mix of cultures

mezclar *VERB* [17] ❶ **to mix** ❷ **to mix up**; has mezclado todos los papeles you've mixed up all the papers

mezclarse *REFLEXIVE VERB* [17] mezclarse en algo to get mixed up in something

mezquita *NOUN FEM* **mosque**

mi *ADJECTIVE* **my**; mis amigos my friends

mí *PRONOUN* ❶ **me**; detrás de mí behind me, se olvidaron de mí they forgot about me ❷ (*as indirect object*) me lo dio a mí he gave it to me ❸ a mí me gusta I like it, a mí me parece que ... I think that ... ❹ mí mismo/misma myself, sé cuidar de mí misma I can look after

myself ❺ por mí ... as far as I'm
concerned

micrófono *NOUN MASC* **microphone**

microondas *NOUN MASC (does not
change in the plural)*, **microwave
(oven)**

microscopio *NOUN MASC*
microscope

mida, **midiendo**, **midió**, **mido**,
etc VERB ▸ SEE **medir**

miedo *NOUN MASC* ❶ fear; tener
miedo to be scared, tengo
mucho miedo I'm really scared,
tengo miedo de intentarlo I'm
afraid of trying, ¡qué miedo! how
frightening!, miedo a algo fear of
something ❷ me da miedo la altura
I'm afraid of heights, les da miedo
ir solos they are afraid of going on
their own ❸ pasamos un rato de
miedo *(informal)* we had a great
time

miedoso, **miedosa** *ADJECTIVE* es muy
miedoso he's afraid of everything

miel *NOUN FEM* **honey**

miembro *NOUN MASC* ❶ **member**
❷ **limb**

mienta, **miento**, *etc VERB*
▸ SEE **mentir**

mientras *ADVERB* **meanwhile**;
mientras tanto in the meantime,
mientras tanto él estaba esperando
en la estación in the meantime he
was waiting at the station

mientras *CONJUNCTION* ❶ while;
pon la mesa mientras yo hago la
comida lay the table while I cook
the meal ❷ as long as; mientras yo
viva as long as I'm alive

miércoles *NOUN MASC* **Wednesday**;
el miércoles on Wednesday,
el miércoles por la mañana on

Wednesday morning, los miércoles
on Wednesdays

miga *NOUN FEM* **crumb**

mil *NUMBER* **thousand**; mil doscientos
one thousand two hundred

milagro *NOUN MASC* **miracle**

milenio *NOUN MASC* **millennium**

milésimo, **milésima** *ADJECTIVE*
thousandth

mili *NOUN FEM (informal)* **military
service**

milímetro *NOUN MASC* **milimetre**

militar *NOUN MASC & FEM* **soldier**

militar *ADJECTIVE* **military**

millón *NUMBER* **million**; un millón de
euros a million euros, un millón de
gracias thank you ever so much

millonario, **millonaria** *NOUN MASC,
FEM* **millionaire**

mimado, **mimada** *ADJECTIVE* **spoilt**
(child)

mina *NOUN FEM* **mine**; una mina de
carbón a coalmine

mineral *NOUN MASC ADJECTIVE* **mineral**

minero, **minera** *NOUN MASC, FEM*
miner

minero *ADJECTIVE* **mining**

mini *NOUN FEM (informal)* **mini**

minifalda *NOUN FEM* **miniskirt**

mínimo¹ *NOUN MASC* **minimum**

mínimo², **mínima** *ADJECTIVE*
minimum; no me importa lo más
mínimo I couldn't care less

ministerio *NOUN MASC* **ministry**

ministro, **ministra** *NOUN MASC, FEM*
minister

a
b
c
d
e
f
g
h
i
j
k
l
m
n
ñ
o
p
q
r
s
t
u
v
w
x
y
z

minoría NOUN FEM **minority**

mintamos, **mintió**, *etc VERB*
▸ SEE **mentir**

minúscula[1] NOUN FEM **small letter**
(not capital)

minúsculo, **minúscula**[2] ADJECTIVE
tiny

minusválido, **minusválida** NOUN
MASC, FEM **disabled person**

minusválido ADJECTIVE **disabled**

minuto NOUN MASC **minute**

mío, **mía** ADJECTIVE **mine**; un amigo
mío a friend of mine

mío PRONOUN **mine**; el mío es verde
mine is green

miope ADJECTIVE **shortsighted**

mirada NOUN FEM **look**; una mirada
alegre a happy look, dirigir una
mirada a to look at, me dirigió una
mirada she looked at me, bajar la
mirada to look down

mirar VERB [17] ❶ **to look**; miré
afuera I looked outside, mira en el
cajón look in the drawer ❷ mirar
algo to look at something, miró
el cuardro con interés he looked
at the picture with interest, me
miró he looked at me ❸ **to watch**;
mirar la tele to watch TV ❹ mirar
fijamente to stare

mirarse REFLEXIVE VERB [17] mirarse en
el espejo to look at yourself in the
mirror, mirarse las manos to look at
your hands

mirlo NOUN MASC **blackbird**

misa NOUN FEM **mass**; ir a misa to go
to mass

miserable ADJECTIVE ❶ **miserable**
❷ **stingy**

miseria NOUN FEM ❶ **misery**
❷ **poverty** ❸ **pittance**

misil NOUN MASC **missile**

mismo[1] ADVERB ❶ **right**; ahora
mismo right now, en ese mismo
momento right at that moment,
está ahí mismo it's right there, al
lado mismo de casa right next to
the house ❷ **just**; lo mismo que
yo just like me, eso mismo dije yo
that's just what I said

mismo[2], **misma** ADJECTIVE ❶ **same**;
al mismo tiempo at the same time,
llevan los mismos zapatos they
have the same shoes, lo mismo
the same ❷ **very**; en este mismo
lugar in this very spot ❸ yo mismo
I myself, lo vi yo mismo I saw it
myself, lo dijo ella misma she said
it herself

mismo PRONOUN ❶ el mismo the
same one, he usado la misma I've
used the same one, Sara tiene los
mismos Sara has the same ones
❷ da lo mismo it doesn't matter,
me da lo mismo el color I don't
mind which colour

misterio NOUN MASC **mystery**

misterioso, **misteriosa** ADJECTIVE
mysterious

mitad NOUN FEM ❶ **half**; la mitad
del pastel half the cake, a mitad
de precio half-price ❷ **halfway**;
a mitad de camino paramos a
comer we stopped halfway to eat,
llenar algo hasta la mitad to half
fill something, lo he leído hasta la
mitad I'm halfway through reading
it ❸ cortar algo por la mitad to cut
something in two

mito NOUN MASC **myth**

mixto, **mixta** ADJECTIVE **mixed**

mobiliario *NOUN MASC* **furniture**;
mobiliario de cocina kitchen
fittings

mochila *NOUN FEM* **backpack**

mocos *PLURAL NOUN MASC* tener mocos
to have a runny nose

moda *NOUN FEM* **fashion**; la moda
juvenil young fashion, estar de
moda to be in fashion, pasarse de
moda to go out of fashion, siempre
va a la última moda he's always
wearing the latest fashion

modales *PLURAL NOUN MASC* **manners**;
tener buenos modales to have
good manners

modelo[1] *NOUN MASC* **model**;
utilizar algo como modelo to use
something as a model

modelo[2] *NOUN MASC & FEM* **model**
(fashion)

moderno, moderna *ADJECTIVE*
❶ **modern** ❷ **trendy**

modesto, modesta *ADJECTIVE*
❶ **modest** ❷ **humble**

modificar *VERB* [31] **to change**

modisto, modista *NOUN MASC,
FEM* ❶ **dressmaker** ❷ **(fashion)
designer**

modo *NOUN MASC* ❶ **way**; lo haré a mi
modo I'll do it my way, a mi modo
de ver to my way of thinking, no
hubo modo there was no way (of
doing it) ❷ lo hizo de cualquier
modo he did it any old way ❸ de
cualquier modo in any case, I'll phone you first ❹ ¡de
ningún modo! no way! ❺ de todos
modos anyway, de todos modos
no iba a comprarlo I wasn't going
to buy it anyway ❻ de modo que
so ❼ en cierto modo somehow

❽ modo de empleo instructions
for use

mohoso, mohosa *ADJECTIVE* **mouldy**

mojado, mojada *ADJECTIVE* **wet**

mojar *VERB* [17] **to wet**

mojarse *REFLEXIVE VERB* [17] **to get
wet**; se me mojó el pelo my hair
got wet

moler *VERB* [38] **to grind**

molestar *VERB* [17] ❶ **to disturb**;
'no molestar' 'do not disturb',
no molestes a tu madre, que
está trabajando don't disturb
your mother, she's working ❷ **to
bother**; perdona que te moleste
sorry to bother you ❸ ¿te molesta
que ponga la tele? do you mind if
I put the TV on? ❹ **to annoy**; me
molesta que no me hayan invitado
I'm annoyed that they haven't
invited me

molestarse *REFLEXIVE VERB* [17] ❶ **to
get upset**; se molestó porque
fuimos sin ella she got upset
because we went without her
❷ molestarse en hacer algo to
bother to do something, no se
molestó en preguntar she didn't
bother to find out

molestia *NOUN FEM* ❶ **trouble**; no es
ninguna molestia it's no trouble at
all, causar molestias a alguien to
inconvenience someone ❷ tomarse
la molestia de hacer algo to take
the trouble to do something
❸ perdone la molestia sorry to
bother you ❹ si no es molestia ... if
you don't mind ...

molesto, molesta *ADJECTIVE*
❶ **annoying** ❷ **uncomfortable**
❸ estar molesto to be upset, sé que
está molesto conmigo I know he's
upset with me

momento *NOUN MASC* **moment**; justo en ese momento right at that moment, dentro de un momento in a moment, ¡un momento! just a moment!, de momento at the moment, en cualquier momento any moment now, en este momento right now

monarquía *NOUN FEM* **monarchy**

monasterio *NOUN MASC* **monastery**

moneda *NOUN FEM* ❶ **coin** ❷ **currency**

monedero *NOUN MASC* **purse**

monja *NOUN FEM* **nun**

monje *NOUN MASC* **monk**

mono, mona *NOUN MASC, FEM* **monkey**

mono *ADJECTIVE* ❶ **cute** *(a puppy or baby, for example)* ❷ **pretty** *(person, garment)*

monopatín *NOUN MASC* **skateboard**

monopatinaje *NOUN MASC* **skateboarding**

monopatinar *VERB* [17] **to skateboard**

monstruo *NOUN MASC* **monster**

montaña *NOUN FEM* ❶ **mountain**; en la montaña in the mountains ❷ la montaña rusa the roller coaster

montañoso, montañosa *ADJECTIVE* **mountainous**

montar *VERB* [17] ❶ **to get on**; montar en el avión to get on the plane ❷ **to get in**; montar en el coche to get in the car ❸ **to ride**; montar a caballo to ride a horse, montar en la moto get on the

motorbike, montar en bicicleta to ride a bike ❹ **to mount** *(a horse)* ❺ **to set up** *(a business or an exhibition)* ❻ **to put up** *(a tent)* ❼ montar claras a punto de nieve to whisk the egg whites until stiff ❽ montar un escándalo *(informal)* to cause a scene

montarse *REFLEXIVE VERB* [17] ❶ **to get on**; se montó en el tren he got on the train ❷ **to get in**; montarse en un coche to get in a car

monte *NOUN MASC* **mountain, scrubland**; monte de piedad pawnbroker's shop

montón *NOUN MASC* ❶ **pile**; puse todas las revistas en un montón I put all the magazines in a pile ❷ un montón de *(informal)* loads of, había un montón de niños there were loads of children, montones de *(informal)* loads of, montones de dinero loads of money ❸ me gusta un montón *(informal)* I like it a lot ❹ del montón *(informal)* ordinary, un cantante del montón an ordinary singer

monumento *NOUN MASC* **monument**

moqueta *NOUN FEM* **fitted carpet**

mora *NOUN FEM* **blackberry**

morado[1] *NOUN MASC* **purple**

morado[2]**, morada** *ADJECTIVE* **purple**

moral *NOUN FEM* ❶ **morals**; no tienen ninguna moral they have no morals ❷ **morale**; estar bajo de moral to feel low

moral *ADJECTIVE* **moral**

morcilla *NOUN FEM* **black pudding**

morder *VERB* [38] **to bite**

mordisco NOUN MASC **bite**; darle un mordisco a algo to bite (on) something

moreno, morena ADJECTIVE ❶ **dark** *(hair)* ❷ es morena she's dark-haired ❸ estar moreno to be tanned, ponerse moreno to get tanned

morir VERB [55] **to die**; morir ahogado to drown, morir en un accidente to be killed in an accident

morirse REFLEXIVE VERB [55] **to die**; me muero de hambre I'm starving, se muere por ir a la playa he's dying to go to the beach

moro, mora NOUN MASC, FEM ❶ **Moor** ❷ **North African**

moro ADJECTIVE **Moorish**

mortal ADJECTIVE ❶ **deadly, lethal** ❷ **fatal**

mosca NOUN FEM **fly**
- por si las moscas *(informal)* just in case
- ¿qué mosca le ha picado? *(informal)* what's got into him? *(literally: 'what fly has bitten him?')*

mosquito NOUN MASC **mosquito**

mostaza NOUN FEM **mustard**

mostrador NOUN MASC ❶ **counter** *(in a shop)* ❷ **bar** *(in a pub)* ❸ **check-in desk**

mostrar VERB [24] **to show**

mostrarse REFLEXIVE VERB [24] mostrarse interesado to show interest, mostrarse amable to be kind, mostrarse contento to be happy

motivo NOUN MASC ❶ **cause**; el motivo del accidente the cause of the accident ❷ **reason**; por motivos personales for personal reasons

moto NOUN FEM **motorbike**; montar en moto to ride a motorbike, montar en la moto to get on the motorbike, moto acuática jetski

motocicleta NOUN FEM **motorbike**

motociclista NOUN MASC & FEM **motorcyclist**

motor NOUN MASC **engine**; motor a reacción jet engine

motora NOUN FEM **motorboat**

motorista NOUN MASC **motorcyclist**

mover VERB [38] **to move**

moverse REFLEXIVE VERB [38] **to move**; no te muevas don't move

móvil NOUN MASC **mobile phone**

movimiento NOUN MASC **movement**

moza NOUN FEM **young girl**

mozo NOUN MASC ❶ **young boy** ❷ mozo de estación porter

muchacha NOUN FEM **girl**

muchacho NOUN MASC **boy**

muchedumbre NOUN FEM **crowd**

mucho¹ ADVERB ❶ **a lot**; lo usan mucho they use it a lot, eso es mucho mejor that's a lot better, salen mucho they go out a lot ❷ **very**; lo siento mucho I'm very sorry, '¿te interesa?' – 'mucho' 'are you interested?' – 'very', trabajar mucho to work very hard, voy a estudiar mucho I'm going to study very hard ❸ mucho antes long before, mucho después long after ❹ como mucho at the most ❺ ni mucho menos far from it

A
B
C
D
E
F
G
H
I
J
K
L
M
N
Ñ
O
P
Q
R
S
T
U
V
W
X
Y
Z

mucho[2] *PRONOUN* ❶ **a lot**; tienes mucho que aprender you have a lot to learn ❷ **much**; no tengo mucho I haven't got much ❸ **many**; no quedan muchas there aren't many left, muchos se sorprendieron many were surprised ❹ *(talking about time)* tardan mucho they are taking a long time, ¿hace mucho que ha llamado? did she call a long time ago?, hace mucho que no sé nada de ella it's a long time since I last heard from her, ya no falta mucho para mi cumpleaños it's not long to my birthday now

mucho[3], **mucha** *ADJECTIVE* ❶ **a lot of**; mucho tiempo a lot of time ❷ **much**; no tienen mucho interés they haven't got much interest ❸ **many**; ¿había muchos niños? were there many children?, muchas veces many times ❹ hacía mucho frío it was very cold, tengo mucho sueño I'm very sleepy ❺ tengo mucha prisa I'm in a real hurry ❻ nos vimos hace mucho tiempo we saw each other a long time ago ❼ muchas gracias thanks a lot, mucho gusto nice to meet you, lo haré con mucho gusto I'd be very pleased to do it

mudanza *NOUN FEM* **removal**; camión de mudanzas removal van, estar de mudanza to be in the process of moving

mudar *VERB* [17] **to move** *(from one house to another)*

mudarse *REFLEXIVE VERB* [17] ❶ **to change one's clothes** ❷ **to move**; mudarse de casa to move house

mudo, muda *ADJECTIVE* **dumb**

mueble *NOUN MASC* **piece of furniture**; muebles furniture

muela *NOUN FEM* **back tooth**; tener dolor de muelas to have toothache

muera, muero, *etc VERB*
▸ SEE **morir**

muerda, muerdo, *etc VERB*
▸ SEE **morder**

muerte *NOUN FEM* **death**; muerte repentina sudden death, estar condenado a muerte to be sentenced to death

muerto, muerta *NOUN MASC, FEM* **dead person**; no ha habido muertos there were no casualties, hubo un muerto one person died

muerto *ADJECTIVE* **dead**; muerto de sed dying of thirst, estoy muerto de frío I'm freezing to death, estoy muerto de hambre I'm starving, estábamos muertos de cansancio we were dead tired

muestra, muestro, *etc VERB*
▸ SEE **mostrar**

mueva, muevo, *etc VERB*
▸ SEE **mover**

mujer *NOUN FEM* ❶ **woman** ❷ **wife**; mi mujer my wife

muleta *NOUN FEM* **crutch**

mulo, mula *NOUN MASC, FEM* **mule**

multa *NOUN FEM* **fine**; me pusieron una multa I was fined

multicolor *ADJECTIVE* **multicoloured**

multicultural *ADJECTIVE* **multicultural**

multiplicación *NOUN FEM* **multiplication**

multiplicar *VERB* [31] **to multiply**

mundial *NOUN MASC* el mundial de fútbol the World Cup

mundial *ADJECTIVE* **world**; un récord mundial a world record, la economía mundial the world economy, de fama mundial world-famous

mundo *NOUN MASC* **world**

municiones *NOUN FEM & PLURAL* **ammunition**

municipal *ADJECTIVE* ❶ **local** ❷ **municipal**

muñeca *NOUN FEM* ❶ **doll**; jugar a las muñecas to play dolls, muñeca de trapo rag doll ❷ **wrist**

muñeco *NOUN MASC* ❶ **toy**; muñeco de peluche soft toy ❷ **puppet**

muralla *NOUN FEM* **wall** *(fortified)*; the Great Wall of China la Gran Muralla de China

murciélago *NOUN MASC* **bat**

muriendo, murió, *etc VERB* ▸ SEE **morir**

murmullo *NOUN MASC* ❶ **whispering**; hablar en un murmullo to whisper ❷ **murmur**

murmurar *VERB* [17] ❶ **to whisper** ❷ **to murmur** ❸ murmurar sobre alguien to gossip about someone, se murmura que … the rumour is …

muro *NOUN MASC* **wall**

músculo *NOUN MASC* **muscle**

museo *NOUN MASC* **museum**; un museo de pintura a gallery, un museo de arte moderno a modern art museum

música¹ *NOUN FEM* **music**; música en directo, música en vivo live music, música pop pop music

musical *ADJECTIVE* **musical**

músico, música² *NOUN MASC, FEM* ❶ **musician** ❷ **composer**

muslo *NOUN MASC* ❶ **thigh** ❷ **leg** *(of a chicken)*

musulmán, musulmana *NOUN MASC, FEM, ADJECTIVE* **Muslim**

mutuo, mutua *ADJECTIVE* **mutual**

muy *ADVERB* ❶ **very**; es muy difícil it's very difficult, está muy bien it's very good, muy bien, sigamos very good, let's continue ❷ **too**; era muy pequeño para entenderlo he was too small to understand it ❸ Muy señor mío Dear sir *(in a letter)*

a
b
c
d
e
f
g
h
i
j
k
l
m
n
ñ
o
p
q
r
s
t
u
v
w
x
y
z

181

A
B
C
D
E
F
G
H
I
J
K
L
M
N
Ñ
O
P
Q
R
S
T
U
V
W
X
Y
Z

nabo NOUN MASC **turnip**

nácar NOUN MASC **mother-of-pearl**

nacer VERB [35] **to be born**; nací en Valencia I was born in Valencia, ¿dónde has nacido? where were you born?

nacido, nacida ADJECTIVE **born**; nacido en Sevilla born in Seville, un niño recién nacido a new-born baby

nacimiento NOUN MASC ❶ **birth**; es ciego de nacimiento he was born blind ❷ **crib** (nativity scene)

nación NOUN FEM **nation**

nacional ADJECTIVE **national**

nacionalidad NOUN FEM **nationality**; ¿de qué nacionalidad eres? what nationality are you?

nada PRONOUN ❶ **nothing**; no hay nada nuevo there's nothing new, no hay nada como ... there's nothing like ... ❷ **anything**; no me queda nada I haven't got anything left, yo no sé nada de eso I don't know anything about that, no me dijeron nada they didn't say anything to me ❸ no tengo nada de dinero I have no money at all ❹ nada más nothing else, solo quiero hablar con ella, nada más I only want to speak to her, nothing else, nada más, gracias that's all thank you ❺ nada más nothing else, no quiero nada más I don't want anything else

❻ nada más que only, no quiero nada más que un kilo I only want one kilo ❼ de nada not at all (to someone who has said thank you) ❽ **love** (in tennis); treinta nada thirty love

nada ADVERB **at all**; no me gusta nada I don't like it at all, no me ayudan nada they don't help me at all

nadar VERB [17] **to swim**

nadie PRONOUN ❶ **nobody**; al final nadie llamó nobody phoned in the end ❷ no se lo dije a nadie I didn't tell anybody

nailon NOUN MASC **nylon**

naipe NOUN MASC **card**

nana NOUN FEM **lullaby**

naranja NOUN FEM **orange**; zumo de naranja orange juice

naranja NOUN MASC **orange** (the colour)

naranja ADJECTIVE **orange** (never changes); unos pantalones naranja orange trousers

naranjada NOUN FEM **orangeade**

naranjo NOUN MASC **orange tree**

narcotraficante NOUN MASC & FEM **drugs trafficker**

narcotráfico NOUN MASC **drugs trade**

nariz NOUN FEM **nose**; sonarse la nariz to blow your nose
• darse de narices con alguien (informal) to bump into someone
• en mis propias narices (informal) right under my nose

nata NOUN FEM **cream**; nata líquida single cream, nata para montar double cream, nata montada whipped cream

natación NOUN FEM **swimming**

natillas PLURAL NOUN FEM **custard**

natural ADJECTIVE **natural**

naturaleza NOUN FEM ❶ **nature**; respetar la naturaleza to respect nature, la naturaleza humana human nature ❷ naturaleza muerta still life

naturalmente ADVERB **naturally**

náusea NOUN FEM **nausea**; tener náuseas to feel sick, el olor me daba náuseas the smell was making me feel sick

nauseabundo, **nauseabunda** ADJECTIVE **nauseating**

navaja NOUN FEM ❶ **penknife** ❷ navaja de afeitar razor

nave NOUN FEM ❶ **ship**; nave espacial spaceship ❷ **premises**; una nave industrial industrial premises

navegador NOUN MASC (Computers) **browser**

navegar VERB [28] ❶ **to navigate** ❷ **to sail**; navegar en Internet to surf the Internet

navegar VERB [28] **to sail**

Navidad NOUN FEM ❶ **Christmas**; el día de Navidad Christmas Day, feliz Navidad Merry Christmas ❷ Navidades Christmas time, pasaré las Navidades con mi hermana I'll spend Christmas with my sister

nazca, **nazco**, etc VERB ▸ SEE **nacer**

neblina NOUN FEM **mist**

necesario, **necesaria** ADJECTIVE **necessary**

necesidad NOUN FEM **need**; no hay necesidad de llamarlos there's no need to call them, en caso de necesidad ... if necessary ...

necesitar VERB [17] ❶ **to need**; no necesitas llevar el pasaporte you don't need to take your passport ❷ 'se necesitan camareros' (on sign) 'waiters wanted'

nectarina NOUN FEM **nectarine**

neerlandés[1] NOUN MASC **Dutch** (the language)

neerlandés[2], **neerlandesa** NOUN MASC, FEM **Dutchman/ Dutchwoman**

neerlandés/neerlandesa ADJECTIVE **Dutch**

nefasto, **nefasta** ADJECTIVE ❶ **disastrous** (consequences) ❷ **awful** (weather or taste in clothes)

negar VERB [30] ❶ **to deny**; lo niega todo he denies everything ❷ **to refuse**; nos negaron su ayuda they refused to help us

negarse REFLEXIVE VERB [30] **to refuse**; se niega a colaborar he refuses to colaborate

negativo, **negativa** ADJECTIVE **negative**

negociación NOUN FEM **negotiation**

negociar VERB [17] **to negotiate**

negocio NOUN MASC ❶ **business**; montar un negocio to set up a business, un viaje de negocios a business trip ❷ negocios business, dedicarse a los negocios to be in business ❸ **deal**; hacer un buen negocio to make a good deal

negro, **negra** NOUN MASC, FEM **black man**, **black woman**

negro *ADJECTIVE* **black**

neozelandés, **neozelandesa** *NOUN* **New Zealander**

neozelandéneozlandesas *ADJECTIVE* **(from) New Zealand**

nervio *NOUN MASC* **nerve**; tengo muchos nervios I'm very nervous
• tener los nervios de punta to be on edge

nervioso, **nerviosa** *ADJECTIVE* **nervous**; ponerse nervioso to get nervous

neumático *NOUN MASC* **tyre**

neumonía *NOUN FEM* **pneumonia**

neumonía atípica *NOUN FEM* **SARS** *(the disease)*

neutro, **neutra** *ADJECTIVE* **❶ neutral ❷ neuter** *(in grammar)*

nevada *NOUN FEM* **snowfall**

nevar *VERB* [29] **to snow**; está nevando it's snowing

nevasca *NOUN FEM* **snow storm**

nevera *NOUN FEM* **fridge**

nevisca *NOUN FEM* **snow flurry**

ni *CONJUNCTION* **❶ not ... even**; ni lo he abierto I haven't even opened it, ni uno de ellos llamó not even one of them called **❷ no ... ni ... neither ... nor**, no vino él ni su hermana neither he nor his sister came, no es mío ni suyo it's not mine and it's not hers either, una casa sin luz ni agua corriente a house with neither water nor electricity, ni uno ni otro neither one nor the other **❸ no es ni grande ni pequeño** it's neither big nor small **❹ ¡ni hablar!** no way!

nicaragüense *NOUN MASC & FEM, ADJECTIVE* **Nicaraguan**

nido *NOUN MASC* **nest**

niebla *NOUN FEM* **fog**; había mucha niebla it was very foggy

nieta *NOUN FEM* **granddaughter**

nieto *NOUN MASC* **❶ grandson ❷ mis nietos** my grandchildren

nieva, **nieve¹**, *etc VERB* ▸ SEE **nevar**

nieve² *NOUN FEM* **❶ snow ❷ batir claras a punto de nieve** to beat eggwhites until stiff
• blanco como la nieve as white as snow

ningún *ADJECTIVE* ▸ SEE **ninguno**

ninguno, **ninguna** *ADJECTIVE* *('ninguno' becomes 'ningún' before a masculine singular noun)* **❶ any**; no trajeron ninguna caja they didn't bring any boxes, no he comprado ningún libro I didn't buy any books, no hay ninguna necesidad there's no need **❷ en ningún momento** never, en ningún lugar nowhere, no lo veo por ningún lado I can't see it anywhere **❸ de ninguna manera** no way

ninguno *PRONOUN* **❶ neither**; ninguno de los dos vale neither of them is suitable, ninguno de los dos me gusta I don't like either of them **❷ none**; ninguno de los que estaban allí none of those who were there, no compró ninguno he didn't buy any of them **❸ nobody**; ninguno lo vio nobody saw him

niña *NOUN FEM* **girl**

niñera *NOUN FEM* **nanny**

niño *NOUN MASC* **❶ boy ❷ child**; van a tener un niño they're going to have a baby ❸ niños children, ropa de niños children's clothes

nitrógeno NOUN MASC **nitrogen**

nivel NOUN MASC ❶ **level**; el nivel del agua the level of the water ❷ **standard**; el nivel de vida the standard of living

no ADVERB ❶ **no**; '¿es tuyo?' – 'no' 'is it yours?' – 'no' ❷ **not**; no es mi amigo he's not my friend, no sabe nadar he can't swim, no se sabe it's not known, no mucho not much, ahí no not there ❸ no comió nada he didn't eat anything, no voy nunca al cine I never go to the cinema, no se parecen en nada they are not similar at all ❹ somos siete ¿no? there are seven of us, aren't there?, tú hablaste con ella, ¿no? you spoke to her, didn't you? ❺ la no violencia non-violence, los nofumadores non smokers ❻ ¡cómo no! of course!

noche NOUN FEM ❶ **evening**, **night**; a las ocho de la noche at eight o'clock in the evening, a las once de la noche at eleven o'clock at night, esta noche this evening, tonight, por la noche in the evening, at night, la noche anterior the previous evening, the night before, el lunes por la noche Monday evening, Monday night, de noche in the evening, at night, buenas noches good evening, goodnight ❷ hacerse de noche to get dark

Nochebuena NOUN FEM **Christmas Eve**

Nochevieja NOUN FEM **New Year's Eve**

nocivo, nociva ADJECTIVE **harmful**

nocturno, nocturna ADJECTIVE ❶ **nocturnal** ❷ **evening**; clases nocturnas evening lessons

nombrar VERB [17] ❶ **to mention** ❷ **to appoint**

nombre NOUN MASC ❶ **name**; ¿qué nombre tiene el grupo? what's the name of the group?, ¿qué nombre le van a poner al niño? what are they going to call the baby?, nombre de pila first name ❷ (on forms) 'nombre' 'first name', 'nombre y apellidos' 'full name' ❸ **noun** (in grammar)

nordeste, noreste NOUN MASC **northeast**

norma NOUN FEM **rule**

normal ADJECTIVE ❶ **normal**; eso es normal that's normal ❷ normal y corriente ordinary

normalmente ADVERB **normally**

noroeste NOUN MASC **northwest**

norte NOUN MASC **north**; hacia el norte northwards, al norte del Madrid to the north of Madrid

norteamericano, norteamericana NOUN MASC, FEM, ADJECTIVE **North American**

Noruega NOUN FEM **Norway**

noruego[1] NOUN MASC **Norwegian** (the language)

noruego[2]**, noruega** NOUN MASC, FEM, ADJECTIVE **Norwegian**

nos PRONOUN ❶ **us**; nos invitaron a la fiesta they invited us to the party ❷ **to us**; nos mintió he lied to us ❸ **ourselves**; nos portamos bien we behaved ourselves ❹ **each other**; siempre nos ayudamos we always help each other ❺ (with reflexive verbs) nos reímos mucho we laugh a lot, vamos a bañarnos let's go for a swim, nos sentamos a la mesa we sat at the table ❻ *(with parts of the body or clothes)* nos quitamos los abrigos we took our coats off, nos limpiamos los pies al entrar we wiped our feet at the door ❼ *(having something done)* el sábado iremos a cortarnos el pelo we'll go and get our hair cut on Saturday

nosotros, nosotras *PRONOUN* ❶ we; lo hicimos nosotras we did it ❷ us; detrás de nosotros behind us ❸ nosotros mismos ourselves

nota *NOUN FEM* ❶ note; tomar nota de algo to write something down, tomar notas to take notes ❷ mark; ¿qué nota has sacado en física? what did you get in physics?, sacar buenas notas to get good marks ❸ nota musical note

notable *ADJECTIVE* noteworthy

notable *NOUN MASC* mark between 70% and 85%

notar *VERB* [17] to notice; te noto preocupado you look worried, se nota que ... you can tell that ...

notario, notaria *NOUN MASC, FEM* notary public

noticia *NOUN FEM* ❶ *(noticia: singular)* una noticia interesante an interesting piece of news, la noticia me sorprendió the news surprised me, dar la noticia a alguien to break the news to someone ❷ *(noticias: plural)* tengo buenas noticias I've got good news, las noticias de las nueve the nine o'clock news

novecientos, novecientas *NUMBER* nine hundred; novecientos veinte nine hundred and twenty

novela *NOUN FEM* novel

noveno, novena *ADJECTIVE* ninth; el noveno piso the ninth floor

noventa *NUMBER* ninety; tiene noventa años she's ninety (years old), noventa y siete ninety-seven, los años noventa the nineties

novia *NOUN FEM* ❶ bride ❷ fiancée ❸ girlfriend

noviazgo *NOUN MASC* ❶ relationship *(romantic)* ❷ engagement *(to marry)*

noviembre *NOUN MASC* November; en noviembre, en el mes de noviembre in November

novillada *NOUN FEM* bullfight for young bulls

novillos *PLURAL NOUN MASC* hacer novillos to play truant

novio *NOUN MASC* ❶ groom ❷ fiancé ❸ boyfriend

nube *NOUN FEM* cloud; un cielo cubierto de nubes a cloudy sky

nublado, nublada *ADJECTIVE* cloudy

nublarse *REFLEXIVE VERB* [17] to cloud over; se nubló por la tarde it clouded over in the afternoon

nuboso, nubosa *ADJECTIVE* cloudy

nuclear *NOUN FEM* nuclear power station

nuclear *ADJECTIVE* nuclear

nudillo *NOUN MASC* knuckle

nudo *NOUN MASC* knot

nuera *NOUN FEM* daughter-in-law

nuestro, nuestra *ADJECTIVE* our; nuestra casa our house, un familiar nuestro a relative of ours

nuestro *PRONOUN* **ours**; la nuestra es verde ours is green, los nuestros están en el salón ours are in the living room, aquel es el nuestro that one is ours

nueve *NUMBER* **❶ nine**; Jaime tiene nueve años Jaime's nine (years old) **❷ ninth** *(in dates)*; hoy estamos a nueve it's the ninth today **❸ nine** *(in clock time)*; son las nueve it's nine o'clock

nuevo, nueva *ADJECTIVE* **❶ new**; mis zapatos nuevos my new shoes **❷** de nuevo once more **❸** ¿qué hay de nuevo? *(informal)* what's new?

nuez *NOUN FEM* **❶ walnut ❷ Adam's apple ❸** nuez moscada nutmeg

número *NOUN MASC* **❶ number**; mi número de teléfono my telephone number **❷ issue** *(of a magazine, for example)* **❸ size**; ¿qué número de zapatos calzas? what size shoes do you take?

numeroso, numerosa *ADJECTIVE* **❶ numerous ❷ large** *(group, audience)*

nunca *ADVERB* **never**; nunca he estado en ese bar I've never been to that bar, nunca más never again, más que nunca more than ever, casi nunca hardly ever

nutritivo, nutritiva *ADJECTIVE* **nourishing**

ñoño, ñoña *ADJECTIVE* no seas ñoño don't be so wet

a
b
c
d
e
f
g
h
i
j
k
l
m
n
ñ
o
p
q
r
s
t
u
v
w
x
y
z

Oo

o *CONJUNCTION* ❶ **or**; antes o después sooner or later, *(note that before a word beginning with 'o', it becomes 'u')* plata u oro silver or gold, *(note that when 'o' appears between numbers, it has an accent)* 11 ó 12 11 or 12 ❷ **o sea** so, ¿o sea que no te importa? so you don't mind?

oasis *NOUN MASC* **oasis**

obedecer *VERB* [35] **to obey**; tienes que obedecerme you must do as I say

obedezca, obedezco, *etc VERB* ▸ SEE **obedecer**

obediencia *NOUN FEM* **obedience**

obediente *ADJECTIVE* **obedient**

obispo *NOUN MASC* **bishop**

objetivo¹ *NOUN MASC* **objective**

objetivo², objetiva *ADJECTIVE* **objective**

objeto *NOUN MASC* **object**; objetos de valor valuables

obligar *VERB* [28] obligar a alguien a hacer algo to make somebody do something

obligarse *REFLEXIVE VERB* [28] obligarse a hacer to force yourself to do

obligatorio, obligatoria *ADJECTIVE* **compulsory**

obra *NOUN FEM* ❶ **deed**; una buena obra a good deed ❷ **play**; una obra de Shakespeare a Shakespeare play ❸ **work**; una obra de arte a work of art ❹ una obra maestra a masterpiece ❺ **building site**; estar en obras to be having some building work done

obrero, obrera *NOUN MASC, FEM* ❶ **worker** ❷ **labourer**

obsceno, obscena *ADJECTIVE* **obscene**

obscuridad *NOUN FEM* **darkness**

obscuro, obscura *ADJECTIVE* **dark**; a obscuras in the dark

observación *NOUN FEM* ❶ **observartion** ❷ **remark**

observador, observadora *NOUN MASC, FEM* **observer**

observador *ADJECTIVE* **observant**

observar *VERB* [17] ❶ **to observe** ❷ **to remark**

observatorio *NOUN MASC* **observatory**

obsesión *NOUN FEM* **obsession**; tiene una obsesión con la limpieza he has an obsession with cleanliness, tiene la obsesión de que la siguen she's obsessed with the idea that she's being followed

obstáculo *NOUN MASC* **obstacle**; superar un obstáculo to overcome an obstacle

obstante *IN PHRASE* no obstante nevertheless

obstinado, obstinada *ADJECTIVE* **obstinate**

obstinarse *REFLEXIVE VERB* [17] obstinarse en hacer to insist on doing

obtendré, **obtendría**, *etc VERB*
  ▶ SEE **obtener**

obtener *VERB* [9] ❶ to obtain
  ❷ obtener un premio to win a prize

obtenga, **obtengo**, **obtuve**, *etc*
  VERB ▶ SEE **obtener**

obvio, **obvia** *ADJECTIVE* **obvious**

oca *NOUN FEM* **goose**

ocasión *NOUN FEM* ❶ occasion
  ❷ opportunity; si hay ocasión if
  there's an opportunity ❸ precios de
  ocasión bargain prices, coches de
  ocasión second-hand cars

ocasionar *VERB* [17] to cause

occidental *ADJECTIVE* **Western**

Occidente *NOUN MASC* **the West**

océano *NOUN MASC* **ocean**

ochenta *NUMBER* **eighty**; tiene
  ochenta años she's eighty (years
  old), ochenta y cinco eighty-five, los
  años ochenta the eighties

ocho *NUMBER* ❶ eight; tiene ocho
  años she's eight (years old)
  ❷ eighth *(in dates)*; estamos a ocho
  it's the eighth today ❸ eight *(in
  clock time)*; son las ocho it's eight
  o'clock

ochocientos, **ochocientas** *NUMBER*
  eight hundred; ochocientos siete
  eight hundred and seven

ocio *NOUN MASC* **spare time**

ocioso, **ociosa** *ADJECTIVE* **idle**

octavo, **octava** *ADJECTIVE* **eighth**; el
  octavo piso the eighth floor

octubre *NOUN MASC* **October**; en
  octubre, en el mes de octubre in
  October

ocupación *NOUN FEM* **occupation**

ocupado, **ocupada** *ADJECTIVE*
  ❶ busy; está muy ocupado he's
  very busy ❷ engaged; la línea
  está ocupada the line is engaged
  ❸ taken; ¿está ocupado este
  asiento? is this seat taken?

ocupar *VERB* [17] ❶ ocupar un asiento
  to have a seat, ocupa el asiento 11b
  he's in seat 11b, ¿quién ocupa esa
  habitación? who's in that room?
  ❷ to occupy *(land or a building)*
  ❸ *(talking about time)* ocupo mi
  tiempo libre leyendo I spend my
  free time reading

ocuparse *REFLEXIVE VERB* [17] ocuparse
  de algo to take care of something

ocurrir *VERB* [19] to happen; me
  ocurrió una cosa muy graciosa
  something really funny happened
  to me, ¿qué le ocurre? what's the
  matter with him?

ocurrirse *REFLEXIVE VERB* [19] ¿se te
  ocurre alguna idea? can you think
  of anything?, se me ocurrió que
  podríamos ... I thought we could ...

odiar *VERB* [17] to hate

odio *NOUN MASC* **hate**, **hatred**

odontólogo, **odontóloga** *NOUN
  MASC, FEM* **dental sugeon**

oeste *NOUN MASC* **west**; hacia el oeste
  westwards, al oeste de Madrid to
  the west of Madrid

ofender *VERB* [18] to offend

ofenderse *REFLEXIVE VERB* [18] to take
  offence

oferta *NOUN FEM* **offer**; estar de/en
  oferta to be on offer

oficial *ADJECTIVE* **official**

oficial *NOUN MASC & FEM* **officer**

oficina *NOUN FEM* **office**; oficina de cambio bureau de change, oficina de objetos perdidos lost property (office), oficina de (información y) turismo tourist (information) office

oficinista *NOUN MASC & FEM* **office worker**

oficio *NOUN MASC* ❶ **trade** ❷ **service** *(in a church)*

ofrecer *VERB* [35] **to offer**

ofrezca, ofrezco, *etc VERB* ▸ SEE **ofrecer**

oído *NOUN MASC* ❶ **ear**; tener dolor de oídos to have earache ❷ tener buen oído to have a good ear

oiga, oigo, *etc VERB* ▸ SEE **oir**

oír *VERB* [56] ❶ **to hear**; no oigo nada I can't hear anything ❷ **listen to**; oír las noticias to listen to the news, oír música to listen to music ❸ ¡oye! hey!

ojalá *EXCLAMATION* ¡ojalá me llame! I hope he rings me!, ¡ojalá pudiera! I wish I could!

ojo *NOUN MASC* ❶ **eye**; tiene los ojos verdes he's got green eyes, ojos claros light-coloured eyes *(blue, green, or grey as opposed to brown)*, con los ojos cerrados with your eyes closed ❷ el ojo de la cerradura the keyhole
• no pegué ojo en toda la noche I didn't sleep a wink all night
• salir por un ojo de la cara *(informal)* to cost an arm and a leg

ojo *EXCLAMATION* ¡ojo! careful!

ola *NOUN FEM* **wave**; una ola de calor a heatwave, una ola de frío a cold spell

ole, olé *EXCLAMATION* **olé**

oler *VERB* [39] **to smell**; oler una flor to smell a flower, oler a algo to smell of something, huele a lavanda it smells of lavender

olimpiadas *PLURAL NOUN FEM* **Olympic Games**

olímpico, olímpica *ADJECTIVE* **Olympic**

oliva *NOUN FEM* **olive**; aceite de oliva olive oil

olivo *NOUN MASC* **olive tree**

olla *NOUN FEM* **pan**; olla a presión pressure cooker

olor *NOUN MASC* **smell**; tiene un olor raro it has a funny smell, tiene olor a almendras it smells of almonds

olvidar *VERB* [17] **to forget**; ¡olvídalo! forget it!

olvidarse *REFLEXIVE VERB* [17] **to forget**; se me olvidó llamarte I forgot to ring you, se me olvidó la cartera I forgot my wallet

ombligo *NOUN MASC* **navel**

omitir *VERB* [19] **to omit**

once *NUMBER* ❶ **eleven**; tiene once años she's eleven (years old) ❷ **eleventh** *(in dates)*; hoy estamos a once it's the eleventh today ❸ **eleven** *(in clock time)*; son las once it's eleven o'clock

onceavo, onceava *ADJECTIVE* **eleventh**

onda *NOUN FEM* **wave**; onda larga long wave
• estar en la onda *(informal)* to be trendy

ondulado, ondulada *ADJECTIVE* **wavy**

ONG *ABBREVIATION FEM* (short for *Organización No Gubernamental*) **NGO**

ONU *ABBREVIATION FEM* (short for *Organización de las Naciones Unidas*) **UN**

opción *NOUN FEM* **option**

opcional *ADJECTIVE* **optional**

ópera *NOUN FEM* **opera**

operación *NOUN FEM* **operation**; ha sufrido una operación he's had an operation

operador, operadora *NOUN MASC, FEM* **operator**

operar *VERB* [17] **❶ to operate on** (*a person*); ¿tendrán que operarlo? will they have to operate on him? **❷ to produce** (*a change*)

operarse *REFLEXIVE VERB* [17] **to have an operation**; se va a operar del corazón she's going to have a heart operation

opinar *VERB* [17] **❶ to think**; opino que ... I think that ..., ¿qué opinas del diseño? what do you think of the design?, prefiero no opinar I prefer not to say what I think **❷ to express an opinion**

opinión *NOUN FEM* **opinion**; ¿cuál es vuestra opinión? what do you think?, cambiar de opinión to change your mind

oponer *VERB* [11] **❶ to raise** (*an objection*) **❷** oponer resistencia to put up a fight

oponerse *REFLEXIVE VERB* [11] oponerse a algo to oppose something, se oponen a cualquier cambio de las reglas they are opposed to any change in the rules

oporto *NOUN MASC* **port**

oportunidad *NOUN FEM* **opportunity**; aprovechar una oportunidad to make the most of an opportunity

oportuno, oportuna *NOUN* **right**, **good**; es un momento oportuno it's the right moment

oposición *NOUN FEM* **❶ opposition ❷** oposiciones competitive public exams for a government job

optar *VERB* [17] optar por algo to opt for something

optativo, optativa *ADJECTIVE* **optional**

óptico, óptica *NOUN MASC & FEM* **optician**

optimismo *NOUN MASC* **optimism**

optimista *NOUN MASC & FEM* **optimist**

optimista *ADJECTIVE* **optimistic**

opuesto, opuesta *ADJECTIVE* **❶ conflicting** (*views or opinions*) **❷ opposite**; venían en dirección opuesta they were coming from the opposite direction

oración *NOUN FEM* **❶ sentence ❷ prayer**

oral *NOUN MASC*

oral *ADJECTIVE* **oral**

orden¹ *NOUN MASC* **order**; en orden alfabético in alphabetical order, en orden de importancia in order of importance, puestos en orden de tamaño arranged according to size, ponlos en orden put them in order, mantener el orden to keep order, poner la habitación en orden to tidy up the room, ¡orden! order!

orden² NOUN FEM **order**; dar una orden to give an order

ordenado, **ordenada** ADJECTIVE **tidy**; es muy ordenado he's very tidy

ordenador NOUN MASC **computer**

ordenar VERB [17] ❶ to tidy up (a room or house) ❷ to put in order; ordenar algo alfabéticamente to put something in alphabetical order ❸ to order; nos ordenó seguir he ordered us to carry on

ordinario, **ordinaria** ADJECTIVE ❶ vulgar ❷ rude (a person) ❸ ordinary, normal (a method or system)

oreja NOUN FEM **ear**

orgánico, **orgánica** ADJECTIVE **organic**

organización NOUN FEM **organization**

organizar VERB [22] to organize

órgano NOUN MASC **organ**

orgullo NOUN MASC **pride**; tiene mucho orgullo he's very proud

orgulloso, **orgullosa** ADJECTIVE **proud**; estar orgulloso de algo to be proud of something

orientación NOUN FEM ❶ ¿qué orientación tiene la casa? which way does the house face? ❷ orientation ❸ bearings ❹ orientación profesional careers guidance

oriental NOUN MASC & FEM **Oriental**

oriental ADJECTIVE ❶ Eastern ❷ Oriental

orientar VERB [17] ❶ to guide ❷ to give guidance to (a young person or student)

orientarse REFLEXIVE VERB [17] to get your bearings

Oriente NOUN MASC **East**; el Lejano Oriente the Far East

original NOUN MASC ADJECTIVE **original**

orilla NOUN FEM ❶ bank; sentados a la orilla del río sitting on the river bank ❷ shore; una casa a orillas del mar a house by the sea

ornamental ADJECTIVE **ornamental**

oro NOUN MASC **gold**; un reloj de oro a gold watch

orquesta NOUN FEM **orchestra**; una orquesta de jazz a jazz band

ortiga NOUN FEM **nettle**

ortografía NOUN FEM **spelling**

oruga NOUN FEM **caterpillar**

os PRONOUN ❶ you (talking to more than one person); os vimos desde la ventana we saw you from the window, ¿os dieron suficiente información? did they give you enough information? ❷ to you; os mintió he lied to you ❸ yourselves; os tenéis que portar bien you must behave yourselves ❹ each other; ¿os conocéis? do you know each other? ❺ (with a reflexive verb) ¿os divertisteis? did you have a good time?, iros a bañar go for a swim ❻ (with parts of the body or clothes) os podéis quitar los abrigos you can take your coats off, ¿os habéis lavado las manos? have you washed your hands? ❼ (having something done) os tenéis que cortar el pelo you have to have your hair cut

osado, **osada** ADJECTIVE **bold**

oscuridad NOUN FEM **darkness**

oscuro, oscura *ADJECTIVE* **dark**; a oscuras in the dark

osito *NOUN MASC* un osito de peluche a teddy bear

oso, osa *NOUN MASC & FEM* **bear**

ostra *NOUN FEM* **oyster**

OTAN *ABBREVIATION FEM (short for Organización del Tratado del Atlántico Norte)* **NATO**

otoño *NOUN MASC* **autumn**

otro, otra *ADJECTIVE* ❶ **another**; ¿te has comprado otro casete? did you buy another cassette?, añade otros dos add another two ❷ **other**; en otros colores in other colours, la otra tarde le vi I saw him the other evening, ¿no tienes ningún otro color? don't you have any other colours? ❸ otra cosa something else, me gustaría comprarle otra cosa I would like to buy her something else, eso es otra cosa diferente that's something different, ¿quieres alguna otra cosa? do you want something else?, no me gusta ninguna otra cosa I don't like anything else ❹ otra vez again, hazlo otra vez do it again

otro *PRONOUN* ❶ **another one**; este no, dame otro not this one, give me another one ❷ **other one**; el otro te queda mejor the other one suits you better, las otras están en el cajón the other ones are in the drawer ❸ *(talking about people)* los otros vendrán en coche the others will come by car, a otros les gustaría other people would like it ❹ *(talking about time)* un mes sí y otro no every other month, de un día para otro from one day to the next

oveja *NOUN FEM* **sheep**

OVNI *ABBREVIATION MASC (short for objeto volante no identificado)* **UFO**

oxidado, oxidada *ADJECTIVE* **rusty**

oxígeno *NOUN MASC* **oxygen**

oyendo, oyó *VERB* ▸ SEE **oír**

ozono *NOUN MASC* **ozone**; la capa de ozono the ozone layer

Pp

pabellón *NOUN MASC* **pavilion**

paciencia *NOUN FEM* **patience**; tener paciencia to be patient

paciente *NOUN MASC & FEM*

paciente *ADJECTIVE* **patient**

padecer *VERB* [35] **to suffer**; padecer de algo to suffer from something

padrastro *NOUN MASC* **stepfather**

padre *NOUN MASC* ❶ **father** ❷ mis padres my parents

padrino *NOUN MASC* ❶ **godfather** ❷ mis padrinos my godparents

padrino de boda *NOUN MASC*; person who gives away the bride and carries out duties of the best man

paella *NOUN FEM* **paella**

paga *NOUN FEM* ❶ **pay** ❷ **pocket money**

pagado, pagada *ADJECTIVE* bien pagado well paid, mal pagado badly paid

pagar *VERB* [28] ❶ **to pay** ❷ **to pay off** *(a debt)* ❸ **to pay for** *(tickets, for example)* ❹ **to repay** *(a favour)*

página *NOUN FEM* **page**

pago *NOUN MASC* **payment**; pago anticipado payment in advance,

pago inicial down payment, pago al contado payment in cash, efectuar un pago to make a payment

país *NOUN MASC* **country**

paisaje *NOUN MASC* **landscape**

País de Gales *NOUN MASC* el País de Gales Wales

Países Bajos *PLURAL NOUN MASC* los Países Bajos the Netherlands

País Vasco *NOUN MASC* el País Vasco the Basque Country

paja *NOUN FEM* ❶ **straw** ❷ pajita drinking straw

pajarita *NOUN FEM* **bow tie**

pájaro *NOUN MASC* **bird**
- matar dos pájaros de un tiro to kill two birds with one stone

Pakistán *NOUN MASC* **Pakistan**

pakistaní *NOUN MASC & FEM, ADJECTIVE* **Pakistani**

pala *NOUN FEM* ❶ **spade** ❷ **shovel** ❸ **bat** *(for table tennis)* ❹ **slice** *(in cooking)*

palabra *NOUN FEM* ❶ **word**; palabra compuesta compound word, no cumplió con su palabra he didn't keep his word ❷ **speech**; el don de la palabra the gift of speech ❸ pedir la palabra to ask permission to speak

palabrota *NOUN FEM* **swearword**; decir palabrotas to swear

palacio *NOUN MASC* **palace**

palanca *NOUN FEM* ❶ **lever**; abrir algo haciendo palanca to lever something open ❷ **crowbar** ❸ palanca de cambios gearstick, palanca de mando joystick

paleta NOUN FEM ❶ palette
❷ spatula *(for cooking)* ❸ trowel
❹ bat *(in table tennis)*

palidecer VERB [35] to go pale

pálido, pálida ADJECTIVE pale

palillo NOUN MASC ❶ chopstick
❷ drumstick ❸ palillo de dientes
toothpick

palma NOUN FEM palm *(of hand)*; dar
palmas to clap your hands

palmera NOUN FEM palm tree

palo NOUN MASC ❶ stick ❷ pole *(for a
tent)* ❸ palo de escoba broomstick

paloma NOUN FEM ❶ dove; la
paloma de la paz the dove of peace
❷ pigeon

palomitas PLURAL NOUN FEM popcorn

pan NOUN MASC bread; un pan de
molde a loaf of bread, una barra
de pan a French loaf, pan integral
wholewheat bread, pan tostado
toast, pan rallado breadcrumbs

pana NOUN FEM corduroy

panadería NOUN FEM bakery

panadero, panadera NOUN MASC,
FEM baker

Panamá NOUN MASC Panama; el Canal
de Panamá the Panama Canal

panameño, panameña NOUN MASC,
FEM, ADJECTIVE Panamanian

pancarta NOUN FEM banner

panceta NOUN FEM belly pork

pandereta NOUN FEM tambourine

pandilla NOUN FEM gang

panecillo NOUN MASC bread roll

pánico NOUN MASC panic

panorama NOUN MASC ❶ panorama
❷ view

pantalla NOUN FEM ❶ screen; la
pantalla grande the big screen
❷ shade *(of a lamp)*

pantalón NOUN MASC trousers; un
pantalón a pair of trousers

pantalones PLURAL NOUN MASC
trousers; un par de pantalones,
unos pantalones a pair of
trousers, pantalones vaqueros
jeans, pantalones cortos shorts,
pantalones de peto dungarees

pantano NOUN MASC ❶ swamp
❷ reservoir

pantanoso, pantanosa ADJECTIVE
swampy, marshy

pantorrilla NOUN FEM calf

panty, panti NOUN MASC tights

pañal NOUN MASC nappy

paño NOUN MASC cloth; un paño
a piece of cloth, un paño de cocina
a dishcloth
• estar en paños menores *(informal)*
to be in your undies

pañuelo NOUN MASC ❶ handkerchief
❷ headscarf ❸ scarf

Papa NOUN MASC Pope

papá NOUN MASC *(informal)* ❶ daddy
❷ mis papás my mum and dad

papagayo NOUN MASC parrot

Papá Noel NOUN MASC Santa Claus

papel NOUN MASC paper; un trozo
de papel a piece of paper, se
encontró un papel en la mesa
he found a piece of paper on the
table, papel aluminio aluminium
foil, papel higiénico toilet paper,
papel pintado wallpaper, papel de
envolver wrapping paper, papel de
lija sandpaper

papelera NOUN FEM **❶ paperbasket ❷ litter bin** (in the street)

papelería NOUN FEM **stationer's**

paperas PLURAL NOUN FEM **mumps**

paquete NOUN MASC **❶ parcel**; mandar un paquete to send a parcel **❷ packet**; un paquete de cigarrillos a packet of cigarettes

par NOUN MASC **❶ pair**; un par de zapatos a pair of shoes **❷ couple**; un par de veces a couple of times **❸ de par en par wide open**

par ADJECTIVE **even**; un número par an even number

para PREPOSITION **❶ for**; es para ti it's for you, sirve para limpiar it's for cleaning, ¿para qué quieres la carpeta? what do you want the folder for?, hay suficiente para todos there's enough for everybody, estará terminado para el doce it'll be finished for the twelfth **❷ to**; se dijo para sí he said to himself, es demasiado difícil para hacerlo it's too difficult to do **❸** (direction) me voy para casa I'm going home, iban para la estación they were going to the station **❹ para que so that**

parabrisas NOUN MASC (does not change in the plural), **windscreen**

paracaídas NOUN MASC (does not change in the plural), **parachute**

parachoques NOUN MASC (does not change in the plural), **bumper**

parada¹ NOUN FEM **stop**; la parada del autobús bus stop, parada de taxis taxi rank

parado, parada² NOUN MASC, FEM **unemployed person**

parado ADJECTIVE **unemployed**

parador NOUN MASC **state-owned hotel**

paraguas NOUN MASC (does not change in the plural), **umbrella**

Paraguay NOUN MASC **Paraguay**

paraguayo, paraguaya NOUN MASC, FEM, ADJECTIVE **Paraguayan**

paraíso NOUN MASC **paradise**

paralelo¹ NOUN MASC **parallel**

paralelo², paralela ADJECTIVE **parallel**; paralelo a algo parallel to something

parapente NOUN MASC **hang gliding**

parar VERB [17] **❶ to stop**; parar de hablar to stop talking, bailamos sin parar toda la noche we didn't stop dancing all night, paré el coche I stopped the car **❷** para un momento hang on a minute **❸ to save**; parar un gol to make a save (in football, hockey) **❹** ir a parar to end up, fueron a parar al hospital they ended up in hospital, ¡no sé a donde vamos a ir a parar! I don't know what the world is coming to!

pararse REFLEXIVE VERB [17] **to stop**; no te pares en medio de la calle don't stop in the middle of the road, se paró a pensar he stopped to think, se me ha parado el reloj my watch has stopped

pararrayos NOUN MASC (does not change in the plural), **lightning conductor**

parasol NOUN MASC **parasol**

parcela NOUN FEM **plot of land**

parche NOUN MASC **patch**

parchís NOUN MASC **ludo**

parecer VERB [35] **❶ to seem**; no parece demasiado complicado it doesn't seem too complicated, parece que ya no vienen it seems they're not coming any more ❷ **to seem like, to look like**; parece de madera it looks as if it's made of wood, esa nube parece un pájaro that cloud looks like a bird, parece que está roto it looks as though it's broken, parece que va a llover it looks like rain ❸ ¿qué te pareció la película? what did you think of the film?, me parece que llegan hoy I think they arrive today, me parece que no I don't think so, le pareció muy mal que no llamasen he thought it was really bad of them not to call ❹ según parece, al parecer apparently

parecerse REFLEXIVE VERB [35] ❶ **to look like**; se parece mucho a su padre she looks very like her father, nos parecemos mucho we look very like each other ❷ **to be like** (in character); se parece mucho a su madre she is very like her mother

parecido¹ NOUN MASC ❶ **similarity**; el parecido era increíble the similarity was incredible ❷ ser bien parecido to be good-looking

parecido², **parecida** ADJECTIVE **similar**

pared NOUN FEM **wall**

pareja NOUN FEM ❶ **pair**; trabajar en pareja to work in pairs ❷ **couple** ❸ mi pareja my partner

paréntesis NOUN MASC (does not change in the plural), **brackets**

parezca, **parezco**, etc VERB ▶ SEE **parecer**

pariente NOUN MASC & FEM **relative**

parking NOUN MASC **car park**

parlamento NOUN MASC **parliament**

paro NOUN MASC ❶ **unemployment**; estar en paro to be unemployed, cobrar el paro to receive unemployment benefit ❷ **strike**; hicieron un paro de 24 horas they went on a 24-hour strike ❸ un paro cardíaco heart failure

parpadear VERB [17] **to blink**

párpado NOUN MASC **eyelid**

parque NOUN MASC ❶ **park**; parque nacional national park, parque infantil play park ❷ parque de atracciones amusement park, parque temático theme park, parque zoológico zoo ❸ parque de bomberos fire station ❹ parque móvil fleet (of cars, lorries etc) ❺ parque eólico wind farm

parquímetro NOUN MASC **parking meter**

párrafo NOUN MASC **paragraph**

parrilla NOUN FEM **grill**; chuletas a la parrilla barbecued chops

parroquia NOUN FEM ❶ **parish** ❷ **parish church**

parte¹ NOUN FEM ❶ **part**; es parte de Asia it's part of Asia, una tercera parte de la herencia a third of the inheritance, la parte antigua de la ciudad the old part of town ❷ **share**; mi parte del trabajo my share of the work ❸ la mayor parte de most of, la mayor parte de los alumnos most of the students ❹ en/por alguna parte somewhere, en/por cualquier parte anywhere, en/por todas partes everywhere ❺ en parte partly, en parte tienen razón they're partly right ❻ en gran parte largely ❼ de un tiempo a esta parte for some time now ❽ ¿de parte de quién? who shall I say is

a
b
c
d
e
f
g
h
i
j
k
l
m
n
ñ
o
p
q
r
s
t
u
v
w
x
y
z

calling? *(on the phone)*, saludos de parte de Juan Juan says hello, felicítalos de mi parte give them my congratulations ❾ yo por mi parte … as far as I'm concerned …

parte² *NOUN MASC* **report**; el parte meteorológico the weather report

partera *NOUN FEM* **midwife**

participación *NOUN FEM* ❶ **participation** ❷ **share in lottery ticket**

participar *VERB* [17] **to participate**

participio *NOUN MASC* **participle**; participio pasado past participle

particular *ADJECTIVE* ❶ **private** *(lesson or teacher)* ❷ **particular** *(feature, for example)* ❸ un colegio particular a fee-paying school ❹ mi teléfono particular my home telephone number, nuestro domicilio particular our home address ❺ es muy particular *(informal)* he's very peculiar

partida *NOUN FEM* **game**; una partida de ajedrez a game of chess

partido *NOUN MASC* ❶ **party** *(political)* ❷ **game, match**

partir *VERB* [19] ❶ **to cut**; partir algo por la mitad to cut something in two ❷ **to break** *(a branch, for example)* ❸ **to crack** *(a nut)* ❹ **to leave** *(a train or person)* ❺ a partir de ese momento from that moment on, a partir de ahora from now on

partirse *REFLEXIVE VERB* [19] **to break** *(a branch, for example)*; la rama se partió the branch broke, me partí un diente I broke a tooth

partitura *NOUN FEM* **score** *(music)*

parto *NOUN MASC* **labour**; estar de parto to be in labour

pasa *NOUN FEM* **raisin**

pasado¹ *NOUN MASC* **past**

pasado², **pasada** *ADJECTIVE* ❶ **last**; el verano pasado last summer ❷ pasados dos días, le llamé after two days, I phoned him ❸ son las diez pasadas it's past ten o'clock, pasado mañana the day after tomorrow ❹ **off**; la leche está pasada the milk is off ❺ quiero el filete muy pasado I want my steak well done

pasaje *NOUN MASC* **ticket**

pasajero, **pasajera** *NOUN MASC, FEM* **passenger**

pasamanos *NOUN MASC (does not change in the plural)* ❶ **banister** ❷ **handrail**

pasaporte *NOUN MASC* **passport**

pasar *VERB* [17] ❶ **to go past**; pasaron por enfrente de mi casa they went past my house, pasar de largo to go straight past, me vió y pasó de largo he saw me and walked straight past me ❷ **to come past**; pasaron por aquí they came past here ❸ **to get past**; no podíamos pasar we couldn't get past ❹ pásate por mi casa por la tarde call round at my house in the evening, el cartero pasa a las diez the postman comes at ten, pasaré por el banco para recoger los impresos I'll call in at the bank to collect the forms ❺ **to go in**; pasaron todos al salón they all went into the living room ❻ **to come in**; pase, por favor please come in ❼ pasar de un lado a otro to go from one side to the other ❽ pasar por to go through, pasar por la aduana to go through customs, el tren no pasa por

Talavera the train does not go through Talavera ❾ pasar algo por algo to put something through something ❿ **to go by**; pasaron tres meses three months went by ⓫ **to pass**; ¿me pasas las tijeras? could you pass me the scissors?, me pasó el balón he passed the ball to me ⓬ **to happen**; ¿qué ha pasado? what's happened?, no le ha pasado nada nothing has happened to him, ¿qué te ha pasado en la mano? what's happened to your hand?, ¿qué te pasa? what's the matter? ⓭ **to spend**; pasaremos las vacaciones en España we'll spend our holidays in Spain, pasé la noche en casa de un amigo I spent the night at a friend's house ⓮ pasarlo bien to have a good time, me lo pasé muy mal en las vacaciones I didn't enjoy myself at all during the holidays ⓯ pasar con to put through, le paso con el Señor Muñoz I'll put you through to Mr Muñoz

pasarse *REFLEXIVE VERB* [17] ❶ **to go off** *(milk or fish)* ❷ **to go bad** *(vegetables or fruit)* ❸ pasarse de un lado a otro to go from one side to the other ❹ **to come (by)**; pásate por la oficina cuando quieras come by my office whenever you want, me pasaré por correos antes de ir a trabajar I'll stop by the post office before going to work ❺ **to go past**; nos pasamos de parada we missed our stop

pasatiempo *NOUN MASC* **pastime**

Pascua *NOUN FEM* ❶ **Easter** ❷ **Christmas**; ¡felices Pascuas! Merry Christmas!

pasear *VERB* [17] ❶ **to go for a walk**; me gusta pasear por la playa I like walking on the beach, sacar al

perro a pasear to take the dog for a walk ❷ pasear en coche to go for a drive, fuimos a pasear en bicicleta we went for a bike ride

pasearse *REFLEXIVE VERB* [17] **to go for a walk**

paseo *NOUN MASC* ❶ **walk**; fuimos a dar un paseo we went for a walk ❷ **stroll** ❸ ir a dar un paseo en coche to go for a drive, ir a dar un paseo en bicicleta to go for a bike ride

pasillo *NOUN MASC* **corridor**

pasión *NOUN FEM* **passion**

pasivo, pasiva *ADJECTIVE* **passive**; un fumador pasivo a passive smoker

paso *NOUN MASC* ❶ **step**; dar un paso adelante to take a step forward, paso a paso step by step ❷ oír pasos to hear footsteps ❸ un paso a nivel a level crossing, un paso elevado a flyover, un paso subterráneo a subway, un paso de peatones a pedestrian crossing, un paso de cebra a zebra crossing ❹ 'ceda el paso' 'give way' ❺ 'prohibido el paso' 'no entry' ❻ te viene de paso, te pilla de paso it's on your way

pasta *NOUN FEM* ❶ **pasta**; prefiero el arroz a la pasta I prefer rice to pasta ❷ **paste** ❸ pastas biscuits ❹ pasta de dientes toothpaste

pastel *NOUN MASC* **cake**

pastelería *NOUN FEM* **cake shop**

pastelero, pastelera *NOUN MASC, FEM* **baker** *(of cakes)*

pastilla *NOUN FEM* ❶ **pill** ❷ una pastilla de jabón a bar of soap

pastor, pastora *NOUN MASC, FEM* **shepherd, shepherdess**

pata¹ NOUN FEM ❶ **leg** ❷ **paw**
- meter la pata (informal) to put your foot in it

patada NOUN FEM **kick**; dar una patada a alguien to kick someone

patata NOUN FEM **potato**; patatas fritas chips, (potato) crisps

paté NOUN MASC **paté**

paternal ADJECTIVE **paternal**

patín NOUN MASC ❶ **roller skate** ❷ **ice skate** ❸ **skateboard** ❹ **pedalo**

patinador, **patinadora** NOUN **skater**

patinaje NOUN MASC ❶ **roller skating** ❷ **ice skating**; patinaje artístico figure skating

patinar NOUN 17 ❶ **to roller skate** ❷ **to ice skate** ❸ **to slip**; patiné en una mancha de aceite I slipped on a patch of oil ❹ **to skid** (a car)

patio NOUN MASC ❶ **patio** ❷ **playground**

pato, **pata**² NOUN MASC, FEM **duck**
- ser un pato (informal) to be very clumsy

patria NOUN FEM **homeland**

patrocinar VERB [17] **to sponsor**

patrón NOUN MASC ❶ **boss** ❷ **landlord**

patrona NOUN FEM **landlady**

patrulla NOUN FEM **patrol**; patrulla de rescate rescue party

patrullera NOUN FEM **patrol boat**

patrullero NOUN MASC ❶ **patrol boat** ❷ **patrol plane** ❸ **patrol car**

pausa NOUN FEM **pause**; hacer una pausa to have a break

pavo, **pava** NOUN MASC, FEM ❶ **turkey** ❷ pavo real peacock

payaso, **payasa** NOUN MASC, FEM **clown**

paz NOUN FEM (PLURAL die **paces**) ❶ **peace** ❷ hacer las paces to make up, nos peleamos pero al final hicimos las paces we had a fight, but we made up in the end ❸ dejar en paz to leave alone, ¡deja mi calculadora en paz! leave my calculator alone!, ¡deja a tu hermano en paz! leave your brother alone!, ¡estos niños nunca me dejan en paz! these children never give me a moment's peace! ❹ en paz descanse rest in peace

PD ABBREVIATION **P.S.** (at the end of a letter)

peaje NOUN FEM **toll**; carretera de peaje toll road

peatón NOUN MASC **pedestrian**

peatonal ADJECTIVE **pedestrian, for pedestrian**

peca NOUN FEM **freckle**

pecado NOUN MASC **sin**

pecho NOUN MASC ❶ **breast**; dar el pecho a un bebé to breastfeed a baby ❷ **chest**

pechuga NOUN FEM **breast**; pechuga de pollo chicken breast

pedal NOUN MASC **pedal**; pedal de arranque kickstart

pedante ADJECTIVE **pompous**

pedazo NOUN MASC **piece**; un pedazo de queso a piece of cheese, hacer pedazos to smash to pieces, hizo pedazos el vaso he smashed the glass to pieces, el jarrón se cayó y se hizo pedazos the vase fell and smashed to pieces

pedir VERB [57] ❶ to ask for; pedir un favor to ask for a favour, pedir ayuda to ask for help, pedir consejo to ask for advice ❷ pedir perdón to apologize ❸ piden medio millón por el cuadro they're asking half a million for the picture, me pidió que le comprase un libro he asked me to buy him a book ❹ pedir hora to ask for an appointment ❺ pedir prestado to ask to borrow, me pidió prestada la moto he asked to borrow my motorbike, pedir dinero prestado to ask to borrow some money, to ask for a loan ❻ to order (in a restaurant); ¿qué vas a pedir? what are you going to order?

pegajoso, pegajosa ADJECTIVE sticky

pegamento NOUN MASC glue

pegar VERB [28] ❶ to hit; me pegó he hit me, pegar una torta a alguien to slap somebody, pegar una patada a alguien to kick somebody, pegar una paliza a alguien to give somebody a beating ❷ pegar un grito to let out a yell ❸ pegar un salto to jump, pegar saltos de alegría to jump for joy ❹ pegarle un susto a alguien to give somebody a fright ❺ to stick; he pegado una foto suya en la pared I've stuck a picture of him on the wall ❻ to glue ❼ (informal) me vas a pegar el resfriado you're going to give me your cold

pegarse REFLEXIVE VERB [28] ❶ to hit each other; empezaron a pegarse they started hitting each other ❷ to stick; este sello no se pega this stamp won't stick

pegatina NOUN FEM sticker

peinado NOUN MASC hairstyle

peinar VERB [17] ❶ to comb ❷ to brush

peinarse REFLEXIVE VERB [17] ❶ to comb your hair ❷ to brush your hair

peine NOUN MASC comb

pela NOUN FEM (informal) penny; no me quedan pelas I haven't got a penny

pelar VERB [17] ❶ to peel (a potato, for example) ❷ pelar a alguien al cero to cut somebody's hair very short

pelarse REFLEXIVE VERB [17] ❶ to peel (from sunburn); se me está pelando la nariz my nose is peeling ❷ (informal) to have your hair cut

peldaño NOUN MASC ❶ step ❷ rung

pelea NOUN FEM ❶ fight ❷ row; tuvo una pelea con su novio she had a row with her boyfriend

pelear VERB [17] ❶ to fight ❷ to quarrel

pelearse REFLEXIVE VERB [17] ❶ to fight; había dos hombres peleándose there were two men fighting ❷ to quarrel; se pelearon por dinero they quarrelled over money, siempre se está peleando con sus padres she's always quarrelling with her parents

película NOUN FEM ❶ film; ¿qué película ponen hoy? what film are they showing today?, una película de terror a horror film, una película de risa a comedy film, una película de suspense a thriller ❷ film (for a camera)

peligro NOUN MASC danger; estar en peligro, correr peligro to be in danger, poner a alguien en peligro to put somebody at risk, fuera de peligro out of danger, un peligro para la salud a health risk, peligro de incendio a fire hazard

peligroso, **peligrosa** *ADJECTIVE* **dangerous**

pelirrojo, **pelirroja** *ADJECTIVE* ❶ **red-haired** ❷ pelo pelirrojo red hair

pellizcar *VERB* [31] **to pinch**

pellizco *NOUN MASC* **pinch**; le di un pellizco en el brazo I pinched her arm

pelo *NOUN MASC* ❶ **hair**; pelo liso/lacio straight hair, pelo rizado curly hair, tengo el pelo negro I've got black hair ❷ un pelo de la barba a whisker ❸ **fur** *(of an animal)*
• salvarse por los pelos *(informal)* to escape by the skin of your teeth
• no se cayó por los pelos he very nearly fell
• ponerle a alguien los pelos de punta *(informal)* to make somebody's hair stand on end
• tomarle el pelo a alguien *(informal)* to pull somebody's leg *(literally: to take somebody's hair)*

pelota *NOUN FEM* **ball**; una pelota de fútbol a football

peluca *NOUN FEM* **wig**

peluche *NOUN MASC* un juguete de peluche a cuddly toy, un osito de peluche a teddy bear

peludo, **peluda** *ADJECTIVE* **hairy**

peluquería *NOUN FEM* **hairdresser's**

peluquero, **peluquera** *NOUN MASC, FEM* **hairdresser**

pena *NOUN FEM* ❶ **shame**; ¡qué pena! what a shame, es una pena que no

puedas venir it's a shame you can't come ❷ **sadness**; me da pena verte llorar it makes me sad to see you cry ❸ Sara me da mucha pena I feel really sorry for Sara ❹ **sentence**; pena de muerte death penalty ❺ valer la pena to be worth it, no vale la pena it's not worth it, vale la pena ver la película the film's worth seeing ❻ penas problems, cuéntame tus penas tell me all your problems
• a duras penas with great difficulty

penalti *NOUN MASC* **penalty**

pendiente *NOUN MASC* **earring**

pendiente *NOUN FEM* **slope**

pendiente *ADJECTIVE* **unresolved**

pene *NOUN MASC* **penis**

penetrar *VERB* [17] **to penetrate**

península *NOUN FEM* **peninsula**

penique *NOUN MASC* **penny**

pensamiento *NOUN MASC* **thought**

pensar *VERB* [29] **to think**; piénsalo bien antes de decidir think about it carefully before deciding anything, pensándolo bien ... on second thoughts ..., pensar en to think about, estaba pensando en ti I was thinking about you, ¿piensas llamarlo? are you thinking of calling him?, pensar mal de alguien to think badly of someone, ¿qué piensas del nuevo entrenador? what do you think of the new coach?

pensión *NOUN FEM* ❶ **pension**; cobrar la pensión to draw your pension, pensión de viudedad widow's pension ❷ **guesthouse** ❸ pensión completa full board, media pensión half board

pensionista NOUN MASC & FEM
pensioner

peor NOUN MASC & FEM el/la peor the
worst one, los/las peores the worst
ones

peor ADJECTIVE ❶ worse; estas son
peores que las de la otra tienda
these are worse than the ones in
the other shop, mucho peor much
worse ❷ worst; mi peor enemigo
my worst enemy, en el peor de los
casos in the worst scenario ❸ peor
para ti it's your loss

peor ADVERB worse; es aún peor it's
even worse, cada vez peor worse
and worse, de mal en peor from bad
to worse, yo bailo peor que tú I'm a
worse dancer than you

pepinillo NOUN MASC gherkin

pepino NOUN MASC cucumber

pequeño, pequeña NOUN MASC, FEM
small boy/small girl

pequeño ADJECTIVE ❶ small; una casa
pequeña a small house, la chaqueta
me está pequeña the jacket's too
small for me ❷ slight; un pequeño
esfuerzo a slight effort ❸ young;
mi hermana pequeña my little
sister

pera NOUN FEM pear

peral NOUN MASC pear tree

percha NOUN FEM ❶ hanger ❷ coat
hook

perder VERB [36] ❶ to lose; he
perdido la cartera I've lost my
wallet, perder la paciencia to lose
patience, perder el conocimiento
to lose consciousness ❷ to miss;
perder el tren to miss the train,
has perdido una gran oportunidad

you've missed a great opportunity
❸ perder la costumbre to get out
of the habit ❹ perder el tiempo to
waste time

perderse REFLEXIVE VERB [36] to get
lost; me he perdido I'm lost, ¿te has
perdido? are you lost?

pérdida NOUN FEM ❶ loss ❷ es una
pérdida de tiempo it's a waste of
time

perdiz NOUN FEM partridge

perdón NOUN MASC pardon

perdón EXCLAMATION excuse me

perdonar VERB [17] ❶ to forgive; no
la he perdonado I haven't forgiven
her ❷ te perdono el castigo I'll
let you off (without a punishment)
❸ ¡perdona!, ¡perdone! sorry!,
(more formal) excuse me!

peregrinación NOUN FEM
pilgrimage; irse de peregrinación
to go on a pilgrimage

perejil NOUN MASC parsley

pereza NOUN FEM laziness

perezoso, perezosa ADJECTIVE lazy

perfeccionar VERB [17] ❶ to
improve ❷ to perfect

perfectamente ADVERB perfectly

perfecto, perfecta ADJECTIVE
perfect

perfil NOUN MASC profile; visto de
perfil from the side

perfume NOUN MASC perfume

perfumería NOUN FEM perfume
shop

periódico NOUN MASC newspaper

Spanish—English

periodismo NOUN MASC **journalism**

periodista NOUN MASC & FEM **journalist**

período, periodo NOUN MASC **period** *(of time)*

periquito NOUN MASC **budgie**

perla NOUN FEM **pearl**

permanecer VERB [35] **❶ to stay** *(in a place)* **❷ to remain**; permanecer callado to remain silent

permanente NOUN FEM **perm**; hacerse la permanente to have your hair permed

permanente ADJECTIVE **permanent**

permanezca, permanezco, *etc* VERB ▶ SEE **permanecer**

permiso NOUN MASC **❶ permission**; darle permiso a alguien para hacer to give someone permission to do **❷** con permiso may I come in?, excuse me *(to get past someone)* **❸ permit**; permiso de trabajo work permit **❹ leave**; estar de permiso to be on leave, un permiso de una semana a week's leave **❺** permiso de conducir driving licence

permitir VERB [19] **❶ to allow**; no nos permitieron pasar they didn't allow us in **❷** no te permito que me contestes I won't have you answering me back **❸** *(when asking permission)* ¿me permite? may I?, ¿me permite una sugerencia? may I make a suggestion? **❹ to make possible**; este proceso permite … this process makes it possible to …

pero CONJUNCTION **but**

perrito NOUN MASC **❶ puppy ❷** perrito caliente hot dog

perro, perra NOUN MASC, FEM **dog**; perro callejero stray dog
• estar de un humor de perros *(informal)* to be in a foul mood

persecución NOUN FEM **❶ pursuit**; salir en persecución de alguien to set off in pursuit of someone **❷ persecution**

perseguir VERB [64] **to pursue**

persiana NOUN FEM **blind**

persistir VERB [19] **to persist**

persona NOUN FEM **❶ person**; una persona importante an important person **❷** personas people, en la sala había diez personas there were ten people in the room

personaje NOUN MASC **❶ character** *(in a book, for example)* **❷ important figure**; un personaje del mundo de la música an important figure in the music world

personal NOUN MASC **staff**

personal ADJECTIVE **personal**

personalidad NOUN FEM **personality**

perspectiva NOUN FEM **❶ perspective ❷ prospect**; hay buenas perspectivas there are good prospects

persuadir VERB [19] **to persuade**

pertenecer VERB [35] **to belong**

pertenezca, pertenezco, *etc* VERB ▶ SEE **pertenecer**

Perú NOUN MASC **Peru**

peruano, peruana NOUN MASC, FEM, ADJECTIVE **Peruvian**

pesa NOUN FEM **weight**; hacer pesas to do weightlifting

pesadilla NOUN FEM **nightmare**

pesado, pesada NOUN MASC, FEM ¡eres un pesado! (informal) you're such a pain!

pesado ADJECTIVE ❶ **heavy** (a box or piece of furniture, for example) ❷ ser muy pesado (informal) to be a pain (a person) ❸ ser muy pesado to be boring (a job or book, for example)

pesar VERB [17] ❶ **to weigh**; peso sesenta kilos I weigh sixty kilos ❷ pesar mucho to be very heavy, puedo llevarlo, pesa poco I can carry it, it's not very heavy, ¿te pesan mucho las bolsas? are the bags too heavy for you?

pesca NOUN FEM **fishing**; ir de pesca to go fishing

pescadería NOUN FEM **fishmonger's**

pescado NOUN MASC **fish**

pescador, pescadora NOUN MASC, FEM **fisherman/fisherwoman**

pescar VERB [31] ❶ **to fish**; ir a pescar to go fishing ❷ **to catch**; no pescamos nada we didn't catch anything

peseta NOUN FEM **peseta** (former Spanish currency replaced by the euro; 500 pesetas = 3.00 euros)

pesimista NOUN MASC & FEM **pessimist**

pesimista ADJECTIVE **pessimistic**

peso NOUN MASC **weight**; perder peso to lose weight, ganar peso to put on weight, peso bruto gross weight, vender al peso to sell by weight

pesquero, pesquera ADJECTIVE **fishing**; la industria pesquera the fishing industry

pestaña NOUN FEM **eyelash**

pétalo NOUN MASC **petal**

petanca NOUN FEM **petanque** (type of bowls)

petardo NOUN MASC **banger**

petróleo NOUN MASC **oil**

petrolero NOUN MASC **oil tanker** (ship)

pez NOUN MASC (PLURAL die peces) **fish** (live); un pez espada a swordfish

piano NOUN MASC **piano**; tocar el piano to play the piano

picado, picada ADJECTIVE ❶ **decayed** (tooth); tengo una muela picada I have a cavity in one of my back teeth ❷ carne picada mince ❸ el mar estaba picado the sea was choppy ❹ (informal) estar picado to be miffed (a person), está picada porque no la llamaste she's a bit miffed that you didn't call her

picadura NOUN FEM **bite, sting**

picante ADJECTIVE **hot** (spicy)

picaporte NOUN MASC **door handle**

picar VERB [31] ❶ **to bite, to sting** ❷ **to mince** (meat) ❸ **to chop** (vegetables) ❹ **to rot** (teeth) ❺ **to be hot** (spicy); esta salsa pica mucho this sauce is too hot ❻ **to itch**; me pica la nariz my nose is itching ❼ me pican los ojos my eyes are stinging

pico NOUN MASC ❶ **beak** ❷ **pick** ❸ **peak** (of a mountain) ❹ **corner** (of a table, for example) ❺ un cuello de pico a V-neck ❻ ... y pico ... and something, fueron tres mil y pico it was three thousand and something, llegaron a las cinco y pico they arrived after five

pida, **pido**, **pidió**, *etc VERB*
▸ SEE **pedir**

pie *NOUN MASC* ❶ **foot**; ir a pie to go on foot ❷ de pie standing, estaban de pie they were standing, ponerse de pie to stand up ❸ **base** *(of a lamp or glass)*

piedra *NOUN FEM* ❶ **stone**; una mesa de piedra a stone table, piedra preciosa precious stone, tener piedras en el riñón to have kidney stones ❷ **flint** *(of a lighter)*

piel *NOUN FEM* ❶ **skin**; tener la piel seca to have dry skin ❷ **peel** ❸ **fur**; un abrigo de pieles a fur coat ❹ **leather**; bolsos de piel leather bags

piensa, **pienso**, *etc VERB*
▸ SEE **pensar**

pierna *NOUN FEM* **leg**

pieza *NOUN FEM* ❶ **piece** ❷ pieza de recambio spare part

pijama *NOUN MASC* **pyjamas**

pila *NOUN FEM* ❶ **pile**; una pila de libros a pile of books ❷ **battery** ❸ **(kitchen) sink**

píldora *NOUN FEM* **pill**

piloto *NOUN MASC & FEM* **pilot**

pimentón *NOUN MASC* ❶ **paprika** ❷ **cayenne pepper**

pimienta *NOUN FEM* **pepper**

pimiento *NOUN MASC* **pepper**; un pimiento rojo a red pepper

pimpón *NOUN MASC* **table tennis**

pincel *NOUN MASC* ❶ **paintbrush** ❷ **make-up brush**

pinchadiscos *NOUN MASC & FEM* *(informal)* **disc jockey**

pinchar *VERB* [17] ❶ **to prick** ❷ **to be prickly** ❸ **to burst** ❹ **to puncture**; creo que hemos pinchado I think we've got a flat tyre ❺ *(informal)* **to give an injection to**

pincharse *REFLEXIVE VERB* [17] ❶ **to burst** ❷ **to puncture**; se me ha pinchado una rueda I've got a flat tyre ❸ **to get miffed**

pinchazo *NOUN MASC* **puncture**; tuvimos un pinchazo we had a puncture

pincho *NOUN MASC* ❶ **small snack bar** ❷ **prickle** *(on a bush)*

pingüino *NOUN MASC* **penguin**

pino *NOUN MASC* **pine tree**; muebles de pino pine furniture

pinta *NOUN FEM* ❶ tiene pinta de oficinista he looks like an office worker, ¡qué pinta más rara! that looks very strange!, la comida tiene muy buena pinta the food looks delicious ❷ **pint**

pintadas *PLURAL NOUN FEM* **graffiti**

pintado, **pintada** *ADJECTIVE* **painted**

pintar *VERB* [17] **to paint**

pintor, **pintora** *NOUN MASC, FEM* **painter**

pintoresco, **pintoresca** *ADJECTIVE* **picturesque**

pintura *NOUN FEM* ❶ **painting**; pintura al óleo oil painting ❷ **pinturas crayons**

pinza *NOUN FEM* ❶ **clothes peg** ❷ **hairgrip** ❸ **pincer** ❹ **dart**; pantalón con pinzas trousers with pleats

pinzas *PLURAL NOUN FEM* **tweezers**

piña NOUN FEM ❶ pineapple ❷ pine cone

pipa NOUN FEM pipe; fumar en pipa to smoke a pipe

piragua NOUN FEM canoe

piragüismo NOUN MASC canoeing

pirámide NOUN FEM pyramid

Pirineos PLURAL NOUN MASC los Pirineos the Pyrenees

piropo NOUN MASC compliment

pirulí NOUN MASC lillipop

pisar VERB [17] ❶ to step; pisar a alguien to step on somebody's foot ❷ 'prohibido pisar el césped' 'keep off the grass'

piscina NOUN swimming pool; la parte honda de la piscina the deep end of the pool, la parte poco profunda de la piscina the shallow end of the pool

piscis NOUN MASC & FEM Pisces; soy piscis I'm Pisces

Piscis NOUN MASC Pisces

piso NOUN MASC ❶ floor; vivo en el tercer piso I live on the third floor ❷ storey; un edificio de cinco pisos a five-storey building ❸ un autobús de dos pisos a double-decker bus ❹ flat; se han comprado un piso they've bought a flat

pista NOUN FEM ❶ track; seguirle la pista a alguien to be on somebody's trail ❷ racecourse ❸ (tennis) court ❹ pista de hielo ice rink, pista de patinaje skating rink ❺ pista de esquí sky slope ❻ pista de despegue runway

pistacho NOUN MASC pistachio

pistola NOUN FEM gun

pitar VERB [17] ❶ to blow a whistle ❷ to sound the horn, to hoot (in a car)

pito NOUN MASC ❶ whistle; tocar el pito to blow the whistle ❷ horn; tocar el pito to sound the horn

pizarra NOUN FEM ❶ blackboard ❷ slate

placa NOUN FEM ❶ plate, sheet (of metal, for example) ❷ placa de matrícula number plate ❸ badge

placer NOUN MASC pleasure

plan NOUN MASC ❶ plan; hacer planes to make plans, ¿qué planes tienes para las vacaciones? what are your plans for the holidays? ❷ (informal) está en plan tirano he's behaving like a tyrant ❸ (informal) viajar en plan económico to travel on the cheap

plancha NOUN FEM ❶ iron ❷ a la plancha grilled ❸ sheet; una plancha de plástico a sheet of plastic

planchar VERB [17] to iron

planear VERB [17] ❶ to plan ❷ to glide

planeta NOUN MASC planet

planificar VERB [17] to plan

plano¹ NOUN MASC ❶ street map; un plano de Madrid a street map of Madrid ❷ plan (of a building)

plano², **plana** ADJECTIVE flat

planta NOUN FEM ❶ plant ❷ floor; la planta baja the ground floor, la sexta planta the sixth floor

plantar VERB [17] to plant

plástico NOUN MASC **plastic**

plata NOUN FEM **silver**; cubiertos de plata silver cutlery

plataforma NOUN FEM ❶ **platform** ❷ plataforma de lanzamiento launching pad

plátano NOUN MASC **banana**

platillo NOUN MASC **saucer**

plato NOUN MASC ❶ **plate**; plato llano dinner plate, plato de postre dessert plate, lavar los platos to wash the dishes ❷ **dish**; plato del día dish of the day, plato combinado complete meal served on a plate ❸ **course**; tomé pescado de primer/segundo plato I had fish for the first/second course

playa NOUN FEM ❶ **beach** ❷ **seaside**; veranear en la playa to spend your summer holidays at the seaside

playera NOUN FEM **canvas shoe**

plaza NOUN FEM ❶ **square**; plaza mayor main square ❷ **market**; los martes hay plaza there's a market on Tuesdays ❸ **seat** (in a bus or train) ❹ **position** (at work); hay plazas vacantes there are vacancies ❺ plaza de toros bullring

plazo NOUN MASC ❶ **period**; el plazo de entrega acaba el once the deadline is the eleventh ❷ plazo de vencimiento expiry date (of a passport, for example) ❸ a corto plazo in the short term, a largo plazo in the long term ❹ pagar algo a plazos to pay for something in instalments

plegar VERB [30] **to fold**

pleno, plena ADJECTIVE ❶ **full** ❷ en pleno verano in the middle of summer, en pleno centro right in the centre

pliega, pliego, pliegue, etc VERB ▸ SEE **plegar**

plomo NOUN MASC ❶ **lead** ❷ (informal) ser un plomo to be really boring ❸ **fuse**; se han fundido los plomos the fuses have blown

pluma NOUN FEM ❶ **pen** ❷ **feather**

plumier NOUN MASC **pencil case**

plural NOUN MASC **plural**; en plural in the plural

plural ADJECTIVE **plural**

población NOUN FEM **population**

pobre NOUN MASC & FEM **poor person**; los pobres the poor, ¡la pobre! poor thing!

pobre ADJECTIVE **poor**; ¡pobre Jaime! poor Jaime!

pobreza NOUN FEM **poverty**

pocilga NOUN FEM **pigsty**; tu habitación está hecha una pocilga your room is a pigsty

poco¹, poca ADJECTIVE ❶ **little**; con poco esfuerzo with little effort, hay poco pan there's not much bread, es poca cosa it's not much ❷ **few**; había pocas personas there were only a few people, pocos días más tarde a few days later

poco², poca PRONOUN ❶ **little**; basta con poco a little is enough, queda poco there's not much left ❷ **few**; vinieron pocos only a few came, pon unos pocos aquí put a few here ❸ un poco a bit, espera un poco wait a bit, me molesta un poco it's a bit uncomfortable, un poco de sal a bit of salt ❹ (referring to time) hace poco not long ago, hace poco que me escribió he wrote to me not long ago, aún voy a tardar un poco it's going to take me a little while yet, falta poco para las cinco it's not long till five now, dentro de poco soon, poco antes de comer shortly before eating **❺** poco a poco little by little

poco³ *ADVERB* **not very much**; habla poco he doesn't talk very much, soy muy poco paciente I'm very impatient, estaban poco interesados they weren't very interested

poder¹ *NOUN MASC* **power**

poder² *VERB* [10] **❶ to be able to** *(but often translated as 'can' in sentences)*; no puedo levantarlo I can't lift it, no pude ir I couldn't go, pueden hacerlo solos they can do it on their own, lo mejor que puedas the best you can, ¿podrás ayudarme? will you be able to help me?, ¿pudiste encontrarlo? were you able to find it? **❷ may** *(asking permission)*; ¿puedo abrir la ventana? may I open the window?, ¿se puede? may I come in?, ¿podría usar tu ordenador? may I use your computer? **❸** *(possibility)* puede que lleguen más tarde they might come later, puede que se haya roto it might have got broken, podía suceder it could happen, has podido romperlo you could have broken it, '¿crees que se habrán olvidado?' – 'puede ser' 'do you think they might have forgotten?' – 'they might have', puede ser que no lo sepan it might be that they don't know, puede ser que se hayan perdido they might have got lost **❹** *(suggesting)* podrías preguntar you could ask,

podríamos comer fuera we could eat out **❺** *(reproaching)* ¡podrías haberlo dicho! you could have said! **❻** no puedo con tanto trabajo I can't cope with so much work **❼** ¡ya no puedo más! I can't carry on! **❽** si puede ser if possible

poderoso, poderosa *ADJECTIVE* **powerful**

podrá, podré, podría, *etc VERB* ▸ SEE **poder²**

podrido, podrida *ADJECTIVE* **rotten**

poema *NOUN MASC* **poem**

poesía *NOUN FEM* **poetry**

poeta *NOUN MASC & FEM* **poet**

póker *NOUN MASC* **poker** *(card game)*

polaco¹ *NOUN MASC* **Polish** *(the language)*

polaco², polaca *NOUN MASC & FEM* **Pole**

polaco *ADJECTIVE* **Polish**

polémico, polémica *ADJECTIVE* **controversial**; una decisión polémica a controversial decision

policía *NOUN MASC & FEM* **police officer**

policía *NOUN FEM* **police**

policíaco, policíaca *ADJECTIVE* novela policíaca detective novel

polideportivo *NOUN MASC* **sports centre**

polilla *NOUN FEM* **moth**

política *NOUN FEM* **❶ politics ❷ policy** *(of a government)*

político, política *NOUN MASC, FEM* **politician**

político *ADJECTIVE* **political**

póliza

póliza NOUN FEM **policy** *(insurance document)*

pollito, pollita NOUN MASC, FEM **chick**

pollo NOUN MASC **chicken**; pollo asado roast chicken

polo NOUN MASC ❶ **pole**; el Polo Norte the North Pole ❷ **ice-lolly**

Polonia NOUN FEM **Poland**

polución NOUN FEM **pollution**

polvo NOUN MASC ❶ **dust**; quitar el polvo a los muebles to dust the furniture ❷ polvos face powder, polvos de talco talcum powder ❸ estar hecho polvo *(informal)* to be all in, después de la excursión nos quedamos hechos polvo we were worn out after the trip, este sofá está hecho polvo this sofa's a wreck

polvorón NOUN MASC **pastry** *(made with almonds; eaten at Christmas time)*

pomada NOUN FEM **ointment**

pomelo NOUN MASC **grapefruit**

pondría, pondrías, *etc VERB*
▸SEE **poner**

poner VERB [11] ❶ **to put**; ponlo encima de la mesa put it on the table, lo puse en el armario I put it in the wardrobe, pusimos diez euros cada uno we put in ten euros each ❷ *(with food)* ¿te pongo más sopa? shall I serve you more soup? ❸ *(in a restaurant)* ¿qué les pongo? what can I get you?, ¿me pone un café? can I have a coffee please? ❹ **to put on**; le puso la silla al caballo she put the saddle on the horse, no le he puesto camiseta

por

al niño I haven't put a vest on the baby ❺ **to put on** *(radio, hi-fi, etc.)*; poner la tele to put on the telly, poner música to put on some music, pon el volumen más alto turn the volume up ❻ poner el despertador to set the alarm clock, puse el despertador a las ocho I set the alarm clock for eight ❼ poner la mesa to lay the table ❽ **to install** ❾ **to fit** *(a carpet)* ❿ *(with names)* ¿qué nombre le vais a poner al niño? what are you going to call the baby?, le pusieron el apodo de 'el Rubio' they nicknamed him 'Blondy' ⓫ poner una película to show a film, ¿qué ponen en el 'Maxin'? what's on at the 'Maxin'?, poner una obra de teatro to put on a play ⓬ poner una tienda to open a shop, poner un negocio to set up a business ⓭ ¿me pone con el señor Sanz? could you put me through to Mr Sanz? *(on the telephone)* ⓮ poner a alguien nervioso to make somebody nervous, poner a alguien triste to make somebody sad, poner a alguien de mal humor to put somebody in a bad mood ⓯ poner atención to pay attention

ponga, pongo, *etc VERB*
▸SEE **poner**

poni NOUN MASC **pony**

popular ADJECTIVE **popular**

por PREPOSITION ❶ **for**; por esa razón for that reason, por ejemplo for example, me ofrecieron dos mil euros por el coche viejo they offered me two thousand euros for my old car, lo hago por tu bien I'm doing it for your own good ❷ **through**; no entra por la ventana it won't go in through the window, me enteré por mi hermana I heard through my sister, pasamos por Toledo we went through Toledo ❸ by; mandar algo por correo to send something by post, viajar por carretera to travel by road ❹ mide tres metros por cuatro it measures three metres by four, cinco por tres son quince five times three is fifteen ❺ por la mañana in the morning ❻ (place) lo dejé por aquí I left it around here somewhere, viven por la Avenida Mayor they live somewhere around Mayor Avenue, ¿por dónde queda la estación? whereabouts is the station?, por todos lados everywhere ❼ per; treinta euros por persona thirty euros per person, a cien kilómetros por hora at a hundred kilometres an hour ❽ in; por escrito in writing, por adelantado in advance ❾ preguntó por ti he asked after you ❿ lo dijeron por la tele they said so on the TV ⓫ andar por la calle to walk along the road, caerse por la escalera to fall down the stairs ⓬ ¿por qué? why? ⓭ por supuesto of course ⓮ por eso no lo hice that's why I didn't do it ⓯ por cierto by the way

porcentaje NOUN MASC **percentage**

porche NOUN MASC **porch**

porción NOUN FEM ❶ **portion**; una porción de tarta a slice of cake ❷ **share**

porque CONJUNCTION **because**

porrón NOUN MASC **wine bottle** (with a long spout from which you drink, holding it as far away from your mouth as possible)

portada NOUN FEM ❶ **title page** (of a book) ❷ **cover** (of a magazine) ❸ **front page** (of a newspaper)

portaequipajes NOUN MASC (does not change in the plural) ❶ **roof rack** ❷ **luggage rack** (on a train)

portarse REFLEXIVE VERB [17] **to behave**; portarse mal to misbehave, ¡pórtate bien! behave yourself!

portátil ADJECTIVE **portable**

portátil NOUN MASC **laptop (computer)**

portazo NOUN MASC dar un portazo to slam the door

portería NOUN FEM **goal**

portero, portera NOUN MASC, FEM ❶ **goalkeeper** ❷ **caretaker** ❸ **porter** ❹ portero automático entry-phone

portorriqueño, portorriqueña NOUN MASC, FEM, ADJECTIVE **Puerto Rican**

Portugal NOUN MASC **Portugal**

portugués[1] NOUN MASC **Portuguese** (the language)

portugués[2], **portuguesa** NOUN MASC, FEM **Portuguese man/woman**

portugués/portuguesa ADJECTIVE **Portuguese**

porvenir NOUN MASC **future**

posar VERB [17] ❶ **to pose** ❷ **to lay** (hand or object)

posarse REFLEXIVE VERB [17] **to land**

poseer VERB [37] ❶ **to own** ❷ **to hold** (a title or record)

posibilidad NOUN FEM ❶ **possibility**; es una posibilidad it's a possibility ❷ tener posibilidades de hacer to have a good chance of doing, no tienen muchas posibilidades de ganar they don't have much chance of winning, ¿qué posibilidades tienen? what are their chances?

posible ADJECTIVE **possible**; a ser posible if possible, no fue posible impedirlo it was impossible to avoid it

posible ADVERB lo más tarde posible as late as possible, hazlo lo mejor posible do the best you can

posición NOUN FEM ❶ **position**; en quinta posición in fifth place ❷ posición social social status

positivo, positiva ADJECTIVE **positive**

postal NOUN FEM **postcard**

postal ADJECTIVE **postal**

poste NOUN MASC ❶ **post** ❷ **pole**

póster NOUN MASC **poster**

posterior ADJECTIVE ❶ **back**; el asiento posterior the back seat, la parte posterior de la casa the back of the house ❷ **subsequent, later**

postilla NOUN FEM **scab**

postizo, postiza ADJECTIVE **false**; dentadura postiza false teeth

postre NOUN MASC **pudding, dessert**; ¿qué hay de postre? what's for pudding?

potable ADJECTIVE agua potable drinking water

potencial ADJECTIVE **potential**

práctica NOUN FEM **practice**; lo aprenderás con la práctica you'll learn with practice, tener mucha práctica to have a lot of practice, he perdido la práctica I'm out of practice, en la práctica in practice

practicar VERB [31] ❶ **to practise**; practicar el violín to practise the violin ❷ practicar deportes to do sports

práctico, práctica ADJECTIVE **practical**

pradera NOUN MASC **grassland**

prado NOUN MASC **meadow**

precaución NOUN FEM ❶ **precaution**; tomar precauciones to take precautions ❷ **caution**; actuar con precaución to act with caution

precedente ADJECTIVE **previous**

precio NOUN MASC **price**; ¿qué precio tiene? how much is it?, precio fijo fixed price, precios de saldo bargain prices, los precios han subido mucho prices have gone up a lot

precioso, preciosa ADJECTIVE ❶ **beautiful** ❷ **precious**; piedras preciosas precious stones

precipicio NOUN MASC **precipice**

precipitación NOUN FEM ❶ **rush**; hacer algo con mucha precipitación to do something in a rush, salió con mucha precipitación he rushed out ❷ precipitaciones rainfall, habrá precipitaciones moderadas there will be moderate rainfall

precipitarse REFLEXIVE VERB [17] ❶ **to rush**; no te precipites don't rush into anything ❷ precipitarse hacia algo to rush towards something

precisamente ADVERB **precisely**

precisión NOUN FEM **precision**

preciso, precisa ADJECTIVE ❶ **precise** ❷ llegaron en el momento preciso they arrived just in time, en este

preciso momento no puedo
I can't right now ❸ **necessary**; si es
preciso if necessary, no es preciso
pagar por adelantado you don't
have to pay in advance, es preciso
que nos aseguremos we must make
sure

predilecto, **predilecta** *ADJECTIVE*
favourite

preescolar *ADJECTIVE* **preschool**

preferencia *NOUN FEM* ❶ **preference**
❷ **right of way**; yo tenía
preferencia I had right of way
❸ **priority**; tener preferencia to
have priority

preferible *ADJECTIVE* **preferable**; ser
preferible a algo to be preferable to
something

preferido, **preferida** *ADJECTIVE*
favourite

preferir *VERB* [14] **to prefer**; preferir
algo a algo to prefer something to
something, preferiría no tener que
ir I'd rather not have to go

prefiera, **prefiero**, *etc VERB*
▸SEE **preferir**

prefijo *NOUN MASC* ❶ **prefix**
❷ **dialling code**; el prefijo de
España the dialling code for Spain

pregunta *NOUN FEM* **question**; hacer
una pregunta to ask a question

preguntar *VERB* [17] **to ask**;
preguntar acerca de, sobre algo
to ask about something, preguntar
por alguien to ask about someone,
me preguntó por tus padres he
asked me about your parents

preguntarse *REFLEXIVE VERB* [17] **to
wonder**; me pregunto si dice la
verdad I wonder if he's telling the
truth

prejuicio *NOUN MASC* **prejudice**;
tener prejuicios contra to be
prejudiced against

prematuro, **prematura** *ADJECTIVE*
premature

premiar *VERB* [17] premiar a alguien
to give somebody a prize

premio *NOUN MASC* **prize**; dar un
premio a alguien to give someone
a prize, ganar un premio to win
a prize, me tocó un premio en
la rifa I won a prize in the raffle,
¿qué dan de premio? what's the
prize?, premio gordo jackpot *(in the
lottery)*

prender *VERB* [18] ❶ **to catch** *(a
criminal)* ❷ **to light** *(a cigarette or
match)* ❸ prenderle fuego a algo to
set something on fire

prensa *NOUN FEM* la prensa the
press, leer la prensa to read the
newspapers

preocupación *NOUN FEM* **worry**

preocupado, **preocupada**
ADJECTIVE **worried**; estar
preocupado por algo to be worried
about something

preocupante *ADJECTIVE* **worrying**

preocupar *VERB* [17] **to worry**;
me preocupan los exámenes I'm
worried about the exams

preocuparse *REFLEXIVE VERB* [17] **to
get worried**; se preocupó porque
no la llamé she got worried because
I didn't phone her

preparación *NOUN FEM*
❶ **preparation** ❷ **training** *(in
sport)* ❸ un trabajador con muy
buena preparación a highly trained
worker

a
b
c
d
e
f
g
h
i
j
k
l
m
n
ñ
o
p
q
r
s
t
u
v
w
x
y
z

preparar *VERB* [17] **❶ to prepare**; preparar la cena to prepare dinner, preparar un examen to prepare for an exam **❷ to train** *(a player or athlete)* **❸ to coach** *(a student)* **❹** preparar la cuenta to draw up the bill

prepararse *REFLEXIVE VERB* [17] **to get ready**

preparativos *PLURAL NOUN MASC* **preparations**

preposición *NOUN FEM* **preposition**

presa *NOUN FEM* **❶ dam ❷ reservoir ❸ prey ❹** ser presa del terror to be seized with panic

presencia *NOUN FEM* **presence**; en presencia de sus padres in front of his parents

presentación *NOUN FEM* **❶ introduction**; hacer las presentaciones to do the introductions **❷ presentation**

presentador, presentadora *NOUN MASC, FEM* **presenter**

presentar *VERB* [17] **❶ to introduce**; te presento a mi novio this is my boyfriend, les presentó a su jefe he introduced them to his boss **❷ to present** *(a programme, for example)* **❸ to submit** *(an application)*

presentarse *REFLEXIVE VERB* [17] **❶ to introduce yourself ❷ to turn up**; se presentaron sin avisar a nadie they turned up without letting anybody know **❸** presentarse voluntario to volunteer **❹** presentarse a un examen to sit an exam **❺** presentarse a un concurso to enter a competition **❻** presentarse para un cargo to apply for a post **❼** presentarse a la presidencia to run for the presidency

presente *NOUN MASC* **present**

preservativo *NOUN MASC* **condom**

presidencia *NOUN FEM* **presidency**

presidente, presidenta *NOUN MASC, FEM* **president**

presión *NOUN FEM* **❶ pressure ❷** cerveza a presión draught beer

preso, presa *NOUN MASC, FEM* **prisoner**

preso *ADJECTIVE* estar preso to be in prison, meter preso a alguien to send somebody to prison

préstamo *NOUN MASC* **loan**; préstamo hipotecario mortgage

prestar *VERB* [17] **❶ to lend**; le presté dinero para el coche I lent him money for the car **❷** ¿me prestas tu abrigo? can I borrow your coat? **❸** prestar atención to pay attention

prestidigitador, prestidigitadora *NOUN MASC, FEM* **conjurer**

presumido, presumida *NOUN MASC, FEM* es un presumido he's so conceited

presumido *ADJECTIVE* **conceited**

presumir *VERB* [19] **to show off**; presumen de casa grande they like to boast about how big their house is, presume de guapa she thinks she's very good-looking

presupuesto *NOUN MASC* **budget**

pretencioso, pretenciosa *ADJECTIVE* **pretentious**

pretender *VERB* [18] **❶ to try**; ¿qué pretendes conseguir? what are you trying to achieve?, pretendía que pagase yo he was trying to make me pay for it ❷ pretender que alguien haga to expect somebody to do, pretende que yo le ayude he expects me to help him

pretexto NOUN MASC **pretext, excuse**; siempre tiene algún pretexto para no hacerlo he always has some excuse or other not to do it

prevenir VERB [15] ❶ to prevent ❷ to warn

prever VERB [16] to forsee

previsto, prevista ADJECTIVE está previsto que vengan mañana they're due to come tomorrow, a la hora prevista at the scheduled time

primavera NOUN FEM **spring**

primer ADJECTIVE **first**
▸ SEE **primero, primera**

primero¹, primera ADJECTIVE, PRONOUN **first**; primera clase first class, el primero de mayo the first of May, (note that 'primero' becomes 'primer' before a masculine singular noun) primer piso first floor, llegar en primer lugar to finish in first position, en primer lugar, no me interesa first of all, I'm not interested

primero² ADVERB **first**; yo estaba primero I was here first, primero vamos a informarnos first of all, let's find out

primicia NOUN FEM ❶ **scoop** (news story) ❷ **first showing** (of film)

primo, prima NOUN MASC, FEM **cousin**

princesa NOUN FEM **princess**

principal ADJECTIVE **main**

príncipe NOUN MASC **prince**

principiante, principianta NOUN MASC, FEM **beginner**

principio NOUN MASC **beginning**; a principios de mes at the beginning of the month, al principio de la temporada at the beginning of the season, un buen principio a good start

prioridad NOUN FEM **priority**

prisa NOUN FEM ❶ **hurry**; tener prisa to be in a hurry, date prisa, que llegamos tarde hurry up or we'll be late ❷ de prisa fast, hacer algo de prisa to do something fast, a toda prisa in a hurry ❸ correr prisa to be urgent, este trabajo corre prisa this job is urgent

prisión NOUN FEM **prison**

prisionero, prisionera NOUN MASC, FEM **prisoner**

prismáticos PLURAL NOUN MASC **binoculars**

privado, privada ADJECTIVE **private**

privar VERB [17] privar a alguien de algo to deprive somebody of something

privarse REFLEXIVE VERB [17] privarse de algo to deprive yourself of something

privilegiado, privilegiada ADJECTIVE **privileged**

privilegio NOUN MASC **privilege**

probable ADJECTIVE **probable**

probador NOUN MASC **changing room**

probar VERB [24] ❶ to try; prueba a abrirlo con esta llave try opening it with this key, es la primera vez que pruebo la comida tailandesa it's the first time I've tried Thai food, probar no cuesta nada there's no harm in trying ❷ **to taste**; ¿has probado la sopa? have you tasted the soup? ❸ **to test** *(brakes, for example)* ❹ **to prove**; no pudo probar su inocencia he could not prove his innocence

probarse REFLEXIVE VERB [24] **to try on**; ¿quiere probárselo? would you like to try it on?

probeta NOUN FEM **test tube**; niño probeta test-tube baby

problema NOUN MASC **problem**; un problema muy importante a major problem

procedente ADJECTIVE **from**; el vuelo procedente de Londres the flight from London

proceder VERB [18] ❶ proceder de algo to come from something ❷ **to proceed**; procedieron con cautela they proceeded with caution

procesador NOUN MASC procesador de textos word processor

procesión NOUN FEM **procession**

proceso NOUN MASC ❶ **process** ❷ **processing**; proceso de datos data processing

procurar VERB [17] procurar hacer to try to do, procura terminarlo para el viernes try to finish it by Friday

producción NOUN FEM **production**

producir VERB [60] ❶ **to produce**; producir coches to produce cars ❷ **to cause**; la tormenta produjo daños the storm caused damage

producto NOUN MASC ❶ **product** ❷ **production**

productor, **productora** NOUN MASC, FEM **producer**

productor ADJECTIVE **producing**; países productores de petróleo oil-producing countries

produje, **produzca**, etc VERB ▸ SEE **producir**

profe NOUN MASC & FEM **teacher** *(informal)*

profesión NOUN FEM **profession**

profesional ADJECTIVE **professional**

profesor, **profesora** NOUN MASC, FEM ❶ **professor**, **lecturer** ❷ **teacher** *(in a secondary school)*

profundidad NOUN FEM **depth**

profundo, **profunda** ADJECTIVE **deep**

programa NOUN MASC ❶ **programme** ❷ **program**; un programa informático a computer program

programador, **programadora** NOUN MASC, FEM **programmer**

programar VERB [17] **to program** *(a computer)*

progresar VERB [17] **to progress**

progreso NOUN MASC **progress**; hacer progresos to make progress

prohibido, **prohibida** ADJECTIVE **forbidden**; está terminantemente prohibido it's strictly forbidden, 'prohibido fumar' 'no smoking', 'prohibido el paso', 'prohibida la entrada' 'no entry', 'prohibido pisar el césped' 'keep off the grass'

prohibir VERB [58] **to prohibit**; se prohíbe la entrada a menores de dieciséis años no admission to persons under 16

prolongar *VERB* [28] **to prolong**

prolongarse *REFLEXIVE VERB* [28] **to go on** (*a meeting or party, for example*)

promedio *NOUN MASC* **average**; un promedio de quince libras por semana an average of fifteen pounds a week

promesa *NOUN FEM* **promise**; no cumplió con su promesa he didn't keep his promise

prometer *VERB* [18] **to promise**; te lo prometo I promise

prometida *NOUN FEM* **fiancée**

prometido *NOUN MASC* **fiancé**

promoción *NOUN FEM* **promotion**

pronombre *NOUN MASC* **pronoun**

pronóstico *NOUN MASC* ❶ **forecast**; pronóstico del tiempo weather forecast ❷ **prognosis**

pronto¹ *ADVERB* ❶ **soon**; tan pronto como sea posible as soon as possible ❷ **quickly**; respondieron muy pronto they answered very quickly ❸ **early**; se marcharon pronto they left early ❹ de pronto all of a sudden

pronto², **pronta** *ADJECTIVE* **prompt**; una pronta respuesta a prompt reply

pronunciación *NOUN FEM* **pronunciation**

pronunciar *VERB* [17] **to pronounce**

propaganda *NOUN FEM* ❶ **advertising**; hacer propaganda de un producto to advertise a product ❷ **propaganda**

propiedad *NOUN FEM* ❶ **property**; propiedad privada private property ❷ ser propiedad de alguien to belong to somebody

propietario, **propietaria** *NOUN MASC, FEM* **owner**

propina *NOUN FEM* **tip**

propio, **propia** *ADJECTIVE* ❶ **own**; mi propio hermano my own brother ❷ la propia Elena lo admitió Elena herself admitted it

proponer *VERB* [11] ❶ **to suggest**; nos propuso ir a cenar fuera he suggested we went out for dinner ❷ **to propose**; proponer una idea to propose an idea, proponer un trato to make a proposition ❸ **to put forward** (*a candidate*)

proponerse *REFLEXIVE VERB* [11] ❶ **to set yourself a goal**; me propuse encontrar un trabajo I set myself the goal of finding a job, siempre consigue lo que se propone he always achieves what he sets out to do ❷ **to decide**; me propuse ir a verlos I decided to go and see them

proporción *NOUN FEM* ❶ **proportion**; en proporción in proportion ❷ proporciones dimensions

proposición *NOUN FEM* **proposal**

propósito *NOUN MASC* **intention**

prórroga *NOUN FEM* ❶ **extension** ❷ **extra time** (*in sports*)

prospecto *NOUN MASC* ❶ **patient information leaflet** (*supplied with medicine*) ❷ **advertising leaflet**

próspero, **próspera** *ADJECTIVE* ❶ **prosperous** ❷ ¡Próspero Año Nuevo! Happy New Year!

prostituta *NOUN FEM* **prostitute**

protagonista *NOUN MASC, FEM*
❶ leading player ❷ leading character

protección *NOUN FEM* protection

protector, **protectora** *NOUN MASC, FEM* protector

protector *ADJECTIVE* ❶ protective ❷ Sociedad Protectora de Animales Society for the Prevention of Cruelty to Animals

proteger *VERB* [3] to protect

protegerse *REFLEXIVE VERB* [3] to protect yourself

protesta *NOUN FEM* protest; en señal de protesta in protest

protestante *NOUN MASC & FEM*

protestante *ADJECTIVE* Protestant

protestar *VERB* [17] to protest

provecho *NOUN MASC* ❶ benefit; sacar provecho de algo to benefit from something ❷ siempre piensa primero en su propio provecho he always thinks of himself first ❸ ¡buen provecho! enjoy your meal!

proveniente *ADJECTIVE* personas provenientes de otros países people from other countries

proverbio *NOUN MASC* proverb

provincia *NOUN FEM* province

provisional *ADJECTIVE* provisional

provocador, **provocadora** *NOUN MASC, FEM* political agitator

provocador *ADJECTIVE* provocative

provocar *VERB* [31] ❶ to provoke (a person) ❷ to cause (an explosion or fire)

proximidad *NOUN FEM* proximity

próximo, **próxima** *ADJECTIVE* ❶ next; la próxima semana next week ❷ en fecha próxima in the near future

proyecto *NOUN MASC* ❶ project ❷ plan; ¿qué proyectos tienes para el verano? what are your plans for the summer? ❸ tengo varios trabajos en proyecto I've got a few jobs lined up

proyector *NOUN MASC* projector

prudente *ADJECTIVE* sensible; sé prudente conduciendo drive carefully

prueba¹ *NOUN FEM* ❶ proof; no tienen pruebas they have no proof ❷ test ❸ hacer la prueba to try, hice la prueba y funcionó I tried and it worked, haz la prueba de limpiarlo con lejía try cleaning it with bleach ❹ a prueba on trial, trabajadores a prueba people working on a trial basis ❺ a prueba de balas bullet-proof, a prueba de agua waterproof

prueba², **pruebo**, *etc VERB* ▸ SEE **probar**

psicólogo, **psicóloga** *NOUN MASC, FEM* psychologist

psiquiatra *NOUN MASC & FEM* psychiatrist

publicar *VERB* [31] to publish

publicidad *NOUN FEM* ❶ publicity ❷ advertising

público¹ *NOUN MASC* ❶ public ❷ audience

público², **pública** *ADJECTIVE* public

pude, **pudo**, *etc VERB* ▸ SEE **poder**²

pudrir *VERB* [59] to rot

pudrirse *REFLEXIVE VERB* [59] **to rot**

pueblo *NOUN MASC* ❶ **village** ❷ **small town** ❸ **people**; el pueblo español the Spanish people

puente *NOUN MASC* ❶ **bridge** ❷ puente aéreo shuttle service ❸ hacer puente take a long weekend (*usually when the Thursday before or the Tuesday after is a public holiday*)

puerco, puerca *NOUN MASC & FEM* **pig**

puerro *NOUN MASC* **leek**

puerta *NOUN FEM* ❶ **door**; puerta principal main door, puerta giratoria revolving door, puerta trasera back door, quedamos en la puerta del cine we arranged to meet outside the cinema ❷ puerta de embarque gate (*in an airport*) ❸ la puerta del jardin the garden gate

puerto *NOUN MASC* ❶ **port**; un puerto pesquero a fishing port ❷ **harbour**; un puerto deportivo a marina

Puerto Rico *NOUN MASC* **Puerto Rico**

puertorriqueño, puertorriqueña *NOUN MASC, FEM, ADJECTIVE* **Puerto Rican**

pues *CONJUNCTION* ❶ pues bien, como te iba diciendo ... well, as I was telling you ..., pues no estoy seguro I'm not sure now, pues mira, ahora no me acuerdo well, look, I can't remember now ❷ ¡pues no vayas! don't go then!, pues si no te gusta el libro, no lo leas if you don't like the book, don't read it then ❸ ¡pues claro! of course!, ¡pues claro que no! of course not!, '¿lo querías tú?' – '¡pues sí!' 'did you want it?' – 'yes, I did!'

puesto¹ *NOUN MASC* ❶ **position**; llegar en primer puesto to finish in first position, sacar el primer puesto en un examen to come top in an exam ❷ **job**; puestos de trabajo jobs, perdió su puesto de trabajo he lost his job, puestos vacantes vacancies, un puesto fijo a permanent job ❸ **post**; un puesto de socorro a first-aid post ❹ **stall** (*in a market*)

puesto *CONJUNCTION* puesto que since

puesto², puesta *ADJECTIVE* ❶ la mesa estaba puesta the table was laid ❷ llevaba el abrigo puesto I had my coat on

pulga *NOUN FEM* **flea**

pulgada *NOUN FEM* **inch**

pulgar *NOUN MASC* **thumb**

pulir *VERB* [19] **to polish**

pulmón *NOUN MASC* **lung**

pulpo *NOUN MASC* **octopus**

pulsar *VERB* [17] ❶ **to press** (*a key or button*) ❷ **to pluck** (*a string*)

pulsera *NOUN FEM* ❶ **bracelet** ❷ **watchstrap**

pulso *NOUN MASC* ❶ **pulse**; le tomó el pulso he took his pulse ❷ tener buen pulso to have a steady hand, me temblaba el pulso my hand was shaking ❸ levantar algo a pulso to lift something with your bare hands, dibujar algo a pulso to draw something freehand ❹ **arm-wrestling contest**

punta *NOUN FEM* ❶ **point** (*of a knife or needle, for example*); acaba en punta it's pointed ❷ **tip** (*of pencil, tongue, finger, etc.*)
• tener algo en la punta de la lengua (*informal*) **to have something on**

the tip of your tongue ❸ end; a la otra punta del pasillo at the other end of the corridor ❹ las puntas: cortarse las puntas to have your hair trimmed, tener las puntas abiertas to have split ends ❺ sacar punta a un lápiz to sharpen a pencil ❻ la hora punta the rush hour

puntada NOUN FEM **stitch**

puntapié NOUN MASC **kick**; darle un puntapié a algo to kick something

puntería NOUN FEM **aim**; tiene buena puntería he's a good shot

puntilla NOUN FEM ❶ **lace edging** ❷ ponerse de puntillas to stand on tiptoe, andar de puntillas to walk on tiptoe

punto NOUN MASC ❶ **point**; un punto de vista a point of view, es mi punto débil it's my weak point, llevan tres puntos de ventaja they're three points ahead, hasta cierto punto up to a point, punto por punto point by point ❷ **dot**; el punto sobre la 'i' the dot on the 'i' ❸ (in punctuation) punto final full stop, punto y coma semicolon ❹ en punto on the dot, las cinco en punto five o'clock sharp, a las dos en punto at two on the dot, llegar en punto to arrive exactly on time ❺ **stitch**; hacer punto to knit, de punto knitted, una falda de punto a knitted skirt ❻ estar a punto de hacer to be about to do ❼ estar algo en su punto to be just right, la carne está en su punto the meat is just right ❽ batir las claras a punto de nieve beat the egg whites until stiff ❾ punto muerto neutral (gear) ❿ punto negro black spot (for accidents), black head (on skin)

puntocom NOUN FEM una puntocom a dot-com company

puntuación NOUN FEM ❶ **punctuation** ❷ **score** (in sports) ❸ **marks** (in an exam)

puntual ADJECTIVE **punctual**; ser puntual to be always on time, llegaron puntuales they arrived on time

puñetazo NOUN MASC **punch**; me dio un puñetazo he punched me, di un puñetazo en la mesa I banged the table with my fist

puño NOUN MASC ❶ **fist** ❷ **cuff** ❸ **handle** (of a tool)

pupila NOUN FEM **pupil**

pupitre NOUN MASC **desk**

puré NOUN MASC ❶ **purée** ❷ **thick soup**; puré de guisantes pea soup ❸ puré de patatas mashed potatoes

puro[1] NOUN MASC **cigar**

puro[2], **pura** ADJECTIVE ❶ **pure** ❷ la pura verdad the simple truth ❸ de puro aburrimiento out of sheer boredom

púrpura ADJECTIVE **purple**

puse, **puso**, etc VERB ▸ SEE **poner**

puzzle NOUN MASC **jigsaw puzzle**

Qq

que¹ PRONOUN ❶ **who**; el hombre que me lo dijo the man who told me, los que están interesados those who are interested ❷ **which**, **that**; el libro que recomendé the book which I recommended, la marca que me gusta the brand (that) I like ❸ el que prefiero the one (that) I prefer

que² CONJUNCTION ❶ **that**; dijo que no lo necesitaba she said (that) she didn't need it, sé que le gusta I know (that) he likes it, nos pidió que le ayudásemos he asked us to help him *('que' is followed by the subjunctive in certain constructions)* ❷ *(in comparisons)* **than**; es más alto que yo he's taller than me ❸ *(for emphasis)* ¡que te he dicho que sí me gusta! I've already told you that I like it!, ¡que es mío! I'm telling you it's mine!, '¿te importa?' – '¡que no!' 'do you mind?' – 'I've already told you that I don't!' ❹ *(expressing surprise)* ¿que tiene veinte años? she's twenty? ❺ *(expressing a wish)* que te mejores pronto get well soon, que pases unas buenas vacaciones have a nice holiday ❻ *(giving an order)* ¡que te calles! shut up!, que pasen show them in ❼ yo que tú if I were you

qué¹ PRONOUN ❶ **what**; ¿qué es eso? what's that?, ¿a qué te refieres?

what are you referring to? ❷ ¿qué? what? ❸ ¿qué tal? how are you doing?, ¿qué tal va? how's it going?, ¿qué hay de nuevo? what's new? ❹ ¡qué va! no way!

qué² ADJECTIVE ❶ **which**; ¿qué abrigo es el tuyo? which coat is yours? ❷ **what** *(in exclamations)*; ¡qué casa tan grande! what a big house!

qué³ ADVERB ¡qué bonito! how nice!, ¡qué egoísta eres! you're so selfish!

quebradero NOUN FEM **worry**

quebrado NOUN MASC **fraction**

quebrar VERB [29] **to break**

quedar VERB [17] ❶ **to be left**; quedan tres paquetes there are three packets left, ¿te queda dinero? do you have any money left?, no queda leche there's no milk ❷ *(in time expressions)* aún quedan dos días there are still two days to go, quedaban quince minutos para el final de la clase it was still fifteen minutes till the end of the class, ¿cuánto tiempo me queda? how much time do I have left?, aún queda tiempo there's still time ❸ *(with distances)* quedaban quince kilómetros there were still fiteen kilometres to go ❹ *(expressing a person's situation)* quedó viudo he was widowed, quedó ciego tras el accidente he was left blind after the accident, quedaron solos they were left alone, quedar en último lugar to end up last ❺ *(talking about the appearance of something)* así queda mejor it's better like this, queda muy feo con esa tela it's horrible with that material ❻ *(arranging meetings)* quedamos en la plaza we arranged to meet in the square, ¿te apetece quedar? would you like to meet?, ¿quedamos para el sábado? shall we meet on Saturday? ❼ *(when talking about clothes, hairstyles, etc.)* me queda apretado it's too tight on me, ¿te queda bien? does it fit you?, esos pantalones te quedan fenomenal those trousers look great on you, ese color te queda muy bien that colour really suits you ❽ *impressions* quiere quedar bien con mi familia she wants to make a good impression on my family ❾ va a quedar mal si no lo hacemos it will look bad if we don't do it, quedamos muy mal con sus padres we made a bad impression on her parents ❿ quedar en algo to agree on something, quedamos en vernos hoy we agreed to see each other today ⓫ *(talking about location)* **to be**; queda cerca de mi casa it's near my house, queda bastante lejos it's quite a long way away, ¿dónde queda la estación? where is the station?

quedarse *REFLEXIVE VERB* [17] ❶ **to stay**; prefiero quedarme en casa I'd rather stay at home, se quedó en la cama he stayed in bed ❷ *(expressing somebody's situation or state)* quedarse ciego to go blind, quedarse calvo to lose your hair, quedarse sin trabajo to lose your job, quedarse viudo to be widowed, quedarse soltero to stay single, quedarse dormido to fall asleep, quedarse callado to remain silent ❸ quedarse con algo to keep something

queja *NOUN FEM* **complaint**; presentar una queja to make a complaint, presentó una queja al gerente por el mal servicio she made a complaint to the manager about the bad service

quejarse *REFLEXIVE VERB* [17] **to complain**; se quejan de la comida they complain about the food, se quejan de que tardamos mucho they complain about how long we take

quemado, quemada *ADJECTIVE* **burnt**

quemadura *NOUN FEM* **burn**

quemar *VERB* [17] ❶ **to burn** ❷ **to scald** ❸ **to be very hot**; la sopa quema mucho the soup's really hot ❹ quemar un motor to burn out an engine ❺ quemar calorías to burn up calories ❻ ¡cómo quema el sol! the sun's scorching!

quemarse *REFLEXIVE VERB* [17] ❶ **to burn yourself**; me quemé la mano I burnt my hand ❷ **to scald** ❸ **to get burned**; el mantel se quemó un poco the tablecloth got slightly burnt, ¡cómo te has quemado! you've really got burnt! *(in the sun)* ❹ **to burn down**; la casa se quemó toda the house burned down

querer *VERB* [12] ❶ **to want**; ¿qué quieres para tu cumpleaños? what do you want for your birthday?, no quiero ir al cine I don't want to go to the cinema ❷ **to love**; te quiero I love you ❸ *(making an offer)* ¿quieres beber algo? would you like something to drink?, si quieres voy más tarde if you like I'll go later ❹ *(asking for something in a shop, cafe, etc.)* quisiera ver plumas I would like to see some pens, yo quiero un café I'll have a coffee, quisiera reservar una mesa para cuatro I'd like to book a table for four ❺ *(asking somebody to do something)* ¿quieres apagar la tele, por favor? would you mind switching off the television, please?

❻ querer decir to mean, ¿qué quieres decir? what do you mean?

quererse *REFLEXIVE VERB* [17] **to love each other**

querido, querida *ADJECTIVE* **dear**; Querido Pablo Dear Pablo *(starting a letter)*

querrá, querré, querría, *etc VERB* ▸ SEE **querer**

queso *NOUN MASC* **cheese**; queso rallado grated cheese

quiebra *NOUN FEM* **bankruptcy**

quien *PRONOUN* **❶** **who**; no fui yo quien lo dijo it wasn't me who said it, ellos son quienes no quisieron they're the ones who didn't want to *(sometimes not translated)* la persona con quien hablé the person I spoke to **❷** **whom, who**; Isabel, a quien vi ayer Isabel, whom I saw yesterday

quién *PRONOUN* **❶** **who**; ¿quién es? who is it?, ¡quién lo hubiese dicho! who would have said! **❷** **which**; ¿quién de vostros es Carlos? which of you is Carlos? **❸** ¿de quién? whose?, ¿de quién es esta cartera? whose is this wallet?

quienquiera *PRONOUN* **whoever**

quiera, quiere, *etc VERB* ▸ SEE **querer**

quieto, quieta *ADJECTIVE* **still**; ¡estate quieto! keep still!

química¹ *NOUN FEM* **chemistry**

químico, química² *NOUN MASC & FEM* **chemist**

químico *ADJECTIVE* **chemical**

quince *NUMBER* **❶** **fifteen**; tiene quince años he's fifteen (years old) **❷** quince días a fortnight **❸** **fifteenth** *(in dates)*; hoy estamos a quince it's the fifteenth today

quinceañero, quinceañera *NOUN MASC, FEM* **teenager**

quincena *NOUN FEM* una quincena a fortnight, la primera quincena de mayo the first two weeks in May

quiniela *NOUN FEM* **pools coupon**; rellenar una quiniela to fill in a pools coupon, jugar a las quinielas to do the pools

quinientos, quinientas *NUMBER* **five hundred**; quinientos cinco five hundred and five

quinto, quinta *ADJECTIVE* **fifth**; el quinto piso the fifth floor, llegar en quinto lugar to finish in fifth position

quiosco *NOUN MASC* **❶** **news-stand** **❷** el quiosco de los helados the ice cream stand **❸** el quiosco de bebidas the drinks stand **❹** **kiosk**

quiosquero, quiosquera *NOUN MASC, FEM* **❶** **newspaper vendor** **❷** **kiosk vendor**

quirúrgico, quirúrgica *ADJECTIVE* **surgical**

quise, quisiera, quiso, *etc VERB* ▸ SEE **querer**

quitaesmalte *NOUN MASC* **nail varnish remover**

quitanieves *NOUN MASC* **snowplough**

quitar *VERB* [17] **❶** **to take off**; quita los pies de la mesa take your feet off the table, no puedo quitar la tapa I can't get the lid off **❷** le quité los zapatos al niño I took the child's shoes off **❸** quitarle algo

a
b
c
d
e
f
g
h
i
j
k
l
m
n
ñ
o
p
q
r
s
t
u
v
w
x
y
z

a alguien to take something from someone, le quitaron la cartera they took his wallet **4 to take away**; le han quitado el carnet de conducir they've taken his driving licence away, quita esa silla de ahí take that chair away from there **5 to remove**; quitar la suciedad to remove the dirt, quitar el polvo to dust

quitarse *REFLEXIVE VERB* [17] **1 to come out** *(a stain, for example)* **2 to go away** *(a pain)* **3** quitarse algo to take something off, se quitó el abrigo he took his coat off

quizá, quizás *ADVERB* **perhaps**

rábano *NOUN MASC* **radish**
• me importa un rábano *(informal)* I couldn't care less *(literally: it matters a radish to me)*

rabia *NOUN FEM* **1 rabies 2** me da mucha rabia it really annoys me, me da mucha rabia llegar tarde I get very annoyed when I'm late, le dio mucha rabia que no se lo dijeran it really annoyed him that they didn't tell him **3** tenerle rabia a alguien to have it in for someone **4** con rabia angrily

rabo *NOUN MASC* **tail**

racha *NOUN FEM* **1** una racha de mala suerte a spell of bad luck, pasar una mala racha to go through a bad patch, tener una buena racha to be on a winning streak **2 gust** *(of wind)*

racimo *NOUN MASC* **bunch**; un racimo de uvas a bunch of grapes

ración *NOUN FEM* **portion**; una ración de gambas a portion of prawns *(in a tapas bar)*

racionar *VERB* [17] **to ration**

racismo *NOUN MASC* **racism**

racista *NOUN MASC & FEM*

racista *ADJECTIVE* **racist**

radar *NOUN MASC* **radar**

radiación *NOUN FEM* **radiation**

radiactivo, **radiactiva** ADJECTIVE **radioactive**

radiador NOUN MASC **radiator**

radio¹ NOUN FEM **radio**; escuchar la radio to listen to the radio, poner la radio to switch on the radio

radio² NOUN MASC **radius**

radiografía NOUN FEM **X-ray**; hacerse una radiografía to have an X-ray taken

ráfaga NOUN FEM ❶ **gust**; una ráfaga de viento a gust of wind ❷ una ráfaga de ametralladora a burst of machine-gun fire

raíz NOUN FEM ❶ **root**; echar raíces to take root ❷ raíz cuadrada square root ❸ a raíz de as a result of

rallado, **rallada** ADJECTIVE ❶ **grated** ❷ pan rallado breadcrumbs

rallador NOUN MASC **grater**

rallar VERB [17] **to grate**

rama NOUN FEM **branch**
• irse por las ramas to beat about the bush

ramo NOUN MASC ❶ **bunch** (of flowers) ❷ **bouquet**

rampa NOUN FEM **ramp**; rampa de lanzamiento launch pad

rana NOUN FEM **frog**

ranura NOUN FEM **coin slot**

rape NOUN MASC ❶ **monkfish** ❷ llevar el pelo cortado al rape to have your hair closely cropped

rápidamente ADVERB **quickly**

rápido¹ NOUN MASC **express train**

rápido ADVERB **fast**, **quickly**; todo lo rápido que podía as fast as I possibly could

rápido², **rápida** ADJECTIVE ❶ **quick**, **fast**; comida rápida fast food ❷ **rapid**

raqueta NOUN FEM ❶ **racket** ❷ **snowshoe**

raro, **rara** ADJECTIVE ❶ **strange**; ¡qué raro que no hayan llamado! how strange they haven't called! ❷ **rare**; es raro que llueva en esa zona it's rare for it to rain in that area

rascacielos NOUN MASC (does not change in the plural) **skyscraper**

rascar VERB [31] **to scratch**

rascarse REFLEXIVE VERB [31] **to scratch yourself**; se rascó la nariz he scratched his nose

rasgar VERB [28] **to tear**

rasguño NOUN MASC **scratch**

rastrillo NOUN MASC **rake**

rastro NOUN MASC ❶ **trail**; sin dejar rastro without a trace ❷ **flea market**

rata NOUN FEM **rat**

ratero, **ratera** NOUN MASC, FEM ❶ **pickpocket** ❷ **petty thief**

rato NOUN MASC ❶ **while**; tardaré un rato en hacerlo it will take me a while to do it, después de un rato after a while, dentro de un rato in a while, ya hace rato que se han ido they went a while ago, al rato after a while, al poco rato soon afterwards ❷ pasar el rato to kill time ❸ pasar un buen rato to have a good time ❹ ratos libres spare time

ratón NOUN MASC **mouse**

raya NOUN FEM ❶ **line** ❷ **dash** (in punctuation) ❸ **parting** (in your hair); **hacerse la raya** to part your hair ❹ **a rayas** striped, stripy (a dress or material, for example), **una falda a rayas** a stripy skirt ❺ **skate** (fish)

rayar VERB [17] ❶ **to scratch** ❷ **rayar en** to border on, **raya en lo ridículo** it's bordering on the ridiculous

rayo NOUN MASC ❶ **ray**; **un rayo de luz** a ray of light ❷ **flash of lightning** ❸ **un rayo láser** a laser beam ❹ **rayos X** X-rays

raza NOUN FEM ❶ **race** ❷ **breed**; **un perro de raza** a pedigree dog

razón NOUN FEM ❶ **reason**; **por alguna razón** for some reason, **¿por qué razón se enfadó?** why did he get cross?, **con razón** with good reason, **por razones de salud** for medical reasons ❷ **tener razón** to be right, **tienes razón** you're right, **no tienes razón en eso** you're wrong about that, **darle la razón a alguien** to agree that somebody is right ❸ **reason**; **perder la razón** to lose your mind ❹ **razón: 279452** call 279452 for information

razonable ADJECTIVE **reasonable**

reacción NOUN FEM **reaction**

reacio, reacia ADJECTIVE **reluctant**

reactor NOUN MASC ❶ **jet** ❷ **reactor**

real ADJECTIVE ❶ **real** ❷ **true**; **una historia real** a true story ❸ **royal**

realidad NOUN FEM ❶ **reality**; **hacerse realidad** to become true ❷ **en realidad** actually

realista ADJECTIVE ❶ **realistic**; **es muy poco realista** he's very unrealistic ❷ **royalist**

realizador, realizadora NOUN MASC, FEM **producer**

realizar VERB [22] ❶ **to carry out** (a task) ❷ **to make** (a visit or trip) ❸ **to fulfil** (a dream)

realizarse REFLEXIVE VERB [22] ❶ **to come true** (a dream) ❷ **to fulfil yourself**

realmente ADVERB **really**

rebaja NOUN FEM ❶ **reduction**; **hacer una rebaja** to give a reduction, **me hizo una rebaja de diez euros** he gave me a ten euro reduction, **lo rebajó a cuarenta euros** he reduced it to forty euros ❷ **rebajas** sales, **esa tienda está de rebajas** this shop has a sale on

rebajar VERB [17] ❶ **to bring down** (prices) ❷ **to reduce** (an article); **todas las faldas están rebajadas** all the skirts are reduced ❸ **rebajar peso** to lose weight

rebanada NOUN FEM **slice**

rebaño NOUN MASC ❶ **flock** (of sheep) ❷ **herd** (of goats)

rebeca NOUN FEM **cardigan**

rebelarse REFLEXIVE VERB [17] **to rebel**

rebelde NOUN MASC & FEM **rebel**

rebelde ADJECTIVE ❶ **rebel** ❷ **unruly** ❸ **una tos rebelde** a persistent cough

rebelión NOUN FEM **rebellion**

rebobinar VERB [17] **rewind**

rebotar *VERB* [17] ❶ to bounce; la pelota rebotó en el poste the ball bounced off the post ❷ to ricochet

rebuznar *VERB* [17] to bray

recado *NOUN MASC* ❶ message; no han dejado recado they didn't leave a message ❷ errand; hacer un recado to run an errand

recalentar *VERB* [29] reheat

recambio *NOUN MASC* ❶ spare part ❷ refill (for a pen)

recargable *ADJECTIVE* rechargeable

recargar *VERB* [17] ❶ to recharge (batteries, etc) ❷ to top up (mobile phones)

recepción *NOUN FEM* reception

recepcionista *NOUN MASC & FEM* receptionist

receta *NOUN FEM* ❶ recipe ❷ prescription

recetar *VERB* [17] to prescribe

rechazar *VERB* [17] to turn down, to reject

recibidor *NOUN MASC* entrance hall

recibir *VERB* [19] ❶ to receive; he recibido una carta de Lola I've received a letter from Lola ❷ to get; recibí una llamada del editor I got a phone call from the editor ❸ recibir a alguien con los brazos abiertos to welcome somebody with open arms ❹ ir a recibir a alguien to go to meet somebody, fuimos a recibirlos a la estación we went to meet them at the station ❺ (ending a letter) recibe un fuerte abrazo best wishes, reciba un cordial saludo yours sincerely

recibo *NOUN MASC* receipt

reciclar *VERB* [17] recycle

recién *ADVERB* ❶ pasteles recién hechos freshly baked cakes, 'recién pintado' 'wet paint' ❷ un recién nacido a newborn baby, los recién casados the newly-weds, los recién llegados the newcomers

reciente *ADJECTIVE* recent

recientemente *ADVERB* recently

recipiente *NOUN MASC* container

recitar *VERB* [17] to recite

reclamación *NOUN FEM* ❶ complaint; hacer una reclamación to make a complaint ❷ claim; hacer una reclamación al seguro to make a claim on insurance

reclamar *VERB* [17] ❶ to complain ❷ to demand (rights, money)

recoger *VERB* [3] ❶ to pick up; recoge ese papel del suelo pick up that piece of paper off the floor, fui a recogerlos a la estación I went to pick them up from the station ❷ to tidy up; tienes que recoger tu habitación you have to tidy up your room ❸ recoger la mesa to clear the table ❹ to collect (money or signatures) ❺ to pick (fruit or flowers)

recogerse *REFLEXIVE VERB* [3] recogerse el pelo to tie your hair back

recogida *NOUN FEM* collection

recomendación *NOUN FEM* ❶ recommendation ❷ reference (for a job)

recomendar *VERB* [29] to recommend

recompensa *NOUN FEM* reward

recompensar *VERB* [17] **to reward**

reconciliarse *REFLEXIVE VERB* [17] reconciliarse con alguien **to make it up with somebody**

reconocer *VERB* [35] **❶ to recognize**; al principio no la reconocí I didn't recognize her to start with **❷ to admit** *(a mistake)* **❸ to examine** *(a patient)*

reconocimiento *NOUN MASC* **❶** reconocimiento médico **medical examination ❷ reconnaissance**

reconozca, *etc VERB* ▸ SEE **reconocer**

récord *NOUN MASC* **record**

recordar *VERB* [24] **❶ to remember**; si mal no recuerdo if I remember rightly, recuerdo que terminamos a las tres I remember that we finished at three **❷ to remind**; me recuerda mucho a ella he reminds me of her a lot **❸** recordarle a alguien que haga algo **to remind somebody to do something**, recuérdale que traiga los papeles remind him to bring the papers

recorrer *VERB* [17] **❶ to cover** *(a distance)* **❷ to travel around** *(a country)* **❸ to go round** *(an exhibition, museum, etc)*

recreo *NOUN MASC* **break** *(at school)*

recta¹ *NOUN FEM* **straight line**

rectángulo *NOUN MASC* **rectangle**

recto, recta² *ADJECTIVE* **❶ straight ❷ honest**

recto *ADVERB* seguir todo recto **to carry straight on**

recuerda, recuerdo¹, *etc VERB* ▸ SEE **recordar**

recuerdo² *NOUN MASC* **❶ memory**; tengo buenos recuerdos I've got happy memories **❷ souvenir**; 'recuerdo de España' 'souvenir from Spain' **❸** recuerdos **regards**, dale recuerdos a tu hermana de mi parte say hello to your sister from me

recuperar *VERB* [17] **❶ to recover** *(money, strength)* **❷** recuperar tiempo **to make up for lost time**

recuperarse *REFLEXIVE VERB* [17] recuperarse de una enfermedad **to recover from an illness**

recurso *NOUN MASC* **resources**; los recursos naturales **natural resources**

red *NOUN FEM* **❶ net ❷ network ❸** la Red **the Net** *(Internet)*
• caer en las redes de alguien **to fall into sombody's clutches**

redacción *NOUN FEM* **❶ essay ❷ editorial team**

redactor, redactora *NOUN MASC, FEM* **editor**

redondo, redonda *ADJECTIVE* **round**; en números redondos **in round figures**

reducción *NOUN FEM* **reduction**

reducir *VERB* [60] **to reduce**

reduje, reduzca, reduzco, *etc VERB* ▸ SEE **reducir**

reembolsar *VERB* [17] **to refund**

reembolso *NOUN MASC* **refund**

reemplazar *VERB* [22] reemplazar a alguien **to stand in for somebody**

reemplazo *NOUN MASC* **replacement**

referencia *NOUN FEM* **reference**; hacer referencia a to refer to

referirse *REFLEXIVE VERB* [14] referirise a to refer to, se refiere a ti she's referring to you

refiera, **refiero**, **refiramos**, **refirió**, *etc VERB* ▸ SEE **referirse**

reflejar *VERB* [17] **to reflect**

reflejarse *REFLEXIVE VERB* [17] **to be reflected**

reflejo *NOUN MASC* ❶ **reflection** ❷ reflejos highlights ❸ reflejos reflexes

reflexión *NOUN FEM* **reflection**

reflexionar *VERB* [17] **to reflect on**; después de reflexionarlo bien after thinking it over

reforestación *FEM* **reforestation**

reforma *NOUN FEM* ❶ **reform** *(of laws, system, etc)* ❷ **alteration** *(to a house, etc)*; 'cerrado por reformas' 'closed for repairs'

reformar *VERB* [17] ❶ **to reform** *(a law, system, etc)* ❷ **to renovate** *(a house, etc)*; reformarla casa to do up the house

refrán *NOUN MASC* **saying**

refrescante *ADJECTIVE* **refreshing**

refrescar *VERB* [31] **to refresh**

refresco *NOUN MASC* **soft drink**

refrigerio *NOUN MASC* **light refreshments**

refugiado, **refugiada** *NOUN MASC, FEM* **refugee**

refugiarse *REFLEXIVE VERB* [17] refugiarse de to take refuge from

refugio *NOUN MASC* **shelter**; dar refugio a alguien to give somebody shelter, un refugio de montaña a mountain refuge

regadera *NOUN FEM* **watering can**
• estar como una regadera *(informal)* to be raving mad *(literally: to be like a watering can)*

regalar *VERB* [17] ❶ **to give** *(as a present)*; mis padrinos me han regalado un reloj my godparents have bought me a watch, ¿qué vas a regalarle por Navidad? what are you going to get her for Christmas? ❷ **to give away**; me ha regalado su abrigo he's given his coat to me, ¿te gusta? te lo regalo do you like it? you can have it

regalo *NOUN MASC* ❶ **present**; regalo de cumpleaños birthday present ❷ compre dos y llévese uno de regalo buy two and get one free

regañar *VERB* [17] ❶ **to tell off**; mi madre me regañó por llegar tarde my mother told me off because I got home late ❷ **regañar con alguien** to quarrel with somebody, ha regañado con su hermano he's had an argument with his brother

regar *VERB* [30] **to water**

régimen *NOUN MASC* **diet**; ponerse a régimen to go on a diet

región *NOUN FEM* **region**

regional *ADJECTIVE* **regional**

registrar *VERB* [17] ❶ **to search**; nos registraron we were searched, la policía registró la casa the police searched the house ❷ **to go through**; me registró todos los papeles he went through all my papers ❸ **to register** *(a birth, for example)* ❹ **to record** *(temperature)*

registrarse *REFLEXIVE VERB* [17]
❶ **to register** ❷ **to check in**;
she checked in at five o'clock se
registró a las cinco

registro *NOUN MASC* ❶ **register** ❷ el
registro civil the registry office
❸ **search**

regla *NOUN FEM* ❶ **ruler** *(for
measuring)* ❷ **rule**; por regla
general as a general rule ❸ estar
con la regla to have your period

reglamento *NOUN MASC* **regulations**

regresar *VERB* [17] **to return**

regreso *NOUN MASC* **return**

regular *ADJECTIVE* ❶ **regular** ❷ **poor**
(mark) ❸ de tamaño regular
medium-sized ❹ por lo regular as a
general rule

regular *ADVERB* '¿qué tal está tu
padre?' – 'regular' 'how's your
father?' – 'so-so'

regularidad *NOUN FEM* **regularity**;
con regularidad regularly

rehacer *VERB* [7] ❶ rehacer algo to do
something again ❷ rehízo su vida
she rebuilt her life

reina *NOUN FEM* **queen**

reinado *NOUN MASC* **reign**; durante el
reinado del rey Juan Carlos during
the reign of King Juan Carlos

reinar *VERB* [17] **to reign**

reino *NOUN MASC* **kingdom**

Reino Unido *NOUN MASC* **United
Kingdom**

reír *VERB* [61] **to laugh**; echarse a reír
to start laughing

reírse *REFLEXIVE VERB* [61] reírse de
to laugh about, siempre se están
riendo de mí they're always
laughing at me, reírse a carcajadas
to roar with laughter

reja *NOUN FEM* ❶ **railing** ❷ **grille**;
estar entre rejas to be behind bars

relación *NOUN FEM* ❶ **relationship**
❷ relaciones públicas public
relations ❸ **connection**; en
relación con mix with *(people)*

relacionado, relacionada
ADJECTIVE **related**

relacionar *VERB* [17] **to relate**;
relacionar algo con algo to relate
something to something

relacionarse *REFLEXIVE VERB* [17] **to
be related** *(facts, for example)*;
relacionarse con to mix with
(a person)

relajar *VERB* [17] **to relax**

relajarse *REFLEXIVE VERB* [17] **to relax**

relámpago *NOUN MASC* **flash of
lightning**
• como un relámpago like greased
lightning

religión *NOUN FEM* **religion**

religioso, religiosa *ADJECTIVE*
religious

rellenar *VERB* [17] ❶ rellenar un
impreso to fill in a form ❷ **to fill up**
❸ **to stuff** *(a chicken, for example)*

relleno¹ *NOUN MASC* ❶ **filling**
❷ **stuffing**

relleno², rellena *ADJECTIVE* ❶ **filled**
❷ **stuffed** *(peppers, for example)*

reloj *NOUN MASC* ❶ **clock**; un reloj
despertador an alarm clock
❷ **watch**; un reloj de pulsera a

wristwatch, mi reloj va atrasado my watch is slow

relojería *NOUN FEM* **watchmaker's**

remar *VERB* [17] **to row**

remate *NOUN MASC* **❶ smash** (*in tennis*) **❷ finish** (*in football*); un remate de cabeza a header **❸ end** (*of a pole, for example*) **❹ top** (*of a tower, for example*) **❺** y para remate and to cap it all
• loco de remate (*informal*) completely nuts

remediar *VERB* [17] **❶ to remedy ❷** no lo puede remediar he can't help it, no pudimos remediarlo we couldn't do anything about it

remedio *NOUN MASC* **❶ remedy**; remedios naturales natural remedies **❷** si no queda más remedio if there's no other alternative, no queda más remedio que aguantarse we had to put up with it, there was nothing else we could do, no tuvimos más remedio que ir we had no other option but to go, ¡qué remedio me queda! what else can I do!, eso ya no tiene remedio there's nothing we can do about it now

remendar *VERB* [29] **to mend**

remite *NOUN MASC* **return address**

remitente *NOUN MASC & FEM* **sender** (*of a letter*)

remo *NOUN MASC* **oar**

remojar *VERB* [17] **to soak**

remojo *NOUN MASC* poner algo en remojo to soak something

remolacha *NOUN FEM* **beetroot**

remolcar *VERB* [31] **to tow**

remolino *NOUN MASC* **whirlpool**

remolque *NOUN MASC* **❶ trailer ❷** llevar algo a remolque to tow something

remorder *VERB* [38] aún me remuerde la conciencia I still feel guilty about it

remoto, remota *ADJECTIVE* **remote**

remover *VERB* [38] **❶ to stir** (*a sauce, for example*) **❷ to toss** (*a salad*) **❸ to turn over** (*soil*)

remueva, remuevo, *etc VERB* ▸SEE **remover**

renacuajo *NOUN MASC* **tadpole**

rencor *NOUN MASC* guardarle rencor a alguien to bear someone a grudge

rendición *NOUN FEM* **surrender**

rendimiento *NOUN MASC* **performance** (*effectiveness*)

rendir *VERB* [57] **❶** rendirle homenaje a alguien to pay tribute to someone **❷** ayer me rindió mucho en el trabajo I managed to get a lot done yesterday at work

rendirse *REFLEXIVE VERB* [57] **to surrender**

RENFE *ABBREVIATION FEM* (*short for Red Nacional de Ferrocarriles Españoles*) **the Spanish national rail network**

renglón *NOUN MASC* **line**

renovable *ADJECTIVE* **renewable**

renovar *VERB* [17] **❶ to renew** (*a passport, licence*) **❷ to renovate** (*a house, a room*) **❸ to update** (*your clothes*)

renta *NOUN FEM* **❶ rent ❷ income**

a
b
c
d
e
f
g
h
i
j
k
l
m
n
ñ
o
p
q
r
s
t
u
v
w
x
y
z

rentable ADJECTIVE **profitable**

renunciar VERB [17] renunciar a to renounce, to give up, renunciar a un puesto to resign from a job

reñir VERB [17] ❶ to argue; reñircon alguien to argue with somebody ❷ reñira alguien to tell somebody off

reparación NOUN FEM **repair**; taller de reparaciones repair shop

reparar VERB [17] ❶ to repair ❷ to mend

repartir VERB [19] ❶ to deliver ❷ to hand out (leaflets, for example) ❸ to distribute; lo repartiremos entre todos nosotros we'll share it between us

reparto NOUN MASC ❶ delivery; reparto a domicilio home delivery service ❷ distribution; hacer el reparto del dinero to share out the money

repasar VERB [17] ❶ to revise; repasar los apuntes to revise your notes ❷ to check through (a list)

repaso NOUN MASC ❶ revision; dar un repaso a los apuntes to revise your notes ❷ check (for mistakes)

repente IN PHRASE de repente all of a sudden

repentino, repentina ADJECTIVE **sudden**

repetición NOUN FEM **repetition**

repetición de la jugada NOUN FEM **action replay**

repetir VERB [57] to repeat; ¿quieres repetir? would you like a second helping?

repisa NOUN FEM ❶ ledge (of window) ❷ mantelpiece (of chimney)

repita, repitió, repito, etc VERB ►SEE **repetir**

repleto, repleta ADJECTIVE **full up**; estar repleto de algo to be packed with something, una sala repleta de gente a room packed with people

repollo NOUN MASC **cabbage**

reponer VERB [11] ❶ to replace ❷ to repay ❸ reponer fuerzas to get your strength back

reponerse REFLEXIVE VERB [11] to recover; cuando me repuse del susto when I recovered from the shock

reportaje NOUN MASC ❶ article (in a newspaper) ❷ report (on TV)

reportero, reportera NOUN MASC, FEM **reporter**

reposar VERB [17] ❶ to rest ❷ dejar reposar to leave to stand

reposo NOUN MASC **rest**

repostería NOUN FEM **confectionery**

representante NOUN MASC & FEM **representative**

representar VERB [17] ❶ to represent ❷ representar una obra to perform a play, representar un papel to play a part

reproducción NOUN FEM **reproduction**

reproducir VERB [60] to reproduce

reproducirse REFLEXIVE VERB [60] to reproduce

reproductor NOUN MASC **player**; reproductor de MP3 MP3 player

reptil NOUN MASC **reptile**

república NOUN FEM **republic**

República Checa NOUN FEM la República Checa the Czech Republic

repuesto NOUN MASC **spare part**; una rueda de repuesto a spare wheel

repugnante ADJECTIVE **disgusting**

repulsivo, repulsiva ADJECTIVE **repulsive**

reputación NOUN FEM **reputation**

requisito NOUN MASC **requirement**

resaca NOUN FEM **hangover**

resaltar VERB [17] ❶ **to stand out** (colours) ❷ **to stress** (the strong points)

resbaladizo, resbaladiza ADJECTIVE **slippery**

resbalar VERB [17] **to slip**

resbalarse REFLEXIVE VERB [17] **to slip**

rescatar VERB [17] **to rescue**

rescate NOUN MASC **rescue**; una operación de rescate a rescue operation

reserva NOUN FEM ❶ **reservation**; hacer una reserva to make a reservation ❷ **reserve**; jugadores de reserva reserve players, una reserva natural a nature reserve ❸ tengo otro de reserva I have a spare one ❹ tengo mis reservas I have my reservations

reservado, reservada ADJECTIVE **reserved**

reservar VERB [17] ❶ **to reserve** ❷ **to book**

resfriado NOUN MASC **cold**; tener un resfriado to have a cold

resfriarse REFLEXIVE VERB [32] **to catch a cold**

residencia NOUN FEM ❶ **residence**; permiso de residencia residence permit ❷ **hall of residence** ❸ residencia de ancianos old people's home

residir VERB [19] residir en to live in

residuos NOUN MASC **waste**; residuos nucleares nuclear waste, residuos tóxicos toxic waste

resistencia NOUN FEM ❶ **resistance** ❷ **element** (electrical) ❸ tener mucha resistencia to have a lot of stamina

resistir VERB [19] ❶ **to resist** ❷ **to stand** (pain or cold); ¡no puedo resistirlo! I can't stand it!

resistirse REFLEXIVE VERB [19] **to resist**

resolver VERB [45] ❶ **to solve** ❷ **to resolve**

resorte NOUN MASC **spring**

respaldo NOUN MASC ❶ **back** ❷ **backing**

respecto NOUN MASC respecto a ... regarding ...

respetable ADJECTIVE **respectable**

respetar VERB [17] **to respect**

respeto NOUN MASC **respect**

respiración NOUN FEM **breathing**; contener la respiración to hold your breath

respirar VERB [17] **to breathe**

respiratorio, respiratoria ADJECTIVE dificultades respiratorias breathing difficulties

responder VERB [18] ❶ to answer; responder a algo to answer something ❷ to respond ❸ to answer back; ¡a mí no me respondas! don't answer back!

responsabilidad NOUN FEM responsibility

responsable NOUN MASC & FEM ❶ person in charge; el responsable de ventas the person in charge of sales ❷ person responsible

responsable ADJECTIVE responsible

respuesta NOUN FEM ❶ answer ❷ response

restante ADJECTIVE remaining; lo restante the remainder

restar VERB [17] to subtract, to take away

restaurante NOUN MASC restaurant

restaurar VERB [17] to restore

resto NOUN MASC ❶ rest; el resto de los libros the rest of the books ❷ restos remains, los restos del castillo the remains of the castle ❸ restos leftovers (from a meal)

restricción NOUN FEM restriction

restringir VERB [49] to restrict

restringirse REFLEXIVE VERB [49] to restrict yourself

resultado NOUN MASC ❶ result ❷ outcome ❸ dar resultado to work (a plan or an idea)

resultar VERB [17] ❶ to work (a plan or an idea) ❷ así resulta más fácil it's easy this way, resultó imposible convencerlo it was impossible to convince him

resumen NOUN MASC summary

resumir VERB [19] ❶ to summarize ❷ to sum up

retener VERB [9] ❶ to retain ❷ to keep back

retirar VERB [17] ❶ to withdraw ❷ to move back; retira esa silla move that chair back

retirarse REFLEXIVE VERB [17] ❶ to withdraw ❷ to move back

retrasado ADJECTIVE ❶ mental disability ❷ vamos muy retrasados con el trabajo we're very late with the job ❸ me reloj va retrasado my watch is slow

retrasar VERB [17] ❶ to delay (departure) ❷ to postpone ❸ retrasar un reloj to put a clock back

retrasarse REFLEXIVE VERB [17] ❶ to be late; me retrasé diez minutos I was ten minutes late ❷ to fall behind; voy retrasado con mi trabajo I'm behind with my work

retraso NOUN MASC ❶ delay; una media hora de retraso a half-hour delay, llevan retraso they're late ❷ con retraso late, llegaron con retraso they arrived late

retrato NOUN MASC portrait
• ser el vivo retrato de alguien to be the spitting image of somebody

retrovisor NOUN MASC ❶ rear-view mirror ❷ wing mirror

reuma, reúma, reumatismo NOUN MASC rheumatism

reunión NOUN FEM ❶ meeting ❷ gathering ❸ reunion; una reunión de antiguos alumnos a reunion of former pupils

reunir VERB [62] ❶ to gather (information, for example) ❷ to have; reúne los elementos que busco it has everything I'm looking for, no reúne los requisitos necesarios it doesn't satisfy the necessary requirements ❸ reunir dinero to raise money

reunirse REFLEXIVE VERB [62] to meet

revancha NOUN FEM ❶ return game; jugar la revancha to play a rematch ❷ tomarse la revancha to get your own back

revelar VERB [17] ❶ to reveal ❷ to develop (a film)

reventar VERB [17] ❶ to burst (balloons, tyres, etc) ❷ to explode

reverencia NOUN FEM bow, curtsey; hacer una reverencia to bow, to curtsey

reverso NOUN MASC back

revés NOUN MASC ❶ back; el revés de la página the back of the page ❷ inside; el revés del abrigo the inside of the coat ❸ se puso el jersey al revés he put his jumper on inside out, he put his jumper on back-to-front, ese cuadro está al revés that picture's upside down ❹ del revés inside out

revisar VERB [17] ❶ to check ❷ to revise ❸ to service

revisión NOUN FEM ❶ (medical) checkup ❷ revision ❸ service (for a car or a machine)

revisor, revisora NOUN MASC, FEM ticket inspector

revista NOUN FEM magazine

revolución NOUN FEM revolution

revolver VERB [45] ❶ to stir (soup or sauce) ❷ me revolvieron todos los cajones they went through all my drawers, le habían revuelto todos sus papeles they'd left all his papers in a mess

revólver NOUN MASC gun

revuelto, revuelta ADJECTIVE ❶ in a mess; los papeles estaban todos revueltos all the papers were in a mess ❷ rough (sea) ❸ unsettled (weather)

rey NOUN MASC ❶ king ❷ los reyes the king and queen

rezar VERB [22] to pray

ría, rían, etc VERB ▸ SEE **reír**

riada NOUN FEM flood

ribera NOUN FEM riverbank

rico, rica NOUN MASC, FEM rich person; los ricos the rich

rico ADJECTIVE rich

ridículo[1] NOUN MASC hacer el ridículo to make a fool of yourself, dejar a alguien en ridículo to make a fool of somebody

ridículo[2]**, ridícula** ADJECTIVE ridiculous

ríe, ríen, etc VERB ▸ SEE **reír**

riega, riego, riegue, etc VERB ▸ SEE **regar**

rienda NOUN FEM rein

riesgo NOUN MASC risk; correr un riesgo to run a risk, voy a correr el riesgo I'll take the risk, un riesgo para la salud a health hazard

rifa NOUN FEM raffle

riguroso, rigurosa ADJECTIVE rigorous

rímel NOUN MASC **mascara**

rincón NOUN MASC ❶ **corner** (of a room) ❷ estará en algún rincón it must be somewhere ❸ un rincón pintoresco a lovely spot (in the country)

rinoceronte NOUN MASC **rhinoceros**

riña NOUN FEM ❶ **fight**; una riña callejera a street fight ❷ **quarrel**; tuvo una riña con su novio she had a quarrel with her boyfriend

riñón NOUN MASC ❶ **kidney** ❷ tener dolor de riñones to have backache

rió VERB ▸ SEE **reir**

río NOUN MASC **river**; ir río abajo to go downstream

riqueza NOUN FEM **wealth**

risa NOUN FEM ❶ **laugh**; una risa histérica an hysterical laugh ❷ risas laughter, las risas del público the laughter of the audience ❸ me dio risa verlo seeing him made me laugh, de repente le dio la risa suddenly he got the giggles ❹ ¡qué risa! how funny! ❺ morirse de risa (informal) to die laughing

ritmo NOUN MASC **rhythm**; llevar el ritmo to keep time, marcar el ritmo to beat time

rival NOUN MASC & FEM **rival**

rizado, rizada ADJECTIVE **curly**

rizo NOUN MASC **curl**

robar VERB [17] ❶ **to steal**; robarle algo a alguien to steal something from somebody ❷ **to rob**; robar un banco to rob a bank ❸ robar en una casa to burgle a house, les robaron mientras estaban de vacaciones

they were burgled while they were away ❹ **to rip (somebody) off**

roble NOUN MASC **oak**

robo NOUN MASC ❶ **theft** ❷ **robbery** ❸ **burglary** ❹ **break in** ❺ ¡esto es un robo! this is a rip-off!

roca NOUN FEM **rock**
• firme como una roca solid as a rock

rocío NOUN MASC **dew**

rodaja NOUN FEM **slice**; cortar en rodajas to slice

rodar VERB [24] ❶ **to roll** (a ball, for example) ❷ **to turn** (a wheel) ❸ **to shoot** (a film)

rodeado, rodeada ADJECTIVE **surrounded**; rodeado de surrounded by

rodear VERB [17] **to surround**

rodilla NOUN FEM **knee**; ponerse de rodillas to kneel down

rogar VERB [24] ❶ **to beg**; te ruego que me perdones I beg you to forgive me ❷ 'se ruega no fumar' 'no smoking'

rojo¹ NOUN MASC **red**

rojo², roja ADJECTIVE **red**; ponerse rojo to turn red

rollo NOUN MASC ❶ **roll**; un rollo de tela a roll of fabric, un rollo de papel higiénico a toilet roll ❷ **coil** (of rope, wire) ❸ (informal) **bore**; ¡vaya rollo de película! what a boring film! ❹ (informal) **business**

romántico, romántica ADJECTIVE **romantic**

rompecabezas NOUN MASC (does not change in the plural) **puzzle**

romper *VERB* [40] **❶ to break**; vas a romper la silla you're going to break the chair **❷ to tear**; rompió la carta en pedazos he tore up the letter **❸** romper algo en mil pedazos to smash something to pieces

romperse *REFLEXIVE VERB* [40] **to break**; la lámpara se ha roto the lamp has broken, romperse una pierna to break your leg

rompiente *NOUN MASC* **breaker** *(wave)*

ron *NOUN MASC* **rum**

roncar *VERB* [31] **to snore**

ronco, ronca *ADJECTIVE* **hoarse**; quedarse ronco to go hoarse

ronda *NOUN FEM* **❶ round**; esta ronda la pago yo it's my round **❷ patrol**

ronronear *VERB* [31] **to purr**

ropa *NOUN FEM* **❶ clothes**; tengo mucha ropa I have a lot of clothes **❷** cambiarse de ropa to get changed **❸** la ropa sucia the dirty laundry **❹** ropa interior underwear

ropero *NOUN MASC* **wardrobe**

rosa[1] *NOUN FEM* **rose**

rosa[2] *NOUN MASC ADJECTIVE* **pink**

rosado[1]**, rosada** *ADJECTIVE* **pink**

rosado[2] *NOUN MASC* **❶ rosé** *(wine)* **❷ pink**

rosario *NOUN MASC* **rosary**

rosbif *NOUN MASC* **roast beef**

rostro *NOUN MASC* **❶ face ❷ nerve**; ¡vaya rostro que tiene! *(informal)* he's got a nerve!

roto, rota *ADJECTIVE* **❶ broken ❷ torn ❸ worn out** *(shoes)*

rotonda *NOUN FEM* **roundabout**

rotulador *NOUN MASC* **felt-tip pen**

rubio, rubia *ADJECTIVE* **blonde**

ruborizarse *REFLEXIVE VERB* [22] **to blush**

rueda *NOUN FEM* **❶ wheel**; la rueda de repuesto the spare wheel, la rueda delantera the front wheel **❷** una rueda de prensa a press conference

rugir *VERB* [49] **to roar**

ruido *NOUN MASC* **noise**; hacer ruido to make a noise

ruidoso, ruidosa *ADJECTIVE* **noisy**

ruina *NOUN FEM* **❶ ruin**; dejar a alguien en la ruina to ruin somebody, la empresa está en la ruina the company is in a terrible state **❷** ruinas ruins, las ruinas del castillo the ruins of the castle, estar en ruinas to be in ruins
* estar hecho una ruina *(informal)* to be a wreck

ruiseñor *NOUN MASC* **nightingale**

rulo *NOUN MASC* **roller** *(curler)*

Rumania, Rumanía *NOUN FEM* **Romania**

rumano, rumana *NOUN MASC, FEM, ADJECTIVE* **Romanian**

rumbo *NOUN MASC* **❶ course**; poner rumbo a to set a course for, el rumbo que tomaron los acontecimientos the course of events **❷ direction ❸** ir con rumbo a to be heading for **❹** sin rumbo fijo aimlessly

rumor *NOUN MASC* **❶ rumour ❷ murmur**

Rusia *NOUN FEM* **Russia**

a
b
c
d
e
f
g
h
i
j
k
l
m
n
ñ
o
p
q
r
s
t
u
v
w
x
y
z

Spanish—English

A B C D E F G H I J K L M N Ñ O P Q **R** **S** T U V W X Y Z

ruso¹ *NOUN MASC* **Russian** *(the language)*

ruso², **rusa** *NOUN MASC, FEM, ADJECTIVE* **Russian**

ruta *NOUN FEM* **route**

rutina *NOUN FEM* **routine**; por rutina out of habit

Ss

sábado *NOUN MASC* **Saturday**
▶ SEE **domingo**

sábana *NOUN FEM* **sheet** *(for a bed)*

sabático, **sabática** *ADJECTIVE* **sabatical**

saber *NOUN MASC* **knowledge**

saber *VERB* [13] ❶ **to know**; ya lo sé I know, no sabe he doesn't know, sabía que no iba a querer hacerlo I knew he wouldn't want to do it ❷ saber algo de memoria to know something by heart ❸ ¿sabes montar en bicicleta? can you ride a bike?, sabe hablar inglés muy bien she can speak English very well, no sé alemán I can't speak German ❹ **to find out**; lo supe por su hermana I found out through her sister ❺ **to taste**; la comida sabía muy rica the food tasted very nice, ¡qué mal sabe! it tastes disgusting! ❻ saber a to taste of, sabe a fresa it tastes of strawberry

sabiduría *NOUN FEM* **wisdom**

sabio, **sabia** *ADJECTIVE* **wise**

sabor *NOUN MASC* **taste**; sabor a fresa strawberry-flavoured

sabrá, **sabré**, **sabría**, *etc VERB*
▶ SEE **saber**

sabroso, **sabrosa** *ADJECTIVE* **tasty**

sacacorchos *NOUN MASC (does not change in the plural)* **corkscrew**

sacapuntas *NOUN MASC (does not change in the plural)* **pencil sharpener**

sacar *VERB* [31] ❶ **to take out**; sacó su monedero del bolso she took her purse out of her bag, lo saqué de la caja I took it out of the box, sacar la basura to take the rubbish out, sacar al perro a pasear to take the dog for a walk ❷ sacar la pistola to draw a gun ❸ **to get**; sacar entradas to get tickets, aún no he sacado los billetes I haven't got the tickets yet ❹ sacar buenas notas to get good marks, he sacado un siete en matemáticas I got seven (out of ten) in maths ❺ sacar una foto to take a picture ❻ sacar una fotocopia to make a photocopy ❼ sacar un libro to publish a book, sacar un disco to release a record ❽ sacar la lengua to stick your tongue out ❾ **to serve** *(in tennis)*; te toca a ti sacar it's your service ❿ **to kick off** *(in football)*

sacarse *REFLEXIVE VERB* [31] ❶ sacarse una muela to have a tooth out ❷ sacarse una foto to have one's photograph taken, me saqué una foto frente al palacio I had my photograph taken in front of the palace

sacerdote *NOUN MASC* **priest**

saco *NOUN MASC* **sack**; un saco de dormir a sleeping bag

sacrificar *VERB* [31] **to sacrifice**

sacrificio *NOUN MASC* **sacrifice**

sacudida *NOUN FEM* ❶ **shake**; le di una sacudida I gave it a shake ❷ el coche iba dando sacudidas the car was jerking along

sacudir *VERB* [19] ❶ **to shake** ❷ **to shake off**; sacudió las migas del mantel she shook the crumbs off the tablecloth

sacudirse *REFLEXIVE VERB* [19] **to shake off**; se sacudió el polvo de la chaqueta he shook off the dust from his jacket

sagaz *ADJECTIVE* **shrewd**

sagitario *NOUN MASC & FEM* **Sagittarius**; es sagitario she's Sagittarius

Sagitario *NOUN MASC* **Sagittarius**

sagrado, sagrada *ADJECTIVE* ❶ **sacred** ❷ **holy**

sal *NOUN FEM* **salt**; sales de baño bath salts

sala *NOUN FEM* ❶ **room**; una sala de estar a living room, una sala de espera a waiting room ❷ **hall**; una sala de exposiciones an exhibition hall ❸ **ward** *(in a hospital)* ❹ una sala de fiestas a night club

salado, salada *ADJECTIVE* **salted**; está muy salado it's too salty, agua salada salt water

salario *NOUN* ❶ **wages** *(when weekly)* ❷ **salary** *(when monthly)*

salchicha *NOUN FEM* **sausage**

salchichón *NOUN MASC* **salami sausage**

saldar *VERB* [17] ❶ **to settle** *(a debt)* ❷ **to sell off**

saldo *NOUN MASC* ❶ **balance**; saldo positivo credit balance, saldo negativo debit balance ❷ **settlement** ❸ saldos sales, precios de saldo sale prices

saldrá, saldré, saldría, salga, salgo, *etc VERB* ▸ SEE **salir**

salero NOUN MASC ❶ salt cellar
❷ tener mucho salero (informal) to
be very funny

salida NOUN FEM exit

salir VERB [63] ❶ to go out; salen
mucho por la noche they go out a
lot in the evenings ❷ to come out;
salieron uno a uno they came out
one by one ❸ to get out; no pude
salir I couldn't get out ❹ to leave;
el vuelo sale a las cinco the flight
leaves at five ❺ salgo de casa a las
ocho I leave home at eight, no sale
nunca de su habitación he never
leaves his room, salió de la casa
corriendo he ran out of the house,
sal de debajo de la cama come out
from under the bed ❻ salir con
alguien to go out with someone,
sale con mi hermano she's going
out with my brother ❼ salir en la
televisión to appear on television,
la noticia salió en el periódico
the news was in the paper ❽ to
turn out; las cosas salieron mal
things turned out badly, todo salió
como esperábamos everything
turned out as we expected ❾ las
vacaciones nos salieron muy caras
the holidays were very expensive
in the end, si compras tres, sale
más barato it's cheaper if you buy
three ❿ ¿cómo te salieron las cosas
en Inglaterra? how did things turn
out for you in England?, le sale
muy bien la tortilla de patatas
he can cook a really good Spanish
omelette, el retrato te ha salido
perfecto you've done a perfect
portrait, el examen me salió fatal
I did terribly in the exam ⓫ me ha
salido un grano I've got a spot,
le están saliendo canas his hair's
starting to go grey, le salía sangre
de la nariz his nose was bleeding

salirse REFLEXIVE VERB [63] ❶ to leave;
el cantante se ha salido del grupo
the singer has left the group,
salirse del colegio to leave school
❷ to leak ❸ el agua se salió del
fregadero the sink overflowed,
se ha salido la leche the milk has
boiled over ❹ el coche se salió de la
carretera the car went off the road

saliva NOUN FEM saliva

salmón NOUN MASC salmon; salmón
ahumado smoked salmon

salmón ADJECTIVE salmon-pink

salón NOUN MASC ❶ living room
❷ function room ❸ salón de
belleza beauty salon ❹ salón de
actos assembly hall ❺ salón de
fiestas reception room

salpicar VERB [31] to splash

salsa NOUN FEM ❶ sauce; salsa
besamel white sauce ❷ gravy
❸ salsa (music)

saltamontes NOUN MASC
grasshopper

saltar VERB [17] to jump; saltar por
encima de la verja to jump over the
fence, saltar un muro to jump over
a wall, saltar al suelo to jump to the
ground, saltar de la cama to jump
out of bed

saltarse REFLEXIVE VERB [17] ❶ to skip
(a page or an appointment) ❷ se
saltaron un semáforo en rojo they
drove through a red light

salto NOUN MASC jump; dar un salto to
jump, ponerse de pie de un salto to
jump to your feet, levantarse de un
salto de la cama to leap out of bed,
salto de altura high jump

salud NOUN FEM health; estar bien de
salud to be in good health

salud *EXCLAMATION* **cheers!**; ¡a tu salud! cheers!

saludable *ADJECTIVE* **healthy**

saludar *VERB* [17] ❶ **to say hello**; nos saludó con la mano she waved hello to us ❷ 'le saluda atentamente' 'Yours sincerely', 'Yours faithfully' *(ending a letter)*

saludo *NOUN MASC* ❶ **greeting**; te envían sus saludos they send their regards, dale saludos de mi parte give him my regards ❷ Un afectuoso saludo Best wishes

salvadoreño, salvadoreña *NOUN* **Salvadorean**

salvadoreño *ADJECTIVE* **Salvadorean**

salvaje *ADJECTIVE* ❶ **savage** ❷ **wild**

salvaje *NOUN MASC & FEM* **savage**

salvamanteles *NOUN MASC (does not change in the plural)* **table mat**

salvamento *NOUN MASC* **rescue**; bote de salvamento lifeboat, operación de salvamento rescue operation

salvar *VERB* [17] **to save**

salvarse *REFLEXIVE VERB* [17] **to survive**

salvavidas *NOUN MASC (does not change in the plural)* **life jacket**

salvo¹, salva *ADJECTIVE* **safe**

salvo² *PREPOSITION, CONJUNCTION* **except**; salvo que unless

salvo *IN PHRASE* estar a salvo to be out of danger, ponerse a salvo to reach safety

San *ADJECTIVE* **St** (Saint)

sanar *VERB* [17] ❶ **to recover** (patient) ❷ **to heal** (injury)

sandalia *NOUN FEM* **sandal**

sandía *NOUN FEM* **watermelon**

sándwich *NOUN MASC* **sandwich**

sangrar *VERB* [17] **to bleed**

sangre *NOUN FEM* **blood**; te sale sangre you're bleeding

sangría *NOUN FEM* **sangria** *(a fruit punch made with red wine and lemonade)*

sanidad *NOUN FEM* ❶ **health** ❷ **public health**; la sanidad pública the health service

sanitaria, sanitaria *ADJECTIVE* ❶ **health** un control sanitario health inspector ❷ **sanitary** las condiciones sanitarias the sanitary conditions

sano, sana *ADJECTIVE* ❶ **healthy** ❷ sano y salvo safe and sound

San Salvador *NOUN MASC* **San Salvador**

santo¹ *NOUN MASC* **name day** *(in Spain each day of the year is associated with the name of a saint and many people celebrate the day of the saint they are named after)*

santo², santa *NOUN MASC, FEM* **saint**; tener la paciencia de un santo to have the patience of a saint

santo *ADJECTIVE* **holy**

santuario *NOUN* **shrine**

sapo *NOUN MASC* **toad**

saque *NOUN MASC* ❶ **serve** (in tennis) ❷ **kick-off** (in football); saque de banda throw in, saque de esquina corner kick

sarampión *NOUN MASC* **measles**

sarcasmo *NOUN MASC* **sarcasm**

sardina *NOUN FEM* **sardine**

sargento *NOUN MASC & FEM* **sergeant**

sarpullido *NOUN MASC* **rash**; me ha salido un sarpullido I've come out in a rash

sartén *NOUN FEM* **frying pan**

sastre *NOUN MASC & FEM* **tailor**

satélite *NOUN MASC* **satellite**

satén *NOUN MASC* **satin**

satisfacción *NOUN FEM* **satisfaction**

satisfacer *VERB* [7] **to satisfy**; la calidad del producto no nos satisface we are not satisfied with the quality of the product, para satisfacer mi curiosidad to satisfy my curiosity

satisfacerse *REFLEXIVE VERB* [7] **to be satisfied**

satisfecho, satisfecha *ADJECTIVE* **satisfied**; estamos muy satisfechos con los resultados we are very happy with the results

sauce *NOUN MASC* **willow**

saxofón *NOUN MASC* **saxophone**

sazonado, sazonada *ADJECTIVE* **seasoned**

sazonar *VERB* [17] **to season**

se *PRONOUN* ❶ **himself/herself**; se cortó he cut himself/she cut herself ❷ **itself**; se desconecta solo it disconnects itself ❸ **themselves**; ¿se han portado bien? did they behave themselves? ❹ **yourself** *(polite form)*; espero que no se haya hecho daño I hope you haven't hurt yourself ❺ **yourselves** *(polite form)*;

¿se han divertido ustedes? did you enjoy yourselves? ❻ **him/her**; no se lo pregunté I didn't ask him/I didn't ask her ❼ **to him/to her**; se lo mandaré I'll send it to him/I'll send it to her ❽ **them**; cuando les vea se lo preguntaré I'll ask them when I see them ❾ **to them**; cuando les vea se lo daré I'll give it to them when I see them ❿ **you** *(polite form)*; se lo dije a usted ayer I told you yesterday ⓫ **to you** *(polite form)*; se lo di a usted ayer I gave it to you yesterday ⓬ **each other**; se quieren they love each other, se miraron they looked at each other ⓭ *(with parts of your body and personal belongings)*; se lavó las manos he washed his hands/she washed her hands, ¿se ha cortado usted el dedo? have you cut your finger?, se pusieron la ropa they put their clothes on ⓮ *(the infinitives of many verbs in Spanish end in '-se' but are not reflexive in English)* me reí mucho I laughed a lot, se cayó he fell down/she fell down, se han peleado they've had a fight, se levantaron they stood up ⓯ *(used in impersonal phrases)* 'se vende piso' 'flat for sale', se habla inglés English spoken here, se hace así it is done like this, se corta la hoja en dos cut the sheet in two

sé *VERB* ▸ SEE **saber**

secador *NOUN MASC* secador de pelo hairdryer

secadora *NOUN FEM* **dryer**

secar *VERB* [31] **to dry**

secarse *REFLEXIVE VERB* [31] ❶ **to dry**; ¿cuánto tarda en secarse la pintura? how long does the paint take to dry?, la camisa ya se ha secado the shirt's dry already ❷ **to**

dry yourself; secarse el pelo to dry your hair, secarse las lágrimas to dry your tears, sécate las manos con este trapo dry your hands with this cloth ❸ **to dry up**

sección NOUN FEM ❶ **section** ❷ **department**

seco, **seca** ADJECTIVE ❶ **dry**; limpieza en seco dry-cleaning ❷ **dried** *(flowers, for example)*

secretaría NOUN FEM **secretary's office**

secretario, **secretaria** NOUN MASC, FEM **secretary**

secreto[1] NOUN MASC **secret**

secreto[2], **secreta** ADJECTIVE **secret**

secuestrador, **secuestradora** NOUN MASC, FEM ❶ **highjacker** ❷ **kidnapper**

secuestrar VERB [17] ❶ **to kidnap** ❷ **to hijack**

secuestro NOUN MASC ❶ **kidnapping** ❷ **hijacking**

secundario, **secundaria** ADJECTIVE **secondary**

sed NOUN FEM **thirst**; tenían sed they were thirsty, las patatas fritas me dan sed crisps make me thirsty

seda NOUN FEM **silk**

sedal NOUN MASC **fishing line**

sede NOUN FEM la sede de las Olimpiadas the venue for the Olympics, la sede de la compañía the company's head office, la sede del gobierno the seat of government

seguida[1] IN PHRASE en seguida **straight away**, voy en seguida I'll be right there

seguido[1], **seguida**[2] ADJECTIVE ❶ tres días seguidos three days in a row, dan las dos películas seguidas they show both films one after the other, los tres autobuses vinieron seguidos the three buses came one after the other ❷ seguido de **followed by**

seguido[2] ADVERB **straight on**; vaya todo seguido go straight on

seguir VERB [64] ❶ **to follow**; seguir a alguien to follow somebody, seguir una pista to follow a trail, seguir un consejo to follow a piece of advice ❷ **to carry on**, **to continue**; sigamos let's carry on ❸ seguir haciendo to carry on doing, colgué el teléfono y seguí leyendo I put down the telephone and carried on reading ❹ seguir haciendo to be still doing, siguen viviendo en Sevilla they're still living in Seville ❺ **to go on**; siga todo recto go straight on, siga por esta calle go on down this street

según PREPOSITION ❶ **according to**; según la ley according to the law ❷ según parece apparently ❸ según dijo él from what he said

según ADVERB '¿te interesa apuntarte?' – 'según' 'would you be interested in enrolling?' – 'it depends'

según CONJUNCTION **as**; según los vayas terminando as you finish them

segunda[1] NOUN FEM la segunda **second gear**

segundo[1] NOUN MASC ❶ **second**; espera un segundo wait a moment, no tardé ni un segundo en hacerlo it didn't take me a minute to do it ❷ el segundo the main course

segundo², **segunda²** *ADJECTIVE*
❶ second; segunda clase second class, viven en el segundo piso they live on the second floor, llegar en segundo lugar to finish in second position **❷** en segundo plano in the background

seguramente *ADVERB* **probably**; seguramente irán they'll probably go

seguridad *NOUN FEM* **❶ security**; seguridad nacional national security **❷ safety**; por razones de seguridad for safety reasons **❸ certainty**; no lo sé con seguridad I don't know for certain **❹** seguridad social social security

seguro¹ *NOUN MASC* **❶ insurance**; hacerse un seguro to take out insurance, seguro a todo riesgo comprehensive insurance, seguro contra incendios fire insurance, ¿tienes seguro médico? have you got medical insurance? **❷ clasp** *(of a bracelet)* **❸ safety catch** *(on a weapon)* **❹** el Seguro Social Social Security

seguro², **segura** *ADJECTIVE* **❶ safe**; la escalera no es muy segura the ladder isn't very safe, aquí me siento seguro I feel safe here **❷** seguro/segura de sí mismo/mismo, es muy segura de sí misma she's very self-confident **❸ sure**; ¿estás seguro de que se pone así? are you sure this is the way to put it?, estoy completamente seguro I'm absolutely certain **❹ definite**; no es seguro todavía it's not definite yet **❺ reliable**; es un método muy seguro it's a very reliable method

seguro³ *ADVERB* **definitely**; irán seguro they'll definitely go, seguro que no están I bet they're not there

seis *NUMBER* **❶ six**; tiene seis años he's six (years old) **❷ sixth** *(in dates)*; el seis de junio the sixth of June **❸ six** *(in clock time)*; son las seis it's six o'clock

seiscientos, **seiscientas** *NUMBER* **six hundred**; seiscientos dos six hundred and two

selección *NOUN FEM* **❶ selection ❷** la selección nacional the national team

seleccionar *VERB* [17] **to select**

selectividad *NOUN FEM* **university entrance exam**

self-service *NOUN MASC* **self-service restaurant**

sello *NOUN MASC* **❶ stamp ❷** sello discográfico record label

selva *NOUN FEM* **❶ jungle ❷ forest**; la selva tropical the tropical rainforest

semáforo *NOUN MASC* **traffic lights**; saltarse un semáforo en rojo to go through a red light, cuando llegue al semáforo, tuerza a la derecha when you get to the traffic lights, turn right

semana *NOUN FEM* **week**; la próxima semana next week, entre semana during the week, Semana Santa Easter, en Semana Santa at Easter

semanal *ADJECTIVE* **weekly**

semanalmente *ADVERB* **weekly**

sembrar *VERB* [29] **❶ to sow ❷ to plant**

semejante *ADJECTIVE* **similar**; semejante a similar to

semestre *NOUN MASC* **semester**

semifinal *NOUN FEM* **semifinal**

semilla *NOUN FEM* **seed**

sémola NOUN FEM **semolina**

sencillo[1] NOUN MASC ❶ **single** (record) ❷ **single ticket**

sencillo[2], **sencilla** ADJECTIVE ❶ **simple** ❷ **modest**

senda NOUN FEM **path**

senderismo NOUN MASC **trekking**

senderista NOUN MASC & FEM **hiker**

sendero NOUN MASC **path**

seno NOUN MASC ❶ **breast** ❷ **bosom**

sensación NOUN FEM ❶ **feeling**; tengo la sensación de que ... I have the feeling that ..., una sensación de tristeza a feeling of sadness ❷ **sense**; una sensación de pérdida a sense of loss ❸ **sensation**; causar sensación to cause a sensation, su llegada causó sensación her arrival caused a sensation

sensacional ADJECTIVE **sensational**; una noticia sensacional a sensational piece of news

sensatez NOUN FEM **sense**; tener sensatez to be sensible, actuar con sensatez to act sensibly

sensato, **sensata** ADJECTIVE **sensible**

sensibilidad NOUN FEM **sensitivity**

sensible ADJECTIVE ❶ **sensitive** ❷ **noticeable** (difference or change)

sensiblemente ADVERB **considerably**

sentado, **sentada** ADJECTIVE estar sentado to be sitting, estaban sentados cerca de la puerta they were sitting near the door, estábamos sentados a la mesa we were sitting at the table, permanezcan sentados, por favor please remain seated

sentar VERB [29] ❶ **to sit**; senté al niño en su silla I sat the baby on his chair ❷ **to suit**; ese vestido te sienta muy bien that dress suits you, el rojo me sienta fatal red doesn't suit me at all ❸ los pimientos me sientan mal peppers don't agree with me

sentarse REFLEXIVE VERB [29] **to sit down**

sentido NOUN MASC ❶ **sense**; sentido del deber sense of duty, sentido común common sense ❷ no tiene sentido it doesn't make sense, en sentido literal in the literal sense ❸ **consciousness**; perder el sentido to lose consciousness ❹ **direction**; venían en sentido contrario they were coming from the opposite direction, en sentido de las agujas del reloj clockwise, en el sentido contrario al de las agujas del reloj anticlockwise ❺ calle de sentido único one-way street

sentimental ADJECTIVE ❶ **sentimental** ❷ ¿qué tal tu vida sentimental? how's your love life?

sentimiento NOUN MASC ❶ **feeling** ❷ te acompaño en el sentimiento my condolences

sentir VERB [14] ❶ **to feel**; sentir dolor to feel pain, sentir sed to feel thirsty, sentir alegría to feel happy ❷ sentir un ruido to hear a noise ❸ (used to express apology) lo siento mucho I'm very sorry, siento llegar tarde sorry I'm late, sentimos tener que comunicarle que ... we regret to inform you that ...

sentirse REFLEXIVE VERB [14] **to feel**; ¿cómo te sientes? how do you feel?, no se sentía bien y se fue a casa he wasn't feeling well and he went home, me siento un poco cansado I feel a bit tired

seña NOUN FEM ❶ sign; hacer una seña to make a sign, me hizo señas para que entrase he beckoned to me to come in ❷ señas address, ¿quieres darme tus señas? would you like to give me your address?

señal NOUN FEM ❶ sign; señal de tráfico traffic sign ❷ en señal de amistad as a token of friendship ❸ sign; hacer una señal to make a sign, nos estaba haciendo señales she was signalling to us ❹ deposit; dar una señal to pay a deposit

señalar VERB [17] ❶ to point; señaló hacia la casa he pointed to the house, no es de buena educación señalar con el dedo it's bad manners to point at people ❷ to point out; señaló que ... she pointed out that ... ❸ to fix (a date or time)

señalarse REFLEXIVE VERB [17] se señaló la pierna he pointed at his leg

señor NOUN MASC ❶ gentleman; había un señor esperando there was a gentleman waiting ❷ sir; perdone señor, ¿me deja pasar? excuse me sir, could you let me through? ❸ Mr; el señor Puyol Mr Puyol, los señores López Mr and Mrs López, (note that sometimes 'señor' is used in Spanish before somebody's first name as a sign of respect, for example 'el señor Mateo' and also in front of titles) el señor presidente the President ❹ Muy señor mío Dear Sir (in letters) ❺ (for emphasis) no señor, eso no se hace you mustn't do that, sí señor, es verdad yes, that's quite right

señora NOUN FEM ❶ lady; una señora se me acercó a lady came up to me ❷ madam; perdone señora, ¿me deja pasar? excuse me madam, could you let me through? ❸ Mrs, Ms; la señora Frutos Ms Frutos (in Spain, women use their maiden name after they get married and not their husband's surname), Doña Ana Villa, señora de García Mrs Ana García (literally, Ms Ana Villa, marrried to Mr García) (note that sometimes 'señora' is used in Spanish before somebody's first name as a sign of respect, for example 'la señora Juana') ❹ wife; fui de vacaciones con mi señora I went on holiday with my wife ❺ (for emphasis) no señora, no fui yo it was not me, sí señora, es mío it certainly is mine

señorita NOUN FEM ❶ young lady; le ha llamado una señorita a young lady has called you ❷ Miss, Ms; la señorita García Miss García, Ms García ('señorita' is also used to address a teacher), aquí están mis deberes, señorita here's my homework, Miss ❸ (for emphasis) no señorita, no se lo dejo I am certainly not lending it to you

sepa, sepan, etc VERB ▶ SEE **saber**

separación NOUN FEM ❶ gap ❷ separation

separado, separada ADJECTIVE ❶ separated ❷ por separado separately

separar VERB [17] ❶ to separate ❷ to move (something) away; separa la silla de la chimenea move the chair away from the fire

separarse REFLEXIVE VERB [17] ❶ to separate (a couple) ❷ nunca nos hemos separado antes we've never been apart before

septiembre NOUN MASC **September**; en septiembre, en el mes de septiembre in September

séptimo, **séptima** ADJECTIVE **seventh**; el séptimo piso the seventh floor

sequía NOUN FEM **drought**

ser NOUN MASC ser humano human being

ser VERB [1] ❶ **to be**; es muy bonito it's very beautiful, es soltero he's single, es muy simpática she's very friendly, soy bastante alta I'm quite tall, '¿quién es?' – 'soy yo' 'who's that?' – 'it's me', mi madre es médico my mother's a doctor, estas naranjas son buenísimas these oranges are really nice, ¿cuánto es? how much is it?, hoy es once it's the eleventh today, eran las seis y media it was half past six ❷ ser de to be from, mi amiga es de Argentina my friend is from Argentina ❸ el coche es de Juan the car is Juan's, era de mi hermano it was my brother's ❹ ser de to be made of, es de madera it's made of wood, es de metal it's made of metal ❺ (passive use) **to be**; la propuesta ha sido rechazada the proposal has been rejected ❻ cuando sea whenever, como sea however, donde sea wherever ❼ lo que sea whatever ❽ ya sea ... o ... either ... or ..., ya sea por carta o por teléfono either by post or by telephone ❾ o sea, que no lo has terminado so, you haven't finished, dentro de una semana, o sea el próximo jueves in a week, that is, next Thursday ❿ a no ser unless, a no ser que no le interese unless he's not interested

será, **seré**, **sería**, etc VERB ▸ SEE **ser**

serie NOUN FEM ❶ **series**; fabricación en serie mass production ❷ fuera de serie out of this world

serio, **seria** ADJECTIVE ❶ **serious**; ponerse serio to have a serious expression, un problema serio a serious problem ❷ **reliable** (a person) ❸ **reputable** (a company) ❹ lo digo en serio I mean it

seropositiva, **seropositiva** ADJECTIVE **HIV positive**

serpiente NOUN FEM **snake**

servicio NOUN MASC ❶ **service**; servicios públicos public services, servicio incluido service included, servicio de atención al cliente customer services ❷ estar de servicio to be on duty ❸ 'servicios' 'toilets' ❹ servicio militar military service

servilleta NOUN FEM **serviette**

servir VERB [57] ❶ **to serve**; servir la sopa to serve the soup, ¿te sirvo más vino? shall I pour you some more wine? ❷ **to be of use**; estas herramientas ya no sirven these tools are no good any more ❸ servir para algo to be used for, ¿para qué sirve este interruptor? what's this switch for?, esto no nos sirve para abrirlo this is no use for opening it ❹ no sirves para nada you're useless, yo no sirvo para camarera I'm no good as a waitress

servirse REFLEXIVE VERB [57] **to help yourself to**; se sirvió ensalada she helped herself to some salad, sírvete más help yourself to some more

sesenta NUMBER **sixty**; tiene sesenta años he's sixty (years old), sesenta y dos sixty-two, los años sesenta the sixties

sesión NOUN FEM ❶ **session**
❷ **performance**; la sesión de
noche the evening performance,
sesión continua continuous
performance

seta NOUN FEM ❶ **mushroom**
❷ **toadstool**

setecientos, **setecientas** NUMBER
seven hundred; setecientos
ochenta seven hundred and eighty

setenta NUMBER **seventy**; tiene
setenta años he's seventy (years
old), setenta y dos seventy-two, los
años setenta the seventies

seto NOUN MASC **hedge**

severo, **severa** ADJECTIVE ❶ **severe**
(person, punishment) ❷ **harsh**
(climate)

sexista ADJECTIVE **sexist**

sexo NOUN MASC **sex**

sexto, **sexta** ADJECTIVE **sixth**; el sexto
piso the sixth floor

sexual ADJECTIVE **sexual**; tener
relaciones sexuales con alguien
to have sex with someone

si CONJUNCTION ❶ **if**; si yo estuviera
en tu lugar if I were you, si lo
hubiese sabido ... if I had known ...,
si tuviese dinero, lo compraría
if I had the money I would buy it
❷ **whether**; no sé si podré I don't
know whether I'll be able to, tanto
si quiere como si no whether he
wants to or not

sí ADVERB **yes**; sí, es cierto yes, it's true,
'¿lo vas a comprar?' – 'sí' 'are you
going to buy it?' – 'yes I am', '¿es
suyo?' – 'creo que sí' 'is it hers?' –
'I think so', ellos no lo saben, pero
yo sí they don't know, but I do

sí PRONOUN ❶ **himself/herself**; pensó
para sí he thought to himself/she
thought to herself ❷ (polite form)
yourself, (polite form) **yourselves**
❸ **itself**; este problema es, en
sí mismo ... this problem is, in
itself ... ❹ **themselves**; los dos
hermanos lo quieren todo para sí
both brothers want everything for
themselves ❺ sí mismo himself,
sí misma herself, quiere hacerlo
por sí mismo he wants to do it
by himself, quiere hacerlo por sí
misma she wants to do it by herself
❻ sí mismo/sí misma **yourself**
(polite form), sí mismos, sí mismas
yourselves (polite form) ❼ sí mismo
oneself, reírse de sí mismo to laugh
at oneself ❽ entre sí **between
themselves**

Sicilia NOUN FEM **Sicily**

sida NOUN MASC **Aids**

sidra NOUN FEM **cider**

siempre ADVERB ❶ **always**; casi
siempre almost always, desde
siempre always ❷ para siempre
for ever, ¿te vas a quedar allí para
siempre? are you going to stay
there for ever? ❸ como siempre
as usual, la historia de siempre
the usual story ❹ siempre que
whenever, siempre que puedo
whenever I can

sienta, **siento**, etc VERB
▸ SEE **sentar**, **sentir**

sierra NOUN FEM ❶ **saw** ❷ **range of
mountains**; veranean en la sierra
they spend their summer holidays
in the mountains

siesta NOUN FEM **nap**; echarse una
siesta (informal) to have a nap, está
durmiendo la siesta he's having
a nap

siete NUMBER ❶ **seven**; tiene siete años she's seven (years old) ❷ **seventh** (in dates); hoy es siete de abril it's the seventh of April today ❸ **seven** (in clock time); son las siete it's seven o'clock

siga, **sigan**, etc VERB ▸ SEE **seguir**

sigla NOUN FEM **abbreviation**; S.A. son las siglas de sociedad anónima. S.A. is the abbreviation for 'sociedad anónima.'

siglo NOUN MASC **century**; el siglo XIII the 13th century (centuries are always indicated in roman numbers in Spanish), hace un siglo que no nos vemos (informal) we haven't seen each other for ages

significado NOUN MASC **meaning**

significar VERB [31] **to mean**; ¿qué significa esta palabra? what does this word mean?, eso no significa nada para él that doesn't mean anything to him

signo NOUN MASC ❶ **sign**; signo del zodiaco star sign, ¿de qué signo eres? what sign are you? ❷ **mark**; signo de exclamación exclamation mark, signo de interrogación question mark

sigo, **sigue**, etc VERB ▸ SEE **seguir**

siguiente NOUN MASC & FEM el siguiente, por favor next, please

siguiente ADJECTIVE **next**, **following**; al día siguiente ... the next day ...

siguió VERB ▸ SEE **seguir**

sílaba NOUN FEM **syllable**

silbar VERB [17] **to whistle**

silbato NOUN MASC **whistle**; tocar el silbato to blow the whistle

silbido NOUN MASC **whistle**; dar un silbido to whistle

silencio NOUN MASC **silence**

silenciosamente ADVERB **quietly**

silencioso, **silenciosa** ADJECTIVE **quiet**

silla NOUN FEM **chair**; silla de montar saddle (for a horse), una silla de ruedas a wheelchair

sillín NOUN MASC **saddle** (on a bicycle)

sillón NOUN MASC **armchair**

símbolo NOUN MASC **symbol**

similar ADJECTIVE **similar**; similar a similar to

similitud NOUN FEM **similarity**

simio NOUN MASC & FEM **ape**

simpático, **simpática** ADJECTIVE **nice**; me cae simpático I think he's really nice

simple ADJECTIVE ❶ **simple** ❷ **mere**; una simple formalidad a mere formality

simplemente ADVERB **simply**

simplificar VERB [31] **to simplify**

simular VERB [17] ❶ **to feign** ❷ **to fake**

simultáneo, **simultánea** ADJECTIVE **simultaneous**

sin PREPOSITION ❶ **without**; sin esfuerzo without effort, lo hice sin pensar I did it without thinking ❷ agua mineral sin gas still mineral water, cerveza sin alcohol non-alcoholic beer ❸ está sin revisar it hasn't been checked yet, terminó sin amigos he ended up with no friends, nos quedamos sin dinero we ran out of money, estamos sin azúcar we're out of sugar ❹ sin querer unintentionally ❺ sin embargo nevertheless

sinagoga NOUN FEM **synagogue**

sinceramente ADVERB ❶ **sincerely** ❷ **quite honestly**

sinceridad NOUN FEM **sincerity**

sincero, sincera ADJECTIVE **sincere**

sindicalista NOUN MASC & FEM **trade unionist**

sindicato NOUN MASC **trade union**

síndrome NOUN MASC **syndrome**; el síndrome de abstinencia withdrawal symptoms

singular NOUN MASC **singular**; en singular in the singular

siniestro[1] NOUN MASC ❶ **accident** ❷ **disaster**

siniestro[2]**, siniestra** ADJECTIVE **sinister**

sino CONJUNCTION **but**; no verde, sino amarillo not green but yellow

sinónimo NOUN MASC **synonym**

sinónimo ADJECTIVE **synonymous**

sintético, sintética ADJECTIVE **synthetic**

sintieron, sintió, etc VERB ► SEE **sentir**

síntoma NOUN MASC **symptom**

sintonizar VERB [22] **to tune in**

sinvergüenza NOUN MASC & FEM ❶ **swine** ❷ **crook** ❸ **rascal**

siquiera ADVERB ❶ **at least**; dales siquiera un poco de dinero give them at least a bit of money ❷ ni siquiera not even, ni siquiera me di cuenta I didn't even realise

sirena NOUN FEM ❶ **mermaid** ❷ **siren**

sistema NOUN MASC **system**

sitio NOUN MASC ❶ **place**; ponlo otra vez en su sitio put it back in its place ❷ **room**; no tengo sitio en la maleta I haven't got any room in my suitcase, hay sitio para uno más en el coche there's room for one more in the car, hacer sitio to make room ❸ **seat**; hay un sitio al lado de la ventana there's a seat by the window ❹ en cualquier sitio anywhere, en algún sitio somewhere, en ningún sitio nowhere, en otro sitio somewhere else ❺ **siege** ❻ un sitio web a web site

situación NOUN FEM ❶ **situation** ❷ **position**; la situación de la casa es buena the house is in a good position

situado, situada ADJECTIVE **situated**

situar VERB [20] ❶ **to site** (a building) ❷ **to set** (a plot in a novel)

situarse REFLEXIVE VERB [20] ❶ **to be situated** ❷ situarse en primer puesto to reach the first position ❸ situarse bien en la vida to do very well for yourself

smoking NOUN MASC **dinner jacket**

SMS NOUN MASC **message**; enviar un SMS to send a text message

sobaco NOUN MASC **armpit**

sobra IN PHRASE ❶ de sobra to spare, tenemos pan de sobra we have plenty of bread, hay una silla de sobra there's a spare chair ❷ saber algo de sobra to know something full well ❸ **aquí estás de sobra** you're not wanted here, como estaba de sobra me fui I wasn't needed, so I left

sobrar VERB [17] ❶ **nos ha sobrado vino** we had a lot of wine left over, **¿te sobró algo de papel?** did you have any paper left over?, va a sobrar dinero there will be money left over ❷ **le sobraba una entrada** he had a spare ticket ❸ **aquí sobra dinero** there is too much money here, **sobran tres sillas** there are three chairs too many ❹ **nos sobraba un sitio** we'd got an extra place ❺ **nos sobra tiempo** we have plenty of time

sobras PLURAL NOUN FEM **leftovers**

sobre NOUN MASC **envelope**

sobre PREPOSITION ❶ **on**; lo dejó sobre la cama he left it on the bed ❷ **above**; la lámpara que está sobre el sofá the lamp above the sofa, sobre el nivel del mar above sea level ❸ **over**; el puente sobre el río the bridge over the river ❹ **about**; una conferencia sobre literatura a lecture about literature ❺ **sobre todo** especially

sobredosis NOUN FEM **overdose**

sobrenatural ADJECTIVE **supernatural**

sobrepasar VERB [17] **to exceed**

sobrepeso NOUN MASC; tener sobrepeso to be overweight

sobresaliente NOUN MASC **mark between 8.5 and 10 (out of 10)**

sobresaliente ADJECTIVE **outstanding, excellent**

sobresalir VERB [63] ❶ **sobresalir en algo** to excel in something ❷ to overhang ❸ to protrude

sobresalto NOUN MASC **fright**; llevarse un sobresalto to get a fright

sobreviviente NOUN MASC & FEM **survivor**

sobrevivir VERB [19] **to survive**; sobrevivir a algo to survive something

sobrina NOUN FEM **niece**

sobrino NOUN MASC **nephew**; sobrinos nephews, nephews and nieces

sociable ADJECTIVE **sociable**

social ADJECTIVE **social**

socialista NOUN MASC & FEM, ADJECTIVE **socialist**

sociedad NOUN FEM ❶ **society**; la sociedad de consumo the consumer society ❷ sociedad anónima public limited company

socio, socia NOUN MASC, FEM **member**; hacerse socio de algo to join something

sociología NOUN FEM **sociology**

socorrer VERB [18] **to help**

socorrista NOUN MASC & FEM **lifeguard**; ¿hay un socorrista en la playa? is there a lifeguard at the beach?

socorro NOUN MASC **help**; pedir socorro to ask for help

socorro EXCLAMATION **¡socorro!** help!

sofá NOUN MASC **sofa**

sofocar VERB [31] **to put out** (a fire)

sofocarse REFLEXIVE VERB [31] **to get worked up**

a
b
c
d
e
f
g
h
i
j
k
l
m
n
ñ
o
p
q
r
s
t
u
v
w
x
y
z

sois *VERB* ▸ SEE **ser**

soja *NOUN FEM* **soya**

sol *NOUN MASC* **sun**; hacía sol it was sunny, un día de sol a sunny day, al ponerse el sol at sunset, el sol estaba saliendo the sun was rising, sentarse al sol to lie in the sun

solamente *ADVERB* **only**

soldado *NOUN MASC & FEM* **soldier**

soleado, soleada *ADJECTIVE* **sunny**

soledad *NOUN FEM* **loneliness**

soler *VERB* [38] **①** suele salir por las noches he usually goes out in the evenings, suelen verse they usually see each other, no suele importarle he usually doesn't mind **②** solía escribirme de vez en cuando she used to write to me from time to time

solicitar *VERB* [17] **①** to ask for *(permission)* **②** to request *(an interview)* **③** to apply for *(a job)*

solicitud *NOUN MASC* **application**

sólido, sólida *ADJECTIVE* **①** solid **②** sound

solitario, solitaria *ADJECTIVE* **lonely**

solo¹, sola *ADJECTIVE* **①** alone; vive solo he lives alone, cuando me quedé solo when I was left alone **②** lonely; está muy sola she's very lonely, sentirse solo to feel lonely **③** on your own; desde que murió su madre está sola she's been on her own since her mother died **④** by yourself; lo hice sola I did it by myself **⑤** con una sola mano with one hand, sin una sola queja without a single complaint **⑥** un café solo a black coffee, una ginebra sola a straight gin

solo² *ADVERB* **only**

solomillo *NOUN MASC* **fillet steak**

soltar *VERB* [24] **①** to let go of; le solté la mano I let go of his hand, ¡suéltame! let go of me! **②** to release *(a prisoner)* **③** to untie; soltar un nudo to untie a knot **④** soltar al perro to let the dog off the lead **⑤** soltar un grito to let out a cry, soltar una carcajada to let out a laugh, soltar una palabrota to come out with a swearword

soltarse *REFLEXIVE VERB* [24] **①** no te sueltes de la barandilla don't let go of the banister, se soltó de mi mano he let go of my hand **②** soltarse el pelo to let your hair down **③** to come undone *(a knot)*

soltero, soltera *NOUN MASC, FEM* **①** bachelor *(male)* **②** single woman

soltero *ADJECTIVE* **single**

soltura *NOUN FEM* hablar español con soltura to speak Spanish fluently, moverse con soltura to move with ease

soluble *ADJECTIVE* **soluble**

solución *NOUN FEM* **solution**

solucionar *VERB* [17] **①** to solve **②** to settle *(a conflict)*

sombra *NOUN FEM* **①** shadow **②** shade; sentarse en la sombra to sit in the shade, dar sombra to give shade **③** sombra de ojos eye shadow

sombrero *NOUN MASC* **hat**

sombrilla *NOUN FEM* **①** parasol **②** sunshade

sombrío, sombría *ADJECTIVE* **①** dark *(street or room)* **②** gloomy *(face or look)*

somos, son VERB ▸ SEE **ser**

sonar VERB [24] ❶ to sound; suena a hueco it sounds hollow, sonó un ruido there was a noise ❷ to ring (a doorbell or telephone) ❸ el despertador no ha sonado the alarm clock hasn't gone off ❹ me suena mucho su cara her face is very familiar to me, ¿Carlos Ramírez? no me suena Carlos Ramírez? it doesn't ring any bells

sonarse REFLEXIVE VERB [24] sonarse la nariz to blow one's nose

sondeo NOUN MASC survey

sonido NOUN MASC sound

sonreír VERB [61] to smile; me sonrió he smiled at me

sonreírse REFLEXIVE VERB [61] to smile

sonría, sonríe, sonrío, etc VERB ▸ SEE **sonreír**

sonrisa NOUN FEM smile

sonrojarse VERB [17] to blush

soñar VERB [24] to dream

sopa NOUN FEM soup

soplar VERB [17] ❶ to blow ❷ to blow off; soplar el polvo de la mesa to blow the dust off the table ❸ soplarle la respuesta a alguien (informal) to whisper the answer to someone (in an exam)

soportar VERB [17] ❶ to put up with (situation) ❷ to bear (pain or heat) ❸ no puedo soportar a Rafael I can't stand Rafael ❹ to withstand

soporte NOUN MASC support

sorbete NOUN MASC sorbet

sorbo NOUN MASC ❶ sip; beber a sorbos to sip ❷ gulp; beberse algo de un sorbo to drink something in one gulp

sordo, sorda NOUN MASC & FEM deaf person

sordo ADJECTIVE deaf

sordomudo, sordomuda NOUN MASC, FEM deaf mute

sordomudo ADJECTIVE deaf and dumb

sorprendente ADJECTIVE surprising

sorprender VERB [18] to surprise; me sorprende que se retrase I'm surprised he's late

sorprenderse REFLEXIVE VERB [18] to be surprised

sorprendido, sorprendida ADJECTIVE surprised

sorpresa NOUN FEM surprise

soso, sosa ADJECTIVE ❶ dull ❷ bland

soso NOUN bore

sospecha NOUN FEM suspicion; tengo la sospecha de que ... I have a feeling that ...

sospechar VERB [17] to suspect

sospechoso, sospechosa ADJECTIVE suspicious; me parece sospechoso I find it suspicious

sostén NOUN MASC ❶ support ❷ bra

sostener VERB [9] ❶ to support (arch, ceiling, or family) ❷ to bear (a weight or load)

sótano NOUN MASC ❶ basement ❷ cellar

soy VERB ▸ SEE **ser**

Sr. *ABBREVIATION (short for Señor)* **Mr**

Sra. *ABBREVIATION (short for Señora)* **Mrs, Ms**

Sres. *ABBREVIATION (short for Señores)* **Messrs**

Srta. *ABBREVIATION (short for Señorita)* **Miss, Ms**

su *ADJECTIVE* ❶ **his/her**; ¿es su falda como esta? is her skirt like this one?, ahí está Carlos con sus padres there's Carlos with his parents ❷ **its**; el perro duerme en su caseta the dog sleeps in its kennel ❸ **their**; mis padres viven allí y este es su coche my parents live there and that's their car ❹ **your** *(polite form)*; ¿son estos sus zapatos? are these your shoes?

suave *ADJECTIVE* ❶ **soft** ❷ **smooth** ❸ **gentle** *(voice)* ❹ **mild** *(weather)*

suavizante *NOUN MASC* ❶ **fabric softener** ❷ **hair conditioner**

subdesarrollado, **subsesarrollada** *ADJECTIVE* **underdeveloped** *(country)*

subestimar *VERB* [17] **understimate**

subida *NOUN FEM* ❶ **rise** *(in temperature or price, for example)* ❷ **climb**

subir *VERB* [19] ❶ **to go up**; el ascensor está subiendo the lift is going up, subir al tercer piso to go up to the third floor, la temperatura ha subido tres grados the temperature has gone up three degrees ❷ **to come up**; ¡sube! come up! ❸ **to bring up**; sube estas cajas al segundo piso bring these boxes up to the third floor, súbeme un vaso de agua bring a glass of water up for me ❹ **to take up**; ¿le

subo las maletas a su habitación? shall I take the luggage up to your room? ❺ **to put up**; han vuelto a subir el precio de la gasolina they've put up the price of petrol again ❻ subir al tren to get on the train, subir a un coche to get into a car, subir a bordo to board ❼ **to turn up** *(volume)*; subió un poco la música he turned up the music a bit ❽ **to raise**; subir una persiana to raise a blind ❾ **to rise**; el nivel del agua ha subido the water level has risen ❿ **to come in** *(the tide)*

subirse *REFLEXIVE VERB* [19] ❶ subirse al tren to get on the train, subirse a un coche to get into a car, subirse a bordo to board ❷ subirse a un árbol to climb up a tree ❸ subirse los calcetines to pull up your socks

súbitamente *ADVERB* **suddenly**

súbito, súbita *ADJECTIVE* **sudden**

subjuntivo *NOUN MASC* **subjunctive**

submarinismo *NOUN MASC* **scuba diving**

submarinista *NOUN MASC & FEM* **scuba diver**

submarino *NOUN MASC* **submarine**

subrayar *VERB* [17] **to underline**

subsidio *NOUN MASC* ❶ **subsidy** ❷ subsidio de desempleo unemployment benefit, subsidio de invalidez disability allowance

subterráneo¹ *NOUN MASC* **subway**

subterráneo², subterránea *ADJECTIVE* **underground**

subtítulos *PLURAL NOUN MASC* **subtitles**

suburbio *NOUN MASC* ❶ **slum**

area *(on the outskirts of a town)* ❷ **suburb**

subvención *NOUN FEM* **subsidy**

subvencionar *VERB* [17] **to subsidize**

suceder *VERB* [18] ❶ **to happen**; ¿qué le ha sucedido? what's happened to him?, sucedió todo muy rápido it all happened very quickly ❷ **to succeed** *(to the throne)*

suceso *NOUN MASC* ❶ **event** ❷ **incident**; 'página de sucesos' 'accidents and crimes report' *(in a newspaper)*

suciedad *NOUN FEM* ❶ **dirt** ❷ **dirtiness**

sucio, sucia *ADJECTIVE* ❶ **dirty**; tienes la cara sucia your face is dirty ❷ primero hice el trabajo en sucio I did the essay in rough first

sucursal *NOUN FEM* ❶ **branch** *(of a bank)* ❷ **office** *(of a company)*

sudadera *NOUN FEM* **sweatshirt**

Sudamérica *NOUN FEM* **South America**

sudamericano, sudamericana *NOUN MASC, FEM, ADJECTIVE* **South American**

sudar *VERB* [17] **to sweat**

sudeste *NOUN MASC* **southeast**

sudoeste *NOUN MASC* **southwest**

sudor *NOUN MASC* **sweat**

Suecia *NOUN FEM* **Sweden**

sueco¹ *NOUN MASC* **Swedish** *(the language)*

sueco², sueca *NOUN MASC, FEM* **Swede**

sueco *ADJECTIVE* **Swedish**

suegra *NOUN FEM* **mother-in-law**

suegro *NOUN MASC* ❶ **father-in-law** ❷ mis suegros my parents in law

suela¹ *NOUN FEM* **sole**

suela², suelas, *etc VERB* ▸ SEE **soler**

sueldo *NOUN MASC* ❶ **salary** ❷ **wage** ❸ aumento de sueldo pay rise

suelo¹ *NOUN MASC* ❶ **floor** ❷ **ground**; tirarse al suelo to throw yourself to the ground

suelo² *VERB* ▸ SEE **soler**

suelta¹, suelte, suelto¹, *etc VERB* ▸ SEE **soltar**

suelto² *NOUN MASC* **small change**; ¿tienes suelto? do you have any small change?

suelto³, suelta² *ADJECTIVE* ❶ **loose**; el tornillo está suelto the screw is loose ❷ dinero suelto small change

suena, suene, sueno, *etc VERB* ▸ SEE **sonar**

sueña, sueñe sueño¹, *etc VERB* ▸ SEE **soñar**

sueño² *NOUN MASC* ❶ **dream** ❷ tener sueño to be sleepy, tener el sueño ligero to be a light sleeper

suerte *NOUN FEM* **luck**; tener suerte to be lucky, traer mala suerte to bring bad luck, ¡qué mala suerte! what bad luck!

suéter *NOUN MASC* **sweater**

suficiente *NOUN MASC* **pass**

suficiente *ADJECTIVE* **enough**

sufrir *VERB* [19] ❶ **to suffer**; sufre mucho he's suffering a lot ❷ **to have**; sufrir un accidente to have an accident, sufre una grave enfermedad he has a serious illness

sugerencia *NOUN FEM* **suggestion**

a
b
c
d
e
f
g
h
i
j
k
l
m
n
ñ
o
p
q
r
s
t
u
v
w
x
y
z

sugerir *VERB* [14] to suggest

sugestión *NOUN FEM* suggestion

sugiera, sugiero, sugirieron, *etc VERB* ▸ SEE **sugerir**

suicidarse *REFLEXIVE VERB* [17] to commit suicide

suicidio *NOUN MASC* suicide

Suiza *NOUN FEM* Switzerland

suizo, suiza *NOUN MASC, FEM, ADJECTIVE* Swiss

sujetador *NOUN MASC* bra

sujeto, sujeta *ADJECTIVE* ❶ secure; está bien sujeto it's really secure ❷ tener sujeto a to have hold of ❸ estar sujeto a algo to be subject to something

suma *NOUN FEM* ❶ addition ❷ en suma in short

sumar *VERB* [17] to add

supe, supiste, *etc VERB* ▸ SEE **saber**

súper, super *ADJECTIVE (informal)* super

súper *ADVERB (informal)* really; cantan súper bien they sing really well, me lo pasé súper bien I had a great time

superar *VERB* [17] ❶ to overcome *(fear or a problem)* ❷ to get over *(a shock)* ❸ to exceed

superficie *NOUN FEM* surface

superior *ADJECTIVE* ❶ superior; es superior a los demás en calidad it's better quality than all the others ❷ top *(floor or layer)* ❸ upper *(lip)* ❹ higher *(level or class)*

supermercado *NOUN MASC* supermarket

superstición *NOUN FEM* superstition

supersticioso, supersticiosa *ADJECTIVE* superstitious

supervisar *VERB* [17] supervise

supervisor, supervisora *NOUN MASC, FEM* supervisor

superviviente *NOUN MASC & FEM* survivor

suplementario, suplementaria *ADJECTIVE* additional

suplemento *NOUN MASC* supplement

supondrá, supondré, supondría, *etc VERB* ▸ SEE **suponer**

suponer *VERB* [11] to suppose; supongo que sí I suppose so

suponga, supongo, *etc VERB* ▸ SEE **suponer**

supositorio *NOUN MASC* suppository

suprimir *VERB* [19] ❶ to suppress *(news)* ❷ to abolish ❸ to delete

supuesto *IN PHRASE* por supuesto of course

supuse, supuso *VERB* ▸ SEE **suponer**

sur *NOUN MASC* south

Suramérica *NOUN FEM* South America

suramericano, suramericana *NOUN MASC & FEM*

suramericano *ADJECTIVE* South American

sureste *NOUN MASC* southeast

surf *NOUN MASC* surfing; practicar el surf to go surfing

surfista *NOUN MASC & FEM* surfer *(in the sea)*

suroeste NOUN MASC **southwest**

surtido¹ NOUN MASC ❶ **assortment** ❷ **selection**

surtido², surtida ADJECTIVE ❶ **assorted** ❷ una tienda bien surtida a well-stocked shop

surtidor NOUN MASC **petrol pump**

suspender VERB [18] ❶ **to fail**; he suspendido la física I've failed physics ❷ **to suspend** (a payment or service) ❸ suspender un viaje to call off a trip

suspense NOUN MASC **suspense**; película de suspense thriller (film)

suspenso NOUN MASC **fail**; sacar un suspenso en examen to fail an exam

suspirar VERB [17] **to sigh**

suspiro NOUN MASC **sigh**

sustancia NOUN FEM **substance**

sustantivo NOUN MASC **noun**

sustituir VERB [54] ❶ **to replace**; sustituir algo por algo to replace something with something ❷ sustituir a alguien to stand in for someone (at work), to come on as a substitute for someone (in football, for example)

sustituto, sustituta NOUN MASC, FEM ❶ **replacement** ❷ **substitute** ❸ **locum**

susto NOUN MASC **fright**; darle un susto a alguien to give someone a fright, ¡qué susto me llevé! I got such a fright!

sustraer VERB [42] **to subtract**

susurrar VERB [17] **to whisper**

sutil ADJECTIVE **subtle**

suyo, suya ADJECTIVE ❶ **his/hers**; (goes after the noun) un conocido suyo a friend of his/hers; venían con un amigo suyo they came with a friend of theirs ❸ **yours** (polite form)

suyo PRONOUN ❶ **his/hers**; el suyo es gris his/hers is grey, las suyas son mejores his/hers are better ❷ **yours** (polite form) ❸ **theirs**; no es el de mis hijos, el suyo es más grande it's not my children's, theirs is bigger

a
b
c
d
e
f
g
h
i
j
k
l
m
n
ñ
o
p
q
r
s
t
u
v
w
x
y
z

Tt

tabaco NOUN MASC ❶ tobacco ❷ cigarettes; tengo que comprar tabaco I've got to buy some cigarettes

tabaquismo NOUN MASC tobacco addiction

taberna NOUN FEM bar (selling wine)

tabla NOUN FEM ❶ plank ❷ board; una tabla de planchar an ironing board, una tabla de picar a chopping board ❸ tabla de multiplicar multiplication table ❹ tabla de gimnasia circuit training ❺ pleat

tablao NOUN MASC un tablao flamenco a flamenco bar

tablero NOUN MASC ❶ board (for a game); un tablero de damas a draughtboard ❷ noticeboard

tablón NOUN MASC ❶ plank ❷ tablón de anuncios noticeboard

taburete NOUN MASC stool

tacaño, tacaña NOUN MASC, FEM miser

tacaño ADJECTIVE stingy

tachar VERB [17] to cross out

taco NOUN MASC ❶ cue (in billards) ❷ stud (on a sports boot) ❸ (informal) swearword

tacón NOUN MASC heel; zapatos de tacón alto high-heeled shoes, tacón de aguja stiletto heel

táctica NOUN FEM ❶ tactic ❷ tactics

tacto NOUN MASC ❶ sense of touch ❷ feel ❸ tact; fue una falta de tacto it was really tactless

tal ADJECTIVE ❶ such; tal cosa es imposible such a thing is impossible ❷ tenía tal preocupación que ... I was so worried that ..., había tal cantidad de cajas que ... there were so many boxes that ... ❸ en tal caso in that case

tal ADVERB ❶ ¿qué tal estás? (informal) how are you doing?, ¿qué tal van las cosas? (informal) how are things? ❷ tal vez maybe ❸ con tal de que as long as
• son tal para cual one is as bad as the other

talco NOUN MASC talc; polvos de talco talcum powder

talento NOUN MASC talent

TALGO ABBREVIATION MASC (short for Tren Articulado Ligero Goicoechea Oriol) express train

talla NOUN FEM size; ¿qué talla de pantalones tienes? what size of trousers do you take?

taller NOUN MASC ❶ workshop ❷ garage; llevar el coche al taller to take the car to the garage

talón NOUN MASC heel

talonario NOUN MASC chequebook

tamaño NOUN MASC size; hay de todos los tamaños they come in all sizes

también ADVERB too; ella también vive allí she lives there too, 'tengo quince años' – 'yo también' 'I'm fifteen' – 'so am I', 'yo quiero tarta'

– 'yo también' 'I want some cake'
– 'so do I'

tambor *NOUN MASC* **drum**

tampoco *ADVERB* él tampoco irá he won't go either, 'a mí no me gusta'
– 'a mí tampoco' 'I don't like it'
– 'neither do I'

tampón *NOUN MASC* **tampon**

tan *ADVERB* ❶ **so**; no es tan fácil it's not so easy ❷ **such**; es una persona tan egoísta he's such a selfish person ❸ *(in comparisons)* es tan alto como su padre he's as tall as his father, no era tan caro como el otro it wasn't as expensive as the other one ❹ ¡qué casa tan grande! what a big house!

tanque *NOUN MASC* **tank**

tanto¹ *NOUN MASC* ❶ tanto por ciento percentage, gano un tanto por ciento de las ventas I get a percentage on the sales ❷ **point**, **goal**; marcar un tanto to score a point, to score a goal

tanto² *ADVERB* ❶ **so**; tanto mejor so much the better, no corras tanto don't go so fast, se enfadó tanto he got so upset ❷ **so much**; no deberías gastar tanto you shouldn't spend so much ❸ **so often**; yo no les visito tanto I don't visit them all that often ❹ **so long**; lleva tanto hacerlo it takes so long to do ❺ pesa tanto como este it's as heavy as this one

tanto³, tanta *ADJECTIVE* ❶ **so much**; tanto dinero so much money, tanta sal so much salt ❷ **so many**; tantos libros so many books, tantas cajas so many boxes, había tanta gente que no cabíamos there were so many people that there wasn't

room for us ❸ tanto/tanta ... como ... as much ... as ..., no gasta tanta gasolina como el coche viejo it doesn't use as much petrol as the old car ❹ tantos/tantas ... como ... as many ... as ..., no hay tantos alumnos como antes there aren't as many students as before

tanto *PRONOUN* ❶ tanto/tanta so much, no hace falta tanto/tanta we don't need so much ❷ tantos/tantas so many, vinieron tantos que no había sillas libres so many came that there weren't any chairs left ❸ tanto *(referring to time)* so long, no tardes tanto como ayer don't take as long as yesterday, 'me llevará dos días hacerlo' – '¿tanto?' 'it'll take me two days to do it' – 'as long as that?' ❹ por lo tanto therefore ❺ mientras tanto in the meantime, entre tanto in the meantime

tapa *NOUN FEM* ❶ **lid** ❷ **top**; tapa de rosca screw top ❸ **tapa** *(a small snack chosen from a selection in a tapas bar)*; un bar de tapas a tapas bar, comer de tapas to eat tapas for lunch, supper, etc

tapar *VERB* [17] ❶ **to cover** ❷ **to put the top on** ❸ tapar un agujero to fill a hole ❹ **to block** *(a road or door)*

tapón *NOUN MASC* ❶ **cork** ❷ **top** *(of a bottle)* ❸ **plug** *(of a sink or bath)*

taquilla *NOUN FEM* ❶ **box office**; éxito de taquilla box office hit ❷ **ticket office**

tardar *VERB* [17] **to take a long time**; tardó mucho en contestarme she took a long time to answer, ¿cuánto se tarda de Sevilla a Córdoba? how long does it take from Seville to Cordoba?, ¡no tardes! don't be long!, no tardes en volver come back soon, a las cuatro a más tardar at four o'clock at the latest

tarde NOUN FEM **afternoon, evening**; buenas tardes good afternoon, good evening, por la tarde in the afternoon, in the evening

tarde ADVERB **late**; llegar tarde to be late, se hizo tarde it got late, tarde o temprano sooner or later

tarea NOUN FEM ❶ **task** ❷ las tareas de la casa the housework ❸ **homework**

tarifa NOUN FEM ❶ **price list** ❷ tarifa telefónica telephone charges

tarjeta NOUN FEM **card**; una tarjeta (postal) a postcard, una tarjeta de crédito a credit card, una tarjeta telefónica a telephone card, una tarjeta de embarque a boarding card, una tarjeta de cumpleaños a birthday card, una tarjeta de Navidad a Christmas card, una tarjeta de fidelidad a loyalty card, sacarle a alguien la tarjeta amarilla/roja to show somebody the yellow/red card

tarrina NOUN FEM **tub** (for food)

tarro NOUN MASC **jar**

tarta NOUN FEM **cake**; una tarta de cumpleaños a birthday cake, tarta helada ice-cream cake

tartera NOUN FEM **sandwich box**

tasa NOUN FEM ❶ **rate**; la tasa de interés the interest rate, la tasa de desempleo the level of unemployment ❷ **valuation** ❸ **tax**

tatuaje NOUN MASC **tatoo**

tauro NOUN MASC & FEM **taurus**; es tauro he's Taurus

Tauro NOUN MASC **Taurus**

taxi NOUN MASC **taxi**

taxista NOUN MASC & FEM **taxi driver**

taza NOUN FEM ❶ **cup**; taza de café coffee cup, cup of coffee ❷ **(toilet) bowl**

tazón NOUN MASC **bowl**

te PRONOUN ❶ **you**; te quiero I love you, te vi ayer I saw you yesterday ❷ **to you**; te lo mandaré por correo I'll post it to you ❸ *(with parts of the body and personal belongings)* ¿te has cortado el dedo? have you cut your finger?, ¿quieres quitarte los zapatos? do you want to take your shoes off? ❹ *(having things done)* ¿te has cortado el pelo? have you had your hair cut? ❺ **yourself**; cuídate mucho look after yourself ❻ siéntate sit down

té NOUN MASC **tea**; voy a tomar un té I'm going to have a cup of tea

teatro NOUN MASC **theatre**

tebeo NOUN MASC **comic** (for children)

techo NOUN MASC ❶ **ceiling** ❷ techo corredizo/solar sunroof ❸ sin techo homeless

tecla NOUN FEM **key**

teclado NOUN MASC **keyboard**

técnica[1] NOUN FEM **technique**

técnico, técnica[2] NOUN MASC, FEM **technician**

técnico ADJECTIVE **technical**

tecnología NOUN FEM **technology**

teja NOUN FEM **tile**

tejado NOUN MASC **roof**

tejanos *PLURAL NOUN MASC* **jeans**

tejer *VERB* [18] ❶ **to weave** ❷ **to knit**

tela *NOUN FEM* ❶ **fabric**; tela de algodón cotton fabric ❷ **canvas** *(for painting)*

telaraña *NOUN FEM* ❶ **spider's web** ❷ **cobweb** ❸ **spider diagram**

tele *NOUN FEM (informal)* **telly**, **TV**; ver la tele to watch telly, poner la tele to switch on the telly

telediario *NOUN MASC* **television news**

telefonear *VERB* [17] **to telephone**

telefónico, telefónica *ADJECTIVE* **telephone**; conversación telefónica telephone conversation, listín telefónico telephone book

teléfono *NOUN MASC* **telephone**; llamar por teléfono a alguien to phone somebody, no tengo teléfono I'm not on the phone *(I don't have a phone)*, contestar el teléfono to answer the phone, colgar el teléfono to put down the phone, estaba hablando por teléfono I was on the phone, no has colgado bien el teléfono you've left the phone off the hook, teléfono celular/móvil mobile phone

telegrama *NOUN MASC* **telegram**

telenovela *NOUN FEM* **TV series**

telescopio *NOUN MASC* **telescope**

teletrabajo *NOUN MASC* **teleworking**

televisión *NOUN FEM* **television**; ver la televisión to watch television, poner la televisión to switch on the television, hoy ponen una película en la televisión there's a film on the television today

televisor *NOUN MASC* **television set**

tema *NOUN MASC* ❶ **subject** ❷ **topic**

temblar *VERB* [29] ❶ **to shiver** ❷ **to shake**; le temblaban las manos his hands were shaking

temer *VERB* [18] ❶ **to fear** *(danger or punishment)* ❷ temer a alguien to be afraid of somebody

temerse *REFLEXIVE VERB* [18] ❶ **to fear** ❷ me temo que no podré acudir I'm afraid I won't be able to come

temperatura *NOUN FEM* **temperature**; ha bajado la temperatura the temperature has dropped

tempestad *NOUN FEM* **storm**

templado, templada *ADJECTIVE* ❶ **mild** *(climate)* ❷ **warm** ❸ **lukewarm**

temporada *NOUN FEM* **season**; fuera de temporada out of season

temprano¹ *ADVERB* **early**; llegar temprano to arrive early

temprano², temprana *ADJECTIVE* **early**

tendencia *NOUN FEM* **tendency**

tender *VERB* [36] ❶ tender a to tend to, tienden a molestarse they tend to get upset ❷ tender la ropa to hang out the washing

tenderse *REFLEXIVE VERB* [36] **to lie down**; tenderse al sol to lie down in the sun

tendero, tendera *NOUN MASC, FEM* **shopkeeper**

tendrá, tendré, tendría, *etc VERB* ▸SEE **tener**

a
b
c
d
e
f
g
h
i
j
k
l
m
n
ñ
o
p
q
r
s
t
u
v
w
x
y
z

tenedor NOUN MASC **fork**

tener VERB [9] ❶ to have; tengo dos hermanas I've got two sisters, tiene los ojos marrones he's got brown eyes, tener dolor de cabeza to have a headache, no tengo tiempo I haven't got the time, ¿tienes hora? have you got the time?, ha tenido un niño she had a baby ❷ tener sed to be thirsty, tener frío to be cold, ¡qué calor tengo! I'm really hot!, ten cuidado be careful ❸ tener sueño to feel sleepy, tener envidia de alguien to be jealous of somebody ❹ tener que hacer to have to do, no puedo, tengo que estudiar I can't, I have to study, tienes que obedecerme you must do as I tell you, tengo que ir a verla un día I must go and see her one day, tendrían que ayudarme they would have to help me, tendría que ir al banco I should go to the bank ❺ tiene que haberse perdido he must have got lost ❻ tener que ver con alguien, no tiene nada que ver con él it has nothing to do with him ❼ lo tengo hecho I've done it, lo tienen solucionado they've sorted it out, tenía pensado invitarlos I'd thought about inviting them

tenga, tengo, etc VERB ▸ SEE **tener**

teniente NOUN MASC & FEM **lieutenant**

tenis NOUN MASC **tennis**; tenis de mesa table tennis

tenista NOUN MASC & FEM **tennis player**

tensión NOUN FEM ❶ **tension** ❷ **stress** ❸ **blood pressure**; tomarse la tensión to have your blood pressure taken

tentación NOUN FEM **temptation**

tentar VERB [29] **to tempt**

teñir VERB [65] **to dye**

teñirse REFLEXIVE VERB [65] **to dye**; teñirse el pelo to have your hair dyed

tercer ADJECTIVE **third** (see also 'tercero/tercera')

tercero, tercera ADJECTIVE (note that 'tercero' becomes 'tercer' before a masculine singular noun), **third**; la tercera puerta a la derecha the third door on the right, el tercer piso the third floor, llegar en tercer lugar to finish in third position, el Tercer Mundo the Third World

terciopelo NOUN MASC **velvet**

terco, terca ADJECTIVE **stubborn**

terminado, terminada ADJECTIVE **finished**

terminal NOUN FEM ❶ **terminal** ❷ **bus station**

terminal ADJECTIVE **terminal**

terminar VERB [17] ❶ **to finish**; ¿cuándo termina el colegio? when does school finish, aún no he terminado I haven't finished yet, no he terminado de revisarlo I haven't finished checking it ❷ terminar con to finish with, ¿has terminado con el libro? have you finished with the book?, ha terminado con su novio she's broken up with her boyfriend ❸ to end up; terminamos en una discoteca we ended up in a disco, terminó harta she was fed up in the end, terminaron por pelearse they ended up having a fight ❹ to end in; su nombre termina en 'l' her name ends in 'l', termina en punta it's pointed, termina en una cruz it's got a cross at the end

terminarse *REFLEXIVE VERB* [17] **❶ to be over**; la clase se terminó a las cinco the lesson was over at five **❷** se ha terminado la leche we've run out of milk, se me terminó la tinta del boli my pen ran out (of ink)

termo *NOUN MASC* **Thermos**

termómetro *NOUN MASC* **thermometer**

ternera¹ *NOUN FEM* **veal**

ternero, ternera² *NOUN MASC, FEM* **calf**

terraza *NOUN FEM* **❶ balcony ❷ terrace** *(of a café or bar)*

terremoto *NOUN MASC* **earthquake**

terreno *NOUN MASC* **❶ plot of land ❷ field ❸ land**; la casa tiene mucho terreno the house has a lot of land **❹** terreno de juego football pitch

terrible *ADJECTIVE* **terrible**

territorio *NOUN MASC* **territory**

terrón *NOUN MASC* **lump** *(of sugar, earth)*

terror *NOUN MASC* **terror**

terrorismo *NOUN MASC* **terrorism**

terrorista *NOUN MASC & FEM*

terrorista *ADJECTIVE* **terrorist**

tesoro *NOUN MASC* **treasure**

test *NOUN MASC* **❶ test ❷** examen tipo test multiple-choice exam

testamento *NOUN MASC* **will**; hacer testamento to make your will

testigo *NOUN MASC & FEM* **witness**

tétano *NOUN MASC* **tetanus**

tetera *NOUN FEM* **teapot**

texto *NOUN MASC* **text**

ti *PRONOUN* **❶ you**; detrás de ti behind you, se olvidaron de ti they forgot about you, a mí no me dijo nada, ¿y a ti? he hasn't told me anything – has he told you? **❷ to you**; te lo dio a ti he gave it to you **❸** ¿a ti te gusta? do you like it?, ¿a ti qué te parece? what do you think? **❹** ti mismo/misma yourself, sabes cuidar de ti misma you can look after yourself

tía *NOUN FEM* **aunt**

tibio, tibia *ADJECTIVE* **lukewarm**

tiburón *NOUN MASC* **shark**

tiembla, tiemblo, *etc VERB* ▸ SEE **temblar**

tiempo *NOUN MASC* **❶ time**; llegar a tiempo to be on time, tiempo libre spare time, ha pasado mucho tiempo desde entonces it's been a long time since then, hace mucho tiempo que no la veo I haven't seen her for a long time, ¿cuánto tiempo hace que se fueron? how long ago did they go?, al mismo tiempo at the same time, la mayor parte del tiempo most of the time **❷** ¿cada cuánto tiempo? how often?, cada cierto tiempo every so often **❸** por un tiempo for a while **❹** a su debido tiempo in due course **❺** trabajar a tiempo completo to work full time, trabajar a tiempo parcial to work part time **❻** en aquellos tiempos in those days, corren otros tiempos things are different now **❼ weather**; el pronóstico del tiempo the weather forecast, nos hizo buen tiempo we had nice weather **❽** el primer tiempo the first half *(of a match)* **❾ tense** *(in grammar)*

tienda¹ *NOUN FEM* ❶ **shop**; una tienda de discos a record shop, una tienda de recuerdos a souvenir shop, una tienda de comestibles a grocer's ❷ una tienda de campaña a tent

tienda², **tiendo**, *etc VERB*
▸ SEE **tender**

tierno, **tierna** *ADJECTIVE* ❶ **tender** *(meat)* ❷ **affectionate**

tierra *NOUN FEM* ❶ **land**; tierra adentro inland, viajar por tierra to travel overland ❷ **earth** ❸ **ground**; tierra firme solid ground ❹ tomar tierra to land

tiesto *NOUN MASC* **flowerpot**

tigre *NOUN MASC* **tiger**

tijeras *PLURAL NOUN FEM* **scissors**; un par de tijeras/unas tijeras a pair of scissors

timbre *NOUN MASC* **bell**, **doorbell**; tocar el timbre to ring the bell

tímido, **tímida** *ADJECTIVE* **shy**

tinta *NOUN FEM* **ink**

tinto *NOUN MASC* **red wine**

tinto *ADJECTIVE* **red** *(wine)*

tintorería *NOUN FEM* **dry cleaner's**

tiña, **tiñeron**, **tiño**, **tiñó**, *etc VERB*
▸ SEE **teñir**

tío *NOUN MASC* ❶ **uncle** ❷ mis tíos my uncles, my aunt and uncle ❸ *(informal)* **guy**

tiovivo *NOUN MASC* **merry-go-round**

típico, **típica** *ADJECTIVE* **typical**

tipo *NOUN MASC* ❶ **type** ❷ **figure**, **physique**; tiene buen tipo she's got a good figure ❸ tipo de cambio exchange rate, tipo de interés interest rate

tirantes *NOUN MASC & PLURAL* **braces**

tirar *VERB* [17] ❶ **to throw**; tirar algo al suelo to throw something on the floor ❷ tirarle algo a alguien to throw something at somebody, tírame ese boli throw me that pen ❸ **to throw away**; no tires esos papeles don't throw these papers away, tirar algo a la basura to throw something out *(that you no longer want)* ❹ **to pull**; tira un poco más pull a bit more ❺ tirar de algo to pull something, tira de la cuerda cuando yo te diga pull the rope when I tell you ❻ tirarle de las orejas a alguien to tweak somebody's ear *(in Spain you do this when you wish somebody happy birthday)* ❼ **to shoot**; tirar una flecha to shoot an arrow, tirar una bomba to drop a bomb ❽ **to knock over**; tiré una silla sin querer I accidentally knocked a chair over ❾ **to knock down**; tiraron la puerta abajo they knocked the door down

tirarse *REFLEXIVE VERB* [17] tirarse al suelo to throw yourself to the ground, tirarse al agua to dive into the water, tirarse en paracaídas to parachute, to bale out

tirita *NOUN FEM* **sticking plaster**

tiritar *VERB* [17] **to shiver**; tiritar de frío to shiver with cold

tiro *NOUN MASC* ❶ **shot**; disparar un tiro to fire a shot, matar a alguien de un tiro to shoot somebody dead, tiro al blanco target shooting ❷ **shot** *(in sport)*; un tiro a portería a shot at goal, un tiro libre a free kick

tirón *NOUN MASC* **pull**; dar un tirón a algo to pull something
• de un tirón *(informal)* in one go

tisana *NOUN FEM* **herbal tea**

títere *NOUN MASC* ❶ **puppet** ❷ títeres puppet show

título *NOUN MASC* ❶ **title** ❷ **heading** ❸ **degree**; título universitario university degree ❹ **certificate** ❺ título nobiliario title (such as 'duke' or 'duchess')

tiza *NOUN FEM* **chalk**; una tiza a piece of chalk

toalla *NOUN FEM* **towel**

tobillo *NOUN MASC* **ankle**

tobogán *NOUN MASC* **slide**

tocador *NOUN MASC* **dressing table**

tocar *VERB* [31] ❶ **to touch**; me tocó el hombro he touched me on the shoulder, toqué la escultura I touched the sculpture, tocar un tema to touch on a subject ❷ tocar el timbre to ring the bell ❸ tocar la bocina to blow the horn ❹ **to play** (an instrument); tocar el violín to play the violin ❺ tocarle a alguien hacer to be somebody's turn to do, te toca jugar it's your turn to play ❻ les ha tocado un viaje they've won a trip, nunca me ha tocado la lotería I've never won the lottery

tocarse *REFLEXIVE VERB* [31] **to touch**; se tocó la cabeza he touched his head, los dos cables se están tocando the two cables are touching

tocino *NOUN MASC* **bacon**

todavía *ADVERB* ❶ **still**; todavía nos vemos we still see each other ❷ **yet**; todavía no han llegado they haven't arrived yet ❸ **even**; todavía más tarde even later

todo¹, toda *ADJECTIVE* ❶ **all**; todos mis amigos all my friends, viajar por todo el mundo to travel all over the world ❷ **whole**; toda la semana the whole week, se comieron toda la caja de bombones they ate the whole box of chocolates ❸ todos los días every day, hay que revisar todas las carpetas we have to check every folder ❹ a toda velocidad at top speed

todo *PRONOUN* ❶ **everything**; se lo conté todo I told him everything, a pesar de todo despite everything ❷ **all**; todo o nada all or nothing, vinieron todos they all came, todos estábamos de acuerdo we were all in agreement ❸ ante todo above all ❹ con todo even so ❺ de todo everything, tienen de todo they've got everything ❻ sobre todo no te olvides del billete above all, don't forget the ticket, se divirtieron mucho, sobre todo Ana they enjoyed themselves a lot, specially Ana

todo *ADVERB* ❶ **all**; estaba todo nervioso he was all nervous ❷ **completely**; está todo roto it's completely had it ❸ seguir todo derecho to carry straight on

todo² *NOUN MASC* el todo the whole

tomar *VERB* [17] ❶ **to take**; tomar el autobús to take the bus, me tomó del brazo she took me by the arm ❷ **to have**; tomar el desayuno to have breakfast, ¿quieres tomar un café? would you like a coffee? ❸ toma, tu billete here's your ticket ❹ tomar el sol to sunbathe ❺ tomar el aire to get some fresh air ❻ tomar algo en serio to take something seriously, tomar algo a mal to take something the wrong way, tomar algo mal/bien to take something badly/well

tomarse *REFLEXIVE VERB* [17] ❶ **to take**; tomarse unas vacaciones to take some holiday, tomarse la molestia de hacer to take the trouble to do ❷ **to have**; se tomó un helado she had an ice cream ❸ tomarse la tensión to have your blood pressure taken
• tomarle el pelo a alguien *(informal)* **to pull somebody's leg** *(literally: to take somebody's hair)*

tomate *NOUN MASC* **tomato**; salsa de tomate tomato sauce
• ponerse (colorado) como un tomate to go as red as a beetroot

tonelada *NOUN FEM* **ton**

tónica *NOUN FEM* **tonic water**

tono *NOUN MASC* ❶ **tone**; en tono serio in a serious tone ❷ **shade**; telas de tonos suaves materials in soft shades ❸ tono de marcar dial tone, tono de ocupado engaged tone
• fuera de tono inappropriate *(a comment)*

tontería *NOUN FEM* vaya tontería how silly, no te enfades por esa tontería don't get upset over such a silly thing, decir tonterías to talk nonsense

tonto, tonta *NOUN MASC, FEM* **idiot**
• hacerse el tonto *(informal)* to play the fool
• hacer el tonto *(informal)* to act dumb

tonto *ADJECTIVE* **silly**

topo *NOUN MASC* **mole** *(animal)*

torbellino *NOUN MASC* **whirlwind**

torcer *VERB* [41] ❶ **to turn**; tuerce a la derecha al final de la calle turn right at the end of the road, torcer

la esquina to turn the corner, torcer la cabeza to turn your head ❷ **to twist**

torcerse *REFLEXIVE VERB* [41] ❶ **to twist**; torcerse el tobillo to twist your ankle ❷ **to warp**

torcido, torcida *ADJECTIVE* ❶ **twisted**; tiene el tobillo torcido he's twisted his ankle ❷ **crooked**; una línea torcida a crooked line ❸ **bent**

torero, torera *NOUN MASC, FEM* **bullfighter**

tormenta *NOUN FEM* **storm**; tormenta de nieve snowstorm

tormentoso, tormentosa *ADJECTIVE* **stormy**

tornado *NOUN MASC* **tornado**

torneo *NOUN MASC* **tournament**

tornillo *NOUN MASC* **screw**
• le falta un tornillo *(informal)* he's got a screw loose

toro *NOUN MASC* ❶ **bull** ❷ los toros bullfighting, ir a los toros to go to a bullfight, ¿te gustan los toros? do you like bullfighting?

torpe *ADJECTIVE* ❶ **clumsy** ❷ **awkward**

torre *NOUN* ❶ **tower**; torre de alta tensión pylon ❷ **rook, castle** *(in chess)*

torta *NOUN FEM* ❶ **cake** ❷ darle una torta a alguien to slap somebody ❸ me pegué una torta con la farola I banged into the streetlamp *(on foot)*, I crashed into the streetlamp *(in a car)*
• no entiendo ni torta *(informal)* I don't understand a thing

tortilla NOUN FEM **omelette**; tortilla francesa French omelette, tortilla española Spanish omelette, tortilla

tortuga NOUN FEM ❶ **tortoise** ❷ **turtle**

torturar VERB [17] **to torture**

tos NOUN FEM **cough**; tener tos to have a cough, le dio la tos he started coughing

toser VERB [18] **to cough**

tostada NOUN FEM una tostada a piece of toast, tomo tostadas para desayunar I have toast for breakfast

tostador NOUN MASC **toaster**

tostadora NOUN FEM **toaster**

tostar VERB [24] ❶ **to toast** (bread) ❷ **to roast** (coffee)

tostarse REFLEXIVE VERB [24] **to tan, to go brown**

total NOUN MASC **total**; ¿cuánto es el total? how much is the total?, son cinco mil quinientas en total it's five thousand five hundred in total

total ADJECTIVE **total**

totalidad NOUN FEM la totalidad del colegio the whole school, la totalidad de los alumnos all the pupils

tóxico, tóxica ADJECTIVE **tóxico/tóxica**; residuos tóxicos toxic waste

trabajador, trabajadora NOUN MASC, FEM **worker**

trabajador ADJECTIVE **hard-working**

trabajar VERB [17] **to work**; trabaja de camarera she works as a waitress, trabaja de canguro she's a babysitter, trabajar a tiempo completo to work full time, trabajar a tiempo parcial to work part time

trabajo NOUN MASC ❶ **work**; estar sin trabajo to be out of work, trabajo a tiempo completo full-time work, trabajo a tiempo parcial part-time work, el trabajo de la casa the housework ❷ **job**; buscar trabajo to look for a job, quedarse sin trabajo to lose your job, un trabajo fijo a steady job ❸ trabajos manuales handicrafts ❹ **piece of work**; un trabajo sobre la contaminación an essay on pollution

trabalenguas NOUN MASC (does not change in the plural) **tongue twister**

tractor NOUN MASC **tractor**

tradición NOUN FEM **tradition**

tradicional ADJECTIVE **traditional**

traducción NOUN FEM **translation**

traducir VERB [60] **to translate**

traductor, traductora NOUN MASC, FEM **translator**

traduje, traduzca, traduzco, etc VERB ▸ SEE **traducir**

traer VERB [42] ❶ **to bring**; he traído algo de comida I've brought some food, me trae un café, por favor would you bring me a coffee, please?, la traerá en coche a la estación he'll bring her to the station in his car, traer buena suerte to bring good luck, to be lucky ❷ **to carry**; la traía en brazos he was carrying her in his arms

traficante NOUN MASC & FEM **dealer**; traficante de armas arms dealer

tráfico NOUN MASC ❶ **traffic** ❷ **trade**; tráfico de armas arms trade, tráfico de drogas drug dealing

tragaperras NOUN MASC & FEM (does not change in the plural) (informal) **slot machine**

tragar VERB [28] to swallow

tragarse REFLEXIVE VERB [28] to swallow; se tragó un hueso de aceituna he swallowed an olive stone

tragedia NOUN FEM **tragedy**

trágico, trágica ADJECTIVE **tragic**

traición NOUN FEM ❶ treason ❷ una traición an act of treachery

traidor, traidora NOUN MASC & FEM **traitor**

traiga, traigo traje[1], etc VERB ▶ SEE **traer**

traje[2] NOUN MASC ❶ suit ❷ traje de baño swimsuit, swimming trunks ❸ costume; un traje de luces a bullfighter's costume ❹ dress; en traje típico in traditional dress

trama NOUN FEM **plot**

trampa NOUN FEM trap; tenderle una trampa a alguien to set a trap for somebody

trampilla NOUN FEM **trapdoor**

trampolín NOUN MASC ❶ springboard, diving board ❷ trampoline ❸ ski jump

tramposo, tramposa NOUN **cheat**

tranquillo NOUN MASC knack; coger el tranquillo a algo to get the knack of something

tranquilo, tranquila ADJECTIVE ❶ quiet; una calle tranquila a quiet street ❷ relaxed; se le ve tranquilo he looks relaxed, ¡tranquilo! relax! ❸ calm; un ambiente tranquilo

a calm environment ❹ ¡déjame tranquilo! leave me alone! ❺ tengo la conciencia tranquila my conscience is clear

transbordador NOUN MASC ❶ ferry ❷ transbordador espacial space shuttle

transbordar VERB [17] ❶ to transfer (luggage or goods) ❷ to change (trains, for example)

transbordo NOUN MASC change; hacer transbordo to change (trains, buses), haz transbordo en Sol change at Sol

transeúnte NOUN MASC & FEM **passer-by**

transferencia NOUN FEM transfer; transferencia bancaria bank transfer

transformar VERB [17] ❶ to transform ❷ to convert; tranformar algo en algo to convert something into something

transformarse REFLEXIVE VERB [17] ❶ to be transformed ❷ to be converted

transfusión NOUN FEM **transfusion**

transmisión NOUN FEM broadcast; transmisión en directo live broadcast, transmisión en diferido pre-recorded broadcast

transparente ADJECTIVE **transparent**

transportar VERB [17] to transport, to carry (people)

transporte NOUN MASC **transport**

tranvía NOUN MASC **tram**

trapo NOUN MASC cloth; un trapo del polvo a duster, un trapo de cocina a tea towel

tras *PREPOSITION* ❶ **behind**; tras de mí behind me ❷ **after**; hora tras hora hour after hour, tras despedirme, subí al coche after saying goodbye, I got in the car

trasero, trasera *ADJECTIVE* ❶ **back**; la puerta trasera the back door ❷ **rear**; la rueda trasera the rear wheel

traslado *NOUN MASC* **transfer** *(of an employee)*

trasnochar *VERB* [17] **to stay up late**; anoche trasnochamos we had a late night last night

trasplante *NOUN MASC* **transplant**

tratado *NOUN MASC* **treaty**

tratamiento *NOUN MASC* **treatment**; estar en tratamiento to be undergoing medical treatment

tratar *VERB* [17] ❶ **to treat**; no me trataron bien they didn't treat me very well ❷ no trata sus libros con cuidado she's not careful with her books ❸ tratar a alguien de usted to address somebody using the polite 'usted' form, tratar a alguien de tú to address somebody using the less formal 'tú' form ❹ tratar de hacer to try to do, trató de impedirlo he tried to stop it ❺ tratar de algo to be about something, ¿de qué trata la película? what's the film about?

tratarse *REFLEXIVE VERB* [17] ❶ tratarse de algo to be about something ❷ tratarse de usted to address each other using the polite 'usted' form, tratarse de tú to address each other using the less formal 'tú' form

través *IN PHRASE* a través de algo through something *(from one side to the other)*, across something

travieso, traviesa *ADJECTIVE* **naughty**; no seas travieso don't be naughty

trayecto *NOUN MASC* ❶ **journey**; cubrir un trayecto to make a journey ❷ **road** ❸ final de trayecto end of the line *(on public transport)*

trazar *VERB* [22] ❶ **to trace** ❷ **to draw** *(a map)* ❸ **to draw up** *(a plan)*

trece *NUMBER* ❶ **thirteen**; tiene trece años she's thirteen (years old) ❷ **thirteenth** *(in dates)*; el trece de mayo the thirteenth of May

treinta *NUMBER* ❶ **thirty**; tiene treinta años she's thirty (years old), treinta y siente thirty-seven ❷ **thirtieth** *(in dates)*; el treinta de mayo the thirtieth of May

tremendo, tremenda *ADJECTIVE* **tremendous**; una tremenda victoria/derrota a tremendous victory/defeat

tren *NOUN MASC* ❶ **train**; coger el tren to catch the train, ir en tren to go by train, un tren directo a through train, un tren de cercanías a local train, un tren de largo recorrido a long-distance train, un tren de alta velocidad a high-speed train ❷ tren de aterrizaje landing gear ❸ tren de montaje assembly line

trepar *VERB* [17] **to climb**; trepar a un árbol to climb a tree

tres *NUMBER* ❶ **three**; tiene tres años she's three (years old) ❷ **third** *(in dates)*; el tres de mayo the third of May ❸ **three** *(in clock time)*; son las tres it's three o'clock

trescientos, trescientas *NUMBER* **three hundred**; trescientos veinte three hundred and twenty

a
b
c
d
e
f
g
h
i
j
k
l
m
n
ñ
o
p
q
r
s
t
u
v
w
x
y
z

triángulo NOUN MASC **triangle**

tribu NOUN FEM **tribe**

tribunal NOUN MASC ❶ **court** ❷ **tribunal**

trigo NOUN MASC **wheat**

trillizos, **trillizas** PLURAL NOUN MASC, FEM **triplets**

trimestre NOUN MASC ❶ **term** *(in school)* ❷ **quarter** *(three months)*

trineo NOUN MASC **sledge**

Trinidad NOUN FEM **Trinidad**

trinitense ADJECTIVE, NOUN **Trinidadian**

triniteño, **triniteña** ADJECTIVE, NOUN **Trinidadian**

tripa NOUN FEM ❶ *(informal)* **belly** ❷ **gut** ❸ **tripas innards**

triple NOUN MASC **el triple del precio original three times the original price**, **es el triple de ancho it's three times as wide**, **subió al triple it tripled**

triple ADJECTIVE **triple**

triplicarse REFLEXIVE VERB [31] **to triple**; **el precio se ha triplicado the price has tripled**

tripulación NOUN FEM **crew**

tripulante NOUN MASC & FEM **crew member**

triste ADJECTIVE ❶ **sad** ❷ **gloomy**

tristeza NOUN FEM **sadness**

triunfar VERB [17] **to triumph**

triunfo NOUN MASC ❶ **victory** ❷ **triumph**

trivial ADJECTIVE **trivial**

trofeo NOUN MASC **trophy**

trombón NOUN MASC **trombone**

trompeta NOUN FEM **trumpet**

tronar VERB [24] **to thunder**

tronco NOUN MASC ❶ **trunk** ❷ **log**
• **dormir como un tronco to sleep like a log**

trono NOUN MASC **throne**

tropezar VERB [25] **to trip**; **tropezar con algo to trip over something**

tropezarse REFLEXIVE VERB [25] **to trip**; **tropezarse con algo to trip over something**, **to come up against something** *(a problem)*

tropezón NOUN MASC **stumble**; **dar un tropezón to stumble**

trópico NOUN MASC **tropic**

tropiece, **tropiezo**, *etc* VERB ▸ SEE **tropezar**

trotar VERB [17] **to trot**

trozo NOUN MASC **piece**; **un trozo de tela a piece of cloth**

trucha NOUN FEM **trout**

truco NOUN MASC **trick**; **el truco está en hacerlo despacio the trick is to do it slowly**

trueno NOUN MASC **thunder**

tu ADJECTIVE **your**; **tu casa your house**, **tus amigos your friends**

tú PRONOUN ❶ **you**; **tú no lo sabes you don't know it** ❷ **tú mismo/ misma yourself**, **hazlo tú mismo do it yourself** ❸ **tratar a alguien de tú to address somebody using the 'tú' form** *(rather than the more formal 'usted')*

tubo *NOUN MASC* ❶ **tube** ❷ **tubo de escape exhaust pipe**

tuerca *NOUN FEM* **nut**

tuerza, tuerzo, *etc VERB*
▶ SEE **torcer**

tuesta, tueste, tuesto, *etc VERB*
▶ SEE **tostar**

tulipán *NOUN MASC* **tulip**

tumba *NOUN FEM* ❶ **grave** ❷ **tomb**

tumbar *VERB* [17] **to knock down;**
tumbar a alguien de un puñetazo
to floor somebody *(with a punch)*

tumbarse *REFLEXIVE VERB* [17] **to lie down;** se tumbó en el sofá he lay
down on the sofa

tumbona *NOUN FEM* **deckchair**

tunecino, tunecina *NOUN MASC, FEM, ADJECTIVE* **Tunisian**

túnel *NOUN MASC* **tunnel**

Túnez *NOUN MASC* **Tunisia**

turbante *NOUN MASC* **turban**

turco, turca *NOUN MASC, FEM, ADJECTIVE* **Turkish**

turismo *NOUN MASC* ❶ **tourism;**
oficina de turismo tourist office,
hacer turismo to travel around, to
go sightseeing ❷ **saloon car**

turista *NOUN MASC & FEM* **tourist**

turístico, turística *ADJECTIVE* **tourist**

turnarse *REFLEXIVE VERB* [17] **to take turns**

turno *NOUN MASC* ❶ **turn;** tocarle el
turno a alguien to be somebody's
turn, te toca el turno a ti it's your
turn ❷ **shift;** turno de noche night
shift, hacer turnos trabajo to work
shifts

Turquía *NOUN FEM* **Turkey**

turrón *NOUN MASC* **nougat** *(a special
sort traditionally eaten in Spain at
Christmas)*

tutear *VERB* [17] tutear a alguien
to address somebody using the
familiar 'tú' form *(rather than the
more formal 'usted')*

tutearse *REFLEXIVE VERB* [17] **to
address each other using the
familiar 'tú' form** *(see note above)*

tutor, tutora *NOUN MASC, FEM* ❶ **tutor**
❷ **class teacher**

tutoría *NOUN FEM* ❶ **study period**
❷ **tutorship**

tuvo, tuvieron, tuviste, *etc VERB*
▶ SEE **tener**

tuyo, tuya *ADJECTIVE* **yours** *(goes after
the noun)*; un amigo tuyo a friend of
yours, una vecina tuya a neighbour
of yours

tuyo *PRONOUN* **yours**; el tuyo es
verde yours is green, las tuyas son
mejores yours are better

Uu

A
B
C
D
E
F
G
H
I
J
K
L
M
N
Ñ
O
P
Q
R
S
T
U
V
W
X
Y
Z

u *CONJUNCTION* **or** *('o' becomes 'u' before words beginning with 'o-' or 'ho-');* uno u otro one or the other

Ucrania *NOUN FEM* **Ukraine**

ucraniano, ucraniana *NOUN MASC, FEM, ADJECTIVE* **Ukrainian**

Ud. *ABBREVIATION (short for usted)* **you**

Uds. *ABBREVIATION (short for ustedes)* **you**

UE *ABBREVIATION FEM (short for Unión Europea)* **EU**

úlcera *NOUN FEM* **ulcer**

últimamente *ADVERB* **lately**

último, última *NOUN MASC, FEM* el último the last one, esta es la última que queda this is the last one left, coge el último del montón take the one at the bottom of the pile

último *ADJECTIVE* ❶ **last**; el último día fuimos a la playa on the last day we went to the beach ❷ **latest**; su última película her latest film, lo último en equipo audio the latest in audio equipment ❸ **top**; el último libro del montón the book at the bottom of the pile

ultramarinos *NOUN MASC (does not change in the plural),* **grocer's shop**

un, una¹ *INDEFINITE ARTICLE* ❶ **a, an**; un hombre a man, una manzana an apple, tiene un año she's a year old/one year old *('un' is used before feminine nouns starting with stressed 'a' or 'ha')* un ala a wing, un hacha an axe ❷ *PLURAL* **unos/unas some, a few,** compré unos sobres I bought some envelopes, se quedarán unas horas they will stay for a few hours ❸ cuesta unas tres mil euros it costs about three thousand euros, llevará unos treinta minutos hacerlo it'll take about thirty minutes to do it

único, única *NOUN MASC & FEM* el único/la única the only one, el único que funciona the only one that works

único *ADJECTIVE* ❶ **unique** ❷ **only**; su único hijo her only child ❸ talla única one size

unidad *NOUN FEM* ❶ **unit**; unidad de cuidados intensivos, unidad de vigilancia intensiva intensive care unit ❷ **unity**

unido, unida *ADJECTIVE* ❶ **united** ❷ **joined** ❸ **close**; las dos hermanas están muy unidas the two sisters are very close

uniforme *NOUN MASC* **uniform**

uniforme *ADJECTIVE* ❶ **uniform** ❷ **even**

Unión Europea *NOUN FEM* **European Union**

unir *VERB* [19] ❶ **to join** ❷ **to combine**; el diseño une la elegancia con la eficacia the design combines elegance and efficiency ❸ **to merge** *(companies, for example)*

unirse *REFLEXIVE VERB* [19] ❶ **to join together** ❷ **to combine** ❸ **to merge**

universidad NOUN FEM **university**; universidad a distancia open university, universidad laboral technical college, estar en la universidad to be at university

universitario, **universitaria** NOUN MASC, FEM **university student**

universitario ADJECTIVE **university**; profesores universitarios university teachers

universo NOUN MASC **universe**

uno[1], **una** NUMBER ❶ **one**; compré solo uno I bought only one, hay una razón there is one reason ❷ **one** (in clock time); la una one o'clock, es la una it's one o'clock, llegaron a la una they arrived at one o'clock ❸ **first** (in dates); el uno de enero the first of January

uno[2], **una** PRONOUN ❶ **one**; de uno en uno one by one (note that 'uno' becomes 'un' before a masculine singular noun) ❷ unos/unas some, unos saben y otros no some know and some don't

unos, **unas** ▸ SEE **un**, **una**[1], **uno**, **una**[2]

uña NOUN FEM **nail** (of finger, toe); una uña del dedo del pie a toe nail

urbanización NOUN FEM **housing estate**

urbano, **urbana** ADJECTIVE **urban**

urgencia NOUN FEM ❶ **urgency** ❷ (in hospital) 'urgencias' 'accident and emergency', sala de urgencias accident and emergency department

urgente ADJECTIVE ❶ **urgent** ❷ **express** (post)

urgentemente ADVERB **urgently**; quiere verte urgentemente she wants to see you urgently

Uruguay NOUN MASC **Uruguay**

uruguayo, **uruguaya** NOUN MASC, FEM, ADJECTIVE **Uruguayan**

usado, **usada** ADJECTIVE ❶ **used** ❷ **second-hand**; ropa usada second-hand clothes

usar VERB [17] ❶ **to use**; ¿qué champú usas? what shampoo do you use? ❷ **to take** (clothes size)

uso NOUN MASC **use**; instrucciones de uso instructions for use

usted PRONOUN **you** (the formal, polite form: talking to one person); usted mismo/misma yourself

ustedes PRONOUN **you** (the formal, polite form: talking to more than one person); ustedes mismos/mismas yourselves

usual ADJECTIVE **usual**

usuario, **usuaria** NOUN MASC, FEM **user**

utensilio NOUN MASC ❶ **tool** ❷ **utensil**

útil ADJECTIVE **useful**

utilizar VERB [22] **to use**

uva NOUN FEM **grape**; las uvas de la suerte the twelve grapes (one for each month of the year) eaten traditionally in Spain at midnight on New Year's Eve, tomar las uvas to eat grapes (at midnight on New Year's Eve)

Vv

vaca *NOUN FEM* **cow**

vacaciones *PLURAL NOUN FEM* **holiday,
holidays**; irse de vacaciones
to go on holiday, tomarse unas
vacaciones to take a holiday,
las vacaciones de Navidad the
Christmas holidays, estar de
vacaciones to be on holiday

vacante *NOUND FEM* **vacancy**

vacante *ADJECTIVE* **vacant**

vaciar *VERB* [32] **to empty**

vacilar *VERB* [17] **❶ to hesitate**; sin
vacilar without hesitating, vacilaba
entre quedarse o no she was
hesitating whether to stay or not
❷ to falter ❸ (informal) **to joke**;
¡deja de vacilar! stop fooling about!

vacío, vacía *ADJECTIVE* **empty**

vacío *NOUN MASC* **vacuum**

vacuna *NOUN FEM* **vaccine**

vacunar *VERB* [17] **to vaccinate**

vagabundo, vagabunda *NOUN
MASC, FEM* **vagrant**

vagabundo *ADJECTIVE* un perro
vagabundo a stray dog

vago, vaga *NOUN MASC, FEM* **layabout**

vago *ADJECTIVE* **lazy**

vagón *NOUN MASC* **❶ carriage
❷ wagon**

vainilla *NOUN FEM* **vanilla**

valdrá, valdré, valdría, etc VERB
▸ SEE **valer**

vale *NOUN MASC* **❶ voucher ❷ credit
slip**

vale *EXCLAMATION* **okay**; '¿vamos a
cenar fuera?' – '¡vale!' 'shall we go
out for dinner?' – 'okay!'

valer *VERB* [43] **❶ to cost**; ¿cuánto
vale? how much is it?, vale
trescientos cincuenta euros it's
three hundred and fifty euros **❷ to
be worth**; vale bastante dinero
it's worth quite a lot of money
❸ valer la pena to be worth it, no
vale la pena it's not worth it, no
vale la pena enfadarse por ello
it's not worth getting upset about,
vale la pena el esfuerzo it's worth
the effort **❹ to be valid** (a ticket or
coupon) **❺ to be allowed**; no vale
preguntar you can't ask, eso no
vale, tú ya lo habías visto that's not
fair, you'd already seen it

valga, valgo, etc VERB ▸ SEE **valer**

válido, válida *ADJECTIVE* **valid**

valiente *ADJECTIVE* **brave**

valioso, valiosa *ADJECTIVE* **valuable**

valle *NOUN MASC* **valley**

valor *NOUN MASC* **courage**

valorar *VERB* [17] **to value**

vals *NOUN MASC* **waltz**

vamos *VERB* ▸ SEE **ir**

vandalismo *NOUN MASC*
hooliganism

vanidoso, vanidosa *ADJECTIVE* **vain**

vano, vana *ADJECTIVE* **❶ futile
❷ pointless**

vapor *NOUN MASC* **steam**; al vapor steamed

vaquero *NOUN MASC* **jeans**; vaqueros jeans

variable *NOUN FEM* **variable**

variable *ADJECTIVE* **changeable**

variado, **variada** *ADJECTIVE* **varied**

variar *VERB* [32] ❶ to vary ❷ to change

varicela *NOUN FEM* **chicken pox**

variedad *NOUN FEM* **variety**

varios, **varias** *PRONOUN, ADJECTIVE* **several**; varias veces several times

varón *NOUN MASC*

varón *ADJECTIVE* **male**

varonil *ADJECTIVE* **manly**

vasco[1] *NOUN MASC* **Basque** *(the language)*

vasco[2], **vasca** *NOUN MASC, FEM, ADJECTIVE* **Basque**

vasija *NOUN FEM* **vessel**

vaso *NOUN MASC* **glass**; un vaso de agua a glass of water, un vaso de papel a paper cup

Vd. *ABBREVIATION (short for usted)* **you**

Vds. *ABBREVIATION (short for ustedes)* **you**

vecindad *NOUN FEM* **neighbourhood**

vecino, **vecina** *NOUN MASC, FEM* **neighbour**

vecino *ADJECTIVE* **neighbouring**

vegetariano, **vegetariana** *NOUN MASC, FEM, ADJECTIVE* **vegetarian**

vehículo *NOUN MASC* **vehicle**; vehículo espacial spacecraft

veía, **veían**, *etc VERB* ▸ SEE **ver**

veinte *NUMBER* ❶ twenty; tiene veinte años she's twenty (years old), veintidós twenty-two ❷ twentieth *(in dates)*; el veinte de diciembre the twentieth of December ❸ twenty *(in clock time)*; a las veinticinco at twenty-five past

vejez *NOUN FEM* **old age**

vela *NOUN FEM* ❶ candle ❷ sail ❸ sailing ❹ pasar la noche en vela, he pasado toda la noche en vela I've been awake all night

velero *NOUN MASC* **sailing ship**, **sailing boat**

velocidad *NOUN FEM* ❶ speed; el coche iba a mucha velocidad the car was going very fast, disminuir la velocidad to slow down ❷ gear *(in a car)*; la cuarta velocidad fourth gear

vena *NOUN FEM* **vein**

vencedor, **vencedora** *ADJECTIVE* **winning**

vencer *VERB* [44] ❶ to defeat; vencer a alguien to defeat somebody ❷ to win ❸ to overcome ❹ to expire *(a passport, for example)*

vencido, **vencida** *ADJECTIVE* **defeated**

venda *NOUN FEM* **bandage**

vendar *VERB* [17] ❶ to bandage ❷ vendar los ojos a alguien to blindfold somebody

vendaval *NOUN MASC* **gale**

vendedor, **vendedora** *NOUN* ❶ shop assistant ❷ salesman/

saleswoman ❸ seller; un vendedor ambulante a street seller

vender VERB [18] to sell; le he vendido mi coche I've sold him my car, los venden a ciento ochenta euros they're selling them for a hundred and eighty euros, 'se vende' 'for sale'

vendimia NOUN FEM wine harvest

vendrá, **vendré**, **vendría**, *etc VERB* ▸ SEE **venir**

veneno NOUN MASC poison, venom

venenoso, **venenosa** ADJECTIVE poisonous

venezolano, **venezolana** NOUN MASC, FEM, ADJECTIVE Venezuelan

Venezuela NOUN FEM Venezuela

venga, **vengo**, *etc VERB* ▸ SEE **venir**

venganza NOUN FEM revenge

vengarse REFLEXIVE VERB [28] vengarse de alguien to get one's revenge on someone

venir VERB [15] ❶ to come; sus padres no vinieron her parents didn't come, ven a las siete come at seven ❷ venir de to come from, viene de Italia it comes from Italy ❸ venir a hacer to come to do, yo vendré a buscarte I'll come and collect you ❹ venir a por algo to come to fetch something, vengo a por el paquete I've come to fetch the parcel, venir a por alguien to come to collect somebody, yo vendré a buscarte I'll come and collect you ❺ to be; la noticia viene en la primera página the news is on the front page ❻ venirle bien a alguien to suit someone, mañana no les viene bien tomorrow doesn't

suit them, ¿te viene bien quedar en la entrada? is it okay for you if we meet at the entrance?, esta parada de metro me viene muy bien this tube station's very convenient for me ❼ que viene: la semana que viene next week, el domingo que viene next Sunday ❽ ¡venga! come on!

venta NOUN FEM sale; estar en venta to be for sale, 'prohibida su venta' 'not for sale'

ventaja NOUN FEM advantage

ventana NOUN FEM window

ventanilla NOUN FEM ❶ window (in a train or car) ❷ box office ❸ horario de ventanilla opening hours (at a consulate, for example)

ventilación NOUN FEM ventilation

ventilador NOUN MASC fan

ventisca NOUN FEM blizzard

ventoso, **ventosa** ADJECTIVE windy

ver VERB [16] ❶ to see; los vi ayer I saw them yesterday, la vi cogerlo I saw her take it, no veo nada desde aquí I can't see anything from here, no veo bien de lejos I'm shortsighted, ya veo cuál es el problema I can see the problem, ya veremos lo que hacemos we'll see what we do ❷ to watch; ver la tele to watch TV, anoche vimos una película muy buena we watched a very good film last night ❸ to think; lo que ha hecho no lo veo bien I don't think what he's done is right ❹ tener que ver con algo to have something to do with something, eso no tiene nada que ver that has nothing to do with it ❺ a ver, ¿qué te pasa? okay, what's the matter with you?, 'mira lo que he encontrado' – '¿a ver?' 'look what I've found' – 'let's see'

verse REFLEXIVE VERB [16] ❶ **to see yourself**; verse en el espejo to see yourself in the mirror ❷ **to see each other**; se ven todas las semanas they see each other every week ❸ **to meet**; ¿nos vemos a la entrada del cine? shall we meet outside the cinema?
• verse en un aprieto **to find yourself in a tight spot**

veraneante NOUN MASC & FEM **holidaymaker**

veranear VERB [17] veranear en to spend your summer holidays in, veranean en la montaña they spend their summer holidays in the mountains

verano NOUN MASC **summer**

veras IN PHRASE ¡de veras! really!, una moto de veras a real motorbike

verbena NOUN FEM **festival** *(held to celebrate the Saint's Day of a town or village)*, **dance** *(in the open air)*

verbo NOUN MASC **verb**

verdad NOUN FEM ❶ **truth**; dime la verdad tell me the truth, la pura verdad the absolute truth, la verdad, no me acuerdo I don't remember, honestly, la verdad es que ... the truth is that ... ❷ a decir verdad ... to tell the truth ... ❸ de verdad really, de verdad que no me importa I don't mind, really ❹ de verdad real, un amigo de verdad a real friend

verdadero, verdadera ADJECTIVE ❶ **real**; su verdadero nombre his real name, es un verdadero idiota he's a real idiot ❷ **true**; una historia verdadera a true story

verde NOUN MASC ❶ **green**; verde botella bottle-green ❷ los Verdes the Greens *(in politics)*

verde ADJECTIVE ❶ **green**; tiene los ojos verdes she has green eyes, una blusa verde oscuro a dark green blouse ❷ **smutty**; un chiste verde a dirty joke

verdulería NOUN FEM **greengrocer's**

verdura NOUN FEM **vegetable**; cómete la verdura eat your vegetables, un puesto de verduras a vegetable stall

vergonzoso, vergonzosa ADJECTIVE ❶ **timid** ❷ **shameful**

vergüenza NOUN FEM ❶ **shame**; tener vergüenza to be ashamed, ¡qué poca vergüenza tienes! have you no shame at all? ❷ darle vergüenza a alguien to be ashamed, me da vergüenza haberme portado de esa forma I'm ashamed of behaving the way I did ❸ **embarrassment**; pasar vergüenza to feel embarrassed ❹ me da vergüenza hablar en público I feel embarrassed when I have to speak in public

verificar VERB [17] **to check**

verruga NOUN FEM ❶ **wart** ❷ **verruca**

versión NOUN FEM **version**; una película en versión original a film which has not been dubbed *(a foreign film, usually with subtitles)*

verso NOUN MASC ❶ **verse**; en verso in verse ❷ **poem** ❸ **line of a poem**; el tercer verso the third line of the poem

vertedero NOUN MASC **rubbish tip**

vertical ADJECTIVE ❶ **vertical** ❷ **down** *(in crosswords)*; ocho vertical eight down

A
B
C
D
E
F
G
H
I
J
K
L
M
N
Ñ
O
P
Q
R
S
T
U
V
W
X
Y
Z

vertido NOUN MASC ❶ spillage *(of pollutants, etc)* ❷ vertidos effluent

vertiente NOUN FEM slope

vértigo NOUN MASC vertigo; me da vértigo mirar abajo looking down makes me dizzy

vestíbulo NOUN MASC ❶ hall ❷ foyer

vestido¹ NOUN MASC dress; un vestido de noche an evening dress, un vestido de novia a wedding dress

vestido², **vestida** ADJECTIVE dressed; ir bien vestido to be well dressed, iba vestida con un traje azul she was wearing a blue suit, tenemos que ir al colegio vestidos de uniforme we have to wear school uniform

vestir VERB [57] to dress; vestir bien to dress well

vestirse REFLEXIVE VERB [57] ❶ to get dressed; voy a vestirme I'm going to get dressed ❷ to dress; se viste a la última moda she wears the latest fashions, me gusta vestirme de azul I like wearing blue

vestuario NOUN MASC ❶ wardrobe ❷ changing room

veterinario, **veterinaria** NOUN MASC, FEM veterinary surgeon

vez NOUN FEM (PLURAL die veces) ❶ time; la primera vez que fui a Inglaterra the first time I went to England, por última vez for the last time, algunas veces sometimes, ¿has estado alguna vez en Italia? have you ever been to Italy?, a veces sometimes, tal vez perhaps, maybe, de vez en cuando ocasionally, from time to time, de vez en cuando nos manda una carta occasionally he sends us a letter ❷ a la vez at the same time, at once ❸ cada vez each time, cada vez más more and more, hay cada vez más turistas there are more and more tourists ❹ cada vez menos less and less, fewer and fewer ❺ muchas veces often, pocas veces not very often, rara vez seldom ❻ una vez once, dos veces twice, tres veces al año three times a year ❼ otra vez again ❽ en vez de instead of ❾ érase una vez ... once upon a time ...

vía NOUN FEM ❶ track; la vía férrea the railway track ❷ por vía aérea by air, por vía marítima by sea ❸ vía de acceso slip road ❹ Vía Láctea Milky Way

viajar VERB [17] to travel; viajar en avión to travel by plane

viaje NOUN MASC journey, trip; estar de viaje to be away, hacer un viaje to go on a journey, to go on a trip, salir de viaje to go on a journey, to go on a trip, ¡buen viaje! have a good journey!, viaje de negocios business trip, viaje organizado package tour, viaje de novios honeymoon

viajero, **viajera** NOUN MASC, FEM ❶ traveller ❷ passenger

víbora NOUN FEM viper

vibrar VERB [17] to vibrate

vicio NOUN MASC ❶ vice ❷ bad habit; tengo el vicio de morderme las uñas I have the bad habit of biting my nails

víctima NOUN FEM victim; el número de víctimas mortales asciende a 25 the death toll has risen to 25

victoria NOUN FEM victory

vid NOUN FEM vine

vida NOUN FEM **life**; ¡esto es vida! this is the life!, la vida está muy cara the cost of living is very high, una cuestión de vida o muerte a matter of life or death, llevar una vida muy ajetreada to lead a very busy life, ganarse la vida to earn a living

vídeo NOUN MASC **video**; en vídeo on video

videocámara NOUN FEM **video camera**

videojuego NOUN MASC **video game**

vidrio NOUN MASC **glass**

viejo, **vieja** NOUN MASC, FEM **old man/ old woman**

viejo ADJECTIVE **old**

viento NOUN MASC ❶ **wind**; hace viento it's windy ❷ **guy rope** (of tent)

vientre NOUN MASC ❶ **belly** ❷ **womb**

viernes NOUN MASC **Friday**; Viernes Santo Good Friday (see 'domingo' for more examples)

vigésimo, **vigésima** ADJECTIVE **twentieth**

villancico NOUN MASC **Christmas carol**

vinagre NOUN MASC **vinegar**

vine, **viniste**, **vino**, etc VERB ▸ SEE **venir**

vino NOUN MASC **wine**; vino tinto red wine, vino blanco white wine, vino de mesa table wine

viñedo NOUN MASC **vineyard**

violar VERB [17] **to rape**

violencia NOUN FEM **violence**

violento, **violenta** ADJECTIVE ❶ **violent** ❷ **embarrassing** (situation) ❸ **embarrassed**

violeta NOUN FEM

violeta ADJECTIVE **violet**

violín NOUN MASC **violin**; tocar el violín to play the violin

violoncelo, **violonchelo** NOUN MASC **cello**

virar VERB [17] **to swerve**; el coche viró brucamente para esquivar al perro the car swerved sharply to avoid the dog

virgen NOUN FEM **virgin**

virgo NOUN MASC & FEM **Virgo**; es virgo he's Virgo

Virgo NOUN MASC **Virgo**

virtud NOUN FEM **virtue**

virus NOUN MASC **virus**; software anti virus anti-virus software

visado NOUN MASC **visa**

visibilidad NOUN FEM **visibility**

visible ADJECTIVE **visible**

visión NOUN FEM ❶ **vision** ❷ **sight**; perder la visión to lose your sight

visita NOUN FEM ❶ **visit**; una visita al museo a visit to the museum, hacer una visita a alguien to visit somebody ❷ **visitor**; tienes una visita you have a visitor ❸ **hit** (on web site)

visitar VERB [17] **to visit**

víspera NOUN FEM la víspera the day before, la víspera del partido the day before the match

vista¹ NOUN FEM ❶ **eyesight**; tener buena vista to have good eyesight, perder la vista to lose your sight, el sol me hace daño a la vista the sun's hurting my eyes, conocer a alguien de vista to know someone by sight ❷ estar a la vista to be within sight, no estar a la vista to be out of sight ❸ view; el hotel tiene unas vistas preciosas the hotel has beautiful views ❹ con vistas a with a view to ❺ ¡hasta la vista! see you!

vistieron, **vistió**, *etc VERB*
  ▸ SEE **vestir**

visto[1] *VERB* ▸ SEE **ver**

visto[2], **vista**[2] *ADJECTIVE* ❶ clear; está visto que ... it's clear that ... ❷ por lo visto apparently ❸ estar bien visto to be acceptable, está mal visto it's not the done thing ❹ eso está muy visto that's not very original

vitamina *NOUN FEM* vitamin

vitrina *NOUN FEM* shop window

viudo, **viuda** *NOUN FEM* widow/ widower

viva[1] *EXCLAMATION* ¡viva! hurray!, ¡viva la novia! three cheers for the bride!

vivienda *NOUN FEM* ❶ housing; el problema de la vivienda the housing problem ❷ flat, house; un bloque de viviendas a block of flats

vivir *VERB* [19] to live; vive en casa de su hermana she lives with her sister, vive de las traducciones she makes her living from translation, vive de su pensión she lives off her pension

vivo, **viva**[2] *ADJECTIVE* ❶ alive ❷ actuación en vivo live performance

vocabulario *NOUN MASC* vocabulary

vocal *NOUN FEM* vowel

volante *NOUN MASC* steering wheel

volante *ADJECTIVE* flying

volar *VERB* [24] ❶ to fly ❷ to blow up; volar un edificio to blow up a building

volcán *NOUN MASC* volcano

volcar *VERB* [24] ❶ to turn over; el camión volcó the lorry turned over ❷ volcar el contenido de algo to empty something ❸ to knock over

volcarse *REFLEXIVE VERB* [24] ❶ to turn over ❷ volcarse en algo to throw yourself into something

vóleibol, **voleibol** *NOUN MASC* volleyball; jugar al vóleibol to play volleyball

voltereta *NOUN FEM* somersault

volumen *NOUN MASC* volume; subir el volumen to turn up the volume

voluntad *NOUN FEM* ❶ will; fuerza de voluntad will power, lo hice por mi propia voluntad I did it of my own free will ❷ wish
• siempre hace su santa voluntad she always does exactly as she pleases

voluntariamente *ADVERB* voluntarily

voluntario, **voluntaria** *NOUN MASC, FEM* volunteer

voluntario *ADJECTIVE* voluntary

volver *VERB* [45] ❶ to turn; volver la página to turn the page, volvió la cabeza she turned her head, al volver la esquina ... when I turned the corner ... ❷ to come back; aún no ha vuelto he hasn't come back yet, ¿cuándo volverás? when will you come back? ❸ **to go back**; volver al colegio to go back to school, ¿quieres que volvamos a casa? do you want us to go back home?, ha vuelto con su novia he's gone back to his girlfriend ❹ **to be back**; volveré a eso de las siete I'll be back by about seven, no había vuelto a Sevilla desde el verano pasado I hadn't been back to Seville since last summer ❺ **to get back**; ¿cuándo volviste de tu viaje? when did you get back from your trip? ❻ volver a hacer to do again, volví a revisarlo I checked it again, ¡no lo vuelvas a hacer! don't do it again!, tenemos que volver a empezar we have to start again ❼ volver loco a alguien to drive someone mad, me está volviendo loca con tantas preguntas she's driving me mad with all her questions ❽ volver en sí to come round *(recover consciousness)*

volverse *REFLEXIVE VERB* [45] ❶ **to turn around**; me volví para mirar I turned around to see ❷ volverse de espaldas to turn your back, ¡no te vuelvas de espaldas cuando te estoy hablando! don't turn your back on me when I'm talking to you! ❸ volverse boca abajo to turn over onto your stomach, volverse boca arriba to turn over onto your back ❹ **to become**; se ha vuelto muy vanidosa she's turned very vain, la situación se ha vuelto insoportable the situation has become unbearable, volverse loco to go mad

vomitar *VERB* [17] **to be sick**; tener ganas de vomitar to feel sick

vosotros, vosotras *PRONOUN* **you** *(talking to more than one person)*; ¿vosotras queréis ir? do you want

to go?, vosotros mismos/vosotras mismas yourselves

votar *VERB* [17] ❶ **to vote on** *(a measure)* ❷ **to vote for** *(a party, a candidate)*; siempre vota a los verdes she always votes for the Greens, ¿por quién votaste? who did you vote for?

voto *NOUN MASC* ❶ **vote**; un voto a favor a vote for, un voto en contra a vote against, un voto secreto a secret ballot, un voto en blanco a blank ballot paper, un voto de censura a vote of no confidence ❷ **vow**

voy *VERB* ▸ SEE **ir**

voz *NOUN FEM (PLURAL* die **voces**) **voice**; oír voces to hear voices, tener la voz tomada to be hoarse, en voz baja quietly, hablar en voz alta to speak loudly, leer algo en voz alta to read something out loud

vuelo *NOUN MASC* **flight**; un vuelo regular a scheduled flight

vuelta *NOUN FEM* ❶ **turn**; una vuelta a la derecha a turn to the right ❷ **return**; a la vuelta podemos visitar el museo we can visit the museum on our way back, 'vuelta al colegio' 'back to school' *(after the summer holidays)* ❸ dar la vuelta a algo to turn something, dar la vuelta a la página to turn the page, dale la vuelta al cuadro turn the picture round the other way, dar la vuelta a un disco to turn a record over ❹ dar la vuelta a la esquina to turn the corner ❺ dar la vuelta al mundo to go round the world, dar una vuelta a la manzana to go round the block ❻ dar una vuelta to go for a walk, ¿te vienes a dar una vuelta? are you coming for a walk?, dar una vuelta en coche to go for a drive ❼ dar una vuelta alrededor de algo to go around something

vuelva, vuelvo, *etc VERB*
▸SEE **volver**

vuestro, vuestra *ADJECTIVE* **your** *(talking to more than one person)*; vuestra casa your house, un familiar vuestro a relative of yours

vuestro *PRONOUN* **yours**; la vuestra es verde yours is green, los vuestros están en el salón yours are in the living room, aquel es el vuestro that one is yours

vulgar *ADJECTIVE* ❶ **vulgar** ❷ **common**

wáter *NOUN MASC* **toilet**

web *NOUN FEM* ❶ **web page** ❷ **website** ❸ **Web**

whisky *NOUN MASC* **whisky**

windsurf *NOUN MASC* hacer windsurf to go windsurfing

windsurf *NOUN MASC* **windsurfing**

xilófono NOUN MASC **xylophone**

y CONJUNCTION ❶ *('y' becomes 'e' before a word beginning with 'i-' or 'hi-')* **and**; Amanda y yo Amanda and I ❷ *(with numbers and times)* treinta y siete thirty-seven ❸ *(with clock time)* las dos y media half past two, a las diez y cinco at five past ten ❹ ¿y a mí qué? so what's it to me?

ya ADVERB ❶ **already**; ya está hecho it's already done, ¿has comido ya? have you already eaten? ❷ **yet**; ¿han llegado ya? have they arrived yet? ❸ **any more**; ya no importa it doesn't matter any more ❹ **now**; antes no quería, pero ya ha cambiado de idea he didn't want to before but he's changed his mind now, tenemos que decidirnos ya we must decide now ❺ *(in the future)* ya veremos we'll see, ya te contaré I'll tell you about it ❻ *(not translated but used to stress what you are saying)* ya lo sé I know, ya entiendo I understand, ya era hora it's about time too, ¡ya está! that's it!, ¡ya estoy! I'm ready!, ¡ya voy! I'm just coming!, ¡ya lo creo! you bet!, preparados, listos, ¡ya! ready, steady, go! ❼ 'esto es de Juan' – 'ya' 'this is Juan's' – 'I know' ❽ 'yo no he sido' – 'ya, ya' 'it wasn't me' – 'yeah, yeah!' ❾ ya que since, ya que vas a estar aquí since you're going to be here

yate NOUN MASC **yacht**

yedra *NOUN FEM* **ivy**

yegua *NOUN FEM* **mare**

yema *NOUN FEM* ❶ **yolk** ❷ la yema del dedo the fingertip

yerno *NOUN MASC* **son-in-law**

yo *PRONOUN* ❶ **I**; yo no lo sé I don't know ❷ **me**; soy yo it's me ❸ yo mismo/misma myself, lo haré yo mismo I'll do it myself

yoga *NOUN FEM* **yoga**

yogur *NOUN MASC* **yoghurt**

yudo *NOUN MASC* **judo**

Yugoslavia *NOUN FEM* **Yugoslavia**

yugoslavo, yugoslava *NOUN MASC, FEM, ADJECTIVE* **Yugoslavian**

Zz

zanahoria *NOUN FEM* **carrot**

zapatería *NOUN FEM* **shoe shop**

zapatero, zapatera *NOUN MASC, FEM* ❶ **shoemaker** ❷ **shoe repairer's**

zapatilla *NOUN FEM* ❶ **slipper** ❷ **canvas shoe** ❸ zapatilla de deporte trainer ❹ zapatilla de esparto espadrille ❺ zapatilla de ballet ballet shoe

zapato *NOUN MASC* **shoe**; zapato de tacón high heeled shoe, zapato bajo flat shoe

zarzamora *NOUN FEM* **blackberry**

zarzuela *NOUN FEM* **Spanish light opera**

zodíaco, zodiaca *NOUN MASC* **zodiac**

zona *NOUN FEM* **area**; viven en la zona they live locally; zona peatonal pedestrian precinct, zona comercial commercial district

zoo *NOUN MASC* **zoo**

zoológico *NOUN MASC* **zoo**

zorro *NOUN MASC* **fox**

zueco *NOUN MASC* **clog**

zumbar *VERB* [17] **to buzz**

zumo *NOUN MASC* **juice**; zumo de fruta fruit juice, zumo de naranja orange juice

zurdo, zurda *NOUN MASC, FEM* **left-handed person**

VERB TABLES

Spanish verb tables

The following verb tables show you how Spanish verbs are formed. They fall into three categories – main irregular verbs, the three regular verb patterns using **hablar**, **comer**, and **vivir** as models, and other irregular verbs.

Main Spanish irregular verbs (pages 286–301)

The following Spanish verbs are unlike any others – they are irregular. The way that they are formed is given in the following section. When you look up a verb in this dictionary, you will see that it has a number in square brackets ([1], [2] etc.) This number tells you which verb to look up in this section.

[1]	**ser**	to be	[9]	**tener**	to have
[2]	**estar**	to be	[10]	**poder**	to be able
[3]	**coger**	to take	[11]	**poner**	to put
[4]	**dar**	to give	[12]	**querer**	to want, to love
[5]	**decir**	to say, to tell	[13]	**saber**	to know (facts)
[6]	**haber**	to have	[14]	**sentir**	to feel
[7]	**hacer**	to make, to do	[15]	**venir**	to come
[8]	**ir**	to go	[16]	**ver**	to see

Regular Spanish verbs (pages 302–304)

All other Spanish verbs belong to verb families. These are the **-ar**, **-er**, and **-ir** verbs. The ones with regular patterns follow the ones given in full here. In this dictionary, the numbers in square brackets ([17], [18] or [19]) tell you which verb pattern to follow.

-ar verbs	**[17]**	habl<u>ar</u>	to speak, to talk
-er verbs	**[18]**	com<u>er</u>	to eat
-ir verbs	**[19]**	viv<u>ir</u>	to live

Other irregular verbs (pages 305–315)

However, some of the verbs in the **-ar**, **-er**, and **-ir** regular verb families have differences from the regular patterns. These verbs are also numbered in the dictionary to tell you where to find them in this centre section. These verbs follow the regular verb patterns, apart from the forms that are given on pages 305-315.

Reflexive verbs

Many Spanish verbs may also be used reflexively with the appropriate pronouns (**me/te/se/nos/os/se**) for each person. Remember that when a verb is used reflexively its meaning may change, so check carefully in the dictionary. A typical example is **[14] sentir** on page 299.

[1]

ser

to be

*(see the entry **be**
on page 340 for when to use
ser and when to use estar)*

Gerund
siendo
being

Past participle
sido
been

Present indicative

soy   I am
eres
es
somos
sois
son

Imperfect indicative

era   I was *or* I used to be
eras
era
éramos
erais
eran

Past simple indicative

fui   I was
fuiste
fue
fuimos
fuisteis
fueron

Future indicative

seré   I will be
serás
será
seremos
seréis
serán

Conditional

sería   I would be
serías
sería
seríamos
seríais
serían

Present subjunctive

sea   I am
seas
sea
seamos
seáis
sean

Imperfect subjunctive

fuera   I was *or* I were
fueras
fuera
fuéramos
fuerais
fueran

Imperative

sé *(tú)*   be *(singular)*
sea *(usted)*   be *(sing formal)*
seamos *(nosotros)* let us be *or*
                      let's be
sed *(vosotros)*   be *(plural)*
sean *(ustedes)*   be *(pl formal)*

Gerund	**Past participle**	**[2]**	**Verb tables**
estando	estado		
being	been	**Estar**	

Estar
to be
*(see the entry **be** on page 340 for when to use ser and when to use estar)*

Present indicative

estoy I am
estás
está
estamos
estáis
están

Imperfect indicative

estaba I was *or* I used to be
estabas
estaba
estábamos
estabais
estaban

Past simple indicative

estuve I was
estuviste
estuvo
estuvimos
estuvisteis
estuvieron

Future indicative

estaré I will be
estarás
estará
estaremos
estaréis
estarán

Conditional

estaría I would be
estarías
estaría
estaríamos
estaríais
estarían

Present subjunctive

esté I am
estés
esté
estemos
estéis
estén

Imperfect subjunctive

estuviera I was *or* I were
estuvieras
estuviera
estuviéramos
estuvierais
estuvieran

Imperative

está *(tú)*	be *(singular)*
esté *(usted)*	be *(sing formal)*
estemos *(nosotros)*	let us be or let's be
estad *(vosotros)*	be *(plural)*
estén *(ustedes)*	be *(pl formal)*

[3]

coger
to take

Gerund	**Past participle**
cogiendo	cogido
taking	taken

Present indicative

cojo	I take or I am taking
coges	
coge	
cogemos	
cogéis	
cogen	

Imperfect indicative

cogía	I was taking or I used to take
cogías	
cogía	
cogíamos	
cogíais	
cogían	

Past simple indicative

cogí	I took
cogiste	
cogió	
cogimos	
cogisteis	
cogieron	

Future indicative

cogeré	I will take
cogerás	
cogerá	
cogeremos	
cogeréis	
cogerán	

Conditional

cogería	I would take
cogerías	
cogería	
cogeríamos	
cogeríais	
cogerían	

Present subjunctive

coja	I take
cojas	
coja	
cojamos	
cojáis	
cojan	

Imperfect subjunctive

cogiera	I took or I were to take
cogieras	
cogiera	
cogiéramos	
cogierais	
cogieran	

Imperative

coge *(tú)*	take *(singular)*
coja *(usted)*	take *(sing formal)*
cojamos *(nosotros)*	let us take or let's take
coged *(vosotros)*	take *(plural)*
cojan *(ustedes)*	take *(pl formal)*

Gerund
dando
giving

Past participle
dado
given

[4]

dar
to give

Present indicative

doy   I give
das
da
damos
dais
dan

Imperfect indicative

daba   I gave or I used to give
dabas
daba
dábamos
dabais
daban

Past simple indicative

di   I gave
diste
dio
dimos
disteis
dieron

Future indicative

daré   I will give
darás
dará
daremos
daréis
darán

Conditional

daría   I would give
darías
daría
daríamos
daríais
darían

Present subjunctive

dé   I give
des
dé
demos
deis
den

Imperfect subjunctive

diera   I gave or I were to give
dieras
diera
diéramos
dierais
dieran

Imperative

da *(tú)*   give *(singular)*
de *(usted)*   give *(sing formal)*
demos *(nosotros)*   let us give or let's give

dad *(vosotros)*   give *(plural)*
den *(ustedes)*   give *(pl formal)*

[5]

decir
to say *or* to tell

Gerund
diciendo
saying

Past participle
dicho
said

Present indicative

digo   I say *or* I am saying
dices
dice
decimos
decís
dicen

Imperfect indicative

decía   I was saying *or*
       I used to say

decías
decía
decíamos
decíais
decían

Past simple indicative

dije   I said
dijiste
dijo
dijimos
dijisteis
dijeron

Future indicative

diré   I will say
dirás
dirá
diremos
diréis
dirán

Conditional

diría   I would say
dirías
diría
diríamos
diríais
dirían

Present subjunctive

diga   I say
digas
diga
digamos
digáis
digan

Imperfect subjunctive

dijera   I said *or* I were to say
dijeras
dijera
dijéramos
dijerais
dijeran

Imperative

di *(tú)*   say *(singular)*
diga *(usted)*   say *(sing formal)*
digamos *(nosotros)*   let us say *or*
       let's say

decid *(vosotros)*   say *(plural)*
digan *(ustedes)*   say *(pl formal)*

Gerund	**Past participle**	**[6]**
habiendo	habido	**haber**
having	been	to have

Present indicative

he	I have
has	
ha	
hemos	
habéis	
han	

Imperfect indicative

había	I was having or I used to have
habías	
había	
habíamos	
habíais	
habían	

Past simple indicative

hube	I had
hubiste	
hubo	
hubimos	
hubisteis	
hubieron	

Future indicative

habré	I will have
habrás	
habrá	
habremos	
habréis	
habrán	

Conditional

habría	I would have
habrías	
habría	
habríamos	
habríais	
habrían	

Present subjunctive

haya	I have
hayas	
haya	
hayamos	
hayáis	
hayan	

Imperfect subjunctive

hubiera	I had or I were to have
hubieras	
hubiera	
hubiéramos	
hubierais	
hubieran	

Imperative

he *(tú)*	have *(singular)*
haya *(usted)*	have *(sing formal)*
hayamos *(nosotros)*	let us have or let's have
habed *(vosotros)*	have *(plural)*
hayan *(ustedes)*	have *(pl formal)*

[7]
hacer
to make *or* to do

Gerund
haciendo
making *or* doing

Past participle
hecho
made *or* done

Present indicative
hago	I make *or* I am making *or* I do *or* I am doing
haces	
hace	
hacemos	
hacéis	
hacen	

Imperfect indicative
hacía	I was making *or* I used to make *or* I was doing *or* I used to do
hacías	
hacía	
hacíamos	
hacíais	
hacían	

Past simple indicative
hice	I made *or* I did
hiciste	
hizo	
hicimos	
hicisteis	
hicieron	

Future indicative
haré	I will make *or* I will do
harás	
hará	
haremos	
haréis	
harán	

Conditional
haría	I would make *or* I would do
harías	
haría	
haríamos	
haríais	
harían	

Present subjunctive
haga	I make *or* I do
hagas	
haga	
hagamos	
hagáis	
hagan	

Imperfect subjunctive
hiciera	I made *or* I were to make *or* I did *or* I were to do
hicieras	
hiciera	
hiciéramos	
hicierais	
hicieran	

Imperative
haz *(tú)*	make *or* do *(singular)*
haga *(usted)*	make *or* do *(sing formal)*
hagamos *(nosotros)*	let us make *or* let's make *or* let us do *or* let's do
haced *(vosotros)*	make *or* do *(plural)*
hagan *(ustedes)*	make *or* do *(pl formal)*

Gerund	**Past participle**	**[8]**
yendo	ido	**ir**
going	gone	to go

Present indicative

voy	I go *or* I am going
vas	
va	
vamos	
vais	
van	

Imperfect indicative

iba	I was going *or* I used to go
ibas	
iba	
íbamos	
ibais	
iban	

Past simple indicative

fui	I went
fuiste	
fue	
fuimos	
fuisteis	
fueron	

Future indicative

iré	I will go
irás	
irá	
iremos	
iréis	
irán	

Conditional

iría	I would go
irías	
iría	
iríamos	
iríais	
irían	

Present subjunctive

vaya	I go
vayas	
vaya	
vayamos	
vayáis	
vayan	

Imperfect subjunctive

fuera	I went *or* I were to go
fueras	
fuera	
fuéramos	
fuerais	
fueran	

Imperative

ve *(tú)*	go *(singular)*
vaya *(usted)*	go *(sing formal)*
vayamos *(nosotros)*	let us go *or* let's go
id *(vosotros)*	go *(plural)*
vayan *(ustedes)*	go *(pl formal)*

[9]

tener
to have

Gerund
teniendo
having

Past participle
tenido
had

Present indicative

tengo	I have *or* I am having
tienes	
tiene	
tenemos	
tenéis	
tienen	

Imperfect indicative

tenía	I was having *or* I used to have
tenías	
tenía	
teníamos	
teníais	
tenían	

Past simple indicative

tuve	I had
tuviste	
tuvo	
tuvimos	
tuvisteis	
tuvieron	

Future indicative

tendré	I will have
tendrás	
tendrá	
tendremos	
tendréis	
tendrán	

Conditional

tendría	I would have
tendrías	
tendría	
tendríamos	
tendríais	
tendrían	

Present subjunctive

tenga	I have
tengas	
tenga	
tengamos	
tengáis	
tengan	

Imperfect subjunctive

tuviera	I have
tuvieras	
tuviera	
tuviéramos	
tuvierais	
tuvieran	

Imperative

ten *(tú)*	have *(singular)*
tenga *(usted)*	have *(sing formal)*
tengamos *(nosotros)*	let us have *or* let's have
tened *(vosotros)*	have *(plural)*
tengan *(ustedes)*	have *(pl formal)*

Gerund
pudiendo
being able to

Past participle
podido
been able to

[10]
poder
to be able

Present indicative

puedo	I am able to or I can
puedes	
puede	
podemos	
podéis	
pueden	

Imperfect indicative

podía	I was able to or I used to be able to or I could
podías	
podía	
podíamos	
podíais	
podían	

Past simple indicative

pude	I was able to to or I could
pudiste	
pudo	
pudimos	
pudisteis	
pudieron	

Future indicative

podré	I will be able to
podrás	
podrá	
podremos	
podréis	
podrán	

Conditional

podría	I would be able to
podrías	
podría	
podríamos	
podríais	
podrían	

Present subjunctive

pueda	I am able to or I can
puedas	
pueda	
podamos	
podáis	
puedan	

Imperfect subjunctive

pudiera	I was able to or I were able to
pudieras	
pudiera	
pudiéramos	
pudierais	
pudieran	

Imperative

The imperative is not used with **poder**

[11]

poner
to put

Gerund	**Past participle**
poniendo	puesto
putting	put

Present indicative

pongo	I put or I am putting
pones	
pone	
ponemos	
ponéis	
ponen	

Imperfect indicative

ponía	I was putting or I used to put
ponías	
ponía	
poníamos	
poníais	
ponían	

Past simple indicative

puse	I put
pusiste	
puso	
pusimos	
pusisteis	
pusieron	

Future indicative

pondré	I will put
pondrás	
pondrá	
pondremos	
pondréis	
pondrán	

Conditional

pondría	I would put
pondrías	
pondría	
pondríamos	
pondríais	
pondrían	

Present subjunctive

ponga	I put
pongas	
ponga	
pongamos	
pongáis	
pongan	

Imperfect subjunctive

pusiera	I put or I were to put
pusieras	
pusiera	
pusiéramos	
pusierais	
pusieran	

Imperative

pon *(tú)*	put *(singular)*
ponga *(usted)*	put *(sing formal)*
pongamos *(nosotros)*	let us put or let's put
poned *(vosotros)*	put *(plural)*
pongan *(ustedes)*	put *(pl formal)*

Gerund
queriendo
wanting to *or* loving

Past participle
querido
wanted *or* loved

Present indicative

quiero	I want to *or* I love
quieres	
quiere	
queremos	
queréis	
quieren	

Imperfect indicative

quería	I wanted to *or* I used to want to *or* I loved *or* I used to love
querías	
quería	
queríamos	
queríais	
querían	

Past simple indicative

quise	I wanted to *or* I loved
quisiste	
quiso	
quisimos	
quisisteis	
quisieron	

Future indicative

querré	I will want to *or* I will love
querrás	
querrá	
querremos	
querréis	
querrán	

Conditional

querría	I would want to *or* I would love
querrías	
querría	
querríamos	
querríais	
querrían	

Present subjunctive

quiera	I want to *or* I love
quieras	
quiera	
queramos	
queráis	
quieran	

Imperfect subjunctive

quisiera	I wanted to *or* I were to want *or* I loved *or* I were to love
quisieras	
quisiera	
quisiéramos	
quisierais	
quisieran	

Imperative

quiere *(tú)*	want *(singular)*
quiera *(usted)*	want *(sing formal)*
queramos *(nosotros)*	let us put *or* let's put
quered *(vosotros)*	want *(plural)*
quieran *(ustedes)*	want *(pl formal)*

[13]
saber
to know

Gerund
sabiendo
knowing

Past participle
sabido
known

Present indicative

sé	I know
sabes	
sabe	
sabemos	
sabéis	
saben	

Imperfect indicative

sabía	I knew *or* I used to know
sabías	
sabía	
sabíamos	
sabíais	
sabían	

Past simple indicative

supe	I knew
supiste	
supo	
supimos	
supisteis	
supieron	

Future indicative

sabré	I will know
sabrás	
sabrá	
sabremos	
sabréis	
sabrán	

Conditional

sabría	I would know
sabrías	
sabría	
sabríamos	
sabríais	
sabrían	

Present subjunctive

sepa	I know
sepas	
sepa	
sepamos	
sepáis	
sepan	

Imperfect subjunctive

supiera	I knew
supieras	
supiera	
supiéramos	
supierais	
supieran	

Imperative

sabe *(tú)*	know *(singular)*
sepa *(usted)*	know *(sing formal)*
sepamos *(nosotros)*	let us know *or* let's know
sabed *(vosotros)*	know *(plural)*
sepan *(ustedes)*	know *(pl formal)*

Gerund
sintiendo
feeling

Past participle
sentido
felt

[14]

sentir
to feel

Present indicative

siento   I feel
sientes
siente
sentimos
sentís
sienten

Conditional

sentiría   I would feel
sentirías
sentiría
sentiríamos
sentiríais
sentirían

Imperfect indicative

sentía   I felt *or* I used to feel
sentías
sentía
sentíamos
sentíais
sentían

Present subjunctive

sienta   I feel
sientas
sienta
sintamos
sintáis
sientan

Past simple indicative

sentí   I felt
sentiste
sintió
sentimos
sentisteis
sintieron

Imperfect subjunctive

sintiera   I felt *or* I were to feel
sintieras
sintiera
sintiéramos
sintierais
sintieran

Future indicative

sentiré   I will feel
sentirás
sentirá
sentiremos
sentiréis
sentirán

Imperative

siente *(tú)*   feel *(singular)*
sienta *(usted)*   feel *(sing formal)*
sintamos *(nosotros)* let us feel or
                       let's feel
sentid *(vosotros)*   feel *(plural)*
sientan *(ustedes)*   feel *(pl formal)*

[15]

venir
to come

Gerund
viniendo
coming

Past participle
venido
come

Present indicative

vengo — I come *or* I am coming
vienes
viene
venimos
venís
vienen

Imperfect indicative

venía — I was coming *or* I used to come
venías
venía
veníamos
veníais
venían

Past simple indicative

vine — I came
viniste
vino
vinimos
vinisteis
vinieron

Future indicative

vendré — I will come
vendrás
vendrá
vendremos
vendréis
vendrán

Conditional

vendría — I would come
vendrías
vendría
vendríamos
vendríais
vendrían

Present subjunctive

venga — I come
vengas
venga
vengamos
vengáis
vengan

Imperfect subjunctive

viniera — I came *or* I were to come
vinieras
viniera
viniéramos
vinierais
vinieran

Imperative

ven *(tú)* — come *(singular)*
venga *(usted)* — come *(sing formal)*
vengamos *(nosotros)* — let us come *or* let's come
venid *(vosotros)* — come *(plural)*
vengan *(ustedes)* — come *(pl formal)*

Gerund	Past participle	**[16]**
viendo	visto	
seeing	seen	**ver** to see

Present indicative

veo	I see or I am seeing
ves	
ve	
vemos	
veis	
ven	

Imperfect indicative

veía	I saw or I used to see
veías	
veía	
veíamos	
veíais	
veían	

Past simple indicative

vi	I saw
viste	
vio	
vimos	
visteis	
vieron	

Future indicative

veré	I will see
verás	
verá	
veremos	
veréis	
verán	

Conditional

vería	I would see
verías	
vería	
veríamos	
veríais	
verían	

Present subjunctive

vea	I see
veas	
vea	
veamos	
veáis	
vean	

Imperfect subjunctive

viera	I saw or I were to see
vieras	
viera	
viéramos	
vierais	
vieran	

Imperative

ve *(tú)*	see *(singular)*
vea *(usted)*	see *(sing formal)*
veamos *(nosotros)*	let us see or let's see
ved *(vosotros)*	see *(plural)*
vean *(ustedes)*	see *(pl formal)*

[17]
hablar
to talk *or* to speak

regular **-ar**

Gerund	**Past participle**
hab**lando**	hab**lado**
speaking	spoken

Present indicative
hab**lo**   I speak
hab**las**
hab**la**
hab**lamos**
hab**láis**
hab**lan**

Imperfect indicative
hab**laba**   I was speaking *or* I used to
         speak
hab**labas**
hab**laba**
hab**lábamos**
hab**labais**
hab**laban**

Past simple indicative
hab**lé**   I spoke
hab**laste**
hab**ló**
hab**lamos**
hab**lasteis**
hab**laron**

Future indicative
hab**laré**   I will speak
hab**larás**
hab**lará**
hab**laremos**
hab**laréis**
hab**larán**

Conditional
hab**laría**   I would speak
hab**larías**
hab**laría**
hab**laríamos**
hab**laríais**
hab**larían**

Present subjunctive
hab**le**   I speak
hab**les**
hab**le**
hab**lemos**
hab**léis**
hab**len**

Imperfect subjunctive
hab**lara**   I spoke *or* I were to speak
hab**laras**
hab**lara**
hab**láramos**
hab**larais**
hab**laran**

Imperative
hab**la** *(tú)*	speak *(singular)*
hab**le** *(usted)*	speak *(sing formal)*
hab**lemos** *(nosotros)*	let us speak *or* let's speak
hab**lad** *(vosotros)*	speak *(plural)*
hab**len** *(ustedes)*	speak *(pl formal)*

Gerund
comiendo
eating

Past participle
comido
eaten

[18]

comer
to eat

regular **-er**

Present indicative

como — I eat or I am eating
comes
come
comemos
coméis
comen

Imperfect indicative

comía — I was eating or I used to eat
comías
comía
comíamos
comíais
comían

Past simple indicative

comí — I ate
comiste
comió
comimos
comisteis
comieron

Future indicative

comeré — I will eat
comerás
comerá
comeremos
comeréis
comerán

Conditional

comería — I would eat
comerías
comería
comeríamos
comeríais
comerían

Present subjunctive

coma — I eat
comas
coma
comamos
comáis
coman

Imperfect subjunctive

comiera — I ate or I were to eat
comieras
comiera
comiéramos
comierais
comieran

Imperative

come *(tú)*	eat *(singular)*
coma *(usted)*	eat *(sing formal)*
comamos *(nosotros)*	let us eat or let's eat
comed *(vosotros)*	eat *(plural)*
coman *(ustedes)*	eat (pl formal)

[19]
vivir
to live

regular -ir

Gerund	**Past participle**
viv**iendo**	viv**ido**
living	lived

Present indicative

viv**o**	I live or I am living
viv**es**	
viv**e**	
viv**imos**	
viv**ís**	
viv**en**	

Imperfect indicative

viv**ía**	I lived or I used to live
viv**ías**	
viv**ía**	
viv**íamos**	
viv**íais**	
viv**ían**	

Past simple indicative

viv**í**	I lived
viv**iste**	
viv**ió**	
viv**imos**	
viv**isteis**	
viv**ieron**	

Future indicative

viv**iré**	I will live
viv**irás**	
viv**irá**	
viv**iremos**	
viv**iréis**	
viv**irán**	

Conditional

viv**iría**	I would live
viv**irías**	
viv**iría**	
viv**iríamos**	
viv**iríais**	
viv**irían**	

Present subjunctive

viv**a**	I live
viv**as**	
viv**a**	
viv**amos**	
viv**áis**	
viv**an**	

Imperfect subjunctive

viv**iera**	I lived or I were to live
viv**ieras**	
viv**iera**	
viv**iéramos**	
viv**ierais**	
viv**ieran**	

Imperative

viv**e** *(tú)*	live *(singular)*
viv**a** *(usted)*	live *(sing formal)*
viv**amos** *(nosotros)*	let us live or let's live
viv**id** *(vosotros)*	live *(plural)*
viv**an** *(ustedes)*	live *(pl formal)*

[20] actuar - like [17] hablar except:

Present indicative	Present subjunctive
actúo	actúe
actúas	actúes
actúa	actúe
actuamos	actuemos
actuáis	actuéis
actúan	actúen

Imperative
actúa *(tú)*
actúe *(usted)*
actuemos *(nosotros)*
actuad *(vosotros)*
actúen *(ustedes)*

[21] andar - like [17] hablar except:

Past simple indicative	Imperfect subjunctive
anduve	anduviera
anduviste	anduvieras
anduvo	anduviera
anduvimos	anduviéramos
andivisteis	anduvierais
anduvieron	anduvieran

[22] cazar - like [17] hablar except:

Past simple indicative	Present subjunctive
cacé	cace
cazaste	caces
cazó	cace
cazamos	cacemos
cazasteis	cacéis
cazaron	cacen

Imperative
caza *(tú)*
cace *(usted)*
cacemos *(nosotros)*
cazad *(vosotros)*
cacen *(ustedes)*

[23] colgar - like [17] hablar except:

Present indicative	Present subjunctive
cuelgo	cuelgue
cuelgas	cuelgues
cuelga	cuelgue
colgamos	colguemos
colgáis	colguéis
cuelgan	cuelguen

Past simple indicative	Imperative
colgué	cuelga *(tú)*
colgaste	cuelgue *(usted)*
colgó	colguemos *(nosotros)*
colgamos	colgad *(vosotros)*
colgasteis	cuelguen *(ustedes)*
colgaron	

[24] contar - like [17] hablar except:

Present indicative	Present subjunctive
cuento	cuente
cuentas	cuentes
cuenta	cuente
contamos	contemos
contáis	contéis
cuentan	cuenten

Imperative
cuenta *(tú)*
cuente *(usted)*
contemos *(nosotros)*
contad *(vosotros)*
cuenten *(ustedes)*

[25] empezar – like [17] hablar except:

Present indicative	Present subjunctive
empiezo	empiece
empiezas	empieces
empieza	empiece
empezamos	empecemos
empezáis	empecéis
empiezan	empiecen

Past simple indicative	Imperative
empecé	empieza *(tú)*
empezaste	empiece *(usted)*
empezó	empecemos
empezamos	*(nosotros)*
empezasteis	empezad *(vosotros)*
empezaron	empiecen *(ustedes)*

[26] forzar – like [17] hablar except:

Present indicative	Present subjunctive
fuerzo	fuerce
fuerzas	fuerces
fuerza	fuerce
forzamos	forcemos
forzáis	forcéis
fuerzan	fuercen

Past simple indicative	Imperative
forcé	fuerza *(tú)*
forzaste	fuerce *(usted)*
forzó	forcemos *(nosotros*
forzamos	forzad *(vosotros)*
forzasteis	fuercen *(ustedes)*
forzaron	

[27] jugar – like [17] hablar except:

Present indicative	Present subjunctive
juego	juegue
juegas	juegues
juega	juegue
jugamos	juguemos
jugáis	juguéis
juegan	jueguen

Past simple indicative	Imperative
jugué	juega *(tú)*
jugaste	juegue *(usted)*
jugó	juguemos *(nosotros)*
jugamos	jugad *(vosotros)*
jugasteis	jueguen *(ustedes)*
jugaron	

[28] pagar – like [17] hablar except:

Past simple indicative	Present subjunctive
pagué	pague
pagaste	pagues
pagó	pague
pagamos	paguemos
pagasteis	paguéis
pagaron	paguen

	Imperative
	paga *(tú)*
	pague *(usted)*
	paguemos *(nosotros)*
	pagad *(vosotros)*
	paguen *(ustedes)*

[29] pensar - like [17] hablar except:

Present indicative	Present subjunctive
pienso	piense
piensas	pienses
piensa	piense
pensamos	pensemos
pensáis	penséis
piensan	piensen

Imperative
piensa *(tú)*
piense *(usted)*
pensemos *(nosotros)*
pensad *(vosotros)*
piensen *(ustedes)*

[30] regar - like [17] hablar except:

Present indicative	Present subjunctive
riego	riegue
riegas	riegues
riega	riegue
regamos	reguemos
regáis	reguéis
riegan	rieguen

Past simple indicative	Imperative
regué	riega *(tú)*
regaste	riegue *(usted)*
regó	reguemos *(nosotros)*
regamos	regad *(vosotros)*
regasteis	rieguen *(ustedes)*
regaron	

[31] sacar - like [17] hablar except:

Past simple indicative	Imperative
saqué	saca *(tú)*
sacaste	saque *(usted)*
sacó	saquemos *(nosotros)*
sacamos	sacad *(vosotros)*
sacasteis	saquen *(ustedes)*
sacaron	

Present subjunctive
saque
saques
saque
saquemos
saquéis
saquen

[32] vaciar - like [17] hablar except:

Present indicative	Present subjunctive
vacío	vacíe
vacías	vacíes
vacía	vacíe
vaciamos	vaciemos
vaciáis	vaciéis
vacian	vacíen

Imperative
vacía *(tú)*
vacie *(usted)*
vaciemos *(nosotros)*
vaciad *(vosotros)*
vacíen *(ustedes)*

[33] caber – like [18] comer except:

Present indicative	Conditional (present)
quepo	cabría
cabes	cabrías
cabe	cabría
cabemos	cabríamos
cabéis	cabríais
caben	cabrían

Past simple indicative	Present subjunctive
cupe	quepa
cupiste	quepas
cupo	quepa
cupimos	quepamos
cupisteis	quepáis
cupieron	quepan

Future indicative	Imperfect subjunctive
cabré	cupiera
cabrás	cupieras
cabrá	cupiera
cabremos	cupiéramos
cabréis	cupierais
cabrán	cupieran

Imperative
cabe *(tú)*
quepa *(usted)*
quepamos
(nosotros)
cabed *(vosotros)*
quepan *(ustedes)*

[34] caer – like [18] comer except:

Gerund cayendo
Past participle caído

Present indicative	Imperfect subjunctive
caigo	cayera
caes	cayeras
cae	cayera
caemos	cayéramos
caéis	cayerais
caen	cayeran

Past simple indicative	Imperative
caí	cae *(tú)*
caíste	caiga *(usted)*
cayó	caigamos *(nosotros)*
caímos	caed *(vosotros)*
caísteis	caigan *(ustedes)*
cayeron	

Present subjunctive
caiga
caigas
caiga
caigamos
caigáis
caigan

[35] conocer – like [18] comer except:

Present indicative	Present subjunctive
conozco	conozca
conoces	conozcas
conoce	conozca
conocemos	conozcamos
conocéis	conozcáis
conocen	conozcan

Imperative
conoce *(tú)*
conozca *(usted)*
conozcamos
(nosotros)
conoced *(vosotros)*
conozcan *(ustedes)*

[36] entender – like [18] comer except:

Present indicative	Present subjunctive
entiendo	entienda
entiendes	entiendas
entiende	entienda
entendemos	entendamos
entendéis	entendáis
entienden	entiendan

Imperative
entiende *(tú)*
entienda *(usted)*
entendamos
(nosotros)
entended (vosotros)
entiendan (ustedes)

[37] leer – like [18] comer except:

Gerund leyendo
Past participle leído

Past simple indicative	Imperfect subjunctive
leí	leyera
leíste	leyeras
leyó	leyera
leímos	layéramos
leísteis	leyerais
leyeron	leyeran

[38] mover – like [18] comer except:

Present indicative	Present subjunctive
muevo	mueva
mueves	muevas
mueve	mueva
movemos	movamos
movéis	mováis
mueven	muevan

Imperative
mueve *(tú)*
mueva *(usted)*
movamos
(nosotros)
moved *(vosotros)*
muevan *(ustedes)*

[39] oler – like [18] comer except:

Present indicative	Present subjunctive
huelo	huela
hueles	huelas
huele	huela
olemos	olamos
oléis	oláis
huelen	huelan

Imperative
huele *(tú)*
huela *(usted)*
olamos *(nosotros)*
oled *(vosotros)*
huelan *(ustedes)*

[40] romper – like [18[comer except:

Past participle roto

[41] torcer – like [18] comer except:

Present indicative	Present subjunctive
tuerzo	tuerza
tuerces	tuerzas
tuerce	tuerza
torcemos	torzamos
torcéis	torzáis
tuercen	tuerzan

Imperative
tuerce *(tú)*
tuerza *(usted)*
torzamos *(nosotros)*
torced *(vosotros)*
tuerzan *(ustedes)*

irregular -er

[42] traer - like [18] comer except:

Gerund trayendo
Past participle traído

Present indicative	Imperfect subjunctive
traigo	trajera
traes	trajeras
trae	trajera
traemos	trajéramos
traéis	trajerais
traen	trajeran

Present subjunctive	Past simple indicative
traiga	traje
traigas	trajiste
traiga	trajo
traigamos	trajimos
traigáis	trajisteis
traigan	trajeron

Imperative
trae *(tú)*
traiga *(usted)*
traigamos *(nosotros)*
traed *(vosotros)*
traigan *(ustedes)*

[43] valer - like [18] comer except:

Present indicative	Present subjunctive
valgo	valga
vales	valgas
vale	valga
valemos	valgamos
valéis	valgáis
valen	valgan

Future indicative	Imperfect subjunctive
valdré	valiera
valdrás	valieras
valdrá	valiera
valdremos	valiéramos
valdréis	valierais
valdrán	valieran

Conditional (present)	Imperative
valdría	vale *(tú)*
valdrías	valga *(usted)*
valdría	valgamos *(nosotro*
valdríamos	valed *(vosotros)*
valdríais	valgan *(ustedes)*
valdrían	

[44] vencer - like [18] comer except:

Present indicative	Present subjunctive
venzo	venza
vences	venzas
vence	venza
vencemos	venzamos
vencéis	venzáis
vencen	venzan

Imperative
vence *(tú)*
venza *(usted)*
venzamos *(nosotros)*
venced *(vosotros)*
venzan *(ustedes)*

[45] volver - like [18] comer except:

Past participle vuelto

Present indicative	Present subjunctive
vuelvo	vuelva
vuelves	vuelvas
vuelve	vuelva
volvemos	volvamos
volvéis	volváis
vuelven	vuelvan

Imperative
vuelve *(tú)*
vuelva *(usted)*
volvamos *(nosotros)*
volved *(vosotros)*
vuelvan *(ustedes)*

[46] abrir – like [19] vivir except:

Past participle abierto

[47] adquirir – like [19] vivir except:

Present indicative	Present subjunctive
adquiero	adquiera
adquieres	adquieras
adquiere	adquiera
adquirimos	adquiramos
adquirís	adquiráis
adquieren	adquieran

Imperative
adquiere *(tú)*
adquiera *(usted)*
adquiramos
(nosotros)
adquirid *(vosotros)*
adquieran *(ustedes)*

[48] corregir – like [19] vivir except:

Present indicative	Present subjunctive
corrijo	corrija
corriges	corrijas
corrige	corrija
corregimos	corrijamos
corregís	corrijáis
corrigen	corrijan

Past simple indicative	Imperative
corregí	corrige *(tú)*
corregiste	corrija *(usted)*
corrigió	corrijamos
corrigieron	*(nosotros)*
corregisteis	corregid *(vosotros)*
corrigieron	corrijan *(ustedes)*

[49] dirigir – like [19] vivir except:

Present indicative	Present subjunctive
dirijo	dirija
diriges	dirijas
dirige	dirija
dirigimos	dirijamos
dirigís	dirijáis
dirigen	dirijan

Imperative
dirige *(tú)*
dirija *(usted)*
dirijamos *(nosotros)*
dirigid *(vosotros)*
dirijan *(ustedes)*

[50] distinguir – like [19] vivir except:

Present indicative	Present subjunctive
distingo	distinga
distingues	distingas
distingue	distinga
distinguimos	distingamos
distinguís	distingáis
distinguen	distingan

Imperative
distingue *(tú)*
distinga *(usted)*
distingamos
(nosotros)
distinguid *(vosotros)*
distingan *(ustedes)*

[51] dormir – like [19] vivir except:

Gerund durmiendo
Past participle dormido

Present indicative	Past simple indicative
duermo	dormí
duermes	dormiste
duerme	dormid
dormimos	dormimos
dormís	dormisteis
duermen	durmieron

irregular -ir

Imperfect subjunctive	Imperative
durmiera	duerme *(tú)*
durmieras	duerma *(usted)*
durmiera	durmamos
durmiéramos	*(nosotros)*
durmierais	dormid *(vosotros)*
durmieran	duerman *(ustedes)*

Present subjunctive
duerma
duermas
duerma
durmamos
durmáis
duerman

[52] escribir - like [19] vivir except:

Past participle escrito

[53] freír - like [19] vivir except:

Gerund friendo
Past participle frito

Present indicative	Present subjunctive
frío	fría
fríes	frías
fríe	fría
freímos	friamos
freís	friáis
fríen	frían

Past simple indicative	Imperfect subjunctive
freí	friera
freíste	frieras
frio	friera
freímos	friéramos
freísteis	frierais
frieron	frieran

Imperative
fríe *(tú)*
fría *(usted)*
friamos *(nosotros)*
freíd *(vosotros)*
frían *(ustedes)*

[54] huir - like [19] vivir except:

Gerund huyendo
Past participle huido

Present indicative	Present subjunctive
huyo	huya
huyes	huyas
huye	huya
huimos	huyamos
huis	huyáis
huyen	huyan

Past simple indicative	Imperfect subjunctive
huí	huyera
huiste	huyeras
huyó	huyera
huimos	huyéramos
huisteis	huyerais
huyeron	huyeran

Imperative
huye *(tú)*
huya *(usted)*
huyamos *(nosotros)*
huid *(vosotros)*
huyan *(ustedes)*

[55] morir - like [19] vivir except:

Gerund muriendo
Past participle muerto

Present indicative	Present subjunctive
muero	muera
mueres	mueras
muere	muera
morimos	muramos
moris	muráis
mueren	mueran

Past simple indicative	Imperfect subjunctive
morí	muriera
moriste	murieras
murió	muriera
morimos	muriéramos
moristeis	murierais
murieron	murieran

[56] oír - like [19] vivir except:

Gerund oyendo
Past participle oído

Present indicative	Imperfect indicative
oigo	oía
oyes	oías
oye	oía
oímos	oíamos
oís	oíais
oyen	oían

Past simple indicative	Present subjunctive
oí	oiga
oíste	oigas
oyó	oiga
oímos	oigamos
oísteis	oigáis
oyeron	oigan

Future indicative	Imperfect subjunctive
oiré	oyera
oirás	oyeras
oirá	oyera
oiremos	oyéramos
oiréis	oyerais
oirán	oyeran

Conditional (present)	Imperative
oiría	oye *(tú)*
oirías	oiga *(usted)*
oiría	oigamos *(nosotros)*
oiríamos	oíd *(vosotros)*
oiríais	oigan *(ustedes)*
oirían	

[57] pedir - like [19] vivir except:

Present indicative	Present subjunctive
pido	pida
pides	pidas
pide	pida
pedimos	pidamos
pedís	pidáis
piden	pidan

Past simple indicative	Imperfect subjunctive
pedí	pidiera
pediste	pidieras
pidió	pidiera
pedimos	pidiéramos
pedisteis	pidierais
pidieron	pidieran

Imperative
pide *(tú)*
pida *(usted)*
pidamos *(nosotros)*
pedid *(vosotros)*
pidan *(ustedes)*

[58] prohibir - like [19] vivir except:

Present indicative	Present subjunctive
prohíbo	prohíba
prohíbes	prohíbas
prohíbe	prohíba
prohibimos	prohibamos
prohibís	prohibáis
prohíben	prohíban

Imperative
prohíbe *(tú)*
prohíba *(usted)*
prohibamos *(nosotros)*
prohibid *(vosotros)*
prohíban *(ustedes)*

[59] pudrir - like [19] vivir except:

Past participle podrido

[60] reducir - like [19] vivir except:

Present indicative	Present subjunctive
reduzco	reduzca
reduces	reduzcas
reduce	reduzca
reducimos	reduzcamos
reducís	reduzcáis
reducen	reduzcan

Past simple indicative	Imperfect subjunctive
reduje	redujera
redujiste	redujeras
redujo	redujera
redujimos	redujéramos
redujisteis	redujerais
redujeron	redujeran

Imperative
reduce *(tú)*
reduzca *(usted)*
reduzcamos
(nosotros)
reducid *(vosotros)*
reduzcan *(ustedes)*

[61] reír - like [19] vivir except:

Present indicative	Conditional (present)
río	reiría
ríes	reirías
ríe	reiría
reímos	reiríamos
reís	reiríais
ríen	reirían

Imperfect indicative	Present subjunctive
reía	ría
reías	rías
reía	ría
reíamos	riamos
reíais	riáis
reían	rían

Past simple indicative	Imperfect subjunctive
reí	riera
reiste	rieras
rio	riera
reímos	riéramos
reisteis	rierais
rieron	rieran

Future indicative	Imperative
reiré	ríe *(tú)*
reirás	ría *(usted)*
reirá	riamos *(nosotros)*
reiremos	reíd *(vosotros)*
reiréis	rían *(ustedes)*
reirán	

[62] reunir - like [19] vivir except:

Present indicative	Imperative
reúno	reúne *(tú)*
reúnes	reúna *(usted)*
reúne	reunamos
reunimos	*(nosotros)*
reunís	reunid *(vosotros)*
reúnen	reúnan *(ustedes)*

Present subjunctive
reúna
reúnas
reúna
reunamos
reunáis
reúnan

[63] salir - like [19] vivir except:

Present indicative	Present subjunctive
salgo	salga
sales	salgas
sale	salga
salimos	salgamos
salís	salgáis
salen	salgan

Future indicative	Imperfect subjunctive
saldré	saliera
saldrás	salieras
saldrá	saliera
saldremos	saliéramos
saldréis	salierais
saldrán	salieran

Conditional (present)	Imperative
saldría	sal *(tú)*
saldrías	salga *(usted)*
saldría	salgamos *(nosotros)*
saldríamos	salid *(vosotros)*
saldríais	salgan *(ustedes)*
saldrían	

[64] seguir - like [19] vivir except:

Present indicative	Past simple indicative
sigo	seguí
sigues	seguiste
sigue	siguió
seguimos	seguimos
seguís	seguisteis
siguen	siguieron

Present subjunctive	Imperfect subjunctive
siga	siguiera
sigas	siguieras
siga	siguiera
sigamos	siguiéramos
sigáis	siguierais
sigan	siguieran

Imperative
sigue *(tú)*
siga *(usted)*
sigamos *(nosotros)*
seguid *(vosotros)*
sigan *(ustedes)*

[65] teñir - like [19] vivir except:

Gerund tiñendo

Present indicative	Present subjunctive
tiño	tiña
tiñes	tiñas
tiñe	tiña
teñimos	tiñamos
teñís	tiñáis
tiñen	tiñan

Past simple indicative	Imperfect subjunctive
teñí	tiñera
teñiste	tiñeras
tiñó	tiñera
teñimos	tiñéramos
teñisteis	tiñerais
tiñeron	tiñeran

Imperative
tiñe *(tú)*
tiña *(usted)*
tiñamos *(nosotros)*
teñid *(vosotros)*
tiñan *(ustedes)*

Aa

a *DETERMINER* ❶ *(before a noun which is masculine in Spanish)* **un**; **a tree** un árbol ❷ *(before a noun which is feminine in Spanish)* **una**; **a table** una mesa ❸ *(before professions, occupations, etc. 'a' is not translated)* **I'm a doctor** soy médico ❹ **five euros a kilo** cinco euros el kilo ❺ **fifty kilometres an hour** cincuenta kilómetros por hora ❻ **three times a day** tres veces al día

abandon *VERB* **abandonar** [17]

abbey *NOUN* **abadía** *FEM*; **Westminster Abbey** la abadía de Westminster

abbreviation *NOUN* **abreviatura** *FEM*

abide *VERB* **I can't abide ...** no puedo soportar ...

ability *NOUN* ❶ **capacidad** *FEM*; **the ability to do** la capacidad de hacer ❷ **do it to the best of your ability** hazlo lo mejor que puedas, **I did it to the best of my ability** lo hice lo mejor que pude

able *ADJECTIVE* **to be able to do** **poder** [10] **hacer, she wasn't able to come** no pudo venir

abnormal *ADJECTIVE* **anormal**

abolish *VERB* **abolir** [19]

abortion *NOUN* **aborto** *MASC*

about *PREPOSITION* ❶ *(on the subject of)* **sobre**; **a film about Picasso** una película sobre Picasso ❷ **what's it about?** ¿de qué trata? ❸ *(concerning or in relation to)* **acerca de**; **he wants to talk to you about your exam** quiere hablarte acerca de tu examen ❹ **to talk about something** hablar de algo, **what is she talking about?** ¿de qué está hablando? ❺ **to think about something/somebody** pensar en algo/alguien, **I'm thinking about you** estoy pensando en ti

about *ADVERB* ❶ *(approximately)* **there are about sixty people** hay unas sesenta personas ❷ *(when talking about time)* **at about three o'clock** como a las tres, **about three weeks/a month ago** hace cosa de tres semanas/de un mes ❸ **to be about to do** estar a punto de hacer, **I'm (just) about to leave** estoy a punto de marcharme

above *PREPOSITION* ❶ **encima de**; **above the sink** encima del fregadero ❷ **above all** sobre todo

above *ADVERB* **de arriba**; **the flat above** el piso de arriba

abroad *ADVERB* **to go abroad** irse al extranjero, **to live abroad** vivir en el extranjero

abscess *NOUN* **flemón** *MASC*

abseiling *NOUN* **rappel** *MASC*

absent *ADJECTIVE* **ausente**; **to be absent from** faltar a, **he was absent from the lesson** faltó a clase, **she's often absent from meetings** falta a menudo a las reuniones, *(when referring to the present moment, 'to be absent' is translated by the present perfect)* **he's absent from school today** hoy ha faltado a clase

absent-minded *ADJECTIVE*
despistado/despistada

absolute *ADJECTIVE* absoluto/
absoluta; **an absolute disaster**
un desastre absoluto

absolutely *ADVERB* ❶ *(completely)*
totalmente; **I'm absolutely
certain** estoy totalmente segura
❷ *(extremely)* realmente; **it's
absolutely dreadful** es realmente
terrible ❸ **you're absolutely right**
tienes toda la razón ❹ **absolutely!**
¡por supuesto!

absorb *VERB* absorber [18]

abuse *NOUN* ❶ **alcohol abuse**
alcoholismo *MASC*, **drug abuse**
consumo (*MASC*) de drogas ❷ *(violent
treatment of a person)* malos tratos
MASC PLURAL ❸ *(insults)* insultos *MASC
PLURAL*

abuse *VERB* **to abuse somebody**
maltratar [17] a alguien

academic *ADJECTIVE* académico/
académica; **the academic year**
el año académico

accelerate *VERB* acelerar [17]

accelerator *NOUN* acelerador *MASC*

accent *NOUN* acento *MASC*; **she has
a Spanish accent** tiene acento
español

accept *VERB* aceptar [17]

acceptable *ADJECTIVE* aceptable

access *NOUN* acceso *MASC*

access *VERB* **to access something**
obtener [9] acceso a algo

accessory *NOUN* accesorio *MASC*

accident *NOUN* ❶ *(an unfortunate
happening)* accidente *MASC*; **to have
an accident** [9] un accidente,
a road accident un accidente
de carretera, **a car accident** un
accidente de coche ❷ *(chance)*
casualidad *FEM*; **it's no accident**
no es casualidad ❸ **by accident** *(by
chance)* por casualidad *(without
meaning to)* sin querer; **I found
it by accident** lo encontré por
casualidad, **she broke it by accident**
lo rompió sin querer

accident & emergency *NOUN*
urgencias *FEM PLURAL*

accidental *ADJECTIVE* fortuito/
fortuita; **an accidental discovery**
un descubrimiento fortuito

accidentally *ADVERB* ❶ *(without
meaning to)* sin querer;
**I accidentally knocked over his
glass** le tiré el vaso sin querer
❷ *(by chance)* por casualidad;
I accidentally discovered that ...
descubrí por casualidad que ...

accommodation *NOUN*
alojamiento *MASC*; **I'm looking for
accommodation** estoy buscando
alojamiento, **hotel accommodation**
alojamiento en hotel

accompany *VERB* **to accompany
somebody** acompañar [17] a alguien

according *IN PHRASE* **according to**
según, **according to Sophie** según
Sophie

accordion *NOUN* acordeón *MASC*

account *NOUN* ❶ *(in a bank, shop,
or post office)* cuenta *FEM*; **a bank
account** una cuenta bancaria, **to
open an account** abrir [46] una
cuenta, **I have fifty pounds in my**

account tengo cincuenta libras en mi cuenta ❷ *(a description of an experience or event)* relato *MASC* ❸ **on account of** debido a, **the station is closed on account of the strike** la estación está cerrada debido a la huelga ❹ **to take something into account** tener [9] algo en cuenta, **we will take his illness into account** tendremos en cuenta su enfermedad

accountant *NOUN* contable *MASC & FEM*; **she's an accountant** es contable

accuracy *NOUN* precisión *FEM*

accurate *ADJECTIVE* preciso/precisa

accurately *ADVERB* con precisión

accuse *VERB* acusar [17]; **to accuse somebody of something** acusar a alguien de algo, **to accuse somebody of doing something** acusar a alguien de hacer algo, **she accused me of stealing her pen** me acusó de haber robado su pluma

accustomed to *ADJECTIVE* **to be accustomed to something** estar [2] acostumbrado/acostumbrada a algo, **she's accustomed to having lots of homework** está acostumbrada a tener muchos deberes

ace *NOUN* as *MASC*; **the ace of hearts** el as de corazones

ace *ADJECTIVE* de primera *(informal)*; **he's an ace drummer** es un batería de primera

ache *VERB* **my arm aches** me duele el brazo, **my head aches** me duele la cabeza

achieve *VERB* ❶ conseguir [64]; **she's achieved a great deal** consiguió

mucho ❷ **to achieve an ambition** hacer [7] realidad una ambición ❸ **to achieve an aim** lograr [17] un objetivo ❹ **to achieve success** tener [9] éxito

achievement *NOUN* ❶ éxito *MASC*; **it's a great achievement** es un gran éxito ❷ **a sense of achievement** un sentimiento de satisfacción

acid *NOUN* ácido *MASC*

acid rain *NOUN* lluvia *(FEM)* ácida

acne *NOUN* acné *MASC*

acorn *NOUN* bellota *FEM*

acrobat *NOUN* acróbata *MASC & FEM*

across *PREPOSITION* ❶ *(over to the other side of)* **to walk across something** cruzar [22] algo, **we walked across the park** cruzamos el parque, **to run across the road** cruzar la calle corriendo ❷ *(on the other side of)* al otro lado de; **the house across the street** la casa de enfrente ❸ **across from** en frente de, **she was sitting across from me** estaba sentada en frente de mí

acrylic *NOUN* acrílica *FEM*

act *NOUN* acto *MASC*

act *VERB* actuar [20]

acting *NOUN* actuación *FEM*; **she wants to go into acting** quiere ser actriz

action *NOUN* acción *FEM*

action replay *NOUN* repetición *(FEM)* de la jugada

active *ADJECTIVE* activo/activa

activity *NOUN* actividad *FEM*

activity holiday NOUN **vacaciones** (FEM PLURAL) **con actividades programadas**

actor NOUN **actor** MASC; **who's your favourite actor?** ¿quién es tu actor favorito?

actress NOUN **actriz** FEM (PLURAL **actrices**); **who's your favourite actress?** ¿quién es tu actriz favorita?

actual ADJECTIVE ❶ **his actual words** sus palabras textuales ❷ **actual cases** casos reales ❸ **in actual fact** de hecho

actually ADVERB ❶ (in fact, as it happens) la verdad es que; **actually, I've changed my mind** la verdad es que he cambiado de idea, **he's not actually here at the moment** la verdad es que no está aquí en este momento ❷ (really and truly) de verdad; **did she actually say that?** ¿dijo eso de verdad?

acupuncture NOUN **acupuntura** FEM

acute ADJECTIVE ❶ (pain) **agudo/aguda** ❷ **an acute accent** un acento agudo

ad NOUN **anuncio** MASC; **to put an ad in the paper** poner un anuncio en el periódico, **the small ads** los anuncios por palabras

AD ABBREVIATION **d. de C.** (short for después de Cristo); **in 400 AD** en el año 400 d. de C.

adapt VERB ❶ **to adapt something** adaptar [17] algo ❷ **to adapt to something** adaptarse [17] a algo, **she's adapted to the new system** se adaptó al nuevo sistema

adaptor NOUN **adaptador** MASC

add VERB **añadir** [19]; **add three eggs** añadir tres huevos
• **to add something up** sumar [17] algo

addict NOUN ❶ (drug addict) **drogadicto** MASC, **drogadicta** FEM ❷ (of television, chocolate, for example) **adicto** MASC, **adicta** FEM; **she's a telly addict** es una adicta a la televisión ❸ (of sport) **fanático** MASC, **fanática** FEM; **he's a football addict** es un fanático del fútbol

addicted ADJECTIVE ❶ (to drugs, television, computer games, etc.) **adicto/adicta**; **she's addicted to heroin** es adicta a la heroína, **he's addicted to the Net** es un adicto a Internet ❷ (to food) **I'm addicted to tomatoes** los tomates son mi vicio (informal) ❸ **to become addicted to something** (to drugs) hacerse adicto a algo (to television, chocolate) enviciarse con algo

addition NOUN ❶ (adding up) **suma** FEM ❷ **in addition** además ❸ **in addition to** además de

additional ADJECTIVE **adicional**; **additional costs** costes (MASC PLURAL) adicionales

additive NOUN **aditivo** MASC

address NOUN ❶ (of person, house, office) **dirección** FEM; **what's your address?** ¿cuál es tu dirección? ❷ (on a form) **domicilio** MASC ❸ **to change address** cambiar [17] de domicilio

address book NOUN **libreta** (FEM) **de direcciones**

adequate ADJECTIVE **suficiente**

adhesive NOUN **pegamento** MASC

adhesive *ADJECTIVE* adhesivo/
adhesiva; **adhesive tape** cinta *(FEM)*
adhesiva

adjective *NOUN* adjetivo *MASC*

adjust *VERB* ❶ regular [17] *(volume,
temperature)*, ajustar [17] *(height,
width)* ❷ **to adjust to something**
adaptarse [17] a algo

adjustable *ADJECTIVE* regulable

administration *NOUN*
administración *FEM*

admiral *NOUN* admirante *MASC & FEM*

admiration *NOUN* admiración *FEM*

admire *VERB* admirar [17]

admission *NOUN* entrada *FEM*; 'no
admission' prohibida la entrada,
'admission free' entrada gratuita

admit *VERB* ❶ *(confess)* admitir [19];
she admits she lied admite que
mintió ❷ *(concede)* reconocer [35];
I must admit that ... debo
reconocer que ... ❸ *(allow to
enter)* dejar [17] entrar; **to admit
somebody to a restaurant** dejar
entrar a alguien en un restaurante

adolescence *NOUN* adolescencia *FEM*

adolescent *NOUN* adolescente *MASC
& FEM*

adopt *VERB* adoptar [17]

adopted *ADJECTIVE* adoptado/
adoptada

adoption *NOUN* adopción *FEM*

adore *VERB* adorar [17]

Adriatic Sea *NOUN* **the Adriatic Sea**
el mar Adriático

adult *NOUN* adulto *MASC*, adulta *FEM*

adult *ADJECTIVE* adulto/adulta; **the
adult population** la población
adulta

Adult Education *NOUN* educación
(FEM) para adultos

advance *NOUN* avance *MASC*;
advances in technology avances en
tecnología

advance *VERB* avanzar [22]

advanced *ADJECTIVE* avanzado/
avanzada

advantage *NOUN* ❶ ventaja *FEM*;
there are several advantages hay
varias ventajas ❷ **to take advantage
of something** aprovechar [17] algo,
**I took advantage of the sales to
buy myself some shoes** aproveché
las rebajas para comprarme unos
zapatos ❸ **to take advantage of
somebody** *(unfairly)* aprovecharse
[17] de alguien

adventure *NOUN* aventura *FEM*

adventurous *ADJECTIVE* ❶ *(person)*
aventurero/aventurera ❷ *(design,
designer, etc.)* innovador/
innovadora

adverb *NOUN* adverbio *MASC*

advert, **advertisement** *NOUN*
❶ *(on television, in a newspaper)*
anuncio *MASC* ❷ *(small ad in a
newspaper advertising a job, an
article for sale, etc.)* anuncio *MASC*,
por palabras

advertise *VERB* ❶ **to advertise a
product** hacer [7] publicidad de un
producto ❷ **to advertise something
in the newspaper** anunciar [17] algo
en el periódico, **I saw it advertised
on telly** lo vi anunciado en la tele, **I
saw a bike advertised in the paper**

a
b
c
d
e
f
g
h
i
j
k
l
m
n
o
p
q
r
s
t
u
v
w
x
y
z

(in the small ads) vi un anuncio (por palabras) de una bicicleta en el periódico

advertising NOUN publicidad FEM

advice NOUN ❶ consejos MASC PLURAL; **his advice is good** sus consejos son buenos ❷ **a piece of advice** un consejo ❸ **to give somebody advice** aconsejar [17] a alguien, **they gave me good advice** me aconsejaron bien ❹ **to ask for advice about something** pedir [57] consejo sobre algo

advise VERB aconsejar [17]; **to advise somebody to ...** aconsejar a alguien que ... *(followed by the subjunctive)*, **I advised him to study more** le aconsejé que estudiase más, **I advised her not to wait** le aconsejé que no esperase

adviser NOUN asesor MASC, asesora FEM

aerial NOUN antena FEM

aerobics NOUN aerobic MASC; **to do aerobics** hacer [7] aerobic

aeroplane NOUN avión MASC

aerosol NOUN **an aerosol (can)** un aerosol

affair NOUN ❶ asunto MASC; **international affairs** asuntos internacionales ❷ **a love affair** una aventura amorosa

affect VERB afectar [17]

affectionate ADJECTIVE cariñoso/cariñosa

afford VERB **to be able to afford to do** tener [9] dinero para hacer, **I can't afford to go out much** no tengo dinero para salir mucho, **I can't**

afford a new bike no tengo dinero para una bicicleta nueva

afraid ADJECTIVE ❶ **to be afraid** tener [9] miedo, **I'm afraid** tengo miedo ❷ *(with 'of')* **I'm afraid of dogs** me dan miedo los perros, **Dan's afraid of spiders** a Dan le dan miedo las arañas, **he's afraid of flying** le da miedo volar, **she's afraid of failing the exam** le da miedo suspender el examen ❸ **I'm afraid there's no milk left** me temo que no queda leche, **I'm afraid so** me temo que sí, **I'm afraid not** me temo que no

Africa NOUN África FEM

African NOUN africano MASC, africana FEM

African ADJECTIVE africano/africana

after PREPOSITION, ADVERB, CONJUNCTION ❶ *(later in time)* después de; **after 10 o'clock** después de las diez en punto, **after lunch** después de comer, **after school** después del colegio, **after I've finished my homework** después de terminar mis deberes ❷ **soon after** poco después ❸ **the day after tomorrow** pasado mañana
• **to run after somebody** correr [18] tras alguien

after all ADVERB después de todo; **after all, she's only six** después de todo, solo tiene seis años

afternoon NOUN tarde FEM; **this afternoon** esta tarde, **tomorrow afternoon** mañana por la tarde, **yesterday afternoon** ayer por la tarde, **on Saturday afternoon** el sábado por la tarde, **on Saturday afternoons** los sábados por la tarde, **at four o' clock in the afternoon** a las cuatro de la tarde, **every afternoon** todas las tardes

afters NOUN **postre** MASC

aftershave NOUN **loción** (FEM) **para después del afeitado**

afterwards ADVERB **después**; **shortly afterwards** poco después

again ADVERB ❶ (one more time) **otra vez**; **try again** inténtalo otra vez, **I've forgotten it again** se me ha olvidado otra vez, **you should ask again** deberías preguntar otra vez ❷ (with a negative verb) **I don't want to see her again** no quiero volver a verla, **don't do it again** no lo vuelvas a hacer ❸ **never again!** ¡nunca más!

against PREPOSITION **contra**; **against the wall** contra la pared, **to lean against the wall** apoyarse contra la pared, **I'm against the idea** estoy en contra de la idea, **to fight against racism** luchar contra el racismo

age NOUN ❶ **edad** FEM; **at the age of fifteen** a la edad de quince años, **she's the same age as me** tiene mi misma edad, **to be under age** ser menor de edad ❷ **I haven't seen Johnny for ages** hace siglos que no he visto a Johnny (informal), **I haven't been to London for ages** hace un montón de tiempo que no voy a Londres (informal)

agenda NOUN **agenda** FEM

agent NOUN **agente** MASC & FEM

aggressive ADJECTIVE **agresivo/agresiva**

ago ADVERB **an hour ago** hace una hora, **three days ago** hace tres días, **five years ago** hace cinco años, **a long time ago** hace mucho tiempo, **not long ago** no hace mucho (tiempo), **how long ago was it?** ¿cuánto tiempo hace de eso?

agree VERB ❶ **to agree with somebody** estar [2] de acuerdo con alguien, **I agree with Laura** estoy de acuerdo con Laura, **I don't agree** no estoy de acuerdo ❷ **I agree that ...** estoy de acuerdo en que ..., **I agree that it's too late now** estoy de acuerdo en que ya es muy tarde ❸ **to agree to do** [18] hacer, **Steve's agreed to help me** Steve ha aceptado ayudarme ❹ **coffee doesn't agree with me** el café no me sienta bien

agreement NOUN **acuerdo** MASC

agricultural ADJECTIVE **agrícola**

agriculture NOUN **agricultura** FEM

ahead ADVERB ❶ **go ahead!** ¡adelante! ❷ **straight ahead** todo recto, **go straight ahead until you get to the crossroads** sigue todo recto hasta que llegues al cruce ❸ **our team was ten points ahead** nuestro equipo llevaba diez puntos de ventaja, **I'll go ahead** yo voy delante ❹ **to be ahead of time** ir [8] adelantado

aid NOUN ❶ **ayuda** FEM; **aid to developing countries** ayuda a los países en vías de desarrollo ❷ **in aid of** en beneficio de, **in aid of the homeless** en beneficio de la gente sin hogar

Aids NOUN **sida** MASC (short for síndrome de inmunodeficiencia adquirida); **to have Aids** tener [9] el sida

aim NOUN **objetivo** MASC; **their aim is to control pollution** su objetivo es controlar la contaminación

aim VERB ❶ **to aim to do** proponerse [11] hacer, **we're aiming to finish it today** nos proponemos terminarlo hoy ❷ **a campaign aimed at young people** una campaña dirigida a los jóvenes ❸ **to aim a gun at somebody** apuntar [17] una pistola a alguien

air NOUN ❶ aire MASC; **in the open air** al aire libre, **to go out for a breath of air** salir [8] a tomar el aire ❷ **to travel by air** viajar [8] en avión

airbag NOUN airbag MASC

air-conditioned ADJECTIVE con aire acondicionado

air conditioning NOUN aire (MASC) acondicionado

air force NOUN fuerza (FEM) aérea

air hostess NOUN azafata FEM; **she's an air hostess** es azafata

airline NOUN compañía (FEM) aérea

airmail NOUN correo (MASC) aéreo; **by airmail** por correo aéreo

airport NOUN aeropuerto MASC

aisle NOUN (in theatre, on plane) pasillo MASC

alarm NOUN alarma FEM; **a fire alarm** una alarma contra incendios, **a burglar alarm** una alarma antirrobo

alarm clock NOUN reloj (MASC) despertador

album NOUN álbum MASC

alcohol NOUN alcohol MASC

alcoholic NOUN alcohólico MASC, alcohólica FEM

alcoholic ADJECTIVE alcohólico/ alcohólica; **alcoholic drinks** bebidas alcohólicas

alert ADJECTIVE espabilado/ espabilada

alert NOUN **to be on the alert** estar [2] al alerta; **be on the alert for pickpockets** hay que estar al tanto con los carteristas

A levels NOUN selectividad FEM, (Students take 'la selectividad' at the same age as A levels are taken in Britain. You can explain A levels briefly as follows: Son exámenes que se realizan a dos niveles, AS y A2. Los exámenes AS se hacen después de un año de preparación, generalmente en cuatro o cinco asignaturas; los A2 abarcan un número menor de asignaturas que ya se hayan estudiado para el nivel AS. Ambos exámenes se califican desde A (nota máxima), a N (sin calificar). La calificación de los A levels se toma en cuenta para ingresar a la universidad)
▸ SEE **selectividad**

alibi NOUN coartada FEM

alien NOUN ❶ (foreigner) extranjero MASC, extranjera FEM ❷ (from outer space) extraterrestre MASC & FEM

alike ADJECTIVE ❶ parecido/parecida; **they're all alike** son todos parecidos ❷ **to look alike** parecerse [35], **the two brothers look alike** los dos hermanos se parecen

alive ADJECTIVE vivo/viva

all ADJECTIVE, PRONOUN ❶ todo/toda; **all the knives** todos los cuchillos, **all the cups** todas las tazas, **all the time** todo el tiempo, **all day** todo el día ❷ **they've eaten it all** se lo han comido todo, **after all** después de todo, **not at all** de nada *(to somebody who's said 'thank you')*, **they're all there** están todos allí ❸ **it's all I have** es todo lo que tengo ❹ *(in scores)* **three all** tres iguales

all *ADVERB* **completamente**; **all alone** completamente solo, **she's all alone at the moment** ahora está completamente sola

all along *ADVERB* **desde el primer momento**; **I knew it all along** lo supe desde el primer momento

allergic *ADJECTIVE* **alérgico/alérgica**; **to be allergic to something** ser [13] alérgico a algo

allergy *NOUN* **alergia** *FEM*

alligator *NOUN* **caimán** *MASC*

allow *VERB* ❶ **to allow somebody to do** permitir [19] a alguien hacer, **the teacher allowed them to go out** el maestro les permitió salir ❷ *(to do)* **I'm not allowed to go out during the week** no me dejan salir durante la semana, **they are allowed to watch TV in the evenings** les dejan ver la tele por las noches

all right *ADVERB* ❶ *(showing agreement)* **de acuerdo**, **vale** *(informal)*; **'come round to my house around six' – 'all right'** 'ven a mi casa a eso de las seis' – 'de acuerdo', 'ven a mi casa a eso de las seis' – 'vale', **it's all right by me** por mí de acuerdo, por mí vale *(informal)* ❷ *(fine)* **is everything all right?** ¿va todo bien? ❸ *(talking about health, wellbeing)* **bien**; **are you all right?** ¿estás bien?, **she's all right now** ya está bien ❹ *(not bad)* **the meal was all right** la comida no

estuvo mal ❺ **is it all right to leave the door open?** ¿puedo dejar la puerta abierta?

ally *NOUN* **aliado** *MASC*, **aliada** *FEM*

almond *NOUN* **almendra** *FEM*

almost *ADVERB* **casi**; **almost every day** casi cada día, **almost everybody** casi todo el mundo, **she's almost five** tiene casi cinco años

alone *ADJECTIVE* ❶ **solo/sola**; **he lives alone** vive solo ❷ **leave me alone!** ¡déjame en paz! ❸ **leave these papers alone!** ¡deja esos papeles!

along *PREPOSITION* ❶ **a lo largo de**; **there are trees all along the road** hay árboles a lo largo de toda la carretera ❷ *(there is often no direct translation for 'along' so the sentence has to be expressed differently)* **she lives along the street from me** vive en mi misma calle, **to go for a walk along the beach** pasear por la playa, **a bit further along** un poco más adelante

aloud *ADVERB* **en voz alta**; **to read something aloud** leer [37] algo en voz alta

alphabet *NOUN* **alfabeto** *MASC*

alphabetical *ADJECTIVE* **alfabético/alfabética**; **in alphabetical order** por orden alfabético

Alps *PLURAL NOUN* **the Alps** los Alpes

already *ADVERB* **ya**; **they've already left** ya han salido, **it's six o'clock already!** ¡ya son las seis!

Alsatian *NOUN* **pastor** *(MASC)* **alemán**

also *ADVERB* **también**; **I've also invited Karen** he invitado también a Karen

alter VERB cambiar [17]

alternate ADJECTIVE on alternate days un día sí y otro no

alternative NOUN alternativa FEM; we have no alternative no tenemos alternativa

alternative ADJECTIVE otro/otra; to find an alternative solution encontrar otra solución

alternatively ADVERB o bien; alternatively, we could go together on Saturday o bien podríamos ir juntos el sábado

alternative medicine NOUN medicina (FEM) alternativa

although CONJUNCTION aunque; although she's ill, she's willing to help us aunque está enferma, está dispuesta a ayudarnos

altitude NOUN altitud FEM

altogether ADVERB ❶ en total; I've spent thirty pounds altogether he gastado treinta libras en total ❷ (completely) totalmente; I'm not altogether convinced no estoy totalmente convencido

aluminium NOUN aluminio MASC

always ADVERB siempre; I always leave at five siempre salgo a las cinco

am VERB ▸ SEE **be**

a.m. ABBREVIATION de la mañana; at 8 a.m. a las ocho de la mañana

amateur NOUN amateur MASC & FEM (PLURAL amateurs); amateur dramatics teatro (MASC) de amateurs

amaze VERB asombrar [17]; what amazes me is ... lo que me asombra es ...

amazed ADJECTIVE asombrado/asombrada; I was amazed to see her me me quedé asombrado al verla, he'll be amazed to find out se quedará asombrado al enterarse

amazement NOUN asombro MASC; to my amazement she agreed para mi gran sorpresa aceptó

amazing ADJECTIVE increíble; they've got an amazing house tienen una casa increíble, she has an amazing number of friends tiene un número increíble de amigos

ambassador NOUN embajador MASC, embajadora FEM

ambition NOUN ambición FEM

ambitious ADJECTIVE ambicioso/ambiciosa

ambulance NOUN ambulancia FEM

ambulance driver NOUN conductor/conductora (MASC & FEM) de ambulancia

amenities PLURAL NOUN servicios (MASC PLURAL) públicos

America NOUN América FEM

American NOUN americano MASC, americana FEM

American ADJECTIVE americano/americana

ammunition NOUN municiones FEM PLURAL

among, **amongst** PREPOSITION entre;
I found it among my books lo
encontré entre mis libros, **you can
decide amongst yourselves** podéis
decidirlo entre vosotros

amount NOUN ❶ cantidad FEM; **an
enormous amount of bread** una
enorme cantidad de pan, **a huge
amount of work** una enorme
cantidad de trabajo ❷ (of money)
suma FEM; **a large amount of
money** una gran suma de dinero

amount to VERB ascender [36] a; **the
bill amounts to five hundred euros**
la cuenta asciende a quinientos
euros

amp NOUN ❶ amperio MASC
❷ (amplifier) amplificador MASC

amplifier NOUN amplificador MASC

amuse VERB divertir [14]

amusement arcade NOUN salón
(MASC) de juegos recreativos

amusement park NOUN parque
(MASC) de atracciones

amusing ADJECTIVE divertido/
divertida

an DETERMINER ▸ SEE **a**

anaesthetic NOUN anestesia FEM

analyse VERB analizar [22]

analysis NOUN análisis MASC

ancestor NOUN antepasado MASC,
antepasada FEM

anchor NOUN ancla FEM

anchovy NOUN anchoa FEM

ancient ADJECTIVE ❶ (historic)
antiguo/antigua; **an ancient**

abbey una antigua abadía ❷ (very
old) viejísimo/viejísima; **an
ancient pair of jeans** unos vaqueros
viejísimos ❸ **ancient Greece** la
Grecia antigua

and CONJUNCTION ❶ y; **Sean and Anna**
Sean y Anna, **your shoes and socks**
tus calcetines y tus zapatos ('y'
becomes 'e' before a word that
starts with 'i' or 'hi') **Spain and Italy**
España e Italia ❷ (with numbers)
three hundred and six trescientos
seis, **five hundred and thirty-one**
quinientos treinta y uno ❸ **fish and
chips** pescado con patatas fritas
❹ **bigger and bigger** cada vez más
grande

Andalusia NOUN Andalucía FEM

Andalusian NOUN andaluz,
andaluza

Andalusian ADJECTIVE andaluz/
andaluza

angel NOUN ángel MASC

anger NOUN ira FEM

angle NOUN ángulo MASC

angrily ADVERB con enfado

angry ADJECTIVE **to be angry** estar [2]
enfadado/enfadada, **she was angry
with me** estaba enfadada conmigo,
to get angry (about something)
enfadarse [17] (por algo)

animal NOUN animal MASC

ankle NOUN tobillo MASC; **to break
your ankle** romperse [40] el tobillo

anniversary NOUN aniversario
MASC; **a wedding anniversary** un
aniversario de boda

announce VERB anunciar [17]

announcement NOUN anuncio MASC

annoy VERB to be annoyed estar [2] enfadado/enfadada, to get annoyed (about something) enfadarse [17] (por algo), she got annoyed se enfadó

annoying ADJECTIVE ❶ (person) pesado/pesada ❷ (noise or habit) irritante ❸ how annoying! ¡qué rabia!, the whole thing's really annoying todo es un verdadero fastidio

annual ADJECTIVE anual

anorak NOUN anorak MASC (PLURAL anoraks)

anorexia NOUN anorexia FEM

another ADJECTIVE otro/otra; would you like another cup of tea? ¿quieres otra taza de té?, another two years otros dos años, we need another three chairs necesitamos otras tres sillas, I'll come another time vendré en otro momento

answer NOUN ❶ respuesta FEM; the right answer la respuesta correcta, the wrong answer la respuesta equivocada ❷ the answer to a problem la solución a un problema

answer VERB ❶ contestar [17]; he hasn't answered our letter no ha contestado a nuestra carta, to answer the phone contestar el teléfono ❷ to answer the door abrir [46] la puerta

answering machine NOUN contestador (MASC) automático; to leave a message on the answering machine dejar [17] un mensaje en el contestador

ant NOUN hormiga FEM

Antarctic NOUN the Antarctic la Antártida

anthem NOUN the national anthem el himno nacional

antibiotic NOUN antibiótico MASC

anticlockwise ADVERB en el sentido contrario al de las agujas del reloj; it turns anticlockwise gira en el sentido contrario al de las agujas del reloj

antique NOUN antiques las antigüedades

antique ADJECTIVE antiguo/antigua; an antique table una mesa antigua

antique shop NOUN tienda (FEM) de antigüedades

antiseptic NOUN antiséptico MASC

anxious ADJECTIVE preocupado/preocupada

anxiously ADVERB con preocupación

any PRONOUN ❶ (in negative sentences) ninguno/ninguna; I don't want any no quiero ninguno/ninguna ❷ (in questions) alguno/alguna; do you want any? ¿quieres alguno/alguna?

any ADJECTIVE, ADVERB ❶ (when followed by a noun 'any' is not translated) is there any butter? ¿hay mantequilla?, have you got any glasses? ¿tienes vasos?, there isn't any flour no hay harina, I haven't got any glasses no tengo vasos ❷ is there any more? (followed by a singular) ¿queda más? (followed by a plural) ¿quedan más?, there isn't any more butter no me queda más mantequilla, I haven't got any more

glasses no me quedan más vasos ❸ *(referring to time)* **I don't go there any more** ya no voy nunca, **I used to phone her but not any more** solía llamarla, pero ya no

anybody, anyone *PRONOUN* ❶ *(in questions and after 'if')* **alguien**; **does anybody want some tea?** ¿alguien quiere té?, **is anybody home?** ¿hay alguien en casa?, **if anybody wants some beer, it's in the fridge** si alguien quiere cerveza, está en la nevera ❷ **not ... anybody** no ... nadie, **there isn't anybody in her office** no hay nadie en su oficina, **I don't know anybody there** no conozco a nadie allí ❸ *(absolutely anybody)* **cualquiera**; **anybody can go** puede ir cualquiera

anyhow *ADVERB* ▸ SEE **anyway**

anyone *PRONOUN* ▸ SEE **anybody**

anything *PRONOUN* ❶ *(in questions)* **algo**; **is there anything I can do to help?** ¿puedo hacer algo para ayudar? ❷ **not ... anything** no ... nada, **there isn't anything on the table** no hay nada en la mesa ❸ *(anything at all)* **cualquier cosa**; **anything could happen** puede pasar cualquier cosa

anyway, anyhow *ADVERB* **de todos modos**; **anyway, I'll ring you before I leave** de todos modos te llamaré antes de salir

anywhere *ADVERB* ❶ *(in questions)* **have you seen my keys anywhere?** ¿has visto mis llaves por algún lado?, **are you going anywhere tomorrow?** ¿vas a algún lado mañana? ❷ **not ... anywhere** por ningún lado, **I can't find my keys anywhere** no puedo encontrar mis llaves por ningún lado, **I'm not**

going anywhere tonight esta noche no voy a ningún lado ❸ *(absolutely anywhere)* **donde sea**; **put your cases down anywhere** pon las maletas donde sea

apart *ADJECTIVE, ADVERB* ❶ *(separate)* **separado/separada**; **we don't like being apart** no nos gusta estar separados, **they're too far apart** están demasiado separados ❷ **to be two metres apart** estar [2] a dos metros de distancia ❸ **apart from** aparte de, **apart from Judy everybody was there** aparte de Judy, todo el mundo estaba allí

apartheid *NOUN* **apartheid** *MASC*

apartment *NOUN* **apartamento** *MASC*

ape *NOUN* **simio** *MASC & FEM*

apologize *VERB* ❶ **disculparse** [17]; **he apologized for his behaviour** se disculpó por su comportamiento ❷ **to apologize to somebody** pedirle [57] perdón a alguien, **he apologized to Tanya** le pidió perdón a Tanya

apology *NOUN* **disculpa** *FEM*

apostrophe *NOUN* **apóstrofe** *MASC*

apparent *ADJECTIVE* **aparente**

apparently *ADVERB* **al parecer**

appeal *NOUN* ❶ *(call)* **an appeal for calm** un llamamiento a la calma ❷ **an appeal for help** una solicitud de ayuda

appeal *VERB* **to appeal to somebody** atraer [42] a alguien, **horror films don't appeal to me** las películas de miedo no me atraen

appear *VERB* ❶ **aparecer** [35]; **Mick appeared at the door** Mick

apareció en la puerta ❷ to appear
on television salir [63] en televisión
❸ *(seem)* parecer [35]; it appears
that somebody has stolen the key
parece que alguien ha robado la
llave, he appears to be calm parece
que está tranquilo

appendicitis NOUN apendicitis FEM

appendix NOUN apéndice MASC

appetite NOUN apetito MASC; it'll
spoil your appetite te quitará el
apetito

applaud VERB aplaudir [19]

applause NOUN aplausos MASC PLURAL

apple NOUN manzana FEM

apple tree NOUN manzano MASC

applicant NOUN candidato MASC,
candidata FEM

application NOUN a job application
una solicitud de trabajo

application form NOUN impreso
(MASC) de solicitud

apply VERB ❶ to apply for a job
solicitar [17] un trabajo ❷ I've
applied for the course he solicitado
que me admitan en el curso ❸ to
apply to aplicarse [31] a, that
doesn't apply to students eso no se
aplica a los estudiantes

appointment NOUN cita FEM; to
make a dental appointment pedir
[57] cita en el dentista, I've got
a hair appointment at 4 o'clock
tengo cita en la peluquería para las
cuatro

appreciate VERB agradecer
[35]; I appreciate your advice
te agradezco tus consejos, I'd

appreciate it if you could tidy up
afterwards te agradecería que
luego recogieses

apprentice NOUN aprendiz MASC,
aprendiza FEM

apprenticeship NOUN aprendizaje
MASC

approach VERB ❶ *(come near
to)* acercarse [31] a; we were
approaching Madrid nos
acercábamos a Madrid ❷ *(tackle)*
abordar [17] *(a problem, task)*

appropriate ADJECTIVE apropiado/
apropiada

approval NOUN aprobación FEM

approve VERB I don't approve of her
friends me no gustan sus amigos,
I don't approve of his methods no
estoy de acuerdo con sus métodos,
does he approve of the idea? ¿le
parece bien la idea?

approximate ADJECTIVE
aproximado/aproximada

approximately ADVERB
aproximadamente;
approximately fifty people
aproximadamente cincuenta
personas

apricot NOUN albaricoque MASC

apricot tree NOUN albaricoquero
MASC

April NOUN abril MASC; in April en abril

April Fool NOUN inocente MASC & FEM
(see the entry for 'April Fool's Day')

April Fool's Day NOUN el día de
los Santos Inocentes *(the rough
equivalent of April Fool's Day, but on
the 28 December)*

apron NOUN delantal MASC

aquarium NOUN acuario MASC

Aquarius NOUN Acuario MASC; **Sharon's Aquarius** Sharon es Acuario

Arab NOUN árabe MASC & FEM

Arab ADJECTIVE árabe; **the Arab countries** los países árabes

arch NOUN arco MASC

archaelogist NOUN arqueólogo MASC, arqueóloga FEM; **she's an archeologist** es arqueóloga

archaeology NOUN arqueología FEM

archbishop NOUN arzobispo MASC

architect NOUN arquitecto MASC, arquitecta FEM; **he's an architect** es arquitecto

architecture NOUN arquitectura FEM

Arctic NOUN the Arctic el Ártico

are VERB ▸ SEE be

area NOUN ❶ (part of a town) barrio MASC; **a nice area** un buen barrio, **a rough area** un barrio peligroso ❷ (region) zona FEM; **in the Leeds area** en la zona de Leeds ❸ (of square, circle) superficie FEM

Argentina NOUN Argentina FEM

Argentinian NOUN argentino MASC, argentina FEM

Argentinian ADJECTIVE argentino/argentina

argue VERB discutir [19]; **there's no point in arguing** no tiene sentido discutir, **to argue about something** discutir sobre algo, **they're arguing about the result** están discutiendo sobre el resultado

argument NOUN discusión FEM; **to have an argument** discutir [19]

Aries NOUN Aries MASC; **Pauline's Aries** Pauline es Aries

arithmetic NOUN aritmética FEM

arm NOUN brazo MASC; **he took my arm** me cogió del brazo, **to fold your arms** cruzar los brazos, **to go arm in arm** ir [8] del brazo, **to break your arm** romperse [40] el brazo

armchair NOUN sillón MASC

armed ADJECTIVE armado/armada

armpit NOUN axila FEM

arms PLURAL NOUN armas FEM PLURAL

army NOUN ejército MASC; **to join the army** alistarse en el ejército

around PREPOSITION, ADVERB ❶ (with time) alrededor de; **we'll be there around ten** estaremos allí alrededor de las diez ❷ (with amounts, age) **we need around six kilos** necesitamos unos seis quilos, **she's around fifteen** tiene unos quince años ❸ (surrounding) alrededor de; **the countryside around Edinburgh** el campo de alrededor de Edinburgo, **we sat around the table** nos sentamos alrededor de la mesa ❹ (near) por aquí; **is there a post office around here?** ¿hay una oficina de correos por aquí?, **is Phil around?** ¿está Phil por aquí? ❺ (wrapped around) alrededor de; **she had a scarf around her neck** tenía una bufanda alrededor del cuello ❻ **around the corner** a la vuelta de la esquina ❼ **to travel around the world** viajar por el mundo

arrange

arrange VERB to arrange to do quedar [17] en hacer, **we've arranged to see a film on Saturday** quedamos en ver una película el domingo

arrangement NOUN ❶ (of things) **disposición** FEM ❷ (agreement) **acuerdo** MASC

arrest NOUN **he's under arrest** está detenido, **you're under arrest** queda detenido

arrest VERB **arrestar** [17]

arrival NOUN **llegada** FEM

arrive VERB **llegar** [17]; **they arrived at three** llegaron a las tres

arrow NOUN **flecha** FEM

art NOUN ❶ **arte** MASC (PLURAL artes) (note that the plural 'artes' is feminine); **modern art** arte moderno, **the arts** las artes ❷ (school subject) **dibujo** MASC; **the art class** la clase de dibujo

artery NOUN **arteria** FEM

art gallery NOUN (public) **museo** (MASC) **de arte**

artichoke NOUN **alcachofa** FEM

article NOUN **artículo** MASC

artificial ADJECTIVE **artificial**

artist NOUN **artista** MASC & FEM; **he's an artist** es artista

artistic ADJECTIVE **artístico/artística**

art school NOUN **escuela** (FEM) **de Bellas Artes**

as CONJUNCTION, ADVERB ❶ **como**; **as you know** como sabes, **as usual** como siempre, **as I told you** como te dije

ask

❷ (because) **como**; **as there were no trains, we took the bus** como no había trenes, cogimos el autobús ❸ **as ... as** tan ... como; **he's as tall as his brother** es tan alto como su hermano, **you must be as tired as I am** debes estar tan cansado como yo, **I did it as quickly as I could** lo hice tan rápido como pude ❹ **as much ... as** tanto/tanta ... como; **you have as much time as I do** tienes tanto tiempo como yo ❺ **as many ... as** tantos/tantas ... como; **we have as many problems as he does** tenemos tantos problemas como él ❻ **as long as** siempre que (followed by the subjunctive); **we'll go tomorrow, as long as it's a nice day** iremos mañana, siempre que haga buen tiempo ❼ **you can stay for as long as you like** puedes quedarte todo el tiempo que quieras ❽ **as soon as possible** lo más pronto posible ❾ **to work as** trabajar [17] de; **he works as a taxi driver in the evenings** trabaja de taxista por las noches

asbestos NOUN **asbestos** MASC

ash NOUN **ceniza** FEM

ashamed ADJECTIVE **to be ashamed** estar [2] avergonzado, **you should be ashamed of yourself!** ¡debería darte vergüenza!

ashtray NOUN **cenicero** MASC

Asia NOUN **Asia** FEM

Asian NOUN **asiático** MASC, **asiática** FEM

Asian ADJECTIVE **asiático/asiátia**

ask VERB ❶ (inquire) **preguntar** [17]; **you can ask at reception** puedes preguntar en recepción, **to ask**

somebody something preguntarle algo a alguien, **I asked him where he lived** le pregunté dónde vivía ❷ *(request)* pedir [57]; **to ask for something** pedir algo, **I asked for three coffees** pedí tres cafés, **to ask somebody to do** pedirle a alguien que haga *(note that 'que' is followed by subjunctive)*, **ask Danny to give you a hand** pídele a Danny que te eche una mano ❸ **to ask somebody a question** hacerle una pregunta a alguien, **I asked you a question!** ¡te he hecho una pregunta! ❹ **invitar** [17]; **they've asked us to a party at their house** nos han invitado a una fiesta en su casa ❺ **Paul's asked Janie out on Friday** Paul invitó a Janie a salir el viernes

asleep *ADJECTIVE* dormido/dormida; **to be asleep** estar [2] dormido, **the baby's asleep** el niño está dormido, **to fall asleep** quedarse [17] dormido

asparagus *NOUN* espárrago *MASC*

aspirin *NOUN* aspirina *FEM*

assignment *NOUN (at school, college)* tarea *FEM*

assist *VERB* ayudar [17]

assistance *NOUN* ayuda *FEM*

assistant *NOUN* ❶ *(at work)* ayudante *MASC & FEM* ❷ **a shop assistant** un dependiente/una dependienta

association *NOUN* asociación *FEM*

assorted *ADJECTIVE* variado/variada

assortment *NOUN* surtido *MASC*

assume *VERB* suponer [11]

assure *VERB* asegurar [17]; **I assure you** te lo aseguro

asterisk *NOUN* asterisco *MASC*

asthma *NOUN* asma *FEM*; **she has asthma** tiene asma

astonishing *ADJECTIVE* asombroso/asombrosa; **her knowledge is astonishing** sus conocimientos son asombrosos

astrologer *NOUN* astrólogo *MASC*, astróloga *FEM*

astrology *NOUN* astrología *FEM*

astronaut *NOUN* astronauta *MASC & FEM*

astronomer *NOUN* astrónomo *MASC*, astrónoma *FEM*

astronomy *NOUN* astronomía *FEM*

at *PREPOSITION* ❶ *(in a place)* en; **at home** en casa, **at school** en el colegio, **at my office** en mi oficina, **I'll be at work** estaré en el trabajo ❷ *(talking about the time)* a; **at eight o'clock** a las ocho ❸ **at night** por la noche, **I'll be there at the weekend** estaré allí el fin de semana ❹ **at Emma's house** en casa de Emma, **she's at her brother's this evening** esta noche está en casa de su hermano, **at the hairdresser's** en la peluquería ❺ **at last** por fin, **he's found a job at last** por fin ha encontrado un trabajo ❻ *(in email addresses)* arroba *FEM*; **john.smith@easycom.com** john-punto-smith-arroba-easycom-punto-com

athlete *NOUN* atleta *MASC & FEM*

athletic *ADJECTIVE* atlético/atlética

athletics NOUN atletismo MASC

Atlantic NOUN the Atlantic el Atlántico

atlas NOUN atlas MASC

atmosphere NOUN atmósfera FEM

atom NOUN átomo MASC

atomic ADJECTIVE atómico/atómica

attach VERB ❶ (fasten) sujetar [17] ❷ (tie) atar [17] ❸ (glue) pegar [28]

attached ADJECTIVE to be attached to (be fond of) tenerle cariño a

attachment NOUN ❶ (to letter) documento (MASC) adjunto ❷ (in e-mail) archivo (MASC) adjunto

attack NOUN ataque MASC

attack VERB atacar [31]

attacker NOUN agresor MASC, agresora FEM

attempt NOUN intento MASC; at the first attempt al primer intento

attempt VERB to attempt to do intentar [17] hacer

attend VERB asistir [19] a; to attend a class asistir a clase

attention NOUN atención FEM; to pay attention to prestar atención a, I wasn't paying atttention no estaba prestando atención

attic NOUN desván MASC

attitude NOUN actitud FEM

attract VERB atraer [42]

attraction NOUN atracción FEM

attractive ADJECTIVE atractivo/atractiva

aubergine NOUN berenjena FEM

auction NOUN subasta FEM

audience NOUN público MASC

August NOUN agosto MASC

aunt, **auntie** NOUN tía FEM

au pair NOUN au pair MASC & FEM; I'm looking for a job as an au pair estoy buscando un trabajo de au pair

Australia NOUN Australia FEM

Australian NOUN australiano MASC, australiana FEM

Australian ADJECTIVE australiano/australiana

Austria NOUN Austria FEM

Austrian NOUN austriaco MASC, austriaca FEM

Austrian ADJECTIVE austriaco/austriaca

author NOUN autor MASC, autora FEM

autobiography NOUN autobiografía FEM

autograph NOUN autógrafo MASC

automatic ADJECTIVE automático/automática

automatically ADVERB automáticamente

autumn NOUN otoño MASC

availability NOUN disponibilidad FEM

available ADJECTIVE disponible

avalanche NOUN avalancha FEM

avenue NOUN avenida FEM

average NOUN ❶ media FEM; **above average** por encima de la media ❷ **on average** como promedio

average ADJECTIVE medio/media; **of average height** de estatura media

avocado NOUN aguacate MASC

avoid VERB evitar [17]; **she avoided me** me evitó, **to avoid doing** evitar hacer, **I avoid speaking to him** evito hablar con él

awake ADJECTIVE **to be awake** estar [2] despierto/despierta, **is Lola awake?** ¿está despierta Lola?

award NOUN premio MASC; **to win an award** ganar [17] un premio

aware ADJECTIVE **to be aware of a problem** ser [1] consciente de un problema, **to become aware of something** darse [4] cuenta de algo, **as far as I'm aware** que yo sepa, **to be aware of a noise** oír [56] un ruido

away ADVERB ❶ **to be away** estar [2] fuera, **I'll be away next week** estaré fuera la próxima semana ❷ **to go away** irse [8], **Laura's gone away for a week** Laura se ha ido por una semana, **go away!** ¡vete! ❸ **to run away** escaparse [17], **the thieves ran away** los ladrones se escaparon ❹ **the school is two kilometres away** el colegio está a dos kilómetros, **how far away is it?** ¿a qué distancia está?, **not far away** no muy lejos, **a long way away** muy lejos ❺ **to put something away** guardar [17] algo, **I'll just put my books away** voy a guardar mis libros ❻ **to give something away** regalar [17] algo, **she's given away**

all her tapes ha regalado todas sus cintas

away match NOUN partido (MASC) fuera de casa

awful ADJECTIVE ❶ horrible; **the film was awful!** la película era horrible ❷ (ill) **I feel awful** me siento fatal ❸ (guilty) **I feel awful about it** me siento muy culpable ❹ **an awful lot of** un montón de ❺ **how awful!** ¡qué horror!

awkward ADJECTIVE ❶ difícil; **it's an awkward situation** es una situación difícil, **it's a bit awkward** es un poco delicado, **an awkward child** un niño difícil ❷ **an awkward question** una pregunta comprometida

axe NOUN hacha FEM (even though 'hacha' is feminine , it takes 'el' and 'un' in the singular)

Bb

baby NOUN bebé MASC

babysit VERB hacer [7] de canguro

babysitter NOUN canguro MASC & FEM

babysitting NOUN hacer [7] de canguro

bachelor NOUN soltero MASC

back NOUN ❶ (of a person or garment) espalda FEM; **to do something behind somebody's back** hacer [7] algo a espaldas de alguien ❷ (of an animal) lomo MASC ❸ (of a piece of paper or your hand) dorso MASC; **on the back** en el dorso ❹ (of a car, a plane, or a hall) fondo MASC; **we have seats at the back** tenemos asientos al fondo, **the children are at the back of the room** los niños que están al fondo de la habitación ❺ (of a building) parte (FEM) de atrás; **a garden at the back of the house** un jardín en la parte de atrás de la casa ❻ (of a chair or sofa) respaldo MASC ❼ (in football or hockey) defensa MASC & FEM

back ADJECTIVE ❶ trasero/trasera (a wheel or seat); **the back seat of the car** el asiento trasero del coche ❷ **the back garden** el jardín de atrás, **the back gate** la verja de atrás

back ADVERB ❶ **to go back** volver [45], **to go back to school** volver al colegio, **Lisa's gone back to London** Lisa ha vuelto a Londres ❷ **to come back** volver [45], **they've come back from Italy** han vuelto de Italia, **she's back at work** ha vuelto al trabajo, **Sue's not back yet** Sue no ha vuelto aún, **she went by bus and walked back** fue en autobús y volvió andando ❸ **to phone back** volver [45] a llamar, **I'll ring back later** te volveré a llamar más tarde ❹ **to give something back to somebody** devolverle [45] algo a alguien, **I gave him back his cassettes** le devolví sus cintas, **give it back!** ¡devuélvemelo!

back VERB ❶ apoyar [17] (a candidate) ❷ apostar [24] por (a horse)
• **to back up** (on a computer) **to back up a file** hacer [7] una copia de seguridad de un archivo
• **to back somebody up** apoyar [17] a alguien

backache NOUN dolor (MASC) de espalda

backbone NOUN columna (FEM) vertebral

back door NOUN ❶ (of a building) puerta (FEM) de atrás ❷ (of a car) puerta (FEM) trasera

backfire VERB (turn out badly) salir [63] mal

background NOUN ❶ (of a person) origen MASC ❷ (of events or a situation) contexto MASC ❸ (in a picture or view) fondo MASC; **the trees in the background** los árboles del fondo ❹ **background music** música de fondo, **background noise** ruido de fondo

backhand NOUN revés MASC

backing NOUN (moral support) apoyo MASC

backpack NOUN mochila FEM

backpack VERB to go backpacking viajar con mochila

back seat NOUN asiento (MASC) trasero

backside NOUN trasero MASC

backstroke NOUN estilo (MASC) espalda; to swim backstroke nadar a espalda

back to front ADVERB al revés; your jumper's back to front te has puesto el jersey al revés

backup NOUN ❶ (support) apoyo MASC ❷ (in computing) a backup disk un disco de seguridad

backwards ADVERB (to lean or fall) hacia atrás

bacon NOUN bacon MASC; bacon and eggs huevos con bacon

bad ADJECTIVE ❶ (not good) malo/ mala ('malo' becomes 'mal' before a masculine singular noun) a bad moment un mal momento, it's bad for your health es malo para la salud ❷ grave (an accident, a mistake); a bad accident un accidente grave ❸ fuerte (a headache, a cold); a bad cold un resfriado fuerte ❹ (rotten) podrido/ podrida; a bad apple una manzana podrida, to go bad estropearse [17] ❺ (rude) bad language lenguaje grosero ❻ (naughty) malo/mala; bad dog! ¡(perro) malo! ❼ to be bad at something dárcele [4] algo mal a alguien; I'm bad at physics se me da mal la física ❽ it's not bad no está mal; his new film's not bad su nueva película no está mal
• too bad! (I'm sorry for you) ¡qué rabia!, (I don't care) ¡y a mí qué!

badge NOUN ❶ (pin-on) chapa FEM ❷ a policeman badge una placa de policía

badly ADVERB ❶ mal; he writes badly escribe mal, I slept badly dormí mal, my exam went badly el examen me fue mal ❷ badly hurt gravemente herido ❸ the car was badly damaged el coche quedó muy estropeado

bad-mannered ADJECTIVE maleducado/maleducada

badminton NOUN bádminton MASC; to play badminton jugar al bádminton

bad-tempered ADJECTIVE ❶ (answer, look) malhumorado/ malhumorada ❷ to be bad-tempered (for a while) estar de mal humor, (always) tener mal genio

bag NOUN ❶ (plastic, paper) bolsa FEM ❷ (handbag) bolso MASC

baggage NOUN equipaje MASC

baggage allowance NOUN franquicia (FEM) de equipaje

baggage reclaim NOUN recogida (FEM) de equipaje

bagpipes PLURAL NOUN gaita FEM; to play the bagpipes tocar la gaita

bags PLURAL NOUN maletas FEM PLURAL; to pack your bags hacer las maletas
• to have bags under your eyes tener ojeras

Bahamas PLURAL NOUN the Bahamas las Bahamas, the Bahama Islands las islas Bahamas

Bahamian NOUN bahameño MASC, bahameña FEM

Bahamian ADJECTIVE bahameño/bahameña

bake VERB to bake a cake hacer [7] un pastel, to bake potatoes asar [17] patatas

baked ADJECTIVE ❶ (fruit or vegetables) asado/asada; baked apples manzanas asadas, a baked potato una patata asada ❷ (fish) al horno

baked beans PLURAL NOUN judías (FEM PLURAL) en salsa de tomate

baker NOUN panadero MASC, panadera FEM; to go to the baker's ir a la panadería

bakery NOUN panadería FEM

balance NOUN ❶ equilibrio MASC; to lose your balance perder el equilibrio ❷ (money in your bank account) saldo MASC

balanced ADJECTIVE equilibrado/equilibrada

balcony NOUN balcón MASC

bald ADJECTIVE calvo/calva

Balearic Islands PLURAL NOUN las Islas Baleares

ball NOUN ❶ (for tennis or golf) pelota FEM ❷ (for football or volleyball) balón MASC ❸ (of string or wool) ovillo MASC

ballet NOUN ballet MASC

ballet dancer NOUN bailarín (MASC) de ballet, bailarina (FEM) de ballet

ballet shoe NOUN zapatilla (FEM) de ballet

balloon NOSUN globo MASC

ballot NOUN votación FEM

ballpoint (pen) NOUN boli MASC (informal) bolígrafo MASC

ban NOUN prohibición FEM; to put a ban on smoking prohibir fumar

ban VERB prohibir [58]

banana NOUN plátano MASC; a banana yoghurt un yogur de plátano

band NOUN ❶ (playing music) grupo MASC; a rock band un grupo de rock ❷ a jazz band (big) una orquesta de jazz, (small) un conjunto de jazz ❸ a brass band una banda de música ❹ a rubber band una goma elástica

bandage NOUN venda FEM

bandage VERB vendar [17]

bang NOUN ❶ (noise) estallido MASC ❷ (of a window) golpe MASC ❸ (of a door) portazo MASC

bang VERB ❶ (to hit) golpear [17] (a drum, for example); he banged his fist on the table golpeó la mesa con el puño ❷ (to knock) dar [4] golpes a; to bang on the door dar golpes a la puerta, I banged my head on the door me di un golpe en la cabeza con la puerta, I banged into the table me choqué con la mesa ❸ to bang the door aporrear [17] la puerta

bang EXCLAMATION (like a gun) ¡pum!

bangle NOUN pulsera FEM

banister(s), **bannister(s)** PLURAL NOUN barandilla FEM (SINGULAR)

bank NOUN ❶ (for money) banco MASC; I'm going to the bank voy al banco ❷ (of a river or lake) orilla FEM

bank account NOUN cuenta (FEM) bancaria

bank balance NOUN saldo MASC

bank card NOUN tarjeta (FEM) bancaria

bank holiday NOUN día (MASC) festivo

banking NOUN banca FEM

banknote NOUN billete (MASC) de banco

bank statement NOUN extracto (MASC) de cuenta

baptize VERB bautizar [22]

bar NOUN ❶ (selling drinks) bar MASC; Janet works in a bar Janet trabaja en un bar ❷ (the counter in a bar) barra FEM; on the bar en la barra ❸ a bar of chocolate una tableta de chocolate ❹ a bar of soap una pastilla de jabón ❺ (made of wood or metal) barra FEM; a metal bar una barra de metal ❻ (in music) compás MASC

bar VERB (to block physically) bloquear [17]; to bar someone's way bloquear el paso a alguien

Barbadian NOUN barbadense MASC & FEM

Barbadian ADJECTIVE barbadense

barbecue NOUN barbacoa FEM; there's a barbecue tonight hay una barbacoa esta noche

barbecue VERB to barbecue a chicken asar [17] un pollo a la parrilla, barbecued chicken pollo a la parrilla

barbed wire NOUN alambre (MASC) de púas

bare ADJECTIVE desnudo/desnuda

barefoot ADJECTIVE descalzo/descalza; to be barefoot estar descalzo/descalza

bargain NOUN (a good buy) ganga FEM; I got a bargain conseguí una ganga, it's a bargain! ¡es una ganga!

barge NOUN barcaza FEM

bark NOUN ❶ (of a tree) corteza FEM ❷ (of a dog) ladrido MASC

bark VERB ladrar [17]

barley NOUN cebada FEM

barmaid NOUN camarera FEM

barman NOUN camarero MASC

barn NOUN granero MASC

barometer NOUN barómetro MASC

barrel NOUN tonel MASC

barrier NOUN barrera FEM

base NOUN base FEM

baseball NOUN baloncesto MASC

based ADJECTIVE ❶ to be based on estar basado en, the film is based on a true story la película está basada en una historia real ❷ to be based in (a company) tener su base en, (a person) vivir en, he's based in Bristol vive en Bristol

basement NOUN sótano MASC; in the basement en el sótano

bash NOUN ❶ golpe MASC; it's got a bash on the bumper tiene un golpe en el guardabarros ❷ I'll have a bash voy a probar

bash VERB I bashed my head me di un golpe en la cabeza

a
b
c
d
e
f
g
h
i
j
k
l
m
n
o
p
q
r
s
t
u
v
w
x
y
z

basic *back* **be**

basic ADJECTIVE ❶ básico/básica; **basic knowledge** conocimientos básicos ❷ **the basic facts** los hechos fundamentales ❸ **basic salary** sueldo base ❹ (not luxurious) sencillo/sencilla; **the flat's a bit basic** el piso es bastante sencillo

basically ADVERB ❶ fundamentalmente; **it's basically all right** fundamentalmente está bien ❷ **basically, I don't really want to go** en pocas palabras, no quiero ir

basics NOUN rudimentos MASC PLURAL

basin NOUN (washbasin) lavabo MASC

basis NOUN ❶ base FEM; **on the basis of** en base a ❷ **on a regular basis** regularmente

basket NOUN ❶ cesta FEM; **a shopping basket** una cesta de la compra, **a linen basket** una cesta de ropa sucia ❷ **a waste-paper basket** una papelera

basketball NOUN baloncesto MASC; **to play basketball** jugar al baloncesto

Basque NOUN ❶ (the language) euskera MASC, vasco MASC ❷ (person) vasco MASC, vasca FEM

Basque ADJECTIVE vasco/vasca; **the Basque Country** el País vasco, Euskadi MASC

bass NOUN ❶ bajo MASC; **to play bass** tocar el bajo ❷ **a double bass** un contrabajo

bass drum NOUN bombo MASC

bass guitar NOUN bajo MASC

bassoon NOUN fagot MASC; **to play the bassoon** tocar el fagot

bat NOUN ❶ (for cricket or baseball) bate MASC ❷ (for table tennis) paleta FEM ❸ (animal) murciélago MASC

batch NOUN lote MASC; **a batch of letters** un lote de cartas

bath NOUN ❶ baño MASC; **I was in the bath** estaba en el baño ❷ (bathtub) bañera FEM; **the bath's pink** la bañera es rosa ❸ **to have a bath** bañarse [17]

bathe VERB ❶ lavar [17] (a wound) ❷ (go swimming) bañarse [17]

bathroom NOUN cuarto (MASC) de baño

bath towel NOUN toalla (FEM) de baño

batter NOUN ❶ (for frying) rebozado MASC; **fish in batter** pescado rebozado ❷ (for pancakes) masa FEM

battery NOUN ❶ (for a torch or radio, for example) pila FEM ❷ (for a car) batería FEM

battle NOUN batalla FEM

bay NOUN ❶ (on coast) bahía FEM; **the Bay of Biscay** el Golfo de Vizcaya ❷ (for bus) dársena FEM

B.C. ABBREVIATION a.de C. (short for antes de Cristo)

be VERB ❶ (referring to permanent characteristics) ser [1]; **it's beautiful** es precioso, **she's very tall** es muy alta, **honey is sweet** la miel es dulce ❷ (referring to changeable emotions and situations) estar [2]; **she's angry** está enfadada, **I'm tired** estoy cansada, **the soup is cold** la sopa está fría, **this cake is too sweet** este pastel está demasiado dulce ❸ (in a place) estar [2]; **Melanie is in the**

kitchen Melanie está en la cocina, **¿where's the butter?** ¿dónde está la mantequilla?, **when we were in France** cuando estábamos en Francia **❹ there is** hay, **there are** hay, **there's more here** aquí hay más, **there are two children outside** hay dos niños fuera, **is there any problem?** ¿hay algún problema? **❺** *(with jobs and professions)* **ser** [1] *(note that 'a' is not translated)*; **she's a teacher** es profesora, **he's a taxi driver** es taxista **❻** *(marital status)* **estar** [2], **es** [1]; **she's married** está casada, **he's single** está/es soltero **❼** *(in clock times)* **ser** [1]; **it's one o'clock** es la una en punto, **it's half past five** son las cinco y media **❽** *(for days of the week and dates)* **ser** [1]; **what day is it today?** ¿qué día es hoy?, **it's Tuesday today** hoy es martes, **it's the twentieth of May** es veinte de mayo **❾** *(talking about age)* **tener** [9]; **to be fifteen** tener quince años, **how old are you?** ¿cuántos años tienes?, **Samuel's two** Samuel tiene dos años **❿** *(feeling cold, hot, hungry)* **tener** [9]; **I'm hot** tengo calor, **I'm cold** tengo frío, **I'm hungry** tengo hambre **⓫** *(talking about weather)* **it's cold today** hoy hace frío, **it's a nice day** hace buen día **⓬** *(to a country or town)* **estar** [2]; **I've never been to Paris** nunca he estado en París, **have you been to Spain before?** ¿has estado en España antes? **⓭ to be loved** ser [1] amado *(but note that often the passive is translated by the third person plural)*, **he has been killed** lo han matado *(literally: they have killed him)*

beach NOUN **playa** FEM; **on the beach** en la playa

bead NOUN **cuenta** FEM

beak NOUN **pico** MASC

beam NOUN **❶** *(of light)* **rayo** FEM **❷** *(for a roof)* **viga** FEM

bean NOUN **alubia** FEM, **judía** FEM; **baked beans** alubias en salsa de tomate, **green beans** judías verdes

bear NOUN **oso** MASC

bear VERB **❶ soportar** [17]; **I can't bear him** no puedo soportarlo, **I can't bear the idea** no puedo soportar la idea **❷ to bear something in mind** tener [9] algo en cuenta, **I'll bear it in mind** lo tendré en cuenta

beard NOUN **barba** FEM

bearded ADJECTIVE **barbudo/barbuda**

bearings PLURAL NOUN **to get your bearings** orientarse [17]

beast NOUN **❶** *(animal)* **bestia** FEM **❷ you beast!** ¡bruto!

beat NOUN **ritmo** MASC

beat VERB **❶** *(defeat)* **ganarle a** [17]; **we beat them!** ¡les hemos ganado!, **he beat me at chess** me ganó al ajedrez **❷** *(hit repeatedly)* **golpear** [17] **❸ batir** [19]; **to beat the eggs** batir los huevos **❹ you can't beat a good meal** no hay nada mejor que una buena comida
• **to beat somebody up** darle [4] una paliza a alguien *(informal)*

beautician NOUN **esteticista** MASC & FEM

beautiful ADJECTIVE **precioso/preciosa**; **a beautiful day** un día precioso, **how beautiful!** ¡qué precioso!

beautifully ADVERB
maravillosamente

beauty NOUN belleza FEM

beauty spot NOUN (for tourists)
lugar (MASC) pintoresco

because CONJUNCTION ❶ porque;
because it's you porque eres tú,
because it's cold porque hace frío
❷ because of a causa de, because of
the accident a causa del accidente

become VERB ❶ hacerse [7]; I want
to become a lawyer quiero
hacerme abogado, she became
famous se hizo famosa, we became
friends nos hicimos amigos
❷ ('become' with an adjective is
sometimes translated by a reflexive
verb in Spanish) to become bored
aburrirse [19], to become tired
cansarse [17]

bed NOUN ❶ cama FEM; a double bed
una cama de matrimonio, in bed en
la cama, to go to bed ir a la cama
❷ (flower bed) macizo MASC

bedclothes PLURAL NOUN ropa (FEM)
de cama (singular)

bedding NOUN ropa (FEM) de cama

bedroom NOUN habitación FEM; my
bedroom window la ventana de mi
habitación

bedside table NOUN mesilla (FEM)
de noche

bedsit, bedsitter NOUN habitación
(FEM) amueblada de aquiler

bedspread NOUN colcha FEM

bedtime NOUN it's bedtime es hora
de acostarse

bee NOUN abeja FEM

beech NOUN haya FEM

beef NOUN carne (FEM) de vaca;
a roast of beef un rosbif

beefburger NOUN hamburguesa FEM

beer NOUN cerveza FEM; two beers
please dos cervezas, por favor,
a beer can una lata de cerveza

beetle NOUN escarabajo MASC

beetroot NOUN remolacha FEM

before PREPOSITION, ADVERB ❶ antes
de; before Monday antes del lunes
❷ before somebody antes que
alguien, he left before me se fue
antes que yo ❸ the day before el
día anterior, the day before the
wedding el día anterior a la boda,
the day before yesterday anteayer,
the week before la semana anterior
❹ (already) ya; I've seen him before
somewhere ya le he visto en algún
sitio, I had seen the film before
ya había visto la película, she'd
never tried before nunca lo había
intentado antes

before CONJUNCTION ❶ antes de;
before doing antes de hacer, I
closed the windows before leaving
cerré las ventanas antes de salir,
phone before you leave llámame
antes de salir ❷ antes de que
(followed by the subjunctive); phone
me before they leave llámame
antes de que salgan, oh, before I
forget ... ah, antes de que se me
olvide ...

beforehand ADVERB antes; phone
beforehand llama antes

beg VERB ❶ (ask for money) mendigar [28] ❷ (ask) suplicarle a [31]; she begged me not to leave me suplicó que no me marchase, I beg your pardon perdone

begin VERB ❶ empezar [25]; the meeting begins at ten la reunión empieza a las diez, the words beginning with P las palabras que empiezan con P ❷ to begin to do empezar a hacer, I'm beginning to understand empiezo a comprender

beginner NOUN principiante MASC & FEM

beginning NOUN ❶ principio MASC; at the beginning al principio, at the beginning of the holidays al principio de las vacaciones ❷ (with 'day', 'week', 'month', 'year') at the beginning of a principios de, at the beginning of the month a principios de mes

behalf NOUN on behalf of en nombre de

behave VERB ❶ portarse [17]; he behaved badly se portó mal ❷ to behave yourself portarse bien, behave yourselves! ¡portaos bien!

behaviour NOUN comportamiento MASC

behind NOUN trasero MASC

behind PREPOSITION detrás de; behind the sofa detrás del sofá, behind them detrás de ellos

behind ADVERB ❶ detrás; you go behind tú vas detrás, the car behind el coche de detrás ❷ to leave something behind olvidarse algo, I've left my keys behind me he olvidado las llaves, to stay behind quedarse ❸ (not making progress)

he's behind in class va retrasado en clase

beige ADJECTIVE beige (does not change); beige socks calcetines beige

Belgian NOUN, ADJECTIVE belga MASC & FEM

Belgium NOUN FEM, Bélgica

belief NOUN creencia FEM; his political beliefs sus creencias políticas

believe VERB ❶ creer [37]; I believe you te creo, they believed what I said se creyeron lo que dije, I don't believe you! ¡no te creo! ❷ to believe in creer en, to believe in ghosts creer en fantasmas, to believe in God creer en Dios

bell NOUN ❶ (in a church) campana FEM ❷ (on a door) timbre MASC; ring the bell! ¡toca el timbre! ❸ (for a cat or toy) cascabel MASC
• that name rings a bell ese nombre me suena

belong VERB ❶ to belong to ser [1] de, that belongs to Lucy eso es de Lucy ❷ to belong to a club pertenecer [35] a un club ❸ (go) ir [8]; that chair belongs in the study esa silla va en el estudio, where does this vase belong? ¿adónde va este jarrón?

belongings PLURAL NOUN pertenencias FEM PLURAL; all my belongings are in London todas mis pertenencias están en Londres

below PREPOSITION debajo de; below the window debajo de la ventana, the flat below yours el piso de debajo del tuyo

below ADVERB **abajo**; **shouts came from below** se oyeron gritos abajo, **the flat below** el piso de abajo

belt NOUN **cinturón** MASC

bench NOUN **banco** MASC

bend NOUN (in a road, river) **curva** FEM

bend VERB ❶ (to make a bend in) **doblar** [17] (your arm or leg, or a wire) ❷ (to curve) (a road or path) **torcer** [41]; **the road bends to the right** la carretera tuerce a la derecha ❸ **to bend down** agacharse [17], **she bent down to look** se agachó para mirar

beneath PREPOSITION **bajo**

benefit NOUN ❶ **beneficio** MASC ❷ **unemployment benefit** subsidio (MASC) de desempleo

bent ADJECTIVE **doblado/doblada**

beret NOUN **boina** FEM

berry NOUN **baya** FEM

berth NOUN **litera** FEM

beside PREPOSITION (next to) **al lado de**; **it's beside the table** está al lado de la mesa, **she was sitting beside me** estaba sentada a mi lado
• **that's beside the point** eso no viene al caso

besides ADVERB **además**; **besides, it's too late** además, es demasiado tarde, **four dogs, and six cats besides** cuatro perros y además seis gatos

best ADJECTIVE ❶ **mejor**; **it's the best** es el mejor, **that's the best car** ese coche es el mejor, **the best song of the album** la mejor canción del álbum, **she's my best friend** es mi

mejor amiga ❷ **she's the best at tennis** es la mejor jugando al tenis, **he's the best at English** es el mejor en inglés, **the best thing to do is to phone them** lo mejor es llamarlos por teléfono, **its the best I can do** es lo más que puedo hacer, **I did my best to help her** hice todo lo posible para ayudarla

best ADVERB ❶ **mejor**; **he plays best** es el que mejor juega, **best of all** lo mejor de todo ❷ **I like Barcelona best** Barcelona es la ciudad que más me gusta

best man NOUN **padrino** (MASC) **de boda**

bet NOUN **apuesta** FEM

bet VERB **apostar** [24]; **to bet on a horse** apostar por un caballo, **I bet you he'll forget!** ¡te apuesto algo a que se le olvida!

better ADJECTIVE ❶ **mejor**; **she's found a better flat** ha encontrado un piso mejor, **this road's better than the other one** esta calle es mejor que la otra, **this pen writes better** esta pluma escribe mejor ❷ **even better** todavía mejor, **it's even better than before** es todavía mejor que antes ❸ (less ill) **to be better** estar [2] mejor, **to feel better** sentirse [14] mejor, **I feel better** hoy me siento mejor ❹ **to get better** mejorar [17], **my Spanish is getting better** mi español está mejorando, **I hope you get better soon** espero que te mejores pronto ❺ **so much the better** mucho mejor, **the sooner the better** cuanto antes mejor

better ADVERB **you/she/etc had better** más vale que (followed by the subjunctive), **you'd better phone at once** más vale que llames ahora mismo, **he'd better not go** más vale que no vaya, **I'd better go now** más vale que me vaya ahora

better off ADJECTIVE ❶ (richer) **they're better off than us** tienen más dinero que nosotros ❷ (more comfortable) mejor; **you'd be better off in bed** estarás mejor en la cama

between PREPOSITION ❶ entre; **between London and Dover** entre Londres y Dover, **I'll go sometime between Monday and Friday** iré entre el lunes y el viernes, **between you and me** entre tú y yo ❷ **it's closed between 2 and 5** está cerrado de dos a cinco

beware VERB beware of the dog! ¡cuidado con el perro!

beyond PREPOSITION ❶ (in space and time) **beyond the border** más allá de la frontera ❷ **it's beyond me!** ¡no lo entiendo!

Bible NOUN the Bible la Biblia

bicycle NOUN bicicleta FEM; **by bicycle** en bicicleta

bicycle lane NOUN carril (MASC) de bicicletas

big ADJECTIVE ❶ grande; **a big house** una casa grande, **big cities** ciudades grandes, **it's too big for me** es demasiado grande para mí, ('grande' becomes 'gran' when it comes before a singular noun) **a big disappointment** una gran desilusión ❷ (older) mayor; **my big sister** mi hermana mayor

bigheaded ADJECTIVE creído/creída; **to be bigheaded** ser un creído/una creída

big screen NOUN pantalla (FEM) grande

big toe NOUN dedo (MASC) gordo del pie

bike

❶ (with pedals) bici FEM; **by bike** en bici ❷ (with motor) moto FEM; **by bike** en moto

bikini NOUN bikini MASC

bilingual ADJECTIVE bilingüe

bill NOUN ❶ (in a restaurant) cuenta FEM; **can I have the bill, please?** ¿me trae la cuenta por favor? ❷ (for gas, electricity, or in a hotel) factura FEM

billiards NOUN billar MASC; **to play billiards** jugar al billar

billion NOUN mil millones MASC PLURAL

bin NOUN ❶ (dustbin) cubo (MASC) de la basura ❷ (wastepaper bin) papelera FEM

binoculars PLURAL NOUN prismáticos MASC PLURAL

biochemistry NOUN bioquímica FEM

biography NOUN biografía FEM

biologist NOUN biólogo MASC, biólogo FEM

biology NOUN biología FEM

bird NOUN ❶ (small) pájaro MASC ❷ (large) ave FEM (even though 'ave' is feminine, it takes 'el' and 'un' in the singular)

birdwatching NOUN to go birdwatching ir [8] a observar pájaros

Biro NOUN boli MASC (informal)

a
b
c
d
e
f
g
h
i
j
k
l
m
n
o
p
q
r
s
t
u
v
w
x
y
z

birth   **blank**

birth NOUN **nacimiento** MASC

birth certificate NOUN **certificado** (MASC) **de nacimiento**

birth control NOUN **control** (FEM) **de la natalidad**

birthday NOUN **cumpleaños** MASC (does not change in the plural); **a birthday present** un regalo de cumpleaños, **happy birthday!** ¡feliz cumpleaños!

birthday party NOUN **fiesta** (FEM) **de cumpleaños**

biscuit NOUN **galleta** FEM

bishop NOUN **obispo** MASC

bit NOUN ❶ (small piece) **trozo** MASC; **a bit of string** un trozo de cordón, **a bit of chocolate** un trozo de chocolate ❷ (small quantity) **a bit of** un poco de, **a bit of sugar** un poco de azúcar, **with a bit of luck** con un poco de suerte, **to have a bit of trouble with something** tener un pequeño problema con algo ❸ (in a book or film, for example) **trozo** MASC; **this bit's brilliant!** ¡este trozo es genial! ❹ **to fall to bits** hacerse pedazos ❺ **a bit of news** una noticia, **a bit of advice** un consejo ❻ **a bit** un poco, **wait a bit!** ¡espera un poco!, **a bit hot** un poco caliente, **a bit early** un poco pronto ❼ (for a horse) **bocado** MASC
• **bit by bit** poco a poco

bite NOUN ❶ (snack) **bocado** MASC; **I'll just have a bite before I go** voy a tomar un bocado antes de irme ❷ (from an insect) **picadura** FEM; **a mosquito bite** una picadura de mosquito ❸ (from a dog) **mordisco** MASC; **it gave me a bite** me dio un mordisco

bite VERB ❶ (a person or a dog) **morder** [38]; **to bite your nails** morderse las uñas ❷ (an insect) **picar** [31]

bitter ADJECTIVE (taste) **amargo/ amarga**

black ADJECTIVE ❶ **negro/negra**; **my black jacket** mi chaqueta negra, **to turn black** volerse negro/negra ❷ **a Black man** un negro, **a Black woman** una negra ❸ **a black coffee** un café solo

blackberry NOUN **mora** FEM

blackbird NOUN **mirlo** MASC

blackboard NOUN **pizarra** FEM

blackcurrant NOUN **grosella** (FEM) **negra**

black eye NOUN **ojo** (MASC) **morado**

black pudding NOUN **morcilla** FEM

blade NOUN **hoja** FEM

blame NOUN ❶ **culpa** FEM; **to put the blame on somebody** echarle la culpa a alguien ❷ **to take the blame for something** asumir la responsabilidad de algo

blame VERB **culpar** [17]; **to blame somebody for something** culpar a alguien de algo, **they blamed him for the accident** lo culparon por el accidente, **she is to blame for it** ella tiene la culpa, **I blame the parents!** ¡yo culpo a los padres!, **I don't blame you!** ¡no me extraña!

blank NOUN (empty space) **espacio** (MASC) **en blanco** (on a form, for instance)

blank ADJECTIVE ❶ (a page or piece of paper, or a cheque, or a screen)

en blanco *(a tape or disk)*, **virgen**
❷ **my mind went blank** me quedé
en blanco

blanket NOUN **manta** FEM

blast NOUN ❶ *(an explosion)*
explosión FEM ❷ *(of air)* **ráfaga** FEM
❸ **to play music at full blast** poner
la música a todo volumen

blaze NOUN **incendio** MASC

blaze VERB **arder** [18]

blazer NOUN **blázer** MASC

bleach NOUN **lejía** FEM

bleed VERB **sangrar** [17]; **my nose is
bleeding** me está sangrando la nariz

blend NOUN **mezcla** FEM

blend VERB **mezclar** [17]

blender NOUN **batidora** FEM

bless VERB **bendecir** [5]; **bless you!**
(after a sneeze) ¡Jesús!

blind NOUN *(in a window)* **persiana**
FEM

blind ADJECTIVE **ciego/ciega**; **to go
blind** quedarse ciego/ciega

blindness NOUN **ceguera** FEM

blink VERB *(a person)* **pestañear** [17]

blister NOUN **ampolla** FEM

blizzard NOUN **tormenta** *(FEM)* **de
nieve**

block NOUN ❶ **bloque** MASC; **a block
of flats** un bloque de pisos, **an office
block** un bloque de oficinas ❷ *(a
group of buildings)* **manzana** FEM; **to
run (or drive) round the block** dar la
vuelta a la manzana

block VERB ❶ **bloquear** [17] *(an exit
or a road)* ❷ **atascar** [31] *(a drain
or a hole)*; **the sink's blocked** el
fregadero está atascado

blog NOUN **el blog** MASC

blond ADJECTIVE **rubio/rubia**

blood NOUN **sangre** FEM

blood test NOUN **análisis** *(MASC)* **de
sangre**

blossom NOUN **flor** FEM; **to be in
blossom** estar [2] en flor

blot NOUN **borrón** MASC

blouse NOUN **blusa** FEM

blow NOUN **golpe** MASC

blow VERB ❶ *(the wind or a person)*
soplar [17] ❷ **to blow off/away**
salir [63] volando, **my hat blew off**
mi sombrero salió volando ❸ *(in an
explosion)* **the bomb blew a hole in
the wall** la bomba hizo un agujero
en la pared ❹ **to blow your nose**
sonarse [24] la nariz
• **to blow something out** *(a candle or
flames)* **apagar** [28] algo
• **to blow up** *(explode)* **explotar** [17]
• **to blow something up** **inflar** [17]
algo *(a balloon or tyre)*, **hacer** [7]
volar algo *(a building or car)*; **they
blew up the president's residence**
hicieron volar la residencia del
presidente

blow-dry NOUN **brushing** MASC;
to have a blow-dry hacerse [7] el
brushing

blue ADJECTIVE **azul**; **blue eyes** ojos
azules

bluebell NOUN **jacinto** *(MASC)*
silvestre

a
b
c
d
e
f
g
h
i
j
k
l
m
n
o
p
q
r
s
t
u
v
w
x
y
z

blues | **bombing**

blues PLURAL NOUN (jazz) blues MASC (SINGULAR)

blunder NOUN metedura (FEM) de pata

blunt ADJECTIVE ❶ (a knife or scissors) desafilado/desafilada ❷ (a pencil) sin punta ❸ (a person) directo/directa

blurred ADJECTIVE ❶ (vision or image) borroso/borrosa ❷ (photo) movido/movida

blush VERB ponerse [11] colorado

board NOUN ❶ (plank) tabla FEM ❷ (blackboard) pizarra FEM ❸ (notice board) tablón (MASC) de anuncios ❹ (for a board game) tablero MASC; a chess board un tablero de ajedrez ❺ (accommodation) full board pensión completa, half board media pensión, board and lodging comida y alojamiento ❻ on board a bordo, on board the ferry a bordo del ferry

board VERB embarcarse [31]

boarder NOUN (in a school) interno MASC, interna FEM

board game NOUN juego (MASC) de mesa

boarding NOUN embarque MASC

boarding card NOUN tarjeta (FEM) de embarque

boarding school NOUN internado MASC

boast VERB presumir [19]; he was boasting about his new bike estaba presumiendo de su nueva bici

boat NOUN ❶ (in general) barco MASC ❷ (rowing boat) barca FEM

body NOUN ❶ cuerpo MASC ❷ (corpse) cadáver MASC

bodybuilding NOUN culturismo MASC

bodyguard NOUN guardaespaldas MASC & FEM

boil NOUN (swelling) furúnculo MASC

boil VERB ❶ hervir [14]; the water's boiling el agua está hirviendo, I'm going to boil some water voy a hervir un poco de agua ❷ to boil vegetables cocer [41] verduras, to boil an egg cocer un huevo
• to boil over salirse [63]

boiled egg NOUN huevo (MASC) pasado por agua

boiler NOUN ❶ (for central heating) caldera FEM ❷ (for central heating) calentador MASC

boiling ADJECTIVE ❶ (water) hirviendo ❷ it's boiling hot today! ¡hoy hace un calor espantoso!

Bolivia NOUN Bolivia FEM

Bolivian NOUN boliviano MASC, boliviana FEM

Bolivian ADJECTIVE boliviano/boliviana

bolt NOUN ❶ (large) cerrojo MASC ❷ (small) pestillo MASC

bolt VERB (a door) cerrar [29] con cerrojo

bomb NOUN bomba FEM

bomb VERB bombardear [17]

bombing NOUN ❶ (in a war) bombardeo MASC ❷ (a terrorist attack) atentado (MASC) terrorista

bone NOUN ❶ hueso MASC ❷ (of a fish) espina FEM

bonfire NOUN hoguera FEM

bonnet NOUN (of a car) capó MASC

bony ADJECTIVE ❶ (fish) lleno/llena de espinas ❷ (body) huesudo/huesuda

boo VERB abuchear [17]; the crowd booed the referee el público abucheó al árbitro

book NOUN ❶ (that you read) libro MASC; a book about dinosaurs un libro sobre los dinosaurios, a biology book un libro de biología ❷ an exercise book un cuaderno ❸ a book of tickets un taco de billetes, a book of stamps un librito de sellos

book VERB reservar [17]; I booked a table for 8 o'clock reservé una mesa para las ocho

bookcase NOUN estantería FEM

booking NOUN reserva FEM

booking office NOUN taquilla FEM

booklet NOUN folleto MASC

bookshelf NOUN estante MASC

bookshop NOUN librería FEM

boot NOUN ❶ (item of clothing) bota FEM; walking boots botas de montaña, wellington boots botas de agua ❷ (short fashion boot) botín MASC ❸ (of a car) maletero MASC

border NOUN (between countries) frontera FEM; we crossed the border at Irún cruzamos la frontera en Irún

bore NOUN ❶ (a boring person) pesado MASC, pesada FEM (informal) ❷ (a nuisance) what a bore! ¡qué rollo! (informal)

bored ADJECTIVE aburrido/aburrida; to be bored estar aburrido, I'm bored estoy aburrido, to get bored aburrirse [19]

boring ADJECTIVE aburrido/aburrida

born VERB to be born nacer [35], she was born in June nació en junio

borrow VERB can I borrow your bike? ¿me prestas tu bici?, to borrow something from someone pedirle algo prestado a alguien (literally, to ask somebody for something on loan), I'll borrow some money from Dad le pediré dinero prestado a papá

boss NOUN jefe MASC, jefa FEM

bossy ADJECTIVE mandón/mandona (informal)

both PRONOUN, ADJECTIVE los/las, dos; they both came vinieron los dos, they're both sold los dos están vendidos, both sisters were there las dos hermanas estaban allí, both my feet mis dos pies

both CONJUNCTION both ... and tanto ... como, both at home and at school tanto en casa como en colegio, both in summer and in winter tanto en verano como en el invierno

bother NOUN problemas FEM PLURAL; I've had a lot of bother with the car he tenido muchos problemas con el coche, it's no bother no es ningún problema, without any bother sin ningún problema, it's too much bother no merece la pena molestarse

a
b
c
d
e
f
g
h
i
j
k
l
m
n
o
p
q
r
s
t
u
v
w
x
y
z

A
B
C
D
E
F
G
H
I
J
K
L
M
N
O
P
Q
R
S
T
U
V
W
X
Y
Z

bother VERB ❶ (disturb) **molestar** [17]; **I'm sorry to bother you** siento molestarte ❷ (worry) **preocuparse** [17]; **that doesn't bother me at all** no me preocupa en absoluto. **don't bother about dinner** no te preocupes de la cena ❸ (take the trouble) **molestarse** [17]; **she didn't even bother to come** ni siquiera se molestó en venir. **don't bother!** ¡no te molestes!

bottle NOUN **botella** FEM

bottle bank NOUN **contenedor** (MASC) **de botellas**

bottle opener NOUN **abrebotellas** MASC (does not change in the plural)

bottom NOUN ❶ (of a page, a hill, a wall, or steps) **pie** MASC; **at the bottom of the ladder** al pie de la escalera. **at the bottom of the page** al pie de la página ❷ (of a bag, a hole, a stretch of water, a street, or a garden) **fondo** MASC; **at the bottom of the lake** en el fondo del lago ❸ (of a list) **final** MASC ❹ (of a bottle) **culo** MASC ❺ (buttocks) **trasero** MASC

bottom ADJECTIVE ❶ (lowest) **de abajo**; **the bottom shelf** el estante de abajo ❷ (a team, or place) **último/última** ❸ **the bottom sheet** la sábana bajera. **the bottom flat** el piso bajo

bounce VERB **rebotar** [17]

bouncer NOUN **gorila** MASC (informal)

bound ADJECTIVE **he's bound to be late** seguro que llega tarde. **that was bound to happen** eso tenía que pasar

boundary NOUN **línea** (FEM) **divisoria**

bow NOUN ❶ (in a shoelace or ribbon) **lazo** MASC ❷ (for playing the violin or shooting arrows) **arco** MASC

bowl NOUN ❶ (for cereal) **bol** MASC ❷ (larger, for mixing) **cuenco** MASC ❸ (for washing up) **barreño** MASC ❹ **a salad bowl** una ensaladera. **a fruit bowl** un frutero

bowl VERB **lanzar** [22] (a ball)

bowling NOUN (tenpin) **bolos** MASC PLURAL; **to go bowling** ir a jugar a los bolos

bow tie NOUN **pajarita** FEM

box NOUN ❶ **caja** FEM; **a box of chocolates** una caja de bombones. **a cardboard box** una caja de cartón ❷ (of matches) **cajetilla** FEM ❸ (on a form) **recuadro** MASC

boxer NOUN ❶ (fighter) **boxeador** MASC ❷ (dog) **bóxer** MASC

boxer shorts PLURAL NOUN **calzoncillos** MASC PLURAL

boxing NOUN ❶ **boxeo** MASC ❷ **a boxing match** un combate de boxeo

Boxing Day NOUN **fiesta del 26 de diciembre**

box office NOUN **taquilla** FEM

boy NOUN **niño** MASC; **a little boy** un niño pequeño

boyfriend NOUN **novio** MASC

bra NOUN **sujetador** MASC

brace NOUN (for teeth) **aparato** (MASC) **de los dientes**

bracelet NOUN **pulsera** FEM

braces PLURAL NOUN (for trousers) **tirantes** MASC PLURAL

bracket NOUN **in brackets** entre paréntesis

brain NOUN cerebro MASC

brainwave NOUN idea *(FEM)* genial

brake NOUN freno MASC

brake VERB frenar [17]

bramble NOUN zarzamora FEM

branch NOUN ❶ *(of a tree)* rama FEM ❷ *(of a shop, company or bank)* sucursal FEM; **our Oxford branch** nuestra sucursal de Oxford

brand NOUN marca FEM

brand new ADJECTIVE nuevo/nueva

brandy NOUN coñac MASC

brass NOUN ❶ *(the metal)* latón MASC; **a brass candlestick** un candelabro dorado ❷ *(in an orchestra)* **the brass** los metales

brass ADJECTIVE de latón

brass band NOUN banda *(FEM)* de música

brave ADJECTIVE valiente

Brazil NOUN Brasil MASC

Brazilian NOUN brasileño MASC, brasileña FEM

Brazilian ADJECTIVE brasileño/brasileña

bread NOUN pan MASC; **a slice of bread** una rebanada de pan

break NOUN ❶ *(a short rest)* descanso MASC; **a fifteen-minute break** un descanso de quince minutos, **to take a break** descansar un rato ❷ *(in school)* recreo MASC ❸ **the Christmas break** las vacaciones de Navidad

break VERB ❶ romper [40]; **he broke a glass** rompió un vaso ❷ **to break your leg** romperse una pierna, **I broke my arm** me rompí un brazo ❸ **to break your promise** romper una promesa, **to break the rules** infringir [49] las reglas, **you mustn't break the rules** no debes infringir las reglas ❹ **to break a record** batir [19] un récord ❺ **to break the news** dar [4] la noticia
- **to break down** estropearse [17]; **the car broke down** el coche se estropeó
- **to break in the thief broke in through the window** el ladrón se metió en la casa por la ventana, **the house was broken into** entraron ladrones en la casa
- **to break out** ❶ *(a fire)* declararse [17] ❷ *(a war or a storm)* estallar [17] ❸ *(a prisoner)* escaparse [17]
- **to break up** ❶ *(a family)* separarse [17] ❷ *(a couple)* romper [40] ❸ *(a crowd or clouds)* dispersarse [17] ❹ *(for the holidays)* **we break up on Thursday** empezamos las vacaciones el jueves

breakdown NOUN ❶ *(of a vehicle)* avería FEM; **we had a breakdown on the motorway** tuvimos una avería en la autopista ❷ *(in talks or negotiations)* ruptura FEM ❸ *(a nervous collapse)* crisis *(FEM)* nerviosa; **to have a (nervous) breakdown** sufrir una crisis nerviosa

breakdown truck NOUN grúa *(FEM)* de recogiola en carretera

breakfast NOUN desayuno MASC; **to have breakfast** desayunar [17], **we have breakfast at eight** desayunamos a las ocho

a
b
c
d
e
f
g
h
i
j
k
l
m
n
o
p
q
r
s
t
u
v
w
x
y
z

A B C D E F G H I J K L M N O P Q R S T U V W X Y Z

break-in NOUN robo MASC

breast NOUN ❶ (a woman's) pecho MASC ❷ (of a chicken or other fowl) pechuga FEM

breaststroke NOUN braza FEM

breath NOUN aliento MASC; **out of breath** sin aliento, **to get one's breath** recobrar el aliento, **to take a deep breath** respirar hondo

breathe VERB respirar [17]

breathing NOUN respiración FEM

breed NOUN (of animal) raza FEM

breed VERB ❶ criar [32] (animals) ❷ (to have babies) reproducirse [60]; **rabbits breed fast** los conejos se reproducen mucho

breeze NOUN brisa FEM

brewery NOUN cervecería FEM

bribe NOUN soborno MASC

bribe VERB sobornar [17]

brick NOUN ladrillo MASC; **a brick wall** una pared de ladrillo

bride NOUN novia FEM; **the bride and groom** los novios, el novio y la novia

bridegroom NOUN novio MASC

bridesmaid NOUN dama (FEM) de honor

bridge NOUN ❶ (over a river) puente MASC; **a bridge over the Thames** un puente sobre el Támesis ❷ (card game) bridge MASC; **to play bridge** jugar al bridge

bridle NOUN brida FEM

brief ADJECTIVE breve

briefcase NOUN maletín MASC

briefly ADJECTIVE brevemente

briefs PLURAL NOUN calzoncillos MASC PLURAL

bright ADJECTIVE ❶ (star, light) brillante ❷ (colour) vivo/viva; **bright green socks** calcetines de un verde vivo ❸ **bright sunshine** un sol radiante ❹ (clever) inteligente; **she's not very bright** no es muy inteligente
• **to look on the bright side** ver el lado bueno de las cosas

brighten up VERB **the weather's brightening up** el tiempo está aclarando

brilliant ADJECTIVE ❶ (very clever) brillante; **a brilliant surgeon** un brillante cirujano, **he's brilliant at maths** es genial para las matemáticas ❷ (wonderful) fenomenal (informal); **the party was brilliant!** ¡la fiesta estuvo fenomenal!

bring VERB ❶ traer [42]; **they brought a present** trajeron un regalo, **bring your camera** trae tu cámara, **it brings good luck** trae buena suerte, **she's bringing all the children** trae a todos los niños ❷ **to bring something back** devolver [45] algo ❸ **to bring up** criar [32] (children), **he was brought up by his aunt** lo crió su tía

bristle NOUN cerda FEM

Britain NOUN Gran Bretaña FEM

British PLURAL NOUN **the British** los británicos

British ADJECTIVE británico/británica; **the British Isles** las islas británicas

broad ADJECTIVE (wide) ancho/ancha

broad bean NOUN haba FEM

broadcast NOUN emisión FEM

broadcast VERB emitir [19] (a programme)

broccoli NOUN brécol MASC

brochure NOUN folleto MASC

broke ADJECTIVE to be broke (no money) no tener un duro (informal)

broken ADJECTIVE roto/rota; the window's broken la ventana está rota, to have a broken leg tener una pierna rota

bronchitis NOUN bronquitis FEM

bronze NOUN bronce MASC

bronze ADJECTIVE de bronce

brooch NOUN broche MASC

broom NOUN ❶ (for sweeping) escoba FEM ❷ (bush) retama FEM

brother NOUN hermano MASC; my little brother mi hermano pequeño, my mother's brother el hermano de mi madre

brother-in-law NOUN cuñado MASC

brown ADJECTIVE ❶ marrón (NEVER CHANGES); brown shoes zapatos marrón ❷ castaño/castaña (hair or eyes) ❸ (tanned in the sun) moreno/morena; to go brown ponerse moreno/morena

brown bread NOUN pan (MASC) integral

brown sugar NOUN azúcar (MASC & FEM) moreno/morena

bruise NOUN ❶ (on a person) moratón MASC ❷ (on fruit) magulladura FEM

brush NOUN ❶ (for your hair, clothes, nails, or shoes) cepillo MASC; my hair brush mi cepillo del pelo ❷ (for sweeping) escoba FEM ❸ (paintbrush) brocha FEM

brush VERB ❶ cepillar [17] (your hair or shoes); to brush your hair cepillarse el pelo, she brushed her hair se cepilló el pelo ❷ to brush your teeth limpiarse [17] los dientes, I'm going to brush my teeth voy a limpiarme los dientes

Brussels NOUN Bruselas FEM

Brussels sprouts NOUN coles (FEM PLURAL) de Bruselas

bubble NOUN burbuja FEM

bubble bath NOUN gel (MASC) de baño

bucket NOUN cubo MASC

buckle NOUN hebilla FEM

bud NOUN brote MASC

Buddhism NOUN budismo MASC

Buddhist NOUN budista MASC & FEM

budget NOUN presupuesto MASC

budgie NOUN periquito MASC

buffet NOUN ❶ (on train) bar MASC ❷ (meal) buffet MASC

buffet car NOUN coche (MASC) restaurante

bug NOUN ❶ (insect) bicho MASC (informal) ❷ (virus) virus MASC; a stomach bug un virus en el estómago

build VERB construir [54]

builder NOUN albañil MASC & FEM

A
B
C
D
E
F
G
H
I
J
K
L
M
N
O
P
Q
R
S
T
U
V
W
X
Y
Z

building NOUN edificio MASC

building site NOUN solar MASC

building society NOUN sociedad FEM de crédito hipotecario

built-in ADJECTIVE empotrado/empotrada

built-up ADJECTIVE urbanizado/urbanizada; a built-up area una zona urbanizada

bulb NOUN ❶ (for a light) bombilla FEM ❷ (that you plant) bulbo MASC

bulky ADJECTIVE voluminoso/voluminosa

bull NOUN toro MASC

bulldozer NOUN bulldozer MASC

bullet NOUN bala FEM

bulletin NOUN boletín MASC; a news bulletin boletín de noticias

bullfight NOUN corrida (FEM) de toros

bullfighter NOUN torero MASC, torera FEM

bullfighting NOUN los toros; do you like bullfighting? ¿te gustan los toros?

bullring NOUN plaza (FEM) de toros

bully NOUN bravucón MASC, bravucona FEM; he's a bully es un bravucón

bully VERB intimidar [17]

bum NOUN (bottom) trasero MASC (informal)

bump NOUN ❶ a bump on the head un chichón en la cabeza ❷ a bump in the road un bache en la carretera ❸ (jolt) sacudida FEM ❹ (noise) golpe MASC

bump VERB ❶ (bang) darse [4] un golpe; I bumped my head me di un golpe en la cabeza ❷ to bump into something chocarse [31] con algo, I bumped into the table me choqué con la mesa ❸ to bump into somebody (meet by chance) encontrarse [24] con alguien

bumper NOUN parachoques MASC (does not change in the plural)

bumpy ADJECTIVE ❶ lleno/llena de baches (road) ❷ con muchas sacudidas (plane landing)

bun NOUN ❶ (for a burger) panecillo MASC ❷ (sweet) bollo MASC

bunch NOUN ❶ (of flowers) ramo MASC ❷ (of carrots, radishes or keys) manojo MASC ❸ a bunch of grapes un racimo de uvas

bundle NOUN ❶ (of clothes) fardo MASC ❷ (of papers, letters) paquete MASC

bungalow NOUN casa (FEM) de una planta

bunk NOUN (on a train or boat) litera FEM

bunk beds PLURAL NOUN literas FEM PLURAL

bureau NOUN ❶ (agency) agencia FEM ❷ (desk) escritorio MASC

bureau de change NOUN casa (FEM) de cambio

burger NOUN hamburguesa FEM

burglar NOUN ladrón MASC, ladrona FEM

burglar alarm NOUN alarma (FEM) antirobo

burglary NOUN robo MASC

burn NOUN quemadura FEM

burn VERB quemar [17]; **I've burned the rubbish** he quemado la basura, **she burnt herself on the grill** se quemó en la parrilla, **you'll burn your finger!** ¡te vas a quemar el dedo!, **Mum's burnt her cake** a mamá se le ha quemado el pastel, **I burn easily** (in the sun) me quemo fácilmente

burnt ADJECTIVE quemado/quemada

burst VERB ❶ estallar [17] (a balloon) ❷ reventar [29] (a tyre or pipe); **a burst tyre** una rueda con un reventón ❸ **to burst out laughing** echarse [17] a reír, **to burst into tears** echarse [17] a llorar ❹ **to burst into flames** empezar [25] a arder

bury VERB enterrar [29]

bus NOUN ❶ (for urban transport) autobús MASC, bus MASC; **we'll take the bus** cogeremos el autobús, **we missed the bus** perdimos el autobús, **on the bus** en el autobús, **a bus ticket** un billete de autobús ❷ (coach) autocar MASC; **to go to London by bus** ir [8] a Londres en autocar

bus driver NOUN conductor (MASC) de autobús, conductora (FEM) de autobús

bush NOUN arbusto MASC

business NOUN ❶ (commercial dealings) negocios MASC PLURAL; **he's in Leeds on business** está en Leeds de viaje de negocios, **a business letter** una carta de negocios ❷ (firm or company) negocio MASC; **small businesses** las pequeñas empresas ❸ **mind your own business!** ¡no te metas en lo que no te importa!, **that's my business!** ¡eso es asunto mío!

business class NOUN clase (FEM) preferente

businessman NOUN hombre (MASC) de negocios

business trip NOUN viaje (MASC) de negocios

businesswoman NOUN mujer (FEM) de negocios

bus lane NOUN carril (MASC) bus

bus pass NOUN abono (MASC) de autobús

bus route NOUN línea (FEM) de autobús

bus shelter NOUN marquesina FEM

bus station NOUN estación (FEM) de autobús

bus stop NOUN parada (FEM), del autobús

bust NOUN busto MASC

busy ADJECTIVE ❶ ocupado/ocupada (a person); **don't disturb him, he's busy** no lo molestes, está ocupado ❷ ajetreado/ajetreada (a day or week); **a very busy day** un día muy ajetreado ❸ (full of cars or people) muy concurrido/concurrida (a road); **the shops were busy** las tiendas estaban muy concurridas ❹ (phone) **the line's busy** está comunicando

but CONJUNCTION ❶ pero; **small but strong** pequeño pero fuerte, **I'll**

try, but it's difficult lo intentaré, pero es difícil ❷ **not … but …** sino …, **not Thursday but Friday** no el jueves sino el viernes

but *PREPOSITION* ❶ menos; **anything but that** cualquier cosa menos eso, **everyone but Leah** todos menos Leah ❷ **the last but one** el penúltimo

butcher *NOUN* carnicero *MASC*, carnicera *FEM*; **the butcher's** la carnicería

butter *NOUN* mantequilla *FEM*

butter *VERB* untar [17] con mantequilla

buttercup *NOUN* botón (*MASC*) de oro

butterfly *NOUN* mariposa *FEM*

button *NOUN* botón *MASC*; **the record button** el botón de grabar

buttonhole *NOUN* ojal *MASC*

buy *NOUN* **a good buy** una buena compra, **a bad buy** una mala compra

buy *VERB* comprar [17]; **I bought the cinema tickets** compré las entradas para el cine, **to buy something for somebody** comprarle algo a alguien, **Sarah bought him a sweater** Sarah le compró un jersey, **to buy something from someone** comprarle algo a alguien, **he bought his bike from Tim** le compré a Tom su bici

buyer *NOUN* comprador *MASC*, compradora *FEM*

buzz *VERB* (*a fly or bee*) zumbar [17]

buzzer *NOUN* timbre *MASC*

by *PREPOSITION* ❶ por; **by telephone** por teléfono, **the thief came in by the window** el ladrón entró por la ventana, **eaten by a dog** comido por un perro, **it's two metres by four** mide dos metros por cuatro, **by mistake** por equivocación, **they pay by the hour** pagan por hora, **written by Lorca** escrito por Lorca ❷ (*travel*) en; **to come by bus** venir en autobús, **to leave by train** salir en tren, **by bike** en bicicleta ❸ (*near*) al lado de; **by the fire** al lado del fuego, **by the sea** al lado del mar, **close by** cerca ❹ (*before*) para; **it'll be ready by Monday** estará listo para el lunes, **Kevin was back by four** Kevin estaba de vuelta para las cuatro ❺ **they should have finished by now** ya deberían haber terminado ❻ **by yourself** solo/sola, **I was by myself in the house** estaba solo en la casa, **she did it by herself** lo hizo sola ❼ **to take somebody by the hand** coger a alguien de la mano ❽ **by the way** por cierto ❾ **to go by** pasar

bye *EXCLAMATION* adiós; **bye for now!** ¡hasta luego!

bypass *NOUN* carretera (*FEM*) de circunvalación

Cc

cab NOUN ❶ taxi MASC; **to call a cab** llamar un taxi ❷ *(on a lorry)* cabina FEM

cabbage NOUN repollo MASC

cabin NOUN ❶ *(on lorry, plane)* cabina FEM ❷ *(on ship)* camarote MASC

cable NOUN cable MASC

cable car NOUN funicular MASC

cable television NOUN televisión *(FEM)* por cable

cactus NOUN cactus MASC

café NOUN cafetería FEM

cage NOUN jaula FEM

cagoule NOUN canguro MASC

cake NOUN pastel MASC; **would you like a piece of cake?** ¿quieres un trozo de pastel?

calculate VERB calcular [17]

calculation NOUN cálculo MASC

calculator NOUN calculadora FEM

calendar NOUN calendario MASC

calf NOUN ❶ *(animal)* ternero MASC, ternera FEM ❷ *(of your leg)* pantorrilla FEM

call NOUN *(telephone)* llamada FEM; **I had several calls this morning;** he tenido varias llamadas esta mañana, **thank you for your call** gracias por llamar, **a phone call** una llamada de teléfono, **to give somebody a call** llamar [17] a alguien

call VERB ❶ *(telephone)* llamar [17]; **to call a taxi** llamar un taxi, **to call the doctor** llamar al médico, **call this number** llama a este número, **thank you for calling** gracias por llamar, **I'll call you back later** te llamo más tarde ❷ *(name)* **they've called the baby Julie** le han puesto Julie al bebé ❸ **to be called** llamarse [17], **she has a brother called Dan** tiene un hermano que se llama Dan, **what's he called?** ¿cómo se llama?
- **to call in** pasar [17]; **I'll call in on my way back** pasaré por tu casa cuando vuelvo

call box NOUN cabina *(FEM)* telefónica

calm ADJECTIVE calma FEM

calm VERB calmar [17]
- **to calm down** calmarse; **he's calmed down a bit** se ha calmado un poco
- **to calm somebody down** calmar a alguien; **I tried to calm her down** intenté calmarla

calmly ADVERB con calma

calorie NOUN caloría FEM

camcorder NOUN videocámara FEM

camel NOUN camello MASC

camera NOUN ❶ *(for photos)* cámara *(FEM)* de fotos ❷ *(film or TV camera)* cámara FEM

cameraman NOUN cámara MASC & FEM

camp NOUN campamento MASC

camp VERB acampar [17]

A
B
C
D
E
F
G
H
I
J
K
L
M
N
O
P
Q
R
S
T
U
V
W
X
Y
Z

campaign NOUN campaña FEM

camper NOUN campista MASC & FEM

camper van NOUN caravana FEM

camping NOUN camping MASC; **to go camping** ir de camping, **we're going camping in Andalusia this summer** nos vamos de camping a Andalucía este verano

campsite NOUN camping MASC

can¹, can NOUN ❶ lata FEM; **a can of tomatoes** una lata de tomates ❷ (for petrol or oil) bidón MASC

can², can VERB ❶ poder [10]; **I can't be there before ten** no puedo estar allí antes de las diez, **you can leave your bag here** puedes dejar tu bolsa aquí, **can you open the door, please?** ¿me abres la puerta por favor?, **can I help you?** ¿qué desea?, **they couldn't come** no pudieron venir, **you could ring back tomorrow** podrías volver a llamar mañana, **you could have told me** me lo podrías haber dicho ❷ (with hear, see, remember, find, 'can' is not translated) **can you hear me?** ¿me oyes?, **I can't see her** no la veo, **I can't remember** no me acuerdo, **I can't find my keys** no me encuentro mis llaves ❸ (know how to) saber [13]; **she can't drive** no sabe conducir, **can you play the piano?** ¿sabes tocar el piano?

Canada NOUN Canadá MASC

Canadian NOUN canadiense MASC & FEM

Canadian ADJECTIVE canadiense

canal NOUN canal MASC

canary NOUN canario MASC

Canary Islands NOUN **the Canary Islands** las Islas Canarias

cancel VERB cancelar [17]; **the concert's been cancelled** han cancelado el concierto

cancer NOUN cáncer MASC; **to have lung cancer** tener cáncer de pulmón

Cancer NOUN Cáncer MASC; **I'm Cancer** soy Cáncer

candidate NOUN candidato MASC, candidata FEM

candle NOUN vela FEM

candlestick NOUN candelabro MASC

candyfloss NOUN algodón (MASC) de azúcar

canned ADJECTIVE en lata; **canned tomatoes** tomates en lata

cannon NOUN cañón MASC

cannot VERB ▶ SEE **can²**

canoe NOUN piragua FEM

canoeing NOUN piragüismo MASC; **to go canoeing** hacer piragüismo, **I like canoeing** me gusta hacer piragüismo

can-opener NOUN abrelatas FEM (does not change in the plural)

canteen NOUN cantina FEM

canvas NOUN ❶ (fabric) lona FEM ❷ (painting) lienzo MASC

cap NOUN ❶ (hat) gorro MASC; **a baseball cap** un gorro de béisbol ❷ (on a bottle or tube) tapón MASC

capable ADJECTIVE capaz

capacity NOUN capacidad FEM

capital NOUN ❶ *(city)* **capital** FEM; **Madrid is the capital of Spain** Madrid es la capital de España ❷ *(letter)* **mayúscula** FEM; **in capitals** en mayúsculas

capitalism NOUN **capitalismo** MASC

Capricorn NOUN **Capricornio** MASC; **Linda's Capricorn** Linda es Capricornio

captain NOUN ❶ *(of a ship or a team)* **capitán** MASC, **capitana** FEM ❷ *(of a plane)* **comandante** MASC & FEM

captivity NOUN **cautiverio** MASC; **to keep someone in captivity** mantener [9] a alguien en cautiverio

capture VERB **capturar** [17]

car NOUN **coche** MASC; **a car crash** un accidente de coche, **to park the car** aparcar el coche, **we're going by car** vamos en coche

caramel NOUN **caramelo** MASC

caravan NOUN **caravana** FEM

card NOUN ❶ *(for a card game)* **carta** FEM; **a card game** un juego de cartas, **to have a game of cards** jugar a las cartas ❷ *(greetings, phone, bank)* **tarjeta** FEM; **a birthday card** una tarjeta de cumpleaños

cardboard NOUN **cartón** MASC

cardigan NOUN **rebeca** FEM

cardphone NOUN **teléfono** *(MASC)* **de tarjeta**

care NOUN ❶ **cuidado** MASC; **he took care opening it** tuvo cuidado al abrirlo ❷ **to take care to do** asegurarse [17] de hacer ❸ **to take care of somebody** cuidar a alguien ❹ **take care!** *(be careful)* ¡cuidado!, *(when saying goodbye)* ¡cuídate!

care VERB ❶ **to care about** preocuparse [17] por, **to care about pollution** preocuparse por la contaminación ❷ **she doesn't care** a ella no le importa, **I couldn't care less!** ¡no me importa en absoluto!

career NOUN **carrera** FEM

careful ADJECTIVE ❶ **cuidadoso/ cuidadosa**; **try to be more careful** procura ser más cuidadoso ❷ **a careful driver** un conductor/una conductora prudente ❸ **be careful!** ¡ten cuidado!

carefully ADVERB ❶ **read the instructions carefully** lea las instrucciones atentamente, **listen carefully** escuchad atentamente ❷ *(handle)* **con cuidado**; **she put the vase down carefully** colocó el jarrón con cuidado ❸ **drive carefully!** ¡conduce con precaución!

careless ADJECTIVE ❶ **he's very careless** no pone atención en lo que hace ❷ **this is careless work** este trabajo está hecho sin cuidado, **a careless mistake** una falta de atención ❸ **careless driving** conducción negligente

caretaker NOUN *(in block of flats)* **portero** MASC, **portera** FEM

car ferry NOUN **ferry** MASC

cargo NOUN **carga** FEM

car hire NOUN **alquiler** *(MASC)* **de coches**

Caribbean¹ NOUN **the Caribbean** el Caribe, **the Caribbean Sea** el mar Caribe

Caribbean² NOUN **caribeño** MASC, **caribeña** FEM

Caribbean ADJECTIVE **caribeño/ caribeña**

caricature NOUN **caricatura** FEM

carnation NOUN **clavel** MASC

carnival NOUN **carnaval** MASC

car park NOUN **aparcamiento** MASC

carpenter NOUN **carpintero** MASC, **carpintera** FEM

carpentry NOUN **carpintería** FEM

carpet NOUN ❶ *(fitted)* **moqueta** FEM ❷ *(loose)* **alfombra** FEM

car phone NOUN **teléfono** *(MASC)* **de automóvil**

car radio NOUN **radio** *(MASC)* **de coche**

carriage NOUN **vagón** MASC

carrier bag NOUN **bolsa** FEM

carrot NOUN **zanahoria** FEM

carry VERB ❶ **llevar** [17]; **she was carrying a parcel** llevaba un paquete ❷ *(vehicle, plane)* **transportar** [17]; **the coach was carrying schoolchildren** el autobús transportaba colegiales
• **to carry on** seguir [64]; **they carried on talking** siguieron hablando

carrycot NOUN **cuna** *(FEM)* **portátil**

carsick ADJECTIVE **to be carsick** **marearse** [17] **al viajar en coche**

cart NOUN **carro** MASC

carton NOUN **envase** MASC

cartoon NOUN ❶ *(a film)* **dibujos** *(MASC PLURAL)* **animados** ❷ *(a comic strip)* **tira** *(FEM)* **cómica** ❸ *(an amusing drawing)* **chiste** MASC

cartridge NOUN ❶ *(for a pen)* **recambio** MASC ❷ *(for a gun)* **cartucho** MASC

carve VERB **trinchar** [17] *(meat)*

case¹ NOUN ❶ *(suitcase)* **maleta** FEM; **to pack a case** hacer una maleta ❷ *(for wine bottles for example)* **caja** FEM ❸ *(for spectacles or small things)* **estuche** MASC

case² NOUN ❶ **caso** MASC; **a case of flu** un caso de gripe, **in that case** en ese caso, **that's not the case** no se trata de eso ❷ **in case** en caso, **in case he's late** en caso de que llegue tarde, **check first, just in case** asegúrate, por si acaso ❸ **in any case** de todas formas, **in any case, it's too late** de todas formas, es demasiado tarde

cash NOUN ❶ *(money in general)* **dinero** MASC; **I haven't any cash on me** no llevo dinero encima ❷ *(money rather than card)* **dinero** *(MASC)* **en efectivo**; **to pay in cash** pagar en efectivo, **£50 in cash** cincuenta libras en efectivo

cash card NOUN **tarjeta** *(FEM)* **de cajero automático**

cash desk NOUN **caja** FEM; **pay at the cash desk** pagar en caja

cash dispenser NOUN **cajero** *(MASC)* **automático**

cashew NOUN **anacardo** MASC

cashier NOUN **cajero** MASC, **cajera** FEM

cash point NOUN **cajero** *(MASC)* **automático**

cassette NOUN **cinta** *(FEM)* **de cassette**

cast NOUN los actores MASC PLURAL; **the cast were on stage** los actores estaban en el escenario

castle NOUN ❶ castillo MASC ❷ (in chess) torre FEM

casual ADJECTIVE informal

casualty NOUN ❶ (in an accident) víctima FEM ❷ (hospital department) urgencias FEM PLURAL; **he's in casualty** está en urgencias

cat NOUN gato MASC (female) gata FEM
• **it's raining cats and dogs** está lloviendo a cántaros (literally: it's raining in jugfuls)

Catalan NOUN ❶ (the language) catalán MASC ❷ (person) catalán MASC, catalana FEM

Catalan ADJECTIVE catalán/catalana

catalogue NOUN catálogo MASC

Catalonia NOUN Cataluña FEM

catastrophe NOUN catástrofe FEM

catch NOUN ❶ (on a door) pestillo MASC ❷ (a drawback) trampa FEM; **what's the catch?** ¿dónde está la trampa?

catch VERB ❶ coger [3]; **Tom caught the ball** Tom cogió la pelota, **you can't catch me!** ¡no me coges!, **can you catch hold of the branch?** ¿puedes coger la rama? ❷ **to catch somebody doing** coger [3] a alguien haciendo, **he was caught stealing money** lo cogieron robando dinero ❸ coger [3] (a bus or plane); **did Tim catch his bus?** ¿cogió Tim el autobús? ❹ coger [3] (an illness); **he's caught chickenpox** ha cogido la varicela, **I've caught a cold** he cogido un resfriado ❺ (fishing or hunting) **to catch a fish** pescar [31] un pez, **to catch a mouse** cazar [22] un ratón ❻ oír [56] (what somebody says); **I didn't catch your name** no he oído tu nombre
• **to catch up with somebody** alcanzar [22] a alguien

category NOUN categoría FEM

catering NOUN catering MASC

caterpillar NOUN oruga FEM

cathedral NOUN catedral FEM; **Seville cathedral** la catedral de Sevilla

Catholic NOUN católico MASC, católica FEM

Catholic ADJECTIVE católico/católica

cattle PLURAL NOUN ganado MASC (singular)

cauliflower NOUN coliflor FEM; **cauliflower cheese** coliflor con besamel

cause NOUN causa FEM; **the cause of the accident** la causa del accidente, **for a good cause** por una buena causa

cause VERB causar [17]; **to cause problems** causar problemas

caution NOUN cautela FEM

cautious ADJECTIVE cauteloso/cautelosa

cave NOUN cueva FEM

caving NOUN espeleología FEM; **to go caving** hacer espeleología

CD NOUN disco (MASC) compacto, CD MASC

CD player NOUN compacto MASC

ceiling NOUN techo MASC; **on the ceiling** en el techo

celebrate VERB celebrar [17]; **I'm celebrating my birthday** estoy celebrando mi cumpleaños

celebrity NOUN famoso MASC, famosa FEM

celery NOUN apio MASC

cell NOUN célula FEM

cellar NOUN sótano MASC

cello NOUN violonchelo MASC; **to play the cello** tocar [31] el violonchelo

cement NOUN cemento MASC

cemetery NOUN cementerio MASC

cent NOUN ❶ (in the euro system) céntimo MASC ❷ (in the dollar system) centavo MASC

centenary NOUN centenario MASC

centigrade ADJECTIVE centígrado MASC; **ten degrees centigrade** diez grados centígrados

centimetre NOUN centímetro MASC

central ADJECTIVE central; **central London** el centro de Londres, **the office is very central** la oficina está en pleno centro

Central America NOUN América (FEM) Central

central heating NOUN calefacción (FEM) central

centre NOUN centro MASC; **in the centre of** en el centro de, **in the town centre** en el centro de la ciudad, **a shopping centre** un centro comercial

century NOUN siglo MASC; **in the twentieth century** en el siglo veinte, **the sixth century** el siglo seis, **the twenty-first century** el siglo veintiuno

cereal NOUN breakfast cereal cereales (MASC PLURAL) para el desayuno, **to have cereal for breakfast** desayunar cereales

ceremony NOUN ceremonia FEM

certain ADJECTIVE ❶ (sure) seguro/ segura; **are you certain of the address?** ¿estás seguro de las señas?, **I'm certain of it** estoy seguro, **to be certain that ...** estar seguro de que ..., **Nicky's certain (that) you're wrong** Nicky está segura de que estás equivocado, **nobody knows for certain** nadie lo sabe con seguridad ❷ (particular) cierto/cierta; **a certain number of** un cierto número de

certainly ADVERB certainly ¡por supuesto!, **certainly not** desde luego que no

certificate NOUN certificado MASC; **a birth certificate** un certificado de nacimiento

chain NOUN cadena FEM

chair NOUN ❶ (upright) silla FEM; **a kitchen chair** una silla de cocina ❷ (with arms) butaca FEM

chair lift NOUN telesilla FEM

chalet NOUN ❶ (in the mountains) chalet MASC ❷ (in a holiday camp) bungalow MASC

chalk NOUN tiza FEM

challenge NOUN **reto** MASC; **the exam was a real challenge** el examen fue un verdadero reto

champion NOUN **campeón/ campeona** MASC & FEM; **world champion** campeón del mundo

chance NOUN ❶ (an opportunity) **ocasión** FEM; **to have the chance to do** tener [9] ocasión de hacer, **if you have the chance to go to New York** si tienes ocasión de ir a Nueva York, **I haven't had the chance to write to him** no he tenido ocasión de escribirle ❷ (likelihood) **posibilidad** FEM; **there's a chance that she'll pass** existe la posibilidad de que apruebe ('de que' is followed by the subjunctive), **there's little chance of winning** hay pocas posibilidades de ganar ❸ (luck) **by chance** por casualidad, **do you have her address, by any chance?** ¿tienes sus señas por casualidad?

change NOUN ❶ **cambio** MASC; **a change of plan** un cambio de planes, **they've made some changes to the house** han hecho algunos cambios en la casa, **it makes a change from hamburgers** por lo menos, es algo distinto a las hamburguesas ❷ **a change of clothes** una muda de ropa ❸ (cash) **cambio** MASC; **I haven't any change** no tengo cambio, **keep the change** quédese con el cambio ❹ **for a change** para variar, **for a change, let's eat out** vamos a comer fuera, para variar

change VERB ❶ (transform completely) **cambiar** [17]; **it changed my life** cambió mi vida, **Liz never changes** Liz no cambia ❷ (to switch from one thing to another) **cambiar** [17] **de**; **we changed trains at Crewe**

cambiamos de tren en Crewe, **she's changed her address** ha cambiado de dirección, **to change your mind** cambiar de opinión, **to change the subject** cambiar de tema, **they changed places** se cambiaron de sitio, **to change colour** cambiar de color ❸ (to swap for another) **cambiar** [17]; **have you changed the towels?** ¿has cambiado las toallas? ❹ (to exchange in a shop) **cambiar** [17]; **can I change it for the larger size?** ¿puedo cambiarlo por una talla más grande? ❺ (to change your clothes) **cambiarse** [17]; **Mike's gone up to change** Mike ha ido a cambiarse, **I must change my shirt** tengo que cambiarme de camisa

changing room NOUN ❶ (for sport or swimming) **vestuario** MASC ❷ (in a shop) **probador** MASC

channel NOUN ❶ (on TV) **canal** MASC; **to change channels** cambiar [17] de canal ❷ **the Channel** el Canal de la Mancha

Channel Tunnel NOUN **Eurotúnel** MASC

chaos NOUN **caos** MASC; **it was chaos!** ¡fue un caos!

chapel NOUN **capilla** FEM

chapter NOUN **capítulo** MASC; **in chapter two** en el capítulo número dos

character NOUN ❶ (personality) **carácter** MASC; **a house with a lot of character** una casa con mucho carácter ❷ (in a book, play, or film) **personaje** MASC; **the main character** el personaje principal

a
b
c
d
e
f
g
h
i
j
k
l
m
n
o
p
q
r
s
t
u
v
w
x
y
z

characteristic NOUN **característica** FEM

charcoal NOUN ❶ (for burning) **carbón** (MASC) **vegetal** ❷ (for drawing) **carboncillo** MASC

charge NOUN ❶ (what you pay) **precio** MASC; admission charge precio de admisión, there's no charge es gratis, an extra charge un suplemento ❷ to be in charge ser responsable, who's in charge? ¿quién es el responsable?, to be in charge of something/somebody estar a cargo de algo/alguien, who's in charge of these children? ¿quién está a cargo de estos niños? ❸ to be on a charge of theft estar acusado de robo

charge VERB ❶ (ask payment) **cobrar** [17]; they charge ten pounds an hour cobran diez libras la hora, how much do you charge for one day? ¿cuánto cobráis por un día?, we don't charge, it's free no cobramos, es gratis, they didn't charge me for the drinks no me cobraron las bebidas ❷ to charge somebody with acusar [17] a alguien de (a crime)

charity NOUN **organización** (FEM) **benéfica**

charm NOUN **encanto** MASC

charming ADJECTIVE **encantador/encantadora**

chart NOUN ❶ (table) **tabla** FEM ❷ the weather chart el mapa del tiempo ❸ the charts las listas de éxitos, number one in the charts número uno en las listas de éxitos

charter flight NOUN **vuelo** (MASC) **chárter**

chase NOUN **persecución** FEM; a car chase una persecución en coche

chase VERB **perseguir** [64] (a person or animal)

chat NOUN **charla** FEM; to have a chat with somebody charlar con alguien

chatroom NOUN **chat** MASC

chat show NOUN **programa** (MASC) **de entrevistas**

chatter VERB ❶ (talk) **cotorrear** [17] (informal) ❷ my teeth are chattering me castañetean los dientes

cheap ADJECTIVE **barato/barata**; cheap shoes zapatos baratos, that's very cheap! ¡eso es muy barato!

cheaply ADVERB to buy/sell cheaply comprar/vender barato, to eat/dress cheaply comer/vestir con poco dinero

cheap-rate ADJECTIVE **de tarifa reducida**; a cheap-rate phone call una llamada de teléfono de tarifa reducida

cheat NOUN **tramposo** MASC, **tramposa** FEM

cheat VERB **engañar** [17]

check NOUN ❶ (in a factory or at border controls) **control** MASC ❷ (by a doctor) **examen** (MASC) **médico** ❸ (in chess) check! ¡jaque!

check VERB (to make sure) **comprobar** [24]; he checked the time comprobó la hora, check they're all back comprueba que ya han llegado todos, check with your father pregunta a tu padre
• to check in ❶ (for a flight) facturar [17] el equipaje ❷ (at a hotel)

registrarse [17]; **she checked in at five o'clock** se registró a las cinco
• **to check out** irse [17]

check-in NOUN **facturación** (FEM) de equipajes

checkout NOUN **caja** FEM; **at the checkout** en caja

checkup NOUN **chequeo** MASC

cheek NOUN ❶ (part of face) **mejilla** FEM ❷ (nerve) **what a cheek!** ¡qué cara! (informal)

cheeky ADJECTIVE ❶ (mischievous) **descarado/descarada** ❷ (rude) **impertinente**

cheer NOUN ❶ **three cheers for Tom!** ¡tres hurras por Tom! ❷ (when you have a drink) **cheers!** ¡salud!

cheer VERB (to shout hurray) **vitorear** [17]
• **to cheer on** animar [17]
• **to cheer somebody up** animar [17] a alguien; **cheer up!** ¡ánimo!

cheerful ADJECTIVE **alegre**

cheese NOUN **queso** MASC; **blue cheese** queso azul, **a cheese sandwich** un sandwich de queso

cheesecake NOUN **tarta** (FEM) de queso

chef NOUN **chef** MASC & FEM

chemical NOUN **producto** (MASC) **químico**

chemist NOUN ❶ **farmacéutico** MASC, **farmacéutica** FEM ❷ **chemist's** farmacia FEM, **at the chemist's** en la farmacia ❸ (scientist) **químico** MASC, **química** FEM

chemistry NOUN **química** FEM

cheque NOUN **cheque** MASC; **to pay by cheque** pagar [28] con cheque, **to write a cheque** extender [18] un cheque

chequebook NOUN **talonario** (MASC) de cheques

cherry NOUN **cereza** FEM

chess NOUN **ajedrez** MASC; **to play chess** jugar [27] al ajedrez

chessboard NOUN **tablero** (MASC) de ajedrez

chest NOUN ❶ (part of the body) **pecho** MASC ❷ (box) **arcón** MASC

chestnut NOUN **castaña** FEM

chestnut tree NOUN **castaño** MASC

chest of drawers NOUN **cómoda** FEM

chew VERB **masticar** [31] (food)

chewing gum NOUN **chicle** MASC

chick NOUN (of a hen) **pollito** MASC

chicken NOUN **pollo** MASC; **roast chicken** pollo asado, **chicken thighs** muslos de pollo

chickenpox NOUN **varicela** FEM

chicory NOUN **endivia** FEM

chief NOUN **jefe** MASC, **jefa** FEM; **the chief of police** el jefe de policía

child NOUN (boy) **niño** MASC (girl) **niña** FEM; **Jenny's children** los niños de Jenny

childish ADJECTIVE **infantil**

childminder NOUN **niñero** MASC, **niñera** FEM

Chile NOUN **Chile** MASC

a
b
c
d
e
f
g
h
i
j
k
l
m
n
o
p
q
r
s
t
u
v
w
x
y
z

Chilean NOUN chileno MASC, chilena FEM

Chilean ADJECTIVE chileno/chilena

chilled ADJECTIVE (drink) frío/fría

chilli NOUN chile MASC

chilly ADJECTIVE frío/fría (a room or the weather); **it's chilly today** hoy hace fresco

chimney NOUN chimenea FEM

chimpanzee NOUN chimpancé MASC

chin NOUN barbilla FEM

china NOUN porcelana FEM; **a china plate** un plato de porcelana

China NOUN China FEM

Chinese NOUN ❶ the Chinese (people) los chinos ❷ (language) chino MASC

Chinese ADJECTIVE chino/china; **a Chinese man** un chino, **a Chinese woman** una china, **a Chinese meal** una comida china

chip NOUN ❶ (fried potato) patata (FEM) frita; **I'd like some chips** quiero unas patatas fritas ❷ (microchip) chip MASC ❸ (in glass or china) desportilladura FEM

chipped ADJECTIVE desportillado/desportillada

chives NOUN cebolletas FEM PLURAL

chocolate NOUN ❶ chocolate MASC; **a chocolate ice-cream** un helado de chocolate, **hot chocolate** chocolate caliente, **milk chocolate** chocolate con leche, **dark chocolate** chocolate sin leche ❷ a chocolate un bombón, **a box of chocolates** una caja de bombones

choice NOUN elección FEM; **freedom of choice** libertad de elección, **it was a good choice** fue una buena elección, **you have a choice of two flights** puede elegir entre dos vuelos, **I had no choice** no tuve más remedio

choir NOUN coro MASC

choke NOUN (on a car) estárter MASC

choke VERB atragantarse [17]; **she choked on a bone** se atragantó con un hueso

choose VERB elegir [48]; **you chose well** elegiste bien, **Cathy chose the red one** Cathy eligió el rojo, **it's hard to choose from all these colours** es difícil elegir entre todos estos colores

chop NOUN chuleta FEM; **a lamb chop** una chuleta de cordero

chop VERB ❶ cortar [17] (wood) ❷ cortar [17] en trozos pequeños (vegetables or meat) ❸ picar [31] (onion)

chopstick NOUN palillo (MASC) para comida china

chord NOUN acorde MASC

chorus NOUN ❶ (of a song) estribillo MASC ❷ (a group of singers) coro MASC

Christ NOUN Cristo

christening NOUN bautizo MASC

Christian NOUN, ADJECTIVE cristiano/cristiana

Christianity NOUN cristianismo MASC

Christian name NOUN nombre (MASC) de pila

Christmas NOUN Navidad FEM; **at Christmas** en Navidad, **Happy Christmas!** ¡Feliz Navidad!

Christmas card NOUN tarjeta (FEM) de Navidad

Christmas carol NOUN villancico MASC

Christmas Day NOUN día (MASC) de Navidad

Christmas dinner NOUN cena (FEM) de Navidad

Christmas Eve NOUN Nochebuena FEM; **on Christmas Eve** en Nochebuena

Christmas present NOUN regalo (MASC) de Navidad

Christmas tree NOUN árbol (MASC) de Navidad

chunk NOUN trozo MASC

church NOUN iglesia FEM; **to go to church** ir a la iglesia

churchyard NOUN cementerio MASC

chute NOUN (for sliding down) tobogán MASC

cider NOUN sidra FEM

cigar NOUN puro MASC

cigarette NOUN cigarrillo MASC; **to light a cigarette** encender un cigarrillo

cinema NOUN cine MASC; **to go to the cinema** ir al cine

circle NOUN círculo MASC; **to sit in a circle** sentarse en círculo, **to go round in circles** dar vueltas

circuit NOUN (racing track) pista FEM

circular ADJECTIVE circular

circumference NOUN circunferencia FEM

circumstances PLURAL NOUN **under the circumstances** en estas circunstancias

circus NOUN circo MASC

citizen NOUN ciudadano MASC, ciudadana FEM

city NOUN ciudad FEM; **the city of Seville** la ciudad de Sevilla

city centre NOUN centro (MASC) de la ciudad; **in the city centre** en el centro de la ciudad

civilian NOUN civil MASC & FEM

civilization NOUN civilización FEM

civil servant NOUN funcionario MASC, funcionaria FEM; **she's a civil servant** es funcionaria

civil service NOUN administración (FEM) pública

civil war NOUN guerra (FEM) civil

claim NOUN ❶ (statement) afirmación FEM ❷ (on insurance) reclamación FEM; **to make a claim on insurance** hacer [7] una reclamación al seguro

claim VERB asegurar [17]; **he claimed to know** aseguró saberlo

clap VERB ❶ aplaudir [19]; **everyone clapped** todo el mundo aplaudió ❷ **to clap your hands** dar [4] palmadas

clapping NOUN aplausos MASC PLURAL

clarinet NOUN clarinete MASC; **to play the clarinet** tocar [31] el clarinete

clash NOUN (violent incident) **choque** MASC

clash VERB ❶ (rival groups) **chocar** [31] ❷ (colours) **desentonar** [17]; **the curtains clash with the wallpaper** las cortinas desentonan con el papel pintado

clasp NOUN (of a necklace) **broche** MASC

class NOUN **clase** FEM; **she's in the same class as me** está en la misma clase que yo, **an art class** una clase de arte, **in class** en clase, **a social class** una clase social

classic ADJECTIVE **clásico/clásica**

classical ADJECTIVE **clásico/clásica**; **classical music** música clásica

classmate NOUN **compañero** (MASC), **de clase**, **compañera** (FEM) **de clase**

classroom NOUN **clase** FEM

claw NOUN ❶ (of a cat or dog) **zarpa** FEM ❷ (of a crab) **pinza** FEM

clay NOUN ❶ (for modelling) **arcilla** FEM ❷ **a clay court** (in tennis) una pista de tierra batida

clean ADJECTIVE ❶ **limpio/limpia**; **a clean shirt** una camisa limpia, **my hands are clean** tengo las manos limpias ❷ (germ-free) **puro/pura** (air or water)

clean VERB ❶ **limpiar** [17]; **I cleaned the whole house** limpié toda la casa ❷ **to clean your teeth** lavarse [17] los dientes, **I'm going to clean my teeth** voy a lavarme los dientes

cleaner NOUN ❶ (in a public place) **limpiador** MASC, **limpiadora** FEM ❷ (a cleaning lady) **señora** (FEM) **de**

la limpieza ❸ **a dry cleaner's** una tintorería

cleaning NOUN **to do the cleaning** hacer [7] la limpieza

cleanser NOUN ❶ (for the house) **producto** (MASC) **de limpieza** ❷ (for your face) **crema** (FEM) **limpiadora**

clear ADJECTIVE ❶ (that you can see through) **transparente**; **clear glass** cristal transparente ❷ (cloudless) **despejado/despejada** ❸ (easy to understand) **claro/clara**; **clear instructions** instrucciones claras, **is that clear?** ¿está claro?, **it's clear that …** está claro que …

clear VERB ❶ **sacar** [31] (papers, rubbish, or clothes); **have you cleared your stuff out of your room?** ¿has sacado todas tus cosas de tu habitación? ❷ **recoger** [3] (a table); **can I clear the table?** ¿puedo recoger la mesa? ❸ **despejar** [17] (a road or path) ❹ (fog or smoke) **disiparse** [17]; **and then the fog cleared** y entonces la niebla se disipó ❺ **to clear your throat** aclararse [17] la voz
• **to clear something up** recoger [3]; **I'll just clear up my books** voy a recoger mis libros

clearly ADJECTIVE ❶ (to think, speak, or hear) **con claridad** ❷ (obviously) **claramente**; **she was clearly worried** estaba claramente preocupada

clementine NOUN **clementina** FEM

clever ADJECTIVE ❶ **inteligente**; **their children are all very clever** todos sus hijos son muy inteligentes ❷ (ingenious) **ingenioso/ingeniosa**; **a clever idea** una idea ingeniosa

click NOUN **clic** MASC; **a double click** un doble clic

click VERB **hacer** [7] **clic en**; **click on the icon twice** haz clic dos veces en el icono

client NOUN **cliente** MASC & FEM

cliff NOUN **acantilado** MASC

climate NOUN **clima** MASC

climb VERB ❶ **subir** [19] (stairs) ❷ **escalar** [17] (a hill or a tree); **we climbed Mont Blanc** escalamos el Mont Blanc

climber NOUN **alpinista** MASC & FEM

climbing NOUN **alpinismo** MASC; **they go climbing in Italy** practican el alpinismo en Italia

clinic NOUN ❶ (in a hospital) **consultorio** MASC ❷ (a private hospital) **clínica** FEM

clip NOUN ❶ (from a film) **clip** MASC ❷ (for your hair) **horquilla** FEM

clip VERB ❶ (to cut) **cortar** [17] ❷ (to fasten) **sujetar** [17] **con un clip**

cloakroom NOUN (for coats) **guardarropa** MASC

clock NOUN **reloj** MASC; **an alarm clock** un reloj despertador, **to put the clocks forward an hour** adelantar los relojes una hora, **to put the clocks back** atrasar los relojes

clock radio NOUN **radiodespertador** MASC

clockwise ADVERB **en el sentido de las agujas del reloj** MASC; **it turns clockwise** gira en el sentido de las agujas del reloj, **anticlockwise** en el sentido contrario al de las agujas del reloj

clog NOUN **zueco** MASC

close¹ ADJECTIVE, ADVERB ❶ (result) **reñido/reñida** ❷ (relation) **cercano/cercana** ❸ (friend or relationship) **she's a close friend of mine** es muy amiga mía, **they are very close** están muy unidos ❹ (near) **cerca**; **the station's very close** la estación está muy cerca, **she lives close by** vive cerca, **not very close** no muy cerca, **close to the cinema** cerca del cine

close² VERB **cerrar** [29]; **close your eyes!** ¡cierra los ojos!, **she closed the door** cerró la puerta, **the post office closes at six** la oficina de correos cierra a las seis
- **to close down** (a shop or factory) **cerrar** [29]

closed ADJECTIVE **cerrado/cerrada**; **'closed on Mondays'** 'cerrado los lunes'

closely ADVERB **de cerca**; **to examine something closely** examinar [17] algo de cerca

closing date NOUN **fecha** (FEM) **límite**; **the closing date for entries** la fecha límite para inscribirse

closing-down sale NOUN **liquidación** (FEM) **por cierre de negocio**

closing time NOUN **hora** (FEM) **de cierre**

cloth NOUN ❶ (for the floor or wiping surfaces) **bayeta** FEM ❷ (for polishing) **trapo** (MASC) **del polvo** ❸ (for drying up) **paño** (MASC) **de cocina** ❹ (fabric by the metre) **tela** FEM

clothes PLURAL NOUN **ropa** FEM
(SINGULAR); **to put your clothes on**
ponerse [11] **la ropa**, **to take your**
clothes off **quitarse** [17] **la ropa**, **to**
change your clothes **cambiarse** [17]
de ropa

clothes hanger NOUN **percha** FEM

clothes line NOUN **cuerda** (FEM) **de**
tender

clothes peg NOUN **pinza** (FEM) **para**
tender

cloud NOUN **nube** FEM
• **to cloud over** **nublarse** [17]; **it**
clouded over in the afternoon **se**
nubló por la tarde

cloudy ADJECTIVE **nublado/nublada**

clove NOUN ❶ **clavo** MASC ❷ **a clove of**
garlic **un diente de ajo**

clown NOUN **payaso** MASC, **payasa** FEM

club NOUN ❶ (association) **club** MASC;
he's in the football club **está en el**
club de fútbol ❷ (in cards) **trébol**;
the four of clubs **el cuatro de**
tréboles ❸ (golfing iron) **palo** (MASC)
de golf

clue NOUN ❶ **pista** FEM; **they have**
a few clues **tienen unas cuantas**
pistas
• **I haven't a clue** **no tengo ni idea**
❷ (in a crossword) **clave** FEM

clumsy ADJECTIVE **torpe**

clutch NOUN (in a car) **embrague** MASC

clutch VERB **to clutch something**
tener [9] **algo firmemente**
agarrado

coach NOUN ❶ (bus) **autobús** MASC;
by coach **en autobús**, **on the coach**
en el autobús, **to travel by coach**

viajar en autobús ❷ (sports trainer)
entrenador MASC, **entrenadora** FEM
❸ (railway carriage) **vagón** MASC

coach station NOUN **estación** (FEM)
de autobuses

coach trip NOUN **excursión** (FEM)
en autobús; **to go on a coach trip**
hacer una excursión en autobús

coal NOUN **carbón** MASC

coal mine NOUN **mina** (FEM) **de**
carbón

coal miner NOUN **minero** MASC,
minera FEM

coarse ADJECTIVE **basto/basta**

coast NOUN **costa** FEM; **on the east**
coast **en la costa este**

coat NOUN ❶ (that you wear) **abrigo**
MASC ❷ **a coat of paint** **una capa de**
pintura

coat hanger NOUN **percha** FEM

cobweb NOUN **telaraña** FEM

cocaine NOUN **cocaína** FEM

cockerel NOUN **gallo** MASC

cocoa NOUN (drink) **chocolate** MASC
(powder) **cacao** MASC

coconut NOUN **coco** MASC

cod NOUN **bacalao** MASC

code NOUN ❶ **código** MASC; **the**
highway code **el código de la**
circulación ❷ **the dialling code for**
Barcelona **el prefijo de Barcelona**

coffee NOUN **café** MASC; **a cup of coffee**
un café, **a black coffee, please** **un**
café solo, por favor, **a white coffee**
un café con leche

coffee break *NOUN* pausa *(FEM)* para el café

coffee cup *NOUN* taza *(FEM)* de café

coffee machine *NOUN* ❶ *(vending machine)* máquina *(FEM)* de café ❷ *(electric)* cafetera *(FEM)* eléctrica

coffee pot *NOUN* cafetera *FEM*

coffee table *NOUN* mesa *(FEM)* de centro

coffin *NOUN* ataúd *MASC*

coin *NOUN* moneda *FEM*; **a pound coin** una moneda de una libra

coincidence *NOUN* coincidencia *FEM*

Coke™ *NOUN* Coca-Cola *FEM*; **two Cokes please** dos Coca-Colas, por favor

colander *NOUN* colador *MASC*

cold *NOUN* ❶ *(cold weather)* frío *MASC*; **I don't want to go out in this cold** no quiero salir con este frío, **come in out of the cold** entra, que hace frío, **she was shivering with cold** estaba temblando de frío ❷ *(illness)* resfriado *MASC*; **to have a cold** estar resfriado/resfriada, **Carol's got a cold** Carol está resfriada, **a bad cold** un fuerte resfriado

cold *ADJECTIVE* ❶ frío/fría; **your hands are cold** tienes las manos frías, **cold milk** leche fría ❷ *(weather, temperature)* **it's cold today** hoy hace frío, **it's cold in the kitchen** hace frío en la cocina ❸ *(feeling)* **I'm cold** tengo frío, **he was feeling very cold** tenía mucho frío

cold sore *NOUN* calentura *FEM*

collapse *VERB* ❶ *(a roof or a wall)* derrumbarse [17] ❷ *(a person)* **he collapsed in his office** sufrió un desmayo en su oficina

collar *NOUN* ❶ *(on a garment)* cuello *MASC* ❷ *(for a dog)* collar *MASC*

collarbone *NOUN* clavícula *FEM*

colleague *NOUN* compañero *MASC*, compañera *FEM*

collect *VERB* ❶ *(as a hobby)* coleccionar [17]; **I collect stamps** colecciono sellos ❷ recoger [3] *(a person or a thing)*; **she collects the children from school** ella recoge a los niños del colegio, **to collect in the exercise books** recoger los cuadernos ❸ cobrar [17] *(fares or money)* ❹ reunir [62] *(data or information)*

collection *NOUN* ❶ *(of stamps etc.)* colección *FEM* ❷ *(of money)* colecta *FEM*

collector *NOUN* coleccionista *MASC & FEM*

college *NOUN* ❶ *(for higher education)* colegio *(MASC)* universitario; **to go to college** ir a la universidad ❷ *(for vocational training)* escuela *(FEM)* de formación profesional ❸ *(a school)* instituto *MASC*

collie *NOUN* collie *MASC & FEM*

collision *NOUN* choque *MASC*

Colombia *NOUN* Colombia *FEM*

Colombian *NOUN* colombiano *MASC*, colombiana *FEM*

Colombian *ADJECTIVE* colombiano/ colombiana

a
b
c
d
e
f
g
h
i
j
k
l
m
n
o
p
q
r
s
t
u
v
w
x
y
z

colonel   comedy

colonel NOUN **coronel** MASC

colour NOUN **color** MASC; **what colour is your car?** ¿de qué color es tu coche?, **what colour is it?** ¿de qué color es?, **do you have it in a different colour?** ¿lo tiene en otros colores?

colour VERB (with paints or crayons) **colorear** [17]; **to colour something red** colorear algo de rojo

colour blind ADJECTIVE **daltónico/daltónica**

colour film NOUN (for a camera) **carrete** (MASC) **de color**

colourful ADJECTIVE **de colores**

colouring book NOUN **libro** (MASC) **para colorear**

colour supplement NOUN **suplemento** (MASC) **a color**

column NOUN **columna** FEM

comb NOUN **peine** MASC

comb VERB **to comb your hair** peinarse [17], **I'll just comb my hair** voy a peinarme

combination NOUN **combinación** FEM

combine VERB **combinar** [17] (two separate things); **they don't combine well** no combinan bien

come VERB **venir** [15]; **come quick!** ¡ven rápido!, **come and see!** ¡ven a ver!, **Nick came by bike** Nick vino en bici, **did Jess come to school yesterday?** ¿vino Jess ayer a clase?, **can you come over for a coffee?** ¿puedes venir a tomar un café?, **the bus is coming** ya viene el autobús, **come on!** ¡venga!, **coming!** ¡ya voy!

- **to come apart** deshacerse [7]; **it came apart in my hands** se deshizo en mis manos
- **to come back** volver [45]; **she's coming back to collect us** volverá para recogernos
- **to come down** bajar [17] (the stairs or the street)
- **to come for** venir [15] a por (a person); **my father's coming for me** mi padre va a venir a por mí
- **to come from** ser [1] de; **Ian comes from Scotland** Ian es de Escocia, **the wine comes from Spain** el vino es español
- **to come in** entrar [17]; **come in!** ¡adelante!, **she came into the kitchen** entró en la cocina
- **to come off** ❶ (a button) desprenderse [18], (a handle) soltarse [24] ❷ (a lid) **I can't get the lid to come off** no puedo quitar la tapa
- **to come out** salir [63]; **they came out when I called** salieron cuando los llamé, **the song's coming out soon** la cancion va a salir pronto, **the sun hasn't come out yet** el sol no ha salido aún
- **to come to** ❶ (get to) llegar [28] a; **when you come to the church turn right** gira a la derecha cuando llegues a la iglesia ❷ (add up to) **it comes to 150 euros** suma ciento cincuenta euros
- **to come up** subir [19]; **can you come up a moment?** ¿puedes subir un momento?
- **to come up to somebody** acercarse [31] a alguien

comedian NOUN **cómico** MASC, **cómica** FEM

comedy NOUN **comedia** FEM

372

comfortable ADJECTIVE **cómodo/cómoda**; this chair's really comfortable esta silla es muy cómoda, to feel comfortable (a person) estar cómodo/cómoda, are you comfortable there? ¿estás cómodo ahí?

comfortably ADVERB **cómodamente**

comic NOUN (magazine) **cómic** MASC

comic strip NOUN **tira** (FEM) **cómica**

comma NOUN **coma** FEM

command NOUN **orden** FEM

comment NOUN (in a conversation) **comentario** MASC; he made some rude comments about my friends hizo unos comentarios groseros sobre mis amigos

commentary NOUN **crónica** FEM; the commentary of the match la crónica del partido

commentator NOUN **comentarista** MASC & FEM; a sports commentator un comentarista deportivo

commercial NOUN **anuncio** (MASC) **de televisión**

commercial ADJECTIVE **comercial**

commit VERB ❶ **cometer** [18] (a crime) ❷ to commit yourself **comprometerse** [18]

committee NOUN **comité** MASC

common ADJECTIVE ❶ **corriente**; it's a common problem es un problema corriente ❷ in common **en común**, they have nothing in common no tienen nada en común

common sense NOUN **sentido** (MASC) **común**

communicate VERB **comunicar** [31]

communication NOUN ❶ (message, letter etc) **comunicación** FEM ❷ (in transport) communications are good las comunicaciones son buenas

communion NOUN **comunión** FEM

communism NOUN **comunismo** MASC

communist NOUN **comunista** MASC & FEM

community NOUN **comunidad** FEM; the European Community la comunidad europea

commute VERB to commute between Oxford and London **viajar** [17] todos los días de Oxford a Londres para ir a trabajar

commuter NOUN trains full of commuters trenes llenos de personas que van a trabajar (Spanish does not have a word for 'commuters' so it has to be explained as 'people travelling to work')

compact disc NOUN **disco** (MASC) **compacto**

compact disc player NOUN **compacto** MASC

company NOUN ❶ **compañía** FEM; an insurance company una compañía de seguros, she's set up a company ha montado una compañía, an airline company una compañía aérea, a theatre company una compañía de teatro ❷ to keep somebody company **hacer** [7] compañía a alguien, the dogs keep me company los perros me hacen compañía

comparatively ADVERB
relativamente

compare VERB comparar [17]; **if you compare the Spanish with the English** si comparas los españoles con los ingleses, **our house is small compared with yours** nuestra casa es pequeña comparada con la tuya

comparison NOUN comparación FEM; **in comparison with** en comparación con

compartment NOUN compartimento MASC

compass NOUN brújula FEM

compatible ADJECTIVE (computing) compatible

compensation NOUN indemnzación FEM

compete VERB ❶ **to compete in something** participar [17] en algo (race, event) ❷ **to compete for something** competir [57] (jobs, places), **thirty people are competing for the job** treinta personas compiten por el puesto

competent ADJECTIVE competente

competition NOUN ❶ (in a magazine or at school) concurso MASC; **a poetry competition** un concurso de poesía ❷ (in sports) competición FEM; **a fishing competition** una competición de pesca ❸ (in business) competencia FEM

competitor NOUN ❶ (in sports) participante MASC & FEM ❷ (in business) competidor MASC, competidora FEM

complain VERB quejarse [17]; **we complained about the hotel and the meals** nos quejamos del hotel y de las comidas

complaint NOUN queja FEM; **to make a complaint** presentar [17] una queja, **she made a complaint to the manager about the bad service** presentó una queja al gerente por el mal servicio

complete ADJECTIVE completo/completa; **the complete collection** la colección completa

complete VERB (to finish) terminar [17]

completely ADVERB completamente

complexion NOUN cutis MASC

complicated ADJECTIVE complicado/complicada

complication NOUN complicación FEM; **there were complications** hubo complicaciones

compliment NOUN cumplido MASC; **to pay somebody a compliment** hacer [7] un cumplido a alguien

compose VERB componer [11]; **composed of** compuesto de

composer NOUN compositor MASC, compositora FEM

comprehension NOUN comprensión FEM; **a comprehension test** un ejercicio de comprensión

compulsory ADJECTIVE obligatorio/obligatoria

computer NOUN ordenador MASC; **to work on a computer** trabajar en ordenador

computer engineer NOUN técnico (MASC) en informática, técnica (FEM) en informática

computer game NOUN juego (MASC) de ordenador

computer program NOUN programa (MASC) informático

computer programmer NOUN programador (MASC), programadora FEM

computer science NOUN informática FEM

computing NOUN informática FEM

conceited ADJECTIVE engreído/engreída

concentrate VERB concentrarse [17]; **I can't concentrate** no puedo concentrarme, **I was concentrating on the film** me estaba concentrando en la película

concentration NOUN concentración FEM

concern NOUN (worry) preocupación FEM; **there is no cause for concern** no hay razón para preocuparse

concern VERB ❶ (to affect) concernir [14]; **this doesn't concern you** esto no te concierne ❷ **as far as I'm concerned** por mi parte

concert NOUN ❶ concierto MASC; **to go to a concert** ir [8] a un concierto ❷ **a concert ticket** una entrada para un concierto

conclusion NOUN conclusión FEM

concrete NOUN cemento MASC; **a concrete floor** un suelo de cemento

condemn VERB condenar [17]

condition NOUN condición FEM; **in good condition** en buenas condiciones, **weather conditions** condiciones meteorológicas, **the conditions of sale** las condiciones de venta, **on one condition** con una condición, **on condition that you let me pay** a condición de que me dejes pagar

conditional NOUN condicional MASC

conditioner NOUN (for your hair) suavizante MASC

condom NOUN condón MASC

conduct NOUN conducta FEM

conduct VERB dirigir [49] (an orchestra or a piece of music)

conductor NOUN ❶ (of an orchestra) director (MASC) de orquesta, directora (FEM) de orquesta ❷ (on bus) cobrador MASC, cobradora FEM

cone NOUN ❶ (for ice cream) cucurucho MASC ❷ (for traffic) cono MASC

confectionery NOUN dulces FEM PLURAL; **she works in a confectionery shop** trabaja en una confitería

conference NOUN conferencia FEM

confess VERB confesar [29]

confession NOUN confesión FEM

confidence NOUN ❶ (self-confidence) seguridad (FEM) en sí mismo; **he has a lot of confidence** tiene mucha seguridad en sí mismo, **you're lacking in confidence** te falta seguridad en ti mismo ❷ (faith in somebody else) confianza FEM; **to have confidence in somebody** tener [9] confianza en alguien

confident ADJECTIVE ❶ (sure of yourself) seguro de sí mismo, segura de sí misma; **you look very confident** pareces muy seguro de ti mismo, **she's a confident young woman** es una joven segura de sí misma ❷ (sure that something will happen) **to be confident that** estar [2] seguro de que, **I'm confident that it will work out all right** estoy seguro de que saldrá bien

confirm VERB confirmar [17]; **we'll confirm the date** confirmaremos la fecha

confuse VERB confundir [19]; **I confuse him with his brother** lo confundo con su hermano

confused ADJECTIVE ❶ (unclear) confuso/confusa; **he gave us a confused story** contó una historia muy confusa ❷ confundido/ confundida; **now I'm completely confused** ahora estoy completamente confundida, **I'm confused about the holiday dates** no estoy segura de las fechas de las vacaciones ❸ **to get confused** confundirse [19], **she got confused** se confundió

confusing ADJECTIVE poco claro/ clara; **the instructions are confusing** las instrucciones son poco claras

confusion NOUN confusión FEM

congratulate VERB felicitar [17]; **I congratulated Tim on his success** felicité a Tim por su éxito, **we congratulate you on winning** te felicitamos por haber ganado

congratulations PLURAL NOUN enhorabuena FEM; **congratulations on the baby!** ¡enhorabuena por el bebé!

conjurer NOUN mago MASC, maga FEM

connect VERB (to plug in to the mains) conectar [17] (a dishwasher or TV, for example)

connection NOUN conexión FEM; **a faulty connection** una conexión defectuosa, **Sally missed her connection** Sally perdió su conexión, **there's no connection between his letter and my decision** no hay relación entre su carta y mi decisión

conscience NOUN conciencia FEM; **to have a guilty conscience** no tener la conciencia tranquila

conscious ADJECTIVE consciente

consequence NOUN consecuencia FEM

consequently ADVERB por consiguiente

conservation NOUN (of nature) protección (FEM) del medio ambiente

conservative NOUN, ADJECTIVE conservador/conservadora

conservatory NOUN jardín (MASC) de invierno

consider VERB ❶ (to give thought to) considerar [17] (a suggestion or idea) ❷ (to think you might do) plantearse [17]; **we're considering buying a flat** estamos planteándonos comprar un piso ❸ **all things considered** bien considerado

considerable ADJECTIVE considerable; **a considerable number of students** un número considerable de estudiantes

considerate ADJECTIVE **considerado/considerada** *(a person)*

consideration NOUN **consideración** FEM

considering PREPOSITION **teniendo en cuenta; considering her age** teniendo en cuenta su edad, **considering he did it all himself** teniendo en cuenta que lo hizo todo él solo

consist VERB **to consist of** consistir [19] en

consistent ADJECTIVE **constante**

consonant NOUN **consonante** FEM

constant ADJECTIVE **constante**

constantly ADVERB **constantemente**

constipated ADJECTIVE **estreñido/estreñida**

construct VERB **construir** [54]

construction NOUN **construcción** FEM

consul NOUN **cónsul** MASC

consulate NOUN **consulado** MASC

consult VERB **consultar** [17]

consumer NOUN **consumidor** MASC, **consumidora** FEM

consumption NOUN **consumo** MASC

contact NOUN **contacto** MASC; **to be in contact with somebody** estar en contacto con alguien, **we've lost contact** hemos perdido contacto, **Rob has contacts in the music business** Rob tiene contactos en el mundo de la música

contact VERB **ponerse** [11] **en contacto con; I'll contact you tomorrow** me pondré en contacto contigo mañana

contact lens NOUN **lentilla** FEM

contain VERB **contener** [9]

container NOUN **recipiente** MASC

contaminate VERB **contaminar** [17]

contemporary ADJECTIVE **contemporáneo/contemporánea**

contents PLURAL NOUN **contenido** MASC; **the contents of my suitcase** el contenido de mi maleta

contest NOUN ❶ **concurso** MASC ❷ *(in sport)* **competición** FEM

contestant NOUN **concursante** MASC & FEM

context NOUN **contexto** MASC

continent NOUN **continente** MASC; **on the Continent** en Europa continental

continental ADJECTIVE **a continental holiday** unas vacaciones en Europa continental

continue VERB ❶ **continuar** [20]; **we continued our journey** continuamos con nuestro viaje, **'to be continued'** 'continuará' ❷ **to continue doing** seguir [64] haciendo, **Jill continued talking** Jill siguió hablando

continuous ADJECTIVE **continuo/continua; continuous assessment** evaluación *(FEM)* **continua**

contraception NOUN **anticoncepción** FEM

contraceptive NOUN **anticonceptivo** MASC

contract NOUN **contrato** MASC

contradict VERB contradecir [5]

contradiction NOUN contradicción FEM

contrary NOUN the contrary lo contrario, on the contrary al contrario

contrast NOUN contraste MASC

contribute VERB contribuir [54] (money)

contribution NOUN (to charity or an appeal) contribución FEM

control NOUN (of a crowd or animals) control MASC; the police have lost control la policía ha perdido el control, everything's under control todo está bajo control

control VERB ❶ controlar [17] (a crowd, animals, or a fire, for example) ❷ to control oneself controlarse [17]

controversial ADJECTIVE controvertido/controvertida; a controversial decision una decisión controvertida

convenient ADJECTIVE ❶ práctico/ práctica; frozen vegetables are very convenient las verduras congeladas son muy prácticas ❷ to be convenient for somebody venirle [15] bien a alguien, if that's convenient for you si te va bien ❸ the house is convenient for shops and schools la casa está bien situada respecto a tiendas y colegios

convent NOUN convento MASC

conventional ADJECTIVE ❶ convencional ❷ (person) tradicional

conversation NOUN conversación FEM

convert VERB convertir [14]; we're going to convert the garage into a workshop vamos a convertir el garaje el un taller

convince VERB convencer [44]; I'm convinced you're wrong estoy convencido de que estás equivocado

convincing ADJECTIVE convincente

cook NOUN cocinero MASC, cocinera FEM

cook VERB ❶ cocinar [17]; who's cooking tonight? ¿quién cocina esta noche?, I like cooking me gusta cocinar ❷ cocer [41] (vegetables, pasta, etc); cook the carrots for five minutes cuece las zanahorias durante cinco minutos ❸ hacer [7] (a meal); Fran's busy cooking supper Fran está haciendo la cena ❹ (food) hacerse [7]; the sausages are cooking las salchichas se están haciendo, is the chicken cooked? ¿está hecho el pollo?

cooker NOUN cocina FEM; an electric cooker una cocina eléctrica, a gas cooker una cocina de gas

cookery NOUN cocina FEM

cookery book NOUN libro (MASC) de cocina

cooking NOUN cocina FEM; Italian cooking la cocina italiana, home cooking la comida casera, to do the cooking cocinar [27]

cool NOUN ❶ (coldness) fresco MASC; stay in the cool quedarse [17] al fresco ❷ (calm) calma FEM; to lose one's cool perder [36] la calma, he kept his cool mantuvo la calma

cool ADJECTIVE ❶ (cold) **fresco/fresca**; **a cool drink** una bebida fresca, **it's cool inside** dentro hace fresco ❷ (laid-back) **tranquilo/tranquila** ❸ **to be cool** (a person) **estar en la onda** (informal), **he's so cool** está muy en la onda (informal) ❹ (trendy) **molón/molona** (informal) (a car or a jacket)

cool VERB **to cool (down) enfriarse** [32]

cooperate VERB **cooperar** [17]

cop NOUN **poli** MASC & FEM (informal)

cope VERB ❶ (to manage) **defenderse** [36]; **she copes well** se defiende bien ❷ **to cope with ocuparse** [17] de (children or work), **I'll cope with the dishes** yo me ocupo de los platos ❸ **hacer** [7] **frente a** (problems); **she's had a lot to cope with** ha tenido que hacer frente a muchos problemas, **he can't cope any more** ya no puede más

copper NOUN **cobre** MASC

copy NOUN ❶ **copia** FEM; **make ten copies of this letter** haz diez copias de esta carta ❷ (of a book) **ejemplar** MASC

copy VERB **copiar** [17]; **I copied (down) the address** copié las señas

cord NOUN (for a blind, for example) **cordón** MASC

cordless telephone NOUN **teléfono** (MASC) **inalámbrico**

core NOUN (of an apple or a pear) **corazón** MASC

cork NOUN ❶ (in a bottle) **tapón** MASC ❷ (material) **corcho** MASC

corkscrew NOUN **sacacorchos** MASC (does not change in the plural)

corn NOUN ❶ (wheat) **trigo** MASC ❷ (sweetcorn) **maíz** MASC

corner NOUN ❶ (of street or page) **esquina** FEM; **at the corner of the street** en la esquina de la calle, **it's just round the corner** está a la vuelta de la esquina, **in the bottom right-hand corner of the page** en la esquina inferior derecha de la página ❷ (of room or cupboard) **rincón** MASC; **in a corner of the kitchen** en un rincón de la cocina ❸ **out of the corner of your eye** por el rabillo del ojo ❹ (in football) **córner** MASC

cornflakes NOUN **copos** (MASC PLURAL) **de maíz**

Cornwall NOUN **Cornualles** MASC

corpse NOUN **cadáver** MASC

correct ADJECTIVE ❶ **correcto/correcta**; **the correct sum** la cantidad total correcta, **the correct answer** la respuesta correcta, **the correct choice** la elección adecuada ❷ **yes, that's correct** sí, así es

correct VERB **corregir** [48]

correction NOUN **corrección** FEM

correctly ADVERB **correctamente**; **have you filled in the form correctly?** ¿has rellenado el formulario correctamente?

correspond VERB **corresponder** [18]

corridor NOUN **pasillo** MASC

cosmetics PLURAL NOUN **cosméticos** MASC PLURAL

cost NOUN **coste** MASC; **the cost of a new computer** el coste de un nuevo ordenador, **the cost of living** el coste de la vida

cost VERB **costar** [24]; **how much does it cost?** ¿cuánto cuesta?, **the tickets cost ten pounds** las entradas cuestan diez libras, **it costs too much** cuesta demasiado caro

Costa Rica NOUN **Costa Rica** FEM

Costa Rican NOUN **costarricense** (MASC & FEM)

Costa Rican ADJECTIVE **costarricense**

costume NOUN ❶ (fancy dress) **disfraz** MASC ❷ (for an actor) **traje** MASC

cosy ADJECTIVE (a room) **acogedor/ acogedora**; **it's cosy by the fire** se está muy bien al lado del fuego

cot NOUN **cuna** FEM

cottage NOUN **casita** (FEM) **en el campo**

cotton NOUN ❶ (fabric) **algodón** MASC; **a cotton shirt** una camisa de algodón ❷ (thread) **hilo** MASC

cotton wool NOUN **algodón** (MASC) **en rama**

couch NOUN **sofá** MASC

cough NOUN **tos** FEM; **a nasty cough** una tos mala, **to have a cough** tener [9] tos

cough VERB **toser** [18]

could VERB ❶ **poder** [10]; **if he could pay** si pudiese pagar, **I couldn't open it** no podía abrirlo, **they couldn't smoke there** no podían fumar allí, **she did all she could** hizo todo lo que pudo ❷ (knew how to) **he couldn't drive** no sabía conducir, **I couldn't swim** no sabía nadar ❸ (with see, hear, smell, remember, or understand, 'could' is

not translated) **I could hear a police car** oí un coche de policía, **she couldn't see anything** no veía nada ❹ (talking about a possibility) **they could be home by now** puede que ya estén en casa, **you could be right** puede que tengas razón ❺ (in 'if' sentences 'could' is translated by the subjunctive) **I would buy it if I could afford it** lo compraría si pudiese, **I could have gone if I'd wanted** hubiese podido ir si hubiese querido ❻ (asking permission or suggesting) **could I speak to David?** ¿podría hablar con David?, **you could try telephoning** podrías intentar llamar por teléfono

council NOUN **consejo** MASC; **the town council** el ayuntamiento

councillor NOUN **concejal** MASC, **concejala** FEM; **her uncle is a councillor** su tío es concejal

count VERB ❶ (reckon up) **contar** [24]; **I counted my money** conté mi dinero, **thirty-five not counting the children** treinta y cinco sin contar a los niños ❷ **to count as considerarse** [17] como, **children over twelve count as adults** los niños mayores de doce años se consideran como adultos ❸ (to be allowed) **that doesn't count** eso no vale

counter NOUN ❶ (in a shop) **mostrador** MASC ❷ (in a café) **barra** FEM ❸ (in a post office or bank) **ventanilla** FEM ❹ (for board games) **ficha** FEM

country NOUN ❶ (Spain, Britain, etc) **país** MASC; **a foreign country** un país extranjero, **from another country** de otro país ❷ (not town) **campo** MASC; **to live in the country** vivir en el campo, **a country walk** un paseo por el campo, **a country road** un camino rural

country dancing NOUN **baile** (MASC) **folklórico**

countryside NOUN **campo** MASC

county NOUN **condado** MASC

couple NOUN ❶ (a pair) **pareja** FEM; **a married couple** una pareja de casados ❷ **a couple of** un par de, **a couple of times** un par de veces, **I've got a couple of things to do** tengo que hacer un par de cosas

courage NOUN **valor** MASC

courgette NOUN **calabacín** MASC

courier NOUN ❶ (on a package holiday) **guía** MASC & FEM ❷ (delivery service) **mensajería** FEM; **by courier** por mensajería

course NOUN ❶ (lessons) **curso** MASC; **a beginners' course** un curso para principiantes, **a computer course** un curso de informática, **to go on a course** asistir a un curso ❷ (part of a meal) **plato** MASC; **the main course** el plato principal ❸ **a golf course** un campo de golf ❹ (of course) claro, **yes, of course!** ¡sí, claro!, **he's forgotten, of course** se ha olvidado, claro

court NOUN ❶ (for tennis, squash, or basketball) **cancha** FEM ❷ (of law) **tribunal** MASC

courtyard NOUN **patio** MASC

cousin NOUN **primo** MASC, **prima** FEM; **my cousin Sonia** mi prima Sonia

cover NOUN ❶ (for a book) **tapa** FEM ❷ (for a duvet or cushion) **funda** FEM; **a duvet cover** una funda de edredón

cover VERB ❶ **cubrir** [46]; **to cover the wound** cubrir la herida, **the ground was covered with snow** el suelo estaba cubierto de nieve, **he was covered in mud** estaba cubierto de barro ❷ (your face or eyes) **cubrirse** [46]; **she covered her face** se cubrió la cara

cow NOUN **vaca** FEM; **mad cow disease** la enfermedad de las vacas locas

coward NOUN **cobarde** MASC & FEM

cowboy NOUN **vaquero** MASC

crab NOUN **cangrejo** MASC

crack NOUN ❶ (in a wall) **grieta** FEM ❷ (in a cup or plate) **raja** FEM ❸ (a cracking noise) **crujido** MASC

crack VERB ❶ (to make a crack in) **hacer** [7] **una raja en** (a cup or a window) ❷ **fracturar** [17] (a bone) ❸ (break open) **cascar** [31] (a nut or an egg) ❹ (split by itself: ice, for example) **rajarse** [17] ❺ (make a noise) (a twig) **crujir** [19]

cracker NOUN (biscuit) **galleta** (FEM) **salada**

crackle VERB **crujir** [19]

craft NOUN (at school) **trabajos** (MASC PLURAL) **manuales**

crafty ADJECTIVE **astuto/astuta**; **that was very crafty of her** eso fue muy astuto por su parte

cramp NOUN **calambre** MASC; **I've got cramp in my leg** tengo un calambre en la pierna

crane NOUN **grúa** FEM

crash NOUN ❶ (an accident) **accidente** MASC; **a car crash** un accidente de coche ❷ (smashing noise) **estrépito**

MASC; **a crash of broken glass** un estrépito de cristales rotos

crash VERB ❶ (a car or plane) **tener [9] un accidente; the plane crashed** el avión tuvo un accidente ❷ **to crash into something** chocar [31] con algo, **the car crashed into a tree** el coche chocó con un árbol

crash course NOUN **curso** (MASC) **intensivo**

crash helmet NOUN **casco** MASC

crate NOUN ❶ (for china) **cajón** (MASC) **para embalar** ❷ (for bottles or fruit) **caja** FEM

crawl NOUN (in swimming) **crol** MASC

crawl VERB ❶ (a person, a baby) **ir [8] a gatas** ❷ (cars in a jam) **ir [8] muy despacio; we were crawling along** íbamos muy despacio

crayon NOUN ❶ (wax) **pintura** (FEM) **de cera** ❷ (coloured pencil) **lápiz** (MASC) **de color**

craze NOUN **fiebre** FEM; **the craze for computer games** la fiebre de los juegos de ordenador

crazy ADJECTIVE **loco/loca; to go crazy** volverse loco/loca, **to be crazy about someone** estar loco/loca por alguien, **he's crazy about football** le encanta el fútbol

creak VERB (a hinge) **chirriar [32]**, (a floorboard) **crujir [19]**

cream NOUN ❶ (dairy cream) **nata** FEM; **strawberries and cream** fresas con nata ❷ (for hands, face, etc.) **crema** FEM

cream cheese NOUN **queso** (MASC) **para untar**

crease NOUN **arruga** FEM

creased ADJECTIVE **arrugado/ arrugada**

create VERB **crear [17]**

creative ADJECTIVE **creativo/creativa** (a person)

creature NOUN **criatura** FEM

creche NOUN **guardería** FEM

credit NOUN **crédito** MASC; **to buy something on credit** comprar algo a crédito

credit card NOUN **tarjeta** (FEM) **de crédito**

crew NOUN ❶ (on a ship or plane) **tripulación** FEM ❷ (rowing or filming) **equipo** MASC

crew cut NOUN **corte** (MASC) **de pelo al rape**

cricket NOUN ❶ (game) **críquet** MASC; **to play cricket** jugar [27] al críquet ❷ (insect) **grillo** MASC

cricket bat NOUN **bate** (MASC) **de críquet**

crime NOUN ❶ **delito** MASC; **theft is a crime** el robo es un delito ❷ (murder) **crimen** MASC ❸ (within society) **crimen** MASC; **the fight against crime** la lucha contra el crimen

criminal NOUN **criminal** MASC & FEM

criminal ADJECTIVE **criminal**

crisis NOUN **crisis** FEM

crisp NOUN **patata** (FEM) **frita; a packet of (potato) crisps** un paquete de patatas fritas

crisp ADJECTIVE **crujiente**

critical ADJECTIVE ❶ **crítico/crítica** *(a remark or somebody's condition)* ❷ **decisivo/decisiva** *(a moment)*

criticism NOUN **crítica** FEM

criticize VERB **criticar** [31]

Croatia NOUN **Croacia** FEM

crockery NOUN **vajilla** FEM

crocodile NOUN **cocodrilo** MASC

crook NOUN *(criminal)* **granuja** MASC & FEM

crooked ADJECTIVE **torcido/torcida**; **a crooked line** una línea torcida

crop NOUN **cosecha** FEM

cross NOUN **cruz** FEM

cross ADJECTIVE **enfadado/enfadada**; **she's very cross** está muy enfadada, **I'm cross with you** estoy enfadada contigo, **to get cross** enfadarse [17]

cross VERB ❶ *(to cross over)* **cruzar** [22]; **to cross the road** cruzar la calle ❷ **to cross your legs** cruzar las piernas ❸ **to cross into Spain** pasar [17] a España ❹ *(to cross each other)* **cruzarse** [22]; **the two roads cross here** las dos carreteras se cruzan aquí
• **to cross out** tachar [17] *(a word or sentence)*

cross-Channel ADJECTIVE **a cross-Channel ferry** un ferry que cruza el Canal de la Mancha

cross-country NOUN ❶ **cross** MASC ❷ **cross-country skiing** esquí *(MASC)* de fondo

crossing NOUN ❶ *(from one place to another)* **travesía** FEM; **a Channel crossing** una travesía por el Canal de la Mancha ❷ **a pedestrian crossing** un cruce de peatones, **a level crossing** un paso a nivel

cross-legged ADJECTIVE **to sit cross-legged** sentarse con las piernas cruzadas

crossroads NOUN **cruce** MASC; **at the crossroads** en el cruce

crossword NOUN **crucigrama** MASC; **to do the crossword** hacer el crucigrama

crouch VERB **ponerse** [11] **en cuclillas**

crow NOUN **cuervo** MASC
• **as the crow flies** en línea recta

crow VERB *(a cock)* **cacarear** [17]

crowd NOUN **multitud** FEM; **in the crowd** en la multitud, **a crowd of 5,000** una multitud de cinco mil personas

crowd VERB **to crowd into** *(or onto)* **aglomerarse** [17] en *(a room or bus, for example)*, **we all crowded into the train** nos aglomeramos en el tren

crowded ADJECTIVE **lleno/llena de gente**

crown NOUN **corona** FEM

crude ADJECTIVE ❶ *(rough and ready)* **rudimentario/rudimentaria** ❷ *(vulgar)* **grosero/grosera**

cruel ADJECTIVE **cruel**

cruelty NOUN **crueldad** FEM; **they were treated with great cruelty** los trataron con gran crueldad

cruise NOUN **crucero** MASC; **to go on a cruise** ir de crucero

crumb *NOUN* miga *FEM*

crumple *VERB* arrugar [28]

crunchy *ADJECTIVE* crujiente

crush *VERB* aplastar [17]

crust *NOUN* corteza *FEM*

crutch *NOUN* muleta *FEM*; **to be on crutches** andar con muletas

cry *NOUN* grito *MASC*

cry *VERB* ❶ *(weep)* llorar [17] ❷ *(call out)* gritar [17]

crystal *NOUN* cristal *MASC*

cub *NOUN* ❶ *(animal)* cachorro *MASC* ❷ *(scout)* lobato *MASC*

Cuba *NOUN* Cuba *FEM*

Cuban *NOUN* cubano *MASC*, cubana *FEM*

Cuban *ADJECTIVE* cubano/cubana

cube *NOUN* cubo *MASC*; **an ice cube** un cubito de hielo

cubic *ADJECTIVE* *(for measurements)* cúbico/cúbica; **three cubic metres** tres metros cúbicos

cubicle *NOUN* ❶ *(in a changing room)* vestuario *MASC* ❷ *(in a public lavatory)* cubículo *MASC*

cuckoo *NOUN* cuco *MASC*

cucumber *NOUN* pepino *MASC*

cuddle *NOUN* **to give somebody a cuddle** dar [4] un abrazo a alguien

cuddle *VERB* abrazar [22]

cue *NOUN* *(billiards, pool, snooker)* taco *MASC*

cuff *NOUN* *(on a shirt)* puño *MASC*

cul-de-sac *NOUN* callejón *(MASC)* sin salida

culture *NOUN* cultura *FEM*

cunning *ADJECTIVE* astuto/astuta

cup *NOUN* ❶ *(for drinking)* taza *FEM*; **a cup of tea** una taza de té ❷ *(a trophy)* copa *FEM*

cupboard *NOUN* armario *MASC*; **in the kitchen cupboard** en el armario de la cocina

cup tie *NOUN* partido *(MASC)* de copa

cure *NOUN* cura *FEM*

cure *VERB* curar [17]

curiosity *NOUN* curiosidad *FEM*

curious *ADJECTIVE* curioso/curiosa

curl *NOUN* rizo *MASC*

curl *VERB* rizar [22] *(hair)*

curly *ADJECTIVE* rizado/rizada

currant *NOUN* pasa *(FEM)* de Corinto

currency *NOUN* moneda *FEM*; **foreign currency** moneda extranjera

current *NOUN* *(of electricity or water)* corriente *FEM*

current *ADJECTIVE* actual *(a situation, for example)*

current affairs *NOUN* sucesos *(MASC PLURAL)* de actualidad

curriculum *NOUN* ❶ *(national)* plan *(MASC)* de estudios ❷ *(for a single course)* programa *(MASC)* de estudios

curry NOUN curry MASC; **chicken curry** curry de pollo

cursor NOUN cursor MASC

curtain NOUN cortina FEM

cushion NOUN cojín MASC

custard NOUN ❶ (runny) natillas FEM, (plural) ❷ (baked) flan MASC

custom NOUN costumbre MASC

customer NOUN cliente MASC, clienta FEM; **customer services** atención al cliente

customs PLURAL NOUN aduana FEM; **to go through customs** pasar por la aduana

customs hall NOUN aduana FEM

customs officer NOUN agente (MASC & FEM) de aduana

cut NOUN (injury or haircut) corte MASC

cut VERB ❶ cortar [17]; **I've cut the bread** he cortado el pan, **you'll cut yourself!** ¡te vas a cortar!, **Kevin's cut his finger** Kevin se ha cortado el dedo, **to cut the grass** cortar la hierba ❷ **to get your hair cut** cortarse el pelo, **Ayesha's had her hair cut** Ayesha se ha cortado el pelo ❸ **to cut prices** bajar [17] los precios
- **to cut down something** cortar [17] algo (a tree)
- **to cut down on something to cut down on fats** consumir [19] menos grasas
- **to cut out something** ❶ recortar [17] algo (a shape, a newspaper article) ❷ suprimir [19] algo (sugar, fatty food, etc)
- **to cut up something** cortar [17] algo en trocitos (food)

cute ADJECTIVE mono/mona

cutlery NOUN cubertería FEM

CV NOUN currículum (MASC) vitae

cycle NOUN (bike) bicicleta FEM

cycle VERB montar [17] en bicicleta; **do you like cycling?** ¿te gusta montar en bicicleta?, **we cycle to school** vamos al colegio en bicicleta

cycle lane NOUN carril (MASC) de bicicletas

cycle race NOUN carrera (FEM) de ciclismo

cycling NOUN ciclismo MASC

cycling holiday NOUN vacaciones (FEM PLURAL) en bicicleta

cyclist NOUN ciclista MASC & FEM

cylinder NOUN cilindro MASC; **a gas cylinder** una bombona

Dd

dad NOUN ❶ (father) **padre** MASC; **Anna's dad** el padre de Ana, **my dad works in a bank** mi padre trabaja en un banco ❷ (daddy) **papá**; **Dad's not home yet** papá no ha llegado a casa aún

daffodil NOUN **narciso** MASC

daily ADJECTIVE **diario/diaria**; **his daily visit** su visita diaria

daily ADVERB **a diario**; **she visits him daily** le visita a diario

dairy products PLURAL NOUN **productos** (MASC PLURAL) **lácteos**

daisy NOUN **margarita** FEM

dam NOUN **presa** FEM

damage NOUN **daño** MASC; **the damage is done** el daño ya está hecho, **there's no damage** no ha habido daños

damage VERB **dañar** [17]

damn NOUN **he doesn't give a damn** le importa un comino (informal)

damn EXCLAMATION **damn!** ¡maldita sea! (informal)

damp NOUN **humedad** FEM; **because of the damp** a causa de la humedad

damp ADJECTIVE **húmedo/húmeda**

dance NOUN **baile** MASC; **a folk dance** un baile folklórico

dance VERB **bailar** [17]; **I like dancing** me gusta bailar

dancer NOUN **bailarín** MASC, **bailarina** FEM

dancing NOUN **baile** MASC; **I love dancing** me encanta bailar

dancing class NOUN **clase** (FEM) **de baile**; **to go to dancing classes** ir a clase de baile

dandruff NOUN **caspa** FEM

danger NOUN **peligro** MASC; **to be in danger** estar en peligro, **out of danger** fuera de peligro

dangerous ADJECTIVE **peligroso/ peligrosa**; **it's dangerous to drive so fast** es peligroso conducir tan rápido

Danish NOUN **danés** MASC, **danesa** FEM

Danish ADJECTIVE **danés/danesa**

dare VERB ❶ **atreverse** [18]; **to dare to do** atreverse a hacer, **I didn't dare suggest it** no me atreví a sugerirlo, **how dare you!** ¡cómo te atreves! ❷ **don't you dare tell her I'm here!** ¡no se te ocurra decirle que estoy aquí! ❸ **I dare you!** ¡a que no te atreves! (informal), **I dare you to tell him!** ¡a que no te atreves a decírselo! (informal)

daring ADJECTIVE **osado/osada**; **that was a bit daring!** ¡eso ha sido un poco osado!

dark NOUN **in the dark** en la oscuridad, **to be afraid of the dark** tener miedo de la oscuridad, **after dark** de noche

dark ADJECTIVE ❶ (colour or room) **oscuro/oscura**; **a dark blue suit**

un traje azul oscuro, **she has dark brown hair** tiene el pelo castaño oscuro, **the kitchen's a bit dark** la cocina es un poco oscura, **it's dark in here** está oscuro aquí ❷ **it's dark already** ya es de noche, **to get dark** oscurecer, **it gets dark around five** oscurece a eso de las cinco

darkness NOUN oscuridad FEM

darling NOUN querido MASC, querida FEM; **see you later, darling!** ¡te veo luego querido!

dart NOUN dardo MASC; **to play darts** jugar a los dardos

data NOUN información FEM

database NOUN base (FEM) de datos

date NOUN ❶ fecha FEM; **the date of the meeting** la fecha de la reunión, **to fix a date for** fijar una fecha para ❷ **what's the date today?** ¿qué día es hoy? ❸ (when you go out) **I have a date with Jerry on Sunday** he quedado para salir con Jerry el domingo ❹ **out of date** (passport, driving licence, etc) caducado/caducada, (technology, method, information, etc) anticuado/anticuada ❺ (fruit) dátil MASC

date of birth NOUN fecha (FEM) de nacimiento

daughter NOUN hija FEM; **Tina's daughter** la hija de Tina

daughter-in-law NOUN nuera FEM

dawn NOUN amanecer MASC

day NOUN ❶ día MASC; **three days later** tres días más tarde, **it rained all day** llovió todo el día, **it's going to be a nice day tomorrow** mañana va a hacer buen día ❷ **the day after** al día siguiente, **the day after the** wedding el día después de la boda, **the day after tomorrow** pasado mañana, **my sister's arriving the day after tomorrow** mi hermana llega pasado mañana ❸ **the day before** el día anterior, **the day before the wedding** el día antes de la boda, **the day before yesterday** anteayer, **my sister arrived the day before yesterday** mi hermana llegó anteayer ❹ **every day** todos los días

day off NOUN día (MASC) libre

dead ADJECTIVE muerto/muerta; **her father's dead** su padre ha muerto

dead ADVERB (really) super (informal); **he's dead nice** es super majo, **it's dead easy** es super fácil, **it was dead good** fue genial, **you're dead right** tienes toda la razón, **she arrived dead on time** llegó justo a la hora

dead end NOUN callejón (MASC) sin salida

deadline NOUN fecha (FEM) límite

deaf ADJECTIVE sordo/sorda; **to go deaf** quedarse sordo/sorda

deafening ADJECTIVE ensordecedor/ensordecedora

deal NOUN ❶ (involving money) negocio MASC; **it's a good deal** es un buen negocio ❷ (pact) trato MASC; **I'll make a deal with you** voy a hacer un trato contigo, **it's a deal!** ¡trato hecho! ❸ **a great deal of** mucho/mucha, **I don't have a great deal of time** no tengo mucho tiempo, **a great deal of energy** mucha energía ❹ **a great deal** mucho, **it has improved a great deal** ha mejorado mucho

deal VERB (in cards) repartir [19]
• **to deal with something** ocuparse

[17] de algo; **Linda deals with the accounts** Linda se ocupa de las cuentas, **I'll deal with it as soon as possible** me ocuparé de ello tan pronto como sea posible

dear *ADJECTIVE* ❶ querido/querida; **Dear Jo** Querida Jo ❷ *(expensive)* caro/cara

death *NOUN* muerte *FEM*; **after his father's death** después de la muerte de su padre
- **you'll frighten him to death** vas a matarlo del susto
- **I'm bored to death** me muero de aburrimiento
- **I'm sick to death of his complaining** estoy harta de sus quejas

death penalty *NOUN* pena *(FEM)* de muerte

debate *NOUN* debate *MASC*

debate *VERB* debatir [19]

debt *NOUN* deuda *FEM*; **to get into debt** endeudarse [17]

decade *NOUN* década *FEM*

decaffeinated *ADJECTIVE* descafeinado/descafeinada

deceive *VERB* engañar [17]

December *NOUN* diciembre *MASC*

decent *ADJECTIVE* decente; **a decent salary** un sueldo decente, **a decent meal** una comida decente, **he seems a decent enough guy** parece un tipo decente

decide *VERB* decidir [19]; **to decide to do** decidir hacer, **she's decided to buy a car** ha decidido comprarse un coche, **they've decided not to go on holiday** han decidido non irse de vacaciones

decimal *ADJECTIVE* decimal

decimal point *NOUN* decimal *MASC*

decision *NOUN* decisión *FEM*; **the right decision** la decisión acertada, **the wrong decision** la decisión errónea, **to make a decision** tomar una decisión

deck *NOUN* *(on a ship)* cubierta *FEM*

deckchair *NOUN* tumbona *FEM*

declare *VERB* declarar [17]

decorate *VERB* ❶ adornar [17]; **to decorate the Christmas tree** adornar el árbol de Navidad ❷ *(a room) (with paint)* pintar [17] *(with wallpaper)* empapelar [17]

decoration *NOUN* ❶ decoración *FEM* ❷ *(ornament)* adorno *MASC*

decorator *NOUN* pintor *MASC*, pintora *FEM*

decrease *NOUN* disminución *FEM*; **a decrease in the number of** una disminución en el número de

decrease *VERB* disminuir [54]

deduct *VERB* deducir [60]

deep *ADJECTIVE* profundo/profunda; **a deep feeling of gratitude** un profundo sentimiento de gratitud, **the river is very deep here** aquí el río es muy profundo, **how deep is the swimming pool?** ¿qué profundidad tiene la piscina?, **a hole two metres deep** un agujero de dos metros de profundidad

deep end *NOUN* *(of a swimming pool)* **the deep end** la parte honda de la piscina

deep freeze *NOUN* congelador *MASC*

deeply *ADVERB* profundamente

deer *NOUN* ciervo *MASC*

defeat *NOUN* derrota *FEM*

defeat *VERB* derrotar [17]

defect *NOUN* defecto *MASC*

defence *NOUN* defensa *FEM*

defend *VERB* defender [36]

defender *NOUN* ❶ *(of cause)* defensor *MASC*, defensora *FEM* ❷ *(in football)* defensa *MASC & FEM*

define *VERB* definir [19]

definite *ADJECTIVE* ❶ *(clear)* claro/ clara; **a definite improvement** una clara mejora, **a definite advantage** una clara ventaja, **it's a definite possibility** es claramente una posibilidad ❷ *(certain)* seguro/ segura; **it's not definite yet** aún no es seguro ❸ *(exact)* preciso/ precisa; **a definite answer** una respuesta precisa, **I don't have a definite idea of what I want** no tengo una idea precisa de lo que quiero

definite article *NOUN* artículo *(MASC)* definido

definitely *ADVERB* ❶ *(when giving your opinion about something)* sin ninguna duda; **the blue one is definitely the biggest** el azul es sin ninguna duda el más grande, **your French is definitely better than mine** hablas francés mejor que yo sin ninguna duda, **'are you sure you like this one better?' – 'definitely'** ¿estás seguro de que te gusta más éste?' – 'segurísimo' ❷ *(for certain)* **she's definitely going to be there** es seguro que va a estar aquí, **I'm**

definitely not going es seguro que no voy, **she definitely said she would do it** dijo que seguro que lo haría

definition *NOUN* definición *FEM*

degree *NOUN* ❶ grado *MASC*; **thirty degrees** treinta grados ❷ **a university degree** un título universitario

delay *NOUN* retraso *MASC*; **a two-hour delay** un retraso de dos horas

delay *VERB* retrasar [17]; **the flight was delayed by bad weather** el mal tiempo retrasó el vuelo, **the decision has been delayed until Thursday** retrasaron la decisión hasta el jueves

deliberate *ADJECTIVE* deliberado/ deliberada

deliberately *ADVERB* a propósito; **you did it deliberately** lo hiciste a propósito, **he left it there deliberately** lo dejó allí a propósito

delicate *ADJECTIVE* delicado/delicada

delicatessen *NOUN* charcutería *FEM*

delicious *ADJECTIVE* delicioso/ deliciosa

delighted *ADJECTIVE* encantado/ encantada; **they're delighted with their new flat** están encantados con su nuevo piso, **I'm delighted to hear you can come** estoy encantado de saber que puedes venir

deliver *VERB* ❶ *(goods)* entregar [28]; **the person who delivered the parcel** la persona que entregó el paquete ❷ *(mail)* repartir [19]

delivery *NOUN* entrega *FEM*

demand NOUN petición FEM

demand VERB exigir [49]

democracy NOUN democracia FEM

democratic ADJECTIVE democrático/democrática

demolish VERB destruir [54]

demonstrate VERB ❶ demostrar [24] (a theory or a skill) ❷ hacer [7] una demostración de (a machine, product, or technique) ❸ (protest) manifestarse [29]; **to demonstrate against something** manifestarse en contra de algo

demonstration NOUN ❶ (of machine, product, technique) demostración FEM ❷ (protest) manifestación FEM

demonstrator NOUN (in protest) manifestante MASC & FEM

denim NOUN tela (FEM) vaquera; **a denim jacket** una chaqueta vaquera

Denmark NOUN Dinamarca FEM

dense ADJECTIVE denso/densa

dent NOUN abolladura FEM

dent VERB abollar [17]

dental ADJECTIVE ❶ dental; **dental hygiene** higiene (FEM) dental ❷ **a dental appointment** una cita con el dentista

dental floss NOUN hilo (MASC) dental

dental surgeon NOUN cirujano (MASC) dentista, cirujana (FEM) dentista

dentist NOUN dentista MASC & FEM; **my mum's a dentist** mi madre es dentista

deny VERB negar [30]

deodorant NOUN desodorante MASC

depart VERB salir [63]

department NOUN ❶ (in school, university) departamento MASC; **the language department** el departamento de idiomas ❷ (in a shop) sección FEM; **the men's department** la sección de caballeros

department store NOUN grandes almacenes MASC PLURAL

departure NOUN salida FEM

departure gate NOUN puerta (FEM) de embarque

departure lounge NOUN sala (FEM) de embarque

depend VERB **to depend on** depender [18] de, **it depends on the price** depende del precio, **it depends on what you want** depende de lo que tú quieras (note that 'que' is followed by the subjunctive), **it depends** depende

deposit NOUN ❶ (when renting, hiring, or making a booking) depósito MASC; **to pay a deposit** pagar un depósito ❷ (when buying something) entrada FEM

depressed ADJECTIVE deprimido/deprimida

depressing ADJECTIVE deprimente

depth NOUN profundidad FEM

deputy NOUN segundo MASC, segunda FEM

deputy head NOUN subdirector MASC, subdirectora FEM

descend VERB descender [36]

describe *VERB* describir [52]

description *NOUN* descripción *FEM*

desert *NOUN* desierto *MASC*

desert island *NOUN* isla (*FEM*) desierta

deserve *VERB* merecer [35]

design *NOUN* diseño *MASC*; **the design of the plane** el diseño del avión, **fashion design** diseño de moda, **a floral design** un diseño de flores

design *VERB* diseñar [17]

designer *NOUN* diseñador *MASC*, diseñadora *FEM*

desire *NOUN* deseo *MASC*

desire *VERB* desear [17]

desk *NOUN* ❶ (*in office or at home*) escritorio *MASC* ❷ (*pupil's*) pupitre *MASC* ❸ **the reception desk** la recepción, **the information desk** información *FEM*

despair *NOUN* desesperación *FEM*

desperate *ADJECTIVE* ❶ desesperado/ desesperada; **a desperate attempt** un intento desesperado ❷ **to be desperate to do** estar [2] deseando hacer, **I'm desperate to see you** estoy deseando verte

despise *VERB* despreciar [17]

dessert *NOUN* postre *MASC*; **what's for dessert?** ¿qué hay de postre?

destination *NOUN* destino *MASC*

destroy *VERB* destruir [54]

destruction *NOUN* destrucción *FEM*

detached house *NOUN* casa (*FEM*) no adosada

detail *NOUN* detalle *MASC*

detailed *ADJECTIVE* detallado/ detallada

detective *NOUN* ❶ (*police*) agente *MASC & FEM* ❷ **a private detective** un detective privado/una detective privada

detective story *NOUN* novela (*FEM*) policiaca

detention *NOUN* (*in school*) **to be in detention** estar [2] castigado/ castigada

detergent *NOUN* detergente *MASC*

determined *ADJECTIVE* decidido/ decidida; **he's determined to leave** está decidido a irse

detour *NOUN* rodeo *MASC*

develop *VERB* ❶ (*a film*) revelar [17]; **to get a film developed** revelar un carrete de fotos ❷ desarrollarse [17]; **how children develop** cómo se desarrollan los niños

developing country *NOUN* país (*MASC*) en vías de desarrollo

development *NOUN* desarrollo *MASC*

devil *NOUN* diablo *MASC*

devoted *ADJECTIVE* ❶ (*couple or family*) unido/unida ❷ (*admirer*) ferviente

dew *NOUN* rocío *MASC*

diabetes *NOUN* diabetes *FEM*

diabetic *NOUN* diabético *MASC*, diabética *FEM*

diabetic *ADJECTIVE* diabético/ diabética; **to be diabetic** ser diabético/diabética

diagnosis *NOUN* diagnóstico *MASC*

a
b
c
d
e
f
g
h
i
j
k
l
m
n
o
p
q
r
s
t
u
v
w
x
y
z

diagonal ADJECTIVE diagonal

diagram NOUN diagrama MASC

dial VERB marcar [31]; dial 00 34 for Spain marca 00 34 para España

dialling tone NOUN tono (MASC) de marcar

dialogue NOUN diálogo MASC

diameter NOUN diámetro MASC

diamond NOUN ❶ diamante MASC ❷ (in cards) diamonds diamantes, the jack of diamonds la jota de diamantes ❸ (shape) rombo MASC

diarrhoea NOUN diarrea FEM; to have diarrhoea tener [9] diarrea

diary NOUN ❶ (for dates) agenda FEM; I've noted the date of the meeting in my diary he anotado la fecha de la reunión en mi agenda ❷ (personal) diario (MASC) íntimo; to keep a diary tener [9] un diario íntimo

dice NOUN dado MASC; to throw the dice tirar [17] los dados

dictation NOUN dictado MASC

dictionary NOUN diccionario MASC; to look up a word in the dictionary buscar [31] una palabra en el diccionario

did VERB ▶ SEE do

die VERB ❶ morir [55]; my grandmother died in January mi abuela murió en enero ❷ to be dying to do something estar [2] deseando hacer algo, I'm dying to see them! ¡estoy deseando verlos!
• **die out** desaparecer [35]; the tradition is dying out la tradición está desapareciendo

diesel NOUN ❶ diesel MASC ❷ a diesel engine un motor diesel, a diesel car un diesel

diet NOUN ❶ dieta FEM; to have a healthy diet llevar una dieta saludable ❷ (slimming or special) régimen MASC; to be on a diet estar a régimen, to go on a diet ponerse a régimen, a salt-free diet un régimen sin sal

difference NOUN ❶ diferencia FEM; I can't see any difference between the two no puedo ver ninguna diferencia entre los dos, what's the difference between ...? ¿qué diferencia hay entre ...? ❷ it makes a difference eso cambia las cosas, it makes no difference da lo mismo, it makes no difference what I say da lo mismo lo que yo diga

different ADJECTIVE distinto/distinta; the two sisters are very different las dos hermanas son muy distintas, she's very different from her sister es muy distinta a su hermana

difficult ADJECTIVE difícil; it's really difficult es muy difícil, it's difficult to decide es difícil decidir

difficulty NOUN ❶ dificultad FEM ❷ I had difficulty finding your house me resultó difícil encontrar tu casa

dig VERB cavar [17]; to dig a hole cavar [17] un agujero

digestion NOUN digestión FEM

digital ADJECTIVE digital; a digital watch un reloj digital

dignity NOUN dignidad FEM

dim ADJECTIVE ❶ tenue; a dim light una luz tenue ❷ she's a bit dim es un poco tonta (informal)

dimension NOUN dimensión FEM

din NOUN ruido MASC; **they were making a dreadful din** estaban haciendo un ruido enorme, **stop making such a din!** ¡deja de hacer tanto ruido!

dinghy NOUN ❶ **a sailing dinghy** un bote ❷ **a rubber dinghy** un bote neumático

dining room NOUN comedor MASC; **in the dining room** en el comedor

dinner NOUN ❶ (evening meal) cena FEM; **to have dinner** cenar [17], **to invite somebody to dinner** invitar [17] a alguien a cenar ❷ (midday meal) comida FEM; **to have dinner** comer [18], **to have school dinner** comer [18] en el colegio

dinner party NOUN cena FEM

dinner time NOUN ❶ (evening) hora (FEM) de cenar ❷ (midday) hora (FEM) de comer

dinosaur NOUN dinosaurio MASC

diploma NOUN diploma MASC

direct ADJECTIVE directo/directa; **a direct flight** un vuelo directo

direct ADVERB directo; **the bus goes direct to the airport** el autobús va directo al aeropuerto

direct VERB ❶ (a programme, film, play or traffic) dirigir [49] ❷ (give directions to) indicarle [31] el camino a; **I directed them to the station** les indiqué el camino a la estación

direction NOUN ❶ dirección FEM; **in the direction of the church** en dirección a la iglesia, **in the other direction** en la otra dirección ❷ **to**

ask somebody for directions pedir a alguien que te indique el camino ❸ **directions for use** instrucciones (FEM PLURAL), de uso

directly ADVERB ❶ (to go, fly, deal or ask) directamente ❷ (at once) inmediatamente ❸ **directly afterwards** inmediatamente después

director NOUN director MASC, directora FEM, (of a company, programme, film or play)

directory NOUN guía (FEM) telefónica; **to be ex-directory** no estar en la guía telefónica

dirt NOUN suciedad FEM

dirty ADJECTIVE sucio/sucia; **my hands are dirty** tengo las manos sucias, **to get something dirty** ensuciar [17] algo, **I got the floor dirty** ensucié el suelo, **you'll get your dress dirty** te vas a ensuciar el vestido, **to get dirty** ensuciarse [17], **the curtains get dirty quickly** las cortinas se ensucian rápido

disability NOUN discapacidad FEM; **does he have a disability?** ¿tiene alguna discapacidad?

disabled ADJECTIVE discapacitado/discapacitada; **disabled people** los discapacitados

disadvantage NOUN ❶ desventaja FEM ❷ **to be at a disadvantage** estar en desventaja

disagree VERB **I disagree** no estoy de acuerdo, **I disagree with James** no estoy de acuerdo con James

disappear VERB desaparecer [35]

disappearance NOUN desaparición FEM

disappointed *ADJECTIVE*
decepcionado/decepcionada; **I was disappointed with my marks** mis notas me decepcionaron

disappointment *NOUN* decepción *FEM*

disaster *NOUN* desastre *MASC*; **it was a complete disaster** fue un completo desastre

disastrous *ADJECTIVE* desastroso/desastrosa

disc *NOUN* ❶ **a compact disc** un disco compacto ❷ **a slipped disc** una hernia de disco

discipline *NOUN* disciplina *FEM*

disc-jockey *NOUN* disc-jockey *MASC & FEM*

disco *NOUN* ❶ baile *MASC*; **they're having a disco** tienen un baile ❷ *(club)* discoteca *FEM*

disconnect *VERB* desconectar [17]; **have you disconnected the electricity?** ¿has desconectado la electricidad?

discount *NOUN* descuento *MASC*

discourage *VERB* ❶ *(depress)* desanimar [17] ❷ **to discourage somebody from doing** convencer a alguien de que no haga *(note that 'que no' is followed by the subjunctive)*, **I tried to discourage her from buying it** intenté convencerla de que no lo comprase

discover *VERB* descubrir [46]

discovery *NOUN* descubrimiento *MASC*

discreet *ADJECTIVE* discreto/discreta

discrimination *NOUN* discriminación *FEM*; **racial discrimination** discriminación racial

discuss *VERB* ❶ *(a subject or topic)* hablar [17] de; **to discuss politics** hablar [17] de política, **I'm going to discuss it with Phil** voy a hablarlo con Phil ❷ *(a problem or plan)* discutir [19]

discussion *NOUN* discusión *FEM*

disease *NOUN* enfermedad *FEM*

disgraceful *ADJECTIVE* vergonzoso/vergonzosa

disguise *NOUN* disfraz *MASC*; **to be in disguise** ir disfrazado

disguise *VERB* disfrazar [22]; **to disguise oneself as something** disfrazarse [22] de algo, **disguised as a woman** disfrazado de mujer

disgust *NOUN* ❶ *(indignation)* indignación *FEM* ❷ *(physical revulsion)* asco *MASC*

disgusted *ADJECTIVE* ❶ *(indignant)* indignado/indignada ❷ *(physically sick)* asqueado/asqueada

disgusting *ADJECTIVE* asqueroso/asquerosa

dish *NOUN* ❶ *(plate or food)* plato *MASC*; **to do the dishes** lavar [17] los platos, **he cooked my favourite dish** cocinó mi plato favorito ❷ *(serving dish)* fuente *FEM*; **a large white dish** una fuente grande blanca

dishcloth *NOUN* *(for drying up)* paño *(MASC)* de cocina

dishonest *ADJECTIVE* deshonesto/deshonesta

dishonesty NOUN falta (FEM) de honradez

dish towel NOUN paño (MASC) de cocina

dishwasher NOUN lavaplatos MASC (does not change in the plural)

disinfect VERB desinfectar [17]

disinfectant NOUN desinfectante MASC

disk NOUN disco MASC; **a floppy disk** un disquete, **the hard disk** el disco duro, **the disk drive** la disquetera

diskette NOUN disquete MASC

dislike VERB **I dislike sport** no me gusta el deporte, **he dislikes my friends** no le gustan mis amigos

dismay NOUN consternación FEM

dismiss VERB despedir [57] (an employee)

disobedient ADJECTIVE desobediente

disobey VERB desobedecer [35]; **she disobeyed the rules** desobedeció el reglamento

display NOUN ❶ exposición FEM; **a handicrafts display** una exposición de artesanía, **to be on display** estar expuesto ❷ **a window display** un escaparate ❸ **a firework display** fuegos (MASC PLURAL) artificiales

display VERB exponer [11]

disposable ADJECTIVE desechable

dispute NOUN ❶ (quarrel) disputa FEM ❷ (argument) polémica FEM

disqualify VERB descalificar [31]

dissolve VERB disolver [45]

distance NOUN distancia FEM; **from a distance** de lejos, **in the distance** a lo lejos, **it's within walking distance** se puede ir andando

distant ADJECTIVE distante

distinct ADJECTIVE claro/clara

distinctly ADVERB ❶ claramente ❷ **it's distinctly odd** es realmente raro

distract VERB distraer [42]

distribute VERB distribuir [54]

distribution NOUN distribución FEM

district NOUN ❶ (in town) barrio MASC; **a poor district of Barcelona** un barrio pobre de Barcelona ❷ (in the country) región FEM

disturb VERB molestar [17]; **sorry to disturb you** perdona que te moleste, **do not disturb** se ruega no molestar

ditch NOUN zanja FEM

ditch VERB **to ditch somebody** plantar [17] a alguien (informal)

dive NOUN zambullida FEM

dive VERB tirarse [17]; **to dive into the water** tirarse al agua

diver NOUN (deep-sea) submarinista MASC & FEM

diversion NOUN (for traffic) desvío MASC

divide VERB dividir [19]

diving NOUN ❶ (from a board) saltos (MASC PLURAL) de trampolín ❷ (from the surface of the water) submarinismo MASC

a
b
c
d
e
f
g
h
i
j
k
l
m
n
o
p
q
r
s
t
u
v
w
x
y
z

A
B
C
D
E
F
G
H
I
J
K
L
M
N
O
P
Q
R
S
T
U
V
W
X
Y
Z

diving board NOUN **trampolín** MASC

division NOUN **división** FEM

divorce NOUN **divorcio** MASC

divorce VERB **divorciarse** [17]; **they divorced in Mexico** se divociaron en México

divorced ADJECTIVE **divorciado/ divorciada**; **my parents are divorced** mis padres están divorciados

DIY NOUN **bricolaje** MASC; **to do DIY** hacer [7] bricolaje, **a DIY shop** una tienda de bricolaje

dizzy ADJECTIVE **to feel dizzy** estar [2] mareado/mareada, **I feel dizzy** estoy mareado

DJ NOUN **disc-jockey** MASC & FEM

do VERB ❶ **hacer** [7]; **what are you doing?** ¿qué estás haciendo?, **I'm doing my homework** estoy haciendo mis deberes, **what have you done with the hammer?** ¿qué has hecho con el martillo? ❷ (in questions, 'do' is not translated) **did Maria go to the party?** ¿fue María a la fiesta?, **do you want some strawberries?** ¿quieres fresas?, **when does it start?** ¿cuándo empieza?, **how did you open the door?** ¿cómo has abierto la puerta? ❸ (in negative sentences) (the negative in Spanish is formed adding 'no' before the verb) **I don't like this kind of music** no me gusta este tipo de música, **Rosie doesn't like spinach** a Rosie no le gustan las espinacas, **you didn't shut the door** no has cerrado la puerta, **it doesn't matter** no importa ❹ (when it refers back to another verb, 'do' is not translated) **'do you live here?'**

– 'yes, I do' ¿vives aquí?' – 'sí', **she has more money than I do** tiene más dinero que yo, **'I live in Oxford' – 'so do I'** 'vivo en Oxford' – 'yo también', **'I didn't phone Gemma' – 'neither did I'** 'no he llamado a Gemma' – 'yo tampoco' ❺ **don't you?, doesn't he?** etc. ¿no?, **you know Helen, don't you?** conoces a Helen, ¿no?, **she left on Thursday, didn't she?** se marchó el jueves, ¿no? ❻ **that'll do** así basta, **it'll do like that** así vale

- **do with** ❶ **tener** [9] que ver con; **it has nothing to do with him** no tiene nada que ver con él ❷ **I could do with a rest** me vendría bien un descanso

- **to do something up** ❶ **atar** [17] (shoes); **I did my shoes up** me até los zapatos ❷ **abrochar** [17] (cardigan, jacket); **do your jacket up** abróchate la chaqueta ❸ **arreglar** [17] (house)

- **to do without something** **arreglarse** [17] sin algo; **we can do without knives** nos arreglaremos sin cuchillos

doctor NOUN **médico** MASC & FEM; **her mother's a doctor** su madre es médico

document NOUN **documento** MASC

documentary NOUN **documental** MASC

dodgems PLURAL NOUN **the dodgems** los cochecitos de choque

dog NOUN **perro** MASC, **perra** FEM

do-it-yourself NOUN **bricolage** MASC

dole NOUN **paro** MASC; **to be on the dole** estar en el paro

doll NOUN **muñeca** FEM

dollar NOUN **dólar** MASC

dolphin NOUN **delfín** MASC

dominate VERB **dominar** [17]

Dominican NOUN **dominicano** MASC, **dominicana** FEM

Dominican ADJECTIVE **dominicano/dominicana**

Dominican Republic NOUN **República Dominicana** FEM

domino NOUN **ficha** (FEM) **de dominó**; **to play dominoes jugar al dominó**

donation NOUN **donación** FEM

donkey NOUN **burro** MASC

don't ▸ SEE **do**

door NOUN **puerta** FEM; **to open the door abrir** [46] **la puerta**, **to shut the door cerrar** [29] **la puerta**

doorbell NOUN **timbre** MASC; **to ring the doorbell tocar** [31] **el timbre**, **there's the doorbell llaman a la puerta**

doorstep NOUN **umbral** (MASC) **de la puerta**

dormitory NOUN **dormitorio** MASC

dot NOUN ❶ (written) **punto** MASC ❷ (on fabric) **lunar** MASC ❸ **at ten on the dot a las diez en punto**

double ADJECTIVE, ADVERB ❶ **doble**; **a double helping una ración doble**, **a double whisky un whisky doble**, **a double room una habitación doble**, **a double bed una cama de matrimonio** ❷ **el doble**; **double the time el doble de tiempo**, **double the price el doble del precio**

double bass NOUN **contrabajo** MASC; **to play the double bass tocar** [31] **el contrabajo**

double-breasted ADJECTIVE **a double-breasted jacket una chaqueta cruzada**

double-decker bus NOUN **autobús** (MASC) **de dos pisos**

double glazing NOUN **doble ventana** FEM

doubles NOUN (in tennis) **dobles** MASC PLURAL; **to play a game of doubles jugar un partido de dobles**

doubt NOUN **duda** FEM; **there's no doubt about it no hay ninguna duda al respecto**, **I have my doubts tengo mis dudas**

doubt VERB **to doubt something dudar** [17] **algo**, **I doubt it lo dudo**, **I doubt that dudo que** (note that 'que' is followed by the subjunctive), **I doubt they'll do it dudo que lo hagan**

doubtful ADJECTIVE ❶ **it's doubtful that no es seguro que** (note that 'que' is followed by the subjunctive), **it's doubtful that she'll want to no es seguro que quiera** ❷ **to be doubtful about doing dudar** [17] **si hacer**, **I'm doubtful about inviting them together estoy dudando si invitarlos a los dos juntos**

dough NOUN **masa** FEM

doughnut NOUN **donut** MASC

down ADVERB, PREPOSITION ❶ **abajo**; **he's down in the cellar está abajo, en el sótano** ❷ **down the road** (nearby) **un poco más allá**, **there's a chemist's just down the road hay una farmacia un poco más allá** ❸ **to**

go down bajar [17], **I went down to the kitchen** bajé a la cocina, **to walk down the street** bajar la calle, **to run down the stairs** bajar corriendo la escalera ❹ **to come down** bajar [17], **she came down from her bedroom** bajó de la habitación ❺ **to sit down** sentarse [29], **she sat down on the sofa** se sentó en el sofá

downstairs ADVERB ❶ abajo; **she's downstairs in the sitting-room** está abajo en el salón, **the dog sleeps downstairs** el perro duerme abajo ❷ (after a noun) de abajo; **the flat downstairs** el piso de abajo, **the people downstairs** la gente de abajo

doze VERB dormitar [17]

dozen NOUN docena FEM; **a dozen eggs** una docena de huevos

drag NOUN **what a drag!** ¡qué rollo! (informal), **she's a bit of a drag** es un poco pesada (informal)

drag VERB arrastrar [17]

dragon NOUN dragón MASC

drain NOUN ❶ (plughole) desagüe MASC ❷ (in street) alcantarilla FEM

drain VERB escurrir [19] (vegetables)

drama NOUN ❶ (subject) arte (MASC) dramático ❷ **he made a big drama about it** montó una escena por eso (informal)

dramatic ADJECTIVE dramático/dramática

draught NOUN corriente (FEM) de aire

draughts NOUN damas FEM PLURAL; **to play draughts** jugar a las damas

draw NOUN ❶ (in a match) empate MASC; **it was a draw** fue un empate ❷ (lottery) sorteo MASC

draw VERB ❶ dibujar [17]; **I can't draw horses** no sé dibujar caballos, **she can draw really well** dibuja muy bien ❷ **to draw a picture** hacer [7] un dibujo ❸ **to draw the curtains** correr [18] las cortinas ❹ **to draw a crowd** atraer [42] a una multitud ❺ (in a match) empatar [17]; **we drew three all** empatamos a tres ❻ **to draw lots for something** echar [17] algo a suertes

drawback NOUN inconveniente MASC

drawer NOUN cajón MASC

drawing NOUN dibujo MASC

drawing pin NOUN chincheta FEM

dreadful ADJECTIVE terrible

dreadfully ADVERB ❶ (to sing or act) espantosamente ❷ **I'm dreadfully late** llego tardísimo, **I'm dreadfully sorry** lo siento muchísimo

dream NOUN sueño MASC; **to have a dream** tener [9] un sueño, **I had a horrible dream last night** tuve un sueño horrible anoche

dream VERB soñar [24]; **to dream about something** soñar con algo

drenched ADJECTIVE empapado/empapada; **to get drenched** empaparse [17], **I got drenched on the way home** me empapé yendo a casa

dress NOUN **vestido** MASC

dress VERB **vestir** [57]; **to dress a child** vestir a un niño
• **to dress up** disfrazarse [22]; **to dress up as a vampire** disfrazarse de vampiro

dressed ADJECTIVE ❶ **vestido/vestida**; **is Tom dressed?** ¿está Tom vestido?, **she was dressed in black trousers and a yellow shirt** iba vestida con unos pantalones negros y una blusa amarilla ❷ **to get dressed** vestirse [57]

dresser NOUN (for dishes) **aparador** MASC

dressing gown NOUN **bata** FEM

dressing table NOUN **tocador** MASC

drier NOUN **a hair drier** un secador de pelo, **a tumble drier** una secadora

drift NOUN **a snow drift** una ventisca de nieve

drill NOUN ❶ (tool) **taladradora** FEM ❷ (in homework) **ejercicio** MASC

drink NOUN ❶ **bebida** FEM; **a hot drink** una bebida caliente, **a cold drink** un refresco ❷ **would you like a drink?** ¿te apetece beber algo? ❸ **to go out for a drink** salir [63] a tomar una copa (informal)

drink VERB **beber** [18]; **he drank a glass of water** bebió un vaso de agua

drive NOUN ❶ **to go for a drive** ir [8] a dar una vuelta en coche ❷ (up to a house) **entrada** (FEM) para coches

drive VERB ❶ **conducir** [60]; **she drives very fast** conduce muy rápido, **to drive a car** conducir [60] un coche, **I'd like to learn to drive**

me gustaría aprender a conducir, **can you drive?** ¿sabes conducir? ❷ **ir** [8] en coche; **we drove to Seville** fuimos en coche a Sevilla ❸ **to drive somebody (to a place)** llevar [17] en coche a alguien (a un sitio), **Mum drove me to the station** mamá me llevó en coche a la estación, **to drive somebody home** llevar [17] a alguien a casa en coche
• **she drives me mad!** ¡me saca de quicio!

driver NOUN ❶ (of a car, taxi or bus) **conductor** MASC, **conductora** FEM ❷ (of a racing car) **piloto** MASC & FEM

driving instructor NOUN **instructor** (MASC) **de autoescuela**, **instructora** (FEM) **de autoescuela**

driving lesson NOUN **clase** (FEM) **de conducir**

driving licence NOUN **permiso** (MASC) **de conducir**

driving school NOUN **autoescuela** FEM

driving test NOUN **examen** (MASC) **de conducir**; **to take your driving test** presentarse [17] al examen de conducir, **Jenny's passed her driving test** Jenny ha aprobado el examen de conducir

drop NOUN **gota** FEM

drop VERB ❶ **I dropped my glasses** se me cayeron las gafas, **careful, don't drop it!** ¡cuidado, que no se te caiga! ❷ (a course, subject or topic) **dejar** [17]; **I'm going to drop history next year** voy a dejar la historia el próximo año ❸ **dejar** [17] (a person); **could you drop me at the station?** ¿me podrías dejar en la estación? ❹ **drop it!** ¡déjalo ya!

A
B
C
D
E
F
G
H
I
J
K
L
M
N
O
P
Q
R
S
T
U
V
W
X
Y
Z

drought NOUN **sequía** FEM

drown VERB **ahogarse** [28]; **she drowned in the lake** se ahogó en el lago

drug NOUN ❶ (medicine) **medicina** FEM ❷ (illegal) **drugs** las drogas, **to be on drugs** drogarse [28]

drug abuse NOUN **consumo** (MASC) **de drogas**

drug addict NOUN **drogadicto** MASC, **drogadicta** FEM

drug addiction NOUN **drogadicción** FEM

drum NOUN ❶ **tambor** MASC ❷ **drums** batería FEM, **to play drums** tocar [31] la batería

drum kit NOUN **batería** FEM

drummer NOUN **batería** MASC & FEM

drunk NOUN **borracho** MASC, **borracha** FEM

drunk ADJECTIVE **borracho/borracha**

dry ADJECTIVE **seco/seca**

dry VERB ❶ **secar** [31]; **to dry the dishes** secar los platos ❷ **to let something dry** dejar que algo se seque, **it took ages to dry** tardó muchísimo en secarse ❸ **to dry oneself** secarse [31], **to dry your hair** secarse [31] el pelo, **I'm going to dry my hair** me voy a secar el pelo

dry cleaner's NOUN **tintorería** FEM

dryer NOUN ► SEE **drier**

dual carriageway NOUN **autovía** FEM

dubbed ADJECTIVE **a dubbed film** una película doblada

duck NOUN **pato** MASC, **pata** FEM

due ADJECTIVE, ADVERB ❶ **to be due to do** tener [9] que hacer, **we're due to leave on Thursday** tenemos que salir el jueves, **Paul's due back soon** Paul tiene que volver pronto ❷ **what time is the train due?** ¿cuándo llega el próximo tren? ❸ **due to** debido a, **the match has been cancelled due to bad weather** el partido ha sido cancelado debido al mal tiempo

duke NOUN **duque** MASC

dull ADJECTIVE ❶ **dull weather** tiempo gris, **it's a dull day today** hoy hace un día muy gris ❷ (boring) **aburrido/aburrida**

dumb ADJECTIVE ❶ **mudo/muda**; **to be deaf and dumb** ser sordomudo/ sordomuda ❷ (stupid) **tonto/tonta**; **he asked some dumb questions** hizo unas preguntas muy tontas

dummy NOUN (for a baby) **chupete** MASC

dump VERB ❶ **tirar** [17] (rubbish) ❷ **plantar** [17] (a person) (informal); **she's dumped her boyfriend** ha plantado a su novio

dune NOUN **duna** FEM

dungarees PLURAL NOUN **pantalón** (MASC) **de peto**

dungeon NOUN **mazmorra** FEM

during PREPOSITION **durante**; **during the night** durante la noche, **I saw her during the holidays** la vi durante las vacaciones

dusk NOUN anochecer MASC; **at dusk** al anochecer

dust NOUN polvo MASC

dust VERB quitar [17] el polvo; **to dust the table** quitarle el polvo a la mesa

dustbin NOUN cubo (MASC) de la basura; **to put something in the dustbin** tirar [17] algo al cubo de la basura

dustman NOUN basurero MASC

dusty ADJECTIVE cubierto/cubierta de polvo

Dutch NOUN ❶ (language) holandés MASC ❷ **the Dutch** (people) los holandeses

Dutch ADJECTIVE holandés/holandesa

duty NOUN ❶ deber MASC; **to have a duty to do** tener [9] el deber de hacer, **you have a duty to inform us** tienes el deber de informarnos ❷ **to be on duty** (a nurse or doctor) estar [2] de guardia (a policeman) estar [2] de servicio, **to be on night duty** tener [9] el turno de noche

duty-free ADJECTIVE libre de impuestos; **the duty-free shops** las tiendas libres de impuestos, **duty-free purchases** artículos libres de impuestos

duvet NOUN edredón MASC

duvet cover NOUN funda (FEM) de edredón

dwarf NOUN enano MASC, enana FEM

dye NOUN tinte MASC

dye VERB teñir [65]; **to dye your hair** teñirse [65] el pelo, **I'm going to dye my hair pink** me voy a teñir el pelo de rosa

dynamic ADJECTIVE dinámico/dinámica

dyslexia NOUN dislexia FEM

dyslexic ADJECTIVE disléxico/disléxica

a
b
c
d
e
f
g
h
i
j
k
l
m
n
o
p
q
r
s
t
u
v
w
x
y
z

Ee

each ADJECTIVE **cada**; **each time** cada vez, **curtains for each window** cortinas para cada ventana

each PRONOUN **cada uno/una**; **my sisters each have a computer** mis hermanas tienen un ordenador cada una, **she gave us an apple each** nos dio una manzana a cada uno, **each of you** cada uno de vosotros, **we each bought a book** cada uno de nosotros compró un libro, **the tickets cost ten pounds each** las entradas cuestan diez libras cada una

each other PRONOUN *('each other' is usually translated using a reflexive pronoun)* **they love each other** se quieren, **we know each other** nos conocemos, **do you often see each other?** ¿os veis a menudo?

eagle NOUN **águila** FEM *(even though 'águila' is feminine, it takes 'el' and 'un' in the singular)*

ear NOUN **oreja** FEM

earache NOUN **to have earache** tener dolor de oídos

earlier ADVERB ❶ *(a while ago)* hace un rato; **your brother phoned earlier** tu hermano llamó hace un rato ❷ *(not as late)* más temprano; **we should have started earlier** deberíamos haber empezado más temprano, **earlier in the morning** por la mañana temprano

early ADVERB ❶ *(in the morning)* temprano; **I get up early** me levanto temprano, **it's too early** es demasiado temprano ❷ *(for an appointment)* pronto; **we're early, the train doesn't leave until ten** hemos llegado pronto, el tren no sale hasta las diez, **Grandma likes to be early** a la abuela le gusta llegar pronto

early ADJECTIVE ❶ *(one of the first)* primero/primera; **in the early months** en los primeros meses ❷ **to have an early lunch** comer temprano, **Jan's having an early night** Jan se ha acostado temprano, **we're making an early start** vamos a salir temprano ❸ **in the early afternoon** a primera hora de la tarde, **in the early hours** de madrugada

earn VERB **ganar** [17] *(money)*; **Richard earns four pounds an hour** Richard gana cuatro libras por hora

earnings PLURAL NOUN **ingresos** MASC PLURAL

earphones PLURAL NOUN **auriculares** MASC PLURAL

earring NOUN **pendiente** MASC

earth NOUN **tierra** FEM; **life on earth** la vida en la tierra
- **what on earth are you doing?** ¿qué demonios estás haciendo?

earthquake NOUN **terremoto** MASC

easily ADVERB ❶ *(to do something)* con facilidad ❷ *(by far)* con mucho; **he's easily the best** es con mucho el mejor

east NOUN **este** MASC; **in the east** en el este

east ADJECTIVE, ADVERB **the east side** el lado este, **an east wind** un viento del este, **east of Seville** al este de Sevilla

Easter NOUN Semana (FEM) Santa; **they're coming at Easter** vienen en Semana Santa

Easter Day NOUN Domingo (MASC) de Pascua

Easter egg NOUN huevo (MASC) de Pascua

Eastern Europe NOUN Europa (FEM) del Este

easy ADJECTIVE fácil; **it's easy!** ¡es fácil!, **it was easy to decide** fue fácil decidir

eat VERB ❶ comer [18]; **he was eating a banana** estaba comiendo un plátano, **we're going to have something to eat** vamos a comer algo ❷ tomar [17] (a meal); **we were eating breakfast** estábamos tomando el desayuno ❸ **to eat out** comer [18] fuera

EC NOUN CE FEM, Comunidad (FEM) Europea

echo NOUN eco MASC

echo VERB hacer [7] eco

eclipse NOUN eclipse MASC

ecological ADJECTIVE ecológico/ ecológica

ecologist NOUN ecologista MASC, ecologista FEM

ecology NOUN ecología FEM

economic ADJECTIVE ❶ (relating to economics) económoco/ económica ❷ (profitable) rentable

economical ADJECTIVE económico/ económica (way of doing something); **it's more economical to buy a big one** sale más económico comprar uno grande

economics NOUN economía FEM

economy NOUN economía FEM

Ecuador NOUN Ecuador MASC

Ecuadorian NOUN ecuatoriano MASC, ecuatoriana FEM

Ecuadorian ADJECTIV ecuatoriano/ ecuatoriana

eczema NOUN eczema MASC

edge NOUN ❶ (of table, plate, or cliff) borde MASC; **the edge of the table** el borde de la mesa ❷ (of river or lake) orilla FEM; **at the edge of the lake** en la orilla del lago ❸ **to be on edge** estar nervioso

edible ADJECTIVE comestible

Edinburgh NOUN Edimburgo MASC

edit VERB editar [17]

editor NOUN (of a newspaper) redactor MASC, redactora FEM

educate VERB (a teacher) educar [31]

education NOUN educación FEM

educational ADJECTIVE educativo/ educativa

effect NOUN efecto MASC; **the effect of the accident** el efecto del accidente, **to have an effect on** afectar [17] a, **it had a good effect on the whole family** afectó positivamente a toda la familia, **special effects** efectos especiales

effective ADJECTIVE eficaz

a b c d e f g h i j k l m n o p q r s t u v w x y z

efficient ADJECTIVE eficiente

effort NOUN esfuerzo MASC; **to make an effort** hacer [7] un esfuerzo, **Jess made an effort to help us** Jess hizo un esfuerzo para ayudarnos, **he didn't even make the effort to apologize** ni sí quiera se molestó en disculparse, **it's not worth the effort** no merece la pena

e.g. ABBREVIATION p.ej.

egg NOUN huevo MASC; **a dozen eggs** una docena de huevos, **a fried egg** un huevo frito, **two boiled eggs** dos huevos pasados por agua, **a hard-boiled egg** un huevo duro, **scrambled eggs** huevos revueltos

egg-cup NOUN huevera FEM

eggshell NOUN cáscara (FEM) de huevo

egg-white NOUN clara (FEM) de huevo

egg-yolk NOUN yema (FEM) de huevo

eight NUMBER ocho MASC; **Rosie's eight** Rosie tiene ocho años, **it's eight o'clock** son las ocho

eighteen NUMBER dieciocho; **Kate's eighteen** Kate tiene dieciocho años

eighth NOUN ❶ (fraction) **an eighth** una octava parte ❷ **the eighth of July** el ocho de julio

eighth ADJECTIVE octavo/octava; **on the eighth floor** en la octava planta

eighties PLURAL NOUN **the eighties** los años ochenta, **in the eighties** en los años ochenta

eighty NUMBER ochenta MASC; **she's eighty** tiene ochenta años, **eighty-five** ochenta y cinco

Eire NOUN Irlanda MASC & FEM

either PRONOUN ❶ (one or the other) **choose either (of them)** elige cualquiera (de los dos), **I don't like either (of them)** no me gusta ninguno (de los dos) ❷ (both) **either is possible** las dos cosas son posibles

either CONJUNCTION ❶ **either ... or** o ... o, **you either pay or return it** o pagas o lo devuelves, **I'll phone either Thursday or Friday** llamaré o el jueves o el viernes ('o' becomes 'u' before a word starting with 'o' or 'ho') **either one or the other** o uno u otro ❷ (with a negative) **he doesn't want to go either** él tampoco quiere ir, **I don't know them either** yo tampoco los conozco

elastic NOUN elástico MASC

elastic ADJECTIVE elástico/elástica

elastic band NOUN goma (FEM) elástica

elbow NOUN codo MASC

elder ADJECTIVE mayor; **her elder brother** su hermano mayor

elderly ADJECTIVE **an elderly man** un anciano, **an elderly woman** una anciana, **an elderly couple** una pareja de ancianos, **the elderly** los ancianos

eldest ADJECTIVE mayor; **her eldest brother** su hermano mayor

elect VERB elegir [48]; **she has been elected** ha sido elegida

election NOUN elecciones FEM PLURAL; **in the election** en las elecciones, **to call a general election** convocar [31] elecciones generales

electric ADJECTIVE eléctrico/eléctrica

electrical ADJECTIVE eléctrico/eléctrica

electrician NOUN electricista MASC & FEM

electricity NOUN electricidad FEM; **to turn off the electricity** desconectar [17] la corriente

electronic ADJECTIVE electrónico/electrónica

electronic mail NOUN correo (MASC) electrónico

electronics NOUN electrónica FEM

elegant ADJECTIVE elegante

element NOUN elemento MASC

elephant NOUN elefante MASC

eleven NUMBER once MASC; **Josh is eleven** Josh tiene once años, **it's eleven o'clock** son las once

eleventh NOUN **the eleventh of May** el once de mayo

eleventh ADJECTIVE onceavo/onceava; **on the eleventh floor** en la onceava planta

eliminate VERB eliminar [17]

else ADVERB ❶ (in questions and negative sentences) más; **who else?** ¿quién más?, **what else?** ¿qué más?, **nothing else** nada más, **I don't want anything else** no quiero nada más ❷ **somebody else** otra persona, **somebody else must have done it** lo ha debido hacer otra persona ❸ **something else** otra cosa, **would you like something else?** ¿quieres otra cosa? ❹ **everybody else** todos los demás, **everything else** todo lo demás ❺ **somewhere else** en otra

parte ❻ **or else** si no, **hurry up, or else we'll be late** date prisa, que si no vamos a llegar tarde

e-mail NOUN correo (MASC) electrónico

embankment NOUN ❶ (by a river) muro (MASC) de contención ❷ (by a railway) terraplén MASC

embarrassed ADJECTIVE **I was terribly embarrassed** me daba mucha vergüenza, **she feels a bit embarrassed** le da un poco de vergüenza

embarrassing ADJECTIVE violento/violenta (situation or silence); **how embarrassing!** ¡qué vergüenza!

embarrassment NOUN vergüenza FEM

embassy NOUN embajada FEM; **the Spanish Embassy** la embajada española

embroider VERB bordar [17]

embroidery NOUN bordado MASC

emergency NOUN ❶ emergencia FEM; **in an emergency, break the glass** en caso de emergencia, rompa el cristal, **it's an emergency!** ¡es una emergencia! ❷ (medical) urgencia FEM; **an emergency operation** una operación de urgencia

emergency exit NOUN salida (FEM) de emergencia

emergency landing NOUN aterrizaje (MASC) forzoso

emotion NOUN emoción FEM

emotional ADJECTIVE ❶ (person) **to be emotional** estar [2] emocionado/emocionada, **to get emotional**

a b c d e f g h i j k l m n o p q r s t u v w x y z

emocionarse [17], **she got quite emotional** se emocionó mucho ❷ *(a speech or an occasion)* **emotivo/emotiva**

emperor NOUN **emperador** MASC

emphasis NOUN **énfasis** MASC

emphasize VERB **recalcar** [31]; **he emphasized that it wasn't compulsory** recalcó que no era obligatorio

empire NOUN **imperio** MASC; **the Roman Empire** el imperio romano

employ VERB ❶ *(have in employment)* **emplear** [17] ❷ *(give work to)* **dar** [4] un trabajo a

employee NOUN **empleado** MASC, **empleada** FEM

employer NOUN **patrón** MASC, **patrona** FEM

employment NOUN **empleo** MASC

empress NOUN **emperatriz** FEM

empty ADJECTIVE **vacío/vacía**; **an empty bottle** una botella vacía, **the room was empty** la habitación estaba vacía

empty VERB **vaciar** [32]; **I emptied the teapot into the sink** vacié la tetera en el fregadero

enchanting ADJECTIVE **encantador/encantadora**

enclose VERB *(in a letter)* **adjuntar** [17]; **please find enclosed a cheque** se adjunta un cheque

encore NOUN **bis** MASC; **encore!** ¡otra!

encourage VERB **animar** [17]; **to encourage somebody to do** animar a alguien a hacer, **Mum encouraged**

me to try again mamá me animó a intentarlo otra vez

encouragement NOUN **ánimo** MASC

encouraging ADJECTIVE **alentador/alentadora**

encyclopedia NOUN **enciclopedia** FEM

end NOUN ❶ *(last part)* **final** MASC; **at the end of the film** al final de la película, **by the end of the day** al final del día, **in the end I went home** al final me fui a casa ❷ **at the end of the year** a finales de año, **Sally's coming at the end of June** Sally viene a finales de junio ❸ **'The End'** *(in a book or film)* 'Fin' ❹ *(of a table, garden, or stick, for example)* **extremo** MASC; **hold the other end** sujeta el otro extremo ❺ *(of a street or road)* **final** MASC; **at the end of the street** al final de la calle ❻ *(of a football pitch)* **lado** MASC; **to change ends** cambiar [17] de lado

end VERB ❶ *(put an end to)* **poner** [11] fin a *(an arrangement)*; **they've ended the strike** han puesto fin a la huelga ❷ *(to come to an end)* **terminar** [17]; **the day ended with a dinner** el día terminó con una cena
• **to end up** terminar [17]; **we ended up taking a taxi** terminamos cogiendo un taxi, **Ross ended up in San Francisco** Ross terminó en San Francisco

endangered ADJECTIVE **en peligro**; **an endangered species** una especie en en vías de extinción

ending NOUN **final** MASC

endless ADJECTIVE **interminable**

enemy *NOUN* enemigo *MASC*, enemiga *FEM*; **to make enemies** hacer [7] enemigos

energetic *ADJECTIVE* energético/ energética

energy *NOUN* energía *FEM*

engaged *ADJECTIVE* ❶ *(to be married)* prometido/prometida; **they're engaged** están prometidos, **to get engaged** prometerse [18] ❷ *(a phone)* comunicando; **it's engaged, I'll ring later** está comunicando, llamaré más tarde ❸ *(a toilet)* ocupado/ocupada

engagement *NOUN* *(to marry)* compromiso *MASC*

engagement ring *NOUN* anillo *(MASC)* de compromiso

engine *NOUN* ❶ *(in a car)* motor *MASC* ❷ *(locomotive)* locomotora *FEM*

engineer *NOUN* ❶ *(who does repairs)* técnico *MASC & FEM* ❷ *(who builds roads and bridges)* ingeniero *MASC*, ingeniera *FEM*

England *NOUN* Inglaterra *FEM*; **I'm from England** soy inglés

English *NOUN* ❶ *(the language)* inglés *MASC*; **do you speak English?** ¿hablas inglés?, **he answered in English** contestó en inglés ❷ *(English people)* **the English** los ingleses

English *ADJECTIVE* ❶ *(of or from England)* inglés/inglesa; **the English team** el equipo inglés ❷ **an English lesson** una clase de inglés, **our English teacher** nuestro profesor de inglés

English Channel *NOUN* **the English Channel** el Canal de la Mancha

Englishman *NOUN* inglés *MASC*

Englishwoman *NOUN* inglesa *FEM*

enjoy *VERB* ❶ disfrutar [17]; **did you enjoy the party?** ¿disfrutaste de la fiesta?, **we really enjoyed the concert** disfrutamos mucho del concierto ❷ **I enjoy swimming** me gusta nadar, **do you enjoy living in York?** ¿te gusta vivir en York? ❸ **to enjoy youself** divertirse [14], **we really enjoyed ourselves** nos divertimos muchísimo, **did you enjoy yourself?** ¿te divertiste?

enjoyable *ADJECTIVE* agradable

enlarge *VERB* ampliar [32]

enlargement *NOUN* *(of a photo)* ampliación *FEM*

enormous *ADJECTIVE* enorme

enough *ADVERB, PRONOUN* ❶ suficiente; **there's enough for everyone** hay suficiente para todos, **is there enough bread?** ¿hay pan suficiente?, **there weren't enough books** no había libros suficientes ❷ *(with an adjective or adverb)* lo suficientemente; **big enough** lo suficientemente grande, **slowly enough** lo suficientemente despacio ❸ **that's enough** ya basta

enquire *VERB* informarse [17]; **I'm going to enquire about the trains** voy a informarme sobre los trenes

enquiry *NOUN* **to make enquiries about something** pedir [57] información sobre algo

enrol *VERB* matricularse [17]; **I want to enrol on the course** quiero matricularme en el curso

enter VERB ❶ (go inside) **entrar** [17] **en** (a room or building); **we all entered the church** todos entramos en la iglesia ❷ **to enter for** presentarse [17] a (an exam), tomar [17] parte en (a race or competition)

entertain VERB ❶ (keep amused) **entretener** [9]; **something to entertain the children** algo para entretener a los niños ❷ (have people round) **invitar** [17] **a gente**; **they don't entertain much** no invitan a mucha gente

entertaining NOUN **they do a lot of entertaining** invitan a mucha gente

entertaining ADJECTIVE **entretenido/ entretenida**

entertainment NOUN (fun) **entretenimiento** MASC; **there wasn't much entertainment in the evenings** por las noches no había mucho entretenimiento

enthusiasm NOUN **entusiasmo** MASC

enthusiast NOUN **to be a rugby enthusiast** ser [1] un apasionado/ una apasionada del rugby

enthusiastic ADJECTIVE **entusiasta**

entire ADJECTIVE **entero/entera**; **the entire class** la clase entera

entirely ADVERB **completamente**

entrance NOUN **entrada** FEM

entry NOUN (the way in) **entrada** FEM; **'no entry'** 'prohibida la entrada'

entry phone NOUN **portero** (MASC) **automático**

envelope NOUN **sobre** MASC

envious ADJECTIVE **envidioso/ envidiosa**; **he's envious of my**

exam results tiene envidia de las notas de mis exámenes

environment NOUN **medio** (MASC) **ambiente**

environmental ADJECTIVE **medioambiental**

environment-friendly ADJECTIVE **ecológico/ecológica**

envy NOUN **envidia** FEM

epidemic NOUN **epidemia** FEM

epileptic NOUN **epiléptico** MASC, **epiléptica** FEM

episode NOUN **episodio** MASC

equal ADJECTIVE **igual**; **in equal quantities** en cantidades iguales

equal VERB **ser** [1] **igual a**

equality NOUN **igualdad** FEM

equalize VERB **empatar** [17]; **they equalized in the last minute** empataron en el último minuto

equally ADJECTIVE (to share) **en partes iguales**; **we divided it equally** lo dividimos en partes iguales

equator NOUN **ecuador** MASC

equip VERB **equipar** [17]; **well equipped for the walk** bien equipado para la marcha

equipment NOUN ❶ (for sport) **artículos** (MASC PLURAL) **deportivos** ❷ (in office or lab) **material** MASC

equivalent ADJECTIVE **to be equivalent to** ser [1] equivalente a

error NOUN ❶ (in spelling or typing) **falta** FEM; **a spelling error** una falta de ortografía ❷ (in maths or on a computer) **error** MASC

escalator NOUN escalera (FEM) mecánica

escape NOUN (from prison) fuga FEM

escape VERB ❶ (a person) fugarse [28] ❷ (an animal) escaparse [17]

escort NOUN escolta FEM; **a police escort** una escolta policial

especially ADJECTIVE especialmente

essay NOUN redacción FEM; **an essay on pollution** una redacción sobre la contaminación

essential ADJECTIVE esencial; **it's essential to reply quickly** es esencial responder rápidamente

estate NOUN ❶ (a housing estate) urbanización FEM ❷ (a big house and grounds) propiedad FEM

estate agent's NOUN agencia (FEM) inmobiliaria

estate car NOUN coche (MASC) ranchera

estimate NOUN ❶ (a quote for work) presupuesto MASC ❷ (a rough guess) cálculo (MASC) aproximado

estimate VERB ❶ calcular [17] ❷ **the estimated time of arrival** la hora prevista de llegada

etc. ABBREVIATION etc

ethnic ADJECTIVE étnico/étnica; **an ethnic minority** una minoría étnica

EU ABBREVIATION EU FEM, Unión (FEM) Europea

euro NOUN euro MASC; **the euro is divided into a hundred cents** el euro se divide en cien céntimos

Europe NOUN Europa FEM

European NOUN europeo MASC, europea FEM

European ADJECTIVE europeo/europea

European Union NOUN Unión (FEM) Europea

eurozone NOUN eurozona FEM

evaporate VERB evaporarse [17]

eve NOUN **Christmas Eve** Nochebuena FEM, **New Year's Eve** Nochevieja FEM

even¹ ADVERB ❶ incluso; **even I could do it** incluso yo podría hacerlo ❷ (in comparisons) **even more difficult** aún más difícil, **even faster** aún más rápido, **even more than** aún más que, **I liked the song even more than their last one** la canción me gustó aún más que la anterior ❸ (in negative sentences or after 'without') ni siquiera; **even Lisa didn't like it** ni siquiera a Lisa le gustó, **without even asking** sin ni siquiera preguntar, **not even** ni siquiera, **I don't like animals, not even dogs** no me gustan los animales, ni siquiera los perros ❹ **even if** incluso si, **even if they arrive** incluso si llegan ❺ **even so** aun así, **even so, we had a good time** aun así lo pasamos bien ❻ **even though** aunque

even² ADJECTIVE ❶ (a surface or layer) plano/plana ❷ (a number) par; **six is an even number** seis es un número par ❸ (with the same score) igualado/igualada; **Lee and Tony are even** Lee y Tony están igualados

evening NOUN ❶ (before dark) tarde FEM (after dark) noche FEM; **this evening** (before dark) esta tarde (after dark) esta noche, **at six o'clock**

in the evening a las seis de la tarde, **at ten in the evening** a las diez de la noche, **tomorrow evening** mañana por la tarde, mañana por la noche, **on Thursday evening** el jueves por la tarde, el jueves por la noche, **the evening before** la tarde anterior, la noche anterior, **every evening** cada tarde, cada noche, **good evening** buenas tardes, buenas noches, **I work in the evening(s)** trabajo por las noches ❷ **the evening meal** la cena ❸ *(event)* velada *FEM*; **an evening with Pavarotti** una velada con Pavarotti

evening class *NOUN* **clase** *(FEM)* **nocturna**

event *NOUN* ❶ *(a happening)* **acontecimiento** *MASC* ❷ *(in athletics)* **prueba** *FEM*; **track events** pruebas de atletismo

eventful *ADJECTIVE* **lleno de incidentes**

eventually *ADVERB* **finalmente**

ever *ADVERB* ❶ *(at any time)* **alguna vez**; **have you ever been to Spain?** ¿has estado alguna vez en España?, **have you ever noticed that?** ¿lo notaste alguna vez?, **hardly ever** casi nunca, **no-one ever came** nunca vino nadie, **more slowly than ever** más despacio que nunca ❷ *(always)* **siempre**; **as cheerful as ever** tan contento como siempre, **the same as ever** como siempre ❸ **ever since** desde entonces, **and it's been raining ever since** y ha estado lloviendo desde entonces

every *ADJECTIVE* ❶ **todos/todas**; **every house has a garden** todas las casas tienen jardín, **every day** todos los días, **every Monday** todos los lunes, **I've seen every one of his**

films he visto todas sus películas ❷ *(repetition)* **cada**; **every ten kilometres** cada diez kilómetros, **every time** cada vez ❸ **every now and then** de vez en cuando, **every second day** un día sí y otro no

everybody, **everyone** *PRONOUN* **todo el mundo**; **everybody knows that ...** todo el mundo sabe que ..., **everyone else** todos los demás

everything *PRONOUN* **todo**; **everything's ready** está todo listo, **everything's fine** está todo bien, **everything else** todo lo demás, **everything you said** todo lo que dijiste

everywhere *ADVERB* **there was mud everywhere** había barro por todas partes, **everywhere she went** a todos los sitios a los que fue, **everywhere else is closed** todos los demás sitios están cerrados

evidently *ADVERB* **obviamente**

evil *NOUN* **mal** *MASC*

evil *ADJECTIVE* **malvado/malvada**

exact *ADJECTIVE* **exacto/exacta**; **the exact amount** la cantidad exacta, **it's the exact opposite** es exactamente lo contrario

exactly *ADVERB* **exactamente**; **they're exactly the same age** tienen exactamente la misma edad, **yes, exactly** exacto

exaggerate *VERB* **exagerar** [17]

exaggeration *NOUN* **exageración** *FEM*

exam *NOUN* **examen** *MASC*; **a history exam** un examen de historia, **to sit an exam** presentarse [17] a un examen, **to pass an exam** aprobar

[24] un examen, **to fail an exam** suspender [18] un examen

examination NOUN examen MASC

examine VERB examinar [17]

examiner NOUN examinador MASC, examinadora FEM

example NOUN ejemplo MASC; **for example** por ejemplo, **to set a good example** dar [4] buen ejemplo

excellent ADJECTIVE excelente

except PREPOSITION excepto; **except in March** excepto en marzo, **except Tuesdays** excepto los martes, **except when it rains** excepto cuando llueve

exception NOUN excepción FEM; **without exception** sin excepción, **with the exception of** con la excepción de

exchange NOUN ❶ *(of information or students)* intercambio MASC; **an exchange visit** un viaje de intercambio ❷ **in exchange for his help** a cambio de su ayuda

exchange VERB cambiar [17]; **can I exchange this shirt for a smaller one?** ¿puedo cambiar esta camisa por una más pequeña?

exchange rate NOUN tipo (MASC) de cambio

excited ADJECTIVE ❶ *(happy)* entusiasmado/entusiasmada; **they're really excited about the idea** están entusiasmados con la idea ❷ *(noisy, boisterous)* alborotado/alborotada; **the children were too excited** los niños estaban demasiado alborotados ❸ **to get excited** *(happy)* entusiasmarse [17] *(boisterous)*

alborotarse [17], **the dogs get excited when they hear the car** los perros se alborotan cuando oyen el coche

excitement NOUN emoción FEM

exciting ADJECTIVE emocionante; **a really exciting film** una película realmente emocionante

exclamation mark NOUN signo *(MASC)* de admiración

excursion NOUN excursión FEM

excuse NOUN excusa FEM; **Gary has a good excuse** Gary tiene una buena excusa, **that's no excuse** eso no es excusa, **to make excuses** poner [11] excusas

excuse VERB *(apologizing)* **excuse me!** ¡perdón!

exercise NOUN ejercicio MASC; **a maths exercise** un ejercicio de matemáticas, **physical exercise** ejercicio físico

exercise book NOUN cuaderno MASC; **my Spanish exercise book** mi cuaderno de español

exhaust (pipe) NOUN tubo *(MASC)* de escape

exhausted ADJECTIVE agotado/ agotada

exhaust fumes NOUN gases *(MASC PLURAL)* del tubo de escape

exhibition NOUN exposición FEM; **the Cézanne exhibition** la exposición de Cézanne

exist VERB existir [19]

exit NOUN salida FEM

A B C D E F G H I J K L M N O P Q R S T U V W X Y Z

expect VERB ❶ esperar [17] *(guests or a baby)*; **we're expecting about thirty people** esperamos unas treinta personas ❷ esperarse [17] *(something to happen)*; **I didn't expect that** no me esperaba eso, **I didn't expect it at all** no me lo esperaba en absoluto ❸ *(to suppose)* suponer [11]; **I expect you're tired** supongo que estarás cansado, **I expect she'll bring her boyfriend** supongo que traerá a su novio, **yes, I expect so** supongo que sí

expedition NOUN expedición FEM

expel VERB **to be expelled** *(from school)* ser [1] expulsado

expenses NOUN gastos MASC PLURAL

expensive ADJECTIVE caro/cara; **those shoes are too expensive for me** esos zapatos son demasiado caros para mí, **the most expensive hotels** los hoteles más caros

experience NOUN experiencia FEM

experienced ADJECTIVE con experiencia

experiment NOUN experimento MASC; **to do an experiment** hacer [7] un experimento

expert NOUN experto MASC, experta FEM; **he's a computer expert** es un experto en ordenadores

expire VERB caducar [31]

expiry date NOUN fecha *(FEM)* de caducidad

explain VERB explicar [31]

explanation NOUN explicación FEM

explode VERB explotar [17]

explore VERB explorar [17]

explosion NOUN explosión FEM

export VERB exportar [17]

export NOUN exportación FEM; **wool is the most important export** el artículo de exportación más importante es la lana

export VERB exportar [17]; **Russia exports a lot of timber and oil** Rusia exporta mucha madera y petróleo

exposure NOUN *(of a film)* exposición FEM; **a 24-exposure film** un carrete de veinticuatro fotos

express NOUN *(a train)* rápido MASC

express VERB ❶ expresar [17] ❷ **to express yourself** expresarse [17]

expression NOUN expresión FEM

extend VERB ampliar [32] *(a building)*

extension NOUN ❶ *(to a house)* ampliación FEM ❷ *(telephone)* extensión FEM; **can I have extension 2347 please?** ¿me puede poner con la extensión veintitrés cuarenta y siete, por favor? *(note that in spoken Spanish telephone numbers are usually said in pairs; this also applies to long numbers)*

extension lead NOUN alargador MASC

extension number NOUN número *(MASC)* de extensión

extinct ADJECTIVE extinto/extinta; **to become extinct** extinguirse [50]

extinguish *VERB* apagar [28]

extinguisher *NOUN* (fire extinguisher) extintor *MASC*

extra *ADJECTIVE, ADVERB* ❶ they gave us some extra homework nos dieron más deberes ❷ you have to pay extra tiene que pagar un suplemento, **to charge extra for something** cobrar [17] un suplemento por algo, **wine is extra** el vino se cobra aparte, **at no extra charge** sin coste suplementario ❸ extra hot super picante, **extra large** super grande

extraordinary *ADJECTIVE* extraordinario/extraordinaria

extra-special *ADJECTIVE* super especial

extra time *NOUN* (in football) prórroga *FEM*

extravagant *ADJECTIVE* derrochador/derrochadora (a person)

extreme *NOUN* extremo *MASC*; **to go to extremes** llevar [17] las cosas al extremo

extreme *ADJECTIVE* extremo/ extrema

extremely *ADVERB* extremely difficult dificilísimo, **extremely fast** rapidísimo

eye *NOUN* ojo *MASC*; **a girl with blue eyes** una niña con ojos azules, **shut your eyes!** ¡cierra los ojos!
- **to keep an eye on something** vigilar [17] algo
- **to make eyes at somebody** hacerle [7] ojitos a alguien (informal)

eyebrow *NOUN* ceja *FEM*

eyelash *NOUN* pestaña *FEM*

eyelid *NOUN* párpado *MASC*

eyeliner *NOUN* delineador (MASC) de ojos

eye make-up *NOUN* maquillaje (MASC) de ojos

eye shadow *NOUN* sombra (FEM) de ojos

eyesight *NOUN* vista *FEM*

a
b
c
d
e
f
g
h
i
j
k
l
m
n
o
p
q
r
s
t
u
v
w
x
y
z

fabric NOUN tela FEM

fabulous ADJECTIVE fabuloso/fabulosa

face NOUN ❶ (of a person) cara FEM; **on your face** en la cara ❷ **to pull a face** hacer [7] muecas ❸ (of a clock or watch) esfera FEM

face VERB ❶ (a person) enfrentarse [17] a ❷ (to be opposite) estar [2] frente a; **the hotel faces the sea** el hotel está frente al mar ❸ **it faces south** está orientado hacia el sur ❹ **I can't face going back** no soporto la idea de volver

face cloth NOUN toalla (FEM) de cara

facilities PLURAL NOUN ❶ **sports facilities** instalaciones (FEM PLURAL) deportivas ❷ **the flat has cooking facilities** el piso tiene cocina

fact NOUN hecho MASC; **in fact** de hecho, **is that a fact?** ¿es eso cierto?

factory NOUN fábrica FEM

fail VERB ❶ suspender [18] (a test or exam); **I failed my driving test** he suspendido el examen de conducir, **three students failed** tres estudiantes suspendieron ❷ **to fail to do** no hacer, **he failed to contact us** no se puso en contacto con nosotros
• **without fail** sin falta; **ring me without fail** llámame sin falta

failure NOUN ❶ fracaso MASC; **it was a terrible failure** fue un fracaso terrible ❷ **a power failure** un apagón

faint ADJECTIVE ❶ **to feel faint** sentirse [14] mareado/mareada ❷ (slight) ligero/ligera; **a faint smell of gas** un ligero olor a gas, **I haven't the faintest idea** no tengo ni la más remota idea ❸ (a voice or sound) débil

faint VERB desmayarse [17]; **Lisa fainted** Lisa se desmayó

fair NOUN feria FEM

fair ADJECTIVE ❶ (not unfair) justo/justa; **it's not fair!** ¡no es justo! ❷ (hair) rubio/rubia; **he's fair-haired** tiene el pelo rubio ❸ (skin) blanco/blanca ❹ (fairly good) bastante bueno/buena

fairground NOUN parque (MASC) de atracciones

fairly ADVERB (quite) bastante; **she's fairly happy** es bastante feliz

fairy NOUN hada FEM, (even though 'hada' is feminine, it takes 'el' and 'un' in the singular)

fairy tale NOUN cuento (MASC) de hadas

faith NOUN ❶ (trust) confianza FEM; **to have faith in somebody** tener confianza en alguien ❷ (religious belief) fe FEM

faithful ADJECTIVE fiel

faithfully ADVERB **yours faithfully** le saluda atentamente

fall NOUN caída FEM; **to have a fall** sufrir [19] una caída

fall VERB ❶ caerse [34]; **mind, you'll fall** cuidado, te vas a caer, **Tony fell off his bike** Tony se cayó de la bici, **she fell downstairs** se cayó por las escaleras, **my jacket fell on the floor** mi chaqueta se cayó al suelo ❷ *(the temperature or prices)* bajar [17]; **it fell to minus eleven last night** la temperatura bajó a once grados bajo cero anoche

false ADJECTIVE falso/falsa; **a false passport** un pasaporte falso; **a false alarm** una falsa alarma

false teeth PLURAL NOUN dentadura *(FEM SINGULAR)* postiza

fame NOUN fama FEM

familiar ADJECTIVE familiar; **your face is familiar** tu cara me es familiar

family NOUN familia FEM; **a family of six** una familia de seis personas, **Ben's one of the family** Ben es uno de la familia, **the Bunting family** la familia Bunting

family name NOUN apellido MASC

famous ADJECTIVE famoso/famosa

fan NOUN ❶ *(of a pop group)* fan MASC & FEM *(informal)*; **Sarah's an Oasis fan** Sarah es fan de Oasis ❷ *(of a team)* hincha MASC & FEM; **Martin's a Chelsea fan** Martin es hincha del Chelsea ❸ *(electric, for cooling)* ventilador MASC ❹ *(that you hold in your hand)* abanico MASC

fanatic NOUN fanático MASC, fanática FEM

fancy NOUN **the picture took his fancy** se encaprichó del cuadro

fancy ADJECTIVE *(equipment)* sofisticado/sofisticada, *(hotel)* de lujo

fancy VERB ❶ *(to want)* **do you fancy a coffee?** ¿te apetece un café?, **I don't fancy going out** no me apetece salir ❷ **I really fancy him** me gusta mucho ❸ **(just) fancy that!** ¡imagínate!, **fancy you being here!** ¡qué casualidad que estés aquí!

fancy dress NOUN disfraz MASC; **in fancy dress** disfrazado/disfrazada, **a fancy-dress party** una fiesta de disfraces

fantastic ADJECTIVE estupendo/estupenda *(informal)*; **really? that's fantastic!** ¿de verdad?¡ eso es estupendo!, **a fantastic holiday** unas vacaciones estupendas

far ADVERB, ADJECTIVE ❶ lejos; **it's not far** no está lejos, **is it far to Cordoba?** ¿está muy lejos Córdoba?, **how far is it to Granada?** ¿a qué distancia está Granada?, **he took us as far as Bilbao** nos llevó hasta Bilbao ❷ **by far** con mucho, **the prettiest by far** es con mucho la más bonita ❸ *(much)* mucho; **far better** mucho mejor, **far faster** mucho más rápido ❹ **far too many people** demasiada gente, **far too much noise** demasiado ruido ❺ **so far** hasta ahora, **so far everything's going well** hasta ahora todo va bien, **as far as I know** que yo sepa

fare NOUN precio *(MASC)* del billete; **half fare** medio billete MASC, **full fare** billete *(MASC)* entero, **the return fare to Barcelona** el billete de ida y vuelta a Barcelona

Far East NOUN Lejano Oriente MASC

farm NOUN granja FEM

farmer NOUN agricultor MASC, agricultora FEM

farmhouse   **feed**

farmhouse NOUN casa (FEM) de labranza

farming NOUN agricultura FEM

farthest ADJECTIVE más lejano/más lejana; **the farthest hill** la colina más lejana

farthest PRONOUN lo más lejos; **the farthest we went** lo más lejos que fuimos aquel día

fascinating ADJECTIVE fascinante

fashion NOUN moda FEM; **in fashion** de moda, **out of fashion** pasado/pasada de moda

fashionable ADJECTIVE de moda

fashion model NOUN modelo MASC & FEM

fashion show NOUN desfile (MASC) de modas

fast ADJECTIVE ❶ rápido/rápida; **a fast car** un coche rápido ❷ **my watch is fast** mi reloj adelanta, **you're ten minutes fast** vas diez minutos adelantado

fast ADVERB ❶ rápido; **she swims very fast** nada muy rápido ❷ **to be fast asleep** estar [2] profundamente dormido

fast food NOUN comida (FEM) rápida

fat NOUN grasa FEM

fat ADJECTIVE gordo/gorda; **a fat man** un hombre gordo, **to get fat** engordar [17]

fatal ADJECTIVE (accident) fatal

father NOUN padre MASC; **my father's office** la oficina de mi padre

Father Christmas NOUN Papá (MASC) Noel

father-in-law NOUN suegro MASC

father's day NOUN día (MASC) del padre

fault NOUN ❶ (responsibility) culpa FEM; **it's Steve's fault** es culpa de Steve, **it's not my fault** no es culpa mía ❷ (in tennis) falta FEM

favour NOUN ❶ (a kindness) favor MASC; **to do somebody a favour** hacerle [7] un favor a alguien, **can you do me a favour?** ¿me haces un favor?, **to ask a favour of somebody** pedirle [57] un favor a alguien ❷ **to be in favour of something** estar [2] a favor de algo

favourite ADJECTIVE favorito/favorita; **my favourite band** mi grupo favorito

fear NOUN miedo MASC

fear VERB temer [18]

feather NOUN pluma FEM

feature NOUN ❶ (of your face) rasgo MASC; **to have delicate features** tener [9] rasgos delicados ❷ (of a machine, product, etc.) característica FEM

February NOUN febrero MASC; **in February** en febrero

fed up ADJECTIVE **I'm fed up** estoy harto/harta (informal), **I'm fed up with working every day** estoy harta de trabajar todos los días

feed VERB dar [4] de comer a; **have you fed the dog?** ¿has dado de comer al perro?

feel VERB ❶ sentirse [14]; **I feel tired** me siento cansada, **I don't feel well** no me siento bien ❷ sentir [14]; **I didn't feel a thing** no sentí nada ❸ **to feel afraid** tener [9] miedo, **to feel cold** tener [9] frío, **to feel thirsty** tener [9] sed ❹ **I feel like some chocolate** me apetece un poco de chocolate, **do you feel like a walk?** ¿te apetece dar un paseo?, **I don't feel like it** no me apetece ❺ **to feel like doing** tener [9] ganas de hacer, **I feel like going to the cinema** tengo ganas de ir al cine ❻ (touch) tocar [31]

feeling NOUN ❶ (in your mind) sentimiento MASC; **a feeling of embarrassment** un sentimiento de vergüenza, **to show your feelings** de mostrar los sentimientos, **to hurt somebody's feelings** herir [14] los sentimientos de alguien ❷ (in your body) sensación FEM; **a dizzy feeling** una sensación de mareo ❸ (impression) impresión FEM; **I have the feeling James doesn't like me** tengo la impresión de que no le caigo bien a James

felt-tip (pen) NOUN rotulador MASC

female NOUN (animal) hembra FEM

female ADJECTIVE ❶ femenino/ femenina (person, population) ❷ hembra (animal, insect)

feminine ADJECTIVE femenino/ femenina

feminist NOUN, ADJECTIVE feminista MASC & FEM

fence NOUN valla FEM

fern NOUN helecho MASC

ferry NOUN ferry MASC

fetch VERB ir [8] a por; **Tom's fetching the children** Tom ha ido a por los niños, **fetch me the other knife!** ¡vete a por el otro cuchillo!

fever NOUN fiebre FEM

few ADJECTIVE, PRONOUN ❶ pocos/ pocas; **few people think that ...** pocos piensan que ... ❷ **a few** (followed by a noun) algunos/ algunas, **a few weeks earlier** algunas semanas antes, **in a few minutes** dentro de algunos minutos ❸ **a few** (by itself) unos cuantos/ unas cuantas, **have you any tomatoes? we want a few for the salad** ¿tienes tomates? queremos unos cuantos para la ensalada, **a few more books** unos cuantos libros más ❹ **quite a few** bastantes, **there were quite a few questions** hubo bastantes preguntas

fewer ADJECTIVE menos; **there are fewer tourists this year** hay menos turistas este año, **fewer than six** menos de seis

fiancé NOUN prometido MASC

fiancée NOUN prometida FEM

fiction NOUN ficción FEM

field NOUN campo MASC; **a field of wheat** un campo de trigo, **a football field** un campo de fútbol

fifteen NUMBER quince MASC; **Lara's fifteen** Lara tiene quince años

fifth NOUN ❶ (fraction) **a fifth** una quinta parte ❷ **the fifth of January** el cinco de enero

fifth ADJECTIVE quinto/quinta; **on the fifth floor** en la quinta planta

fifties PLURAL NOUN **the fifties** los años cincuenta, **in the fifties** en los años cincuenta

fifty NUMBER cincuenta MASC; **she's fifty** tiene cincuenta años, **fifty-five** cincuenta y cinco

fig NOUN higo MASC

fight NOUN ❶ (a scuffle or in boxing) **pelea** FEM ❷ (in war or against illness or poverty) **lucha** FEM

fight VERB ❶ (in war or against poverty or a disease) **luchar** [17] ❷ (to quarrel) **pelear** [17]; **they're always fighting** siempre se están peleando

figure NOUN ❶ (number) cifra FEM; **a four-figure number** un número de cuatro cifras ❷ (body shape) figura FEM ❸ (a person) personaje MASC; **a public figure** un personaje público

file NOUN ❶ (for records of a person or case) **archivo** MASC ❷ (in computer system) **fichero** MASC ❸ (ring binder) **archivador** MASC ❹ (cardboard folder for documents) **carpeta** FEM ❺ **a nail file** una lima

file VERB ❶ **archivar** [17] (documents) ❷ **to file your nails** limarse [17] las uñas

fill VERB **llenar** [17]; **she filled my glass** me llenó el vaso
• **to fill in** rellenar [17] (a form)

filling NOUN ❶ (of pie) **relleno** MASC ❷ (in tooth) **empaste** MASC

film NOUN ❶ (in a cinema) **película** FEM; **shall we go and see a film?** ¿vamos a ver una película?, **the new film about Picasso** la nueva película sobre Picasso ❷ (for a camera) **carrete** (MASC) **de fotos; a**

24-exposure colour film un carrete de color de veinticuatro fotos

film star NOUN **estrella** (FEM) **de cine**

filthy ADJECTIVE **asqueroso/ asquerosa** (informal)

final NOUN (in sport) **final** FEM

final ADJECTIVE ❶ (definite) **final; the final result** el resultado final ❷ (last) **último/última; the final instalment** el último plazo

finally ADVERB **finalmente**

find VERB **encontrar** [24]; **did you find your passport?** ¿has encontrado tu pasaporte?, **I can't find my keys** no puedo encontrar mis llaves
• **to find out** ❶ (to enquire) informarse [17]; **I don't know, I'll find out** no lo sé, me informaré ❷ **to find something out** descubrir [46] algo (the facts or an answer), **when Lucy found out the truth** cuando Lucy se enteró de la verdad

fine NOUN **multa** FEM

fine ADJECTIVE ❶ **bien; 'how are you?' – 'fine, thanks'** '¿cómo estás?' – 'bien, gracias', **ten o'clock? yes, that's fine** ¿a las diez? sí, está bien, **Friday will be fine** el viernes está bien ❷ (very good) **muy bueno/ buena; she's a fine athlete** es muy buena atleta ❸ (weather or a day;) **bueno/buena; if it's fine** si hace buen tiempo ❹ (not coarse or thick) **fino/fina; in fine wool** de lana fina

finely ADJECTIVE (chopped or grated) **muy fino/fina**

finger NOUN **dedo** MASC
• **I'll keep my fingers crossed for you** te deseo suerte

fingernail NOUN uña FEM

finish NOUN ❶ (end) final MASC ❷ (in a race) llegada FEM

finish VERB ❶ terminar [17]; **wait, I haven't finished** espera, no he terminado, **when does school finish?** ¿cuándo termina el colegio?, **have you finished the book?** ¿has terminado el libro? ❷ **to finish doing** terminar [17] de hacer, **have you finished telephoning?** ¿has terminado de llamar por teléfono?
- **to finish with** terminar [17] con; **have you finished with the computer?** ¿has terminado con el ordenador?

finishing line NOUN meta FEM

Finland NOUN Finlandia FEM

Finn NOUN Finlandés MASC, Finlandesa FEM

Finnish NOUN (the language) finlandés MASC

Finnish ADJECTIVE finlandés/finlandesa

fire NOUN ❶ (in a grate) fuego MASC; **to light the fire** encender [36] el fuego ❷ (accidental) incendio MASC ❸ **to catch fire** prenderse [18] fuego, **to be on fire** estar [2] ardiendo

fire VERB (to shoot) disparar [17]; **to fire at somebody** disparar a alguien

fire alarm NOUN alarma (FEM) contra incendios

fire brigade NOUN cuerpo (MASC) de bomberos

fire engine NOUN coche (MASC) de bomberos

fire escape NOUN escalera (FEM) de incendios

fire extinguisher NOUN extintor MASC

firefighter NOUN bombero MASC & FEM

fireplace NOUN chimenea FEM

fire station NOUN estación (FEM) de bomberos

fireworks PLURAL NOUN fuegos (MASC PLURAL) artificiales

firm NOUN (business) empresa FEM

firm ADJECTIVE firme

first NOUN **the first of May** el primero de mayo

first PRONOUN, ADJECTIVE, ADVERB ❶ primero/primera; **Susan's the first** Susan es la primera, **the first of May** el primero de Mayo, **for the first time** por primera vez, **Christy got here first** Christy llegó aquí la primera, **Ben came first in the 200 metres** Ben llegó el primero en los doscientos metros ❷ (to begin with) primero; first, **I'm going to make some tea** primero voy a hacer té, **first of all** en primer lugar ❸ **at first** al principio, **at first he didn't want to** al principio no quería

first aid NOUN primeros auxilios MASC PLURAL

first aid kit NOUN botiquín (MASC) de primeros auxilios

first class ADJECTIVE, ADVERB de primera (a ticket, carriage, or hotel); **a first-class compartment** un compartimento de primera, **he always travels first class** siempre viaja en primera

first floor NOUN **primera planta** FEM; **on the first floor** en la primera planta

firstly ADVERB **en primer lugar**

first name NOUN **nombre** (MASC) **de pila**

fir tree NOUN **abeto** MASC

fish NOUN ❶ (as a meal) **pescado** MASC; **do you like fish?** ¿te gusta el pescado? ❷ (in the sea) **pez** MASC (PLURAL **peces**)

fish VERB **pescar** [31]; **Dad was fishing for trout** papá estaba pescando truchas

fish and chips NOUN **pescado** (MASC) **con patatas fritas**

fisherman NOUN **pescador** MASC

fishing NOUN **pesca** FEM; **fishing is my favourite sport** la pesca es mi deporte favorito, **I love fishing** me encanta pescar, **to go fishing** ir a pescar

fishing rod NOUN **caña** (FEM) **de pescar**

fishing tackle NOUN **aparejos** (MASC PLURAL) **de pesca**

fist NOUN **puño** MASC

fit NOUN **ataque** MASC; **an epileptic fit** un ataque epiléptico, **I had a fit** me dio un ataque, **your dad'll have a fit when he sees your hair!** ¡a tu padre le va a dar un ataque cuando te vea el pelo!

fit ADJECTIVE (healthy) **en forma**; **I feel really fit** me siento muy en forma, **to keep fit** mantenerse [9] en forma

fit VERB ❶ (a garment or shoes) **estar** [2] **bien** (a person); **this skirt doesn't fit me** esta falda no me está bien, **does it fit you okay?** ¿te está bien? ❷ (go into) **entrar** [17] en; **will my cases all fit in the car?** ¿entrarán todas mis maletas en el coche? ❸ (install) **poner** [11]

fitness NOUN **estado** (MASC) **físico**; **fitness training** entrenamiento MASC

fitted carpet NOUN **moqueta** FEM

five NUMBER **cinco** MASC; **Oskar's five** Oskar tiene cinco años, **it's five o'clock** son las cinco

fix VERB ❶ (repair) **arreglar** [17]; **Mum's fixed the computer** mamá ha arreglado el ordenador ❷ (to decide on) **fijar** [17]; **to fix a date** fijar [17] una fecha, **at a fixed price** a un precio fijo ❸ **preparar** [17] (a meal)

fizzy ADJECTIVE **con gas**; **fizzy water** agua con gas

flag NOUN **bandera** FEM

flame NOUN **llama** FEM

flan NOUN ❶ (savoury) **quiche** MASC; **an onion flan** un quiche de cebolla ❷ (sweet) **tarta** FEM

flap VERB (a flag or sail) **agitarse** [17]

flash NOUN ❶ **a flash of lightning** un relámpago ❷ (of light) **destello** MASC ❸ **to do something in a flash** hacer [7] algo a la velocidad del rayo ❹ (on a camera) **flash** MASC

flash VERB ❶ (a light) **destellar** [17] ❷ **to flash by or past** pasar [17] como un rayo ❸ **to flash your headlights** hacer [7] señas con los faros del coche

flask N ❶ *(insulated bottle)* **termo** MASC ❷ *(container)* **frasco** MASC

flat NOUN **piso** MASC; **a third-floor flat** un piso en la tercera planta

flat ADJECTIVE ❶ **plano/plana**; **flat shoes** zapatos planos, **a flat surface** una superficie plana ❷ *(landscape)* **llano/llana** ❸ **a flat tyre** una rueda pinchada

flatmate NOUN **compañero** *(MASC)*, **compañera** *(FEM)* **de piso**

flavour NOUN **sabor** MASC; **the sauce had no flavour** la salsa no tenía sabor, **what flavour of ice cream would you like?** ¿de qué sabor quieres el helado?

flavour VERB **sazonar** [17]; **vanilla-flavoured** con sabor a vainilla

flea NOUN **pulga** FEM

fleet N ❶ *(of ships)* **flota** FEM ❷ *(of vehicles)* **parque** *(MASC)* **móvil**

flight NOUN ❶ **vuelo** MASC; **a charter flight** un vuelo chárter, **the flight from Moscow is delayed** el vuelo procedente de Moscú lleva retraso ❷ **a flight of stairs** un tramo de escalera, **four flights of stairs** cuatro tramos de escalera

flight attendant NOUN **auxiliar** *(MASC & FEM)* **de vuelo**

fling VERB **lanzar** [22]

flipper NOUN *(for a swimmer)* **aleta** FEM

flirt VERB **flirtear** [17]

float VERB **flotar** [17]

flood NOUN ❶ *(of water)* **inundación** FEM; **the floods in the south** las inundaciones del sur ❷ *(of letters or complaints)* **avalancha** FEM ❸ **to be in floods of tears** estar [2] llorando a mares *(literally: to be weeping oceans)*

flood VERB **inundar** [17]

floodlight NOUN **foco** MASC

floor NOUN ❶ **suelo** MASC; **on the floor** en el suelo, **to sweep the floor** barrer [18] ❷ *(a storey)* **planta** FEM; **on the second floor** en la segunda planta

florist NOUN **florista** MASC & FEM

florist's NOUN **floristería** FEM

flour NOUN **harina** FEM

flower NOUN **flor** FEM; **a bunch of flowers** un ramo de flores

flower VERB **florecer** [35]

flu NOUN **gripe** FEM; **to have flu** tener [9] la gripe

fluent ADJECTIVE **she speaks fluent Italian** habla italiano con fluidez

fluently ADVERB **con fluidez**

fluid NOUN **fluido** MASC

flush VERB ❶ *(to go red)* **enrojecer** [35] ❷ **to flush the lavatory** tirar [17] de la cadena

flute NOUN **flauta** FEM; **to play the flute** tocar [30] la flauta

fly NOUN **mosca** FEM

fly VERB ❶ *(a bird, an insect, or a plane)* **volar** [24] ❷ *(in a plane)* **ir** [8] **en avión**; **we flew to Edinburgh** fuimos en avión a Edimburgo, **we**

flew from Gatwick salimos desde Gatwick ❸ hacer [7] volar *(a kite)* ❹ *(to pass quickly) (time)* pasar [17] volando

foam NOUN ❶ *(foam rubber)* goma *(FEM)* espuma; a foam mattress un colchón de goma espuma ❷ *(on a drink)* espuma *FEM*

focus NOUN to be in focus estar [2] enfocado, to be out of focus estar [2] desenfocado

focus VERB enfocar [31] *(a camera)*

fog NOUN niebla *FEM*

foggy ADJECTIVE it was foggy había niebla, a foggy day un día de niebla

foil NOUN *(kitchen foil)* papel *(MASC)* de aluminio

fold NOUN doblez *MASC*

fold VERB doblar [17]; to fold something up doblar algo

folder NOUN carpeta *FEM*

follow VERB seguir [64]; follow me! ¡sígueme!, followed by a dinner seguido de una cena, do you follow me? ¿me sigues?

following ADJECTIVE siguiente; the following year el año siguiente

fond ADJECTIVE ❶ to be fond of somebody tenerle [9] cariño a alguien, I'm very fond of him le tengo mucho cariño ❷ I'm fond of dogs me gustan los perros

food NOUN comida *FEM*; to buy food comprar [17] comida, I like Italian food me gusta la comida italiana

food poisoning NOUN intoxicación *(FEM)* alimenticia

fool NOUN idiota *MASC & FEM*

foot NOUN ❶ pie *MASC*; he stepped on my foot me pisó el pie, Lucy came on foot Lucy vino a pie, at the foot of the stairs al pie de las escaleras ❷ *(of animal)* pata *FEM*

football NOUN ❶ *(the game)* fútbol *MASC*; to play football jugar [27] al fútbol ❷ *(ball)* balón *(MASC)* de fútbol

footballer NOUN futbolista *MASC & FEM*

footpath NOUN sendero *MASC*

for PREPOSITION ❶ para; a present for my mother un regalo para mi madre, petrol for the car gasolina para el coche, sausages for lunch salchichas para comer, it's for cleaning es para limpiar, what's it for? ¿para qué es? ❷ *(in time expressions in the past or future, 'for' is not usually translated)* I studied Spanish for four years estudié español cuatro años, I'll be away for four days estaré fuera cuatro días, I've been waiting here for an hour llevo esperando aquí una hora, my brother's been living in London for three years mi hermano lleva tres años viviendo en Londres ❸ *(cost or amount)* por; I sold my bike for fifty pounds vendí mi bicicleta por cincuenta libras ❹ what's the Spanish for 'bee'? ¿cómo se dice 'bee' en español?

forbid VERB prohibir [58]; to forbid somebody to do something prohibir [58] a alguien hacer algo, I forbid you to go out te prohíbo salir

forbidden *ADJECTIVE* prohibido/
prohibida

force *NOUN* fuerza *FEM*

force *VERB* forzar [26]; **to force
somebody to do** forzar a alguien
a hacer

forecast *NOUN* *(weather forecast)*
pronóstico *MASC*

forehead *NOUN* frente *FEM*

foreign *ADJECTIVE* extranjero/
extranjera; **in a foreign country**
en un país extranjero

foreigner *NOUN* extranjero *MASC*,
extranjera *FEM*

forest *NOUN* bosque *MASC*

forever *ADVERB* ❶ para siempre;
I'd like to stay here forever me
gustaría quedarme aquí para
siempre ❷ *(non-stop)* siempre; **he's
forever asking questions** siempre
está preguntando

forgery *NOUN* falsificación *FEM*

forget *VERB* olvidarse [17]; **I forget his
name** se me ha olvidado su nombre,
we've forgotten the bread! ¡se nos
ha olvidado el pan!, **to forget to
do** olvidarse [17] de hacer, **I forgot
to phone** se me olvidó llamar por
teléfono, **to forget about something**
olvidarse [17] de algo

forgetful *ADJECTIVE* olvidadizo/
olvidadiza

forgive *VERB* perdonar [17]; **I
forgave him** lo perdoné, **to forgive
somebody for doing** perdonar
[17] a alguien que *(followed by
subjunctive)*, **I forgave her for losing
my ring** la perdoné por perderme
el anillo

fork *NOUN* tenedor *MASC*

form *NOUN* ❶ formulario *MASC*; **to fill
in a form** rellenar [17] un formulario
❷ *(shape or kind)* forma *FEM*; **in the
form of** bajo forma de ❸ **to be on
form** estar [2] en forma ❹ *(school
class)* clase *FEM* ❺ *(school year)*
curso *MASC*

form *VERB* formar [17]

formal *ADJECTIVE* formal *(invitation,
event, complaint, etc)*

former *ADJECTIVE* antiguo/antigua
(goes before the noun); **a former
pupil** un antiguo alumno

formula *NOUN* fórmula *FEM*

fortnight *NOUN* quince días *MASC
PLURAL*; **we're going to Spain for
a fortnight** vamos quince días a
España

fortress *NOUN* fortaleza *FEM*

fortunate *ADJECTIVE* afortunado/
afortunada

fortunately *ADVERB*
afortunadamente

fortune *NOUN* fortuna *FEM*; **to make a
fortune** hacer [7] una fortuna

forty *NUMBER* cuarenta *MASC*; **he's
forty** tiene cuarenta años, **forty-five**
cuarenta y cinco

forward *NOUN* *(in sport)* delantero
MASC & FEM

forward *ADVERB* **a seat further
forward** un asiento de más
adelante, **to move forward** ir [8]
hacia adelante

foster child *NOUN* hijo *(MASC)*
acogido, hija *(MASC)* acogida

foster family NOUN familia (FEM) de acogida

foul NOUN (in sport) falta FEM

foul ADJECTIVE asqueroso/asquerosa (smell or taste); **the weather's foul** el tiempo es horroroso

fountain NOUN fuente FEM

fountain pen NOUN pluma FEM

four NUMBER cuatro MASC; **Simon's four** Simon tiene cuatro años, **it's four o'clock** son las cuatro

fourteen NUMBER catorce MASC; **Susie's fourteen** Susie tiene catorce años

fourth NOUN ❶ (fraction) a fourth un cuarto ❷ the fourth of July el cuatro de julio

fourth ADJECTIVE cuarto/cuarta; **on the fourth floor** en la cuarta planta

fox NOUN zorro MASC

fracture NOUN fractura FEM

fragile ADJECTIVE frágil

frame NOUN (of picture or photograph) marco MASC

France NOUN Francia FEM

frantic ADJECTIVE ❶ (desperate) desesperado/desesperada (efforts or a search) ❷ (very upset) **Mum was frantic with worry** mamá estaba muerta de preocupación

freckle NOUN peca FEM

free ADJECTIVE ❶ (when you don't pay) gratis; **the bus is free** el autobús es gratis, **a free ticket** un billete gratis ❷ (not occupied) libre; **are you free on Thursday?** ¿estás libre el jueves?

❸ sugar-free sin azúcar, **lead-free** sin plomo

free VERB ❶ (a person) poner [11] en libertad ❷ (an animal) soltar [24]

freedom NOUN libertad FEM

free gift NOUN regalo MASC

free kick NOUN tiro (MASC) libre

freeze VERB ❶ (in a freezer) congelar [17]; **frozen peas** guisantes congelados ❷ (in cold weather) helarse [29] (person or ground)

freezer NOUN congelador MASC

freezing NOUN **three degrees below freezing** tres grados bajo cero

freezing ADJECTIVE **I'm freezing** ¡estoy helado! (informal), **it's freezing outside!** ¡fuera hace un frío que pela! (informal)

French NOUN ❶ (the language) francés MASC ❷ (the people) the French los franceses

French ADJECTIVE francés/francesa

French beans PLURAL NOUN judías (FEM PLURAL) verdes

French fries PLURAL NOUN patatas (FEM PLURAL) fritas

Frenchman NOUN francés MASC

French stick NOUN baguette FEM

French window NOUN cristalera FEM

Frenchwoman NOUN francesa FEM

frequently NOUN frecuentemente, a menudo

fresh ADJECTIVE fresco/fresca; **fresh eggs** huevos frescos, **I'm going out**

for some fresh air voy fuera a tomar un poco el aire

Friday NOUN **viernes** MASC (PLURAL **viernes**); **last Friday** el pasado viernes, **on Friday** el viernes, **I'll phone you on Friday evening** te llamaré el viernes por la tarde, **on Fridays** los viernes, **closed on Fridays** cerrado los viernes, **every Friday** cada viernes, **Good Friday** Viernes Santo

fridge NOUN **nevera** FEM; **put it in the fridge** ponlo en la nevera

friend NOUN **amigo** MASC, **amiga** FEM; **a friend of mine** un amigo mío/una amiga mía, **to make friends** hacer [7] amigos, **he made friends with Danny** se hizo amigo de Danny

friendly ADJECTIVE ❶ (a person) **simpático/simpática** ❷ (a letter or gesture) **amable**

friendship NOUN **amistad** FEM

fries PLURAL NOUN **patatas** (FEM PLURAL) **fritas**

fright NOUN **susto** MASC; **to get a fright** asustarse [17], **to give somebody a fright** asustar [17] a alguien, **you gave me a fright!** ¡me has asustado!

frighten VERB **asustar** [17]

frightened ADJECTIVE **to be frightened** estar [2] **asustado/ asustada**, **I'm frightened of asking her** me da miedo preguntarle, **Martin's frightened of snakes** a Martin le dan miedo las serpientes

frightening ADJECTIVE **espantoso/ espantosa**

fringe NOUN (of hair) **flequillo** MASC

frog NOUN **rana** FEM

from PREPOSITION ❶ **de**; **a letter from Tom** una carta de Tom, **100 metres from the cinema** a cien metros del cine, **he comes from Dublin** es de Dublín, **from seven o'clock onwards** de las siete en adelante ❷ **from ... to ...** de ... a ..., **from Monday to Friday** de lunes a viernes, **the train from London to Liverpool** el tren de Londres a Liverpool, **from here to the wall** de aquí a la pared ❸ (starting from) **desde**; **tickets from ten pounds** entradas desde diez libras, **from today** desde hoy ❹ **two years from now** dentro de dos años, **from then on** a partir de entonces

front NOUN ❶ (of a car, train, envelope, or queue) **parte** (FEM) **de delante**; **sitting in the front** sentado en la parte de delante, **the address is on the front** las señas están en la parte de delante, **from the front** por delante ❷ (of a building) **fachada** FEM ❸ (of a garment) **delantera** MASC ❹ **the front of the class** el frente de la clase ❺ **in front of** delante de, **in front of the TV** delante de la televisión, **in front of me** delante de mí

front ADJECTIVE ❶ **delantero/ delantera**; **the front seat** (of a car) el asiento delantero ❷ **in the front row** en la fila de delante

front door NOUN **puerta** (FEM) **de la calle**

frontier NOUN **frontera** FEM

frost NOUN **helada** FEM

425

English—Spanish

A B C D E F G H I J K L M N O P Q R S T U V W X Y Z

frosty ADJECTIVE ❶ it was frosty this morning había helada esta mañana ❷ cubierto/cubierta de escarcha *(windscreen, grass, etc)*

frown VERB fruncir [66] el ceño

frozen ADJECTIVE *(in a freezer)* congelado/congelada; a frozen pizza una pizza congelada

fruit NOUN fruta FEM; fruit juice zumo *(MASC)* de fruta

fruit salad NOUN macedonia *(FEM)* de frutas

frustrating ADJECTIVE frustrante

fry VERB freír [53]; we fried the fish freímos el pescado, a fried egg un huevo frito

frying pan NOUN sartén FEM

fuel NOUN *(for a vehicle or plane)* combustible MASC

full ADJECTIVE ❶ lleno/llena; this glass is full este vaso está lleno, the train was full of tourists el tren estaba lleno de turistas, I'm full estoy lleno ❷ completo/completa *(a hotel or flight)* ❸ *(top)* at full speed a toda velocidad, at full volume a todo volumen ❹ *(complete)* todo/toda; the full story toda la historia ❺ to write your name out in full escribir [52] su nombre completo

full stop NOUN punto MASC

full-time ADJECTIVE a tiempo completo MASC; a full-time job un trabajo a tiempo completo

full time NOUN final *(MASC)* de partido

fully ADJECTIVE completamente

fun NOUN to have fun divertirse [14], have fun! ¡que te diviertas!, we had fun catching the ponies nos divertimos atrapando a los poneys, skiing is fun esquiar es divertido, I do it for fun lo hago para divertirme, to make fun of somebody reírse [61] de alguien

funds NOUN fondos MASC PLURAL

funeral NOUN ❶ *(ceremony)* funeral MASC ❷ *(burial)* entierro MASC

funfair NOUN feria FEM

funny ADJECTIVE ❶ *(when you laugh)* gracioso/graciosa; how funny you are! ¡qué gracioso eres!, a funny story una historia graciosa ❷ *(strange)* raro; that's funny, I'm sure I paid qué raro, estoy seguro de que pagué, a funny noise un ruido raro

fur NOUN ❶ *(on an animal)* pelaje MASC ❷ *(for a coat)* piel FEM; a fur coat un abrigo de piel

furious ADJECTIVE furioso/furiosa; she was furious with Steve estaba furiosa con Steve

furniture NOUN muebles MASC PLURAL; to buy some furniture comprar muebles, a piece of furniture un mueble

further ADVERB further than the station más allá de la estación, ten kilometres further on diez kilómetros más adelante, further forward más adelante, further back más atrás, further in más adentro

fuse NOUN fusible MASC

fuss *NOUN* escándalo *MASC*; **to make a fuss** montar [17] un escándalo, **to make a fuss about the bill** montar [17] un escándalo a causa de la factura

fussy *ADJECTIVE* ❶ *(about how things are done)* quisquilloso/quisquillosa; **to be fussy about something** ser [1] muy quisquilloso/quisquillosa para algo ❷ *(about food)* maniático/maniática; **to be fussy about food** ser [1] muy maniático/maniática para la comida

future *NOUN* futuro *MASC*; **in the future** en el futuro, **in future** en el futuro, **in future, ask me first** en el futuro, pregúntame antes

Gg

gadget *NOUN* aparato *MASC*

gain *VERB* ganar [17]; **in order to gain time** para ganar tiempo, **to gain weight** ganar peso

galaxy *NOUN* galaxia *FEM*

gale *NOUN* vendaval *MASC*

Galicia *NOUN* Galicia *FEM*

Galician *NOUN* ❶ *(the language)* gallego *MASC* ❷ *(person)* gallego *MASC*, gallega *FEM*

Galician *ADJECTIVE* gallego/gallega

gallery *NOUN* **an art gallery** *(public)* un museo de pintura, *(private)* una galería de arte

gambling *NOUN* juego *MASC*

game *NOUN* ❶ juego *MASC*; **a board game** un juego de mesa, *(to be good at games)* **Jack's very good at games** Jack es muy buen deportista ❷ **a game of** una partida de, **a game of cards** una partida de cartas, **to play cards** jugar [27] a las cartas ❸ partido *MASC*; **a game of football** un partido de fútbol

gang *NOUN* ❶ panda *FEM* *(of friends)*; **all the gang were there** toda la panda estaba allí ❷ banda *FEM* *(of criminals)*

gangster *NOUN* gángster *MASC & FEM*

gap   genius

gap *NOUN* ❶ *(hole)* **hueco** *MASC* ❷ *(in time)* **intervalo** *MASC*; **a two-year gap** un intervalo de dos años ❸ **an age gap** una diferencia de edad

gap year *NOUN* **año** *(MASC)* **libre** antes de entrar a la universidad

garage *NOUN* **garaje** *MASC*

garden *NOUN* **jardín** *MASC*

gardener *NOUN* **jardinero** *MASC*, **jardinera** *FEM*; **he's a gardener** es jardinero

gardening *NOUN* **jardinería** *FEM*

garlic *NOUN* **ajo** *MASC*

garment *NOUN* **prenda** *FEM*

gas *NOUN* **gas** *MASC*

gas cooker *NOUN* **cocina** *(FEM)* **de gas**

gas fire *NOUN* **estufa** *(FEM)* **de gas**

gas meter *NOUN* **contador** *(MASC)* **de gas**

gate *NOUN* ❶ *(garden)* **verja** *FEM* ❷ *(field)* **portillo** *MASC* ❸ *(at the airport)* **puerta** *(FEM)* *(de embarque)*

gather *VERB* ❶ *(people)* **juntarse** [17]; **a crowd gathered** se juntó una multitud ❷ **recoger** [3] *(fruit, vegetables, flowers)* ❸ **as far as I can gather** según tengo entendido

gay *ADJECTIVE* **gay** *(homosexual)*

GCSEs *NOUN PLURAL*
(You can explain GCSEs briefly as follows: Son exámenes que se realizan alrededor de los 16 años y abarcan hasta 12 asignaturas. Se califican desde A-star (nota máxima), a N (sin calificar). Muchos

alumnos estudian para los A levels después de hacer los GCSEs)
▸ *SEE* **A levels**

gear *NOUN* ❶ *(in a car)* **marcha** *FEM*; **to change gear** cambiar [17] de marcha, **in third gear** en tercera ❷ *(equipment)* **equipo** *MASC*; **camping gear** equipo de acampada ❸ **fishing gear** aparejos *(MASC PLURAL)* de pesca ❹ *(things)* **cosas** *FEM PLURAL*; **I've left all my gear at Gary's** he dejado todas mis cosas en casa de Gary

gear lever *NOUN* **palanca** *(FEM)* **de cambio**

gel *NOUN* **gel** *MASC*; **hair gel** gel para el pelo

Gemini *NOUN* **Géminis** *MASC PLURAL*; **Steph's Gemini** Steph es Géminis

gender *NOUN* *(of a word)* **género** *MASC*; **what is the gender of 'casa'?** ¿de qué género es 'casa'?

general *ADJECTIVE* **general**; **in general** en general

general *NOUN* **general** *MASC*; **General Jackson** el general Jackson

general election *NOUN* **elecciones** *(FEM PLURAL)* **generales**

general knowledge *NOUN* **cultura** *(FEM)* **general**

generally *ADVERB* **generalmente**

generation *NOUN* **generación** *FEM*

generous *ADJECTIVE* **generoso/ generosa**

genetics *NOUN* **genética** *FEM*

genius *NOUN* **genio** *MASC*; **Lisa, you're a genius!** Lisa, ¡eres un genio!

gentle ADJECTIVE ❶ (person, voice or nature) **dulce** ❷ (breeze, murmur, heat) **suave**

gentleman NOUN **caballero** MASC; **ladies and gentlemen** señoras y caballeros

gently ADVERB ❶ (talk) **dulcemente** ❷ (touch) **suavemente** ❸ (handle) **con cuidado**

gents NOUN **servicios** (MASC PLURAL) de caballeros, (sign) **Caballeros**; **where's the gents?** ¿dónde están los servicios de caballeros?

genuine ADJECTIVE ❶ (real) **auténtico/auténtica**; **a genuine diamond** un diamante auténtico ❷ **sincero/sincera** (person); **she's very genuine** es muy sincera

geography NOUN **geografía** FEM

geology NOUN **geología** FEM

geometry NOUN **geometría** FEM

germ NOUN **germen** MASC

German NOUN ❶ **alemán** MASC, **alemana** FEM ❷ (language) **alemán** MASC

German ADJECTIVE **alemán/alemana**

Germany NOUN **Alemania** FEM

get VERB ❶ (to obtain) **I got fifteen for my maths exam** saqué un quince en el examen de matemáticas, **where did you get that jacket?** ¿de dónde has sacado esa chaqueta? ❷ (as a present) **I got a bike for my birthday** me regalaron una bicicleta por mi cumpleaños ❸ (a parcel or letter) **recibir** [19]; **I got your letter yesterday** recibí tu carta ayer ❹ (a job) **conseguir** [64]; **Fred's got a job** Fred ha conseguido un trabajo

❺ (fetch) **ir** [8] **a buscar**; **go and get some bread** vete a buscar pan, **I'll get your bag for you** voy a buscar tu bolso ❻ (to buy) **comprar** [17]; **I got a nice shirt in the sales** compré una camisa muy bonita en las rebajas ❼ **to have got tener** [9], **he's got lots of money** tiene mucho dinero, **she's got long hair** tiene el pelo largo ❽ **to have got to do tener** [9] **que hacer**, **I've got to phone before midday** tengo que llamar antes del mediodía ❾ **to get to llegar** [28] **a**, **when we got to London** cuando llegamos a Londres, **to get here/there llegar** [28], **we got here this morning** llegamos esta mañana, **what time did they get there?** ¿a qué hora llegaron? ❿ (become) **to get tired cansarse** [17], **she was getting worried** se estaba preocupando, **it's getting late** se está haciendo tarde, **I'm getting hungry** me está entrando hambre ⓫ **to get your hair cut cortarse** [17] **el pelo**

- **to get back volver** [45]; **Mum gets back at six** mamá vuelve a las seis
- **to get something back we got the money back** nos devolvieron el dinero, **did you get your books back?** ¿te devolvieron los libros?
- **to get into something entrar** [17] (a vehicle); **he got into the car** entró en el coche
- **to get off something bajarse** [17] **de**; **I got off the train at Banbury** me bajé del tren en Banbury
- **to get on how's Amanda getting on?** ¿cómo le va a Amanda?
- **to get on something subir** [19] **a** (vehicle); **she got on the train at Reading** subió al tren en Reading
- **to get on with somebody llevarse** [17] **bien con alguien**; **she doesn't get on with her brother** no se lleva

bien con su hermano

- **to get out of something** salir [63] de algo *(vehicle)*; **Laura got out of the car** Laura salió del coche
- **to get something out** sacar [31] algo; **Robert got his guitar out** Robert sacó la guitarra
- **to get together** verse [16]; **we must get together soon** tenemos que vernos pronto
- **to get up** levantarse [17]; **I get up at seven** me levanto a la siete

ghost NOUN **fantasma** MASC

giddy ADJECTIVE **mareado/mareada**; **I'm feeling giddy** me siento mareado/mareada

gift NOUN ❶ **regalo** MASC; **a Christmas gift** un regalo de Navidad ❷ **to have a gift for something** estar [2] dotado/dotada para, **Jo has a real gift for languages** Jo está realmente dotada para los idiomas

gig NOUN **concierto** MASC

gigabyte NOUN **gigabyte** MASC; **a fifty gigabyte hard disk** un disco duro de cinquenta gigabytes

gin NOUN **ginebra** FEM

ginger NOUN **jengibre** MASC

gipsy NOUN **gitano** MASC, **gitana** FEM

giraffe NOUN **jirafa** FEM

girl NOUN ❶ **niña** FEM; **three boys and four girls** tres niños y cuatro niñas, **a little girl** una niña pequeña, **when I was a little girl** cuando yo era pequeña ❷ *(a teenager or young woman)* **chica** FEM; **an eighteen-year-old girl** una chica de dieciocho años

girlfriend NOUN ❶ *(in relationship)* **novia** FEM; **Darren's girlfriend** la novia de Darren ❷ *(female friend)* **amiga** FEM; **Lizzie and her girlfriends have gone to the cinema** Lizzie y sus amigas han ido al cine

give VERB **dar** [4]; **to give something to somebody** darle [4] algo a alguien, **I'll give you my address** te daré mis señas, **give me the key** dame la llave, **I gave Sandy the books** le di los libros a Sandy, **Yasmin's dad gave her the money** el padre de Yasmin le dio el dinero
- **to give something away** regalar [17] algo; **she's given away all her books** ha regalado todos sus libros
- **to give something back to somebody** devolverle [45] algo a alguien; **I gave her back the keys** le devolví las llaves
- **to give in** ceder [18]; **she gave in in the end** al final cedió
- **to give up** rendirse [57]; **I give up!** ¡me rindo!
- **to give up doing** dejar [17] de hacer; **she's given up smoking** ha dejado de fumar

glacier NOUN **glaciar** MASC

glad ADJECTIVE **to be glad to** alegrarse [17], **I'm glad to hear he's better** me alegra saber que está mejor, **I'm glad to be back** me alegro de haber vuelto

glamorous ADJECTIVE ❶ *(life, job)* **con mucho glamour** ❷ *(woman)* **elegante**

glass NOUN ❶ *(for drinking)* **vaso** MASC; **a glass of water** un vaso de agua ❷ *(material)* **cristal** MASC; **a glass table** una mesa de cristal

glasses *PLURAL NOUN* **gafas** *FEM PLURAL*; **to wear glasses** llevar [17] gafas

global *ADJECTIVE* **global**

global warming *NOUN* **calentamiento** *(MASC)* **global**

globe *NOUN* **globo** *(MASC)* **terráqueo**

gloomy *ADJECTIVE* ❶ *(expression)* **lúgubre** ❷ *(weather)* **gris**

glory *NOUN* **gloria** *FEM*

glove *NOUN* **guante** *MASC*; **a pair of gloves** un par de guantes

glue *NOUN* **pegamento** *MASC*

go *NOUN* ❶ *(in a game)* **whose go is it?** ¿a quién le toca?, **it's my go** me toca a mí ❷ **to have a go at doing** intentar [17] hacer, **I'll have a go at mending it for you** intentaré arreglártelo

go *VERB* ❶ **ir** [8]; **we're going to London tomorrow** mañana vamos a Londres, **Mark's gone to the dentist's** Mark ha ido al dentista, **to go for a walk** ir [8] a dar un paseo, **to go shopping** ir [8] de compras ❷ *(with another verb)* **to go to do it** ir [8] a hacer, **I'm going to make some tea** voy a hacer té, **he was going to phone me** él iba a llamarme ❸ *(leave)* **irse** [8]; **Pauline's already gone** Pauline ya se ha ido, **we're going on holiday tomorrow** nos vamos de vacaciones mañana ❹ *(a train or plane)* **salir** [63]; **the train goes at seven** el tren sale a las siete ❺ *(time)* **pasar** [17]; **the time goes quickly** el tiempo pasa rápido ❻ *(an event)* **ir** [8]; **did the party go well?** ¿qué tal fue la fiesta? ❼ *(a pain)* **pasarse** [17]; **my headache's gone** se me ha pasado el dolor de cabeza

• **to go away** irse [8]; **go away!** ¡vete!

• **to go back** volver [45]; **I'm going back to Madrid in March** vuelvo a Madrid en marzo, **I'm not going back there again!** ¡no voy a volver nunca!, **I went back home** volví a casa

• **to go down** ❶ **bajar** [17]; **she's gone down to the kitchen** ha bajado a la cocina, **to go down the stairs** bajar las escaleras, **prices have gone down** los precios han bajado ❷ *(tyre, balloon, airbed)* **desinflarse** [17]

• **to go in** entrar [17]; **he went in and shut the door** entró y cerró la puerta

• **to go into** entrar [17]; **Fran went into the kitchen** Fran entró en la cocina, **this file won't go into my bag** esta carpeta no entra en mi bolsa

• **to go off** ❶ *(bomb)* **estallar** [17] ❷ *(alarm clock)* **sonar** [24]; **my alarm clock went off at six** mi despertador sonó a las seis ❸ *(fire or burglar alarm)* **dispararse** [17]; **the fire alarm went off** la alarma contra incendios se disparó

• **to go on** ❶ **pasar** [17]; **what's going on?** ¿qué pasa? ❷ **to go on doing** seguir [64] haciendo, **she went on talking** siguió hablando ❸ **to go on about something** hablar [17] de algo, **he's always going on about his dog** siempre está hablando de su perro

• **to go out** ❶ **salir** [63]; **I'm going out tonight** voy a salir esta noche, **she went out of the kitchen** salió de la cocina ❷ **to be going out with somebody** salir [63] con alguien, **she's going out with my brother** está saliendo con mi hermano ❸ *(light, fire)* **apagarse** [28]; **the light went out** la luz se apagó

• **to go past something** pasar [17]

por algo; **we went past your house** pasamos por tu casa
- **to go round to go round to somebody's house** ir [8] a casa de alguien, **I went round to Fred's last night** anoche fui a casa de Fred
- **to go round something ❶** recorrer [18] *(building, park, garden)* ❷ visitar [17] *(museum, monument)*
- **to go through** pasar [17] por; **the train went through York** el tren pasó por York, **you can go through my office** puedes pasar por mi oficina
- **to go up** subir [19]; **she's gone up to her room** ha subido a su habitación, **to go up the stairs** subir las escaleras, **the price of petrol has gone up** el precio de la gasolina ha subido

goal NOUN gol MASC; **to score a goal** marcar un gol, **to win by three goals to two** ganar [17] por tres goles a dos

goalkeeper NOUN portero MASC, portera FEM

goat NOUN cabra FEM; **goat's cheese** queso *(MASC)* de cabra

god NOUN dios MASC

God NOUN Dios MASC; **to believe in God** creer en Dios

godchild NOUN ahijado MASC, ahijada FEM

goddaughter NOUN ahijada FEM

goddess NOUN diosa FEM

godfather NOUN padrino MASC

godmother NOUN madrina FEM

godparent NOUN padrino MASC, madrina FEM; **my godparents** mis padrinos

godson NOUN ahijado MASC

goggles PLURAL NOUN **swimming goggles** gafas *(FEM PLURAL)* de natación, **skiing goggles** gafas *(FEM PLURAL)* de esquí

go-karting NOUN karting MASC; **to go go-karting** hacer karting

gold NOUN oro MASC; **a gold bracelet** una pulsera de oro

goldfish NOUN pececito MASC (rojo)

golf NOUN golf MASC; **to play golf** jugar [31] al golf

golf club NOUN ❶ *(place)* club *(MASC)* de golf ❷ *(iron)* palo *(MASC)* de golf

golf course NOUN campo *(MASC)* de golf

golfer NOUN golfista MASC & FEM

good NOUN **to do somebody good** irle [15] bien a alguien, **it will do you good** te irá bien

good ADJECTIVE ❶ bueno/buena *('bueno' becomes 'buen' before a masculine singular noun)* **she's a good teacher** es una buena profesora, **a good deal** un buen negocio, **be good!** ¡sé bueno!, **to feel good** sentirse [14] bien ❷ **to be good for you** ser [1] bueno para la salud, **tomatoes are good for you** los tomates son muy buenos para la salud ❸ **she's good at art** se la da bien el arte, **I'm good at cooking** se me da bien cocinar ❹ *(kind)* amable; **she's been very good to me** ha sido muy amable conmigo ❺ bien; **it smelled good** olía bien, **it**

tastes good sabe bien, **his Spanish is very good** habla español muy bien, **good!** *(well done)* ¡muy bien! ❻ **for good** para siempre, **I've stopped smoking for good** he dejado de fumar para siempre

good afternoon EXCLAMATION buenas tardes

goodbye EXCLAMATION adiós

good evening EXCLAMATION ❶ *(up to eight or nine)* buenas tardes ❷ *(from nine onwards)* buenas noches

Good Friday NOUN Viernes *(MASC)* Santo

good-looking ADJECTIVE guapo/ guapa; **Maya's boyfriend's really good-looking** el novio de Maya es muy guapo

good morning EXCLAMATION buenos días

goodness EXCLAMATION ¡Dios mío!; **for goodness sake!** ¡por Dios!

goodnight EXCLAMATION buenas noches

goods PLURAL NOUN artículos MASC PLURAL

goods train NOUN tren *(MASC)* de mercancías

goose NOUN ganso MASC

goose pimples NOUN carne *(FEM)* de gallina

gorgeous ADJECTIVE precioso/ preciosa; **a gorgeous dress** un vestido precioso, **it's a gorgeous day** un día precioso

gorilla NOUN gorila MASC

gosh EXCLAMATION ¡Dios mío!

gossip NOUN ❶ *(person)* cotilla MASC & FEM ❷ *(news)* cotilleo MASC; **what's the latest gossip?** ¿qué hay de nuevo?

gossip VERB cotillear [17]

government NOUN gobierno MASC

grab VERB ❶ agarrar [17]; **she grabbed my arm** me agarró el brazo ❷ **to grab something from somebody** arrebatarle [17] algo a alguien, **he grabbed the book from me** me arrebató el libro

graceful ADJECTIVE elegante

grade NOUN *(mark)* notas FEM PLURAL; **to get good grades** sacar [31] buenas notas

gradual ADJECTIVE gradual

gradually ADVERB poco a poco; **the weather got gradually better** el tiempo mejoró poco a poco

graffiti PLURAL NOUN grafitti MASC PLURAL

grain NOUN grano MASC

grammar NOUN gramática FEM

grammar school NOUN colegio MASC

grammatical ADJECTIVE gramatical; **a grammatical error** un error gramatical

gramme NOUN gramo MASC

gran NOUN abuelita FEM

grandchildren PLURAL NOUN nietos MASC PLURAL

granddad NOUN abuelito (informal) MASC

granddaughter NOUN nieta FEM

grandfather NOUN abuelo MASC

grandma NOUN abuelita (informal) FEM

grandmother NOUN abuela FEM

grandpa NOUN abuelito (informal) MASC

grandparents PLURAL NOUN abuelos MASC PLURAL

grandson NOUN nieto MASC PLURAL

granny NOUN abuelita (informal) FEM

grape NOUN a grape una uva, to buy some grapes comprar uvas, a bunch of grapes un racimo de uvas

grapefruit NOUN pomelo MASC

graph NOUN gráfico MASC

graphic designer NOUN diseñador (MASC) gráfico, diseñadora (FEM) gráfica

graphics NOUN gráficos MASC PLURAL

grass NOUN ❶ hierba FEM; he was sitting on the grass estaba sentado en la hierba ❷ (lawn) césped MASC; to cut the grass cortar [17] el césped

grasshopper NOUN saltamontes MASC (PLURAL saltamontes)

grate VERB rallar [17]; grated cheese queso rallado

grateful ADJECTIVE agradecido/ agradecida

grater NOUN rallador MASC

grave NOUN tumba FEM

gravel NOUN grava FEM

graveyard NOUN cementerio MASC

gravity NOUN gravedad FEM

gravy NOUN salsa (FEM) del asado

grease NOUN grasa FEM

greasy ADJECTIVE ❶ (hands or surface) grasiento/grasienta ❷ (hair, skin or food) graso/grasa; to have greasy skin tener [9] la piel grasa, I hate greasy food no soporto la comida grasa

great ADJECTIVE ❶ gran (PLURAL grandes); a great poet un gran poeta, a great opportunity una gran oportunidad, great expectations grandes esperanzas ❷ (terrific) estupendo/estupenda; it was a great party! ¡fue una fiesta estupenda!, great! ¡estupendo! ❸ a great deal of un montón de, a great many muchos/muchas, there are a great many things still to be done aún quedan muchas cosas por hacer

Great Britain NOUN Gran Bretaña FEM

Greece NOUN Grecia FEM

greedy ADJECTIVE (with food) glotón/ glotona

Greek NOUN ❶ (person) griego MASC, griega FEM ❷ (language) griego MASC

Greek ADJECTIVE griego/griega

green NOUN ❶ (colour) **verde** MASC; **a pale green** un verde pálido ❷ **greens** (vegetables) **verduras** FEM PLURAL ❸ **the Greens** (ecologists) **los verdes** (informal)

green ADJECTIVE ❶ **verde**; **a green door** una puerta verde ❷ **ecologista**; **the Green Party** el partido ecologista

greengrocer NOUN **verdulero** MASC, **verdulera** FEM; **the greengrocer's** la verdulería

greenhouse NOUN **invernadero** MASC

greenhouse effect NOUN **efecto** (MASC) **invernadero**

greetings PLURAL NOUN **Season's Greetings** Feliz Navidad

greetings card NOUN **tarjeta** (FEM) **de felicitación**

grey ADJECTIVE ❶ **gris**; **a grey skirt** una falda gris ❷ (hair) **canoso/canosa**; **to have grey hair** tener el pelo canoso

greyhound NOUN **galgo** MASC

grid NOUN ❶ (grating) **parrilla** FEM ❷ (network) **red** FEM

grief NOUN **dolor** MASC

grill NOUN (of a cooker) **grill** MASC

grill VERB **to grill something** hacer [7] algo al grill, **I grilled the sausages** hice las salchichas al grill

grin NOUN **sonrisa** FEM

grin VERB **sonreír** [61]

grip VERB **agarrar** [17]

grit NOUN (for roads) **arenilla** FEM

groan NOUN ❶ (of pain) **gemido** MASC ❷ (of disgust, boredom) **gruñido** MASC

groan VERB ❶ (in pain) **gemir** [57] ❷ (in disgust, boredom) **refunfuñar** [17]

grocer NOUN **tendero** MASC, **tendera** FEM; **my dad's a grocer** mi padre es tendero

groceries PLURAL NOUN **cosas** (FEM PLURAL) **de comer**; **to buy some groceries** comprar [17] cosas de comer

grocer's NOUN **tienda** (FEM) **de comestibles**

groom NOUN (bridegroom) **novio** MASC

gross ADJECTIVE ❶ **a gross injustice** una flagrante injustica ❷ **a gross error** un grave error ❸ (disgusting) **repugnante**; **the food was gross!** ¡la comida era repugnante!

ground NOUN ❶ **suelo** MASC; **to sit on the ground** sentarse [29] en el suelo, **to throw something on the ground** tirar [17] algo al suelo ❷ (for sport) **campo** MASC; **a football ground** un campo de fútbol

ground ADJECTIVE **molido/molida**; **ground coffee** café (MASC) molido

ground floor NOUN **planta** (FEM) **baja**; **they live on the ground floor** viven en la planta baja

group NOUN **grupo** MASC

grow VERB ❶ (plant, hair or person) **crecer** [35]; **your hair's grown!** te ha crecido el pelo, **my little sister's grown a lot this year** mi hermana pequeña ha crecido mucho este año

❷ cultivar [17] *(fruit, vegetables)*; **our neighbour grows strawberries** nuestro vecino cultiva fresas **❸ to grow a beard** dejarse [17] barba **❹ to grow old** envejecer [35]
• **to grow up** crecer [35]; **the children are growing up** los niños están creciendo, **she grew up in Scotland** creció en Escocia

growl VERB gruñir [65]

grown-up NOUN adulto MASC, adulta FEM

growth NOUN crecimiento MASC

grudge NOUN **to bear a grudge against somebody** guardarle [17] rencor a alguien, **she bears me a grudge** me guarda rencor

gruesome ADJECTIVE horrible

grumble VERB refunfuñar [17]; **she's always grumbling** siempre está refunfuñando, **to grumble about something** refunfuñar por algo

guarantee NOUN garantía FEM; **a year's guarantee** una garantía de un año

guarantee VERB garantizar [22]

guard NOUN **❶ a prison guard** un guardia de prisiones **❷** *(on a train)* jefe *(MASC)* de tren, jefa *(FEM)* de tren **❸ a security guard** un guardia de seguridad

guard VERB vigilar [17]

guard dog NOUN perro *(MASC)* guardián

guardian NOUN tutor MASC, tutora FEM

Guatemalan NOUN guatemalteco MASC, guatemalteca FEM

Guatemalan ADJECTIVE guatemalteco/guatemalteca

guess NOUN **have a guess!** ¡adivina!, **it's a good guess** lo has adivinado

guess VERB **❶** adivinar [17]; **guess who I saw last night!** ¡adivina a quién vi anoche!, **you'll never guess!** ¡no lo vas a adivinar nunca!, **guess what!** ¿sabes qué? **❷** *(suppose)* suponer [11]; **I guess so** supongo que sí

guest NOUN **❶** invitado MASC, invitada FEM; **we've got guests coming tonight** tenemos invitados esta noche **❷** *(in a hotel)* cliente MASC & FEM **❸ a paying guest** un huésped de pago

guide NOUN **❶** *(book, girl guide)* guía FEM **❷** *(person)* guía MASC & FEM

guidebook NOUN guía FEM

guide dog NOUN perro *(MASC)* lazarillo

guideline NOUN pauta FEM

guilty ADJECTIVE culpable; **to feel guilty** sentirse [14] culpable

guinea pig NOUN *(pet)* cobaya *(FEM)*, *(in an experiment)* conejillo *(MASC)* de indias

guitar NOUN guitarra FEM; **to play the guitar** tocar [31] la guitarra, **on the guitar** a la guitarra

guitarist NOUN guitarrista MASC & FEM

gum NOUN **❶** *(in mouth)* encía FEM **❷** *(chewing gum)* chicle MASC

gun NOUN ❶ pistola FEM ❷ (rifle) fusil MASC

guy NOUN tipo MASC (informal); **he's a nice guy** es un tipo muy majo, **a guy from Newcastle** un tipo de Newcastle

guy rope NOUN viento (MASC) de un tienda de campaña

gym NOUN ❶ (gymnasium) gimnasio MASC; **to go to the gym** ir [8] al gimnasio ❷ (gymnastics) gimnasia FEM

gymnasium NOUN gimnasio MASC

gymnast NOUN gimnasta MASC & FEM

gymnastics NOUN gimnasia FEM

gym shoe NOUN zapatilla (FEM) de gimnasia

habit NOUN costumbre FEM; **to have a habit of doing** tener [9] la costumbre de hacer, **it's a bad habit** es una mala costumbre

hail NOUN granizo MASC

hailstone NOUN granizo MASC

hailstorm NOUN granizada FEM

hair NOUN ❶ pelo MASC; **to have short hair** tener [9] el pelo corto, **to brush your hair** cepillarse [17] el pelo, **to wash your hair** lavarse [17] el pelo, **to have your hair cut** cortarse [17] el pelo, **she's had her hair cut** se ha cortado el pelo ❷ **a hair** (from the head) un pelo (from the body) un vello

hairbrush NOUN cepillo (MASC) del pelo

haircut NOUN ❶ corte (MASC) de pelo; **I like your new haircut** me gusta tu nuevo corte de pelo ❷ **to have a haircut** cortarse [17] el pelo

hairdresser NOUN peluquero (MASC), peluquera FEM; **she's a hairdresser** es peluquera, **at the hairdresser's** en la peluquería

hair drier NOUN secador (MASC) de pelo

hair gel NOUN gel (MASC) para el cabello

hairslide NOUN pasador MASC

a
b
c
d
e
f
g
h
i
j
k
l
m
n
o
p
q
r
s
t
u
v
w
x
y
z

hairspray NOUN laca (FEM) del pelo

hairstyle NOUN peinado MASC

hairy ADJECTIVE peludo/peluda

Haiti NOUN Haití MASC

Haitian NOUN haitiano MASC, haitiana FEM

Haitian ADJECTIVE haitiano/haitiana

half NOUN, PRONOUN ❶ mitad FEM; **half of** la mitad de, **I gave him half of the money** le di la mitad del dinero ❷ **to cut something in half** cortar algo por la mitad ❸ (as a fraction) medio; **three and a half** tres y medio, **she's five and a half** tiene seis años y medio ❹ (in time) media; **half an hour** media hora, **an hour and a half** una hora y media, **it's half past three** son las tres y media ❺ **half a** medio/media, **half a litre** medio litro, **half an apple** media manzana ❻ **half the people** la mitad de la gente, **half the time he's not here** la mitad del tiempo no está aquí

half hour NOUN media hora FEM; **every half hour** cada media hora

half price ADJECTIVE, ADVERB a mitad de precio; **half-price CDs** compactos a mitad de precio, **I bought it half price** lo compré a mitad de precio

half-time NOUN descanso MASC; **at half-time** en el descanso

halfway ADVERB ❶ a mitad de camino; **halfway between Madrid and Barcelona** a mitad de camino entre Madrid y Barcelona ❷ **to be halfway through** ir [8] por la mitad de, **I'm halfway through my homework** voy por la mitad de los deberes

hall NOUN ❶ (in a house) entrada FEM ❷ (public) salón MASC; **the village hall** el salón de actos del pueblo ❸ **a concert hall** una sala de conciertos

ham NOUN ❶ (cooked) jamón (MASC) de York ❷ (cured) jamón (MASC) serrano

hamburger NOUN hamburguesa FEM

hammer NOUN martillo MASC

hammock NOUN hamaca FEM

hamster NOUN hámster MASC

hand NOUN ❶ mano FEM; **to have something in your hand** tener [9] algo en la mano, **to be holding hands** (two people) ir [8] cogidos de la mano, **they were holding hands** iban cogidos de la mano ❷ **to give somebody a hand** echar [17] una mano a alguien, **can you give me a hand to move the table?** ¿puedes echarme una mano para mover la mesa?, **do you need a hand?** ¿necesitas que te echen una mano? ❸ **on the other hand ...** por otro lado ... ❹ (of a watch or clock) manecilla FEM; **the hour hand** la manecilla de las horas

hand VERB **to hand something to somebody** pasarle [17] algo a alguien, **I handed him the keys** le pasé las llaves

handbag NOUN bolso MASC

handbrake NOUN freno (MASC) de mano

handcuffs PLURAL NOUN esposas FEM PLURAL

handful NOUN **a handful of** un puñado de

handkerchief NOUN pañuelo MASC

handle NOUN ❶ (of a door) picaporte MASC ❷ (of a drawer) tirador MASC ❸ (on a cup or basket) asa FEM ❹ (of a knife, tool, or pan) mango MASC

handle VERB ❶ encargarse [28] de; Gina handles the accounts Gina se encarga de la contabilidad ❷ she's good at handling people se le da muy bien tratar con la gente

handlebars PLURAL NOUN manillar MASC

hand luggage NOUN equipaje (MASC) de mano

handsome ADJECTIVE guapo; he's a very handsome guy es un tipo muy guapo

handwriting NOUN letra FEM

handy ADJECTIVE ❶ práctico/práctica; this little knife's very handy este cuchillito es muy práctico ❷ a mano; I always keep a notebook handy siempre guardo un cuaderno a mano

hang VERB colgar [23]; we hung the mirror on the wall colgamos el espejo en la pared, there was a mirror hanging on the wall había un espejo colgado en la pared

• to hang on esperar [17]; hang on a second! ¡espera un poco!
• to hang up (on the phone) colgar [23]; she hung up on me me colgó
• to hang something up colgar [23] algo; you can hang your coat up in the hall puedes colgar el abrigo en la entrada

hangover NOUN resaca FEM; to have a hangover tener [9] resaca

happen VERB ❶ pasar [17]; what's happening? ¿qué pasa?, what happened to him? ¿qué le pasó?, it happened in June pasó en junio ❷ what's happened to the can-opener? ¿dónde se ha metido el abridor? ❸ if you happen to see Jill si ves a Jill

happily ADVERB ❶ alegremente; she smiled happily sonrió alegremente ❷ (willingly) con mucho gusto; I'll happily do it for you lo haré por ti con mucho gusto

happiness NOUN felicidad FEM

happy ADJECTIVE feliz; a happy child un niño feliz, happy birthday! ¡feliz cumpleaños!

harbour NOUN puerto MASC

hard ADJECTIVE ❶ duro/dura ❷ (difficult) difícil; a hard question una pregunta difícil, it's hard to know … es difícil saber …

hard ADVERB mucho; to study hard estudiar [17] mucho, to try hard esforzarse [26] mucho, to work hard trabajar [17] duro

hard-boiled egg NOUN huevo (MASC) duro

hard disk NOUN (in a computer) disco (MASC) duro

hardly ADVERB ❶ apenas; I can hardly hear him apenas puedo oírle ❷ hardly any casi nada, there's hardly any milk casi no hay nada de leche ❸ hardly ever casi nunca, I hardly ever see them casi nunca los veo ❹ there was hardly anybody no había casi nadie

hard up *ADJECTIVE* **to be hard up** estar [2] mal de dinero *(informal)*

harm *NOUN* **it won't do you any harm** no te va a pasar nada

harm *VERB* **to harm somebody** hacerle [7] daño a alguien, **a cup of coffee won't harm you** una taza de café no te va a hacer daño

harvest *NOUN* cosecha *FEM*; **to get the harvest in** hacer [7] la cosecha

hat *NOUN* sombrero *MASC*

hate *VERB* odiar [17]; **I hate geography** odio la geografía

hatred *NOUN* odio *MASC*

haunted *ADJECTIVE* embrujado/ embrujada

have *VERB* ❶ tener [9]; **Anna has three brothers** Anna tiene tres hermanos, **how many sisters do you have?** ¿cuántas hermanas tienes? ❷ **to have got** tener [9], **we've got a dog** tenemos un perro, **what have you got in your hand?** ¿qué tienes en la mano? ❸ *(to form past tenses, verbs in Spanish take 'haber')* **I've finished** he terminado, **have you seen the film?** ¿has visto la película, **Rosie hasn't arrived yet** Rosie aún no ha llegado, **he had left** se había ido *(in question tags 'have' is not translated)*, **you've done this before, haven't you?** tú has hecho esto antes, ¿no? ❹ **to have to do** tener [9] que hacer, **I have to phone my mum** tengo que llamar a mi madre ❺ tomar [17] *(food or drink)*; **we had a coffee** tomamos un café, **what will you have?** ¿qué vais a tomar?, **I'll have an omelette** voy a tomar una tortilla ❻ **to have a shower** ducharse [17], **to have a bath**

bañarse [17] ❼ **to have lunch** comer [18], **to have dinner** *(in the evening)* cenar [17] ❽ **to have a party** dar [4] una fiesta ❾ *(for illnesses)* tener [9]; **he has cancer** tiene cáncer, **I had flu** tuve la gripe ❿ *(for aches)* **she has stomachache** le duele el estómago, **I had a terrible headache** me dolía mucho la cabeza ⓫ **I'm going to have my hair cut** voy a cortarme el pelo, **she's had her TV repaired** ha arreglado la tele

hawk *NOUN* halcón *MASC*

hay *NOUN* heno *MASC*

hay fever *NOUN* fiebre *(FEM)* del heno

hazelnut *NOUN* avellana *FEM*

he *PRONOUN* ❶ *('he', like other subject pronouns, is generally not translated in Spanish; the form of the verb tells you whether the subject of the verb is 'he/she/it', you, they', etc., so 'he' is only translated for emphasis)* **he lives in Newcastle** vive en Newcastle, **he's a student** es estudiante, **he's a very good teacher** es muy buen profesor, **here he is!** ¡aquí está! ❷ *(for emphasis)* él; **he did it** lo hizo él

head *NOUN* ❶ cabeza *FEM*; **he had a cap on his head** tenía un sombrero en la cabeza, **at the head of the queue** a la cabeza de la cola ❷ *(of school)* director *MASC*, directora *FEM* ❸ *(when tossing a coin)* **'heads or tails?' – 'heads'** ¿cara o cruz?' – 'cara'
• **to head for something** dirigirse [49] a; **Liz headed for the door** Liz se dirigió a la puerta

headache NOUN **I've got a headache** me duele la cabeza

headlight NOUN **faro** MASC

headline NOUN **titular** MASC; **to hit the headlines** aparecer [35] en los titulares

headmaster NOUN **director** MASC

headmistress NOUN **directora** FEM

headphones PLURAL NOUN **auriculares** MASC PLURAL

headquarters N PLURAL ❶ (of organization) **sede** FEM ❷ (military) **cuartel** (MASC) **general**

headteacher NOUN **director** MASC, **directora** FEM

health NOUN **salud** FEM

health centre NOUN **centro** (MASC) **médico**

healthy ADJECTIVE ❶ (person) **to be healthy** estar [2] sano ❷ **a healthy diet** una dieta sana

heap NOUN **montón** MASC; **I've got heaps of things to do** tengo montones de cosas que hacer

hear VERB **oír** [56]; **I can't hear you** no te oigo, **I can't hear anything** no oigo nada, **I hear you've bought a dog** he oído que te has comprado un perro
* **to hear about something** enterarse [17] de algo; **have you heard about the concert?** ¿te has enterado de lo del concierto?
* **to hear from somebody have you heard from Amanda?** ¿sabes algo de Amanda?, **I haven't heard from them** no sé nada de ellos

hearing aid NOUN **audífono** MASC

heart NOUN ❶ **corazón** MASC ❷ (in cards) **hearts** corazones (MASC PLURAL), **the jack of hearts** la jota de corazones
* **to learn something by heart** aprender [18] algo de memoria

heart attack NOUN **ataque** (MASC) **al corazón**

heat NOUN **calor** MASC

heat VERB ❶ **calentarse** [29]; **the soup's heating** la sopa se está calentando ❷ **to heat something** calentar [29] algo, **I'll go and heat the soup** voy a calentar la sopa

heater NOUN **estufa** FEM

heating NOUN **calefacción** FEM

heaven NOUN **cielo** MASC

heavy ADJECTIVE ❶ **pesado/pesada**; **a heavy bag** una bolsa pesada, **to be heavy** pesar [17] mucho, **my rucksack's really heavy** mi mochila pesa mucho ❷ (busy) **ocupado/ ocupada**; **I've got a heavy day tomorrow** mañana tengo un día muy ocupado ❸ **heavy rain** lluvia fuerte

hectic ADJECTIVE **a hectic day** un día muy ajetreado

hedge NOUN **seto** MASC

hedgehog NOUN **erizo** MASC

heel NOUN ❶ (of foot) **talón** MASC ❷ (of shoe) **tacón** MASC

height NOUN ❶ (of a person) **estatura** FEM ❷ (of a building) **altura** FEM ❸ (of a mountain) **altitud** FEM

helicopter NOUN **helicóptero** MASC

hell NOUN **infierno** MASC; **it's hell here!** ¡esto es un infierno!

hello EXCLAMATION ❶ (greeting) hola ❷ (on the telephone) ¿dígame?

helmet NOUN casco MASC

help NOUN ayuda FEM; do you need any help? ¿necesitas ayuda?

help VERB ❶ ayudar [17]; to help somebody to do ayudar [17] a alguien a hacer, can you help me move the table? ¿me ayudas a mover la mesa? ❷ to help yourself to something servirse [57] algo, help yourselves to vegetables serviros verdura, help yourself! ¡sírvete! ❸ help! ¡socorro!

helping NOUN porción FEM; would you like a second helping? ¿quieres repetir?

hem NOUN dobladillo MASC

hen NOUN gallina FEM

her PRONOUN ❶ la; I know her la conozco, I saw her last week la vi la semana pasada (with an infinitive or when telling someone to do something, 'la' joins onto the verb) I can hear her puedo oírla, listen to her! ¡escúchala!, (but when telling someone NOT to do something, 'la' comes before the verb) don't push her! ¡no la empujes! ❷ (to her) le; I gave her my address le di mis señas ('le' becomes 'se' before pronouns 'lo' or 'la') I lent it to her se lo dejé ❸ (after a preposition, in comparisons, or after the verb 'to be') ella; with her con ella, without her sin ella, he's older than her él es mayor que ella, it was her era ella

her ADJECTIVE ❶ (before a singular noun) su; her brother su hermano, her house su casa ❷ (before a plural noun) sus; her children sus niños

❸ (with parts of the body) el, la, los, las; she had a glass in her hand tenía un vaso en la mano, she's washing her hands se está lavando las manos

herb NOUN hierba FEM

herd NOUN ❶ (of cattle) manada FEM ❷ (of goats) rebaño MASC

here ADVERB ❶ aquí; not far from here no lejos de aquí, and here they are! ¡aquí están!, Tom isn't here at the moment Tom no está aquí en este momento ❷ (giving something) here it is toma, here's my address toma mis señas, here you are toma

hero NOUN héroe MASC

heroin NOUN heroína FEM

heroine NOUN heroína FEM

hers PRONOUN ❶ (referring to a singular noun) el suyo/la suya; I took my hat and she took hers yo cogí mi sombrero y ella cogió el suyo, I phoned my mum and Donna phoned hers llamé a mi madre y Donna llamó a la suya ❷ (referring to a plural noun) los suyos/las suyas; I've invited my parents and Karen's invited hers yo he invitado a mis padres y Karen a los suyos, I showed her my photos and she showed me hers yo le enseñé mis fotos y ella me enseñó las suyas

herself PRONOUN ❶ (as reflexive) se; she's hurt herself se ha hecho daño, she washed herself se lavó ❷ (for emphasis) ella misma; she said it herself lo dijo ella misma ❸ she did it by herself lo hizo ella sola

hesitate VERB dudar [17]; to hesitate to do dudar en hacer

heterosexual NOUN heterosexual MASC & FEM

hi EXCLAMATION hola

hiccups PLURAL NOUN to have the hiccups tener [9] hipo

hidden ADJECTIVE escondido/escondida

hide VERB ❶ (person) esconderse [18]; she hid behind the door se escondió detrás de la puerta ❷ to hide something esconder [18] algo, who's hidden the chocolate? ¿quién ha escondido el chocolate?

hide-and-seek NOUN to play hide-and-seek jugar [27] al escondite

hi-fi NOUN equipo (MASC) de alta fidelidad

high ADJECTIVE ❶ alto/alta; on a high shelf en una estantería alta, the wall is very high la pared es muy alta, how high is the wall? ¿qué altura tiene la pared?, the wall is two metres high la pared tiene dos metros de altura ❷ (number, price, temperature) alto/alta; food prices are very high el precio de la comida es muy alto ❸ at high speed a alta velocidad ❹ high winds vientos fuertes

Highers, Advanced Highers NOUN PLURAL selectividad FEM (Students take 'la selectividad' at the same age as Advanced Highers in Scotland. You can explain Highers and Advanced Highers briefly as follows: Son exámenes que se hacen en hasta cinco asignaturas, en el penúltimo año de la educación secundaria. Algunos alumnos también se presentan al Advanced Highers en el último años que pueden abarcar

hasta tres asignaturas que ya se hayan estudiado para el nivel de los Highers)
▸ SEE **selectividad**

high-heeled ADJECTIVE de tacón alto; high-heeled shoes zapatos de tacón alto

high jump NOUN salto (MASC) de altura

hijacking NOUN secuestro MASC

hiking NOUN senderismo MASC

hilarious ADJECTIVE divertidísimo/divertidísima

hill NOUN ❶ (low) colina FEM (higher) montaña FEM ❷ (sloping street or road) to go up the hill subir la cuesta

him PRONOUN ❶ lo; I know him lo conozco, I saw him last week lo vi la semana pasada (with an infinitive or when telling someone to do something, 'lo' joins onto the verb) I can't hear him no puedo oírlo, listen to him! ¡escúchalo!, (but when telling someone NOT to do something, 'lo' comes before the verb) don't push him! ¡no lo empujes! ❷ (to him) le; I gave him my address le di mis señas ('le' becomes 'se' before pronouns 'lo' or 'la') I lent it to him se lo dejé ❸ (after a preposition, in comparisons, or after the verb 'to be') él; with him con él, without him sin él, she's older than him ella es mayor que él, it was him era él

himself PRONOUN ❶ (as a reflexive) se; he's hurt himself se hizo daño ❷ (for emphasis) él mismo; he said it himself lo dijo él mismo ❸ he did it by himself lo hizo él solo

hip NOUN **cadera** FEM

hire NOUN **alquiler** MASC; **car hire** alquiler de coches, **for hire** se alquila

hire VERB **alquilar** [17]; **we're going to hire a car** vamos a alquilar un coche

his ADJECTIVE ❶ (before a singular noun) **su**; **his brother** su hermano, **his house** su casa ❷ (before a plural noun) **sus**; **his children** sus niños ❸ (with parts of the body) **el, la, los, las**; **he had a glass in his hand** tenía un vaso en la mano, **he's washing his hands** se está lavando las manos

his PRONOUN ❶ (referring to a singular noun) **el suyo/la suya**; **I took my hat and he took his** yo cogí mi sombrero y él cogió el suyo, **I phoned my mum and Danny phoned his** llamé a mi madre y Danny llamó a la suya ❷ (referring to a plural noun) **los suyos/las suyas**; **I've invited my parents and Steve's invited his** yo he invitado a mis padres y Steve a los suyos, **I showed him my photos and he showed me his** yo le enseñé mis fotos y él me enseño las suyas

historic ADJECTIVE **histórico/histórica**

history NOUN **historia** FEM

hit NOUN (song) **éxito** MASC; **their latest hit** su último éxito, **the film is a huge hit** la película es un gran éxito

hit VERB ❶ **golpear** [17]; **to hit the ball** golpear la pelota ❷ **to hit your head on something** darse [4] un golpe en la cabeza con algo ❸ **chocar** [31] **con**; **the car hit a tree** el coche chocó con el árbol ❹ **she was hit by a car** la atropelló un coche

hitch NOUN **problema** MASC; **there's been a slight hitch** ha habido un pequeño problema

hitch VERB **to hitch a lift** hacer [7] dedo (informal)

hitchhike VERB **hacer** [7] **dedo** (informal); **we hitchhiked to Valencia** hicimos dedo hasta Valencia

hitchhiker NOUN **autoestopista** MASC & FEM

hitchhiking NOUN **autostop** MASC

HIV-negative ADJECTIVE **seronegativo/seronegativa**

HIV-positive ADJECTIVE **seropositivo/ seropositiva**

hobby NOUN **pasatiempo** MASC

hockey NOUN **hockey** MASC; **to play hockey** jugar al hockey

hockey stick NOUN **palo** (MASC) **de hockey**

hold VERB ❶ **sostener** [9]; **to hold something in your hand** sostener algo en la mano, **can you hold the torch?** ¿puedes sostener la linterna? ❷ (contain) **contener** [9]; **a jug which holds a litre** una jarra que contiene un litro ❸ **to hold a meeting** celebrar [17] una reunión ❹ **can you hold the line, please** no se retire, por favor ❺ **hold on!** (wait) ¡un momento!, (on telephone) ¡no cuelgue!
- **to hold somebody up** (delay) entretener [9] a alguien; **I don't want to hold you up** no quiero entretenerte, **I was held up at the dentist's** me entretuve en el dentista
- **to hold something up** (raise)

levantar [17]; **he held up his glass** levantó su vaso

hold-up NOUN ❶ (delay) retraso MASC ❷ (traffic jam) atasco MASC ❸ (robbery) atraco MASC

hole NOUN agujero MASC

holiday NOUN ❶ vacaciones FEM PLURAL; **where are you going for your holiday?** ¿dónde vas de vacaciones?, **have a good holiday!** ¡que pases unas buenas vacaciones!, **to be away on holiday** estar de vacaciones, **to go on holiday** irse de vacaciones, **the school holidays** las vacaciones escolares ❷ **a public holiday** un día de fiesta, **Monday's a holiday** el lunes es fiesta

Holland NOUN Holanda FEM

hollow ADJECTIVE hueco/hueca

holly NOUN acebo MASC

holy ADJECTIVE santo/santa

home NOUN casa FEM; **I was at home** estaba en casa, **to stay at home** quedarse [17] en casa, **make yourself at home** ponte cómodo

home ADVERB a casa; **Susie's gone home** Susie se ha ido a casa, **I'll call in and see you on my way home** te iré a visitar de camino a mi casa, **to get home** llegar [28] a casa, **we got home at midnight** llegamos a casa a media noche

homeless ADJECTIVE sin hogar; **the homeless** la gente sin hogar

homemade ADJECTIVE casero/casera; **homemade cakes** pasteles caseros

home match NOUN **to play a home match** jugar [27] en casa

homeopathic ADJECTIVE homeopático/homeopática

homesick ADJECTIVE **to be homesick** tener [9] morriña

homework NOUN deberes MASC PLURAL; **I did my homework** hice mis deberes, **my Spanish homework** mis deberes de español

homosexual NOUN, ADJECTIVE homosexual

Honduran NOUN hondureño MASC, hondureña FEM

Honduran ADJECTIVE hondureño/ hondureña

Honduras NOUN Honduras FEM

honest ADJECTIVE ❶ honrado/ honrada ❷ **to be honest ...** para serte sincero ...

honestly ADVERB sinceramente

honesty NOUN honradez FEM

honey NOUN miel FEM

honeymoon NOUN luna (FEM) de miel

honour NOUN honor MASC

hood NOUN capucha FEM

hook NOUN ❶ (in clothes) corchete MASC ❷ (for fishing) anzuelo MASC ❸ (for hanging pictures or clothes) gancho MASC ❹ **to take the phone of the hook** descolgar [23] el teléfono

hooligan NOUN gamberro MASC, gamberra FEM

hooray EXCLAMATION ¡hurra!

hoover *VERB* pasar [17] la aspiradora por; **I hoovered my bedroom** pasé la aspiradora por mi habitación

Hoover *NOUN* aspirador *MASC*, aspiradora *FEM*

hope *NOUN* esperanza *FEM*; **to give up hope** perder [36] la esperanza

hope *VERB* esperar [17]; **hoping to see you on Friday** esperando verte el domingo, **here's hoping!** ¡esperemos!, **I hope so** espero que sí, **I hope not** espero que no, **we hope you'll be able to come** esperamos que puedas venir (*'espero que' is followed by the subjunctive*)

hopeless *ADJECTIVE* **to be hopeless at something** ser [1] un negado para algo (*informal*), **I'm hopeless at geography** soy un negado para la geografía

horizon *NOUN* horizonte *MASC*

horn *NOUN* ❶ (*of an animal*) cuerno *MASC* ❷ (*of a car*) bocina *FEM*; **to sound your horn** tocar [31] la bocina ❸ (*musical instrument*) trompa *FEM*; **to play the horn** tocar [31] trompa

horoscope *NOUN* horóscopo *MASC*

horrible *ADJECTIVE* ❶ horrible; **the weather was horrible** el tiempo era horrible, **she's really horrible!** ¡es realmente horrible! ❷ **he was really horrible to me** me trató muy mal

horrific *ADJECTIVE* horroroso/horrorosa; **a horrific accident** un accidente horroroso

horror *NOUN* horror *MASC*

horror film *NOUN* película (*FEM*) de terror

horse *NOUN* caballo *MASC*

horse racing *NOUN* carreras (*FEM PLURAL*) de caballos

hose *NOUN* manguera *FEM*

hospital *NOUN* hospital *MASC*; **to be in hospital** estar [2] en el hospital, **to be taken into hospital** ser [1] hospitalizado

hospitality *NOUN* hospitalidad *FEM*

host *NOUN* anfitrión *MASC*, anfitriona *FEM*; **my host family is very nice** la familia que me hospeda es muy amable

hostage *NOUN* rehén *MASC*

hostel *NOUN* **youth hostel** albergue (*MASC*) juvenil

hostess *NOUN* azafata *FEM*; **an air hostess** una azafata de vuelo

hot *ADJECTIVE* ❶ caliente; **a hot drink** una bebida caliente, **be careful, the plates are hot!** ¡cuidado! los platos están calientes ❷ (*a person*) **to be hot** tener [9] calor, **I'm hot** tengo calor, **I'm very hot** tengo mucho calor, **I'm too hot** tengo demasiado calor ❸ (*the weather or temperature in a room*) **it's hot** hace calor, **it's hot today** hace calor hoy, **it's very hot in the kitchen** hace mucho calor en la cocina ❹ **a hot climate** un clima cálido ❺ (*food: spicy*) picante; **this curry's too hot for me** este curry es demasiado picante para mí

hot dog *NOUN* perrito (*MASC*) caliente

hotel NOUN hotel MASC

hour NOUN hora FEM; **two hours later** dos horas más tarde, **we waited for two hours** esperamos dos horas, **two hours ago** hace dos horas, **to be paid by the hour** cobrar [17] por hora, **I earn six pounds an hour** gano seis libras por hora, **every hour** cada hora, **half an hour** media hora, **a quarter of an hour** un cuarto de hora, **an hour and a half** una hora y media

hourly ADJECTIVE **there is an hourly bus** hay un bus que sale cada hora

hourly ADVERB **the trains leave hourly** los trenes salen cada hora

house NOUN casa FEM; **I'm at Judy's house** estoy en casa de Judy, **I'm going to Judy's house tonight** voy a casa de Judy esta noche, **I phoned from Judy's house** llamé desde casa de Judy

housework NOUN tareas (FEM PLURAL) de la casa; **to do the housework** hacer [7] las tareas de la casa

hovercraft NOUN aerodeslizador MASC

how ADVERB ❶ cómo; **how did you do it?** ¿cómo lo hiciste?, **how are you?** ¿cómo estás?, **I know how to do it** sé cómo hacerlo ❷ **how was the party?** ¿qué tal fue la fiesta? ❸ **how much?** ¿cuánto?, **how much money do you have?** ¿cuánto dinero tienes?, **how much is it?** ¿cuánto cuesta? ❹ **how many?** ¿cuántos?, **how many brothers do you have?** ¿cuántos hermanos tienes? ❺ **how old are you?** ¿cuántos años tienes?, **how heavy is it?** ¿cuánto pesa? ❻ **how far is it?** ¿a qué distancia está?, **how far is it to Bilbao?** ¿a qué

distancia está Bilbao? ❼ **how long will it take?** ¿cuánto tardará?, **how long have you known her?** ¿cuánto tiempo hace que la conoces? ❽ *(in exclamations)* qué; **how nice!** ¡qué bonito!

however ADVERB sin embargo

hug NOUN **to give somebody a hug** darle [4] un abrazo a alguien, **she gave me a hug** me dio un abrazo

huge ADJECTIVE enorme

hum VERB tararear [17] *(a person)*

human ADJECTIVE humano/humana

human being NOUN ser (MASC) humano

humour NOUN humor MASC; **to have a sense of humour** tener [9] sentido del humor

hundred NUMBER ❶ cien; **a hundred** cien, **about a hundred** unos/unas cien, **about a hundred people** unas cien personas, **hundreds of people** cientos de personas ❷ *(for numbers 101 to 199)* ciento; **one hundred and six** ciento seis ❸ *(for numbers 200 to 999)* **two hundred** doscientos/doscientas, **two hundred and ten** doscientos diez, **six hundred** seiscientos/seiscientas

Hungary NOUN Hungría FEM

hunger NOUN hambre FEM *(even though 'hambre' is feminine, it takes 'el' and 'un')*

hungry ADJECTIVE **to be hungry** tener [9] hambre, **I'm hungry** tengo hambre

hunt VERB cazar [22] *(animals)*
• **hunt for** *(search for)* buscar

hurricane *NOUN* hurracán *MASC*

hurry *NOUN* **to be in a hurry** tener [9] prisa, **I'm in a hurry** tengo prisa

hurry *VERB* darse [4] prisa; **I must hurry** debo darme prisa, **we hurried home** nos dimos prisa para llegar a casa, **hurry up!** ¡date prisa!

hurt *VERB* **❶ to hurt somebody** hacer [7] daño a alguien, **you're hurting me!** me estás haciendo daño, **that hurts!** ¡eso hace daño! **❷ my back hurts** me duele la espalda, **my legs hurt** me duelen las piernas **❸ to hurt yourself** hacerse [7] daño, **did you hurt yourself?** ¿te has hecho daño? **❹ to hurt your hand** hacerse [7] daño en la mano, **I hurt my arm** me hice daño en el brazo

husband *NOUN* marido *MASC*

hymn *NOUN* himno *MASC*

hypermarket *NOUN* hipermercado *MASC*

hyphen *NOUN* guión *MASC*

hypnotize *VERB* hipnotizar [25]

I *PRONOUN* **❶** *(like other subject pronouns, 'I' is generally not translated; in Spanish the form of the verb tells you whether the subject of the verb is 'I, we, they', etc., so 'I' is only translated for emphasis)* **I am Scottish** soy escocés, **I have two sisters** tengo dos hermanas **❷** *(for emphasis)* yo; **I did it** lo hice yo, **I went but Robert didn't** yo fui pero Robert no, **Tony and I** Tony y yo

Iberia *NOUN* Iberia *FEM*

Iberian *ADJECTIVE* ibérico/ibérica

ice *NOUN* hielo *MASC*

iceberg *NOUN* iceberg *MASC*

ice cream *NOUN* helado *MASC*; **a chocolate ice cream** un helado de chocolate

ice-cube *NOUN* cubito *(MASC)* de hielo

ice hockey *NOUN* hockey *(MASC)* sobre hielo

ice rink *NOUN* pista *(FEM)* de hielo

ice-skating *NOUN* patinaje *(MASC)* sobre hielo; **to go ice-skating** ir [8] a patinar sobre hielo

icing *NOUN* azúcar *(MASC)* glaseado

icon *NOUN* icono *MASC*

icy *ADJECTIVE* **❶** cubierto/cubierta de hielo *(a road)* **❷** *(very cold)* helado/

helada; **an icy wind** un viento helado

idea NOUN idea FEM; **what a good idea!** ¡qué buena idea!, **I've no idea** no tengo ni idea

ideal ADJECTIVE ideal

identical ADJECTIVE idéntico/idéntica; **identical twins** gemelos *(male, or male and female)*, gemelas *(female only)*

identity card NOUN carné *(FEM)* de identidad

idiot NOUN idiota MASC & FEM

idiotic ADJECTIVE idiota

i.e. ABBREVIATION *(in writing)* i.e., *(in speech)* esto es

if CONJUNCTION ❶ si; **if Sue's there** si Sue está allí, **if it rains** si llueve, **if not** si no *(when talking about something that might or might not happen, 'si' is followed by the subjunctive)* **if I won the lottery** si ganase la lotería ❷ **if only ...** ojalá ..., **if only you'd told me** ojalá me lo hubieses dicho ❸ **even if** incluso si, **even if it snows** incluso si nieva ❹ **if I were you ...** yo que tú ..., **if I were you, I'd forget it** yo que tú me olvidaría del asunto

ignore VERB ❶ ignorar [17] *(a person)* ❷ no hacer [7] caso de *(what somebody says)*; **just ignore it** no hagas caso

ill ADJECTIVE enfermo/enferma; **to fall ill, to be taken ill** enfermar [17], **to feel ill** sentirse [14] mal

illegal ADJECTIVE ilegal

illness NOUN enfermedad FEM

illustrated ADJECTIVE ilustrado/ilustrada

illustration NOUN ilustración FEM

imagination NOUN imaginación FEM; **to show imagination** demostrar [24] imaginación

imaginative ADJECTIVE imaginativo/imaginativa

imagine VERB imaginar [17]; **imagine that you're very rich** imagina que eres muy rico, **you can't imagine how hard it was!** ojalá me lo ¡no puedes imaginarte lo difícil que fue!

imitate VERB imitar [17]

imitation NOUN imitación FEM

immediate ADJECTIVE inmediato/inmediata

immediately ADVERB inmediatamente; **I rang them immediately** los llamé inmediatamente, **immediately before** justo antes, **immediately after** justo después

immigrant NOUN inmigrante MASC & FEM

immigration NOUN inmigración FEM

impact NOUN impacto MASC

impatience NOUN impaciencia FEM

impatient ADJECTIVE ❶ impaciente ❷ **to get impatient with somebody** impacientarse [17] con alguien

impatiently ADVERB con impaciencia

imperfect NOUN *(of a verb)* imperfecto MASC; **in the imperfect** en imperfecto

import NOUN **importación** FEM

import VERB **importar** [17]

importance NOUN **importancia** FEM

important ADJECTIVE **importante**

impossible ADJECTIVE **imposible**; **it's impossible to find a telephone** es imposible encontrar un teléfono

impressed ADJECTIVE **impresionado/impresionada**

impression NOUN **impresión** FEM; **to make a good impression on somebody** causar [17] una buena impresión a alguien, **I got the impression he was hiding something** me dio la impresión de que estaba ocultando algo

improve VERB **mejorar** [17]; **to improve something** mejorar [17] algo, **the weather is improving** el tiempo está mejorando

improvement NOUN ❶ (a change for the better) **mejora** FEM ❷ (gradual progress) **progreso** MASC (in schoolwork, for example)

in PREPOSITION, ADVERB ❶ **en**; **in Spain** en España, **in Spanish** en español, **in Barcelona** en Barcelona, **in my pocket** en mi bolsillo, **in the newspaper** en el periódico, **in my class** en mi clase, **I was in the bath** estaba en el baño, **a house in the country** una casa en el campo, **in school** en el colegio, **in town** en la ciudad, **in the photo** en la foto ❷ **in pencil** a lápiz, **in twos** de dos en dos ❸ (wearing) **de**; **the girl in the pink shirt** la chica de la falda rosa, **he was in a suit** llevaba un traje, **dressed in white** vestida de blanco ❹ (with month, season, or year) **in May** en mayo, **in 1998** en

mil novecientos noventa y ocho, **in winter** en invierno ❺ (with parts of the day) **in the morning** por la mañana, **in the night** por la noche, **at eight in the morning** a las ocho de la mañana ❻ **I'll phone you in ten minutes** te llamaré dentro de diez minutos, **she did it in five minutes** lo hizo en cinco minutos ❼ (after superlative) **de**; **the tallest boy in the class** el chico más alto de la clase, **the biggest city in the world** la ciudad más grande del mundo ❽ **in time** con el tiempo ❾ **in the sun** al sol, **in the rain** bajo la lluvia ❿ **to come in** entrar [17], **to go in** entrar [17], **we went into the cinema** entramos en el cine, **to run in** entrar [17] corriendo ⓫ **to be in** (at home, around) estar [2], **Mick's not in at the moment** Mick no está en este momento

include VERB **incluir** [54]; **dinner is included in the price** la cena está incluida en el precio, **service included** servicio incluido

including PREPOSITION **incluido**; **50 pounds including VAT** cincuenta libras IVA incluido, **everyone, including children** todo el mundo incluidos los niños, **including Sundays** incluidos los domingos, **not including Sundays** sin incluir los domingos

income NOUN **ingresos** MASC PLURAL

income tax NOUN **impuesto** (MASC) **sobre la renta**

inconvenient ADJECTIVE ❶ **poco conveniente** (a place or an arrangement) ❷ **inoportuno/inoportuna** (a time)

increase NOUN **aumento** MASC (in price, for example)

increase *VERB* aumentar [17]; **the price has increased by ten pounds** el precio ha aumentado diez libras

incredible *ADJECTIVE* increíble

incredibly *ADVERB* *(very)* increíblemente; **the film's incredibly boring** la película es increíblemente aburrida

indeed *ADVERB* ❶ *(to emphasize)* **she's very pleased indeed** está contentísima, **I'm very hungry indeed** tengo muchísima hambre, **thank you very much indeed** muchísimas gracias ❷ *(certainly)* **'can you hear his radio?' – 'indeed I can!'** ¿oyes su radio?' – 'ya lo creo', **'do you like it?' – 'I do indeed!'** ¿te gusta?' – 'sí, muchísimo'

indefinite article *NOUN* *(in grammar)* artículo *(MASC)* indefinido

independence *NOUN* independencia *FEM*

independent *ADJECTIVE* ❶ *(a country or person)* independiente ❷ **an independent school** una escuela privada

index *NOUN* índice *MASC*

index finger *NOUN* dedo *(MASC)* índice

India *NOUN* India *FEM*

Indian *NOUN* *(of India)* indio *MASC*, india *FEM*

Indian *ADJECTIVE* *(of India)* indio/india

indigestion *NOUN* indigestión *FEM*; **to have indigestion** tener [9] indigestión

indirect *ADJECTIVE* indirecto/indirecta

individual *NOUN* individuo *MASC*

individual *ADJECTIVE* ❶ individual *(a serving or a contribution, for example)* ❷ **individual tuition** clases *(FEM PLURAL)* particulares

indoor *ADJECTIVE* **an indoor swimming pool** una piscina cubierta, **an indoor plant** una planta de interior

indoors *ADVERB* dentro; **it's cooler indoors** hace más fresco dentro, **to go indoors** entrar [17], **to stay indoors** quedarse [17] dentro

industrial *ADJECTIVE* industrial

industrial estate *NOUN* zona *(FEM)* industrial

industry *NOUN* industria *FEM*; **the advertising industry** la industria de la publicidad

inevitable *ADJECTIVE* inevitable

inevitably *ADVERB* inevitablemente

inexperienced *ADJECTIVE* inexperto/inexperta

infected *ADJECTIVE* infectado/infectada

infection *NOUN* infección *FEM*; **an eye infection** una infección de ojos, **a throat infection** anginas *FEM PLURAL*

infectious *ADJECTIVE* infeccioso/infecciosa

infinitive *NOUN* infinitivo *MASC*; **in the infinitive** en infinitivo

inflation *NOUN* inflación *FEM*

influence *NOUN* influencia *FEM*; **to be a good influence on somebody** ser [1] una buena influencia para alguien

inform *VERB* informar [17]; **to inform somebody that** informar a alguien de que, **they informed us that there was a problem** nos informaron de que había un problema, **to inform somebody of something** informar a alguien de algo

informal *ADJECTIVE* ❶ informal *(a meal or event, for example)* ❷ *(language)* familiar; **an informal expression** una expresión familiar

information *NOUN* información *FEM*; **I need some information about flights to Madrid** necesito información sobre vuelos a Madrid, **a piece of information** un dato

information desk *NOUN* mostrador *(MASC)* de información

information office *NOUN* oficina *(FEM)* de información

information technology, **IT** *NOUN* informática *FEM*

infuriating *ADJECTIVE* exasperante

ingredient *NOUN* ingrediente *MASC*

initials *PLURAL NOUN* iniciales *FEM PLURAL*; **put your initials here** pon tus iniciales aquí

injection *NOUN* inyección *FEM*; **to give somebody an injection** ponerle [11] una inyección a alguien

injure *VERB* herir [14]

injured *ADJECTIVE* herido/herida

injury *NOUN* herida *FEM*

ink *NOUN* tinta *FEM*

in-laws *PLURAL NOUN* suegros *MASC PLURAL*

innocent *ADJECTIVE* inocente

insane *ADJECTIVE* loco/loca

inscription *NOUN* inscripción *FEM*

insect *NOUN* insecto *MASC*; **an insect bite** una picadura de insecto

insert *VERB* insertar [17]

inside *NOUN* interior *MASC*; **the inside of the oven** el interior del horno

inside *PREPOSITION* dentro de; **inside the cinema** dentro del cine

inside *ADVERB* dentro; **she's inside, I think** creo que está dentro, **to go inside** entrar [17]

inside out *ADJECTIVE, ADVERB* del revés; **your jumper's inside out** llevas el jersey del revés

insist *VERB* ❶ insistir [19]; **if you insist** si insistes, **to insist on doing** insistir en hacer, **he insisted on paying** insistió en pagar ❷ **to insist that** insistir en que, **Ruth insisted I was wrong** Ruth insistió en que yo estaba equivocada

inspection *NOUN* inspección *FEM*

inspector *NOUN* inspector *MASC*, inspectora *FEM*

inspiration *NOUN* inspiración *FEM*

install *VERB* instalar [17]

instalment *NOUN* ❶ *(of a TV or radio serial)* episodio *MASC* ❷ *(payment)* plazo *MASC*; **to pay by instalments** pagar [28] a plazos

instance *NOUN* **for instance** por ejemplo

instant *NOUN* **instante** *MASC*; **come here this instant!** ¡ven aquí ahora mismo!

instant *ADJECTIVE* ❶ **instantáneo/ instantánea** *(coffee or soup)* ❷ *(immediate)* **inmediato/ inmediata** *(an effect or a success, for example)*

instead *ADVERB* ❶ **Ted couldn't go, so I went instead** Ted no pudo ir, así que fui yo en su lugar, **we didn't go to the concert, we went to Lucy's instead** no fuimos al concierto, fuimos a casa de Lucy ❷ **instead of** en vez de, **instead of pudding I had cheese** en vez de dulce tomé queso, **instead of playing tennis we went swimming** en vez de jugar al tenis nos fuimos a nadar

instinct *NOUN* **instinto** *MASC*

instruct *VERB* **to instruct somebody to do** ordenar [17] a alguien que haga (*'que' is followed by the subjunctive*), **the teacher instructed us to stay together** la profesora nos ordenó que nos quedásemos juntos

instructions *PLURAL NOUN* **instrucciones** *FEM PLURAL*; **follow the instructions on the packet** siga las instrucciones del paquete, **'instructions for use'** 'modo de empleo'

instructor *NOUN* ❶ **monitor** *MASC*, **monitora** *FEM*; **my skiing instructor** mi monitor de esquí ❷ **profesor** *MASC*, **profesora** *FEM*; **my driving instructor** mi profesor de conducir

instrument *NOUN* **instrumento** *MASC*; **to play an instrument** tocar [31] un instrumento

insulin *NOUN* **insulina** *FEM*

insult *NOUN* **insulto** *MASC*

insult *VERB* **insultar** [17]

insurance *NOUN* **seguro** *MASC*; **travel insurance** seguro de viaje, **fire insurance** seguro contra incendios, **do you have medical insurance?** ¿tienes seguro médico?

intelligence *NOUN* **inteligencia** *FEM*

intelligent *ADJECTIVE* **inteligente**

intend *VERB* ❶ **querer** [12]; **as I intended** como yo quería ❷ **to intend to do** tener [9] pensado hacer, **we intend to spend the night in Rome** tenemos pensado pasar la noche en Roma

intensive *ADJECTIVE* **intensivo/ intensiva**; **an intensive course** un curso intensivo, **in intensive care** en cuidados intensivos

intention *NOUN* **intención** *FEM*; **I have no intention of paying** no tengo ninguna intención de pagar

interest *NOUN* ❶ *(hobby)* **afición** *FEM*; **what are your interests?** ¿qué aficiones tienes? ❷ *(keenness)* **interés** *MASC*; **she showed interest** mostró interés

interest *VERB* **interesar** [17]; **that doesn't interest me** eso no me interesa

interested *ADJECTIVE* **Sean's very interested in cooking** *(to fiddle with it)* a Sean le interesa mucho la cocina

interesting *ADJECTIVE* **interesante**

interfere *VERB* ❶ **to interfere with something** *(to fiddle with it)* tocar [31] algo, **don't interfere with my computer!** ¡no toques mi ordenador! ❷ **to interfere in**

a
b
c
d
e
f
g
h
i
j
k
l
m
n
o
p
q
r
s
t
u
v
w
x
y
z

entrometerse [18] en *(someone else's affairs)*

interior *ADJECTIVE* interior

interior designer *NOUN* interiorista *MASC & FEM*

international *ADJECTIVE* internacional

Internet *NOUN* Internet *FEM*; **on the Internet** en Internet *('Internet' is never used with 'the' or 'a/an')*

interpreter *NOUN* intérprete *MASC & FEM*

interrupt *VERB* interrumpir [19]

interruption *NOUN* interrupción *FEM*

interval *NOUN* intermedio *MASC (in a play or concert)*

interview *NOUN* entrevista *FEM*; **a job interview** una entrevista de trabajo, **a TV interview** una entrevista en la tele

interview *VERB* entrevistar [17] *(on TV, radio)*

interviewer *NOUN* entrevistador *MASC*, entrevistadora *FEM*

into *PREPOSITION* ❶ dentro; **I put the cat into his basket** puse al gato dentro de su cesta ❷ **to go into** entrar, entrar [17] a, **he's gone into the bank** ha entrado al banco ❸ **to get into** entrar [17] en *(car)*, **we all got into the car** entramos todos en el coche ❹ **to go into town** ir [8] a la ciudad, **Mum's gone into town** mamá se ha ido a la ciudad, **to get into bed** meterse [18] a la cama ❺ **to translate into Spanish** traducir [60] al español, **to change pounds into euros** cambiar [17] libras a euros

introduce *VERB* presentar [17]; **she introduced me to her brother** me presentó a su hermano, **can I introduce you to my mother?** ¿te puedo presentar a mi madre?

introduction *NOUN (in a book)* introducción *FEM*

invade *VERB* invadir [19]

invalid *NOUN* inválido *MASC*, inválida *FEM*

invasion *NOUN* invasión *FEM*

invent *VERB* inventar [17]

invention *NOUN* invento *MASC*

inverted commas *PLURAL NOUN* comillas *FEM PLURAL*; **in inverted commas** entre comillas

investigation *NOUN* investigación *FEM*; **an investigation into the fire** una investigación sobre el fuego

invisible *ADJECTIVE* invisible

invitation *NOUN* invitación *FEM*; **an invitation to dinner** una invitación a cenar

invite *VERB* invitar [17]; **Kirsty invited me to lunch** Kirsty me invitó a comer, **he's invited me out on Tuesday** me ha invitado a salir el martes

invoice *NOUN* factura *FEM*

involve *VERB* ❶ suponer [11]; **it involves a lot of work** supone mucho trabajo ❷ *(consist in)* **what does the job involve?** ¿en qué consiste el trabajo? ❸ **to be involved in** tomar [17] parte en, **I am involved in the new project** estoy tomando parte en el nuevo proyecto

Iran NOUN Iran MASC

Iraq NOUN Irak MASC

Ireland NOUN Irlanda FEM; **the Republic of Ireland** la República Irlandesa

iris NOUN lirio MASC

Irish NOUN ❶ (the language) irlandés MASC ❷ (the people) **the Irish** los irlandeses

Irish ADJECTIVE irlandés/irlandesa

Irishman NOUN irlandés

Irish Sea NOUN mar (MASC) de Irlanda

Irishwoman NOUN irlandesa FEM

iron NOUN ❶ (for clothes) plancha FEM ❷ (the metal) hierro MASC

iron VERB planchar [17]

ironing NOUN **to do the ironing** planchar [17]

ironing board NOUN tabla (FEM) de planchar

irregular ADJECTIVE irregular

irresponsible ADJECTIVE irresponsable

irritating ADJECTIVE irritante

Islam NOUN Islam MASC

Islamic ADJECTIVE islámico/islámica

island NOUN isla FEM

isolated ADJECTIVE aislado/aislada

Israel NOUN Israel MASC

Israeli NOUN israelí MASC & FEM

Israeli ADJECTIVE israelí

issue NOUN ❶ (something you discuss) tema MASC; **a political issue** un tema político ❷ (of a magazine) número MASC

issue VERB distribuir [54]

it PRONOUN ❶ ('it' like other subject pronouns is generally not translated; in Spanish the form of the verb tells you whether the subject of the verb is 'he/she/it, we, they', etc) **'where is my bag?' – 'it's in the kitchen'** ¿dónde está mi bolso?' – 'está en la cocina', **read this book, it's great** lee este libro, es genial, **'how old is your car?' – 'it's five years old'** ¿cuántos años tiene tu coche?' – 'cinco' ❷ (as the object of the verb) lo/la; **where's my book? I've lost it** ¿dónde está mi libro? lo he perdido, **give me the suitcase, I'll carry it** dame la maleta, yo la llevo (with a verb in the infinitive or when telling somebody to do something, 'lo' or 'la' join onto the verb) **I've finished the letter, I only have to sign it** he terminado la carta, solo me queda firmarla, **it's your money, take it** es tu dinero, cógelo (but when telling somebody NOT to do something, 'lo' or 'la' goes before the verb) **it's an expensive vase, don't break it** es un jarrón caro, no lo rompas ❸ **who is it?** ¿quién es?, **it's me** soy yo, **what is it?** ¿qué es? ❹ **yes, it's true** sí, es verdad, **it doesn't matter** no importa ❺ **it's raining** está lloviendo, **it's a nice day** hace buen día, **it's very cold here** hace mucho frío aquí, **it's two o'clock** son las dos ❻ (after a preposition) **I don't want to talk about it** no quiero hablar de ello, **the box goes behind it** la caja va detrás

English—Spanish

A
B
C
D
E
F
G
H
I
J
K
L
M
N
O
P
Q
R
S
T
U
V
W
X
Y
Z

IT NOUN *(short for information technology)* **informática** FEM

Italian NOUN ❶ *(the language)* **italiano** MASC ❷ *(person)* **italiano** MASC, **italiana** FEM

Italian ADJECTIVE ❶ **italiano/italiana**; **Italian food** la comida italiana ❷ de italiano *(a teacher or a lesson)*; **my Italian class** mi clase de italiano

italics NOUN **cursiva** FEM; **in italics** en cursiva

Italy NOUN **Italia** FEM

itch VERB ❶ *(a garment)* **picar** [31]; **this sweater itches** este jersey pica ❷ *(a part of the body)* **my back is itching** me pica la espalda, **I'm itching all over** me pica todo el cuerpo

item NOUN **artículo** MASC

its ADJECTIVE ❶ *(before a singular noun)* **su**; **its ear** su oreja ❷ *(before a plural noun)* **sus**; **its toys** sus juguetes

itself PRONOUN ❶ *(as a reflexive)* **se**; **the cat is washing itself** el gato se está lavando ❷ **by itself** solo/sola, **he left the dog by itself** dejó al perro solo

ivory NOUN **marfil** MASC

ivy NOUN **hiedra** FEM

jack NOUN ❶ *(in cards)* **jota** FEM; **the jack of clubs** la jota de tréboles ❷ *(for a car)* **gato** MASC

jacket NOUN ❶ **chaqueta** FEM ❷ *(casual)* **americana** FEM

jagged ADJECTIVE **dentado/dentada**

jail NOUN **cárcel** FEM

jail VERB **meter** [18] **en la cárcel**

jam NOUN ❶ *(that you eat)* **mermelada** FEM; **raspberry jam** mermelada de frambuesa ❷ **a traffic jam** un atasco (de tráfico)

Jamaica NOUN **Jamaica** FEM

Jamaican NOUN **jamaicano** MASC, **jamaicana** FEM

Jamaican ADJECTIVE **jamaicano/jamaicana**

January NOUN **enero** MASC

Japan NOUN **Japón** MASC

Japanese NOUN ❶ *(the language)* **japonés** MASC ❷ *(person)* **japonés** MASC, **japonesa** FEM; **the Japanese** los japoneses

Japanese ADJECTIVE **japonés/japonesa**

jar NOUN **bote** MASC; **a jar of jam** un bote de mermelada

jazz NOUN jazz MASC

jealous ADJECTIVE celoso/celosa

jealousy NOUN celos MASC PLURAL

jeans NOUN vaqueros MASC PLURAL; **my jeans** mis vaqueros, **a pair of jeans** unos vaqueros

jelly NOUN ❶ (clear jam) jalea FEM ❷ (dessert) gelatina FEM

jellyfish NOUN medusa FEM

jersey NOUN ❶ (sweater) jersey MASC ❷ (for football) camiseta FEM

Jesus NOUN Jesús MASC; **Jesus Christ** Jesucristo

Jew NOUN judío MASC, judía FEM

jewel NOUN joya FEM

jeweller NOUN joyero MASC, joyera FEM

jeweller's NOUN joyería FEM

jewellery NOUN joyas FEM PLURAL

Jewish ADJECTIVE judío/judía

jigsaw NOUN rompecabezas (MASC) puzzle MASC

job NOUN ❶ (paid work) trabajo MASC; **a job as a secretary** un trabajo de secretaria, **he's got a job** tiene un trabajo, **out of a job** sin trabajo, **what's your job?** ¿en qué trabajas? ❷ (a task) tarea FEM; **it's not an easy job** no es una tarea fácil, **she made a good job of it** lo hizo muy bien

jobless ADJECTIVE en paro

jog VERB **to go jogging** hacer [7] footing

join VERB ❶ (become a member of) hacerse [7] socio de; **I've joined the judo club** me he hecho socio del club de judo ❷ (to meet up with) **you go ahead, I'll join you later** id vosotros, yo voy más tarde, **we are going for a meal, do you want to join us?** vamos a salir a comer, ¿quieres venirte con nosotros? ❸ **to join two things together** unir [19] dos cosas ❹ **to join a queue** ponerse [11] a la cola

• **to join in** ❶ participar [17]; **Ruth never joins in** Ruth nunca participa ❷ **to join in something** tomar [17] parte en algo, **won't you join in the game?** ¿no quieres tomar parte en el juego?

joiner NOUN carpintero MASC, carpintera FEM

joint NOUN ❶ (of meat) corte MASC; **a joint of beef** un corte de carne ❷ (in your body) articulación FEM ❸ **the joint winner of the Nobel Prize** uno de los ganadores del Premio Nobel

joke NOUN ❶ (a funny story) chiste MASC; **to tell a joke** contar [24] un chiste ❷ (directed against somebody) broma FEM; **to play a joke on somebody** gastarle [17] una broma a alguien

joke VERB bromear [17]; **you must be joking!** ¡estás bromeando!

joker NOUN (in cards) comodín MASC

journalism NOUN periodismo MASC

journalist NOUN periodista MASC & FEM; **Sean's a journalist** Sean es periodista

journey NOUN viaje MASC; **our journey to Turkey** nuestro viaje a Turquía, **a bus journey** un viaje en autobús

joy NOUN alegría FEM

joystick NOUN *(for computer games)* mando MASC

Judaism NOUN judaismo MASC

judge NOUN juez MASC, jueza FEM

judge VERB juzgar [28]

judgement NOUN ❶ *(sense)* juicio MASC ❷ *(judge's decision)* sentencia FEM

judo NOUN judo MASC; **he does judo** hace judo

jug NOUN jarra FEM *(big)*, jarrita FEM *(small)*

juggle VERB hacer [17] malabarismos

juice NOUN zumo MASC; **two orange juices, please** dos zumos de naranja, por favor

juicy ADJECTIVE jugoso/jugosa

jukebox NOUN máquina *(FEM)* de discos

July NOUN julio MASC

jumble sale NOUN mercadillo *(MASC)* de beneficencia

jumbo jet NOUN jumbo MASC

jump NOUN salto MASC; **a parachute jump** un salto en paracaídas

jump VERB saltar [17]

jumper NOUN jersey MASC

junction NOUN ❶ *(of roads)* cruce MASC ❷ *(on railway)* empalme MASC

June NOUN junio MASC

jungle NOUN selva FEM

junior ADJECTIVE **a junior school** una escuela primaria, **the juniors** los alumnos de primaria

junk NOUN ❶ *(rubbish)* basura FEM ❷ *(discarded things)* trastos *(MASC PLURAL)* viejos

junk food NOUN comida *(FEM)* basura

jury NOUN jurado MASC

just ADVERB ❶ justo; **just on time** justo a tiempo, **just after the church** justo después de misa, **it's just what I need** es justo lo que necesito ❷ **to have just done** acabar [17] de hacer, **Tom has just arrived** Tom acaba de llegar, **Helen had just called** Helen acaba de llamar ❸ **I'm just finishing the ironing** estoy terminando de planchar ❹ *(only)* solo; **just for fun** solo por pasarlo bien, **he's just a child** es solo un niño, **there's just me and Justine** solo estamos Justine y yo ❺ **just as** igual de, **it's just as good as the other** es igual de bueno que el otro, **it's just as possible** es igualmente posible ❻ **just coming!** ¡ahora mismo voy!

justice NOUN justicia FEM

Kk

kangaroo *NOUN* **canguro** *MASC*

karate *NOUN* **kárate** *MASC*

kebab *NOUN* **brocheta** *FEM*

keen *ADJECTIVE* ❶ *(enthusiastic)* **you don't look too keen** no pareces muy entusiasmado, **they were keen on the idea** estaban interesados en la idea, **he's not keen on fish** no le gusta el pescado ❷ *(committed)* **he's a keen photographer** le encanta la fotografía

keep *VERB* ❶ **quedarse** [17] **con**; **I kept the letter** me quedé con la carta, **keep the change** quédese con el cambio ❷ **to keep something for someone** guardarle [17] algo a alguien, **will you keep my seat?** ¿me guardas el sitio?, **to keep a secret** guardar [17] un secreto ❸ **to keep somebody waiting** hacer [7] esperar a alguien ❹ *(to store)* **guardar**; **I keep my bike in the garage** guardo mi bici en el garaje, **where do you keep the saucepans?** ¿dónde guardas las cacerolas? ❺ **to keep on doing** seguir [64] haciendo, **she kept on talking** siguió hablando, **keep straight on** siga todo recto ❻ **to keep on doing** *(time after time)* no parar de hacer, **he keeps on ringing me up** no para [17] de llamarme ❼ **keep calm!** ¡no te pongas nervioso!, **keep still!** ¡estate quieto!,

keep out of the sun no te pongas al sol ❽ **to keep a promise** mantener [9] una promesa

kerb *NOUN* **bordillo** *(MASC)* **de la acera**

ketchup *NOUN* **ketchup** *MASC*

kettle *NOUN* **hervidora** *FEM*; **to put the kettle on** enchufar la hervidora *(electric)*

key *NOUN* ❶ *(for a lock)* **llave** *FEM*; **a bunch of keys** un manojo de llaves ❷ *(on a piano or typewriter)* **tecla** *FEM*

keyboard *NOUN* *(for a piano or a computer)* **teclado** *MASC*

keyhole *NOUN* **ojo** *(MASC)* **de la cerradura**

kick *NOUN* *(from a person or a horse)* **patada** *FEM*; **to give somebody a kick** darle [4] una patada a alguien
• **to get a kick out of doing** disfrutar [17] haciendo

kick *VERB* **to kick somebody** darle [4] una patada a alguien, **to kick the ball** darle [4] una patada al balón
• **to kick off** empezar [25]

kick-off *NOUN* **saque** *(MASC)* **inicial**

kid *NOUN* **niño** *MASC*, **niña** *(FEM)* *(child)*; **Dad's looking after the kids** papá está cuidando de los niños

kidnap *VERB* **secuestrar** [17]

kidnapper *NOUN* **secuestrador** *MASC*, **secuestradora** *FEM*

kidney *NOUN* **riñón** *MASC*

kill *VERB* **matar** [17]; **she was killed in an accident** se mató en un accidente

killer NOUN (murderer) asesino MASC, asesina FEM

kilo NOUN kilo MASC; **a kilo of sugar** un kilo de azúcar, **five euros a kilo** cinco euros el kilo

kilogramme NOUN kilogramo MASC

kilometre NOUN kilómetro MASC

kilt NOUN falda (FEM) escocesa

kind NOUN tipo MASC; **it's a kind of fruit** es un tipo de fruta, **all kinds of people** todo tipo de personas

kind ADJECTIVE amable; **Marion was very kind to me** Marion fue muy amable conmigo

kindness NOUN amabilidad FEM

king NOUN rey MASC; **King Juan Carlos** el rey Juan Carlos, **the king of hearts** el rey de corazones

kingdom NOUN reino MASC; **the United Kingdom** el Reino Unido

kiosk NOUN ❶ (for newspapers or snacks) quiosco MASC ❷ (for a phone) cabina FEM

kiss NOUN beso MASC; **to give somebody a kiss** darle [4] un beso a alguien

kiss VERB besar [17]; **kiss me!** ¡bésame!, **to kiss somebody goodbye** darle [4] un beso de despedida a alguien, **we kissed each other** nos besamos

kit NOUN ❶ (of tools) a tool kit una caja de herramientas, **a first-aid kit** un botiquín ❷ (clothes) equipo MASC; **where's my gym kit?** ¿dónde está mi equipo de gimnasia? ❸ (for making a model, a piece of furniture, etc) kit MASC

kitchen NOUN cocina FEM; **the kitchen table** la mesa de la cocina

kitchen roll NOUN papel (MASC) de cocina

kite NOUN (toy) cometa FEM; **to fly a kite** hacer [7] volar una cometa

kitten NOUN gatito MASC, gatita FEM

kiwi fruit NOUN kiwi MASC

knack NOUN tranquillo MASC

knee NOUN rodilla FEM; **to be on your knees** estar [2] de rodillas

kneel VERB (to kneel down) arrodillarse [17], (to be on your knees) estar [2] de rodillas

knickers PLURAL NOUN bragas FEM PLURAL

knife NOUN cuchillo MASC

knight NOUN (in chess) caballo MASC

knit VERB hacer [7] punto

knitting NOUN punto MASC

knob NOUN pomo MASC (on a door), tirador MASC (on a drawer)

knock NOUN golpe MASC; **a knock on the head** un golpe en la cabeza, **a knock at the door** un golpe en la puerta

knock VERB ❶ (to bang) darse [4] un golpe; **I knocked my arm on the table** me di un golpe en el brazo con la mesa ❷ **to knock at the door** llamar [17] a la puerta
• **to knock down** ❶ (in a traffic accident) atropellar [17] (a person) ❷ (to demolish) derribar [17] (an old building)
• **to knock out** ❶ (to make unconscious) dejar [17] sin sentido

❷ *(in sport, to eliminate)* eliminar [17]

knocker *NOUN* aldaba *FEM*

knot *NOUN* nudo *MASC*; **to tie a knot in something** hacer [7] un nudo a algo

know *VERB* ❶ *(facts)* saber [13]; **do you know where Tim is?** ¿sabes dónde está Tim?, **I know they've moved house** sé que se han cambiado de casa, **he knows it by heart** se lo sabe de memoria, **yes, I know** sí, ya lo sé, **you never know!** ¡nunca se sabe! ❷ *(be personally acquainted with)* conocer [35] *(a person, place, book, or music, for example)*; **do you know that song?** ¿conoces esa canción?, **all the people I know** toda la gente que conozco, **I don't know his mother** no conozco a su madre ❸ **to know how to do** saber [13] hacer, **Steve knows how to make paella** Steve sabe hacer paella ❹ **to know about** estar [2] al corriente de *(the latest news)* ❺ **to know about** saber [13] de *(a subject, machines)*, **Lindy knows about computers** Lindy sabe de ordenadores

knowledge *NOUN* conocimientos *MASC PLURAL*; **scientific knowledge** conocimientos científicos

knuckle *NOUN* nudillo *MASC*

koala *NOUN* koala *MASC*

Koran *NOUN* Corán *MASC*

kosher *ADJECTIVE* kosher

lab *NOUN* laboratorio *MASC*

label *NOUN* etiqueta *FEM*

laboratory *NOUN* laboratorio *MASC*

Labour *NOUN* los laboristas *MASC PLURAL*; **to vote for Labour** votar [17] por los laboristas, **the Labour Party** el partido laborista

lace *NOUN* ❶ *(for a shoe)* cordón *MASC*; **to do up your laces** atarse los cordones ❷ *(fabric)* encaje *MASC*

lad *NOUN* chaval *MASC (informal)*

ladder *NOUN* ❶ *(for climbing)* escalera *FEM* ❷ *(in your tights)* carrera *FEM*

ladies *NOUN (lavatory)* servicio *(MASC)* de señoras; *(sign)* **'Ladies'** 'Señoras'

lady *NOUN* señora *FEM*; **ladies and gentlemen** señoras y señores

lager *NOUN* cerveza *(FEM)* rubia

laid-back *ADJECTIVE* relajado/relajada

lake *NOUN* lago *MASC*

lamb *NOUN* cordero *MASC*; **a leg of lamb** una pierna de cordero

lamp *NOUN* lámpara *FEM*

lamp-post *NOUN* farola *FEM*

lampshade *NOUN* pantalla *FEM*

a b c d e f g h i j **k** **l** m n o p q r s t u v w x y z

land NOUN ❶ tierra FEM ❷ *(property)* a piece of land un terreno, **he has land** tiene tierras

land VERB ❶ *(plane, passenger)* aterrizar [22] ❷ *(leave a ship)* desembarcar [31]

landing NOUN ❶ *(on the stairs)* descansillo MASC ❷ *(of a plane)* aterrizaje MASC ❸ *(from a boat)* desembarco MASC

landlady NOUN ❶ *(of rented house)* casera FEM ❷ *(of pub)* dueña FEM

landlord NOUN ❶ *(of rented house)* casero MASC ❷ *(of pub)* dueño MASC

lane NOUN ❶ *(in the country)* camino MASC ❷ *(of a motorway or road)* carril MASC; **bus lane** carril de autobuses

language NOUN ❶ *(Spanish, Italian, etc.)* idioma MASC; **a foreign language** un idioma extranjero ❷ *(way of speaking)* lenguaje MASC; **scientific language** lenguaje científico ❸ **bad language** palabrotas FEM PLURAL, **to use bad language** decir [5] palabrotas

language lab NOUN laboratorio *(MASC)* de idiomas

language school NOUN academia *(FEM)* de idiomas

lap NOUN ❶ *(your knees)* rodillas FEM PLURAL; **on my lap** en mis rodilla ❷ *(in races)* vuelta FEM

laptop NOUN ordenador *(MASC)* portátil

laser NOUN láser MASC; **a laser beam** un rayo láser, **a laser printer** una impresora láser

last ADJECTIVE ❶ último/última; **the last time** la última vez, **the last thing I did** lo último que hice ❷ **last week** la semana pasada, **last night** *(in the evening)* ayer por la tarde, *(in the night)* anoche

last ADVERB ❶ *(in final position) (to arrive or leave)*; **Rob arrived last** Rob llegó el último, **I came last in the race** llegué en último lugar en la carrera ❷ *(most recently)* **I last saw him in May** la última vez que lo vi fue en mayo ❸ **at last!** ¡por fin!

last VERB durar [17]; **the play lasted two hours** la obra duró dos horas

late ADJECTIVE, ADVERB ❶ tarde; **we're late** llegamos tarde, **they arrived late** llegaron tarde, **to be late for something** llegar [28] tarde a algo, **we were late for the film** llegamos tarde a la película ❷ **to be late** *(a bus or train)* llegar [28] con retraso, **the train was an hour late** el tren llegó con una hora de retraso ❸ *(late in the day)* tarde; **we got up late** nos levantamos tarde, **it's getting late** se está haciendo tarde, **late last night** ayer por la noche ya tarde, **too late!** ¡demasiado tarde!

later ADVERB más tarde; **I'll explain to you later** te lo explicaré más tarde, **later that same day** ese mismo día más tarde, **no later than Thursday** no más tarde del jueves, **see you later!** ¡hasta luego!

latest ADJECTIVE último/última; **the latest news** las últimas noticias

latest NOUN **at the latest** a más tardar, **the latest in audio equipment** lo último en equipo de audio

Latin NOUN latín MASC

Latin America NOUN América (FEM) Latina

Latin American ADJECTIVE latinoamericano/ latinoamericana

laugh NOUN risa FEM; **to do something for a laugh** hacer [7] algo por divertirse

laugh VERB ❶ reírse [61]; **everybody laughed** todo el mundo se rió ❷ **to laugh at** reírse [61] de, **I tried to explain but they laughed at me** intenté explicarlo pero se rieron de mí

laughter NOUN risas FEM PLURAL

launch NOUN ❶ (of product, spacecraft) lanzamiento MASC ❷ (of ship) botadura FEM

launch VERB ❶ (product, spacecraft) lanzar [22] ❷ (ship) botar [17]

launderette NOUN lavandería FEM

laundry NOUN lavandería FEM

lavatory NOUN servicio (MASC), aseo MASC

lavender NOUN lavanda FEM

law NOUN ❶ ley FEM; **it's against the law** es ilegal ❷ (subject of study) derecho MASC

lawn NOUN césped MASC

lawnmower NOUN cortacésped MASC

lawyer NOUN abogado MASC, abogada FEM

lay VERB poner [11]; **she laid the card on the table** puso la tarjeta en la mesa, **to lay the table** poner la mesa

lay-by NOUN área (FEM) de reposo (even though 'área' is a feminine, it takes 'el' and 'un' in the singular); **a lay-by** un área de reposo

layer NOUN capa FEM

laziness NOUN pereza FEM

lazy ADJECTIVE perezoso/perezosa

lead NOUN ❶ (when you are ahead) **to be in the lead** llevar [17] la delantera, **Sam's in the lead** Sam lleva la delantera, **we have a lead of three points** llevamos una ventaja de tres puntos ❷ (electric) cable MASC ❸ (for a dog) correa FEM; **on a lead** con correa

lead ADJECTIVE (a role or a singer) principal

lead VERB ❶ llevar [17]; **the path leads to the sea** el sendero lleva al mar ❷ **to lead the way** ir [8] delante ❸ (in a competition) llevar [17] la delantera ❹ **this will lead to problems** esto traerá problemas, **to lead to an accident** causar [17] un accidente

leader NOUN ❶ (of a gang) cabecilla MASC & FEM ❷ (of a political party) líder MASC & FEM ❸ (in a competition) primero MASC, primera FEM

lead-free petrol NOUN gasolina (FEM) sin plomo

lead singer NOUN cantante (MASC & FEM) principal

leaf NOUN hoja FEM

leaflet NOUN folleto MASC

league NOUN (in sport) liga FEM

lean ADJECTIVE (meat) magro/magra

a
b
c
d
e
f
g
h
i
j
k
l
m
n
o
p
q
r
s
t
u
v
w
x
y
z

lean VERB ❶ to lean on something apoyarse [17] en algo ❷ (prop) apoyar [17]; lean the ladder against the tree apoya la escalera en el árbol ❸ (a person) echarse [17]; lean forward a bit échate para delante un poco ❹ to lean out of the window asomarse [17] por la ventana

leap year NOUN año (MASC) bisiesto

learn VERB aprender [18]; to learn Russian aprender ruso, to learn to drive aprender a conducir

learner driver NOUN she's a learner driver está aprendiendo a conducir

least ADVERB, DETERMINER, PRONOUN ❶ menos; the least expensive hotel el hotel menos caro, the least expensive glasses las gafas menos caras, Tony has the least money Tony es el que menos dinero tiene, I like the blue shirt least la camisa azul es la que menos me gusta ❷ (slightest) más mínimo/más mínima; I haven't the least idea no tengo ni la más mínima idea, he didn't show the least interest no mostró el más mínimo interés ❸ at least (at a minimum) por lo menos, there must be at least twenty people debe haber por lo menos veinte personas ❹ at least (at any rate) al menos, at least, that's what I think al menos eso creo

leather NOUN cuero MASC; a leather jacket una chaqueta de cuero

leave VERB ❶ (go away) irse [8]; they're leaving tomorrow se van mañana, we left at six se fueron a las seis ❷ (go away from) irse [8] de; I left the office at five me fui de la oficina a las cinco ❸ (go out of) salir [63] de; she left the cinema at ten

salió del cine a las diez ❹ (abandon) dejar [17] a (family or partner); he left his wife dejó a su mujer ❺ (deposit) dejar [17]; you can leave your coats in the hall podéis dejar los abrigos en la entrada ❻ (forget) dejarse [17]; he left his umbrella on the train se dejó el paraguas en el tren ❼ to leave school dejar [17] los estudios, Guy left school at sixteen Guy dejó los estudios a los dieciséis años ❽ be left quedar [17], there are two cakes left quedan dos pasteles, we have ten minutes left nos quedan diez minutos, I don't have any money left no me queda dinero

lecture NOUN ❶ (at university) clase FEM ❷ (public) conferencia FEM

lecturer NOUN profesor MASC, profesora FEM

ledge NOUN ❶ (of window) repisa FEM ❷ (on cliff) saliente MASC

leek NOUN puerro MASC

left NOUN izquierda FEM; to drive on the left conducir [60] por la izquierda, turn left at the church tuerce a la izquierda en la iglesia, on my left a mi izquierda

left ADJECTIVE izquierdo/izquierda; his left foot su pie izquierdo

left-click NOUN clic (MASC) con el botón izquierdo

left-click VERB hacer [7] clic con el botón izquierdo; left-click the icon haz clic en el icono con el botón izquierdo

left-hand NOUN the left-hand side la parte izquierda

left-handed ADJECTIVE zurdo/zurda

left luggage office NOUN
consigna FEM

leftovers PLURAL NOUN sobras FEM
PLURAL

leg NOUN ❶ (of a person) pierna FEM;
my left leg mi pierna izquierda, to
break your leg romperse [40] una
pierna ❷ (of a table, chair, or animal)
pata FEM ❸ (in cooking) a leg of
chicken un muslo de pollo, a leg of
lamb una pierna de cordero
• to pull somebody's leg tomarle [17]
el pelo a alguien (literally: to take
somebody's hair)

legal ADJECTIVE legal

legend NOUN ❶ (story) leyenda FEM
❷ (star, personality) leyenda FEM

leggings PLURAL NOUN leggings MASC
PLURAL

leisure NOUN tiempo (MASC) libre; in
my leisure time en mi tiempo libre

leisure centre NOUN polideportivo
MASC

lemon NOUN limón MASC; a lemon
yoghurt un yogur de limón

lemonade NOUN ❶ (made with
lemons) limonada FEM ❷ (fizzy drink)
gaseosa FEM

lemon juice NOUN zumo (MASC) de
limón

lend VERB dejar [17]; to lend
something to somebody dejarle
algo a alguien, I lent Judy my bike le
dejé mi bici a Judy, will you lend it
to me? ¿me lo dejas?

length NOUN ❶ (of fabric, board,
etc.) largo MASC ❷ (of film, play)
duración FEM ❸ (of book, list)
extensión FEM

lens NOUN ❶ (in a camera) lente
FEM ❷ (in spectacles) cristal MASC
❸ contact lenses lentillas FEM PLURAL

Lent NOUN Cuaresma FEM

lentil NOUN lenteja FEM

Leo NOUN Leo MASC; I'm Leo soy Leo

leotard NOUN malla FEM

lesbian NOUN lesbiana FEM

less PRONOUN, DETERMINER, ADVERB
❶ menos; Richard eats less Richard
come menos, less time menos
tiempo, less interesting menos
interesante, less quickly than us
menos rápido que nosotros ❷ less
than menos de, less than a kilo
menos de un kilo, less than three
hours menos de tres horas ❸ less
than (in comparisons) menos que,
you spend less than me gastas
menos que yo

lesson NOUN clase FEM; the history
lesson la clase de historia, a driving
lesson una clase de conducir, to
take tennis lessons tomar [17]
clases de tenis

let[1] VERB ❶ (allow) dejar [17]; will you
let me go alone? ¿me dejas ir sola?,
the police let us through la policía
me dejó pasar, let me help you
déjame que te ayude, she lets me
borrow her bike me deja que coja
su bici prestada, let me see (show
me) déjame ver ❷ (as a suggestion
or a command) let's go! ¡vámonos!,
let's not talk about it no hablemos
de ello, let's see, if Tuesday is the
third ... vamos a ver, si el martes
es el tres ..., let's eat out vamos a
comer fuera
• to let off ❶ tirar [17] (fireworks)
❷ hacer [7] estallar (a bomb)

a
b
c
d
e
f
g
h
i
j
k
l
m
n
o
p
q
r
s
t
u
v
w
x
y
z

❸ *(to excuse from)* **perdonar** [17] *(homework or task)*; **I'll let you off doing the dishes** te perdono que no laves los platos

let² *VERB (to rent out)* **alquilar** [17]; **'flat to let'** 'se alquila apartamento'

lethal *ADJECTIVE* **mortal**

letter *NOUN* ❶ **carta** *FEM*; **a letter for you from Delia** una carta de Delia para ti ❷ *(of alphabet)* **letra** *FEM*; **M is the letter after L** M es la letra que viene depués de L

letterbox *NOUN* **buzón** *MASC*

lettuce *NOUN* **lechuga** *FEM*

leukaemia *NOUN* **leucemia** *FEM*

level *NOUN* **nivel** *MASC*; **at street level** a nivel de la calle

level *ADJECTIVE* ❶ **plano/plana** *(a shelf or floor)* ❷ **llano/llana** *(ground)*

level crossing *NOUN* **paso** *(MASC)* **a nivel**

lever *NOUN* **palanca** *FEM*

liar *NOUN* **mentiroso** *MASC*, **mentirosa** *FEM*

liberal *ADJECTIVE* **liberal**; **the Liberal Democrats** los demócratas liberales

liberty *NOUN* **libertad** *FEM*

Libra *NOUN* **Libra** *FEM*; **Sean's Libra** Sean es Libra

librarian *NOUN* **bibliotecario** *MASC*, **bibliotecaria** *FEM*; **Mark's a librarian** Mark es bibliotecario

library *NOUN* **biblioteca** *FEM*; **the public library** la biblioteca pública

licence *NOUN* ❶ *(for driving or fishing)* **permiso** *MASC*; **a driving licence** un permiso de conducir ❷ *(for a TV)* **licencia** *FEM*

lick *VERB* **lamer** [18]

lid *NOUN* **tapa** *FEM*; **she took the lid off** quitó la tapa

lie *NOUN* **mentira** *FEM*; **to tell lies** decir [5] mentiras

lie *VERB* ❶ *(to be stretched out)* **estar** [2] **tumbado**; **Jimmy was lying on the bed** Jimmy estaba tumbado en la cama ❷ **to lie down** **tumbarse** [17] *(for a little while)*, **come and lie down in the sun** ven y a tumbarte al sol ❸ *(object)* **estar** [2]; **my coat lay on the bed** mi abrigo estaba sobre la cama ❹ *(not to tell the truth)* **mentir** [14]

lieutenant *NOUN* **teniente** *MASC & FEM*

life *NOUN* **vida** *FEM*; **all her life** toda su vida, **full of life** lleno/llena de vida, **that's life!** ¡así es la vida!

lifebelt *NOUN* **salvavidas** *MASC (does not change in the plural)*

lifeboat *NOUN* **bote** *(MASC)* **salvavidas**

lifeguard *NOUN* **socorrista** *MASC & FEM*; **is there a lifeguard at the pool?** ¿hay un socorrista en la piscina?

life jacket *NOUN* **chaleco** *(MASC)* **salvavidas**

life-style *NOUN* **estilo** *(MASC)* **de vida**

lift *NOUN* ❶ **ascensor** *MASC*; **let's take the lift** vamos a coger el ascensor ❷ *(a ride)* **to give somebody a lift to the station** **llevar** [17] a alguien a la estación, **Tom gave me a lift home**

Tom me llevó a casa, **can you give me a lift?** ¿me puedes llevar?

lift VERB **levantar** [17]

light NOUN ❶ *(electric)* **luz** FEM; **can you turn the light on?** ¿puedes encender la luz?, **to turn off the light** apagar la luz, **are your lights on?** *(on a car)* ¿tienes las luces encendidas? ❷ *(streetlight)* **farola** FEM ❸ *(on a machine)* **piloto** MASC ❹ **traffic lights** semáforo MASC, **the lights were green** el semáforo estaba en verde ❺ **have you got a light?** ¿tienes fuego?

light ADJECTIVE ❶ *(in colour)* **claro/clara**; **light blue eyes** ojos azul claro ❷ *(not night)* **it gets light at six** se hace de día a las seis ❸ *(not heavy)* **ligero/ligera**; **a light sweater** un jersey fino

light VERB **encender** [36] *(the oven, the fire, a match, or a cigarette)*; **we lit a fire** encendimos un fuego

light bulb NOUN **bombilla** FEM

lighter NOUN **encendedor** MASC

lightning NOUN **relámpago** MASC; **a flash of lightning** un relámpago, **the tree was struck by lightning** cayó un rayo en el árbol

light switch NOUN **interruptor** *(MASC)* de la luz

like¹ PREPOSITION, CONJUNCTION ❶ **como**; **like me** como yo, **like this** como esto, **like a duck** como un pato, **like I said** como dije (yo), **what's it like?** ¿cómo es?, **what was the weather like?** ¿qué tiempo hizo? ❷ **to look like** parecerse [35] a, **Cindy looks like her father** Cindy se parece a su padre

like² VERB ❶ **I like fish** me gusta el pescado, **I don't like dogs** no me gustan los perros, **Mum likes travelling** a mamá le gusta viajar, **she likes my brother** le gusta mi hermano, **I like Picasso best** el que más me gusta es Picasso ❷ **I would like** quiero, **would you like a coffee?** ¿quieres un café?, **what would you like to eat?** ¿qué quieres comer?, **yes, if you like** sí, si tú quieres

likely ADJECTIVE **probable**; **it's not very likely** no es muy probable, **she's likely to phone** es probable que llame

lime NOUN **lima** FEM *(fruit)*

limit NOUN **límite** MASC; **the speed limit** el límite de velocidad

line NOUN ❶ **línea** FEM; **a straight line** una línea recta, **to draw a line** trazar [22] una línea ❷ **a railway line** *(from one place to another)* una línea de ferrocarril, **on the railway line** *(the track)* en la vía férrea ❸ *(queue)* **cola** FEM; **to stand in line** hacer [7] cola ❹ *(telephone)* **línea** FEM; **the line's bad** no se oye bien, **hold the line, please** no cuelgue, por favor

linen NOUN **lino** MASC; **a linen jacket** una chaqueta de lino

link NOUN **conexión** FEM; **what's the link between the two?** ¿qué conexión hay entre los dos?

link VERB **conectar** [17] *(two places)*; **the terminals are linked by a shuttle service** las terminales están conectadas por un servicio de enlace

lion NOUN **león** MASC

lip NOUN **labio** MASC

lip-read VERB **leer** [37] **los labios**

lipstick NOUN **lápiz** (MASC) **de labios**

liquid NOUN **líquido** MASC

liquid ADJECTIVE **líquido/líquida**

liquidizer NOUN **licuadora** FEM

list NOUN **lista** FEM

listen VERB **escuchar** [17]; **I wasn't listening** no estaba escuchando, **to listen to** escuchar [17], **listen to the music** escucha la música, **you're not listening to me** no me estás escuchando

literature NOUN **literatura** FEM

litre NOUN **litro** MASC; **a litre of milk** un litro de leche

litter NOUN (rubbish) **basura** FEM

litter bin NOUN **papelera** FEM

little ADJECTIVE, PRONOUN ❶ (small) **pequeño/pequeña**; **a little boy** un niño pequeño, **a little break** una pequeña pausa ❷ (not much) **poco/poca**; **we have very little time** tenemos muy poco tiempo ❸ **a little** un poco, **we have a little money** tenemos un poco de dinero, **just a little, please** solo un poco, por favor, **it's a little late** es un poco tarde, **a little more** un poco más, **a little less** un poco menos
• **little by little** poco a poco

live[1] VERB **vivir** [19]; **Susan lives in York** Susan vive en York, **they live at number 57** viven en el número cincuenta y siete, **they live together** viven juntos

live[2] ADJECTIVE ❶ **en directo** (a broadcast); **a live concert** un concierto en directo ❷ (alive) **vivo/viva**

liver NOUN **hígado** MASC

living NOUN **to earn a living** ganarse [17] la vida

living room NOUN **salón** MASC

load NOUN ❶ (on a lorry) **cargamento** MASC ❷ **a bus-load of tourists** un autobús lleno de turistas ❸ **loads of** un montón de (informal), **loads of people** un montón de gente, **they've got loads of money** tienen un montón de dinero

load VERB **cargar** [28]

loaf NOUN **a loaf of bread** un pan, **a loaf of wholemeal bread** un pan integral

loan NOUN **préstamo** MASC

loan VERB **prestar** [17]

lobster NOUN **langosta** FEM

local NOUN ❶ (a pub) **our local** el bar de nuestro barrio ❷ **the locals** (people) la gente del lugar

local ADJECTIVE **the local library** la biblioteca del barrio, **the local newspaper** el periódico local

locally ADVERB **en la zona**

lock NOUN ❶ (with a key) **cerradura** FEM ❷ (on a canal) **esclusa** FEM

lock VERB **to lock the door** cerrar [29] la puerta con llave, **the door was locked** la puerta estaba cerrada con llave

locker NOUN **armario** MASC

locker room NOUN **vestuario** MASC

lodger NOUN **inquilino** MASC, **inquilina** FEM

loft NOUN **desván** MASC

log NOUN **tronco** MASC

logical ADJECTIVE **lógico/lógica**

lollipop NOUN **piruleta** FEM

London NOUN **Londres** MASC; **to London** a Londres, **the London streets** las calles de Londres

Londoner NOUN **londinense** MASC & FEM

loneliness NOUN **soledad** FEM

lonely ADJECTIVE ❶ **solitario/solitaria**; **she has a lonely life** tiene una vida solitaria ❷ **to feel lonely** sentirse solo

long ADJECTIVE, ADVERB ❶ **largo/larga**; **a long film** una película larga, **a long illness** una enfermedad larga, **it's five metres long** mide cinco metros de largo, **how long is the corridor?** ¿cuánto mide el pasillo de largo?, **how long is the play?** ¿cuánto dura la obra?, **it's been a long day** ha sido un día muy largo ❷ **a long time** mucho tiempo, **he stayed for a long time** se quedó mucho tiempo, **it's an hour long** dura una hora, **I've been here for a long time** he pasado mucho tiempo aquí, **a long time ago** hace mucho tiempo, **this won't take long** esto no llevará mucho tiempo, **I won't be long** no tardo mucho ❸ **how long?** ¿cuánto tiempo?, **how long have you been here?** ¿cuánto tiempo llevas aquí? ❹ **a long way** muy lejos, **we're a**

long way from the cinema estamos muy lejos del cine ❺ **all night long** toda la noche

long VERB **to long to do** anhelar [17] hacer, **I'm longing to see you** anhelo verte

longer ADVERB **no longer** ya no, **he doesn't work here any longer** ya no trabaja aquí, **I no longer know** ya no lo sé, **they no longer live here** ya no viven aquí

long jump NOUN **salto** (MASC) **de longitud**

longlife milk NOUN **leche** (FEM) **uperizada**

loo NOUN **váter** MASC (informal)

look NOUN ❶ (a glance) **mirada** FEM; **to have a look at something** mirar [17] algo ❷ **to have a look round the town** visitar [17] la ciudad, **to have a look round the shops** ver [16] tiendas ❸ **to have a look for** buscar [31] (something you've lost)

look VERB ❶ **mirar** [17]; **I wasn't looking** no estaba mirando, **to look out of the window** mirar por la ventana ❷ **to look at** mirar [17], **Andy was looking at the photos** Andy estaba mirando las fotos ❸ (to seem) **parecer** [35]; **Melanie looked pleased** Melanie parecía contenta, **you look well** tienes buen aspecto, **he looks ill** tiene mal aspecto, **the salad looks delicious** la ensalada tiene un aspecto delicioso ❹ **to look like** parecerse [35] a, **Sally looks like her aunt** Sally se parece a su tía, **they look like each other** se parecen, **it looks like rain** parece que va a llover ❺ **what does the house look like?** ¿cómo es la casa?

loose   **love**

- to look after cuidar [17]; **Dad's looking after the baby** papá está cuidando del niño, **I'll look after your luggage** yo te cuido el equipaje
- to look for buscar [31]; **I'm looking for the keys** estoy buscando las llaves
- to look forward to something **I'm looking forward to the holidays** estoy deseando que lleguen las vacaciones, **she's looking forward to the trip** está deseando ir de viaje
- to look out *(to be careful)* tener [9] cuidado; **look out, it's hot!** ¡cuidado, está caliente!
- to look something up buscar [17] algo *(in a dictionary or directory)*; **you can look it up in the dictionary** puedes buscarlo en el diccionario

loose ADJECTIVE ❶ *(a screw or knot)* flojo/floja ❷ *(a garment)* amplio/amplia ❸ loose change cambio MASC
- I'm at a loose end no sé qué hacer

lorry NOUN camión MASC

lorry driver NOUN camionero MASC, camionera FEM

lose VERB ❶ perder [36]; **we lost** perdimos, **we lost the match** perdimos el partido, **Sam's lost his watch** Sam ha perdido su reloj ❷ to get lost perderse [36], **we got lost in the woods** nos perdimos en el bosque

loss NOUN pérdida FEM

lost ADJECTIVE perdido/perdida; **I'm lost** me he perdido, **are you lost?** ¿te has perdido?

lost property NOUN objetos *(MASC PLURAL)* perdidos

lot NOUN ❶ a lot mucho, **Jason eats a lot** Jason come mucho, **I spent a lot** gasté mucho, **your house is a lot bigger than ours** tu casa es mucho más grande que la nuestra ❷ a lot of mucho/mucha *(PLURAL* muchos/muchas*)*, **a lot of coffee** mucho café, **lots of people** mucha gente, **a lot of books** muchos libros, **'what are you doing tonight?' – 'not a lot'** ¿qué haces esta noche?' – 'no mucho'

lottery NOUN lotería FEM; **to win the lottery** ganar [17] la lotería

loud ADJECTIVE ❶ fuerte; **a loud banging** unos golpes fuertes, **a loud shout** un grito fuerte, **the radio is very loud** la radio está muy fuerte ❷ in a loud voice en voz alta, **to say something out loud** decir algo en voz alta

loudspeaker NOUN altavoz MASC

lounge NOUN ❶ *(in a house or hotel)* salón MASC ❷ *(in an airport)* **the departure lounge** la sala de embarque

love NOUN ❶ amor MASC; **to be in love with somebody** estar [2] enamorado de alguien, **she's in love with Jake** está enamorada de Jake ❷ **Gina sends her love** Gina manda recuerdos ❸ **with love from Charlie** con cariño de Charlie, **lots of love, Ann** con mucho cariño: Ann ❹ *(in tennis)* cero MASC

love VERB ❶ querer [12] *(a person)*; **I love you** te quiero ❷ **she loves London** le encanta Londres, **I'd love to come** me encantaría venir, **I love dancing** me encanta bailar, **Wayne loves seafood** a Wayne le encanta el marisco

lovely *ADJECTIVE* ❶ *(to look at)* **precioso/preciosa**; **a lovely house** una casa preciosa ❷ **it's a lovely day** hace un día muy bueno, **we had lovely weather** tuvimos un tiempo muy bueno ❸ **I had a lovely time at their house** lo pasé muy bien en su casa ❹ **it's lovely to see you!** ¡qué alegría verte! ❺ *(food, meal)* **riquísimo/riquísima**

lover *NOUN* **amante** *MASC & FEM*

low *ADJECTIVE* **bajo/baja**; **a low table** una mesa baja, **at a low price** a un precio bajo, **in a low voice** en voz baja

lower *ADJECTIVE* *(not as high)* **inferior**

loyalty *NOUN* **lealtad** *FEM*; **a loyalty card** una tarjeta de fidelidad

luck *NOUN* **suerte** *FEM*; **good luck!** ¡buena suerte!, **bad luck!** ¡qué mala suerte!, **with a bit of luck** con un poco de suerte

luckily *ADVERB* **afortunadamente**; **luckily for them** afortunadamente para ellos

lucky *ADJECTIVE* ❶ **to be lucky** *(a person)* **tener** [9] **suerte**, **we were lucky** tuvimos suerte ❷ **to be lucky** *(bringing luck)* **traer** [42] **suerte**, **it's supposed to be lucky** se supone que trae suerte, **my lucky number** mi número de la suerte

luggage *NOUN* **equipaje** *MASC*

lump *NOUN* ❶ **bulto** *MASC (on the body)* ❷ **terrón** *MASC (of sugar)* ❸ **trozo** *MASC (of cheese)*

lunch *NOUN* **comida** *FEM*; **to have lunch** comer [18], **we had lunch in Oxford** comimos en Oxford

lunch break *NOUN* **descanso** *(MASC)* **para comer**

lunch hour, **lunch time** *NOUN* **hora** *(FEM)* **de comer**

Luxembourg *NOUN* **Luxemburgo** *MASC*

luxurious *ADJECTIVE* **lujoso/lujosa**

luxury *NOUN* **lujo** *MASC*; **a luxury hotel** un hotel de lujo

lyrics *PLURAL NOUN* **letra** *FEM*

a
b
c
d
e
f
g
h
i
j
k
l
m
n
o
p
q
r
s
t
u
v
w
x
y
z

Mm

macaroni NOUN **macarrones** MASC PLURAL

machine NOUN **máquina** FEM

machinery NOUN **maquinaria** FEM

mad ADJECTIVE ❶ **loco/loca**; **she's completely mad!** ¡está completamente loca! ❷ *(angry)* **enfadado/enfadada**; **to be mad with somebody** estar enfadado/enfadada con alguien, **my mum will be mad!** ¡mamá se pondrá hecha una furia! *(informal)* ❸ **she's mad about horses** le encantan los caballos

madam NOUN **señora** FEM

madness NOUN **locura** FEM

magazine NOUN **revista** FEM

maggot NOUN **gusano** MASC

magic NOUN **magia** FEM

magic ADJECTIVE ❶ **mágico/mágica**; **a magic wand** una varita mágica ❷ *(great)* **fantástico/fantástica**

magician NOUN **mago** MASC, **maga** FEM

magnet NOUN **imán** MASC

magnifying glass NOUN **lupa** FEM

maid NOUN **criada** FEM; **is there a maid service?** ¿ha asistenta?

maiden name NOUN **nombre** *(MASC)* **de soltera**

mail NOUN **correo** MASC; **e-mail** *(electronic mail)* **correo** *(MASC)* **electrónico**

mail order NOUN **to buy something by mail order** comprar [17] algo por correo, **a mail order catalogue** un catálogo de venta por correo

main ADJECTIVE **principal**; **the main entrance** la entrada principal

main course NOUN **plato** *(MASC)* **principal, segundo plato** MASC

mainly ADVERB **principalmente**

main road NOUN **carretera** *(FEM)* **principal**

major ADJECTIVE **muy importante**; **a major problem** un problema muy importante

major NOUN **comandante** MASC & FEM

Majorca NOUN **Mallorca** FEM

majority NOUN **mayoría** FEM

make NOUN **marca** FEM; **what make is your bike?** ¿de qué marca es tu bici?

make VERB ❶ **hacer** [7]; **I made an omelette** hice una tortilla, **she made her bed** hizo su cama, **he made me wait** me hizo esperar, **she makes me laugh** me hace reír, **to make a phone call** hacer una llamada de teléfono, **I have to make a few phone calls** tengo que hacer varias llamadas de teléfono ❷ **fabricar** [31]; **they make computers** fabrican ordenadores, **'made in Spain'** 'fabricado en España' ❸ **that makes me hungry** eso me da hambre, **it made me sleepy** me dio sueño ❹ *(sad, happy)* to make somebody sad poner [11] triste a alguien, **it made me sad** me puso triste, **to make somebody happy** hacer [7] feliz a alguien, **it made him really annoyed** le dio mucha rabia, **it makes me so angry** me da tanta rabia ❺ ganar [17] *(money)*; **he makes forty pounds a day** gana cuarenta libras al día, **to make a living** ganarse [17] la vida ❻ *(force)* **to make somebody do ...** obligar [28] a alguien a hacer ..., **she made him give the money back** le obligó a devolver el dinero ❼ **to make a meal** preparar [17] una comida ❽ *(add up to)* sumar [17]; **two and three make five** dos y tres suman cinco ❾ **I can't make it tonight** no puedo venir esta noche

• **to make something up** ❶ inventarse [17] algo; **she made up an excuse** se inventó una excusa ❷ **to make it up** *(after a quarrel)* hacer [7] las paces, **they've made it up now** han hecho las paces ahora

make-up NOUN maquillaje MASC; **to put on your make-up** ponerse [11] el maquillaje, **Jo's putting on her make-up** Jo se está poniendo el maquillaje, **I don't wear make-up** yo no uso maquillaje

male ADJECTIVE ❶ *(animal)* macho; **a male rat** una rata macho ❷ *(of a man)* masculino/masculina; **a male voice** una voz masculina ❸ *(sex: on a form)* varón

male chauvinist NOUN machista MASC

mall NOUN centro *(MASC)* comercial

mammal NOUN mamífero MASC

man NOUN hombre MASC; **modern man is taller than his ancestors** el hombre moderno es más alto que sus antepasados

manage VERB ❶ dirigir [49] *(business, team)*; **she manages a travel agency** ella dirige una agencia de viajes ❷ *(cope)* arreglárselas [17]; **I can manage** puedo arreglármelas ❸ **to manage to do** conseguir [64] hacer, **I didn't manage to get in touch with her** no conseguí ponerme en contacto con ella

management NOUN ❶ dirección FEM; **the management of the company** la dirección de la empresa ❷ *(management staff)* directivos MASC PLURAL

manager NOUN ❶ *(of a company or a bank)* director MASC, directora FEM ❷ *(of a shop or restaurant)* encargado MASC, encargada FEM ❸ *(in sport and entertainment)* manager MASC & FEM

manageress NOUN encargada FEM

managing director NOUN consejero *(MASC)* delegado, consejera *(FEM)* delegada

mango NOUN mango MASC

maniac NOUN loco MASC, loca FEM; **she drives like a maniac** conduce como una loca

mankind NOUN humanidad FEM

manner NOUN ❶ **in a manner of speaking** por así decirlo ❷ **to have good manners** tener [9] buena educación, **it's bad manners to talk like that** no es de es buena educación hablar así

mansion NOUN mansión FEM

mantelpiece NOUN repisa *(FEM)* de la chimenea

manual NOUN manual MASC

a
b
c
d
e
f
g
h
i
j
k
l
m
n
o
p
q
r
s
t
u
v
w
x
y
z

manufacture VERB **fabricar** [31]

manufacturer NOUN **fabricante** MASC

many DETERMINER, PRONOUN
❶ **muchos/muchas**; **does she have many friends?** ¿tiene muchos amigos?, **there aren't many onions left** no quedan muchas cebollas, **not many** no muchos/muchas, **many of them forgot** muchos de ellos se olvidaron, **many people** mucha gente ❷ **very many** muchos/muchas, **there aren't very many glasses** no hay muchos vasos ❸ **so many** tantos/tantas, **I have so many things to do!** ¡tengo tantas cosas que hacer!, **I've never eaten so many cakes** nunca he comido tantos pasteles ❹ **as many as** todos los que/todas las que, **you can take as many as you like** puedes llevarte todos los que quieras ❺ **too many** demasiados/demasiadas, **I've got too many things to do** tengo demasiadas cosas que hacer, **that's far too many!** ¡ésos son demasiados!, **there were too many people** había demasiada gente ❻ **how many?** ¿cuántos?/¿cuántas?, **how many are there?** ¿cuántos hay?, **how many sisters have you got?** ¿cuántas hermanas tienes?, **how many are there left?** ¿cuántos quedan? ❼ **as many as** tantos/tantas como, **there aren't as many as before** no hay tantos como antes, **she got as many points as I did** consiguió tantos puntos como yo

map NOUN ❶ **mapa** MASC; **a road map** un mapa de carreteras ❷ (of a town) **plano** MASC

marathon NOUN **maratón** MASC & FEM

marble NOUN ❶ **mármol** MASC; **a marble fireplace** una chimenea de mármol ❷ **canica** FEM; **to play marbles** jugar [27] a las canicas

march NOUN (demonstration) **manifestación** FEM

march VERB (demonstrators) **manifestarse** [29]

March NOUN **marzo** MASC

mare NOUN **yegua** FEM

margarine NOUN **margarina** FEM

margin NOUN **margen** MASC

marijuana NOUN **marihuana** FEM

mark NOUN ❶ (at school) **nota** FEM; **I got a good mark for my Spanish homework** he sacado una buena nota en los deberes de español, **what mark did you get for Spanish?** ¿que nota sacaste en español? ❷ (stain) **mancha** FEM

mark VERB (correct) **corregir** [48]

market NOUN **mercado** MASC

marketing NOUN **marketing** MASC

marmalade NOUN **mermelada** (FEM) **de naranja**

marriage NOUN **matrimonio** MASC (relationship)

married ADJECTIVE **casado/casada**; **to be married** estar [2] casado/casada, **he's married** está casado, **they've been married for twenty years** llevan casados veinte años, **a married couple** un matrimonio

marry VERB ❶ **to marry somebody** casarse [17] con alguien, **she married a Spaniard** se casó con un español ❷ **to get married** casarse

[17], **they got married in July** se casaron en julio

marvellous *ADJECTIVE* maravilloso/ maravillosa; **the weather's marvellous** el tiempo es maravilloso, **how marvellous!** ¡qué maravilla!

marzipan *NOUN* mazapán *MASC*

mascara *NOUN* rímel *MASC*

masculine *NOUN* (in Spanish and other grammars) masculino *MASC*; **in the masculine** en masculino

mash *VERB* triturar [17] (vegetables)

mashed potatoes *NOUN* puré (*MASC*) de patatas

mask *NOUN* máscara *FEM*

mass *NOUN* ❶ **a mass of** un montón de ❷ **masses of** un montón de, **they've got masses of money** tienen un montón de dinero, **there's masses left over** queda un montón ❸ (religious) misa *FEM*; **to go to mass** ir [8] a misa

massacre *NOUN* matanza *FEM*

massage *NOUN* masaje *MASC*

massive *ADJECTIVE* enorme

mat *NOUN* ❶ (doormat) felpudo *MASC* ❷ (bathmat) alfombrilla *FEM* ❸ (for hot dish) salvamanteles *MASC* (does not change in the plural)

match *NOUN* ❶ cerilla *FEM*; **a box of matches** una caja de cerillas ❷ (sports) partido *MASC*; **a football match** un partido de fútbol, **to watch the match** ver [16] el partido, **to win the match** ganar [17] el partido, **to lose the match** perder [36] el partido

match *VERB* hacer [7] juego con; **the jacket matches the skirt** la chaqueta hace juego con la falda

mate *NOUN* amigo *MASC*, amiga *FEM*; **I'm going out with my mates tonight** voy a salir esta noche con mis amigos

material *NOUN* ❶ (fabric) tela *FEM* ❷ (information) material *MASC*; **teaching materials** material educativo ❸ (substance) materia *FEM*; **raw materials** materias primas

mathematics *NOUN* matemáticas *FEM PLURAL*

maths *NOUN* matemáticas *FEM PLURAL*; **I like maths** me gustan las matemáticas, **Anna's good at maths** a Anna se le dan bien las matemáticas

matter *NOUN* **what's the matter?** ¿qué pasa?

matter *VERB* ❶ importar [17]; **the things that matter** lo que importa, **it matters a lot to me** me importa mucho ❷ **it doesn't matter** no importa, **it doesn't matter if it rains** no importa que llueva ❸ **it doesn't matter** (whether one thing or another) da lo mismo, **you can write it in Spanish or French, it doesn't matter** puedes escribirlo en español o en francés, da lo mismo

mattress *NOUN* colchón *MASC*

maximum *NOUN* máximo *MASC*

maximum *ADJECTIVE* máximo/ máxima

may | **measure**

may VERB ❶ she may be ill puede que esté enferma, we may go to Spain puede que vayamos a España ❷ *(asking permission)* may I close the door? ¿puedo cerrar la puerta?

May NOUN mayo MASC

maybe ADVERB quizás; maybe not quizás no, maybe he's forgotten quizás se ha olvidado, maybe they've got lost quizás se han perdido

mayonnaise NOUN mayonesa FEM

mayor NOUN alcalde MASC, alcaldesa FEM

mayoress NOUN alcaldesa FEM

me PRONOUN ❶ me; she knows me me conoce, she gave me the documents me dio los documentos ❷ *(with an infinitive or when telling someone to do something, 'me' joins onto the verb)* can you help me, please? ¿puedes ayudarme por favor?, listen to me! ¡escúchame!, wait for me! ¡espérame!, *(but when telling someone NOT to do something, 'me' comes before the verb)* don't push me! ¡no me empujes! ❸ *(after a preposition)* mí; behind me detrás de mí, they left without me se fueron sin mí, with me conmigo, I took her with me la traje conmigo ❹ *(in comparisons or after the verb 'to be')* yo; she's older than me es mayor que yo, it's me soy yo, me too! ¡yo también! ❺ excuse me! ¡perdona!

meadow NOUN prado MASC

meal NOUN comida FEM; they have three meals a day hacen tres comidas al día

mean VERB ❶ querer [12] decir; what do you mean? ¿qué quieres decir?, what does that mean? ¿qué quiere decir eso?, that's not what I meant eso no es lo que quería decir ❷ *(imply)* suponer [11]; that means that I'll have to do it again eso supone que voy a tener que hacerlo otra vez ❸ to mean to do tener [9] la intención de, I meant to phone my mother tenía la intención de llamar a mi madre ❹ she was meant to be here at six se supone que ella tenía que estar aquí a las seis, this is meant to be easy se supone que esto es fácil

mean ADJECTIVE ❶ *(with money)* tacaño/tacaña ❷ *(nasty)* she's really mean to her brother trata muy mal a su hermano, what a mean thing to do! ¡qué maldad!

meaning NOUN significado MASC

means NOUN ❶ medio MASC; a means of transport un medio de transporte, by means of por medio de ❷ a means of doing una forma de hacer, we have no means of contacting him no tenemos forma de contactar con él ❸ by all means por supuesto

meantime ADVERB for the meantime por ahora, in the meantime mientras tanto

meanwhile ADVERB mientras tanto; meanwhile she was waiting at the station mientras tanto ella estaba esperando en la estación

measles NOUN sarampión MASC

measure VERB medir [57]

measurements PLURAL NOUN ❶ (of a room or an object) **medidas** FEM PLURAL; **the measurements of the room** las medidas de la habitación ❷ (of a person) **medida** FEM; **my waist measurement** mi medida de cintura

meat NOUN **carne** FEM

Mecca NOUN **La Meca** FEM

mechanic NOUN **mecánico** MASC, **mecánica** FEM; **he's a mechanic** es mecánico

medal NOUN **medalla** FEM; **the gold medal** la medalla de oro

media NOUN **the media** los medios de comunicación

medical NOUN **revisión** (FEM) **médica**; **to have a medical** someterse [18] a una revisión médica

medical ADJECTIVE **médico/médica**; **on medical grounds** por razones de salud

medicine NOUN ❶ **medicamento** MASC ❷ (science) **medicina** FEM; **she's studying medicine** está estudiando medicina, **alternative medicine** medicina alternativa

medieval ADJECTIVE **medieval**

Mediterranean NOUN **the Mediterranean** el Mediterráneo

medium ADJECTIVE **mediano/ mediana**

medium-sized ADJECTIVE **de tamaño mediano**

meet VERB ❶ (by chance) **encontrarse** [24] **con**; **I met Rosie outside the baker's** me encontré con Rosie en la puerta de la panadería ❷ (by appointment) **haber** [6] **quedado (con)**; **we're meeting at six** hemos quedado a las seis, **I'm meeting him at the museum** he quedado con él en el museo, **shall we meet after work?** ¿quedamos después del trabajo? ❸ (get to know) **conocer** [35] a; **I met a Spanish girl last week** conocí a una chica española la semana pasada, **have you met Oskar?** ¿conoces a Oskar? ❹ **Tom, meet Ann** Tom, te presento a Ann, **pleased to meet you!** ¡encantado/ encantada! ❺ (off a train, bus, plane) **recoger** [3]; **my dad's meeting me at the station** mi padre va a ir a recogerme a la estación

meeting NOUN **reunión** FEM; **there's a meeting a ten o'clock** hay una reunión a las diez, **she's in a meeting** está en una reunión

megabyte NOUN **megabyte** MASC

melon NOUN **melón** MASC

melt VERB ❶ (snow, butter, ice cream) **derretirse** [57]; **it melts in your mouth** se derrite en la boca ❷ **to melt something** derretir [57] algo, **melt the butter in a saucepan** derretir la mantequilla en una sartén

member NOUN ❶ (of party or committee) **miembro** MASC & FEM; **she's a member of the Labour Party** es miembro del partido laborista ❷ (of club) **socio** MASC, **socia** FEM

Member of Parliament NOUN **diputado** MASC, **diputada** FEM

memorial NOUN **monumento** MASC; **a war memorial** un monumento a los caídos

memorize <> micophone

memorize VERB to memorize something aprender [18] algo de memoria

memory NOUN ❶ (of a person or computer) memoria FEM; you have a good memory! ¡tienes buena memoria!, I have a bad memory tengo mala memoria ❷ (of the past) recuerdo MASC; I have good memories of my stay in Spain tengo buenos recuerdos de mi estancia en España

mend VERB arreglar [17]

mental ADJECTIVE mental; a mental illness una enfermedad mental, a mental hospital un hospital psiquiátrico

mention VERB mencionar [17]

menu NOUN ❶ (in restaurant) carta FEM, menú MASC; what's on on the menu? ¿qué hay en la carta?, have you got a set menu? ¿tienen un menú del día? ❷ (in computer program) menú MASC

merge VERB ❶ (documents) fusionar [17] ❷ (roads) confluir [54]

meringue NOUN merengue MASC

merit NOUN mérito MASC

merry ADJECTIVE ❶ alegre; Merry Christmas Feliz Navidad ❷ (from drinking) achispado/achispada (informal)

merry-go-round NOUN tiovivo MASC

mess NOUN desorden MASC; my papers are in a mess mis papeles están desordenados, don't make a mess! ¡no desordenes nada!, what a mess! ¡qué desastre! (informal)
• to mess about hacer [7] el tonto;

stop messing about! ¡deja de hacer el tonto!
• to mess about with something jugar [27] con algo; it's dangerous to mess about with matches es peligroso jugar con cerillas
• to mess something up desordenar [17] algo; you've messed up all my papers ¡me has desordenado todos mis papeles!

message NOUN mensaje MASC; a telephone message un recado

messenger NOUN mensajero MASC, mensajera FEM

messy ADJECTIVE ❶ it's a messy job es un trabajo sucio ❷ he's a messy eater se ensucia mucho comiendo, her writing's really messy escribe sin poner cuidado

metal NOUN metal MASC

meter NOUN ❶ (electricity, gas, taxi) contador MASC; to read the meter leer [37] el contador ❷ a parking meter un parquímetro

method NOUN método MASC

Methodist NOUN metodista MASC & FEM; I'm a Methodist soy metodista

metre NOUN metro MASC

metric ADJECTIVE métrico/métrica

Mexican NOUN mexicano MASC, mexicana FEM

Mexican ADJECTIVE mexicano/mexicana

Mexico NOUN Méjico MASC

microchip NOUN microchip MASC

microphone NOUN micrófono MASC

478

microscope NOUN microscopio MASC

microwave oven NOUN microondas MASC (does not change in the plural)

midday NOUN mediodía MASC; **at midday** al mediodía

middle NOUN ❶ medio MASC; **in the middle of the room** en medio de la habitación ❷ **in the middle of the night** en mitad de la noche, **in the middle of the day** alrededor del mediodía, **in the middle of the year** a mediados de año ❸ **to be in the middle of doing** estar [2] haciendo, **when she phoned I was in the middle of washing my hair** cuando llamó estaba lavándome el pelo

middle-aged ADJECTIVE de mediana edad; **a middle-aged woman** una mujer de mediana edad

middle-class ADJECTIVE de clase media; **a middle-class family** una familia de clase media

Middle-East NOUN Oriente (MASC) Medio

middle finger NOUN dedo (MASC) corazón

midge NOUN mosquito (MASC) pequeño

midnight NOUN medianoche FEM; **at midnight** a medianoche

Midsummer's Day NOUN la noche de San Juan

midwife NOUN comadrona FEM

might VERB **I might invite Jo** puede que invite a Jo, **Amanda might know** puede que Amanda lo sepa, **he might have forgotten** puede que se haya olvidado, **'are you going to phone him?' – 'I might'** ¿vas a llamarlo? – 'quizás'

migraine NOUN jaqueca FEM

mike NOUN micro MASC (informal)

mild ADJECTIVE ❶ suave (soap or cheese) ❷ templado/templada (climate); **it's quite mild today** hoy no hace frío

mile NOUN ❶ milla FEM, (in Spain distances are measured in kilometres; to convert miles roughly to kilometres, multiply by 8 and divide by 5); **the village is ten miles from Oxford** el pueblo está a dieciseis kilómetros de Oxford ❷ **it's miles better!** ¡es mil veces mejor! (informal)

mileage NOUN distancia (FEM) en millas; **what's the mileage on your car?** ¿cuántas millas ha hecho tu coche?

milk NOUN leche FEM; **full-cream milk** leche entera, **skimmed milk** leche desnatada, **semi-skimmed milk** leche semidesnatada

milk VERB ordeñar [17]

milk chocolate NOUN chocolate (MASC) con leche

milkman NOUN lechero MASC

milkshake NOUN batido MASC

millennium NOUN milenio MASC

millimetre NOUN milímetro MASC

million NOUN millón MASC; **a million people** un millón de personas, **two million people** dos millones de personas

millionaire NOUN millonario MASC, millonaria FEM

mince *NOUN* **mince** *mince* **carne** *(FEM)* **picada**

mind *NOUN* ❶ **mente** *FEM*; **a logical mind** una mente lógica ❷ **it crossed my mind that ...** se me pasó por la cabeza que ... ❸ **to change your mind** cambiar [17] de opinión, **I've changed my mind** he cambiado de opinión ❹ **to make up your mind** decidirse [19], **I can't make up my mind** no puedo decidirme

mind *VERB* ❶ **cuidar** [17]; **can you mind my bag for me?** ¿me cuidas el bolso?, **could you mind the baby for ten minutes?** ¿puedes cuidar del niño diez minutos? ❷ **do you mind if ...?** ¿te importa que ...?, **do you mind if I close the door?** ¿te importa que cierre la puerta?, **I don't mind** no me importa, **never mind!** ¡no importa! ❸ **I don't mind the heat** no me molesta el calor ❹ **mind the step!** ¡cuidado con el escalón!

mine¹ *NOUN* **mina** *FEM*; **a coal mine** una mina de carbón

mine² *PRONOUN* ❶ *(referring to a singular noun)* **el mío/la mía**; **she took her hat and I took mine** ella cogió su sombrero y yo cogí el mío, **Tessa phoned her mum and I phoned mine** Tessa llamó a su madre y yo llamé a la mía ❷ *(referring to a plural noun)* **los míos/las mías**; **Karen's invited her parents and I've invited mine** Karen ha invitado a sus padres y yo a los míos, **she showed me her photos and I showed her mine** ella me enseñó sus fotos y yo le enseñé las mías

miner *NOUN* **minero** *MASC*, **minera** *FEM*

mineral water *NOUN* **agua** *(FEM)* **mineral**

minibus *NOUN* **microbús** *MASC*

minimum *NOUN* **mínimo** *MASC*

minimum *ADJECTIVE* **mínimo/mínima**; **the minimum age** la edad mínima

miniskirt *NOUN* **minifalda** *FEM*

minister *NOUN* ❶ *(in government)* **ministro** *MASC*, **ministra** *FEM* ❷ *(of a church)* **pastor** *MASC*, **pastora** *FEM*

minor *ADJECTIVE* **menor**

minority *NOUN* **minoría** *FEM*

mint *NOUN* ❶ *(herb)* **menta** *FEM* ❷ *(sweet)* **caramelo** *(MASC)* **de menta**

minus *PREPOSITION* ❶ **menos**; **seven minus three is four** siete menos tres es cuatro ❷ **it was minus ten this morning** esta mañana hacía diez grados bajo cero

minute *NOUN* **minuto** *MASC*; **it's five minutes' walk from here** está a cinco minutos andando de aquí, **I'll be ready in two minutes** en dos minutos estoy lista, **just a minute!** ¡un momento!

miracle *NOUN* **milagro** *MASC*

mirror *NOUN* ❶ **espejo** *MASC*; **I looked at myself in the mirror** me miré al espejo ❷ *(rearview mirror in a car)* **retrovisor** *MASC*

misbehave *VERB* **portarse** [17] **mal**

mischief *NOUN* **to get up to mischief** **hacer** [7] **travesuras**

mischievous *ADJECTIVE* **travieso/traviesa**

miser NOUN avaro/avara

miserable ADJECTIVE ❶ triste; he was miserable without her estaba triste sin ella, I feel really miserable today hoy tengo el ánimo por los suelos ❷ it's miserable weather un tiempo deprimente ❸ she gets paid a miserable wage le pagan un sueldo miserable

misery NOUN miseria FEM; he was in misery estaba muy triste

miss VERB ❶ perder [36]; she missed her train perdió el tren, I missed the film me perdí la película, to miss an opportunity perder una oportunidad ❷ the ball missed the goal la pelota no entró en la portería, you missed! ¡fallaste! ❸ faltar [17] a; he's missed several classes ha faltado a varias clases ❹ I miss you te echo de menos, she's missing her sister echa de menos a su hermana, I miss Madrid echo de menos Madrid

Miss NOUN señorita FEM (usually abbreviated to 'Srta'); Miss Jones la señorita Jones

missile NOUN misil MASC

missing ADJECTIVE ❶ the missing piece la pieza que falta, the missing documents los documentos que faltan, the missing link el eslabón perdido ❷ faltar [17], there's a plate missing falta un plato, there are three forks missing faltan tres tenedores, is there anybody missing? ¿falta alguien? ❸ to go missing desaparecer [35], several things have gone missing lately han desaparecido varias cosas últimamente, three people have gone missing han desaparecido tres personas

mist NOUN neblina FEM

mistake NOUN ❶ error MASC; by mistake por error, it was my mistake fue un error mío ❷ falta FEM; a spelling mistake una falta de ortografía, you've made lots of mistakes has cometido muchas faltas ❸ to make a mistake (be mistaken) cometer [18] un error, sorry, I made a mistake perdona, he cometido un error

mistake VERB confundir [19]; I mistook you for your brother te confundí con tu hermano

mistaken ADJECTIVE to be mistaken estar [2] equivocado/equivocada, you're mistaken estás equivocado

mistletoe NOUN muérdago MASC

misunderstand VERB entender [36] mal; I misunderstood lo entendí mal

misunderstanding NOUN malentendido MASC; there's been a misunderstanding hay un malentendido

mix NOUN ❶ mezcla FEM; a good mix of people una buena mezcla de gente ❷ a cake mix un preparado para hacer un pastel

mix VERB ❶ mezclar [17]; mix all the ingredients together mezclar todos los ingredientes ❷ to mix with tratarse [17] con, she mixes with lots of interesting people se trata con mucha gente interesante
• to mix up ❶ desordenar [17], you've mixed up all my papers has desordenado todos mis papeles ❷ (confuse) confundir [19] (confuse) I get him mixed up with his brother lo confundo con su hermano,

you've got it all **mixed up!** ¡te has confundido!

mixed ADJECTIVE **variado/variada**; a mixed programme un programa variado

mixed salad NOUN **ensalada** (FEM) **mixta**

mixer NOUN **batidora** FEM

mixture NOUN **mezcla** FEM; it's a mixture of jazz and rock es una mezcla de jazz y rock

moan VERB (complain) **quejarse** [17]; stop moaning! ¡deja de quejarte!

mobile home NOUN **caravana** (FEM) **fija**

mobile phone NOUN **teléfono** (MASC) **móvil, móvil** MASC

mock NOUN (mock exam) **examen** (MASC) **de práctica**

mock VERB **burlarse** [17] **de**; stop mocking me! ¡deja de burlarte de mí!

model NOUN ❶ (type) **modelo** MASC; the latest model el último modelo ❷ (fashion model) **modelo** MASC & FEM; she's a model es modelo ❸ (of a plane, car, etc.) **maqueta** FEM; he makes models construye maquetas, a model of Westminster Abbey una maqueta de la abadía de Westminster

model aeroplane NOUN **aeromodelo** MASC

model railway NOUN **ferrocarril** (MASC) **de juguete**

modem NOUN **módem** MASC

moderate ADJECTIVE **moderado/ moderada**

modern ADJECTIVE **moderno/ moderna**

modernize VERB **modernizar** [22]

modern languages NOUN **lenguas** (FEM PLURAL) **modernas**

moisturizer NOUN ❶ (lotion) **loción** (FEM) **hidratante** ❷ (cream) **crema** (FEM) **hidratante**

mole NOUN ❶ (animal) **topo** MASC ❷ (on skin) **lunar** MASC

moment NOUN **momento** MASC; he'll be here in a moment llegará en cualquier momento, at any moment en cualquier momento, at the moment en este momento, at the right moment en el momento preciso, for the moment de momento

monarchy NOUN **monarquía** FEM

Monday NOUN **lunes** MASC (does not change in the plural); on Monday el lunes, I'm going out on Monday voy a salir el lunes, see you on Monday! ¡te veo el lunes!, on Mondays los lunes, the museum is closed on Mondays el museo cierra los lunes, every Monday todos los lunes, last Monday el lunes pasado, next Monday el próximo lunes

money NOUN **dinero** MASC; I don't have enough money no tengo suficiente dinero, to make money hacer [7] dinero, they gave me my money back (in a shop) me devolvieron el dinero

money box NOUN **hucha** FEM

mongrel NOUN **chucho** MASC (informal)

monitor NOUN (on computer)
monitor MASC

monkey NOUN ❶ mono MASC ❷ you
little monkey! ¡diablillo! (informal)

monster NOUN monstruo MASC

month NOUN mes MASC; in the month
of May en el mes de mayo, this
month este mes, next month el
próximo mes, we're leaving next
month nos vamos el próximo mes,
last month el mes pasado, every
month todos los meses, in two
months' time dentro de dos meses,
at the end of the month a final de
mes

monthly ADJECTIVE mensual; a
monthly payment una mensualidad

monument NOUN monumento MASC

mood NOUN humor MASC; to be in
a good mood estar [2] de buen
humor, to be in a bad mood estar
[2] de mal humor, I'm not in the
mood no estoy de humor

moody ADJECTIVE temperamental

moon NOUN luna FEM; by the light of
the moon a la luz de la luna
• to be over the moon estar loco/loca
de contento (literally: to be mad with
happiness)

moonlight NOUN luz (FEM) de la
luna; by moonlight a la luz de la
luna

moped NOUN ciclomotor MASC

moral NOUN moraleja FEM; the
moral of the story la moraleja de
la historia

moral ADJECTIVE moral

morals PLURAL NOUN moralidad FEM

more ADVERB, ADJECTIVE

more PRONOUN ❶ más; more
interesting más interesante, more
easily más fácilmente, a little more
milk un poco más de leche, a few
more glasses unos cuantos vasos
más, would you like some more
cake? ¿quieres más pastel?, we
need three more necesitamos tres
más ❷ more ... than más ... que, the
book's more interesting than the
film el libro es más interesante que
la película, he eats more than me
come más que yo ❸ more and more
cada vez más, books are getting
more and more expensive los libros
están cada vez más caros, it takes
more and more time lleva cada vez
más tiempo ❹ more or less más o
menos, it's more or less finished
está más o menos terminado ❺ any
more más, I don't want any more
no quiero más, I don't like it any
more ya no me gusta

morning NOUN mañana FEM; this
morning esta mañana, tomorrow
morning mañana por la mañana,
yesterday morning ayer por la
mañana, in the morning por la
mañana, she doesn't work in
the morning no trabaja por las
mañanas, on Friday mornings los
viernes por la mañana, at six o'clock
in the morning a las seis de la
mañana, I spent the whole morning
doing the washing-up me pasé
toda la mañana lavando los platos

Morocco NOUN Marruecos MASC

mortgage NOUN hipoteca FEM

Moscow NOUN Moscú MASC

A B C D E F G H I J K L **M** N O P Q R S T U V W X Y Z

Moslem NOUN musulmán MASC, musulmana FEM

mosque NOUN mezquita FEM

mosquito NOUN mosquito MASC; **a mosquito bite** una picadura de mosquito

most ADJECTIVE, ADVERB, PRONOUN
❶ *(followed by a plural noun)* la mayoría de; **most children like chocolate** a la mayoría de los niños les gusta el chocolate, **most of my friends** la mayoría de mis amigos ❷ *(followed by a singular noun)* casi todo; **they've eaten most of the chocolate** se han comido casi todo el chocolate ❸ **most of the time** la mayor parte del tiempo, **most of it is clear** la mayor parte está claro ❹ **the most** *(followed by adjective)* más, **the most interesting film** la película más interesante, **the most exciting story** la historia más emocionante, **the most boring books** los libros más aburridos ❺ **the most** *(followed by noun)* **I've got the most time** soy el que más tiempo tiene ❻ *(after averb)* **what I hate most is the noise** lo que más odio es el ruido

mother NOUN madre FEM; **my mother** mi madre, **Kate's mother** la madre de Kate

mother-in-law NOUN suegra FEM

Mother's Day NOUN día *(MASC)* de la Madre *(in Spain, the first Sunday in May)*

motivated ADJECTIVE motivado/ motivada

motivation NOUN motivo MASC

motor NOUN motor MASC

motorbike NOUN motocicleta FEM

motorboat NOUN motora FEM

motorcyclist NOUN motociclista MASC & FEM

motorist NOUN automovilista MASC & FEM

motor racing NOUN carreras *(FEM PLURAL)* de coches

motorway NOUN autopista FEM

mouldy ADJECTIVE mohoso/mohosa

mountain NOUN montaña FEM; **in the mountains** en las montañas

mountain bike NOUN bicicleta *(FEM)* de montaña

mountaineer NOUN montañero MASC, montañera FEM

mountaineering NOUN montañismo MASC; **to go mountaineering** hacer [7] montañismo

mountainous ADJECTIVE montañoso/montañosa

mouse NOUN ratón MASC *(both the animal and for a computer)*

mousse NOUN mousse FEM; **chocolate mousse** mousse de chocolate

moustache NOUN bigote MASC

mouth NOUN boca FEM

mouthful NOUN bocado MASC *(of food)* **trago** MASC *(of drink)*

mouth organ NOUN armónica FEM; **to play the mouth organ** tocar [31] la armónica

move *NOUN* ❶ *(to a different house)* **mudanza** *FEM* ❷ *(in a game)* **your move!** ¡tu turno!

move *VERB* ❶ **moverse** [38]; **she didn't move** no se movió ❷ **move up a bit** córrete un poco ❸ *(an object)* **cambiar** [17] **de sitio**; **you've moved the picture** has cambiado el cuadro de sitio, **can you move your bag, please?** ¿puedes correr tu bolsa, por favor? ❹ **mover** [38] *(an object or part of the body)*; **she moved her hand** movió la mano ❺ *(car, traffic)* **avanzar** [22]; **the traffic was moving slowly** el tráfico avanzaba lentamente ❻ **to move forward** avanzar [22]; **he moved forward a step** avanzó un paso ❼ *(move house)* **mudarse** [17]; **we're moving on Tuesday** nos mudamos el martes, **they've moved house** se han mudado de casa, **they've moved to Spain** se han ido a vivir en España ❽ *(emotionally)* **conmover** [38]; **it really moved me** me conmovió de verdad, **to be moved** estar [2] conmovido/conmovida

• **to move in** mudarse [17]; **when are you moving in?** ¿cuándo se mudan?
• **to move out** mudarse [17]; **I'm moving out at the end of the month** me mudo a finales del mes

movie *NOUN* **película** *FEM*; **to go to the movies** ir [8] al cine

moving *ADJECTIVE* ❶ **en marcha**; **a moving vehicle** un vehículo en marcha ❷ *(emotionally)* **conmovedor/conmovedora**; **it's a very moving film** es una película muy conmovedora

MP *NOUN* **diputado** *MASC*, **diputada** *FEM*; **she's an MP** es diputada

Mr *NOUN* **Señor** *(usually abbreviated to 'Sr.')*; **Mr Angus Brown** el Sr. Angus Brown

Mrs *NOUN* **Señora** *(usually abbreviated to 'Sra.')*; **Mrs Mary Hendry** la Sra. Mary Hendry

Ms *NOUN* **Señora** *(usually abbreviated to 'Sra.'; note that there is no direct equivalent to 'Ms' in Spanish, but 'Señora' may be used whether a woman is married or not)*

much *ADVERB, PRONOUN, DETERMINER* ❶ **mucho**; **she doesn't eat much** no come mucho, **we don't go out much** no salimos mucho, **much more** mucho más, **much shorter** mucho más bajo ❷ *(followed by a noun)* **mucho/mucha**; **we don't have much time** no tenemos mucho tiempo, **there isn't much butter left** no queda mucha mantequilla ❸ **very much** mucho, **I don't watch television very much** no veo mucho la tele, **thank you very much** muchas gracias ❹ **very much** *(followed by a noun)* **mucho/mucha**, **there isn't very much milk** no queda mucha leche ❺ **not much** *(referring to a verb)* **no mucho**, **'do you go out?' – 'not much'** ¿sales? – 'no mucho' ❻ **not much** *(referring to a noun)*, **no mucho/no mucha**, **'did you add salt?' – 'yes, but not much'** ¿has puesto sal? – 'sí, pero no mucha' ❼ **so much** tanto, **we liked it so much!** ¡nos gustó tanto!, **I have so much to do!** ¡tengo tanto que hacer!, **you shouldn't have given me so much** no deberías haberme dado tanto ❽ **as much as** tanto como, **you can take as much as you like** puedes coger tanto como quieras ❾ **too much** demasiado, **that's far too much!** ¡eso es demasiado! ❿ **too much** *(followed by noun)* demasiado/demasiada, **too much ink** demasiada tinta ⓫ **how much?** ¿cuánto?, **how much is it?** ¿cuánto cuesta?, **how much do you want?** ¿cuánto quieres? ⓬ **how much?** *(followed by a noun)* ¿cuánto?/¿cuánta?, **how much milk do you want?** ¿cuánta leche quieres?

mud *NOUN* **barro** *MASC*

muddle *NOUN* **desorden** *MASC*; **to be in a muddle** estar [2] todo desordenado

muddy *ADJECTIVE* **lleno de barro/ llena de barro**; **your boots are all muddy** tus botas están llenas de barro, **a muddy road** una carretera llena de barro

mug *NOUN* **taza** *(FEM)* **alta**; **a mug of coffee** una taza alta de café

mug *VERB* **to mug somebody** atracar [31] a alguien, **my brother was mugged in the park** atracaron a mi hermano en el parque

mugging *NOUN* **atraco** *MASC*

multiplication *NOUN* **multiplicación** *FEM*

multiply *VERB* **multiplicar** [31]; **to multiply six by four** multiplicar seis por cuatro

mum, mummy *NOUN* ❶ **madre** *FEM*; **Tom's mum** la madre de Tom, **I'll ask my mum** preguntaré a mi madre ❷ *(within the family or as a name)* **mamá** *FEM*; **Mum's not back yet** mamá no ha vuelto todavía

mumps *NOUN* **paperas** *FEM PLURAL*

murder *NOUN* **asesinato** *MASC*

murder *VERB* **asesinar** [17]

murderer *NOUN* **asesino** *MASC*, **asesina** *FEM*

muscle *NOUN* **músculo** *MASC*

museum *NOUN* **museo** *MASC*; **to go to the museum** ir [8] al museo

mushroom *NOUN* **champiñón** *MASC*

music *NOUN* **música** *FEM*; **pop music** música pop, **classical music** música clásica

musical *NOUN* **musical** *MASC*

musical *ADJECTIVE* ❶ **a musical instrument** un instrumento musical ❷ **they're a very musical family** toda la familia tiene dotes para la música

musician *NOUN* **músico** *MASC*, **música** *FEM*

Muslim *NOUN* **musulmán** *MASC*, **musulmana** *FEM*

mussel *NOUN* **mejillón** *MASC*

must *VERB* ❶ *(expressing obligation)* **tener** [9] **que** *(stronger)*, **deber** [18]; **you must be there at eight** tienes que estar allí a las ocho, **debes estar allí a las ocho** ❷ *(expressing probability)* **deber** [18]; **you must be tired** debes estar cansado, **it must be five o'clock** deben ser las cinco en punto, **he must have forgotten** debe haberse olvidado

mustard *NOUN* **mostaza** *FEM*

my *ADJECTIVE* ❶ *(before a singular noun)* **mi**; **my book** mi libro, **my sister** mi hermana ❷ *(before a plural noun)* **mis**; **my children** mis hijos ❸ *(with parts of the body)* **el/la/los/las**; **I had**

a glass in my hand tenía un vaso en la mano, **I'm washing my hands** me estoy lavando las manos

myself *PRONOUN* ❶ *(as a reflexive)* me; **I've hurt myself** me he hecho daño ❷ **I said it myself** lo dije yo mismo ❸ *(for emphasis)* yo; **by myself** yo solo/yo sola, **I did it by myself** lo hice yo solo/yo sola

mysterious *ADJECTIVE* misterioso/misteriosa

mystery *NOUN* ❶ misterio *MASC* ❷ *(book)* novela *(FEM)* de misterio

nail *NOUN* ❶ *(on finger or toe)* uña *FEM*; **to bite your nails** morderse [38] las uñas ❷ *(metal)* clavo *MASC*

nailbrush *NOUN* cepillo *(MASC)* de uñas

nailfile *NOUN* lima *(FEM)* de uñas

nail scissors *NOUN* tijeras *(FEM PLURAL)* de uñas

nail varnish *NOUN* esmalte *(MASC)* de uñas

nail varnish remover *NOUN* quitaesmalte *MASC*

name *NOUN* ❶ nombre *MASC*; **I've forgotten her name** se me ha olvidado su nombre, **what's your name?** ¿cómo te llamas?, **my name's Lily** me llamo Lily ❷ *(of a book or film)* título *MASC*

nanny *NOUN* niñera *FEM*

napkin *NOUN* servilleta *FEM*

nappy *NOUN* pañal *MASC*

narrow *ADJECTIVE* estrecho/estrecha; **a narrow street** una calle estrecha

nasty *ADJECTIVE* ❶ *(mean)* cruel; **they were nasty to him** fueron crueles con él, **that was a nasty thing to do** eso fue una crueldad ❷ *(unpleasant)* desagradable; **that's a nasty job** ese es un trabajo desagradable ❸ *(bad)* repugnante; **a nasty smell** un olor repugnante

nation NOUN nación FEM

national ADJECTIVE nacional

national anthem NOUN himno (MASC) nacional

nationality NOUN nacionalidad FEM

national park NOUN parque (MASC) nacional

Nativity scene NOUN belén MASC

natural ADJECTIVE natural

naturally ADVERB naturalmente

nature NOUN naturaleza FEM

nature reserve NOUN reserva (FEM) natural

naughty ADJECTIVE malo/mala

nausea NOUN náuseas FEM PLURAL

navel NOUN ombligo MASC

navigate VERB navegar [28]

navy NOUN marina FEM; my uncle's in the navy mi tío está en la marina

navy-blue ADJECTIVE azul marino; navy-blue gloves guantes azul marino

near ADJECTIVE cercano/cercana; the nearest shop la tienda más cercana

near ADVERB, PREPOSITION ❶ cerca; they live quite near viven bastante cerca, to come nearer acercarse [31] ❷ near (to) cerca de, near the station cerca de la estación

nearby ADVERB cerca; there's a park nearby hay un parque cerca

nearly ADVERB casi; nearly empty casi vacío, we're nearly there ya casi hemos llegado

neat ADJECTIVE ❶ (well-organized) ordenado/ordenada; a neat desk un pupitre ordenado ❷ arreglado/arreglada (your clothes, or the way you look); she always looks very neat siempre va muy arreglada ❸ muy cuidado/muy cuidada (a garden)

necessarily ADVERB not necessarily no necesariamente

necessary ADJECTIVE necesario/necesaria; if necessary si es necesario

neck NOUN cuello MASC (of a person or garment)

necklace NOUN collar MASC

nectarine NOUN nectarina FEM

need NOUN necesidad FEM; there's no need, I've done it already no hay necesidad, ya lo he hecho, there's no need to wait no hay necesidad de esperar

need VERB ❶ necesitar [17]; we need bread necesitamos pan, they need help necesitan ayuda, everything you need todo lo que necesites ❷ (to have to) tener [9] que; I need to drop in at the bank tengo que pasarme por el banco, she'll need to check tendrá que comprobarlo ❸ you needn't decide today no hace falta que decidas hoy, you needn't wait no hace falta que esperes

needle NOUN aguja FEM

negative NOUN (of a photo) negativo MASC

neglected ADJECTIVE descuidado/descuidada

neighbour NOUN **vecino** MASC, **vecina** FEM; **we're going round to the neighbours'** vamos a casa de los vecinos

neighbourhood NOUN **barrio** MASC; **a nice neighbourhood** un barrio agradable

neither CONJUNCTION ❶ **neither … nor** ni … ni, **I have neither the time nor the money** no tengo ni tiempo ni dinero ❷ **neither do I** yo tampoco, **'I didn't go' – 'neither did I'** 'no fui' – 'yo tampoco' ❸ (with 'gustar') **'I don't like fish' – 'neither do I'** 'no me gusta el pescado' – 'ni a mí tampoco', **''I didn't like the film' – 'neither did Kirsty'** 'no me gustó la película' – 'ni a Kirsty tampoco', **'which do you like?' – 'neither'** '¿cuál te gusta?' – 'ninguno'

nephew NOUN **sobrino** MASC

nerve NOUN ❶ (in the body) **nervio** MASC ❷ **to lose one's nerve** perder [36] el valor ❸ **you've got a nerve!** ¡vaya cara que tienes! (informal)

• **he gets on my nerves** me pone los nervios de punta (informal)

nervous ADJECTIVE **nervioso/ nerviosa**; **to feel nervous** (before a performance or an exam) estar nervioso

nervous breakdown NOUN **crisis** (FEM) **nerviosa**

nest NOUN **nido** MASC

net NOUN **red** FEM

Netherlands NOUN **the Netherlands** los Países Bajos

nettle NOUN **ortiga** FEM

network NOUN **red** FEM

neutral NOUN (in a gearbox) **punto** (MASC) **muerto**; **to be in neutral** estar [2] en punto muerto

neutral ADJECTIVE ❶ (impartial) **neutral** ❷ (colour) **neutro**

never ADJECTIVE ❶ **nunca**; **Ben never smokes** Ben no fuma nunca, **I've never seen the film** no he visto nunca la película, **'have you ever been to Spain?' – 'no, never'** ¿has estado alguna vez en España?' – 'no, nunca' ❷ **never again!** ¡nunca jamás! ❸ **never mind** no importa

nevertheless ADVERB **sin embargo**

new ADJECTIVE **nuevo/nueva**; **have you seen their new house?** ¿has visto su casa nueva?, **Debbie's new boyfriend** el nuevo novio de Debbie, **it's a new car** es un coche nuevo

news PLURAL NOUN ❶ (everyday gossip) **noticia** FEM; **a piece of good news** una buena noticia, **have you heard the news?** ¿te has enterado de la noticia?, **any news?** ¿hay alguna noticia? ❷ (on TV or radio) **noticias** FEM PLURAL; **the midday news** las noticias del mediodía

newsagent NOUN **vendedor** (MASC) **de periódicos, vendedora** (FEM) **de periódicos**; **at the newsagent's** en la tienda de periódicos

newspaper NOUN **periódico** MASC

newsreader NOUN **presentador** MASC, **presentadora** FEM

New Year NOUN **Año** (MASC) **Nuevo**; **Happy New Year!** ¡Feliz Año Nuevo!

New Year's Day NOUN **día** (MASC) **de Año Nuevo**

New Year's Eve NOUN **Nochevieja** FEM

New Zealand NOUN **Nueva Zelanda** FEM

New Zealander NOUN **neozelandés** MASC, **neozelandesa** FEM

next ADJECTIVE ❶ (*following*) **próximo/próxima**; **the next train is at ten** el próximo tren sale a las diez, **next week** la próxima semana, **next Thursday** el próximo jueves, **next year** el próximo año, **the next time I see you** la próxima vez que te vea ❷ (*following*) **siguiente**; **the next day** el día siguiente, **at the next stop** en la siguiente parada ❸ (*next-door*) **in the next room** en la habitación de al lado

next ADVERB ❶ (*afterwards*) **luego**; **what did he say next?** ¿qué dijo luego? ❷ (*now*) **ahora**; **what shall we do next?** ¿qué hacemos ahora? ❸ **next to** al lado de, **the girl next to Pat** la chica que está al lado de Pat, **it's next to the baker's** está al lado de la panadería

next door ADVERB **al lado**; **they live next door** viven al lado, **the girl next door** la chica de al lado

Nicaraguan NOUN **nicaragüense** MASC & FEM

Nicaraguan ADJECTIVE **nicaragüense**

nice ADJECTIVE ❶ (*pleasant*) **agradable**; **we had a very nice evening** pasamos una tarde muy agradable, **Brighton's a very nice town** Brighton es una ciudad muy agradable, **have a nice time!** ¡que lo pases bien! ❷ (*attractive to look at*) **bonito/bonita** (*an object or place*); **that's a nice dress** ese vestido es

bonito ❸ (*attractive to look at*) **guapo/guapa** (*a person*); **you look nice in that dress** estás muy guapa con ese vestido ❹ (*kind, friendly*) **majo/maja** (*informal*); **she's really nice** es muy maja (*informal*) ❺ **to be nice to somebody** ser [1] bueno/buena con alguien, **she's been very nice to me** ha sido muy buena conmigo ❻ (*tasting good*) **rico/rica**; **the food was really nice** la comida estaba muy rica ❼ (*weather*) **bueno/buena**; **it's a nice day** hace buen día, **we had nice weather** tuvimos buen tiempo

nick VERB (*steal*) **mangar** [28] (*informal*)

nickname NOUN **apodo** MASC

niece NOUN **sobrina** FEM

night NOUN **noche** FEM; **what are you doing tonight?** ¿qué haces esta noche?, **see you tonight!** ¡hasta esta noche!, **I saw Greg last night** anoche vi a Greg, **it's cold at night** hace frío por la noche, **to stay the night with somebody** pasar [17] la noche con alguien

night club NOUN **club** (MASC) **nocturno**

nightie NOUN **camisón** MASC

nightmare NOUN **pesadilla** FEM; **to have a nightmare** tener [9] una pesadilla

night-time NOUN **noche** FEM

nil NOUN **cero** MASC; **they won four-nil** ganaron cuatro a cero

nine NUMBER **nueve** MASC; **Jake's nine** Jake tiene nueve años, **it's nine o'clock** son las nueve

nineteen _NUMBER_ diecinueve _MASC_; **Jonny's nineteen** Jonny tiene diecinueve años

nineties _PLURAL NOUN_ **the nineties** los años noventa, **in the nineties** en los años noventa

ninety _NUMBER_ noventa _MASC_; **he's ninety** tiene noventa años, **ninety-five** noventa y cinco

ninth _NOUN_ ❶ _(fraction)_ **a ninth** una novena parte ❷ **the ninth of June** el nueve de junio

ninth _ADJECTIVE_ noveno/novena; **on the ninth floor** en la novena planta

nitrogen _NOUN_ nitrógeno _MASC_

no _ADVERB_ no; **I said no** he dicho que no, **no thank you** no, gracias

no _ADJECTIVE_ ❶ **we've got no bread** no tenemos pan, **no problem!** ¡sin problema! ❷ _(on a notice)_ **'no smoking'** 'prohibido fumar', **'no parking'** 'prohibido aparcar'

nobody _PRONOUN_ nadie; **'who's there?' – 'nobody'** '¿quién está ahí?' – 'nadie', **there's nobody in the kitchen** no hay nadie en la cocina, **nobody knows me** nadie me conoce, **nobody answered** no contestó nadie

nod _VERB_ _(to say yes)_ asentir [14] con la cabeza; **he nodded** asintió con la cabeza

noise _NOUN_ ruido _MASC_; **to make a noise** hacer [7] ruido

noisy _ADJECTIVE_ ruidoso/ruidosa

none _PRONOUN_ ❶ _(not one)_ niguno/ ninguna; **'how many students failed the exam?' – 'none'** '¿cuántos estudiantes suspendieron?' –

'ninguno', **none of the girls knows him** ninguna de las chicas lo conoce ❷ **there's none left** no queda nada, **there are none left** no queda ninguno/ninguna

nonsense _NOUN_ tonterías _FEM_, _(plural)_; **to talk nonsense** decir [5] tonterías, **nonsense! she's at least thirty** ¡tonterías! tiene por lo menos treinta años

non-smoker _NOUN_ no fumador _MASC_, no fumadora _FEM_

non-stop _ADJECTIVE_ directo/directa _(a train or flight)_

non-stop _ADVERB_ **she talks non-stop** habla sin parar

noodles _PLURAL NOUN_ fideos _MASC_ _PLURAL_

noon _NOUN_ mediodía _MASC_; **at (twelve) noon** a mediodía

no-one _PRONOUN_ nadie; **'who's there?' – 'no-one'** '¿quién está ahí?' – 'nadie', **there's no-one in the kitchen** no hay nadie en la cocina, **no-one knows me** nadie me conoce, **no-one answered** nadie contestó

nor _CONJUNCTION_ ❶ **neither ... nor** ni ... ni, **I have neither the time nor the money** no tengo ni tiempo ni dinero ❷ **nor do I** yo tampoco, **'I didn't go' – 'nor did I'** 'no fui' – 'yo tampoco' ❸ _(with 'gustar')_ **'I don't like fish' – 'nor do I'** 'no me gusta el pescado' – 'ni a mí tampoco', **"I didn't like the film' – 'nor did Kirsty'** 'no me gustó la película' – 'ni a Kirsty tampoco'

normal _ADJECTIVE_ normal

normally _ADVERB_ normalmente

north _NOUN_ norte _MASC_; **in the north** en el norte

a b c d e f g h i j k l m n o p q r s t u v w x y z

north ADJECTIVE, ADVERB **norte** *(never changes)*; **the north side** la parte norte, **a north wind** un viento del norte, **north of Madrid** al norte de Madrid

North America NOUN **Norteamérica** FEM

North American NOUN **norteamericano** MASC, **norteamericana** FEM

North American ADJECTIVE **norteamericano/ norteamericana**

northeast NOUN **noreste** MASC

northeast ADJECTIVE **in northeast England** en el noreste de Inglaterra

Northern Ireland NOUN **Irlanda** *(FEM)* **del Norte**

North Pole NOUN **Polo** *(MASC)* **Norte**

North Sea NOUN **the North Sea** el mar del Norte

northwest NOUN **noroeste** MASC

northwest ADJECTIVE **in northwest England** en el noroeste de Inglaterra

Norway NOUN **Noruega** FEM

Norwegian NOUN ❶ *(person)* **noruego** MASC, **noruega** FEM ❷ *(language)* **noruego** MASC

Norwegian ADJECTIVE **noruego/ noruega**

nose NOUN **nariz** FEM; **to blow your nose** sonarse [24] la nariz

nosebleed NOUN **to have a nosebleed** tener [9] una hemorragia nasal

nostril NOUN **fosa** *(FEM)* **nasal**

not ADVERB ❶ **no**; **not on Saturdays** los sábados no, **not all alone!** ¡completamente solo no!, **it's not bad** no está mal, **not at all** *(in no way)* en absoluto, *(after somebody says 'thank you')* de nada, **not yet** todavía no, **of course not!** ¡por supuesto que no! ❷ *(when used with a verb)* **no**; **it's not my car** no es mi coche, **I don't know** no sé, **Sam didn't phone** Sam no llamó, **we decided not to wait** decidimos no esperar ❸ **I hope not** espero que no

note NOUN ❶ *(a short letter)* **nota** FEM; **she left me a note** me dejó una nota ❷ **to take notes** tomar [17] apuntes ❸ *(a banknote)* **billete** MASC; **a ten-pound note** un billete de diez libras ❹ *(in music)* **nota** FEM

notebook NOUN **cuaderno** MASC

notepad NOUN **bloc** MASC

nothing PRONOUN ❶ **nada**; **'what did you say?' – 'nothing'** ¿qué has dicho? – 'nada', **nothing new** nada nuevo, **nothing special** nada especial ❷ *(when used with a verb)* **no ... nada**; **she knows nothing** no sabe nada, **but there was nothing there** pero no había nada allí, **I saw nothing** no vi nada, **there's nothing happening** no está pasando nada, **there's nothing new** no hay nada nuevo ❸ **they do nothing but fight** no hacen más que pelearse

notice NOUN ❶ *(a sign)* **letrero** MASC ❷ **don't take any notice of her!** ¡no le hagas caso! ❸ **to do something at short notice** hacer [7] algo con poca antelación

notice *VERB* notar [17]; **I didn't notice anything** no noté nada

notice board *NOUN* tablón *(MASC)* de anuncios

nought *NOUN* cero *MASC*

noun *NOUN* nombre *MASC*

novel *NOUN* novela *FEM*

novelist *NOUN* novelista *MASC & FEM*

November *NOUN* noviembre *MASC*

now *ADVERB* ❶ ahora; **where is he now?** ¿dónde está ahora?, **they live in the country now** ahora viven en el campo ❷ **he's busy just now** está ocupado en este momento, **I saw her just now in the corridor** acabo de verla en el pasillo ❸ **do it right now!** ¡hazlo ahora mismo! ❹ **now and then** de vez en cuando, **from now on** de ahora en adelante

nowadays *ADVERB* hoy en día; **nowadays they are quite common** hoy en día son bastante comunes

nowhere *ADJECTIVE* ❶ ninguna parte; **nowhere in Spain** en ninguna parte de España, **'where did she go after work?' – 'nowhere'** ¿dónde fue después del trabajo? – 'a ninguna parte' ❷ **there's nowhere to park** no hay sitio donde aparcar

nuclear *ADJECTIVE* nuclear; **a nuclear power station** una central nuclear

nuisance *NOUN* ❶ *(a person)* pesado/pesada; **he's a real nuisance** es un verdadero pesado ❷ **it's a nuisance** es un fastidio

numb *ADJECTIVE* entumecido/entumecida; **my fingers are numb with cold** tengo los dedos entumecidos del frío

number *NOUN* número *MASC*; **I live at number thirty-one** vivo en el número treinta y uno, **my new phone number** mi nuevo número de teléfono, **a large number of visitors** un gran número de visitantes, **the third number is a 7** el tercer número es un siete

number plate *NOUN* matrícula *FEM*

nun *NOUN* monja *FEM*

nurse *NOUN* enfermero *MASC*, enfermera *FEM*; **Janet's a nurse** Janet es enfermera

nursery *NOUN* ❶ *(for children)* guardería *FEM* ❷ *(for plants)* vivero *MASC*

nursery school *NOUN* jardín *(MASC)* de infancia

nursing *NOUN* enfermería *FEM*

nut *NOUN* ❶ *(walnut)* nuez *FEM* ❷ *(almond)* almendra *FEM* ❸ *(peanut)* cacahuete *MASC* ❹ *(for a bolt)* tuerca *FEM*

nylon *NOUN* nylon *MASC*

a
b
c
d
e
f
g
h
i
j
k
l
m
n
o
p
q
r
s
t
u
v
w
x
y
z

Oo

A
B
C
D
E
F
G
H
I
J
K
L
M
N
O
P
Q
R
S
T
U
V
W
X
Y
Z

oak NOUN roble MASC

oar NOUN remo MASC

oasis NOUN oasis MASC

obedient ADJECTIVE obediente

obey VERB obedecer [35] *(a person)*; to obey the rules respetar [17] las reglas

object NOUN objeto MASC

object VERB oponerse [11]; if you don't object si no te opones

objection NOUN objeción FEM

oboe NOUN oboe MASC; to play the oboe tocar [31] el oboe

obsessed ADJECTIVE obsesionado/ obsesionada; she's obsessed with her diet está obsesionada con su dieta

obsession NOUN obsesión FEM; he has an obsession with cleanliness tiene obsesión con la limpieza

obvious ADJECTIVE obvio/obvia

obviously ADVERB evidentemente; the house is obviously empty evidentemente la casa está vacía, 'do you want to come too?' – 'obviously, but it's a bit difficult' '¿tú quieres venir también?' – 'evidentemente, pero es un poco difícil'

occasion NOUN ocasión FEM; a special occasion una ocasión especial

occasional ADJECTIVE he sends us the occasional letter de vez en cuando nos manda una carta

occasionally ADVERB de vez en cuando

occupation NOUN ocupación FEM

occupied ADJECTIVE ocupado/ ocupada

occur VERB ocurrir [19]; the accident occurred on Monday el accidente ocurrió el lunes, it never occurred to me nunca se me había ocurrido

ocean NOUN océano MASC

o'clock ADVERB at ten o'clock a las diez, it's three o'clock son las tres, exactly five o'clock exactamente las cinco en punto

October NOUN octubre MASC

odd ADJECTIVE ❶ *(strange)* raro/rara; that's odd, I'm sure I heard the phone qué raro, estoy seguro de que he oído el teléfono ❷ *(number)* impar; three is an odd number el tres es un número impar

odds and ends PLURAL NOUN cachivaches MASC PLURAL

of PREPOSITION ❶ de *(note that 'de + el' becomes 'del')*; a kilo of tomatoes un kilo de tomates, the end of my work el final de mi trabajo, the beginning of the concert el principio del concierto, the name of the flower el nombre de la flor, the sixth of June el seis de junio, a cup of tea una taza de té ❷ Ray has four horses but he's selling three of them Ray tiene cuatro caballos, pero va a vender tres, **we ate a lot of it** comimos mucho, **a lot of them** muchos/muchas, **some of them** algunos/algunas ❸ **two of us** dos de nosotros, **there are two of us** somos dos, **a friend of mine** un amigo mío ❹ **a bracelet made of silver** una pulsera de plata

off ADVERB, ADJECTIVE, PREPOSITION
❶ (switched off) **apagado/ apagada**; **is the telly off?** ¿está apagada la tele?, **to turn off the lights** apagar [28] la luz ❷ (tap, water, gas) **cerrado/cerrada**; **to turn off the tap** cerrar [29] el grifo ❸ **to be off** (to leave) irse [8], **I'm off** me voy ❹ **a day off** un día libre, **Caro took three days off work** Caro se tomó tres días libres en el trabajo, **Maya's off school today** Maya no ha venido al colegio hoy ❺ **he's off sick** no ha venido al trabajo porque está enfermo ❻ (cancelled) **suspendido/ suspendida**; **the match is off** el partido se ha suspendido ❼ **to be off** (meat or fish) estar malo/mala, **the milk's off** la leche está cortada

offence NOUN ❶ (crime) **delito** MASC ❷ **to take offence** ofenderse [18], **he takes offence easily** se ofende fácilmente

offer NOUN ❶ **oferta** FEM; **a job offer** una oferta de trabajo ❷ **'on (special) offer'** 'de oferta (especial)'

offer VERB ❶ **ofrecer** [35] (a present, a reward, or a job); **he offered her a chair** le ofreció una silla ❷ **to offer to do** ofrecerse [35] a hacer, **Mike offered to drive me to the station** Mike se ofreció a llevarme a la estación

office NOUN **oficina** FEM; **he's still at the office** aún está en la oficina

office block NOUN **bloque** (MASC) **de oficinas**

officer NOUN **oficial** MASC & FEM

official ADJECTIVE **oficial**; **the official version** la versión oficial

off-licence NOUN **tienda** (FEM) **de vinos y licores**

offside ADVERB **fuera de juego**

often ADVERB ❶ **a menudo**; **he's often late** a menudo llega tarde, **I'd like to see Eric more often** me gustaría ver a Eric más a menudo, **do you go often?** ¿vas a menudo? ❷ **how often?** ¿con qué frecuencia?, **how often do you see Rosie?** ¿con qué frecuencia ves a Rosie?

oil NOUN **aceite** MASC; **olive oil** aceite de oliva, **suntan oil** aceite bronceador

oil painting NOUN **óleo** MASC (picture)

ointment NOUN **pomada** FEM

okay ADJECTIVE ❶ (showing agreement) **vale**; **okay, tomorrow at ten** vale, mañana a las diez ❷ (asking or giving permission) **is it okay to use the phone?** ¿puedo usar el teléfono?, **is it okay with you if I don't come till Friday?** ¿te va bien si no vengo hasta el viernes?, **it's okay if you don't want to do it** no pasa nada si no quieres hacerlo ❸ (person) **majo/maja** (informal); **Daisy's okay** Daisy es maja ❹ (nothing special) **the film was okay** la película no estuvo mal ❺ (not ill) **are you okay?** ¿estás bien?, **I've been ill but I'm okay now** he estado enferma, pero ahora estoy bien

old ADJECTIVE ❶ (not young, not new) viejo/vieja; **an old man** un hombre viejo, **an old lady** una señora vieja, **bring some old clothes** trae ropa vieja, **an old friend of mine** un viejo amigo mío, **old people** los ancianos ❷ (previous) antiguo/antigua; **our old car was a Rover** su antiguo coche era un Rover, **their old address** su antigua dirección ❸ (talking about age) **how old are you?** ¿cuántos años tienes?, **James is ten years old** James tiene diez años, **a three-year-old child** un niño de tres años ❹ **my older sister** mi hermana mayor, **she's older than me** es mayor que yo, **he's a year older than me** es un año mayor que yo

old age NOUN vejez FEM

old age pensioner NOUN pensionista MASC & FEM

old-fashioned NOUN ❶ (clothes, music, style) pasado de moda/pasada de moda ❷ (a person) anticuado/anticuada; **my parents are so old-fashioned** mis padres son tan anticuados

olive NOUN aceituna FEM

olive oil NOUN aceite (FEM) de oliva

Olympic Games, Olympics PLURAL NOUN Juegos (MASC PLURAL) Olímpicos

ombudsman NOUN **the ombudsman** el defensor/la defensora del pueblo MASC & FEM

omelette NOUN tortilla FEM; **a cheese omelette** una tortilla de queso

omit VERB omitir [19]

on PREPOSITION ❶ en; **on the desk** en el escritorio, **on the road** en la carretera, **on the beach** en la playa ❷ (in expressions of time) **on March 21st** el 21 de marzo, **he's arriving on Tuesday** llega el martes, **it's shut on Saturdays** cierra los sábados, **on rainy days** los días de lluvia ❸ (for buses, trains, etc.) **she arrived on the bus** llegó en autobús, **I met Jackie on the bus** me encontré con Jackie en el autobús, **I slept on the plane** dormí en el avión, **let's go on our bikes!** ¡vayamos en las bicis! ❹ **on TV** en la tele, **on the radio** en la radio, **on video** en vídeo ❺ **on holiday** de vacacciones, **on strike** de huelga

on ADJECTIVE ❶ (TV, light, oven, radio) **to be on** estar [2] encendido/encendida, **all the lights were on** todas las luces estaban encendidas, **is the radio on?** ¡está encendida la radio?, **I've put the oven on** he encendido el horno ❷ (machine) estar en marcha; **the dishwasher's on** el lavaplatos está en marcha ❸ (happening) **what's on TV?** ¿qué ponen en la tele?, **what's on this week at the cinema?** ¿qué ponen en el cine esta semana?

once ADVERB ❶ una vez; **I've tried once already** ya lo he intentado una vez, **try once more** inténtalo una vez más, **once a day** una vez al día, **more than once** más de una vez, **once upon a time** érase una vez ❷ **at once** (immediately) inmediatamente, **the doctor came at once** el médico vino inmediatamente ❸ **at once** (at the same time) a la vez, **I can't do two things at once** no puedo hacer dos cosas a la vez

one NUMBER ❶ uno/una; **one apple** una manzana (*note that 'uno' becomes 'un' before a masculine singular noun*) **one son** un hijo ❷ **it's one o'clock** es la una

one PRONOUN ❶ uno/una; **if you want a pen I've got one** si quieres un boli yo tengo uno, **one of us** uno de nosotros, **one of my friends** uno de mis amigos, **you never know** uno nunca sabe ❷ **this one** este/esta, **I like that jumper, but this one's cheaper** me gusta ese jersey, pero este es más barato, **do you want this red tie or this one?** ¿quieres esta corbata roja o esta otra? ❸ **that one** ese/esa, **'which video?' – 'that one'** '¿qué vídeo?' – 'ese' ❹ **which one?** ¿cuál?, **'my foot's hurting' – 'which one?'** 'me duele el pie' – '¿cuál?' ❺ **another one** otro/otra, **I've already had a coffee, but I'll have another one** ya he tomado un café pero voy a tomar otro, **I liked the shirt so much that I bought another one** me gustó tanto la camisa que compré otra

one's ADJECTIVE **to pay for one's car** pagar su coche, **to wash one's hands** lavarse las manos

oneself PRONOUN ❶ (*as a reflexive*) se; **to wash oneself** lavarse, **to hurt oneself** hacerse daño ❷ (*for emphasis*) uno mismo/una misma; **one has to do everything oneself** lo tiene que hacer todo uno mismo

one-way street NOUN calle (FEM) de sentido único

onion NOUN cebolla FEM

only ADJECTIVE único/única; **the only free seat** el único sitio libre, **the only thing to do** lo único que se puede hacer, **I am an only child** soy hijo único

only ADVERB, CONJUNCTION ❶ (*with a verb*) solo; **they've only got two bedrooms** solo tienen dos habitaciones, **Anne's only free on Fridays** Anne solo tiene libres los viernes, **there are only three left** solo quedan tres, **'how long did they stay?' – 'only two days'** '¿cuánto tiempo se quedaron?' – 'solo dos días' ❷ (*but*) pero; **I'd walk, only it's raining** iría andando, pero está lloviendo ❸ **I've only just seen it** acabo de verlo

onto PREPOSITION sobre

open NOUN **in the open** al aire libre

open ADJECTIVE ❶ (*not shut*) abierto/ abierta; **the door's open** la puerta está abierta, **the baker's isn't open** la panadería no está abierta ❷ **in the open air** al aire libre

open VERB ❶ abrir [46]; **can you open the door for me?** ¿me puedes abrir la puerta?, **Sam opened his eyes** Sam abrió los ojos, **the banks open at nine** los bancos abren a las nueve ❷ (*by itself*) abrirse [46]; **the door opened slowly** la puerta se abrió lentamente

open-air ADJECTIVE al aire libre; **an open-air swimming pool** una piscina al aire libre

opener NOUN abridor MASC

opening NOUN ❶ (*space*) abertura FEM ❷ (*opportunity*) oportunidad FEM

opera NOUN ópera FEM

operate VERB ❶ (*a machine*) manejar [17] ❷ (*on a patient, organ*) operar [17]; **will they have to operate** ¿tendrán que operarlo?

operation NOUN **operación** FEM; **she's had an operation** le han operado

opinion NOUN **opinión** FEM; **in my opinion** en mi opinión

opinion poll NOUN **encuesta** (FEM) **de opinión**

opponent NOUN **oponente** MASC & FEM

opportunity NOUN **oportunidad** FEM; **to have the opportunity of doing** tener [9] la oportunidad de hacer, **I took the opportunity to visit the museum** aproveché la oportunidad para visitar el museo

opposed ADJECTIVE **to be opposed to something** oponerse [11] a algo, **they are opposed to any change in the rules** se oponen a cualquier cambio de las reglas

opposite NOUN **the opposite** lo contrario, **no, quite the opposite** no, todo lo contrario

opposite ADJECTIVE ❶ **opuesto/opuesta** (*a direction, side, or view, for example*); **she went off in the opposite direction** se fue en la dirección opuesta ❷ (*facing*) **de enfrente**; **in the house opposite** en la casa de enfrente

opposite ADVERB **enfrente**; **they live opposite** viven enfrente

opposite PREPOSITION **enfrente de**; **opposite the station** enfrente de la estación

opposition NOUN **oposición** FEM

optician NOUN **oculista** MASC & FEM

optimistic ADJECTIVE **optimista**

or CONJUNCTION ❶ **o** (*note that 'o' becomes 'u' before a word starting with 'o-' or 'ho-'*); **English or Spanish?** ¿inglés o español?, **yesterday or today?** ¿ayer u hoy? ❷ (*in negatives*) **I don't have a cat or a dog** no tengo ni un gato ni un perro, **not in June or July** ni en junio ni en julio ❸ (*or else*) **si no**; **phone Mum, or she'll worry** llama a mamá, si no se va a preocupar

oral NOUN (*an exam*) **oral** MASC; **the Spanish oral** el oral de español

orange NOUN (*the fruit*) **naranja** FEM; **an orange juice** un zumo de naranja

orange ADJECTIVE **naranja** (*never changes*); **my orange socks** mis calcetines naranja

orchard NOUN **huerto** FEM

orchestra NOUN **orquesta** FEM

order NOUN ❶ (*arrangement*) **orden** MASC; **in the right order** ordenado/ordenada, **the books are in the right order** los libros están ordenados, **in the wrong order** desordenado/desordenada, **in alphabetical order** en orden alfabético ❷ (*command*) **orden** FEM; **that's an order** es una orden ❸ (*in a restaurant or café*) **can I take your orders?** ¿les tomo la nota? ❹ '**out of order**' 'no funciona' ❺ **in order to do** para hacer, **we hurried in order to be on time** nos dimos prisa para llegar a tiempo

order VERB ❶ (*in a restaurant or a shop*) **pedir** [57]; **we ordered steaks** pedimos filetes ❷ **llamar** [17] **a** (*a taxi*)

ordinary ADJECTIVE **normal**

organ NOUN (the instrument) **órgano** MASC; **to play the organ** tocar [31] el órgano

organic ADJECTIVE **biológico/ biológica** (food)

organization NOUN **organización** FEM

organize VERB **organizar** [22]

original ADJECTIVE **original**; **the original version was better** la versión original era mejor, **it's a really original novel** es una novela realmente original

originally ADVERB **al principio**; **originally we wanted to take the car** al principio queríamos llevar el coche

Orkneys PLURAL NOUN **the Orkneys** las órcadas FEM PLURAL

ornament NOUN **adorno** MASC

orphan NOUN **huérfano** MASC, **huérfana** FEM

other ADJECTIVE ❶ (before a singular noun) **otro/otra**; **the other day** el otro día, **we took the other road** cogimos la otra carretera, **the other one** el otro/la otra, **I don't like this book, give me the other one** no me gusta este libro, dame el otro ❷ **the others** los otros/las otras, **where are the others?** ¿dónde están los otros?, **the other two cars** los otros dos coches ❸ **every other week** una semana sí y otra no ❹ **somebody or other** alguien, **something or other** algo, **somewhere or other** en algún sitio

otherwise ADVERB (in other ways) **aparte de eso**; **the flat's a bit small but otherwise it's lovely** el piso

es pequeño, pero aparte de eso es precioso

otherwise CONJUNCTION (or else) **si no**; **I'll phone home, otherwise they'll worry** voy a llamar a casa, si no van a preocuparse

ought VERB **deber** [18] ('ought' is translated by the conditional tense of 'deber'); **I ought to go now** debería irme ahora, **they ought to know the address** deberían saber las señas, **you oughtn't to have any problems** no deberías tener ningún problema

our ADJECTIVE ❶ (before a singular noun) **nuestro/nuestra**; **our house** nuestra casa ❷ (before a plural noun) **nuestros/nuestras**; **our parents** nuestros padres, **our address** nuestras señas ❸ (with parts of the body) **el/la/los/las**; **we'll go and wash our hands** vamos a lavarnos las manos

ours PRONOUN ❶ (referring to a singular noun) **el nuestro/la nuestra**; **their garden's bigger than ours** su jardín es más grande que el nuestro, **their house is smaller than ours** su casa es más pequeña que la nuestra ❷ (referring to a plural noun) **los nuestros/las nuestras**; **they've invited their friends and we've invited ours** han invitado a sus amigos y nosotros a los nuestros, **they showed us their photos and we showed them ours** ellos nos enseñaron sus fotos y nosotros les enseñamos las nuestras

ourselves PRONOUN ❶ (as a reflexive) **nos**; **we introduced ourselves** nos presentamos ❷ (for emphasis) **nosotros solos/nosotras solas**; **in the end we did it ourselves** al final lo hicimos nosotros solos

out ADVERB ❶ *(outside)* **fuera**; **it's cold out there** hace frío ahí fuera, **out in the rain** bajo la lluvia, **they're out in the garden** están en el jardín ❷ **to go out** salir [63], **he went out of the room** salió de la habitación, **are you going out this evening?** ¿vas a salir esta noche?, **Alison's going out with Danny at the moment** Alison está saliendo ahora con Danny, **he's asked me out** me ha pedido que salga con él ❸ **to be out** *(absent)* no estar [2], **my mum's out** mi madre no está, **when they were out** cuando ellos no estaban ❹ *(light, fire)* **apagado/apagada**; **are all the lights out?** ¿están todas las luces apagadas?, **the fire was out** el fuego estaba apagado ❺ **he threw it out of the window** lo tiró por la ventana, **to drink out of a glass** beber [18] de un vaso, **she took the photo out of her bag** sacó la foto del bolso

outing NOUN **excursión** *FEM*; **to go on an outing** ir [8] de excursión

outline NOUN *(of an object)* **contorno** *MASC*

out-of-date ADJECTIVE ❶ *(no longer valid)* **caducado/caducada**; **my passport's out of date** mi pasaporte está caducado ❷ *(old-fashioned)* **pasado/pasada de moda**; **they played out-of-date music** tocaron música pasada de moda

outside NOUN **parte** *(FEM)* **de fuera**; **it's blue on the outside** la parte de fuera es azul

outside ADJECTIVE **exterior**

outside ADVERB **fuera**; **it's cold outside** hace frío fuera

outside PREPOSITION **fuera de**; **I'll meet you outside the cinema** te veo fuera del cine

outskirts NOUN **afueras** *FEM PLURAL*; **on the outskirts of York** en las afueras de York

outstanding ADJECTIVE **excepcional**

oven NOUN **horno** *MASC*; **I've put it in the oven** lo he puesto en el horno

over PREPOSITION, ADVERB ❶ *(above)* **encima de**; **there's a mirror over the sideboard** hay un espejo encima del aparador ❷ *(involving movement)* **por encima de**; **she jumped over the fence** saltó por encima de la valla, **he threw the ball over the wall** tiró la pelota por encima del muro ❸ **over here** aquí, **the drinks are over here** las bebidas están aquí ❹ **over there** allí, **she's over there talking to Julian** está allí, hablando con Julián ❺ *(more than)* **más de**; **it will cost over a hundred pounds** costará más de cien libras, **he's over sixty** tiene más de sesenta años ❻ *(during)* **durante**; **over the weekend** durante el fin de semana, **over Christmas** durante las Navidades ❼ *(finished)* **when the meeting's over** cuando la reunión haya acabado, **it's all over now** ahora todo ha acabado ❽ **over the phone** por teléfono ❾ **to ask someone over** invitar [17] a alguien, **can you come over on Saturday?** ¿puedes venir el sábado? ❿ **all over the place** por todas partes, **all over the house** por toda la casa

overcast ADJECTIVE **nublado/nublada**

overcrowded ADJECTIVE **abarrotado/abarrotada**

overdose NOUN **sobredosis** FEM

overdraft NOUN **descubierto** MASC

overflow VERB ❶ (water) **derramarse** [17] ❷ (river) **desbordarse** [17]

overseas ADVERB **en el extranjero**; **Dave works overseas** Dave trabaja en el extranjero

overtake VERB **adelantar** [17] (another car)

overtime NOUN **horas** (FEM PLURAL) **extras**; **to work overtime** trabajar [17] horas extras

owe VERB **deber** [18]; **I owe Rick ten pounds** le debo diez libras a Rick

owing ADJECTIVE ❶ (to pay) **a pagar**; **there's five pounds owing** quedan cinco libras a pagar ❷ **owing to** debido a, **owing to the snow** debido a la nieve

owl NOUN **búho** MASC

own ADJECTIVE ❶ **propio/propia** (goes before the noun); **my own computer** mi propio ordenador, **I've got my own room** tengo mi propia habitación ❷ **on your own** solo/ sola, **Annie did it on her own** Annie lo hizo sola

own VERB **tener** [9]

owner NOUN **dueño** MASC, **dueña** FEM

oxygen NOUN **oxígeno** MASC

oyster NOUN **ostra** FEM

ozone layer NOUN **capa** (FEM) **de ozono**

Pp

Pacific NOUN **the Pacific Ocean** el océano (MASC) Pacífico

pack NOUN ❶ **paquete** MASC ❷ **a pack of cards** baraja FEM

pack VERB ❶ **hacer** [7] **las maletas** ❷ **I'll pack my case tonight** voy a hacer la maleta esta noche

package NOUN **paquete** MASC

package holiday, **package tour** NOUN **viaje** (MASC) **organizado**

packed lunch NOUN **comida** (FEM) **preparada desde casa**

packet NOUN ❶ **paquete** MASC; **a packet of biscuits** un paquete de galletas ❷ (bag) **bolsa** FEM; **a packet of crisps** una bolsa de patatas

packing NOUN **to do your packing** hacer [7] las maletas

pad NOUN (of paper) **bloc** MASC

padlock NOUN **cercado** MASC

page NOUN **página** FEM; **on page seven** en la página siete

pain NOUN **dolor** MASC; **to be in pain** tener [9] dolor, **I've got a pain in my leg** me duele la pierna
• **Eric's a real pain (in the neck)** Eric es un verdadero pesado

painkiller NOUN **analgésico** MASC

paint NOUN pintura FEM; 'wet paint' 'recién pintado'

paint VERB pintar [17]; to paint something pink pintar algo de rosa

paintbrush NOUN ❶ (for painting pictures) pincel MASC ❷ (for decorating) brocha FEM

painter NOUN pintor MASC, pintora FEM

painting NOUN (picture) cuadro MASC; a painting by Monet un cuadro de Monet

pair NOUN ❶ par MASC; a pair of socks un par de calcetines, a pair of shoes un par de zapatos, a pair of jeans unos vaqueros, a pair of trousers unos pantalones, a pair of knickers unas bragas, a pair of scissors unas tijeras ❷ (of people) pareja FEM; to work in pairs trabajar [17] en parejas

Pakistan NOUN Pakistán MASC

Pakistani NOUN pakistaní MASC & FEM

Pakistani ADJECTIVE pakistaní

palace NOUN palacio MASC

pale ADJECTIVE pálido/pálida; pale green verde pálido (never changes), pale green curtains cortinas verde pálido, to turn pale palidecer [35]

palm NOUN ❶ (of your hand) palma FEM ❷ (a palm tree) palmera FEM

pan NOUN ❶ (saucepan) cacerola FEM; a pan of water una cacerola de agua ❷ (frying-pan) sartén FEM

pancake NOUN crepe MASC

panel NOUN ❶ (on radio or TV) (for a discussion) panel MASC (for a quiz show) equipo MASC ❷ (for a wall or a bath, for example) panel MASC

panel game NOUN concurso (MASC) por equipos

panic NOUN pánico MASC

panic VERB dejarse [17] llevar por el pánico; don't panic! ¡no pierdas la calma!

panties PLURAL NOUN bragas FEM PLURAL

pantomime NOUN pantomima FEM

pants PLURAL NOUN calzoncillos MASC PLURAL

paper NOUN ❶ papel MASC; a sheet of paper una hoja de papel ❷ a paper hanky un pañuelo de papel ❸ (newspaper) periódico MASC; it was in the paper salió en el periódico

paperback NOUN libro (MASC) en rústica

paperclip NOUN clip MASC

paper towel NOUN toalla (FEM) de papel

parachute NOUN paracaídas MASC (does not change in the plural)

parade NOUN desfile MASC

paradise NOUN paraíso MASC

paragraph NOUN párrafo MASC; 'new paragraph' 'punto y aparte'

Paraguayan NOUN paraguayo MASC, paraguaya FEM

Paraguayan ADJECTIVE paraguayo/paraguaya

parallel ADJECTIVE paralelo/paralela

Paralympics PLURAL NOUN the Paralympic Games los Juegos Paralímpicos

paralysed ADJECTIVE paralizado/
paralizada

parcel NOUN paquete MASC

pardon NOUN **I beg your pardon**
(to someone you know) perdón,
(to show respect) perdone, **pardon?**
(to someone you know) ¿cómo
dices?, *(to show respect)* ¿cómo dice?

parents NOUN **my parents** mis
padres, **a parents' evening** una
reunión de padres

park NOUN ❶ parque MASC; **a theme
park** un parque temático ❷ **a car
park** un aparcamiento

park VERB ❶ aparcar [31]; **you can
park outside the house** puedes
aparcar fuera de la casa ❷ **to park
a car** aparcar [31] un coche, **where
did you park the car?** ¿dónde has
aparcado el coche?

parking NOUN aparcamiento MASC;
'no parking' 'no aparcar'

parking meter NOUN parquímetro
MASC

parking space NOUN sitio (MASC)
para aparcar

parking ticket NOUN multa FEM

parliament NOUN parlamento MASC

parrot NOUN loro MASC

parsley NOUN perejil MASC

part NOUN ❶ parte FEM; **part of the
garden** parte del jardín, **the last
part of the concert** la última parte
del concierto, **that's part of your
job** eso es parte de tu trabajo ❷ **to
take part in something** participar
[17] en algo ❸ *(in a play)* papel MASC

particular ADJECTIVE particular;
nothing in particular nada en
particular

particularly ADVERB especialmente;
not particularly interesting no
especialmente interesante

partly ADVERB en parte

partner NOUN ❶ *(in a game)* pareja
FEM ❷ *(the person you live with)*
compañero MASC, compañera FEM
❸ *(in business)* socio MASC, socia FEM

partridge NOUN perdiz FEM

part-time ADJECTIVE, ADVERB **a tiempo
parcial**; **part-time work** trabajo a
tiempo parcial, **to work part-time**
trabajar [17] a tiempo parcial

party NOUN ❶ fiesta FEM; **a Christmas
party** una fiesta de Navidad, **to
have a birthday party** celebrar [17]
una fiesta de cumpleaños, **we've
been invited to a party at the
Smiths' house** estamos invitados
a una fiesta en casa de los Smith
❷ *(group)* grupo MASC; **a party
of schoolchildren** un grupo de
colegiales, **a rescue party** un equipo
de rescate ❸ *(in politics)* partido
MASC; **the Labour party** el partido
laborista

pass NOUN ❶ *(to let you in)* pase MASC
❷ **a bus pass** un abono de autobús
❸ *(a mountain pass)* paso MASC
❹ *(in an exam)* aprobado MASC; **to
get a pass in history** sacar [31] un
aprobado en historia

pass VERB ❶ *(go past)* pasar [17] por
(a place or building); **we passed
your house** pasamos por tu casa
❷ *(to overtake)* adelantar [17] *(a
car)* ❸ *(give)* pasar [17]; **could you
pass me the paper please?** ¿me

a
b
c
d
e
f
g
h
i
j
k
l
m
n
o
p
q
r
s
t
u
v
w
x
y
z

passenger   **pay**

pasas el papel, por favor? ❹ *(time)* pasar [17]; **the time passed slowly** el tiempo pasaba lentamente ❺ *(in an exam)* aprobar [24]; **did you pass?** ¿aprobaste?, **to pass an exam** aprobar un examen

passenger NOUN pasajero MASC, pasajera FEM

passion NOUN pasión FEM

passionate ADJECTIVE apasionado/apasionada

passive NOUN voz *(FEM)* pasiva

passive ADJECTIVE pasivo/pasiva

Passover NOUN Pascua *(FEM)* judía

passport NOUN pasaporte MASC; **an EU passport** un pasaporte de la Comunidad Europea

password NOUN contraseña FEM

past NOUN pasado MASC; **in the past** en el pasado

past ADJECTIVE ❶ *(recent)* último/última *(goes before the noun)*; **in the past few weeks** en las últimas semanas ❷ *(over)* **winter is past** ya ha pasado el invierno

past PREPOSITION, ADVERB ❶ **to walk or drive past something** pasar [17] por delante de algo, **we went past the school** pasamos por delante del colegio, **Ray went past in his new car** Ray pasó en su coche nuevo ❷ *(the other side of)* pasado/pasada; **it's just past the post office** está justo pasada la oficina de correos ❸ *(talking about time)* **ten past six** las seis y diez, **half past four** las cuatro y media, **a quarter past two** las dos y cuarto

pasta NOUN pasta FEM; **I don't like pasta** no me gusta la pasta

pasteurized ADJECTIVE pasteurizado/pasteurizada

pastry NOUN masa FEM

patch NOUN ❶ *(of colour)* mancha FEM ❷ *(for repairs)* parche MASC

path NOUN camino MASC *(very narrow)* sendero MASC

patience NOUN ❶ paciencia FEM ❷ *(card game)* solitario MASC

patient NOUN paciente MASC & FEM

patient ADJECTIVE paciente

patiently ADVERB pacientemente

patio NOUN patio MASC

patrol NOUN patrulla FEM

patrol car NOUN coche *(MASC)* patrulla

pattern NOUN ❶ *(on wallpaper or fabric)* diseño MASC ❷ *(dressmaking)* patrón MASC ❸ *(knittting)* modelo MASC

pavement NOUN acera FEM; **on the pavement** en la acera

paw NOUN pata FEM

pawn NOUN peón MASC

pay NOUN sueldo MASC

pay VERB ❶ pagar [28]; **I'm paying** yo pago, **to pay cash** pagar al contado ❷ **to pay for something** pagar [28] algo, **Tony paid for the drinks** Tony pagó las bebidas, **it's all paid for** está todo pagado ❸ **to pay by credit card** pagar [28] con tarjeta de crédito, **to pay by cheque** pagar [28] con cheque ❹ **to pay somebody back** *(money)*

504

devolverle [45] dinero a alguien **❺ to pay attention** prestar [17] atención **❻ to pay a visit to somebody** hacer [7] una visita a alguien

payment NOUN pago MASC

pay phone NOUN teléfono *(MASC)* público

PC NOUN *(computer)* PC MASC

pea NOUN guisante MASC

peace NOUN paz FEM

peaceful ADJECTIVE tranquilo/ tranquila *(day, scene)*

peach NOUN melocotón MASC

peacock NOUN pavo *(MASC)* real

peak NOUN *(of a mountain)* pico MASC

peak period NOUN *(for holidays)* temporada *(FEM)* alta

peak rate NOUN *(for phoning)* tarifa *(FEM)* máxima

peak time NOUN *(for traffic)* hora *(FEM)* punta

peanut NOUN cacahuete MASC

peanut butter NOUN mantequilla *(FEM)* de cacahuete

pear NOUN pera FEM

pearl NOUN perla FEM

peasant NOUN campesino MASC, campesina FEM

pebble NOUN guijarro MASC

pedal NOUN pedal MASC

pedal VERB pedalear [17]

pedestrian NOUN peatón MASC, peatona FEM

pedestrian crossing NOUN paso *(MASC)* peatonal

pedestrian precinct NOUN zona *(FEM)* peatonal

pee NOUN **to have a pee** hacer [7] pis *(informal)*

peel NOUN **❶** *(of an apple)* piel FEM **❷** *(of an orange)* cáscara FEM

peel VERB pelar [17] *(fruit, vegetables)*

peg NOUN **❶** *(hook)* gancho MASC **❷** a clothes peg una pinza de la ropa **❸** a tent peg una piqueta

pen NOUN **❶** bolígrafo MASC, boli MASC *(informal)* **❷** *(fountain pen)* pluma FEM **❸** a felt pen un rotulador

penalty NOUN **❶** *(a fine)* multa FEM **❷** *(in football or rugby)* penalty MASC

penalty area NOUN área *(FEM)* de castigo *(even though 'área' is feminine it takes 'el' and 'un')*

pence PLURAL NOUN peniques MASC PLURAL

pencil NOUN lápiz MASC; **to write in pencil** escribir [52] a lápiz

pencil case NOUN estuche *(MASC)* para lápices

pencil sharpener NOUN sacapuntas MASC *(does not change in the plural)*

pendant NOUN colgante MASC

penfriend NOUN amigo *(MASC)* por correspondencia, amiga *(FEM)* por correspondencia; **my Spanish pen-friend is called Cristina** mi amiga, por correspondencia española se llama Cristina

penis NOUN pene MASC

penknife *NOUN* navaja *FEM*

penny *NOUN* penique *MASC*

pension *NOUN* pensión *FEM*

pensioner *NOUN* pensionista *MASC & FEM*

people *PLURAL NOUN* ❶ gente *FEM* (*SINGULAR*); **people round here** la gente de por aquí, **nice people** gente simpática, **people say he's very rich** la gente dice que es muy rico ❷ (*when you're counting them*) persona *FEM*; **ten people** diez personas, **several people** varias personas, **how many people have you asked?** ¿a cuántas personas has preguntado?

pepper *NOUN* ❶ (*spice*) pimienta *FEM* ❷ (*pepper*) pimiento *MASC*; **a green pepper** un pimiento verde

peppermill *NOUN* pimentero *MASC*

peppermint *NOUN* menta *FEM*; **peppermint tea** infusión (*FEM*) de menta

per *PREPOSITION* por; **ten pounds per person** diez libras por persona

per cent *ADVERB* por ciento; **sixty per cent of the students** el sesenta por ciento de los estudiantes

percentage *NOUN* porcentaje *MASC*

percussion *NOUN* percusión *FEM*; **to play percussion** tocar [31] la percusión

perfect *ADJECTIVE* ❶ perfecto/ perfecta; **she speaks perfect English** habla un inglés perfecto ❷ (*ideal*) ideal; **the perfect place for a picnic** el sitio ideal para un picnic

perfectly *ADVERB* perfectamente

perform *VERB* ❶ interpretar [17] (*a piece of music or a role*) ❷ representar [17] (*a play*) ❸ cantar [17] (*a song*)

performance *NOUN* ❶ (*playing or acting*) interpretación *FEM*; **a wonderful performance of Macbeth** una maravillosa interpretación de Macbeth ❷ (*show*) espectáculo *MASC*; **the performance starts at eight** el espectáculo empieza a las ocho ❸ (*the results of a team or company*) actuación *FEM*

performer *NOUN* artista *MASC & FEM*

perfume *NOUN* perfume *MASC*

perhaps *ADVERB* quizás; **perhaps it's in the drawer?** ¿a lo mejor está el cajón?, **perhaps he's missed the train** quizás ha perdido el tren

period *NOUN* ❶ periodo *MASC*; **a two-year period** un periodo de dos años ❷ (*in school*) clase *FEM*; **a forty-five-minute period** una clase de cuarenta y cinco minutos ❸ (*menstruation*) periodo *MASC*; **to have your period** tener [9] el periodo

perm *NOUN* permanente *FEM*

permanent *ADJECTIVE* permanente

permanently *ADVERB* permanentemente

permission *NOUN* permiso *MASC*; **to get permission to do** conseguir [64] permiso para hacer

permit *NOUN* permiso *MASC*

permit *VERB* permitir [19]; **to permit somebody to do** permitir [19] a alguien hacer, **smoking is not**

506

permitted está prohibido fumar, **weather permitting** si el tiempo lo permite

person *NOUN* persona *FEM*; **there's room for one more person** hay sitio para una persona más, **in person** en persona

personal *ADJECTIVE* personal

personality *NOUN* personalidad *FEM*

personally *ADVERB* personalmente; **personally, I'm against it** personalmente, estoy en contra

perspiration *NOUN* sudor *MASC*

persuade *VERB* convencer [44]; **to persuade somebody to do** convencer a alguien para que haga *(note that 'para que' is followed by the subjunctive)*, **we persuaded Tim to wait a bit** convencimos a Tim para que esperara un poco

peseta *NOUN* peseta *FEM* *(former Spanish currency replaced by the euro; 500 pesetas = 3.00 euros)*

pessimistic *ADJECTIVE* pesimista

pest *NOUN* ❶ *(greenfly for example)* plaga *FEM* ❷ *(annoying person)* pesado *MASC*, pesada *FEM*

pester *VERB* fastidiar [17]

pet *NOUN* ❶ animal *(MASC)* de compañía; **do you have a pet?** ¿tienes un animal de compañía?, **a pet dog** un perro de compañía ❷ *(favourite person)* favorito *MASC*, favorita *FEM*; **Julie is teacher's pet** Julie es la favorita de la maestra

petal *NOUN* pétalo *MASC*

pet name *NOUN* apodo *(MASC)* cariñoso

petrol *NOUN* gasolina *FEM*; **to fill up with petrol** llenar [17] de gasolina, **to run out of petrol** quedarse [17] sin gasolina

petrol station *NOUN* gasolinera *FEM*

petticoat *NOUN* enagua *FEM*

pharmacist *NOUN* farmacéutico *MASC*, farmacéutica *FEM*

pharmacy *NOUN* farmacia *FEM*

pheasant *NOUN* faisán *MASC*

philosophy *NOUN* filosofía *FEM*

phone *NOUN* teléfono *MASC*; **she's on the phone** está hablando por teléfono, **I was on the phone to Sophie** estaba hablando por teléfono con Sophie, **you can book by phone** puedes reservar por teléfono

phone *VERB* ❶ llamar [17] por teléfono; **while I was phoning** mientras llamaba por teléfono ❷ **to phone somebody** llamar [17] a alguien, **I'll phone you tonight** te llamaré esta noche

phone book *NOUN* guía *(FEM)* telefónica

phone box *NOUN* cabina *(FEM)* telefónica

phone call *NOUN* llamada *(FEM)* telefónica; **phone calls are free** las llamadas telefónicas son gratis, **to make a phone call** hacer [7] una llamada (telefónica)

phone card *NOUN* tarjeta *(FEM)* telefónica

a
b
c
d
e
f
g
h
i
j
k
l
m
n
o
p
q
r
s
t
u
v
w
x
y
z

phone number NOUN **número** (MASC) **de teléfono**

photo NOUN **foto** FEM; **to take a photo** hacer [7] una foto, **to take a photo of somebody** hacerle [7] una foto a alguien, **I took a photo of their house** hice una foto de su casa

photocopier NOUN **fotocopiadora** FEM

photocopy NOUN **fotocopia** FEM

photocopy VERB **fotocopiar** [17]

photograph NOUN **fotografía** FEM; **to take a photograph** hacer [7] una fotografía, **to take a photograph of somebody** hacerle [7] una fotografía a alguien

photograph VERB **fotografiar** [32]

photographer NOUN **fotógrafo** MASC, **fotógrafa** FEM

photography NOUN **fotografía** FEM

phrase NOUN **frase** FEM

phrase-book NOUN **manual** (MASC) **de conversación**

physicist NOUN **físico** MASC, **física** FEM

physics NOUN **física** FEM

physiotherapist NOUN **fisioterapeuta** MASC & FEM

physiotherapy NOUN **fisioterapia** FEM

pianist NOUN **pianista** MASC & FEM

piano NOUN **piano** MASC; **to play the piano** tocar [31] el piano, **Steve played it on the piano** Steve lo tocó al piano, **a piano lesson** una clase de piano

pick NOUN **take your pick!** ¡escoge!

pick VERB ❶ (to choose) **escoge** [3]; **pick a card** escoger una carta ❷ (for a team) **seleccionar** [17]; **I've been picked for Saturday** me han seleccionado para el sábado ❸ **recoger** [3] (fruit) ❹ **coger** [3] (flowers)

• **to pick up** ❶ (lift) **coger** [3]; **he picked up the papers and went out** cogió los papeles y salió, **to pick up the phone** coger el teléfono ❷ (from the floor) **recoger** [3]; **pick up that piece of paper** recoge ese papel ❸ (collect together) **recoger** [3]; **I'll pick up the toys** voy a recoger los juguetes ❹ (to collect) **recoger** [3]; **I'll pick you up at six** te recogeré a las seis, **I'll pick up the keys tomorrow** recogeré las llaves mañana ❺ (learn) **aprender** [18]; **you'll soon pick it up** lo aprenderás pronto

pickpocket NOUN **carterista** MASC & FEM

picnic NOUN **picnic** MASC; **to have a picnic** hacer [7] un picnic

picture NOUN ❶ (a painting) **cuadro** MASC; **a picture by Picasso** un cuadro de Picasso, **he painted a picture of a horse** pintó un caballo ❷ (a drawing) **dibujo** MASC; **draw me a picture of your house** hazme un dibujo de tu casa ❸ (in a book) **ilustración** FEM; **a book with lots of pictures** un libro con muchas ilustraciones ❹ **the pictures** el cine, **to go to the pictures** ir [8] al cine

pie NOUN ❶ (sweet) **pastel** MASC; **an apple pie** un pastel de manzana ❷ (savoury) **empanada** FEM; **a meat pie** una empanada de carne

piece NOUN ❶ (a bit) trozo MASC; **a big piece of cheese** un trozo grande de queso ❷ (that you fit together) pieza FEM; **the pieces of a jigsaw** las piezas de un rompecabezas, **to take something to pieces** desmontar [17] algo ❸ **a piece of furniture** un mueble, **four pieces of luggage** cuatro maletas, **a piece of information** un dato, **that's a piece of luck!** ¡qué suerte! ❹ (coin) moneda FEM; **a 10p piece** una moneda de diez peniques

pierced ADJECTIVE **to have pierced ears** tener [9] agujeros en las orejas

pig NOUN cerdo MASC, cerda FEM

pigeon NOUN paloma FEM

piggy bank NOUN hucha FEM

pigsty NOUN pocilga FEM; **your room is a pigsty** tu habitación está hecha una pocilga

pigtail NOUN trenza FEM

pile NOUN ❶ (a neat stack) pila FEM; **a pile of plates** una pila de platos ❷ (a heap) montón MASC; **a pile of dirty shirts** un montón de camisas sucias
• **to pile something up** (neatly) apilar [17] algo, (in a heap) amontonar [17] algo

pilgrimage NOUN peregrinación FEM; **to go on a pilgrimage** irse [8] de peregrinación

pill NOUN pastilla FEM; **the pill** (contraceptive) la píldora

pillow NOUN almohada FEM

pillow case NOUN almohadón MASC

pilot NOUN piloto MASC & FEM

pimple NOUN grano MASC

pin NOUN ❶ (for sewing) alfiler MASC ❷ **a three-pin plug** un enchufe de tres clavijas
• **to pin up** ❶ prender [18] con alfileres (a hem) ❷ poner [11] (a notice)

PIN NOUN (short for personal identification number) PIN MASC

pinball NOUN flipper MASC; **to play pinball** jugar [27] al flipper, **a pinball machine** un flipper

pinch NOUN (of salt, for example) pellizco MASC

pinch VERB ❶ (steal) mangar [28] (informal); **somebody's pinched my bike** alguien me ha robado la bici ❷ **to pinch somebody** pellizcar [31] a alguien

pine NOUN pino MASC; **a pine table** una mesa de pino

pineapple NOUN piña FEM

pine cone NOUN piña FEM

ping-pong NOUN ping-pong MASC; **to play ping-pong** jugar [27] al ping-pong

pink ADJECTIVE rosa (never changes); **my pink dress** mi vestido rosa, **pink socks** calcetines rosa

pint NOUN pinta FEM

pip NOUN pepita FEM

pipe NOUN ❶ (for gas or water) tubería FEM ❷ (to smoke) pipa FEM; **he smokes a pipe** fuma en pipa

Pisces NOUN Piscis MASC; **Amanda's Pisces** Amanda es Piscis

pistachio NOUN pistacho MASC

pit NOUN foso MASC

a
b
c
d
e
f
g
h
i
j
k
l
m
n
o
p
q
r
s
t
u
v
w
x
y
z

pitch NOUN **campo** MASC; **a football pitch** un campo de fútbol

pitch VERB **to pitch a tent** montar [17] una tienda

pity NOUN ❶ **lástima** FEM; **what a pity!** ¡qué lástima!, **it would be a pity to miss the beginning** sería una lástima perderse el principio ❷ *(for a person)* **piedad** FEM

pity VERB **to pity somebody** compadecer [35] a alguien

pizza NOUN **pizza** FEM

place NOUN ❶ **sitio** MASC; **in a warm place** en un sitio caliente, **Rome is a wonderful place** Roma es un lugar maravilloso, **all over the place** por todos sitios, **a place for the car** un sitio para el coche, **will you keep my place?** ¿me guardas el sitio?, **to change places** cambiarse [17] de sitio ❷ *(in a race)* **lugar** MASC; **in first place** en primer lugar ❸ **at your place** et tu casa, **we'll go round to Zafir's place** iremos a casa de Zafir ❹ **to take place** tener [9] lugar, **the competition will take place at four** la competición tendrá lugar a las cuatro ❺ **if I was in your place …** si yo estuviese en tu lugar …

place VERB **poner** [11]; **he placed his cup on the table** puso su taza en la mesa

plain ADJECTIVE ❶ **sencillo/sencilla**; **plain cooking** la cocina sencilla ❷ *(unflavoured)* **natural**; **a plain yoghurt** yogur natural ❸ **plain chocolate** chocolate sin leche ❹ *(not patterned)* **liso/lisa**; **plain curtains** cortinas lisas

plait NOUN **trenza** FEM

plan NOUN ❶ **plan** MASC; **what are your plans for this summer?** ¿qué planes tienes para este verano?, **to go according to plan** salir [63] según el plan, **everything went according to plan** todo salió según el plan ❷ *(a map)* **plano** MASC

plan VERB ❶ **planear** [17]; **Ricky's planning a trip to Italy** Ricky está planeando un viaje a Italia, **to plan to do** planear [17] hacer, **we're planning to leave at eight** planeamos salir a las ocho ❷ *(organize)* **organizar** [22]; **I'm planning my day** estoy organizándome el día ❸ *(to design)* **diseñar** [17] *(a house or garden)*; **a well-planned kitchen** una cocina bien diseñada

plane NOUN **avión** MASC; **we went by plane** fuimos en avión

planet NOUN **planeta** MASC

plant NOUN **planta** FEM; **a house plant** una planta de interior

plant VERB **plantar** [17]

plaster NOUN ❶ *(sticking plaster)* **tirita** FEM ❷ *(for walls)* **yeso** MASC ❸ **to have your leg in plaster** tener [9] una pierna escayolada

plastic NOUN **plástico** MASC; **a plastic bag** una bolsa de plástico

plate NOUN **plato** MASC

platform NOUN ❶ *(in a station)* **andén** MASC; **the train arriving at platform six** el tren que llega al andén número seis ❷ *(for lecturing or performing)* **estrado** MASC

play NOUN **obra** FEM; **a play by Shakespeare** una obra de Shakespeare, **our school is putting**

on a play nuestro colegio está preparando una obra

play VERB ❶ (lots) jugar [27]; **the children were playing with a ball** los niños estaban jugando con una pelota, **to play tennis** jugar al tenis, **they were playing cards** estaban jugando a las cartas ❷ (music or an instrument) tocar [31]; **Helen plays the violin** Helen toca el violín, **they play all kinds of music** tocan todo tipo de música ❸ poner [11]; **play me your new song** ponme tu nueva cancion ❹ **who's playing Hamlet?** ¿quién hace el papel de Hamlet?

player NOUN ❶ (in sport) jugador MASC, jugadora FEM; **a football player** un jugador de fútbol ❷ (musician) músico MASC, música FEM

playground NOUN patio (MASC) de recreo

playing card NOUN naipe MASC

playing field NOUN campo (MASC) de juego

playroom NOUN cuarto (MASC) de los juguetes

pleasant ADJECTIVE agradable

please ADVERB por favor; **two coffees, please** dos cafés, por favor, **could you turn the TV off, please?** ¿puedes apagar la tele, por favor?

pleased ADJECTIVE contento/ contenta; **I'm very pleased** estoy muy contento (in the past tense 'ponerse' is used in place of 'estar'), **I was really pleased!** ¡me puse muy contento!, **she was pleased with her present** se puso muy contenta con su regalo, **pleased to meet you!** ¡encantado de conocerte!

pleasure NOUN placer MASC

plenty PRONOUN ❶ (lots) mucho/ mucha; **there's plenty of bread** hay mucho pan, **he's got plenty of experience** tiene mucha experiencia ❷ (with a plural noun) muchos/ muchas; **there are plenty of cases** hay muchos casos, **she's got plenty of ideas** tiene muchas ideas, **there were plenty of them** había muchos ❸ (quite enough) más que suficiente; **we've got plenty of time for a coffee** tenemos tiempo más que suficiente para tomar un café, **thank you, that's plenty!** gracias, esto es más que suficiente

pliers PLURAL NOUN alicates MASC PLURAL

plug NOUN ❶ (electrical) enchufe MASC ❷ (in a bath or sink) tapón MASC; **to pull out the plug** quitar [17] el tapón
• **to plug something in** enchufar [17] algo

plum NOUN ciruela FEM; **a plum tart** una tarta de ciruelas

plumber NOUN fontanero MASC, fontanera FEM; **he's a plumber** es fontanero

plump ADJECTIVE regordete/ regordeta

plural NOUN plural MASC; **in the plural** en plural

plus PREPOSITION más; **three children plus the baby** tres niños más el bebé

p.m. ADVERB (Spanish people usually use 'de la tarde', for times up to approximately 8 p.m. and 'de la noche' for times approximately after 8 p.m.) **at two p.m.** a las dos de la tarde, **at nine p.m.** a las nueve de la noche

poached egg NOUN huevo (MASC) escalfado

pocket NOUN bolsillo MASC

pocket money NOUN ❶ (for children) paga FEM ❷ (for minor purchases) dinero (MASC) para gastos personales

poem NOUN poema MASC

poet NOUN poeta MASC & FEM

poetry NOUN poesía FEM

point NOUN ❶ (tip) punta FEM; the point of a nail la punta de un clavo ❷ (in time) momento MASC; at that point the police arrived en ese momento llegó la policía ❸ to get the point entender [36], I don't get the point no lo entiendo ❹ what's the point of waiting? ¿qué sentido tiene esperar?, there's no point phoning, he's out no tiene sentido llamar, ha salido, that's not the point no se trata de eso ❺ that's a good point! ¡es verdad! ❻ from my point of view desde mi punto de vista ❼ her strong point su punto fuerte ❽ (in scoring) punto MASC; fifteen points to eleven quince puntos a once ❾ (in decimals) (in Spanish, a comma is used for the decimal point, so 6.4 = 6,4) 6 point 4 seis coma cuatro

point VERB ❶ señalar [17]; a notice pointing to the station un cartel señalando hacia la estación, James pointed out the cathedral James señaló la catedral, he pointed at one of the children señaló a uno de los niños ❷ I'd like to point out that I'm paying quisiera dejar claro que pago yo

poison NOUN veneno MASC

poison VERB envenenar [17]

poisonous ADJECTIVE venenoso/ venenosa

poker NOUN ❶ (for fire) atizador MASC ❷ (card game) póker MASC

Poland NOUN Polonia FEM

polar bear NOUN oso (MASC) polar

pole

❶ (for a tent) mástil MASC ❷ the North Pole el Polo Norte

Pole NOUN (a Polish person) polaco MASC, polaca FEM

police NOUN the police la policía, the police are coming ya viene la policía (note that a singular verb is used with 'la policía')

police VERB patrullar [17] (the streets)

police car NOUN coche (MASC) de policía

policeman NOUN policía MASC

police station NOUN comisaría FEM

policewoman NOUN mujer (FEM) policía

policy NOUN ❶ (plan of action) política FEM ❷ (document) póliza FEM

polish NOUN ❶ (for furniture) cera FEM ❷ (for shoes) betún MASC

polish VERB sacar [31] brillo a (shoes or furniture)

Polish NOUN ❶ (language) polaco MASC ❷ (people) the Polish los polacos (plural)

Polish ADJECTIVE polaco/polaca

polite ADJECTIVE educado/educada; **to be polite to somebody** ser [1] educado/educada con alguien

political ADJECTIVE político/política

politician NOUN político MASC, política FEM

politics NOUN política FEM

polluted ADJECTIVE contaminado/contaminada

pollution NOUN contaminación FEM

polo-necked ADJECTIVE de cuello alto; **a polo-necked jumper** un jersey de cuello alto

polythene bag NOUN bolsa (FEM) de plástico

pond NOUN ❶ (natural) laguna FEM ❷ (man-made) estanque MASC

pony NOUN poni MASC

ponytail NOUN cola (FEM) de caballo

poodle NOUN caniche MASC

pool NOUN ❶ (swimming pool) piscina FEM ❷ (in the country) alberca FEM ❸ (puddle) charco MASC ❹ (game) billar (MASC) americano; **to have a game of pool** jugar [27] al billar americano ❺ **the football pools** las quinielas, **to do the pools** hacer [7] las quinielas

poor ADJECTIVE ❶ pobre; **a poor area** una zona pobre, **a poor family** una familia pobre, **poor Tanya's failed her exam** la pobre Tanya suspendió el examen ❷ (bad) malo/mala; **this is poor quality** esto es de mala calidad, **the weather was pretty poor** el tiempo fue bastante malo

pop NOUN pop MASC; **a pop concert** un concierto de pop, **a pop star** una estrella del pop, **a pop song** una canción de pop
- **to pop into** entrar [17] un momento a; **I'll just pop into the bank** voy a entrar un momento en el banco

popcorn NOUN palomitas (FEM PLURAL) de maíz

pope NOUN papa MASC

poppy NOUN amapola FEM

popular ADJECTIVE popular

population NOUN población FEM

porch NOUN porche MASC

pork NOUN cerdo MASC; **a pork chop** una chuleta de cerdo

porridge NOUN gachas FEM PLURAL

port NOUN ❶ (for ships) puerto MASC ❷ (wine) oporto MASC

portable computer NOUN (ordenador) portátil MASC

porter NOUN ❶ (at a station or airport) mozo (MASC) de las maletas ❷ (in a hotel) portero MASC

portion NOUN (of food) ración FEM

portrait NOUN retrato MASC

Portugal NOUN Portugal MASC

Portuguese NOUN ❶ (language) portugués MASC ❷ (a person) portugués MASC, portuguesa FEM

Portuguese ADJECTIVE portugués/portuguesa

posh ADJECTIVE elegante; **a posh house** una casa elegante

position NOUN posición FEM

positive ADJECTIVE ❶ (sure) seguro/segura; **I'm positive he's left**

estoy seguro de que se ha ido ❷ *(enthusiastic)* positivo/positiva; **her reaction was very positive** su reacción fue muy positiva, **try to be more positive** intenta tener una actitud más positiva

possessions PLURAL NOUN pertenencias FEM PLURAL; **all my possessions are in the flat** todas mis pertenencias están en el piso

possibility NOUN posibilidad FEM

possible ADJECTIVE posible; **it's possible** es posible, **if possible** si es posible, **as quickly as possible** tan rápidamente como sea posible

possibly ADVERB ❶ *(maybe)* posiblemente; **'will you be at home at midday?' – 'possibly'** '¿estarás en casa a mediodía?' – 'posiblemente' ❷ *(for emphasis)* **how can you possibly believe that?** pero, ¿cómo puedes creerte eso?, **I can't possibly arrive before Thursday** no puedo llegar antes del jueves de ninguna manera

post NOUN ❶ correo MASC; **to send something by post** mandar [17] algo por correo ❷ *(letters)* **is there any post for me?** ¿hay alguna carta para mí? ❸ *(a pole)* poste MASC ❹ *(a job)* puesto MASC

post VERB **to post a letter** echar [17] una carta al correo, **to post something to somebody** mandarle [17] algo a alguien

postbox NOUN buzón MASC

postcard NOUN postal FEM

postcode NOUN código *(MASC)* postal

poster NOUN ❶ *(for decoration)* póster MASC; **I've bought an Oasis**

poster he comprado un póster de Oasis ❷ *(advertising)* cartel MASC; **I saw a poster for the concert** vi un cartel del concierto

postman NOUN cartero MASC; **has the postman been?** ¿ha venido el cartero?

post office NOUN oficina *(FEM)* de correos

postpone VERB **to postpone something** posponer [11] algo

postwoman NOUN cartera FEM

pot NOUN ❶ *(jar)* tarro MASC; **a pot of honey** un tarro de miel ❷ *(teapot)* tetera FEM; **I'll make a pot of tea** voy ha hacer té ❸ **the pots and pans** los cacharros
• **to take pot luck** probar [24] suerte

potato NOUN patata FEM; **fried potatoes** patatas fritas, **mashed potatoes** puré de patatas

potato crisps PLURAL NOUN patatas *(FEM PLURAL)* fritas de bolsa

pottery NOUN cerámica FEM

pound NOUN ❶ *(money)* libra FEM; **fourteen pounds** catorce libras, **how much is that in pounds?** ¿cuánto es eso en libras? ❷ *(in weight)* libra FEM; **a pound of apples** una libra de manzanas

pour VERB ❶ echar [17] *(liquid)*; **he poured the milk into the pan** echó la leche en la cacerola ❷ servir [57] *(a drink)*; **to pour the tea** servir el té, **I poured him a drink** le serví una bebida
• **it's pouring down** *(with rain)* está lloviendo a cántaros *(literally: it's raining jugfuls)*

poverty NOUN **pobreza** FEM

powder NOUN **polvo** MASC

power NOUN ❶ (electricity) **corriente** (FEM) **eléctrica** ❷ (energy) **energía** FEM; **nuclear power** energía nuclear ❸ (over other people) **poder** MASC; **to be in power** estar en el poder

power cut NOUN **apagón** MASC

powerful ADJECTIVE **poderoso/ poderosa**

power point NOUN **enchufe** MASC

power station NOUN **central** (FEM) **eléctrica**

practical ADJECTIVE **práctico/práctica**

practical joke NOUN **broma** (FEM) **pesada**

practice NOUN ❶ (for sport) **entrenamiento** MASC; **hockey practice** entrenamiento de hockey ❷ (for an instrument) **to do your piano practice** hacer [7] los ejercicios de piano ❸ **to be out of practice** (for a sport) estar desentrenado/desentrenada ❹ **in practice** en la práctica

practise VERB ❶ **practicar** [31] (music, language, etc); **a week in Granada to practise my Spanish** una semana en Granada para practicar mi español ❷ (in a sport) **entrenar** [17]; **the team practises on Wednesdays** el equipo entrena los miércoles

praise VERB **to praise somebody for something** **elogiar** [17] a alguien por algo

pram NOUN **cochecito** (MASC) **de bebé**

prawn NOUN **gamba** FEM

pray VERB **rezar** [22]

prayer NOUN **oración** FEM

precious ADJECTIVE **precioso/ preciosa**

precise ADJECTIVE **preciso/precisa**

prefer VERB **preferir** [14]; **I prefer coffee to tea** prefiero el café al té, **he'd prefer not to see them** preferiría no verlos

pregnancy NOUN **embarazo** MASC

pregnant ADJECTIVE **embarazada**

prejudice NOUN **prejuicio** MASC; **a prejudice** un prejuicio, **to fight against racial prejudice** luchar [17] contra los prejuicios raciales

prejudiced ADJECTIVE **to be prejudiced** tener [9] prejuicios

premiere NOUN **estreno** MASC (of a play or film)

prep NOUN **deberes** MASC PLURAL; **my English prep** mis deberes de inglés

preparation NOUN ❶ **preparación** FEM ❷ **the preparations for** los preparativos para

prepare VERB ❶ **to prepare for something** prepararse para algo ❷ **preparar** [17]; **to prepare somebody for** preparar [17] a alguien para (a surprise or shock), **to be prepared for the worst** estar [2] preparado para lo peor

prepared ADJECTIVE **dispuesto/ dispuesta**; **I'm prepared to pay half** estoy dispuesta a pagar la mitad

preposition NOUN preposición FEM

prescribe VERB recetar [17]

prescription NOUN receta FEM; **on prescription** con receta

present NOUN ❶ *(a gift)* regalo MASC; **to give somebody a present** regalarle [17] algo a alguien ❷ *(the time now)* presente MASC; **in the present (tense)** en presente, **that's all for the present** eso es todo por ahora

present ADJECTIVE ❶ *(attending)* presente; **is Tracy present?** ¿está Tracy presente?, **to be present at** asistir [19] a, **fifty people were present at the funeral** cincuenta personas asistieron al funeral ❷ *(existing now)* actual; **the present situation** la situación actual ❸ **at the present time** en este momento

present VERB ❶ entregar [28] *(a prize)* ❷ *(introduce)* presentar [17]

presenter NOUN *(on TV)* presentador MASC, presentadora FEM

president NOUN presidente MASC, presidenta FEM

press NOUN **the press** la prensa

press VERB ❶ *(to push)* empujar [17]; **press here to open** para abrir, empuje aquí ❷ apretar [29] *(a button or doorbell)*; **she pressed the button** apretó el botón

press conference NOUN conferencia *(FEM)* de prensa

pressure NOUN presión FEM

pressure gauge NOUN manómetro MASC

pressure group NOUN grupo *(MASC)* de presión

pretend VERB **to pretend to do** fingir [49] hacer, **he's pretending not to hear** está fingiendo no oír

pretty ADJECTIVE bonito/bonita; **a pretty dress** un vestido bonito

pretty ADVERB bastante; **it was pretty embarrassing** fue bastante vergonzoso

prevent VERB ❶ evitar [17] *(a war or disaster)* ❷ **to prevent somebody from doing** impedir [57] a alguien hacer, **there's nothing to prevent you from leaving** no hay nada que te impida irte

previous ADJECTIVE anterior

previously ADVERB antes

price NOUN precio MASC; **the price per kilo** el precio por kilo, **clothes have gone up in price** la ropa han subido de precio

price list NOUN lista *(FEM)* de precios

price ticket NOUN etiqueta *(FEM)* del precio

pride NOUN orgullo MASC

priest NOUN sacerdote MASC

primary school NOUN escuela *(FEM)* primaria

prime minister NOUN primer ministro MASC, primera ministra FEM

prince NOUN príncipe MASC; **Prince Charles** el príncipe Carlos

princess NOUN princesa FEM; **Princess Anne** la Princesa Ana

principal NOUN *(of a college)* **rector** MASC, **rectora** FEM

principal ADJECTIVE *(main)* **principal**

print NOUN ❶ *(letters)* **letra** FEM; **in small print** en letra pequeña ❷ *(a photo)* **copia** FEM; **a colour print** una copia a color

printer NOUN *(machine)* **impresora** FEM

print-out NOUN **copia** *(FEM)* **en papel**

prison NOUN **cárcel** FEM; **in prison** en la cárcel

prisoner NOUN **preso** MASC, **presa** FEM

private ADJECTIVE ❶ **privado/ privada**; **a private school** una escuela privada, **'private property'** 'propiedad privada' ❷ **particular** *(lesson)*; **to have private lessons** tener [9] clases particulares

prize NOUN **premio** MASC; **to win a prize** ganar [17] un premio

prize-giving NOUN **entrega** *(FEM)* **de premios**

prizewinner NOUN **ganador** MASC, **ganadora** FEM

probable ADJECTIVE **probable**

probably ADVERB **probablemente**

problem NOUN **problema** MASC; **it's a serious problem** es un problema grave, **no problem!** ¡no hay problema!

procession NOUN ❶ *(at religious festival)* **procesión** FEM ❷ *(parade)* **desfile** MASC

produce NOUN *(food)* **productos** MASC PLURAL

produce VERB ❶ **producir** [60]; **it produces a lot of heat** produce mucho calor ❷ *(show)* **presentar** [17]; **I produced my passport** presenté mi pasaporte

producer NOUN *(of a film or programme)* **productor** MASC, **productora** FEM

product NOUN **producto** MASC

production NOUN ❶ *(of a film)* **producción** FEM ❷ *(of a play or opera)* **puesta** *(FEM)* **en escena**; **a new production of Hamlet** una nueva puesta en escena de Hamlet ❸ *(by a factory)* **producción** FEM

profession NOUN **profesión** FEM

professional NOUN **profesional** MASC & FEM; **he's a professional** es un profesional

professional ADJECTIVE **profesional**; **she's a professional singer** es cantante profesional

professor NOUN **catedrático** MASC, **catedrática** FEM

profit NOUN **beneficios** MASC PLURAL

profitable ADJECTIVE **rentable**

program NOUN **a computer program** un programa de ordenador

programme NOUN **programa** MASC

programmer NOUN **programador** MASC, **programadora** FEM

progress NOUN ❶ **progreso** MASC; **to make progress** *(in your work)* hacer [7] progresos ❷ **to be in progress** estar [2] en curso

English—Spanish

A B C D E F G H I J K L M N O P Q R S T U V W X Y Z

project NOUN ❶ (at school) **trabajo** MASC ❷ (a plan) **proyecto** MASC; **a project to build a bridge** un proyecto para construir un puente

projector NOUN **proyector** MASC

promise NOUN **promesa** FEM; **to make a promise** hacer [7] una promesa, **to break a promise** romper [40] una promesa, **it's a promise!** ¡lo prometo!

promise VERB **to promise to do** prometer [18] hacer, **I've promised to be home by ten** he prometido estar en casa a las diez

promote VERB **ascender** [36]; **she's been promoted** la han ascendido

promotion NOUN **ascenso** MASC

prompt ADJECTIVE **pronto/pronta**; **a prompt reply** una pronta respuesta

pronoun NOUN **pronombre** MASC

pronounce VERB **pronunciar** [17]; **it's hard to pronounce** es difícil de pronunciar

pronunciation NOUN **pronunciación** FEM

proof NOUN **pruebas** FEM PLURAL; **they've got proof** tienen pruebas, **there's no proof that ...** no hay pruebas de que ...

propaganda NOUN **propaganda** FEM

propeller NOUN **hélice** FEM

proper ADJECTIVE ❶ (real, genuine) **de verdad**; **a proper doctor** un médico titulado, **I need a proper meal** necesito una comida de verdad ❷ (correct) **adecuado/adecuada**; **the proper tool** la herramienta adecuada ❸ **in its proper place** en su sitio

properly ADVERB **bien**; **hold it properly** sujétalo bien, **is it properly wrapped?** ¿está bien envuelto?

property NOUN (your belongings) **propiedad** FEM; **'private property'** 'propiedad privada'

propose VERB ❶ (suggest) **proponer** [11] ❷ (marriage) **he proposed to her** le pidió que se casara con él

prostitute NOUN **prostituta** FEM

protect VERB **proteger** [3]

protection NOUN **protección** FEM

protein NOUN **proteína** FEM

protest NOUN **protesta** FEM; **in spite of their protests** a pesar de sus protestas

protest VERB ❶ (to grumble) **protestar** [17]; **he protested, but ...** él protestó, pero ... ❷ (demonstrate) **manifestarse** [29]

Protestant NOUN, ADJECTIVE **protestante** MASC & FEM

protester NOUN **manifestante** MASC & FEM

protest march NOUN **manifestación** FEM

proud ADJECTIVE **orgulloso/orgullosa**

prove VERB **probar** [24]

proverb NOUN **refrán** MASC

provide VERB **proveer** [37]

provided CONJUNCTION **siempre que**; **provided you do it now** siempre que tú lo hagas (note that 'que' is followed by the subjunctive)

province NOUN **provincia** FEM

prune NOUN ciruela (FEM) pasa

PS ABBREVIATION (in letter) PD

psychiatrist NOUN psiquiatra MASC & FEM; **he's a psychiatrist** es psiquiatra

psychological ADJECTIVE psicológico/psicológica

psychologist NOUN psicólogo MASC, psicóloga FEM; **she's a psychologist** es psicóloga

psychology NOUN psicología FEM

PTO ABBREVIATION sigue al dorso

pub NOUN bar MASC

public NOUN **the public** el público, **in public** en público

public ADJECTIVE ❶ público/pública ❷ **the public library** la biblioteca pública

public address system NOUN sistema (MASC) de megafonía

public holiday NOUN día (MASC) de fiesta; **the first of January is a public holiday** el uno de enero es fiesta

publicity NOUN publicidad FEM

public school NOUN colegio (MASC) privado

public transport NOUN transporte (MASC) público

publish VERB publicar [31]

publisher NOUN ❶ (person) editor MASC, editora FEM ❷ (company) editorial FEM

pudding NOUN (dessert) postre MASC; **for pudding we've got strawberries** de postre tenemos fresas

puddle NOUN charco MASC

Puerto Rican NOUN puertorriqueño MASC, puertorriqueña FEM

Puerto Rican ADJECTIVE puertorriqueño/puertorriqueña

puff pastry NOUN hojaldre MASC

pull VERB tirar [17]; **pull hard!** ¡tira fuerte!, **to pull a rope** tirar de una cuerda
• **you're pulling my leg!** ¡me estás tomando el pelo! (literally: you are taking my hair)
• **to pull down** bajar [17] (a blind)
• **to pull in** (at the roadside) parar [17]
• **to pull something out** sacar [31] algo; **he pulled a letter out of his pocket** sacó una carta del bolsillo

pullover NOUN jersey MASC

pulse NOUN pulso MASC; **the doctor took my pulse** el médico me tomó el pulso

pump NOUN ❶ bomba FEM; **a bicycle pump** una bomba de bicicleta ❷ **a petrol pump** un surtidor de gasolina

pump VERB bombear [17]; **they were pumping the water out of the cellar** estaban bombeando el agua del sótano
• **to pump up** inflar [17] (a tyre)

punch NOUN ❶ (in boxing) puñetazo MASC ❷ (drink) ponche MASC

punch VERB ❶ **to punch somebody** darle [4] un puñetazo a alguien, **he punched me** me dio un puñetazo ❷ picar [31] (a ticket)

punctual ADJECTIVE puntual

punctuation NOUN puntuación FEM

a
b
c
d
e
f
g
h
i
j
k
l
m
n
o
p
q
r
s
t
u
v
w
x
y
z

A
B
C
D
E
F
G
H
I
J
K
L
M
N
O
P
Q
R
S
T
U
V
W
X
Y
Z

punctuation mark *NOUN* **signo** *(MASC)* **de puntuación**

puncture *NOUN* **pinchazo** *MASC*; **we had a puncture on the way** tuvimos un pinchazo en el camino

punish *VERB* **castigar** [28]

punishment *NOUN* **castigo** *MASC*

pupil *NOUN* **alumno** *MASC*, **alumna** *FEM*

puppet *NOUN* **títere** *MASC*

puppy *NOUN* **cachorro** *MASC (female)* **cachorra** *FEM*; **a labrador puppy** un cachorro de labrador

pure *ADJECTIVE* **puro/pura**

purple *ADJECTIVE* **morado/morada**

purpose *NOUN* ❶ **propósito** *MASC*; **what was the purpose of her call?** ¿qué propósito tenía su llamada? ❷ **on purpose** a propósito, **she did it on purpose** lo hizo a propósito

purr *VERB* **ronronear** [17]

purse *NOUN* **monedero** *MASC*

push *NOUN* **empujón** *MASC*; **to give something a push** dar [4] un empujón a alguien

push *VERB* ❶ **empujar** [17]; **he pushed me** me empujó ❷ *(to press)* **apretar** [29] *(a bell or button)* ❸ **to push somebody to do** presionar [17] a alguien para que haga *(note that 'que' is followed by the subjunctive)* **his teacher is pushing him to sit the exam** su profesor le está presionando para que se presente al examen

• **to push something away** apartar [17] algo; **she pushed her plate away** apartó su plato

pushchair *NOUN* **sillita** *(FEM)* **de niño**

put *VERB* ❶ **poner** [11]; **you can put the cream in the fridge** puedes poner la nata en la nevera, **where did you put my bag?** ¿dónde has puesto mi bolso?, **put your suitcase here** pon tu maleta aquí, **put your address here** pon tus señas aquí ❷ *(put inside)* **meter** [18]; **I put it in the drawer** lo metí en el cajón

• **to put away** guardar [17]; **I'll put the shopping away** voy a guardar la compra

• **to put back** ❶ **volver** [45] a poner; **I put it back in the drawer** lo volví a poner en el cajón ❷ *(postpone)* **aplazar** [22]; **the meeting has been put back until Thursday** han aplazado la reunión hasta el jueves

• **to put down** poner [11]; **she put the vase down on the table** puso el jarrón en la mesa

• **to put off** ❶ *(postpone)* **aplazar** [22]; **he's put off my lesson till Thursday** ha aplazado mi clase hasta el jueves ❷ **it put me off Chinese food!** ¡hizo que se me quitaran las ganas de tomar comida china! ❸ **to be put off** *(doing something)* **desanimarse** [17], **don't be put off!** ¡no te desanimes!

• **to put on** ❶ **ponerse** [11] *(clothing, make-up)*; **I'll just put my shoes on** voy a ponerme los zapatos ❷ **poner** [11] *(TV, radio)*; **shall we put on the telly?** ¿ponemos la tele? ❸ **he's put on Oasis** ha puesto a Oasis ❸ *(switch on)* **encender** [36] *(a light or heating)*; **could you put the lamp on?** ¿puedes encender la lámpara? ❹ **montar** [17] *(a play)*; **we're putting on a Spanish play** estamos montando una obra española

• **to put out** ❶ *(put outside)* **sacar** [31]; **have you put the rubbish out?** ¿has sacado la basura? ❷ **apagar** [28] *(a fire, light, or cigarette)*; **I've put the lights out** he apagado las luces ❸ **to**

put out your hand extender [36] la mano

- **to put through** pasar [17] con; **I'll put you through to the manager** le paso con el gerente
- **to put up ❶** levantar [17] *(your hand)*; **I put up my hand** levanté la mano **❷** poner [11] *(picture)*; **I've put up some photos in my room** he puesto algunas fotos en mi habitacion **❸** colgar [23] *(a notice)* **❹** subir [19] *(the price)*; **they've put up the price of the tickets** han subido el precio de las entradas **❺** *(for the night)* **can you put me up on Friday?** ¿puedo quedarme a dormir en tu casa el viernes?
- **to put up with something** aguantar [17] algo; **I don't know how she puts up with it** no sé cómo lo aguanta

puzzle NOUN *(jigsaw)* **rompecabezas** MASC, **puzzle** MASC

puzzled ADJECTIVE **confuso/confusa**

pyjamas PLURAL NOUN **pijama** MASC; **a pair of pyjamas** un pijama, **where are my pyjamas?** ¿dónde está mi pijama?

pylon NOUN **torre** *(FEM)* **de alta tensión**

Pyrenees NOUN **the Pyrenees** los Pirineos

quail NOUN **codorniz** FEM

qualification NOUN **❶ título** MASC *(certificate, exam, degree)* **❷ qualifications** titulación FEM, **vocational qualifications** titulación profesional

qualified ADJECTIVE **❶ cualificado/ cualificada**; **she's a qualified ski instructor** es una monitora de esquí cualificada **❷** *(having a degree or a diploma)* **titulado/titulada**; **a qualified architect** un arquitecto titulado

qualify VERB **❶** *(to be eligible)* **tener** [9] **derecho a**; **we don't qualify for a reduction** no tenemos derecho a una reducción **❷** *(in sport)* **clasificarse** [31]

quality NOUN **calidad** FEM; **good quality vegetables** verduras de buena calidad

quantity NOUN **cantidad** FEM

quarantine NOUN **cuarentena** FEM

quarrel NOUN **pelea** FEM; **to have a quarrel** tener [9] una pelea

quarrel VERB **pelearse** [17]; **they're always quarrelling** siempre se están peleando

quarry NOUN **cantera** FEM

quarter NOUN ❶ cuarta parte FEM; **a quarter of the class** una cuarta parte de la clase, **three quarters of the class** tres cuartas partes de la clase ❷ (telling the time) cuarto MASC; **a quarter past ten** las diez y cuarto, **a quarter to ten** las diez menos cuarto, **a quarter of an hour** un cuarto de hora, **three quarters of an hour** tres cuartos de hora, **an hour and a quarter** una hora y cuarto

quarter finals PLURAL NOUN cuartos (MASC PLURAL) de final

quartet NOUN cuarteto MASC; **a jazz quartet** un cuarteto de jazz

quay NOUN muelle MASC

queen NOUN reina FEM; **Queen Elizabeth** la reina Isabel, **the Queen Mother** la reina madre

query NOUN duda FEM; **are there any queries?** ¿hay alguna duda?

question NOUN ❶ pregunta FEM; **to ask a question** hacer [7] una pregunta, **I asked her a question** le hice una pregunta ❷ **it's a question of time** es una cuestión de tiempo, **it's out of the question!** ¡es completamente imposible!

question VERB interrogar [28]

question mark NOUN signo (MASC) de interrogación

questionnaire NOUN cuestionario MASC; **to fill in a questionnaire** rellenar [17] un cuestionario

queue NOUN ❶ (of people) cola FEM; **to stand in a queue** estar [2] en la cola ❷ (of cars) fila FEM

queue VERB hacer [7] cola; **we were queueing for check-in** estábamos haciendo cola para facturar

quick ADJECTIVE ❶ rápido/rápida; **a quick lunch** una comida rápida, **it's quicker on the motorway** es más rápido por la autopista, **to have a quick look at something** echarle [17] un vistazo rápido a algo ❷ **quick! there's the bus!** ¡de prisa, que viene el autobús!, **be quick!** ¡date prisa!

quickly ADVERB rápidamente; **I'll just quickly phone my mother** voy a llamar rápidamente a mi madre

quiet ADJECTIVE ❶ (silent) silencioso/silenciosa; **the children are very quiet** los niños están muy silenciosos ❷ **to keep quiet** no hablar [17], **please keep quiet** por favor, no hablen ❸ (gentle) suave; **some quiet music** una música suave, **in a quiet voice** en voz baja ❹ (peaceful) tranquilo/tranquila; **a quiet street** una calle tranquila, **a quiet day at home** un día tranquilo en casa

quietly ADVERB ❶ (to move) sin hacer ruido; **he got up quietly** se levantó sin hacer ruido ❷ (speak) en voz baja ❸ (read or play) en silencio

quilt NOUN edredón MASC

quite ADVERB ❶ bastante; **it's quite cold outside** hace bastante frío fuera, **that's quite a good idea** es una idea bastante buena, **he sings quite well** canta bastante bien, **quite often** bastante a menudo ❷ **not quite** no ... todavía, **the meat's not quite cooked** la carne no está hecha todavía ❸ **quite a lot of** bastante, **quite a lot of money** bastante dinero, **quite a few people**

bastante gente **❹ quite a lot of** (with a plural noun) bastantes, **I've got quite a lot of friends here** tengo bastantes amigos aquí

quiz NOUN **concurso** MASC

quotation NOUN (from a book) **cita** FEM

quotation marks PLURAL NOUN **comillas** FEM PLURAL; **in quotation marks** entre comillas

quote NOUN **❶** (from a book) **cita** FEM **❷** (estimate) **presupuesto** MASC **❸ in quotes** entre comillas

quote VERB **citar** [17]

Rr

rabbi NOUN **rabino** MASC, **rabina** FEM

rabbit NOUN **conejo** MASC

race NOUN **❶** (a sports event) **carrera** FEM; **a cycle race** una carrera de bicicletas, **to have a race** echar [17] una carrera **❷** (an ethnic group) **raza** FEM

racer NOUN (bike) **bicicleta** (FEM) **de carreras**

racetrack NOUN **❶** (for horses) **pista** (FEM) **de carreras ❷** (for cars) **circuito** MASC **❸** (for cycles) **velódromo** MASC

racial ADJECTIVE **racial**; **racial discrimination** discriminación racial

racing NOUN **carreras** FEM PLURAL

racing car NOUN **coche** (MASC) **de carreras**

racing driver NOUN **piloto** (MASC & FEM) **de carreras**

racism NOUN **racismo** MASC

racist NOUN **racista** MASC & FEM

racist ADJECTIVE **racista**

racket NOUN **❶** (for tennis) **raqueta** FEM **❷** (noise) **jaleo** MASC; **what a racket!** ¡qué jaleo!

radar NOUN **radar** MASC

radiator NOUN **radiador** MASC

radio NOUN radio FEM; **to listen to the radio** escuchar [17] la radio, **to hear something on the radio** oír [56] algo en la radio

radio station NOUN emisora *(FEM)* de radio

radish NOUN rabanito MASC

radius NOUN radio MASC

raffle NOUN rifa FEM

raft NOUN balsa FEM

rag NOUN trapo MASC

rage NOUN furia FEM; **she's in a rage** está furiosa
• **it's all the rage** hace furor *(informal)*

rail NOUN ❶ *(the railway)* **to go by rail** ir [8] en tren ❷ *(on a balcony or bridge)* baranda FEM ❸ *(on stairs)* pasamanos MASC ❹ *(for a train)* raíl MASC

railings NOUN verja FEM

rail strike NOUN huelga *(FEM)* de trenes

railway NOUN ❶ *(the system)* ferrocarril MASC; **the railways** el ferrocarril ❷ **a railway line** una línea de ferrocarril *(from one place to another)* ❸ **on the railway line** en la vía férrea *(the rails)*

railway carriage NOUN vagón *(MASC)* de tren

railway station NOUN estación *(FEM)* de tren; **opposite the railway station** enfrente de la estación de tren

rain NOUN lluvia FEM; **in the rain** bajo la lluvia

rain VERB llover [38]; **it's raining** está lloviendo, **it's going to rain** va a llover

rainbow NOUN arco *(MASC)* iris

raincoat NOUN impermeable MASC

rainfall NOUN precipitaciones FEM PLURAL

rainy ADJECTIVE lluvioso/lluviosa

raise VERB ❶ *(lift up)* levantar [17]; **she raised her head** levantó la cabeza ❷ *(increase)* subir [19] *(a price or a salary)* ❸ **to raise money for something** recaudar [17] dinero para algo ❹ **to raise the alarm** dar [4] la alarma ❺ **to raise somebody's spirits** animar [17] a alguien

raisin NOUN pasa FEM

rally NOUN ❶ *(a meeting)* concentración FEM ❷ *(for sport)* rally MASC ❸ *(in tennis)* peloteo MASC

rambler NOUN excursionista MASC & FEM

rambling NOUN **to go rambling** ir [8] de excursión

ramp NOUN *(for a wheelchair, for example)* rampa FEM

range NOUN ❶ *(a choice)* gama FEM; **in a wide range of colours** en una amplia gama de colores ❷ *(of mountains)* cordillera FEM

rap NOUN rap MASC *(music)*

rape NOUN violación FEM

rape VERB violar [17]

rare ADJECTIVE ❶ poco común; **a rare bird** un pájaro poco común ❷ poco hecho *(a steak)*; **medium-rare** un filete poco hecho

raspberry NOUN **frambuesa** FEM; **raspberry jam** mermelada de frambuesa, **a raspberry tart** una tarta de frambuesas

rat NOUN **rata** FEM

rate NOUN ❶ *(a charge)* **tarifa** FEM; **what are the rates for children?** ¿cuáles son las tarifas para niños?, **reduced rates** tarifas reducidas ❷ **at any rate** en todo caso

rather ADVERB ❶ **bastante**; **I'm rather busy** estoy bastante ocupado ❷ **rather a lot of** bastante, **I've got rather a lot of work** tengo bastante trabajo ❸ **rather a lot of** *(with a plural noun)* bastantes, **there are rather a lot of mistakes** hay bastantes errores ❹ **rather than** en vez de, **in summer rather than winter** en verano más que en invierno ❺ **I'd rather wait** preferiría esperar, **they'd rather come on Thursday** preferirían venir el jueves

raw ADJECTIVE **crudo/cruda**

ray NOUN **rayo** MASC

razor NOUN **máquina** *(FEM)* **de afeitar** *(safety)*

razor blade NOUN **cuchilla** FEM

RE NOUN **religión** FEM

reach NOUN **alcance** MASC; **out of my reach** fuera de mi alcance, **within reach** *(of your hand)* al alcance, **within easy reach of the sea** cerca del mar

reach VERB **llegar** [28]; **when you reach the church** cuando llegues a la iglesia, **to reach the final** llegar [28] a la final

read VERB **leer** [37]; **what are you reading at the moment?** ¿qué estás leyendo en este momento?, **I'm reading a detective novel** estoy leyendo una novela policiaca, **he read out the list** leyó la lista

reading NOUN **lectura** FEM; **I don't much like reading** no me gusta mucho la lectura, **some easy reading for the beach** lectura fácil para la playa

ready ADJECTIVE ❶ **preparado/preparada**; **supper's not ready yet** la cena aún no está preparada ❷ *(person)* **listo/lista**; **are you ready to leave?** ¿estás listo para salir? ❸ **to get ready** *(meal or things)* **preparar** [17], **I'll get your room ready** voy a preparar tu habitación ❹ **to get ready** *(a person)* **prepararse** [17], **I'm getting ready to go out** me estoy preparando para salir, **I was getting ready for bed** estaba preparándome para irme a la cama

real ADJECTIVE **verdadero/verdadera**; **is that his real name?** ¿es ese su verdadero nombre?, **her real father is dead** su verdadero padre está muerto, **he's a real bore** es un verdadero pesado, **it's a real diamond** es un diamante de verdad

realize VERB **darse** [4] **cuenta**; **I hadn't realized** no me había dado cuenta, **to realize (that) ...** darse cuenta de que ..., **I didn't realize (that) he was French** no me di cuenta de que era francés, **do you realize what time it is?** ¿te das cuenta de la hora que es?

really ADVERB ❶ *(truly)* **is it really midnight?** ¿de verdad son las doce de la noche?, **really?** ¿de verdad?, **not really** la verdad es que no ❷ **I**

a
b
c
d
e
f
g
h
i
j
k
l
m
n
o
p
q
r
s
t
u
v
w
x
y
z

really don't know realmente no lo sé ❸ *(extremely) (Spanish uses the superlative of the adjective to express this sense)* **the film was really good** la película fue buenísima

reason *NOUN* razón *FEM*; **the reason for the delay** la razón del retraso, **the reason why I phoned** la razón por la que llamé

reasonable *ADJECTIVE* razonable

rebel *NOUN* rebelde *MASC & FEM*

rebellion *NOUN* rebelión *FEM*

receipt *NOUN* recibo *MASC*

receive *VERB* recibir [19]

receiver *NOUN* auricular *MASC*; **to pick up the receiver** descolgar [23] el teléfono

recent *ADJECTIVE* reciente; **a recent change** un cambio reciente

recently *ADVERB* recientemente

reception *NOUN* ❶ recepción *FEM*; **he's waiting at reception** está esperando en recepción, **a big wedding reception** un gran banqueté de bodas ❷ **to get a good reception** tener [9] buena acogida

receptionist *NOUN* recepcionista *MASC & FEM*

recipe *NOUN* receta *FEM*; **can I have the recipe for your salad?** ¿me puedes dar tu receta de la ensalada?

reckon *VERB* creer [37]; **I reckon it's a good idea** creo que es una buena idea

recognize *VERB* reconocer [35]

recommend *VERB* recomendar [29]; **can you recommend a**

dentist? ¿puedes recomendarme un dentista?, **I recommend the fish soup** recomiendo la sopa de pescado

recommendation *NOUN* recomendación *FEM*

record *NOUN* ❶ récord *MASC*; **it's a world record** es un récord mundial, **record sales** récord de ventas, **the hottest summer on record** el verano más caluroso del que se tienen datos ❷ **to keep a record of something** llevar [17] un registro de algo ❸ *(music)* disco *MASC*; **a Miles Davis record** un disco de Miles Davis ❹ *(office files)* archivo *MASC*; **I'll just check your records** voy a mirar tu ficha ❺ *(of attendance)* registro *MASC*

record *VERB (on tape)* grabar [17]; **they're recording a new album** están grabando un nuevo álbum

recorder *NOUN* ❶ flauta *(FEM)* dulce; **to play the recorder** tocar [31] la flauta dulce ❷ **a video recorder** una cámara de vídeo

recording *NOUN* grabación *FEM*

record player *NOUN* tocadiscos *MASC (does not change in the plural)*

recover *VERB* recuperarse [17]; **she's recovered now** ya se ha recuperado

recovery *NOUN (from an illness)* recuperación *FEM*

recovery vehicle *NOUN* grúa *FEM*

rectangle *NOUN* rectángulo *MASC*

rectangular *ADJECTIVE* rectangular

recycle *VERB* reciclar [17]

red *ADJECTIVE* ❶ rojo/roja; a red shirt una camisa roja, a bright red car un coche rojo vivo ❷ to go red ponerse [11] colorado ❸ *hair* to have red hair ser [1] pelirrojo

Red Cross *NOUN* the Red Cross la Cruz Roja

redcurrant *NOUN* grosella *FEM*; redcurrant jelly jalea de grosellas

reduce *VERB* reducir [60]; they've reduced the price han reducido el precio

reduction *NOUN* rebaja *FEM* (in price)

redundant *ADJECTIVE* he was made redundant lo despidieron por reducción de plantilla

referee *NOUN* (in sport) árbitro *MASC & FEM*

reference *NOUN* referencia *FEM* (for a job); she gave me a good reference me dio una buena referencia

referendum *NOUN* referendum *MASC*

refer to *VERB* referirse [14] a; she's referring to you se refiere a ti

refill *NOUN* ❶ (for pen) recambio *MASC* ❷ (for lighter) carga *FEM*

reflect *VERB* reflejar [17]

reflection *NOUN* ❶ (in a mirror) reflejo *MASC* ❷ (thought) reflexión *FEM*; on reflection pensándolo bien

reflexive *ADJECTIVE* a reflexive verb un verbo reflexivo

refreshing *ADJECTIVE* refrescante

refreshment *NOUN* refresco *MASC*

refrigerator *NOUN* nevera *FEM*

refuge *NOUN* refugio *MASC*; a mountain refuge un refugio (de montaña), to take refuge in refugiarse [17] en

refugee *NOUN* refugiado *MASC*, refugiada *FEM*

refund *NOUN* reembolso *MASC*

refund *VERB* reembolsar [17]

refuse *NOUN* (rubbish) desperdicios *MASC PLURAL*

refuse *VERB* negarse [30]; I refused me negué, he refuses to help se niega a ayudar

regards *PLURAL NOUN* recuerdos *MASC PLURAL*; 'regards to your parents' 'recuerdos a tus padres', Nat sends his regards Nat manda recuerdos

reggae *NOUN* reggae *MASC*

region *NOUN* región *FEM*

regional *ADJECTIVE* regional

register *NOUN* (in school) lista *FEM*

register *VERB* inscribirse [52]

registered letter *NOUN* carta (*FEM*) certificada

registration number *NOUN* número (*MASC*) de matrícula (of a vehicle)

regret *VERB* to regret something arrepentirse [14] de algo

regular *ADJECTIVE* ❶ regular visits visitas frecuentes ❷ habitual (customer)

regularly *ADVERB* regularmente

regulation *NOUN* norma *FEM*

rehearsal *NOUN* ensayo *MASC*

rehearse VERB ensayar [17]

reign NOUN reinado MASC

rein NOUN rienda FEM

reject VERB rechazar [22]

related ADJECTIVE ❶ relacionado/relacionada *(subject or ideas)* ❷ we're not related no somos parientes

relation NOUN pariente MASC & FEM; my relations mis parientes

relationship NOUN relación FEM; we have a good relationship tenemos una buena relación

relative NOUN pariente MASC & FEM; all my relatives todos mis parientes

relax VERB relajarse [17]; I'm going to relax and watch telly tonight esta noche voy a relajarme y ver la tele

relaxation NOUN esparcimiento MASC; tennis is her relaxation el tenis es su esparcimiento

relaxed ADJECTIVE relajado/relajada

relaxing ADJECTIVE relajante

relay race NOUN carrera *(FEM)* de relevos

release NOUN ❶ estreno MASC; this week's new releases los estrenos de esta semana ❷ *(of a prisoner or hostage)* puesta *(FEM)* en libertad

release VERB ❶ sacar [31] *(a record or a video)* ❷ estrenar [17] *(a film)* ❸ poner [11] en libertad *(a person)*

reliable ADJECTIVE ❶ responsable *(person)* ❷ fidedigno/fidedigna *(information)*

relief NOUN alivio MASC; what a relief! ¡qué alivio!

relieved ADJECTIVE aliviado/aliviada; I was relieved to hear you'd arrived fue un alivio oír que habías llegado

religion NOUN religión FEM

religious ADJECTIVE religioso/religiosa; Jane's not religious Jane no es religiosa

reluctant ADJECTIVE reacio/reacia; he's reluctant to go se muestra reacio a ir

rely VERB to rely on somebody contar [24] con alguien, I'm relying on you for Saturday cuento contigo el para sábado

remain VERB permanecer [35]

remark NOUN comentario MASC; to make remarks about hacer [7] comentarios sobre

remember VERB ❶ acordarse [24]; I don't remember no me acuerdo ❷ to remember something acordarse de algo, I can't remember the number no me acuerdo del número ❸ to remember to do acordarse de hacer, remember to shut the door! ¡acuérdate de cerrar la puerta!, I remembered to bring the CDs me acordé de traer los compactos

remind VERB ❶ recordar [24]; to remind somebody to do recordarle a alguien que haga *(note that 'que' is followed by the subjunctive)* remind your mother to pick me up recuérdale a tu madre que me recoja ❷ it reminds me of Paris me recuerda a París, he reminds me of Frank me recuerda a Frank, oh, that reminds me ... ¡ah!, por cierto ...

remove VERB quitar [17]; **he removed his jacket** se quitó la chaqueta, **the chairs had all been removed** habían quitado todas las sillas

renew VERB renovar [24] (a passport or licence)

rent NOUN alquiler MASC

rent VERB alquilar [17]; **Simon's rented a flat** Simon ha alquilado un piso

repair NOUN reparación FEM

repair VERB arreglar [17]; **to get something repaired** arreglar [17] algo, **we've had the television repaired** hemos arreglado la televisión

repay VERB devolver [45]; **he repaid me the money he owed me** me devolvió el dinero que me debía

repeat NOUN repetición (FEM) (of a programme)

repeat VERB repetir [57]

replacement NOUN ❶ (person) sustituto MASC, sustituta FEM ❷ (thing); **when can you find me a replacement?** ¿para cuándo me puedes encontrar otro?

reply NOUN contestación FEM; **I didn't get a reply to my letter** no recibí contestación a mi carta, **there's no reply** no contestan (on the telephone)

reply VERB contestar [17]; **I still haven't replied to the letter** aún no he contestado a la carta

report NOUN ❶ (of an event) informe MASC ❷ (school report) boletín (MASC) de notas

report VERB ❶ informar [17] sobre (a problem or accident) ❷ denunciar [17] (a crime); **we've reported the theft** hemos denunciado sobre el robo ❸ presentarse [17]; **I had to report to reception** tuve que presentarme en recepción

reporter NOUN periodista MASC & FEM

representative NOUN representante MASC & FEM

reproach NOUN reproche MASC

reproach VERB reprochar [17]

republic NOUN república FEM

reputation NOUN ❶ reputación FEM; **a good reputation** una buena reputación ❷ **to have a reputation for something** tener [9] fama de algo, **she has a reputation for honesty** tiene fama de honesta

request NOUN petición FEM; **on request** a solicitud

request VERB pedir [57]

rescue NOUN ❶ rescate MASC ❷ **to come to somebody's rescue** acudir [19] en auxilio de alguien

rescue VERB rescatar [17]; **they rescued the dog** rescataron al perro

rescue party NOUN equipo (MASC) de rescate

rescue worker NOUN socorrista MASC & FEM

research NOUN investigación FEM; **for research into Aids** para la investigación sobre el sida, **to do research** investigar [28]

research VERB **to research into** investigar [28] sobre, **a well-researched programme** un programa bien documentado

resemble VERB **parecerse** [35] a; **she looks like her aunt** se parece a su tía

reservation NOUN *(a booking)* **reserva** FEM; **to make a reservation** hacer [7] una reserva

reserve NOUN ❶ **reserva** FEM; **we have some in reserve** tener [9] algo de reserva ❷ **a nature reserve** una reserva natural ❸ *(for a match)* **reserva** MASC & FEM

reserve VERB **reservar** [17]; **this table is reserved** la mesa está reservada

resident NOUN **residente** MASC & FEM

residential ADJECTIVE **residencial**; **a residential area** un área residencial

resign VERB **dimitir** [19]

resignation NOUN *(from a post)* **dimisión** FEM

resist VERB **resistir** [19] *(an offer or temptation)*; **I can't resist!** ¡no puedo resistirlo!

resit VERB **to resit an exam** volver [45] a presentarse a un examen

resort NOUN ❶ *(for holidays)* **a holiday resort** un c entro turístico, **a ski resort** una estación de esquí, **a seaside resort** un centro turístico costero ❷ **as a last resort** como último recurso

respect NOUN **respeto** MASC

respect VERB **respetar** [17]

respectable ADJECTIVE **respetable**

respectful ADJECTIVE **respetuoso/ respetuosa**

responsibility NOUN **responsabilidad** FEM

responsible ADJECTIVE **responsable**; **he's responsible for the delay** él es el responsable del retraso, **I'm responsible for booking the rooms** soy responsable de reservar las habitaciones, **he's not very responsible** no es muy responsable

rest NOUN ❶ **the rest** el resto, **the rest of the day** el resto del día, **the rest of the bread** el resto del pan ❷ *(the others)* **los otros**; **the rest have gone home** los otros se han ido a casa ❸ **descanso** MASC; **ten days' complete rest** diez días de completo descanso, **to have a rest** descansar [17] ❹ *(a short break)* **to stop for a rest** parar [17] para descansar

rest VERB *(have a rest)* **descansar** [17]

restaurant NOUN **restaurante** MASC

restore VERB **restaurar** [17]

result NOUN ❶ **resultado** MASC; **the exam results** los resultados del examen ❷ **as a result** como consecuencia de ello, **as a result we missed the ferry** como consecuencia de ello perdimos el ferry

retire VERB *(from work)* **jubilarse** [17]; **she retires in June** se jubila en junio, **for retired people** para los jubilados

retirement NOUN **jubilación** FEM

return NOUN ❶ **vuelta** FEM; **the return journey** el viaje de vuelta, **by return of post** a vuelta de correo ❷ **in return** a cambio, **in return for his**

help a cambio de su ayuda
• **many happy returns!** ¡muchas felicidades!

return *VERB* ❶ *(come back or get home)* volver [45]; **he returned ten minutes later** volvió diez minutos más tarde, **to return from holiday** volver de vacaciones, **I'll ask her to phone as soon as she returns** le diré que te llame en cuanto vuelva ❷ *(to give back)* devolver [45]; **Gemma's never returned the video** Gemma no devolvió nunca el vídeo

return fare *NOUN* precio *(MASC)* del billete de ida y vuelta

return ticket *NOUN* billete *(MASC)* de ida y vuelta

reunion *NOUN* reunión *FEM*; **a class reunion** una reunión de excompañeros de clase

revenge *NOUN* venganza *FEM*; **to get one's revenge on someone** vengarse [28] de alguien

reverse *NOUN* ❶ *(of coin)* anverso *MASC* ❷ *(gear)* marcha *(FEM)* atrás ❸ *(of page)* dorso *MASC* ❹ *(opposite)* **the reverse is true** es al contrario

reverse *VERB* ❶ *(in a car)* dar [4] marcha atrás ❷ **to reverse the charges** llamar [17] a cobro revertido

review *NOUN* *(of a book, play, or film)* crítica *FEM*

review *VERB* escribir [52] la crítica de; **the film was well reviewed** la película recibió buenas críticas

revise *VERB* repasar [17]; **Tessa's busy revising for her exams** Tessa está muy ocupada repasando para los exámenes

revision *NOUN* repaso *MASC*

revolting *ADJECTIVE* asqueroso/asquerosa; **the sausages are revolting** las salchichas están asquerosas

revolution *NOUN* revolución *FEM*; **the Fench Revolution** la Revolución Francesa

reward *NOUN* recompensa *FEM*; **a £100 reward** una recompensa de cien libras

reward *VERB* recompensar [17]

rewarding *ADJECTIVE* gratificante

rhubarb *NOUN* ruibarbo *MASC*

rhyme *NOUN* rima *FEM*

rhythm *NOUN* ritmo *MASC*

rib *NOUN* costilla *FEM*

ribbon *NOUN* cinta *FEM*

rice *NOUN* arroz *MASC*; **chicken and rice** pollo y arroz, **rice pudding** arroz con leche

rich *ADJECTIVE* rico/rica; **we're not very rich** no somos muy ricos, **the rich and the poor** los ricos y los pobres

rid *ADJECTIVE* **to get rid of something** deshacerse [7] de algo, **we got rid of the car** nos deshicimos del coche

riddle *NOUN* adivinanza *FEM*

ride *NOUN* **to go for a ride (on a bike)** ir [8] a montar en bicicleta, **to go for a ride (on a horse)** ir [8] a montar a caballo

ride *VERB* ❶ **to learn to ride a bike** aprender [18] a montar en bicicleta, **can you ride a bike?** ¿sabes montar en bicicleta? ❷ **to learn to ride (a horse)** aprender [18] a montar a caballo, **I've never ridden a horse** nunca he montado a caballo

rider *NOUN* ❶ *(of horse)* **jinete** *MASC*, **amazona** *FEM* ❷ *(of bicycle)* **ciclista** *MASC & FEM* ❸ *(of motorbike)* **motorista** *MASC & FEM*

ridiculous *ADJECTIVE* **ridículo/ ridícula**

riding *NOUN* **equitación** *FEM*; **to go riding** hacer [7] equitación

riding school *NOUN* **escuela** *(FEM)* **de equitación**

rifle *NOUN* **rifle** *MASC*

right *NOUN* ❶ *(not left)* **derecha** *FEM*; **on the right** a la derecha, **on my right** a mi derecha ❷ *(to do something)* **derecho** *MASC*; **the right to strike** el derecho a hacer huelga, **you have no right to say that** no tienes derecho a decir eso

right *ADJECTIVE* ❶ *(not left)* **derecho/ derecha**; **my right hand** mi mano derecha ❷ *(correct)* **correcto/ correcta**; **the right answer** la respuesta correcta, **the right telephone number** el teléfono correcto, **is this the right address?** ¿son estas las señas? ❸ **to be right** *(a person)* tener [9] razón, **you see, I was right** ¿ves? tenía yo razón ❹ **you were right to stay at home** hiciste bien en quedarte en casa, **he was right not to say anything** hizo bien en no decir nada ❺ **it's not right to talk like that** no está bien hablar así

right *ADVERB* ❶ *(direction)* **derecha**; **turn right at the lights** gira a la derecha en el semáforo ❷ *(correctly)*

bien; **you're not doing it right** no lo estás haciendo bien ❸ *(completely)* **right at the bottom** al fondo del todo, **right now** ahora mismo, **right at the beginning** justo al principio, **right in the middle** justo en medio ❹ *(okay)* **vale**; **right, let's go** vale, vamos

right click *NOUN* **clic** *(MASC)* **con el botón derecho del ratón**

right-hand *ADJECTIVE* **on the right-hand side** a mano derecha

right-handed *ADJECTIVE* **diestro/ diestra**

ring *NOUN* ❶ *(on the phone)* **to give somebody a ring** llamar [17] a alguien ❷ *(for your finger)* **anillo** *MASC* ❸ *(circle)* **círculo** *MASC* ❹ **there was a ring at the door** llamaron a la puerta

ring *VERB* ❶ *(a bell or phone)* **sonar** [24]; **the phone rang** sonó el teléfono ❷ *(to phone)* **llamar** [17]; **I'll ring you tomorrow** te llamaré mañana, **could you ring for a taxi?** ¿podrías llamar un taxi?
• **to ring back** volver [45] a llamar; **I'll ring you back later** te volveré a llamar más tarde
• **to ring off** colgar [23]

rinse *VERB* **enjuagar** [28]

ripe *ADJECTIVE* **maduro/madura**; **are the tomatoes ripe?** ¿están maduros los tomates?

rip-off *NOUN* **it's a rip-off!** ¡es una estafa!

rise *NOUN* ❶ **subida** *FEM*; **a rise in price** una subida de precio ❷ **a pay rise** un aumento de sueldo

rise VERB ❶ *(the sun)* salir [63]; **when the sun rose** cuando salió el sol ❷ *(prices)* subir [19]

risk NOUN riesgo MASC; **to take risks** arriesgarse [28]

risk VERB arriesgar [28] *(your life or reputation)*; **she risked her life** arriesgó su vida

rival NOUN rival MASC & FEM

river NOUN río MASC

road NOUN ❶ carretera FEM; **the road to London** la carretera de Londres ❷ *(in a town)* calle FEM; **on the other side of the road** al otro lado de la calle ❸ **across the road** enfrente, **they live across the road from us** viven enfrente de nosotros

road accident NOUN accidente *(MASC)* de carretera

road map NOUN mapa *(MASC)* de carreteras

roadside NOUN **by the roadside** al borde de la carretera

road sign NOUN señal *(FEM)* de tráfico

roadworks PLURAL NOUN obras FEM PLURAL

roast NOUN asado MASC

roast ADJECTIVE asado/asada; **roast potatoes** patatas asadas, **roast beef** rosbif MASC

rob VERB ❶ robar [17] *(a person)* ❷ atracar [31] *(a bank)*

robber NOUN **bank robber** atracador/atracadora MASC & FEM

robbery NOUN atraco MASC; **a bank robbery** un atraco a un banco

rock NOUN ❶ *(a big stone)* roca FEM; **she was sitting on a rock** estaba sentada en una roca ❷ *(the material)* piedra FEM ❸ *(music)* rock MASC; **a rock band** un grupo de rock, **to dance rock and roll** bailar [17] rock and roll

rock climbing NOUN escalada *(FEM)* en roca; **to go rock climbing** hacer [7] escalada

rocket NOUN cohete MASC

rocking horse NOUN caballito *(MASC)* de balancín

rock star NOUN estrella *(FEM)* de rock

rocky ADJECTIVE rocoso/rocosa

rod NOUN **a fishing rod** una caña de pescar

role NOUN papel MASC; **to play the role of** interpretar [17] el papel de

roll NOUN ❶ rollo MASC; **a roll of fabric** un rollo de tela, **a toilet roll** un rollo de papel higiénico ❷ **a bread roll** un panecillo
• **to roll something up** *(a carpet)* enrollar [17] algo; **he rolled up his sleeves** se remangó las mangas

rollerblades PLURAL NOUN patines *(MASC PLURAL)* en línea

rollercoaster NOUN montaña *(FEM)* rusa *(literally: Russian mountain)*

roller skates PLURAL NOUN patines MASC PLURAL

Roman Catholic NOUN católico MASC, católica FEM

Roman Catholic ADJECTIVE católico/católica

a
b
c
d
e
f
g
h
i
j
k
l
m
n
o
p
q
r
s
t
u
v
w
x
y
z

romantic | **row**

romantic ADJECTIVE romántico/romántica

roof NOUN tejado MASC

roof rack NOUN baca FEM

rook NOUN ❶ (in chess) torre FEM ❷ (bird) grajo MASC

room NOUN ❶ habitación FEM; **she's in the other room** está en la otra habitación, **it's the biggest room in the house** es la habitación más grande de la casa, **a three-room flat** un piso de tres habitaciones ❷ (a bedroom) habitación MASC; **Lola's in her room** Lola está en su habitación ❸ (space) sitio MASC; **enough room for two** sitio suficiente para dos, **very little room** muy poco sitio

root NOUN raíz FEM

rope NOUN cuerda FEM

rose NOUN rosa FEM

rosebush NOUN rosal MASC

rot VERB pudrirse [59]

rota NOUN lista (FEM) de turnos

rotten ADJECTIVE podrido/podrida

rough ADJECTIVE ❶ (scratchy) áspero/áspera ❷ (vague) aproximado/aproximada; **a rough idea** una idea aproximada ❸ (stormy) **a rough sea** un mar agitado ❹ (difficult) **to have a rough time** pasarlo [17] mal ❺ **to sleep rough** dormir [51] a la intemperie

roughly ADJECTIVE (approximately) aproximadamente; **roughly ten per cent** aproximadamente el diez por ciento, **it takes roughly three hours** lleva aproximadamente tres horas

round NOUN ❶ (in a tournament) vuelta FEM ❷ (of cards) partida FEM ❸ **a round of drinks** una ronda de bebidas, **it's my round** esta ronda la pago yo

round ADJECTIVE redondo/redonda; **a round table** una mesa redonda

round PREPOSITION ❶ alrededor de; **round the city** alrededor de la ciudad, **round my arm** alrededor de mi brazo, **they were sitting round the table** estaban sentados alrededor de la mesa ❷ **to go round the shops** ir [8] de tiendas, **to go round a museum** visitar [17] un museo, **it's just round the corner** está a la vuelta de la esquina

round ADVERB ❶ **to go round to somebody's house** ir [8] a casa de alguien, **we invited Sally round for lunch** invitamos a Sally a comer ❷ **all the year round** todo el año

roundabout NOUN ❶ (for traffic) rotonda FEM ❷ (in a fairground) tiovivo MASC

route NOUN ❶ (that you plan) ruta FEM; **the best route is via Leeds** la mejor ruta es pasando por Leeds ❷ **a bus route** el recorrido de un autobús

row¹ NOUN ❶ fila FEM (of seats); **in the front row** en la primera fila, **in the back row** en la última fila ❷ hilera FEM; **a row of huts** un hilera de cabañas ❸ **four times in a row** cuatro veces seguidas

row² VERB (in a boat) remar [17]; **it's your turn to row** te toca remar, **we rowed across the lake** cruzamos el lago remando

row³ NOUN ❶ *(a quarrel)* **pelea** FEM; **to have a row** pelearse [17], **they've had a row** se han peleado, **I had a row with my parents** me peleé con mis padres ❷ *(noise)* **ruido** MASC; **they are making a terrible row!** ¡están haciendo un ruido terrible!

rowing NOUN **remo** MASC; **to go rowing** practicar [31] el remo

rowing boat NOUN **bote** *(MASC)* **de remos**

royal ADJECTIVE **real**; **the royal family** la familia real

rub VERB **frotar** [17]; **to rub your eyes** frotarse los ojos
• **to rub something out** borrar [17] algo

rubber NOUN ❶ *(an eraser)* **goma** *(FEM)* **de borrar** ❷ *(material)* **goma** *FEM*; **rubber soles** suelas de goma

rubber band NOUN **goma** *(FEM)* **elástica**

rubbish NOUN ❶ *(for the bin)* **basura** FEM ❷ *(nonsense)* **estupideces** FEM PLURAL; **you're talking rubbish!** ¡estás diciendo estupideces!

rubbish ADJECTIVE **the film was rubbish** la película fue una porquería, **they're a rubbish band** es una porquería de grupo

rubbish bin NOUN **cubo** *(MASC)* **de la basura**

rucksack NOUN **mochila** FEM

rude ADJECTIVE ❶ **maleducado/ maleducada** *(a person)* ❷ **that's rude** eso es de mala educación ❸ **a rude joke** una broma grosera, **a rude word** una palabrota

rug NOUN ❶ **alfombra** FEM ❷ *(a blanket)* **manta** *(FEM)* **de viaje**

rugby NOUN **rugby** MASC; **to play rugby** jugar [27] al rugby, **a rugby match** un partido de rugby

ruin NOUN **ruina** FEM; **in ruins** en ruinas

ruin VERB ❶ **estropear** [17]; **you'll ruin your jacket** vas a estropear tu chaqueta ❷ **fastidiar** [17] *(informal) (day, holiday)*; **it ruined my holiday** me fastidió las vacaciones

rule NOUN ❶ **regla** FEM; **the rules of the game** las reglas del juego ❷ **the school rules** el reglamento del colegio ❸ **as a rule** como norma

ruler NOUN **regla** FEM; **I've lost my ruler** he perdido mi regla

rumour NOUN **rumor** MASC

run NOUN ❶ **to go for a run** ir [8] a correr ❷ *(in cricket)* **carrera** FEM ❸ **in the long run** a la larga

run VERB ❶ **correr** [18]; **I ran ten kilometres** corrí diez kilómetros, **he ran across the pitch** cruzó el campo corriendo, **Kitty ran for the bus** Kitty corrió para coger el autobús ❷ *(organize)* **organizar** [22]; **who's running this concert?** ¿quién organiza el concierto? ❸ **dirigir** [49] *(a business)*; **he ran the firm for forty years** dirigió la compañía durante cuarenta años ❹ *(a train or bus)* **circular** [17]; **the buses don't run on Sundays** los autobuses no circulan los domingos ❺ *(to operate)* **hacer** [7] **funcionar**; **to run a bath** preparar [17] un baño
• **to run away** huir [54]
• **to run into** chocar [31] con; **the car ran into a tree** el coche chocó con un árbol

a b c d e f g h i j k l m n o p q r s t u v w x y z

- to run out of something I'm running out of money se me está acabando el dinero
- to run somebody over atropellar [17] a alguien; you'll get run over! ¡te van a atropellar!

runner-up NOUN **segundo** MASC, **segunda** FEM

running NOUN **running is good exercise** correr es un buen ejercicio

runway NOUN **pista** FEM

rush NOUN (a hurry) **to be in a rush** tener [9] prisa, **sorry, I'm in a rush** perdona, tengo prisa

rush VERB ❶ (hurry) **darse** [4] **prisa; I must rush!** ¡tengo que darme prisa! ❷ (run) **she rushed into the street** salió corriendo a la calle, **I rushed into the room** entré corriendo en la habitación ❸ **Louise was rushed to hospital** llevaron a Louise corriendo al hospital

rush hour NOUN **hora** (FEM) **punta; in the rush hour** a la hora punta

Russia NOUN **Rusia** FEM

Russian NOUN ❶ (a person) **ruso** MASC, **rusa** FEM ❷ (the language) **ruso** MASC

Russian ADJECTIVE **ruso/rusa**

rye NOUN **centeno** MASC

Ss

Sabbath NOUN ❶ (Jewish) **sábado** MASC ❷ (Christian) **domingo** MASC

sack NOUN ❶ **saco** MASC ❷ **he got the sack** le despidieron

sack VERB **to sack somebody** despedir [57] a alguien

sacred ADJECTIVE **sagrado/sagrada**

sacrifice NOUN **sacrificio** MASC

sad ADJECTIVE **triste**

saddle NOUN **silla** (FEM) **de montar**

saddlebag NOUN **alforja** FEM (on bike)

safe ADJECTIVE ❶ (out of danger) **seguro/segura; to feel safe** sentirse [14] seguro/segura ❷ (not dangerous) **seguro/segura; the path is safe** el camino es seguro, **it's not safe** no es seguro ❸ (unharmed) **to be safe** estar [2] sano y salvo

safety NOUN **seguridad** FEM

safety belt NOUN **cinturón** (MASC) **de seguridad**

safety pin NOUN **imperdible** MASC

Sagittarius NOUN **Sagitario** MASC; **Kylie's Sagittarius** Kylie es Sagitario

sail NOUN **vela** FEM

sailing NOUN **vela** FEM; **to go sailing** ir [8] a hacer vela, **she does a lot of sailing** practica mucho la vela

sailing boat NOUN bote (MASC) de vela

sailor NOUN marinero MASC

saint NOUN santo MASC, santa FEM

sake NOUN ❶ for your mother's sake por tu madre ❷ for heaven's sake! ¡por el amor de Dios!

salad NOUN ensalada FEM; a tomato salad una ensalada de tomate

salad dressing NOUN aliño (MASC) para la ensalada

salary NOUN sueldo MASC

sale NOUN ❶ (selling) venta FEM; the sale of the house la venta de la casa, 'for sale' 'se vende' ❷ the sales las rebajas, I bought it in the sales lo compré en las rebajas

sales assistant NOUN dependiente MASC, dependienta FEM

salesman NOUN representante MASC; he's a salesman es representante

saleswoman NOUN representante FEM

saliva NOUN saliva FEM

salmon NOUN salmón MASC

salt NOUN sal FEM

salty ADJECTIVE salado/salada

Salvadorean NOUN salvadoreño MASC, salvadoreña FEM

Salvadorean ADJECTIVE salvadoreño/salvadoreña

Salvation Army NOUN Ejército (MASC) de Salvación

same ADJECTIVE ❶ mismo/misma; she said the same thing ella dijo lo mismo, her birthday's the same day as mine su cumpleaños es el mismo día que el mío, at the same time al mismo tiempo, their car's the same as ours su coche es el mismo que el nuestro ❷ (with a plural noun) mismos/mismas; they were wearing the same shoes llevaban los mismos zapatos ❸ to look the same parecer [35] iguales, they all look the same to me a mí todos me parecen iguales

same PRONOUN the same lo mismo, it's not the same no es lo mismo, it's always the same siempre pasa lo mismo

sample NOUN muestra FEM; a free sample una muestra gratuita

sand NOUN arena FEM

sandal NOUN sandalia FEM; a pair of sandals un par de sandalias

sand castle NOUN castillo (MASC) de arena

sandpaper NOUN papel (MASC) de lija

sandwich NOUN sándwich MASC; a ham sandwich un sándwich de jamón

sanitary towel NOUN compresa FEM

Santa Claus NOUN Papá (MASC) Noel

sarcasm NOUN sarcasmo MASC

sarcastic ADJECTIVE sarcástico/sarcástica

sardine NOUN sardina FEM

SARS NOUN síndrome (MASC) respiratorio agudo severo

satchel NOUN cartera FEM

satellite NOUN satélite MASC

a
b
c
d
e
f
g
h
i
j
k
l
m
n
o
p
q
r

s
t
u
v
w
x
y
z

satellite dish NOUN antena (FEM) parabólica

satellite television NOUN televisión (FEM) por vía satélite

satisfactory ADJECTIVE satisfactorio/ satisfactoria

satisfied ADJECTIVE satisfecho/ satisfecha

satisfy VERB satisfacer [7]

satisfying ADJECTIVE ❶ (pleasing) satisfactorio/satisfactoria ❷ a satisfying meal una comida que llena

Saturday NOUN sábado MASC; on Saturday el sábado, I'm going out on Saturday voy a salir el sábado, see you on Saturday! ¡te veo el sábado!, on Saturdays los sábados, the museum is closed on Saturdays el museo cierra los sábados, every Saturday todos los sábados, last Saturday el sábado pasado, next Saturday el próximo sábado, to have a Saturday job trabajar [17] los sábados

sauce NOUN salsa FEM

saucepan NOUN cazo MASC

saucer NOUN platillo MASC

sausage NOUN ❶ salchicha FEM ❷ (salami) salchichón MASC

savage NOUN salvaje MASC & FEM

save VERB ❶ (rescue) salvar [17]; to save somebody's life salvarle la vida a alguien, the doctors saved his life los médicos le salvaron la vida ❷ (money or energy); I've saved £60 he ahorrado sesenta libras, try to save electricity intenta ahorrar electricidad ❸ (put aside)

guardar [17] (food); save the cake for later guarda el pastel para luego ❹ (avoid spending) no gastar [17]; I walk to school to save money voy andando al colegio para no gastar dinero ❺ to save time ahorrar [17] tiempo, we'll take a taxi to save time cogeremos un taxi para ahorrar tiempo ❻ (on a computer) guardar [17]

• to save up ahorrar [17]; I'm saving up to go to Spain estoy ahorrando para ir a España

savings PLURAL NOUN ahorros MASC PLURAL; I've spent all my savings me he gastado todos los ahorros

savoury ADJECTIVE salado/salada; I prefer savoury things to sweet things prefiero lo salado a lo dulce

saw NOUN sierra FEM

saxophone NOUN saxofón MASC; to play the saxophone tocar [31] el saxofón

say VERB ❶ decir [5]; what did you say? ¿qué has dicho?, she says she's tired dice que está cansada, he said to wait here dijo que esperásemos aquí, as they say como se suele decir, that goes without saying eso no hace falta ni decirlo ❷ to say something again repetir [57] algo

saying NOUN refrán MASC; as the saying goes como dice el refrán

scab NOUN costra FEM

scale NOUN ❶ (size) escala FEM; on a large scale en gran escala, the scale of the disaster la escala del desastre ❷ (in music) escala FEM ❸ (of a fish) escama FEM

scales NOUN ❶ balanza FEM; kitchen scales una balanza de cocina

❷ **bathroom scales** una báscula de baño

scalp NOUN **cuero** (MASC) **cabelludo**

scandal NOUN ❶ **escándalo** MASC ❷ (gossip) **chismorreo** MASC

Scandinavia NOUN **Escandinavia** FEM

Scandinavian ADJECTIVE **escandinavo/escandinava**

scanner NOUN **escáner** MASC

scar NOUN **cicatriz** FEM

scarce ADJECTIVE **escaso/escasa**

scarcely ADVERB **apenas**; **I could scarcely see it** apenas lo veía

scare NOUN ❶ **susto** MASC; **to give somebody a scare** darle [4] un susto a alguien ❷ **a bomb scare** una amenaza de bomba

scare VERB **to scare somebody** asustar [17] a alguien, **you scared me!** ¡me has asustado!

scarecrow NOUN **espantapájaros** MASC (does not change in the plural)

scared ADJECTIVE **to be scared** estar [2] asustado/asustada, **I'm scared!** estoy asustado, **to be scared of** tenerle [9] miedo a, **he's scared of dogs** le tiene miedo a los perros

scarf NOUN ❶ (long, warm) **bufanda** FEM ❷ (silky) **foulard** MASC

scary ADJECTIVE **de miedo** (book or film)

scene NOUN ❶ (of an incident or a crime) **escena** FEM; **the scene of the crime** la escena del crimen ❷ (world) **mundo** MASC; **the music scene** el mundo de la música ❸ **scenes of violence** escenas violentas ❹ to

make a scene montar [17] un número (informal)

scenery NOUN ❶ (landscape) **paisaje** MASC ❷ (theatrical) **decorado** MASC

schedule NOUN **programa** MASC

scheduled flight NOUN **vuelo** (MASC) **regular**

scheme NOUN **plan** MASC

scholarship NOUN **beca** FEM

school NOUN **colegio** MASC; **to go to school** ir [8] al colegio, **she's still at school** todavía va al colegio

schoolbook NOUN **libro** (MASC) **de texto**

schoolboy NOUN **colegial** MASC

schoolchildren PLURAL NOUN **colegiales** MASC PLURAL

schoolfriend NOUN **amigo** (MASC), **amiga** (FEM) **del colegio**

schoolgirl NOUN **colegiala** FEM

science NOUN **ciencia** FEM; **I like science** me gustan las ciencias, **the science teacher** el profesor de ciencias

science fiction NOUN **ciencia** (FEM) **ficción**

scientific ADJECTIVE **científico/científica**

scientist NOUN **científico** MASC, **científica** FEM

scissors PLURAL NOUN **tijeras** FEM PLURAL; **a pair of scissors** unas tijeras

scoop NOUN ❶ (of ice-cream) **bola** FEM; **how many scoops would you like?** ¿cuántas bolas quieres? ❷ (in newspaper) **primicia** FEM

score NOUN *(in game)* resultado *MASC*; **the score was three two** el resultado fue tres a dos, **what's the score?** ¿a cómo van?

score VERB ❶ *(goal)* marcar [31]; **Lenny scored a goal** Lenny marcó un gol ❷ *(points)* **I scored three points** conseguí tres puntos ❸ *(keep score)* llevar [17] la puntuación ❹ *(in test or card game)* puntuación *FEM*

Scorpio NOUN Escorpio *MASC*; **Jess is Scorpio** Jess es Escorpio

Scot NOUN escocés *MASC*, escocesa *FEM*; **the Scots** los escoceses

Scotland NOUN Escocia *FEM*; **in Scotland** en Escocia, **Pauline's from Scotland** Pauline es de Escocia

Scots ADJECTIVE escocés/escocesa; **a Scots accent** un acento escocés

Scotsman NOUN escocés *MASC*

Scotswoman NOUN escocesa *FEM*

Scottish ADJECTIVE escocés/escocesa; **a Scottish accent** un acento escocés

scout NOUN explorador *MASC*, exploradora *FEM*

scrambled eggs NOUN huevos *(MASC PLURAL)* revueltos

scrap NOUN **a scrap of paper** un trocito de papel

scrape VERB rayar [17]

scratch NOUN ❶ *(on your skin)* arañazo *MASC* ❷ *(on a surface)* rayón *MASC*
• **to start from scratch** empezar [25] de cero

scratch VERB *(scratch yourself)* rascarse [31]; **to scratch your head** rascarse [31] la cabeza

scream NOUN grito *MASC*

scream VERB gritar [17]

screen NOUN pantalla *FEM*; **on the screen** en la pantalla

screw NOUN tornillo *MASC*

screw VERB atornillar [17]

screwdriver NOUN destornillador *MASC*

scribble VERB garabatear [17]

scrub VERB ❶ fregar [30] *(a saucepan)* ❷ **to scrub your nails** cepillarse [17] las uñas

scuba diving NOUN submarinismo *MASC*

sculptor NOUN escultor *MASC*, escultora *FEM*; **Frazer's a sculptor** Frazer es escultor

sculpture NOUN escultura *FEM*

sea NOUN mar *MASC*

seafood NOUN marisco *MASC*

seagull NOUN gaviota *FEM*

seal NOUN *(animal)* foca *FEM*

seal VERB cerrar [29] *(envelope)*

seaman NOUN marinero *MASC*

search NOUN búsqueda *FEM*

search VERB ❶ *(to look for)* buscar [31]; **I've searched my desk but I can't find the letter** he buscado en mi escritorio pero no encuentro la carta, **to search for something** buscar [31] algo, **I've been searching everywhere for the**

scissors he buscado las tijeras por todas partes ❷ *(a building, a person)* **registrar** [17]; **the police searched the house** la policía registró la casa

seashell NOUN **concha** *(FEM)* **de mar**

seasick ADJECTIVE **to be seasick** estar [2] **mareado/mareada, to get seasick marearse** [17]

seaside NOUN **costa** *FEM*; **at the seaside** en la costa

season NOUN **temporada** *FEM*; **the rugby season** la temporada de rugby, **strawberries are not in season at the moment** ahora no es temporada de fresas, **off-season prices** billetes de fuera de temporada

season ticket NOUN **abono** *(MASC)* **de temporada**

seat NOUN ❶ **asiento** *MASC*; **the front seat** *(in a car)* el asiento delantero, **the back seat** el asiento trasero, **take a seat** toma asiento ❷ *(in a cinema, theatre, etc.)* **localidad** *FEM*; **to book a seat** reservar [17] una localidad ❸ **can you keep my seat?** ¿puedes guardarme el sitio?

seatbelt NOUN **cinturón** *(MASC)* **de seguridad**

second NOUN ❶ *(time unit)* **segundo** *MASC*; **can you wait a second?** ¿puedes esperar un segundo? ❷ **the second of July** el dos de julio

second ADJECTIVE **segundo/segunda; for the second time** por segunda vez, **on the second floor** en la segunda planta

secondary school NOUN **colegio** *(MASC)* **de enseñanza secundaria**

second class ADJECTIVE **de segunda clase** *(a ticket, hotel)*; **a second class team** un equipo de segunda clase

secondhand ADJECTIVE, ADVERB **de segunda mano; a secondhand bike** una bicicleta de segunda mano, **I bought it secondhand** lo compré de segunda mano

secondly ADVERB **en segundo lugar**

secret NOUN **secreto** *MASC*; **to keep a secret** guardar [17] un secreto, **in secret** en secreto

secret ADJECTIVE **secreto/secreta; a secret plan** un plan secreto

secretarial college NOUN **escuela** *(FEM)* **de secretariado**

secretary NOUN **secretario** *MASC*, **secretaria** *FEM*; **she's a secretary** es secretaria, **the secretary's office** la secretaría

secretly ADVERB **en secreto**

sect NOUN **secta** *FEM*

section NOUN **sección** *FEM*

security NOUN **seguridad** *FEM*

security guard NOUN **guarda** *(MASC)* **jurado, guarda** *(FEM)* **jurada; he's a security guard** es guarda jurado

see VERB ❶ **ver** [16]; **I saw Lindy yesterday** vi a Lindy ayer, **have you seen the film?** ¿has visto la película?, **I haven't seen her for ages** hace años que no la veo, **I'll see what I can do** veré lo que puedo hacer, **let's see** a ver ❷ **to be able to see** ver [16], **I can't see anything** no veo nada ❸ **see you!** ¡hasta luego!, **see you on Saturday!** ¡hasta el sábado!, **see you soon!** ¡hasta pronto!, **see you tomorrow!** ¡hasta

mañana! ❹ **to see somebody home** acompañar [17] a alguien a casa
• **to see to something** ocuparse [17] de algo; **Jo's seeing to the drinks** Jo se está ocupando de las bebidas

seed NOUN semilla FEM; **to plant seeds** plantar [17] semillas

seem VERB parecer [35]; **it seems odd to me** me parece raro, **it seems she's left** parece que se ha ido, **he seems a bit shy** parece un poco tímido, **the museum seems to be closed** parece que el museo está cerrado

seesaw NOUN balancín MASC

select VERB seleccionar [17]

selection NOUN selección FEM

self-confidence NOUN confianza (FEM) en sí mismo; **I don't have much self-confidence** no tengo mucha confianza en mí misma

self-confident ADJECTIVE seguro/ segura de sí mismo/misma

self-conscious ADJECTIVE cohibido/ cohibida

self-employed NOUN autónomo MASC, autónoma FEM; **the self-employed** los autónomos

self-employed ADJECTIVE autónomo/autónoma; **to be self-employed** ser [1] autónomo

selfish ADJECTIVE egoísta

self-service ADJECTIVE **a self-service restaurant** un autoservicio

sell VERB vender [18]; **to sell something to somebody** venderle algo a alguien, **I sold him my bike** le vendí mi bici, **the house has been sold** la casa se ha vendido, **the concert's sold out** se han agotado las localidades para el concierto

sell-by date NOUN fecha (FEM) límite de venta

seller NOUN vendedor MASC, vendedora FEM

Sellotape NOUN celo MASC

semi NOUN casa (FEM) adosada; **we live in a semi** vivimos en una casa adosada

semicircle NOUN semicírculo MASC

semicolon NOUN punto (MASC) y coma

semi-detached house NOUN casa (FEM) adosada

semi-final NOUN semifinal FEM

semi-skimmed milk NOUN leche (FEM) semidesnatada

send VERB mandar [17]; **to send something to somebody** mandarle algo a alguien, **I sent her a present for her birthday** le mandé un regalo por su cumpleaños
• **to send somebody back** hacer [7] volver a alguien
• **to send something back** devolver [45] algo

senior citizen NOUN persona (FEM) de la tercera edad

sensation NOUN ❶ (feeling) sensibilidad FEM; **she had no sensation in her fingers** no tenía sensibilidad en los dedos ❷ (impact) sensación FEM; **she caused a sensation** causó sensación

sensational ADJECTIVE sensacional

sense NOUN ❶ sentido MASC; **common sense** sentido común, **it doesn't make sense** no tiene sentido, **it makes sense** tiene sentido, **to have a sense of humour** tener [9] sentido del humor, **she has no sense of humour** no tiene sentido del humor ❷ **the sense of smell** el olfato, **the sense of touch** el tacto

sensible ADJECTIVE sensato/sensata; **she's very sensible** es muy sensata, **it's a sensible decision** es una decisión sensata

sensitive ADJECTIVE sensible; **for sensitive skin** para pieles sensibles

sentence NOUN ❶ frase FEM; **write a sentence in Spanish** escribe una frase en español ❷ (by judge) sentencia FEM

sentence VERB condenar [17]

sentimental ADJECTIVE sentimental

separate ADJECTIVE ❶ aparte; **in a separate pile** en un montón aparte, **on a separate sheet of paper** en una hoja de papel aparte ❷ (different) distinto/distinta; **that's a separate problem** ese es un problema distinto ❸ (individual) separado/separada; **they have separate rooms** tienen habitaciones separadas

separate VERB ❶ separar [17] ❷ (a couple) separarse [17]

separately ADVERB por separado

separation NOUN separación FEM

September NOUN septiembre MASC

sequel NOUN continuación FEM

serial NOUN serie FEM

series NOUN serie FEM; **a television series** una serie de televisión

serious ADJECTIVE ❶ serio/seria; **a serious discussion** una discusión seria, **are you serious?** ¿lo dices en serio? ❷ grave (illness, injury, mistake, problem); **we have a serious problem** tenemos un problema grave

seriously ADVERB ❶ en serio; **seriously, I have to go now** en serio, tengo que irme, **seriously?** ¿en serio? ❷ **to take somebody seriously** tomarse [17] en serio a alguien ❸ gravemente (ill, injured)

servant NOUN criado MASC, criada FEM

serve NOUN (in tennis) saque MASC; **it's my serve** me toca sacar

serve VERB ❶ servir [57]; **can you serve the vegetables, please?** ¿puedes servir la verdura, por favor? ❷ **are you being served?** ¿le atienden? ❸ (in tennis) sacar [31]
• **it serves him right** lo tiene bien merecido

service NOUN ❶ (in a restaurant, from a company, etc.) servicio MASC; **the service is very slow** el servicio es muy lento, **service is included** el servicio está incluido ❷ **the emergency services** los servicios de emergencia ❸ (church) oficio (MASC) religioso ❹ (of a car or machine) revisión FEM

service VERB hacerle [7] una revisión a (a car or a machine)

service charge NOUN servicio MASC; **what's the service charge?** ¿cuánto se cobra por el servicio?

service station NOUN estación (FEM) de servicio

serviette NOUN servilleta FEM

session NOUN sesión FEM

set NOUN ❶ (for playing a game) juego MASC; **a chess set** un juego de ajedrez ❷ (of keys, tools, etc.) juego MASC ❸ **a train set** un tren de juguete ❹ (in tennis) set MASC

set ADJECTIVE **at a set time** a una hora determinada, **a set menu** un menú del día, **a set price** un precio fijo

set VERB ❶ fijar [17] (date, time) ❷ establecer [35] (record) ❸ **to set the table** poner [11] la mesa, **to set the alarm clock** poner [11] el despertador, **I've set my alarm for seven** he puesto el despertador para las siete ❹ **to set a watch** poner [11] el reloj en hora ❺ (the sun) ponerse [11]
- **to set off** salir [63]; **we're setting off at ten** salimos a las diez, **they set off for Barcelona yesterday** salieron ayer para Barcelona
- **to set off something** ❶ tirar [17] (firework) ❷ hacer [7] sonar (alarm)
- **to set out** salir [63]; **they set out for Seville yesterday** salieron ayer para Sevilla

settee NOUN sofá MASC

settle VERB ❶ (a bill) pagar [28] ❷ (a problem) solucionar [17]

seven NUMBER siete MASC; **Khalil's seven** Khalil tiene siete años, **it's seven o'clock** son las siete

seventeen NUMBER diecisiete MASC; **Jason's seventeen** Jason tiene diecisiete años

seventh NOUN ❶ (fraction) **a seventh** una séptima parte ❷ **the seventh of July** el siete de julio

seventh ADJECTIVE séptimo/séptima; **on the seventh floor** en la séptima planta

seventies PLURAL NOUN **the seventies** los años setenta, **in the seventies** en los años setenta

seventy NUMBER setenta MASC; **he's seventy** tiene setenta años, **seventy-five** setenta y cinco

several ADJECTIVE, PRONOUN varios/varias; **I've seen her several times** la he visto varias veces, **I've read several of her novels** he leído varias novelas suyas, **he took several** cogió varios

severe ADJECTIVE ❶ (person) severo/severa ❷ (weather) malo/mala ❸ (injury) grave

Seville NOUN Sevilla FEM

sew VERB coser [18]

sewer NOUN alcantarilla FEM

sewing NOUN costura FEM; **I like sewing** me gusta la costura

sewing machine NOUN máquina (FEM) de coser

sex NOUN ❶ (gender) sexo MASC ❷ (intercourse) relaciones (FEM PLURAL) sexuales; **to have sex with someone** tener [9] relaciones sexuales con alguien

sex education NOUN educación (FEM) sexual

sexism NOUN sexismo MASC

sexist ADJECTIVE **sexista; sexist remarks** comentarios sexistas

sexual ADJECTIVE **sexual**

sexual harassment NOUN **acoso** (MASC) **sexual**

sexuality NOUN **sexualidad** FEM

sexy ADJECTIVE **sexy**

shabby ADJECTIVE **gastado/gastada**

shade NOUN ❶ (of a colour) **tono** MASC; **a pretty shade of green** un bonito tono verde ❷ **in the shade** en la sombra

shadow NOUN **sombra** FEM

shake VERB ❶ (tremble) **temblar** [29]; **my hands are shaking** me tiemblan las manos ❷ **to shake something** agitar [17] algo ❸ **to shake hands with somebody** estrecharle [17] la mano a alguien, **she shook hands with me** me dio la mano, **we shook hands** nos estrechamos la mano ❹ **to shake your head** (meaning no) negar [30] con la cabeza

shall VERB **shall I come with you?** ¿voy contigo?, **shall we stop now?** ¿paramos ya?

shallow ADJECTIVE **poco profundo/ poco profunda; the water's very shallow here** el agua es muy poco profunda aquí

shallow end NOUN (of a swimming pool) **the shallow end** la parte poco profunda de la piscina

shambles NOUN **caos** MASC; **it was a total shambles!** ¡fue un caos total!

shame NOUN ❶ **vergüenza** FEM; **shame on you!** ¡debería darte vergüenza! ❷ **what a shame!** ¡qué

penal, **it's a shame she can't come** ¡qué pena que no pueda venir! (note that 'que' is followed by the subjunctive)

shampoo NOUN **champú** MASC; **I bought some shampoo** compré champú

shamrock NOUN **trébol** MASC

shandy NOUN **clara** FEM; **a shandy** una clara

shape NOUN **forma** FEM; **to be in good shape** estar [2] en buena forma

share NOUN ❶ **parte** FEM; **your share of the money** tu parte del dinero ❷ (in a company) **acción** FEM

share VERB **compartir** [19]; **I'm sharing a room with Emma** comparto una habitación con Emma
• **to share out** repartir [19]

sharp ADJECTIVE ❶ (knife) **afilado/ afilada; this knife isn't very sharp** este cuchillo no está muy afilado ❷ **a sharp pencil** un lápiz con mucha punta ❸ **a sharp bend** una curva cerrada ❹ (clever) **agudo/aguda**

sharpen VERB ❶ **sacarle** [31] **punta a** (a pencil) ❷ **afilar** [17] (a knife)

sharpener NOUN **sacapuntas** MASC PLURAL

shave VERB ❶ (have a shave) **afeitarse** [17]; **he's shaving** se está afeitando ❷ **to shave your legs** afeitarse [17] las piernas, **to shave off your beard** afeitarse [17] la barba

shaving cream NOUN **crema** (FEM) **de afeitar**

shaving foam NOUN **espuma** (FEM) **de afeitar**

she PRONOUN ❶ ('she' like other subject pronouns is generally not translated; in Spanish the form of the verb tells you whether the subject of the verb is 'he/she/it, you, they', etc., so 'she' is only translated for emphasis) **she's in her room** está en su cuarto, **she's a student** es estudiante, **she's a very good teacher** es muy buena profesora, **here she is!** ¡aquí está! ❷ (for emphasis) **ella**; **she did it** lo hizo ella

shed NOUN ❶ cabaña FEM ❷ (in garden) cobertizo MASC

sheep NOUN oveja FEM

sheepdog NOUN perro (MASC) pastor

sheet NOUN ❶ (for a bed) sábana FEM ❷ **a sheet of paper** una hoja de papel, **a blank sheet** una hoja en blanco ❸ (of glass or metal) plancha FEM
• **to be as white as a sheet** estar [2] blanco como el papel

shelf NOUN ❶ (in the home) estante MASC; **a set of shelves** una estantería FEM ❷ (in a shop or a fridge) balda FEM

shell NOUN ❶ (of an egg or a nut) cáscara FEM ❷ (seashell) concha FEM ❸ (explosive) proyectil MASC

shellfish NOUN marisco MASC

shelter NOUN ❶ refugio MASC; **to take shelter from the rain** refugiarse [17] de la lluvia, **in the shelter of** al abrigo de ❷ **a bus shelter** una marquesina

sherry NOUN jerez MASC

Shetland Islands NOUN islas (FEM PLURAL) Shetland

shield NOUN escudo MASC

shift NOUN turno MASC; **the night shift** el turno de noche, **to be on night shift** hacer [7] el turno de noche

shift VERB **to shift something** mover [38] algo

shin NOUN espinilla FEM

shine VERB brillar [17]

shiny ADJECTIVE brillante

ship NOUN ❶ barco MASC; **a passenger ship** un barco de pasajeros ❷ **a sailing ship** un velero

shirt NOUN camisa FEM

shiver VERB temblar [29]

shock NOUN ❶ shock MASC; **it was a shock** fue un shock, **it gave me a shock** me llevé un shock, **in a state of shock** en estado de shock ❷ **an electric shock** una descarga eléctrica, **I got an electric shock** me dio una descarga eléctrica

shock VERB horrorizar [22]

shocked ADJECTIVE horrorizado/horrorizada

shocking ADJECTIVE espantoso/espantosa

shoe NOUN zapato MASC; **a pair of shoes** un par de zapatos

shoelace NOUN cordón (MASC) de zapato

shoe polish NOUN betún MASC

shoe shop NOUN zapatería FEM

shoot VERB ❶ (fire) disparar [17]; **to shoot at somebody** disparar a alguien, **she shot him in the leg** le disparó en la pierna, **he was shot in**

the arm le dispararon en el brazo ❷ *(kill)* **matar** [17] **a tiros; he was shot by terrorists** los terroristas lo mataron a tiros ❸ *(execute)* **fusilar** [17] ❹ *(in football, hockey)* **lanzar** [22] ❺ **to shoot a film** rodar [24] una película

shooting NOUN **tiro** *(MASC)* **al blanco**

shop NOUN **tienda** *FEM*; **a record shop** una tienda de discos, **a shoe shop** una zapatería, **to go round the shops** ir [8] de tiendas

shop assistant NOUN **dependiente** *MASC*, **dependienta** *FEM*; **Brad's a shop assistant** Brad trabaja de dependiente

shopkeeper NOUN **tendero** *MASC*, **tendera** *FEM*

shoplifter NOUN **ladrón** *MASC*, **ladrona** *FEM*

shoplifting NOUN **hurto** *(MASC)* **en las tiendas**

shopping NOUN **compras** *FEM PLURAL*; **can you put the shopping away?** ¿puedes guardar las compras?, **I've got a lot of shopping to do** tengo muchas cosas que comprar, **to go shopping** ir [8] a hacer la compra, *(for fun, to buy clothes or presents)* ir [8] de compras

shopping centre NOUN **centro** *(MASC)* **comercial**

shop window NOUN **escaparate** *MASC*

shore NOUN **orilla** *(FEM)* **del mar**

short ADJECTIVE ❶ **corto/corta; a short dress** un vestido corto, **she has short hair** tiene el pelo corto ❷ *(person)* **bajo/baja** *(in height)*; **he's quite short** es bastante bajo

❸ **a short break** un descanso corto, **a short visit** una visita corta, **to go for a short walk** ir [8] a dar un pequeño paseo, **it's a short walk from the station** es un pequeño paseo desde la estación ❹ **a short time ago** hace poco tiempo ❺ **to be short of** no tener mucho, **we're a bit short of money at the moment** no tenemos mucho dinero en este momento, **we're getting short of time** se nos está acabando el tiempo

shortage NOUN **escasez** *FEM*

shortbread NOUN **galleta** *(FEM)* **de mantequilla**

shortcrust pastry NOUN **pasta** *(FEM)* **quebrada**

short cut NOUN **atajo** *MASC*; **we took a short cut** tomamos un atajo

shorten VERB **acortar** [17]

shortly ADVERB **dentro de poco**

shorts PLURAL NOUN **shorts** *MASC PLURAL*; **a pair of shorts** unos shorts, **my red shorts** mis shorts rojos

short-sighted ADJECTIVE **miope**; **I'm short-sighted** soy miope

shotgun NOUN **escopeta** *FEM*

should VERB ❶ **deber** [18] *('should' is translated by the conditional tense of 'deber')*; **you should ask Simon** deberías preguntárselo a Simon, **the potatoes should be cooked now** las patatas deberían estar hechas ya ❷ *('should have' is translated by the past conditional tense of 'deber')* **you should have told me** deberías habérmelo dicho, **I shouldn't have stayed** no deberías haberte quedado ❸ *('should* meaning 'would' is translated by the conditional tense of the appropriate verb) **I should forget it if I were you** yo en tu lugar me olvidaría del asunto ❹ **I should think** yo diría, **I should think he's forgotten** yo diría que se ha olvidado

shoulder NOUN **hombro** MASC

shoulder bag NOUN **bolso** MASC

shout NOUN **grito** MASC

shout VERB **gritar** [17]; **stop shouting!** ¡deja de gritar!, **they shouted at us to come back** nos gritaron que volviésemos

shovel NOUN **pala** FEM

show NOUN ❶ (on stage) **espectáculo** MASC; **we went to see a show** fuimos a ver un espectáculo ❷ (on TV) **programa** MASC; **he has a TV show** tiene un programa en la tele ❸ (exhibition) **salón** MASC; **the motor show** el salón del automóvil

show VERB ❶ **enseñar** [17]; **to show something to somebody** enseñar a alguien algo, **I'll show you my photos** te enseñaré mis fotos, **to show somebody how to do** enseñar algo a alguien cómo hacer, **he showed me how to make pancakes** me enseñó cómo hacer crepes ❷ **it shows!** ¡ya se ve!
• **to show off** presumir [19]; **stop showing off!** ¡déjate de hacer fanfarronadas!

shower NOUN ❶ (in a bathroom) **ducha** FEM; **to have a shower** ducharse [17] ❷ (of rain) **chaparrón** MASC

show-off NOUN **fanfarrón** MASC, **fanfarrona** FEM

shriek VERB **gritar** [17]

shrimp NOUN **camarón** MASC

shrine NOUN **santuario** MASC

shrink VERB **encoger** [3]

Shrove Tuesday NOUN **martes** (MASC) **de Carnaval**

shrug VERB **to shrug your shoulders** encogerse [3] de hombros

shuffle VERB **to shuffle the cards** barajar [17] las cartas

shut ADJECTIVE **cerrado/cerrada**; **the shops are shut** las tiendas están cerradas

shut VERB **cerrar** [29]; **can you shut the door please?** ¿puedes cerrar la puerta por favor?, **the shops shut at six** las tiendas cierran a las seis
• **to shut up** (be quiet) **callarse** [17]; **shut up!** ¡cállate!

shuttlecock NOUN **volante** MASC

shy ADJECTIVE **tímido/tímida**

shyness NOUN **timidez** FEM

Sicily NOUN **Sicilia** FEM

sick ADJECTIVE ❶ (ill) **enfermo/ enferma** ❷ **to be sick** (vomit) **devolver** [45], **I was sick several times** devolví varias veces, **to feel sick** tener [9] ganas de devolver ❸ **a sick joke** una broma de mal gusto ❹ **to be sick of something** estar [2] harto/harta de algo, **I'm sick of staying at home every night** estoy harto de quedarme en casa todas las noches

sickness NOUN **enfermedad** FEM

side NOUN ❶ **lado** MASC; **on the other side of the street** al otro lado de la calle, **on the wrong side** en el lado equivocado, **I'm on your side** (*I agree with you*) estoy de tu lado ❷ (*edge*) **borde** *MASC*; **at the side of the road** al borde de la carretera, **by the side of the pool** al borde de la piscina, **by the side of the river** a la orilla del río ❸ (*team*) **equipo** *MASC*; **she plays on our side** juega en nuestro equipo ❹ **to take sides** tomar [17] partido ❺ **side by side** uno al lado del otro

sideboard *NOUN* **aparador** *MASC*

siege *NOUN* **sitio** *MASC*

sieve *NOUN* **tamiz** *MASC*

sigh *NOUN* **suspiro** *MASC*

sigh *VERB* **suspirar** [17]

sight *NOUN* ❶ (*notice*) **espectáculo** *MASC*; **it was a marvellous sight** era un espectáculo maravilloso ❷ **at the sight of** a la vista de, **at first sight** a primera vista ❸ (*eyesight*) **vista** *FEM*; **to have poor sight** tener [9] mala vista, **to know somebody by sight** conocer [35] a alguien de vista, **I'd lost sight of them** los había perdido de vista ❹ **to see the sights** visitar [17] los lugares de interés

sightseeing *NOUN* **to do some sightseeing** visitar [17] los lugares de interés

sign *NOUN* ❶ (*notice*) **letrero** *MASC*; **there's a sign on the door** hay un letrero en la puerta ❷ (*trace, indication*) **señal** *FEM* ❸ (*of the Zodiac*) **signo** *MASC*; **what sign are you?** ¿de qué signo eres?

sign *VERB* ❶ **firmar** [17]; **to sign a cheque** firmar un cheque ❷ (*using sign language*) **comunicarse** [31] **por señas**

• **to sign on** (*as unemployed*) inscribirse [17] al paro

signal *NOUN* **señal** *FEM*

signature *NOUN* **firma** *FEM*

significance *NOUN* **importancia** *FEM*

significant *ADJECTIVE* **importante**

sign language *NOUN* **lenguaje** (*MASC*) **de gestos**

signpost *NOUN* **señal** *FEM*

silence *NOUN* **silencio** *MASC*

silent *ADJECTIVE* **silencioso/silenciosa**

silk *NOUN* **seda** *FEM*

silk *ADJECTIVE* **de seda; a silk shirt** una blusa de seda

silky *ADJECTIVE* **sedoso/sedosa**

silly *ADJECTIVE* **tonto/tonta; it was a really silly thing to do** hacer eso fue una verdadera tontería

silver *NOUN* **plata** *FEM*

silver *ADJECTIVE* **de plata; a silver spoon** una cuchara de plata

similar *ADJECTIVE* **parecido/parecida**

similarity *NOUN* **parecido** *MASC*

simple *ADJECTIVE* **sencillo/sencilla**

simplify *VERB* **simplificar** [31]

simply *ADVERB* **sencillamente**

sin *NOUN* **pecado** *MASC*

since *PREPOSITION, ADVERB*

since *CONJUNCTION* ❶ **desde** (*notice that Spanish uses the present tense where English uses 'have done' or 'have been doing'*) **I've been in Madrid since Saturday** llevo en

Madrid desde el sábado, **I've been learning Spanish since last year** estoy aprendiendo español desde el año pasado ❷ *desde que (the same thing happens with tenses here as above)*; **since I have known her** desde que la conozco, **since I've been learning Spanish** desde que estoy aprendiendo español ❸ I haven't seen her since no la he visto desde entonces, **I haven't seen her since Monday** no la he visto desde el lunes, **since when?** ¿desde cuándo? ❹ *(because)* como; **since it was raining, the match was cancelled** como estaba lloviendo, cancelaron el partido

sincere ADJECTIVE sincero/sincera

sincerely ADVERB **Yours sincerely** Atentamente

sing VERB cantar [17]

singer NOUN cantante MASC & FEM

singing NOUN ❶ canto MASC; **a singing lesson** una lección de canto ❷ I like singing me gusta cantar

single NOUN *(ticket)* billete *(MASC)* de ida; **a single to Barcelona** un billete de ida para Barcelona

single ADJECTIVE ❶ *(not married)* soltero/soltera ❷ **a single room** una habitación individual, **a single bed** una cama individual ❸ **not a single ...** ni un solo/ni una sola ..., **I haven't had a single reply** no he tenido ni una sola respuesta ❹ **every single day** todos los días, **every single morning** todas las mañanas

single parent NOUN **she's a single parent** es madre soltera, **a single-parent family** una familia monoparental

singular NOUN singular MASC; **in the singular** en singular

sink NOUN ❶ *(in kitchen)* fregadero MASC ❷ *(in bathroom)* lavabo MASC

sink VERB hundirse [19]

sir NOUN señor MASC; **yes, sir** sí, señor

sister NOUN hermana FEM; **my sister's ten** mi hermana tiene diez años

sister-in-law NOUN cuñada FEM

sit VERB ❶ sentarse [29]; **you can sit on the sofa** puedes sentarte en el sofá, **I can sit on the floor** me puedo sentar en el suelo ❷ **to be sitting** estar [2] sentado, **Leila was sitting on the sofa** Leila estaba sentada en el sofá ❸ **to sit an exam** presentarse [17] a un examen, **she's sitting her driving test on Thursday** se presenta al examen de conducir el jueves
- **to sit down** sentarse [29]; **he sat down on a chair** se sentó en una silla, **do sit down** siéntate

site NOUN ❶ **a building site** una obra ❷ **a camping site** un camping

sitting room NOUN salón MASC

situation NOUN situación FEM

six NUMBER seis MASC; **Tom's six** Tom tiene seis años, **it's six o'clock** son las seis

sixteen NUMBER dieciséis MASC; **Hannah's sixteen** Hannah tiene dieciséis años

sixth NOUN ❶ *(fraction)* **a sixth** una sexta parte ❷ **the sixth of July** el seis de julio

sixth ADJECTIVE sexto/sexta; **on the sixth floor** en el sexto piso

sixties PLURAL NOUN **the sixties** los años sesenta, **in the sixties** en los años sesenta

sixty NUMBER **sesenta** MASC; **she's sixty** tiene sesenta años, **sixty-five** sesenta y cinco

size NOUN ❶ **tamaño** MASC; **it depends on the size of the house** depende del tamaño de la casa ❷ (precise measurements) **medidas** FEM PLURAL; **what size is the window?** ¿qué medidas tiene la ventana? ❸ (in clothes) **talla** FEM; **what size do you take?** ¿qué talla usas? ❹ (of shoes) **número** MASC; **I take a size thirty-eight** calzo el número treinta y ocho

skate NOUN ❶ **an ice skate** un patín de hielo ❷ **a roller skate** un patín de ruedas

skate VERB ❶ (ice-skate) **hacer** [7] **patinaje sobre hielo** ❷ (roller-skate) **hacer** [7] **patinaje sobre ruedas**

skateboard NOUN **monopatín** MASC

skateboarding NOUN **to go skateboarding** patinar [17] con el monopatín

skater NOUN **patinador** MASC, **patinadora** FEM

skating NOUN ❶ (ice) **patinaje** (MASC) **sobre hielo**; **to go skating** ir [8] a patinar sobre hielo ❷ **roller-skating** patinaje (MASC) sobre ruedas, **to go roller-skating** ir [8] a patinar sobre ruedas

skating rink NOUN **pista** (FEM) **de patinaje**

sketch NOUN ❶ (drawing) **boceto** MASC ❷ (comedy routine) **sketch** MASC

ski NOUN **esquí** MASC

ski VERB **esquiar** [32]

ski boot NOUN **bota** (FEM) **de esquí**

skid VERB **derrapar** [17]; **the car skidded** el coche derrapó

skier NOUN **esquiador** MASC, **esquiadora** FEM

skiing NOUN **esquí** MASC; **to go skiing** ir [8] a esquiar

skilful NOUN **habilidoso/habilidosa**

ski lift NOUN **telesquí** MASC

skill NOUN **habilidad** FEM; **it's not one of my skills** no es una de mis habilidades

skimmed milk NOUN **leche** (FEM) **desnatada**

skin NOUN **piel** FEM

skinhead NOUN **cabeza** (MASC) **rapada, cabeza** (FEM) **rapada**

skinny ADJECTIVE **flaco/flaca**

skip NOUN (for rubbish) **contenedor** MASC

skip VERB ❶ **saltarse** [17] (a meal, part of a book); **I skipped a few chapters** me salté algunos capítulos ❷ **to skip a lesson** hacer [7] pellas de una clase (informal)

ski pants NOUN **pantalones** (MASC PLURAL) **de esquí**

skipping rope NOUN **comba** FEM

skirt NOUN **falda** FEM; **a long skirt** una falda larga, **a straight skirt** una falda de tubo, **a mini-skirt** una minifalda

ski suit NOUN **traje** (MASC) **de esquí**

sky *NOUN* **cielo** *MASC*

skyscraper *NOUN* **rascacielos** *MASC* *(does not change in the plural)*

slam *VERB* **cerrar** [29] **de un portazo**; **she slammed the door** cerró la puerta de un portazo

slang *NOUN* **argot** *MASC*

slap *NOUN* ❶ *(on the face)* **bofetada** *FEM* ❷ *(on the leg, bottom)* **azote** *MASC*

slap *VERB* **to slap somebody** *(on the face)* **dar** [4] **una bofetada a alguien**, *(on the leg or bottom)* **dar** [4] **un azote a alguien**

slate *NOUN* **pizarra** *FEM*

slave *NOUN* **esclavo** *MASC*, **esclava** *FEM*

sledge *NOUN* **trineo** *MASC*

sledging *NOUN* **to go sledging ir** [8] **en trineo**

sleep *NOUN* **sueño** *MASC*; **six hours' sleep** seis horas de sueño, **I had a good sleep** dormí bien, **to go to sleep** dormirse [51]

sleep *VERB* **dormir** [51]; **she's sleeping** está durmiendo

sleeping bag *NOUN* **saco** *(MASC)* **de dormir**

sleeping pill *NOUN* **somnífero** *MASC*

sleepy *ADJECTIVE* **to be sleepy tener** [9] **sueño**, **I feel sleepy** tengo sueño, **I was getting sleepy** me estaba entrando sueño

sleeve *NOUN* **manga** *FEM*; **a long-sleeved jumper** un jersey de manga larga, **a short-sleeved shirt** una camisa de manga corta, **to roll up your sleeves** arremangarse [28]

slice *NOUN* ❶ *(of bread, cheese)* **rebanada** *FEM* ❷ *(of meat)* **loncha** *FEM*; **a slice of ham** una loncha de jamón ❸ *(of cake)* **trozo** *MASC* ❹ *(a round slice: of lemon, tomato, etc.)* **rodaja** *FEM*

slice *VERB* **to slice something** **cortar** [17] **algo en rebanadas** *(or 'lonchas', 'trozos', etc, depending on what you are slicing: see noun translations above)*

slide *NOUN* ❶ *(photo)* **diapositiva** *FEM* ❷ *(hairslide)* **pasador** *MASC* ❸ *(for sliding down)* **tobogán** *MASC*

slight *ADJECTIVE* **ligero/ligera**; **there's a slight problem** hay un pequeño problema

slightly *ADVERB* **ligeramente**

slim *ADJECTIVE* **delgado/delgada**

slim *VERB* **adelgazar** [22]; **I'm slimming** estoy adelgazando

slip *NOUN* ❶ *(mistake)* **error** *MASC* ❷ *(petticoat)* **combinación** *FEM*

slip *VERB* ❶ *(slide)* **resbalarse** [17] ❷ **the jar slipped out of my hands** el frasco se me resbaló de las manos ❸ **it slipped my mind** se me olvidó completamente

slipper *NOUN* **zapatilla** *FEM*

slippery *ADJECTIVE* **resbaladizo/ resbaladiza**

slope *NOUN* **cuesta** *FEM*

slow *ADJECTIVE* ❶ **lento/lenta**; **the service is a bit slow** el servicio es un poco lento ❷ **my watch is slow** mi reloj está atrasado
• **to slow down reducir** [60] **la velocidad** *(a car)*

slowly ADVERB **despacio**; **he got up slowly** se levantó despacio, **can you speak more slowly, please?** ¿puedes hablar más despacio, por favor?

slum NOUN **barrio** (MASC) **bajo**

smack NOUN ❶ (on the face) **bofetada** FEM ❷ (on the leg or bottom) **azote** MASC

smack VERB **to smack somebody** (on the face) dar [4] una bofetada a alguien, (on the leg or bottom) dar [4] un azote a alguien

small ADJECTIVE **pequeño/pequeña**; **a small dog** un perro pequeño

smart ADJECTIVE ❶ (well-dressed, posh) **elegante**; **a smart restaurant** un restaurante elegante ❷ (clever) **inteligente**

smash VERB **romper** [40]; **they smashed the window** rompieron la ventana

smashing ADJECTIVE **fantástico/ fantástica**

smell NOUN **olor** MASC; **a nasty smell** un mal olor, **there's a smell of burning** huele a quemado

smell VERB ❶ **oler** [39]; **I can't smell anything** no huelo nada, **I can smell lavender** huele a lavanda ❷ (smell bad) **oler** [39] **mal**; **the drains smell** las alcantarillas huelen mal

smelly ADJECTIVE **apestoso/apestosa**

smile NOUN **sonrisa** FEM

smile VERB **sonreír** [61]

smoke NOUN **humo** MASC

smoke VERB **fumar** [17]; **she doesn't smoke** no fuma, **he smokes a pipe** fuma en pipa

smoked ADJECTIVE **ahumado/ ahumada**; **smoked salmon** salmón ahumado

smoker NOUN **fumador** MASC, **fumadora** FEM

smoking NOUN '**no smoking**' '**prohibido fumar**', **to give up smoking** dejar [17] de fumar

smooth ADJECTIVE ❶ (stone or surface) **liso/lisa**; **a smooth surface** una superficie lisa ❷ (skin) **suave**

SMS NOUN **SMS** MASC; **an SMS message** un mensaje SMS

smuggle VERB **to smuggle something** pasar [17] algo de contrabando

smuggler NOUN ❶ **contrabandista** MASC & FEM ❷ **a drugs smuggler** un/ una traficante de drogas

smuggling NOUN ❶ **contrabando** MASC ❷ **drugs smuggling** tráfico (MASC) de drogas, **arms smuggling** tráfico (MASC) de armas

snack NOUN **tentempié** MASC

snack bar NOUN **cafetería** FEM, **bocatería** FEM

snail NOUN **caracol** MASC

snake NOUN **serpiente** FEM

snap VERB ❶ (break) **romperse** [40] ❷ **to snap your fingers** chasquear [17] los dedos

snatch VERB ❶ **arrebatar** [17]; **to snatch something from somebody** arrebatar algo a alguien, **he snatched my book** me arrebató el libro ❷ (steal) **robar** [17]; **she had**

sneak | **social security**

her bag snatched le robaron el bolso

sneak VERB **to sneak in** entrar [17] a escondidas, **to sneak out** salir [63] a escondidas, **he sneaked up on me** se acercó a mí sin que yo me diese cuenta

sneeze NOUN estornudo MASC

sneeze VERB estornudar [17]

sniff VERB olisquear [17]

snob NOUN esnob MASC & FEM

snobbery NOUN esnobismo MASC

snooker NOUN snooker MASC; **to play snooker** jugar [27] al snooker

snore VERB roncar [31]

snow NOUN nieve FEM

snow VERB nevar [29]; **it's snowing** está nevando, **it's going to snow** va a nevar

snowball NOUN bola (FEM) de nieve

snow drift NOUN montón (MASC) de nieve

snowman NOUN muñeco (MASC) de nieve

snowy ADJECTIVE **it was very snowy** hubo mucha nieve

so CONJUNCTION, ADVERB ❶ tan; **he's so lazy** es tan vago, **the coffee's so hot I can't drink it** este café está tan caliente que no puedo beberlo ❷ **not so** no tan, **our house is like yours, but not so big** nuestra casa es parecida a la tuya pero no tan grande ❸ **so much** (after a verb), **I hate it so much!** ¡lo odio tanto! ❹ **so much** (before a noun) tanto/tanta, **I have so much**

work to do tengo tanto trabajo que hacer ❺ **so many** (before a noun) tantos/tantas, **we've got so many problems** tenemos tantos problemas ❻ (therefore) así que; **he got up late so he missed his train** se levantó tarde así que perdió el tren ❼ (starting a sentence: there is no direct translation) **so what's your name?** ¿y cómo te llamas?, **so what shall we do?** ¿y entonces qué hacemos?, **so what?** ¿y qué? ❽ **so do I, so did I** yo también, '**I live in Leeds' – 'so do I'** 'vivo en Leeds' – 'yo también', **so am I, so was I** yo también, **so do we, so did we** nosotros también, '**I have a headache' – 'so do I'** 'me duele la cabeza' – 'a mí también', '**I like Miró' – 'so do I'** 'me gusta Miró' – 'a mí tambien' ❾ **I think so** creo que sí, **I hope so** espero que sí

soap NOUN ❶ jabón MASC; **a cake of soap** una pastilla de jabón ❷ (soap opera: on TV) telenovela FEM

soap powder NOUN jabón (MASC) en polvo

sober ADJECTIVE **to be sober** estar [2] sobrio/sobria

soccer NOUN fútbol MASC; **to play soccer** jugar [27] al fútbol

social ADJECTIVE social

socialism NOUN socialismo MASC

socialist NOUN socialista MASC & FEM

socialist ADJECTIVE socialista

social security NOUN ❶ asistencia (FEM) social; **to be on social security** recibir [19] asistencia social ❷ **the social security** (the system) la seguridad social

social worker NOUN asistente (MASC & FEM) social; **she's a social worker** es asistente social

society NOUN sociedad FEM

sociology NOUN sociología FEM

sock NOUN calcetín MASC; **a pair of socks** un par de calcetines

sofa NOUN sofá MASC

sofa bed NOUN sofá-cama MASC

soft ADJECTIVE suave
• **to have a soft spot for somebody** tener [9] debilidad por alguien

soft drink NOUN refresco MASC

soft toy NOUN muñeco (MASC) de peluche

software NOUN software MASC

soil NOUN tierra FEM

solar energy NOUN energía (FEM) solar

soldier NOUN soldado MASC & FEM

solicitor NOUN abogado MASC, abogada FEM; **she's a solicitor** es abogada

solid ADJECTIVE ❶ macizo/maciza; **a table made of solid pine** una mesa de pino macizo, **a solid gold ring** un anillo de oro macizo, **solid silver** plata maciza ❷ (not flimsy) sólido/sólida; **a solid structure** una estructura sólida

solo NOUN solo MASC; **a guitar solo** un solo de guitarra

solo ADJECTIVE, ADVERB en solitario; **a solo album** un álbum en solitario, **to play solo** tocar [31] en solitario

soloist NOUN solista MASC & FEM

some DETERMINER, ADVERB ❶ (with a singular noun) un poco de; **would you like some butter?** ¿quieres un poco de mantequilla?, **may I have some salad?** ¿puedo tomar un poco de ensalada?, **can you lend me some money?** ¿puedes prestarme un poco de dinero? ❷ (with a plural noun) unos/unas; **I've bought some apples** he comprado unas manzanas, **we picked some flowers** cogimos unas flores ❸ (referring to something that has already been mentioned, 'some' is not translated) **'would you like butter?' – 'thanks, I've got some'** ¿quieres mantequilla?' – 'gracias ya tengo', **he's eaten some of it** ya ha comido un poco ❹ (certain) algunos/ algunas; **some people think he's wrong** algunas personas piensan que él no tiene razón ❺ **some day** algún día

somebody, someone PRONOUN alguien; **there's somebody in the garden** hay alguien en el jardín

somehow ADVERB ❶ de alguna forma; **I've got to finish this essay somehow** tengo que terminar esta composición de alguna forma ❷ **I somehow think they won't come** no sé por qué, pero creo que no van a venir

somersault NOUN voltereta FEM

something PRONOUN algo; **I've got something to tell you** tengo algo que decirte, **something pretty** algo bonito, **something interesting** algo interesante, **there's something wrong** algo va mal, **their house is really something!** ¡su casa es increíble!, **a guy called Colin something or other** un tipo llamado Colin, o algo así

sometime ADVERB un día de estos; **give me a ring sometime** llámame un día de estos, **I'll ring you sometime next week** te llamaré un día de la semana que viene

sometimes ADVERB a veces; **I sometimes take the train** a veces cojo el tren

somewhere ADVERB en algún sitio; **I've put my bag down somewhere** he puesto mi bolso en algún sitio, **I've met you somewhere before** te he conocido antes en algún sitio

son NOUN hijo MASC

song NOUN canción FEM

son-in-law NOUN yerno MASC

soon ADVERB ❶ pronto; **it will soon be the holidays** pronto llegarán las vacaciones, **see you soon!** ¡hasta pronto!, **it's too soon** es demasiado pronto ❷ **as soon as** tan pronto como, **as soon as she arrives** tan pronto como llegue, **as soon as possible** tan pronto como sea posible

sooner ADVERB ❶ antes; **we should have started sooner** deberíamos haber empezado antes ❷ **I'd sooner wait** prefiero esperar
• **sooner or later** tarde o temprano

soprano NOUN soprano MASC & FEM

sore NOUN llaga FEM

sore ADJECTIVE **he has a sore leg** le duele la pierna, **my arm's sore** me duele el brazo
• **it's a sore point** es un tema delicado

sorry ADJECTIVE ❶ **I'm really sorry** lo siento mucho, **I'm sorry I forgot your birthday** siento haberme olvidado de tu cumpleaños

❷ **sorry to disturb you** perdona que te moleste ❸ **sorry!** ¡perdón! ❹ **sorry?** ¿cómo? ❺ **to feel sorry for somebody** compadecer [35] a alguien ❻ **to say you're sorry** pedir [57] perdón

sort NOUN tipo MASC; **what sort of music do you like?** ¿qué tipo de música te gusta?, **all sorts of** todo tipo de, **for all sorts of reasons** por todo tipo de razones
• **to sort something out** ❶ ordenar [17] algo (room, desk, papers, possessions); **I must sort out my room tonight** tengo que ordenar mi habitación esta noche ❷ solucionar [17] (problem, arrangement); **Liz is sorting it out** Liz se está ocupando de ello

soul NOUN ❶ alma FEM (even though 'alma' is feminine, it takes 'el' and 'un' in the singular); **the soul** el alma ❷ (music) soul MASC

sound NOUN ❶ (noise) ruido MASC; **the sound of voices** el ruido de voces ❷ (volume) volumen MASC; **to turn down the sound** bajar el volumen

sound VERB **it sounds easy** parece fácil, **it sounds as if she's happy** parece que está contenta

sound asleep ADJECTIVE profundamente dormido/dormida

sound effect NOUN efecto (MASC) sonoro

soundtrack NOUN banda (FEM) sonora

soup NOUN ❶ (clear) consomé MASC ❷ (thick) sopa FEM ❸ (pureed) crema FEM; **mushroom soup** crema de champiñones

soup plate NOUN plato (MASC) de sopa

soup spoon NOUN cuchara (FEM) de sopera

sour ADJECTIVE ❶ (taste) agrio/agria ❷ **the milk's gone sour** la leche se ha cortado

south NOUN sur MASC; **in the south** en el sur

south ADJECTIVE, ADVERB sur (never changes); **the south side** la parte sur, **a south wind** un viento del sur, **south of Paris** al sur de París

South Africa NOUN Sudáfrica FEM

South America NOUN Sudamérica FEM

South American NOUN suramericano MASC, suramericana FEM

South American ADJECTIVE suramericano/suramericana

southeast NOUN sureste MASC

southeast ADJECTIVE sureste (never changes); **in southeast England** en el sureste de Inglaterra

South Pole NOUN Polo (MASC) Sur

southwest NOUN suroeste MASC

southwest ADJECTIVE suroeste (never changes); **in southwest England** en el suroeste de Inglaterra

souvenir NOUN recuerdo MASC

soya NOUN soja FEM

space NOUN ❶ (room) sitio MASC; **is there enough space?** ¿hay sitio suficiente?, **there's enough space for two** hay sitio suficiente para dos ❷ (gap) espacio MASC; **leave a space** deja un espacio ❸ (outer space) espacio MASC; **in space** en el espacio

spacecraft NOUN nave (FEM) espacial

spade NOUN ❶ pala FEM ❷ (in cards) pica FEM; **the queen of spades** la reina de picas

spaghetti NOUN espaguetis MASC PLURAL

Spain NOUN España FEM

Spaniard NOUN español MASC, española FEM

spaniel NOUN spaniel MASC

Spanish NOUN ❶ (language) español MASC; **to speak Spanish** hablar [17] español, **say it in Spanish** dilo en español, **I'm learning Spanish** estoy aprendiendo español ❷ **the Spanish** (people) los españoles MASC PLURAL

Spanish ADJECTIVE ❶ español/española; **Pedro's Spanish** Pedro es español ❷ de español (a teacher or lesson); **the Spanish class** la clase de español

spanner NOUN llave (FEM) inglesa

spare ADJECTIVE ❶ (part, battery) de repuesto; **a spare battery** una batería de repuesto ❷ (extra) de más; **we have a spare ticket** tenemos una entrada de más

spare VERB **I can't spare the time** no tengo tiempo para eso, **can you spare a moment?** ¿tienes un momento libre?, **I don't have any money to spare** no me sobra el dinero

spare room NOUN habitación (FEM) de invitados

spare time NOUN tiempo (MASC) libre; **in my spare time** en mi tiempo libre

spare wheel NOUN rueda (FEM) de repuesto

sparrow NOUN gorrión MASC

speak VERB ❶ hablar [17]; **do you speak Spanish?** ¿hablas español?, **spoken Spanish** el español hablado, 'Spanish spoken here' 'aquí se habla español' ❷ **to speak to somebody** hablar [17] con alguien, **she's speaking to Mike** está hablando con Mike, **I've never spoken to her** nunca he hablado con ella, **I'll speak to him about it** hablaré sobre ello con él ❸ **who's speaking?** (on the phone) ¿quién es?, **Mike speaking** soy Mike

speaker NOUN ❶ (on a music system) altavoz MASC ❷ (at a public lecture) conferenciante MASC & FEM ❸ (of a language) **a Spanish speaker** un hablante de español, **an English speaker** un hablante de inglés

spear NOUN lanza FEM

special ADJECTIVE especial

specialist NOUN especialista MASC & FEM

specialize VERB **to specialize in** especializarse [22] en

specially ADVERB especialmente; **not specially** no especialmente, **the poems have been specially chosen for small children** los poemas han sido escogidos especialmente para niños pequeños, **I came specially in order to see you** vine especialmente para verte

spectacles NOUN gafas FEM PLURAL

spectacular ADJECTIVE espectacular

spectator NOUN espectador MASC, espectadora FEM

speech NOUN discurso MASC; **to make a speech** dar [4] un discurso

speechless ADJECTIVE ❶ sin habla; **I was speechless** me quedé sin habla ❷ **to be speechless with rage** quedarse [17] mudo de cólera

speed NOUN velocidad FEM; **what speed was he doing?** ¿a qué velocidad iba?, **a twelve-speed bike** una bici de doce marchas
• **to speed up** acelerar [17]

speeding NOUN **he was fined for speeding** le multaron por exceso de velocidad

speed limit NOUN límite (MASC) de velocidad

spell NOUN ❶ (of time) periodo MASC ❷ (talking about weather) **a cold spell** una ola de frío, **sunny spells** intervalos de sol

spell VERB ❶ (in writing) escribir [52]; **how do you spell it?** ¿cómo se escribe?, **how do you spell your surname?** ¿cómo se escribe tu apellido? ❷ (out loud) deletrear [17]; **shall I spell it for you?** ¿se lo deletreo?

spelling NOUN ortografía FEM; **a spelling mistake** una falta de ortografía

spelling checker NOUN corrector (MASC) ortográfico

spend VERB ❶ gastar [17] (money); **I've spent all my money** me he gastado todo el dinero ❷ pasar [17] (time); **we spent three days**

in Barcelona pasamos tres días en Barcelona, **she spends her time writing letters** pasa el tiempo escribiendo cartas

spice NOUN **especia** FEM

spicy ADJECTIVE **picante**; **I don't like spicy food** no me gustan los platos picantes

spider NOUN **araña** FEM

spill VERB **derramar** [17]; **I've spilled my wine on the carpet** he derramado vino en la alfombra

spinach NOUN **espinacas** FEM PLURAL; **do you like spinach?** ¿te gustan las espinacas?

spire NOUN **aguja** FEM

spirit NOUN ❶ (energy) **brío** MASC ❷ **to get into the spirit of the occasion** entrar [17] en el ambiente

spirits NOUN ❶ (alcohol) **bebidas** (FEM PLURAL) **alcohólicas** ❷ **to be in good spirits** estar [2] de buen humor

spit VERB **escupir** [19]; **to spit something out** escupir algo

spite NOUN ❶ **in spite of** a pesar de, **we decided to go in spite of the rain** decidimos ir a pesar de la lluvia ❷ (nastiness) **maldad** FEM; **to do something out of spite** hacer [7] algo por maldad

spiteful ADJECTIVE ❶ (person) **malo/ mala** ❷ (comment) **malicioso/ maliciosa**

splash NOUN ❶ (noise) **we heard a splash** oímos el ruido de algo que caía al agua ❷ **a splash of colour** un toque de color

splash VERB **salpicar** [31]

splendid ADJECTIVE **espléndido/ espléndida**

splinter NOUN **astilla** FEM

split VERB ❶ (with an axe or a knife) **partir** [19]; **to split a piece of wood** partir un trozo de madera ❷ (come apart) **rajarse** [17]; **the lining has split** el forro se ha rajado ❸ (divide up) **dividirse** [19]; **they split the money between them** se dividieron el dinero entre ellos
• **to split up** ❶ (a married couple or group) **separarse** [17] ❷ **she's split up with her boyfriend** ha roto con su novio

spoil VERB ❶ **arruinar** [17]; **it completely spoiled the evening** arruinó la tarde completamente, **to spoil the surprise** arruinar la sorpresa ❷ **malcriar** [32] (a child)

spoiled ADJECTIVE **malcriado/ malcriada**; **a spoiled child** un niño malcriado

spoilsport NOUN **aguafiestas** MASC & FEM (does not change in the plural)

spokesperson NOUN **portavoz** MASC & FEM

sponge NOUN **esponja** FEM

sponge cake NOUN **bizcocho** MASC

sponsor NOUN **patrocinador** MASC, **patrocinadora** FEM

sponsor VERB **patrocinar** [17]

spooky ADJECTIVE **espeluznante**

spoon NOUN **cuchara** FEM; **a soup spoon** una cuchara sopera, **a teaspoon** una cucharilla

spoonful NOUN (large) **cucharada** FEM, (small) **cucharadita** FEM

sport NOUN deporte MASC; **to be good at sport** tener [9] facilidad para los deportes, **my favourite sport** mi deporte favorito

sports bag NOUN bolsa (FEM) de deportes

sports car NOUN coche (MASC) deportivo

sports centre NOUN polideportivo MASC

sports club NOUN club (MASC) deportivo

sportsman NOUN deportista MASC

sportswear NOUN ropa (FEM) de deporte

sportswoman NOUN deportista FEM

spot NOUN ❶ (in fabric) lunar MASC; **a red tie with black spots** una corbata roja con lunares negros ❷ (on your skin) grano MASC; **I've got spots** tengo granos, **to be covered in spots** estar [2] cubierto de granos ❸ (stain) mancha FEM ❹ (place) sitio MASC; **a beautiful spot** un sitio precioso ❺ (spotlight) foco MASC (in the home) luz (FEM) direccional

spot VERB ❶ divisar [17] (a person or object); **I spotted her in the crowd** la divisé entre la multitud ❷ encontrar [24] (an error)

spotlight NOUN ❶ foco MASC ❷ (in the home) luz (FEM) direccional

spotty ADJECTIVE (pimply) lleno de granos/llena de granos

sprain NOUN esguince MASC

sprain VERB **to sprain your ankle** hacerse [7] un esguince en el tobillo

spray NOUN (spray can) espray MASC

spread VERB ❶ (news or a disease) propagarse [28] ❷ extender [36] (butter, jam, cement, glue, etc)

spring NOUN ❶ (the season) primavera FEM; **in the spring** en primavera, **spring flowers** flores de primavera ❷ (made of metal) muelle MASC ❸ (providing water) manantial MASC

springtime NOUN primavera FEM; **in springtime** en primavera

spring water NOUN agua (FEM) de manantial

sprint NOUN esprint MASC

sprint VERB correr [18] a toda velocidad

sprout NOUN (Brussels sprout) col (FEM) de Bruselas

spy NOUN espía MASC & FEM

spy VERB **to spy on somebody** espiar [32] a alguien

spying NOUN espionaje MASC

square NOUN ❶ (shape) cuadrado MASC ❷ (in a town or village) plaza FEM; **the village square** la plaza del pueblo
• **to go back to square one** volver [45] a empezar de cero

square ADJECTIVE cuadrado/cuadrada; **a square box** una caja cuadrada, **three square metres** tres metros cuadrados, **the room is four metres square** la habitación tiene cuatro metros cuadrados

squash NOUN ❶ (drink) lemon squash limonada FEM, **orange squash** naranjada FEM ❷ (sport) squash MASC; **to play squash** jugar [27] al squash

squeak VERB ❶ (door, hinge) chirriar [32] ❷ (person, animal) chillar [17]

squeeze VERB ❶ apretar [29] (somebody's arm, hand or a toothpaste tube) ❷ exprimir [19] (a lemon or an orange)

squid NOUN calamar MASC

squirrel NOUN ardilla FEM

stab VERB apuñalar [17]

stable NOUN cuadra FEM

stable ADJECTIVE estable

stack NOUN ❶ (pile) montón MASC ❷ stacks of montones de, she's got stacks of CDs tiene montones de compactos

stadium NOUN estadio MASC

staff NOUN ❶ (of a company) personal MASC ❷ (in a school) profesorado MASC

stage NOUN ❶ (for a performance) escenario MASC; on stage en el escenario ❷ (phase) etapa FEM; the earlier stages of the project las primeras etapas del proyecto ❸ at this stage it's hard to know a estas alturas es difícil saberlo

stain NOUN mancha FEM

stain VERB manchar [17]

stainless steel NOUN acero (MASC) inoxidable; a stainless steel sink un fregadero de acero inoxidable

stair NOUN ❶ (step) escalón MASC ❷ stairs escaleras FEM PLURAL, I met her on the stairs me la encontré en las escaleras

staircase NOUN escaleras FEM PLURAL

stale ADJECTIVE (bread) correoso/ correosa

stalemate NOUN (in chess) tablas FEM PLURAL

stall NOUN ❶ (at a market or fair) puesto MASC ❷ the stalls (in a theatre) patio (MASC) de butacas

stamp NOUN sello MASC

stamp VERB ❶ poner [11] sello(s) a (a letter) ❷ to stamp your foot dar [4] una patada en el suelo

stamp album NOUN álbum (MASC) de sellos

stamp collection NOUN colección (FEM) de sellos

stand VERB ❶ estar [2] de pie; several people were standing varias personas estaban de pie ❷ (when you say somebody is standing somewhere, 'standing' is not usually translated) we were standing outside the cinema estábamos delante del cine, I'm standing here waiting for you estoy aquí esperándote ❸ to stand on something pisar [17] algo ❹ (bear) soportar [17]; I can't stand her no la soporto, I can't stand waiting no soporto esperar
- to stand for something (be short for) significar [31]; what does 'plc' stand for? ¿qué significa 'plc'?
- stand up levantarse [17]; everybody stood up todo el mundo se levantó

standard NOUN nivel MASC; the standard of living el nivel de vida

standard ADJECTIVE estándar; the standard price el precio estándar

Standard grades *NOUN PLURAL*
(You can explain Standard grades as follows: Son exámenes que se realizan alrededor de los 16 años y pueden abarcar hasta 7 asignaturas. Se califican desde 1 (nota máxima) hasta 7 (por haber terminado el curso). Muchos alumnos continúan estudiando para los Highers y Advanced Highers después de hacer los Standard grades.) ▸ SEE **Highers**

stands *NOUN (in a stadium)* tribuna *FEM*

staple *NOUN* grapa *FEM*

staple *VERB* grapar [17]; **to staple the pages together** grapar las hojas

stapler *NOUN* grapadora *FEM*

star *NOUN (in the sky or rock star, etc)* estrella *FEM*; **he's a film star** es una estrella de cine

star *VERB* **to star in a film** protagonizar [22] una película

stare *VERB* mirar [17] fijamente; **he was staring at me** me estaba mirando fijamente, **what are you staring at?** ¿qué miras?

star sign *NOUN* signo *(MASC)* del zodíaco; **what star sign are you?** ¿de qué signo eres?

start *NOUN* ❶ principio *MASC*; **at the start** al principio, **at the start of the book** al principio del libro, **from the start** desde el principio, **we knew from the start that it was dangerous** sabíamos desde el principio que era peligroso ❷ **to make a start on something** empezar [25] algo, **I've made a start on my homework** he empezado mis deberes ❸ *(of a race)* salida *FEM*

start *VERB* ❶ empezar [25]; **the film starts at eight** la película empieza a las ocho, **I've started the book** he empezado el libro ❷ **to start doing** empezar [25] a hacer, **I've started learning Spanish** he empezado a aprender español ❸ **to start a business** montar [17] un negocio ❹ **to start a car** arrancar [31] un coche, **she started the car** arrancó el coche, **the car wouldn't start** el coche no arrancaba

starter *NOUN (in a meal)* entrante *MASC*; **what would you like as a starter?** ¿qué quieres de entrante?

starve *VERB* morirse [55] de hambre; **I'm starving!** ¡me muero de hambre!

state *NOUN* ❶ estado *MASC*; **the house is in a very bad state** la casa está en muy mal estado ❷ *(administrative)* estado *MASC*; **the state** el estado ❸ **the States** (los) Estados Unidos, **they live in the States** viven en Estados Unidos

state *VERB* ❶ declarar [17] *(intention, opinion)* ❷ indicar [31] *(address, income, occupation, reason, etc)*

statement *NOUN* declaración *FEM*

station *NOUN* ❶ estación *FEM*; **the railway station** la estación de trenes, **the bus station** la estación de autobuses ❷ **the police station** la comisaría ❸ **a radio station** una emisora de radio, **a TV station** un canal de televisión

stationary *ADJECTIVE* estacionario/estacionaria

stationer's *NOUN* papelería *FEM*

stationery *NOUN* artículos *(MASC PLURAL)* de papelería

statistics NOUN ❶ (subject) estadística FEM ❷ the statistics (figures) las estadísticas

statue NOUN estatua FEM

status NOUN estatus MASC

stay NOUN estancia FEM; our stay in Paris nuestra estancia en París, enjoy your stay! ¡que disfruten de su estancia!

stay VERB ❶ quedarse [17]; I'll stay here me quedaré aquí, how long are you staying? ¿cuánto tiempo te quedas? ❷ (with time) we're going to stay in Berlin for three days vamos a pasar tres días en Berlín ❸ (at somebody's house) to stay with somebody quedarse [17] con alguien, I'm going to stay with my sister this weekend me voy a quedar con mi hermana este fin de semana ❹ (be temporarily lodged) hospedarse [17]; where are you staying? ¿dónde te hospedas?
• to stay in no salir [63]; I'm staying in tonight esta noche no salgo

steady ADJECTIVE ❶ estable; a steady job un trabajo estable ❷ constante; a steady increase un incremento constante ❸ (hand, voice) firme ❹ to hold something steady sostener [9] algo firmemente

steak NOUN filete MASC; steak and chips filete con patatas fritas

steal VERB robar [17]

steam NOUN vapor MASC

steam engine NOUN locomotora (FEM) de vapor

steam iron NOUN plancha (FEM) a vapor

steel NOUN acero MASC

steep ADJECTIVE empinado/empinada; a steep slope una cuesta empinada

steeple NOUN ❶ (spire) aguja FEM ❷ (bell tower) campanario MASC

steering wheel NOUN volante MASC

step NOUN ❶ paso MASC; to take a step forwards dar [4] un paso hacia adelante ❷ (stair) escalón MASC; 'mind the step' 'cuidado con el escalón'
• to step back retroceder [18]
• to step forward avanzar [22]
• to step into entrar [17] en (a lift)

stepbrother NOUN hermanastro MASC

stepdaughter NOUN hijastra FEM

stepfather NOUN padrastro MASC

stepladder NOUN escalera (FEM) de mano

stepmother NOUN madrastra FEM

stepsister NOUN hermanastra FEM

stepson NOUN hijastro MASC

stereo NOUN estéreo MASC

sterling NOUN libra (FEM) esterlina; in sterling en libras esterlinas

stew NOUN estofado MASC

steward NOUN camarero MASC

stewardess NOUN camarera FEM

stick NOUN ❶ palo MASC ❷ a walking stick un bastón ❸ a hockey stick un palo de hockey

stick VERB ❶ (with glue) pegar [28] ❷ (put) poner [11]; stick them on my desk ponlos en mi mesa

sticker NOUN pegatina FEM

sticky ADJECTIVE ❶ pegajoso/pegajosa; my hands are sticky tengo las manos pegajosas ❷ adhesivo/adhesiva; sticky paper papel (MASC) adhesivo

sticky tape NOUN cinta (FEM) adhesiva

stiff ADJECTIVE to feel stiff estar [2] entumecido, to have stiff legs tener [9] las piernas entumecidas, to have a stiff neck tener [9] tortícolis
- to be bored stiff estar más aburrido que una ostra (literally: to be more bored than an oyster)
- to be scared stiff estar muerto de miedo (literally: to be dead from fear)

still ADJECTIVE ❶ quieto/quieta; sit still! ¡siéntate quieto!, keep still! ¡estate quieto! ❷ still mineral water agua (FEM) mineral sin gas

still ADVERB ❶ todavía, aún; do you still live in London? ¿vives todavía en Londres?, ¿vives aún en Londres?, I've still not finished todavía no he terminado, aún no he terminado, he's still working está trabajando todavía, there's still a lot of beer left todavía queda mucha cerveza ❷ better still todavía mejor, aún mejor

sting NOUN aguijón MASC; a wasp sting un aguijón de avispa

sting VERB picar [31]; I was stung by a bee me picó una abeja

stink NOUN peste FEM; what a stink! ¡qué peste!

stink VERB apestar [17]; it stinks of cigarette smoke in here aquí apesta a tabaco

stir VERB remover [38]

stitch NOUN ❶ (in sewing) puntada FEM ❷ (in knitting) punto MASC ❸ (surgical) punto (MASC) de sutura

stock NOUN ❶ (in a shop) estock MASC; to have something in stock tener [9] algo en estock ❷ (supply) reserva FEM; I always have a stock of pencils siempre tengo una reserva de lápices ❸ (for cooking) caldo MASC; chicken stock caldo de pollo

stock VERB (in a shop) vender [18]; they don't stock dictionaries no venden diccionarios

stock cube NOUN pastilla (FEM) de caldo

stock exchange NOUN bolsa (FEM) de valores

stocking NOUN media FEM (de liguero)

stomach NOUN estómago MASC

stomachache NOUN dolor (MASC) de estómago; to have stomachache tener [9] dolor de estómago

stone NOUN ❶ piedra FEM; a stone wall una pared de piedra, to throw a stone tirar [17] una piedra ❷ (in fruit) hueso MASC

stool NOUN taburete MASC

stop NOUN parada FEM; the bus stop la parada del autobús

stop VERB ❶ (person or vehicle) **parar** [17]; he stopped in front of the shop paró enfrente de la tienda, **does the train stop in Cordoba?** ¿para el tren en Córdoba?, **the music stopped** la música paró ❷ (engine or machine) **pararse** [17] ❸ to stop something/somebody **parar** [17] algo/a alguien, she stopped me in the street me paró en la calle ❹ to stop doing **dejar** [17] de hacer, he's stopped smoking ha dejado de fumar, she never stops asking questions nunca deja de hacer preguntas ❺ to stop somebody doing **impedir** [57] a alguien hacer, **there's nothing to stop you going on your own** nada te impide ir solo

stopwatch NOUN **cronómetro** MASC

store NOUN (shop) **tienda** FEM

store VERB ❶ **guardar** [17] ❷ (on a computer) **almacenar** [17]

storey NOUN **piso** MASC; a three-storey house una casa de tres pisos

stork NOUN **cigüeña** FEM

storm NOUN **tormenta** FEM; a snowstorm una tormenta de nieve, a rainstorm una tormenta de lluvia

stormy ADJECTIVE **de tormenta**

story NOUN ❶ **historia** FEM; to tell a story contar [24] una historia ❷ (tale) **cuento** MASC

stove NOUN (cooker) **cocina** FEM

straight ADJECTIVE ❶ **recto/recta**; a straight line una línea recta ❷ to have straight hair tener [9] el pelo liso ❸ (not crooked) **derecho/derecha**; the candle's not straight la vela no está derecha

straight ADVERB ❶ (in direction) **recto**; go straight ahead sigue todo recto ❷ (in time) **directamente**; he went straight to the doctor's fue directamente al médico ❸ straight away **en seguida**

strain VERB ❶ **colar** [17] (vegetables, rice) ❷ **hacerse** [7] un esguince en (a muscle)

strain NOUN **tensión** FEM

strange ADJECTIVE **extraño/extraña**; a strange situation una situación extraña

stranger NOUN **desconocido** MASC, **desconocida** FEM

strangle VERB **estrangular** [17]

strap NOUN ❶ (on camera or watch) **correa** FEM; a watchstrap una correa de reloj ❷ (on case or bag) **asa** FEM ❸ (on a garment) **tirante** MASC ❹ (on a shoe) **tira** FEM

straw NOUN **paja** FEM (both the material and for drinking with); a straw hat un sombrero de paja

strawberry NOUN **fresa** FEM; strawberry jam mermelada de fresa

stream NOUN (small river) **arroyo** MASC

street NOUN **calle** FEM; I met Simon in the street me encontré con Simon en la calle

streetlamp NOUN **farol** MASC

street map NOUN **plano** (MASC) de la ciudad

streetwise ADJECTIVE **avispado/avispada**

strength NOUN **fuerza** FEM

stress | **stuff**

stress NOUN ❶ tensión FEM ❷ (in a word) acento MASC

stress VERB (emphasize) recalcar [31]; **to stress the importance of something** recalcar la importancia de algo

stretch VERB (garment or shoes) dar [4] de sí; **this jumper has stretched** este jersey ha dado de sí

strict ADJECTIVE estricto/estricta

strike NOUN huelga FEM; **to go on strike** ponerse [11] en huelga, **to be on strike** estar [2] en huelga

strike VERB ❶ (hit) golpear [17] (a person) ❷ (clock) dar [4]; **the clock struck six** el reloj dio las seis ❸ (go on strike) ponerse [11] en huelga

striker NOUN ❶ (in football) delantero MASC, delantera FEM ❷ (person on strike) huelguista MASC & FEM

string NOUN ❶ (for tying) cordel MASC ❷ (for a musical instrument) cuerda FEM

strip NOUN tira FEM

strip VERB (undress) desnudarse [17]

strip cartoon NOUN tira (FEM) cómica

stripe NOUN raya FEM

striped ADJECTIVE de rayas

stroke NOUN ❶ (in swimming) brazada FEM ❷ (medical) derrame (MASC) cerebral; **to have a stroke** sufrir [19] un derrame cerebral
• **a stroke of luck** un golpe de suerte

stroke VERB acariciar [17]

strong ADJECTIVE ❶ (person, drink, smell, taste, or feeling) fuerte ❷ (material) resistente ❸ (accent) marcado

struggle NOUN ❶ lucha FEM; **the struggle for independence** la lucha por la independencia, **a power struggle** una lucha por el poder ❷ **it's been a struggle** ha sido muy difícil

struggle VERB ❶ (to obtain something) luchar [17]; **they have struggled to survive** han luchado para sobrevivir ❷ (physically, in order to escape or get something) forcejear [17] ❸ (have difficulty in doing) **I'm struggling to finish my homework** me está costando terminar mis deberes

stubborn ADJECTIVE terco/terca

stuck ADJECTIVE (jammed) atascado/atascada; **the drawer's stuck** el cajón está atascado

stud NOUN ❶ (on a belt or jacket) tachuela FEM ❷ (on a boot) taco MASC ❸ (earring) pendiente (MASC) de bolita

student NOUN estudiante MASC & FEM

studio NOUN estudio MASC

studio flat NOUN estudio MASC

study VERB estudiar [17]; **he's busy studying for his exams** está muy ocupado estudiando para los exámenes, **she's studying medicine** estudia medicina

stuff NOUN ❶ (things) cosas FEM PLURAL; **we can put all that stuff in the attic** podemos poner todas estas cosas en el ático, **you can leave your stuff at my house** puedes dejar tus cosas en mi casa ❷ (substance) cosa FEM

stuff VERB ❶ *(shove)* meter [18]; she stuffed some things into a suitcase metió algunas cosas en una maleta ❷ rellenar [17] *(chicken, turkey, vegetables)*; stuffed aubergines berenjenas rellenas

stuffing NOUN *(for cooking)* relleno MASC

stuffy ADJECTIVE viciado/viciada; it's very stuffy in here aquí dentro falta aire

stunned ADJECTIVE *(amazed)* atónito/atónita

stunning ADJECTIVE sensacional

stunt NOUN *(in a film)* escena *(FEM)* peligrosa

stupid ADJECTIVE estúpido/estúpida; a stupid man un hombre estúpido, that was really stupid eso fue una verdadera estupidez, to do something stupid hacer [7] una estupidez

stutter NOUN to have a stutter tartamudear [17]

stutter VERB tartamudear [17]

style NOUN ❶ estilo MASC; a style of living un estilo de vida, he has his own style tiene su propio estilo ❷ *(fashion)* moda *FEM*; it's the latest style es la última moda

subject NOUN ❶ tema MASC; the subject of my talk el tema de mi charla ❷ *(at school)* asignatura *FEM*; my favourite subject is biology mi asignatura favorita es la biología

submarine NOUN submarino MASC

subscription NOUN suscripción *FEM*; to take out a subscription to suscribirse [52] a

subsidy NOUN subvención *FEM*

substance NOUN sustancia *FEM*

substitute NOUN *(person)* sustituto MASC, sustituta *FEM*

substitute VERB sustituir [54]

subtitled ADJECTIVE *(film)* subtitulado/subtitulada

subtitles PLURAL NOUN subtítulos MASC PLURAL

subtract VERB restar [17]

suburb NOUN barrio *(MASC)* residencial de las afueras; a suburb of Edinburgh un barrio residencial de las afueras de Edimburgo, in the suburbs of London en los barrios residenciales de las afueras de Londres

subway NOUN *(underpass)* paso *(MASC)* subterráneo

succeed VERB ❶ lograr [17]; to succeed in doing lograr hacer, we've succeeded in contacting her hemos logrado contactar con ella ❷ *(be successful)* tener [9] éxito; to succeed in business tener éxito en los negocios

success NOUN éxito MASC; a great success un gran éxito

successful ADJECTIVE ❶ de éxito; he's a successful writer es un escritor de éxito ❷ to be successful in doing lograr [17] hacer

successfully ADVERB satisfactoriamente

such ADJECTIVE, ADVERB ❶ tan; they're such nice people! ¡son gente tan agradable!, I've had such a busy day! ¡he tenido un día tan ocupado!, it's such a long way está tan lejos, it's such a pity es una verdadera lástima ❷ such a lot of tantos/tantas, I've got such a lot of things to tell you! ¡tengo tantas cosas que contarte! ❸ such as como, in big cities such as Glasgow en ciudades grandes como Glasgow ❹ there's no such thing eso no existe

sudden ADJECTIVE repentino/repentina
• all of a sudden de repente

suddenly ADVERB de repente; he suddenly started to laugh de repente empezó a reír, suddenly the light went out de repente se apagó la luz, to die suddenly morir [55] de repente

suede NOUN ante MASC; a suede jacket una chaqueta de ante

suffer VERB sufrir [19]

sugar NOUN azúcar MASC & FEM; would you like sugar? ¿quieres azúcar?, brown sugar azúcar morena

suggest VERB sugerir [14]; he suggested I should speak to you about it sugirió que hablase contigo acerca de ello

suggestion NOUN sugerencia FEM; to make a suggestion hacer [7] una sugerencia

suicide NOUN suicidio MASC; to commit suicide suicidarse [17]

suit NOUN ❶ (man's) traje MASC ❷ (woman's) traje (MASC) de chaqueta

suitable ADJECTIVE ❶ adecuado/adecuada
a suitable hotel un hotel adecuado,

to be suitable for ser [1] adecuado para ❷ (clothing) apropiado/apropiada; I don't have any suitable shoes no tengo zapatos apropiados

suitcase NOUN maleta FEM

sulk VERB enfurruñarse [17]

sum NOUN ❶ cantidad FEM; a sum of money una cantidad de dinero, a large sum una cantidad grande ❷ (calculation) suma FEM
• to sum up resumir [19]

summarize VERB resumir [19]

summary NOUN resumen MASC

summer NOUN verano MASC; in summer en verano, summer clothes ropa (FEM) de verano, the summer holidays las vacaciones de verano

summertime NOUN verano MASC; in summertime en verano

summit NOUN cumbre FEM

sun NOUN sol MASC; in the sun en el sol

sunbathe VERB tomar [17] el sol

sunblock NOUN filtro (MASC) solar

sunburn NOUN quemadura (FEM) solar

sunburned ADJECTIVE ❶ (tanned) moreno/morena ❷ to get sunburned (burned) quemarse [17]

Sunday NOUN domingo MASC; on Sunday el domingo, I'm going out on Sunday voy a salir el domingo, see you on Sunday! ¡hasta el domingo!, on Sundays los domingos, the museum is closed on Sundays el museo cierra los domingos, every Sunday todos los domingos, last Sunday el domingo

pasado, **next Sunday** el próximo
domingo

sunflower NOUN **girasol** MASC;
sunflower oil aceite (MASC) de
girasol

sunglasses PLURAL NOUN **gafas** (FEM
PLURAL) de sol

sunlight NOUN **luz** (FEM) del sol

sunny ADJECTIVE ❶ **it's a sunny day**
hace sol, **it's going to be sunny**
va a hacer sol ❷ (place) **soleado/
soleada**; **in a sunny corner of the
garden** una esquina soleada del
jardín

sunrise NOUN **salida** (FEM) del sol; **at
sunrise** al amanecer

sunroof NOUN **techo** (MASC) solar

sunset NOUN **puesta** (FEM) de sol; **at
sunset** al atardecer

sunshine NOUN **sol** MASC

sunstroke NOUN **insolación** FEM;
to get sunstroke coger [3] una
insolación

suntan NOUN **bronceado** MASC; **to get
a suntan** broncearse [17]

suntan lotion NOUN **loción** (FEM)
bronceadora

suntan oil NOUN **aceite** (MASC)
bronceador

super ADJECTIVE **genial**; **we had a
super time!** ¡lo pasamos genial!

supermarket NOUN **supermercado**
MASC

supernatural ADJECTIVE
supernatural

superstitious ADJECTIVE
supersticioso/supersticiosa

supervise VERB **supervisar** [17]

supervisor NOUN **supervisor** MASC,
supervisora FEM

supper NOUN **cena** FEM; **I had supper
at Sandy's** cené en casa de Sandy

supplement NOUN **suplemento**
MASC

supplies PLURAL NOUN (of food)
provisiones FEM PLURAL

supply NOUN ❶ (stock) **reservas** (FEM
PLURAL) ❷ **to be in short supply**
escasear [17]

supply VERB **suministrar** [17];
the school supplies the paper
el colegio suministra el papel, **to
supply somebody with something**
suministrar algo a alguien

supply teacher NOUN **profesor**
(MASC) **suplente**, **profesora** (FEM)
suplente

support NOUN **apoyo** MASC; **he has a
lot of support** tiene mucho apoyo

support VERB ❶ (back up) **apoyar**
[17]; **her teachers have really
supported her** sus profesoras la han
apoyado mucho ❷ **ser** [1] **hincha
de** (a team); **Graeme supports
Liverpool** Graeme es hincha del
Liverpool ❸ (financially) **to support
a family** mantener [9] una familia

supporter NOUN **hincha** MASC & FEM;
an Arsenal supporter un hincha del
Arsenal

suppose VERB **suponer** [11]; **I
suppose she's forgotten** supongo
que se ha olvidado

supposed ADJECTIVE **to be supposed
to do** tener [9] que, **you're
supposed to wear a helmet** tienes

que usar casco, he was supposed to be here at six tenía que estar aquí a las seis

sure ADJECTIVE ❶ seguro/segura; are you sure? ¿estás seguro?, are you sure you've had enough to eat? ¿seguro que has comido suficiente?, are you sure you saw her? ¿estás seguro de que la viste? ❷ sure! ¡claro!, 'can you shut the door?' – 'sure!' ¿puedes cerrar la puerta?' – '¡por supuesto!'

surely ADVERB surely she couldn't have forgotten! ¡no es posible que se haya olvidado! (note that 'que' is followed by the subjunctive)

surf NOUN rompiente MASC

surf VERB ❶ (in the sea) hacer [7] surfing ❷ (on the Net) navegar [28]

surface NOUN superficie FEM

surfboard NOUN tabla (FEM) de surf

surfer NOUN ❶ (in the sea) surfista MASC & FEM ❷ (on the Net) internauta MASC & FEM

surfing NOUN surfing MASC; to go surfing hacer [7] surfing

surgeon NOUN cirujano MASC, cirujana FEM; she's a surgeon es cirujana

surgery NOUN ❶ (treatment) cirugía FEM; laser surgery cirugía láser, to have surgery operarse [17] ❷ (doctor's) consultorio MASC; the dentist's surgery la consulta del dentista

surname NOUN apellido MASC

surprise NOUN sorpresa FEM; what a surprise! ¡qué sorpresa!

surprised ADJECTIVE sorprendido/ sorprendida; I was surprised to see her me sorprendió verla

surprising ADJECTIVE sorprendente

surrender NOUN rendición FEM

surrender VERB ❶ (to give up) rendirse [57] ❷ entregar [28] (a castle, town)

surround VERB ❶ rodear [17] ❷ to be surrounded by estar [2] rodeado de, she's surrounded by friends está rodeada de amigos

survive VERB sobrevivir [19]

survivor NOUN superviviente MASC & FEM

suspect NOUN sospechoso MASC, sospechosa FEM

suspect ADJECTIVE sospechoso/ sospechosa

suspect VERB sospechar [17]

suspend VERB ❶ (hang) suspender [18] ❷ to be suspended (from school) ser [1] expulsado

suspense NOUN suspense MASC

suspicious ADJECTIVE sospechoso/ sospechosa; to be suspicious of sospechar [17] de, a suspicious parcel un paquete sospechoso, a suspicious-looking individual un individuo de apariencia sospechosa

swallow NOUN (bird) golondrina FEM

swallow VERB tragar [28]

swamp NOUN pantano MASC

swan NOUN cisne MASC

swap VERB ❶ cambiar [17]; **do you want to swap?** ¿quieres que cambiemos?, **he's swapped his bike for a computer** ha cambiado su bici por un ordenador ❷ **to swap seats with somebody** cambiarse [17] de sitio con alguien

swear VERB (use bad language) decir [5] palabrotas; **he swears a lot** dice muchas palabrotas

swearword NOUN palabrota FEM

sweat NOUN sudor MASC

sweat VERB sudar [17]

sweater NOUN suéter MASC

sweatshirt NOUN sudadera FEM

Swede NOUN sueco MASC, sueca FEM

Sweden NOUN Suecia FEM

Swedish NOUN (language) sueco MASC

Swedish ADJECTIVE sueco/sueca

sweep VERB barrer [18]

sweet NOUN ❶ caramelo MASC; **I bought her some sweets** le he comprado unos caramelos ❷ (dessert) postre MASC

sweet ADJECTIVE ❶ (food or smile) dulce; **I try not to eat sweet things** intento no comer cosas dulces ❷ (kind) encantador/encantadora; **she's a really sweet person** es realmente encantadora, **it was really sweet of him** ha sido un detalle encantador ❸ (cute) rico/rica; **he looks really sweet in that hat!** ¡está muy rico con ese sombrero!

sweetcorn NOUN maíz (MASC) tierno

swelling NOUN hinchazón FEM

swerve VERB virar [17] bruscamente; **the car swerved to avoid the dog** el coche viró bruscamente para esquivar al perro

swim NOUN **to go for a swim** ir [8] a nadar

swim VERB nadar [17]; **can he swim?** ¿sabe nadar?, **to swim across something** cruzar [22] algo a nado

swimmer NOUN nadador MASC, nadadora FEM; **she's a strong swimmer** es muy buena nadadora

swimming NOUN natación FEM; **to go swimming** ir [8] a nadar

swimming cap NOUN gorro (MASC) de baño

swimming pool NOUN piscina FEM

swimming trunks NOUN bañador MASC

swimsuit NOUN traje (MASC) de baño

swindle NOUN estafa FEM; **what a swindle!** ¡qué estafa!

swing NOUN columpio MASC

Swiss NOUN (person) suizo MASC, suiza FEM; **the Swiss** los suizos

Swiss ADJECTIVE suizo/suiza

switch NOUN interruptor MASC

switch VERB (change) cambiar [17]; **to switch places** cambiar de sitio
• **to switch something off** apagar [28] algo
• **to switch something on** encender [36] algo

Switzerland NOUN Suiza FEM

English—Spanish

A B C D E F G H I J K L M N O P Q R S T U V W X Y Z

swollen ADJECTIVE **hinchado/hinchada**

swop VERB ▶ SEE **swap**

sword NOUN **espada** FEM

swordfish NOUN **pez** (MASC) **espada**

syllabus NOUN **programa** MASC; **to be on the syllabus estar [2] en el programa**

sympathetic ADJECTIVE **comprensivo/comprensiva**

sympathize VERB **to sympathize with somebody compadecer [35] a alguien, I sympathize with her la compadezco**

sympathy NOUN **compasión** FEM

symphony NOUN **sinfonía** FEM

symphony orchestra NOUN **orquesta** (FEM) **sinfónica**

symptom NOUN **síntoma** MASC

synagogue NOUN **sinagoga** FEM

synthesizer NOUN **sintetizador** MASC

synthetic ADJECTIVE **sintético/sintética**

syringe NOUN **jeringa** FEM

system NOUN **sistema** MASC

table NOUN **mesa** FEM; **on the table en la mesa, to set the table poner [11] la mesa, to clear the table quitar [17] la mesa**

tablecloth NOUN **mantel** MASC

table football NOUN **futbolín** MASC

table mat NOUN **salvamanteles** MASC (doesn't change in the plural)

tablespoon NOUN **cuchara** (FEM) **de servir**; (in recipes) **a tablespoon of flour una cucharada grande de harina**

tablet NOUN **pastilla** FEM

table tennis NOUN **ping-pong** MASC; **to play table tennis jugar [27] al ping-pong**

tackle NOUN ❶ (in football) **entrada** FEM ❷ (in rugby) **placaje** MASC

tackle VERB ❶ (in football or hockey) **entrarle [17] a** ❷ **abordar [17]** (a job or problem)

tact NOUN **tacto** MASC

tactful ADJECTIVE **diplomático/diplomática**; **that wasn't very tactful eso no ha sido muy diplomático**

tactic NOUN **táctica** FEM

tadpole NOUN **renacuajo** MASC

tail NOUN ❶ (of dog, cat) **rabo** MASC ❷ (of horse, fish, bird) **cola** FEM ❸ 'heads or tails?' – 'tails' '¿cara o cruz?' – 'cruz'

tailor NOUN **sastre** MASC

take VERB ❶ **coger** [3]; he took a chocolate cogió un bombón, take my hand cógeme la mano, I took the bus cogí el autobús, who's taken my keys? ¿quién ha cogido mis llaves?, to take a holiday cogerse [3] unas vacaciones ❷ (person or car) **llevar** [17]; I'm taking Jake to the doctor's voy a llevar a Jake al médico, I must take the car to the garage debo llevar el coche al garaje ❸ (carry away) **llevar** [17]; I'll take my camera with me me llevaré la cámara ❹ to take something up(stairs) **subir** [19] algo, could you take these towels up? ¿puedes subir estas toallas? ❺ to take something down(stairs) **bajar** [17] algo, Cheryl's taken the cups down Cheryl ha bajado las tazas ❻ (time: for a task or job) **llevar** [17]; it takes two hours lleva dos horas ❼ (food or medicine) **tomar** [17]; do you take sugar? ¿tomas azúcar? ❽ **aceptar** [17] (a credit card); do you take cheques? ¿aceptan cheques? ❾ **hacer** [7] (an exam); she's taking her driving test tomorrow va a hacer el examen de conducir mañana ❿ what size do you take? ¿qué talla usas?
• to take something apart **desmontar** [17] algo
• to take something back **devolver** [45] algo
• to take off ❶ (a plane) **despegar** [28] ❷ **quitarse** [17] (clothes or shoes); he took off his shirt se quitó la camisa

❸ **rebajar** [17] (money); he took five pounds off the price rebajó cinco libras del precio
• to take out ❶ (from a bag or pocket) **sacar** [31]; Eric took out his wallet Eric sacó su cartera ❷ he's taking me out to lunch me ha invitado a comer fuera, she took me out to the theatre me invitó a ir al teatro

takeaway NOUN ❶ (a meal) **comida** (FEM) **para llevar**; an Indian takeaway comida india para llevar ❷ (where you buy it) **restaurante** (MASC) **que hace comida para llevar**

tale NOUN **historia** FEM

talent NOUN **talento** MASC; to have a talent for something **estar** [2] dotado/dotada para algo

talented ADJECTIVE he's really talented tiene mucho talento

talk NOUN ❶ (a chat) **conversación** FEM; after our talk después de nuestra conversación, I had a talk with Rob about it hablé con Rob acerca de ello ❷ (lecture) **charla** FEM; she's giving a talk on Hungary va a dar una charla sobre Hungría

talk VERB **hablar** [17]; I was talking to Jeevan about football estuve hablando con Jeevan sobre fútbol, what's he talking about? ¿de qué está hablando?, we'll talk about it later hablaremos de ello más tarde

talkative ADJECTIVE **hablador/habladora**; he's not very talkative! ¡no es muy hablador!

tall ADJECTIVE **alto/alta**; she's very tall es muy alta, I'm 1.7 metres tall mido un metro setenta, how tall is she? ¿cuánto mide?, the tallest

a
b
c
d
e
f
g
h
i
j
k
l
m
n
o
p
q
r
s
t
u
v
w
x
y
z

tambourine   **teach**

buildings in the city los edificios
más altos de la ciudad

tambourine NOUN pandereta FEM

tame ADJECTIVE domesticado/
domesticada (an animal)

tampon NOUN tampón MASC

tan NOUN bronceado MASC; to get a
tan broncearse [17]

tan VERB broncearse [17]; I tan easily
me bronceo fácilmente

tangerine NOUN mandarina FEM

tank NOUN ❶ (for petrol or water)
depósito MASC ❷ a fish tank una
pecera ❸ (military) tanque MASC

tanker NOUN ❶ (ship) petrolero MASC
❷ (on road) camión (MASC) cisterna

tanned ADJECTIVE bronceado/
bronceada

tap NOUN ❶ grifo MASC; to turn on the
tap abrir [46] el grifo, to turn off the
tap cerrar [29] el grifo, the hot tap
el grifo del agua caliente ❷ (a pat)
golpecito MASC

tap VERB dar [4] golpecitos

tap-dancing NOUN claqué MASC; to
do tap-dancing hacer [7] claqué

tape NOUN ❶ cinta FEM; my tape of
the Stones mi cinta de los Stones,
I've got it on tape lo tengo en cinta
❷ sticky tape cinta (FEM) adhesiva

tape VERB grabar [17]; I want to tape
the film quiero grabar la película

tape measure NOUN cinta (FEM)
métrica

tar NOUN alquitrán MASC

target NOUN objetivo MASC

tart NOUN tarta FEM; a raspberry tart
una tarta de frambuesas

tartan ADJECTIVE escocés/escocesa; a
tartan skirt una falda escocesa

task NOUN tarea FEM

taste NOUN ❶ (flavour) sabor MASC; the
taste of onions el sabor a cebolla
❷ (judgement) gusto MASC; she has
good taste tiene buen gusto, in bad
taste de mal gusto

taste VERB ❶ saber [13]; the soup
tastes horrible la sopa sabe fatal,
to taste of saber a, it tastes of
strawberries sabe a fresas ❷ do you
want to taste? ¿quieres probarlo?

tasty ADJECTIVE sabroso/sabrosa

tattoo NOUN tatuaje MASC; he's got a
tattoo on his arm tiene un tatuaje
en el brazo

Taurus NOUN Tauro MASC; Jo's Taurus
Jo es Tauro

tax NOUN impuesto MASC

taxi NOUN taxi MASC; by taxi en taxi, to
take a taxi coger [3] un taxi

taxi driver NOUN taxista MASC & FEM

taxi rank NOUN parada (FEM) de
taxis

TB NOUN tuberculosis FEM

tea NOUN ❶ té MASC; a cup of tea una
taza de té, to have tea tomar [17] té,
a herbal tea una infusión ❷ (evening
meal) cena FEM

teabag NOUN bolsita (FEM) de té

teach VERB ❶ enseñar [17]; she's
teaching me Italian me está
enseñando italiano, that'll teach
you! ¡así aprenderás! ❷ (working

as a teacher) dar [4] clases de; **her mum teaches maths** su madre da clases de matemáticas ❸ **to teach yourself something** aprender [18] algo por su cuenta, **Anne taught herself Italian** Anne ha aprendido italiano por su cuenta

teacher NOUN ❶ *(in a secondary school)* profesor MASC, profesora FEM; **my mother's a teacher** mi madre es profesora, **our biology teacher** nuestra profesora de biología ❷ *(in primary school)* maestro MASC, maestra FEM; **she's a primary school teacher** es maestra

teaching NOUN enseñanza FEM

team NOUN equipo MASC; **a football team** un equipo de fútbol, **our team won** nuestro equipo ganó

teapot NOUN tetera FEM

tear¹ NOUN *(a rip)* roto MASC; **I've got a tear in my jeans** tengo un roto en los vaqueros

tear VERB ❶ romper [40]; **you've torn your shirt** te has roto la camisa, **she tore up my letter** rompió mi carta ❷ romperse [40]; **be careful, it tears easily** cuidado, se rompe fácilmente
- **to tear off** ❶ *(carefully)* recortar [17] ❷ *(violently)* arrancar [31]
- **to tear open** ❶ *(carefully)* abrir [46] ❷ *(violently)* rasgar [28]

tear² NOUN *(when you cry)* lágrima FEM; **to be in tears** estar [2] llorando, **to burst into tears** ponerse [11] a llorar

teaspoon NOUN cucharita FEM; *(in recipes)* **a teaspoonful of …** una cucharadita de …

teatime NOUN hora *(FEM)* merendar

tea towel NOUN paño *(MASC)* de cocina

technical ADJECTIVE técnico/técnica

technical college NOUN escuela *(FEM)* politécnica

technician NOUN técnico MASC, técnica FEM

technological ADJECTIVE tecnológico/tecnológica

technology NOUN tecnología FEM; **information technology** informática FEM

teddy bear NOUN osito *(MASC)* de peluche

teenage ADJECTIVE ❶ adolescente; **they have a teenage son** tienen un hijo adolescente ❷ *(films, magazines, etc.)* para adolescentes; **a teenage magazine** una revista para adolescentes

teenager NOUN adolescente MASC & FEM; **a group of teenagers** un grupo de adolescentes

teens PLURAL NOUN adolescencia FEM; **he's in his teens** es un adolescente

tee-shirt NOUN camiseta FEM

telegraph pole NOUN poste *(MASC)* telegráfico

telephone NOUN teléfono MASC; **on the telephone** al teléfono

telephone VERB llamar [17] por teléfono; **I'll telephone the bank** llamaré al banco por teléfono

telephone call NOUN llamada *(FEM)* de teléfono

telephone card NOUN carta (FEM) telefónica

telephone directory NOUN guía (FEM) telefónica

telephone number NOUN número (MASC) de teléfono

television NOUN televisión FEM; she was watching television estaba viendo la televisión, I saw it on television lo vi en televisión

television programme NOUN programa (MASC) de televisión

tell VERB ❶ to tell somebody something decirle [5] algo a alguien, that's what she told me eso es lo que ella me dijo, I told him it was silly le dije que era una tontería, have you told Sara? ¿se lo has dicho a Sara?, I didn't tell anyone no se lo dije a nadie ❷ to tell somebody to do decirle [5] a alguien que haga (note that 'que' is followed by the subjunctive), he told me to do it myself me dijo que lo hiciese solo, she told me not to wait me dijo que no esperase ❸ (explain) decir [5]; can you tell me how to do it? ¿puedes decirme cómo hacerlo? ❹ contar [24] (a story); tell me about your holiday cuéntame qué tal tus vacaciones ❺ (to see) notar [17]; to tell the difference notar la diferencia, you can tell … se nota …, you can tell it's old se nota que es viejo, you can tell she's cross se nota que está enfadada, I can't tell them apart no puedo distinguirlos

telly NOUN tele FEM, (informal); to watch telly ver [16] la tele, I saw her on telly la vi en la tele

temper NOUN to be in a temper estar [2] de mal humor, to lose your temper perder [36] los estribos

temperature NOUN ❶ temperatura FEM; the oven temperature la temperatura del horno ❷ to have a temperature tener [9] fiebre FEM

temporary ADJECTIVE temporal

temptation NOUN tentación FEM

tempted ADJECTIVE tentado/tentada; I'm really tempted to go estoy realmente tentado de ir

tempting ADJECTIVE tentador/tentadora

ten NUMBER diez MASC; Harry's ten Harry tiene diez años, it's ten o'clock son las diez

tend VERB to tend to do tender [36] a hacer, he tends to talk a lot tiende a hablar mucho

tendency NOUN tendencia FEM

tennis NOUN tenis MASC; to play tennis jugar [27] al tenis

tennis ball NOUN pelota (FEM) de tenis

tennis court NOUN cancha (FEM) de tenis

tennis player NOUN jugador/jugadora (MASC & FEM) de tenis

tennis racket NOUN raqueta (FEM) de tenis

tenor NOUN tenor MASC

tenpin bowling NOUN bolos MASC PLURAL; to go tenpin bowling jugar [27] a los bolos

tense NOUN the present tense el presente, **in the future tense** en futuro

tense ADJECTIVE **tenso/tensa**

tent NOUN **tienda** FEM

tenth NOUN ❶ *(fraction)* **a tenth** una décima parte ❷ **the tenth of April** el diez de abril

tenth ADJECTIVE **décimo/décima**; **on the tenth floor** en la décima planta

term NOUN ❶ *(in school)* **trimestre** MASC ❷ **to be on good terms with somebody** llevarse [17] bien con alguien

terminal NOUN **terminal** FEM; **terminal two** la terminal dos, **a computer terminal** una terminal de ordenador

terrace NOUN ❶ *(of a house or hotel)* **terraza** FEM ❷ **the terraces** *(at a stadium)* las gradas

terrible ADJECTIVE **espantoso/ espantosa**; **the weather was terrible** el tiempo fue espantoso

terribly ADVERB ❶ *(very)* **muy**; **not terribly clean** no muy limpio que digamos ❷ *(badly)* **fatal**; **I played terribly** jugué fatal

terrific ADJECTIVE ❶ **increíble**; **at a terrific speed** a una velocidad increíble, **a terrific amount** una cantidad increíble ❷ **terrific!** ¡fenomenal!

terrified ADJECTIVE **aterrorizado/ aterrorizada**

terrify VERB **aterrar** [17]

territory NOUN **territorio** MASC

terrorism NOUN **terrorismo** MASC

terrorist NOUN **terrorista** MASC & FEM

test NOUN ❶ *(in school)* **examen** MASC; **we've got a maths test tomorrow** tenemos un examen de matemáticas mañana ❷ *(of your skills or patience)* **prueba** FEM ❸ *(medical)* **análisis** MASC; **a blood test** un análisis de sangre ❹ **a driving test** un examen de conducir, **she's sitting her driving test on Friday** va a hacer el exámen de conducir mañana, **he passed his driving test** ha aprobado el examen de conducir

test VERB ❶ *(in school)* **examinarse** [17] ❷ **to test something out** probar [24] algo

text NOUN **texto** MASC

text VERB **mandar** [17] un mensaje de texto a; **I'll text you tomorrow** te mandaré un mensaje (de texto) mañana

textbook NOUN **libro** *(MASC)* de texto

text message NOUN **mensaje** *(MASC)* de texto

Thames NOUN **the Thames** el Támesis

than PREPOSITION, CONJUNCTION ❶ **que**; **their new album's better than the last one** su nuevo álbum es mejor que el último, **they have more money than we do** tienen más dinero que nosotros ❷ *(for quantities)* **de**; **more than forty** más de cuarenta, **more than thirty years** más de treinta años

thank VERB **dar** [4] las gracias a

thanks PLURAL NOUN ❶ **gracias** FEM PLURAL; **no thanks** no gracias, **thanks a lot** muchas gracias, **thanks for**

your letter gracias por tu carta
❷ thanks to gracias a, **it was thanks
to Micky** fue gracias a Micky

thank you *EXCLAMATION* **gracias**;
**thank you very much for the
cheque** muchas gracias por el
cheque, **no thank you** no, gracias,
a thank-you letter un carta de
agradecimiento

that *DETERMINER* **❶** *(before a masculine
noun)* **ese**; **that dog** ese perro, **that
blue car** ese coche azul **❷** *(before
a feminine noun)* **esa**; **that woman**
esa mujer **❸** *that one (referring to
a masculine noun)* **ese**, *(referring
to a feminine noun)* **esa**, **'which
cake would you like?' – 'that one,
please'** ¿qué pastel quieres? –
'ese, por favor', **I like all the skirts
but I'm going to buy that one** me
gustan todas las faldas pero voy a
comprar esa

that *ADVERB* **it's not that funny** no es
tan divertido, **their house isn't that
big** su casa no es tan grande

that *PRONOUN* **❶** *(referring to a
masculine noun)* **ese**, *(referring to
a feminine noun)* **esa**; **that's not
his car** ese no es su coche, **that's
my bedroom** esa es mi habitación
❷ eso; **that's not what you told me**
eso no es lo que tú me dijiste, **that's
not true** eso no es cierto, **did you
see that?** ¿has visto eso?, **what's
that?** ¿qué es eso?, **who's that?**
¿quién es?, **where's that?** ¿dónde
está? **❸ que**; **the book that's on the
table** el libro que está en la mesa,
the girl that I saw la chica que yo
vi **❹** *(when the verb is followed by a
preposition)* *(referring to a masculine
noun)* **el que**, *(referring to a feminine
noun)* **la que**; **the drawer that I put
it in** el cajón en el que lo metí

that *CONJUNCTION* **que**; **I knew that he
was wrong** sabía que no tenía razón

thaw *NOUN* **deshielo** *MASC*

the *DETERMINER* **❶** *(before a masculine
noun)* **el**; **the cat** el gato, **the tree** el
árbol *(when 'el' follows 'de', they join
to become 'del')*, **the branches of
the tree** las ramas del árbol, *(when
'el' follows 'a' they join to become
'al')* **we went to the park** fuimos al
parque **❷** *(before a feminine noun)*
la; **the table** la mesa, **the orange** la
naranja **❸** *(before masculine plural
nouns)* **los**; **the plates** los platos
❹ *(before feminine plural nouns)* **las**;
the windows las ventanas

theatre *NOUN* **teatro** *MASC*; **to go to
the theatre** ir [8] al teatro

theft *NOUN* **robo** *MASC*

their *ADJECTIVE* **❶** *(before a singular
noun)* **su**; **their flat** su piso, **their
mother** su madre **❷** *(before a
plural noun)* **sus**; **their presents** sus
regalos **❸** *(with parts of the body)*
el, la, los, las; **they had tatoos
on their arms** tenían tatuajes en
los brazos, **they're washing their
hands** se están lavando las manos

theirs *PRONOUN* **❶** *(when referring to
a singular noun)* **el suyo/la suya**;
our garden's smaller than theirs
nuestro jardín es más pequeño que
el suyo, **our house is bigger than
theirs** nuestra casa es más grande
que la suya **❷** *(when referring to a
plural noun)* **los suyos/las suyas**;
our shoes were newer than theirs
nuestros zapatos eran más nuevos
que los suyos, **our photos were
better that theirs** nuestras fotos
eran mejores que las suyas

them PRONOUN ❶ los/las; **she's got two brothers, but I don't know them** tiene dos hermanos, pero no los conozco, **remember Ann and Lisa? I saw them last week** ¿te acuerdas de Ann y Lisa? las vi la semana pasada ❷ *(with an infinitive or when telling somebody to do something 'los'/'las' join onto the verb)* **I don't want to see them** no quiero verlos, **listen to them!** ¡escúchalos!, *(but when telling someone NOT to do something, 'los' or 'las' comes before the verb)* **don't push them!** ¡no los empujes! ❸ *(to them)* **I gave them my address** les di mis señas *('les' becomes 'se' before pronouns 'lo' or 'la')* **I lent it to them** se lo dejé, *(when giving an order 'se' joins the verb)* **give it back to them** ¡devuélveselo! ❹ *(after a preposition, in comparisons, or after the verb 'to be')* ellos/ellas; **I'll go with them** iré con ellos/ellas, **without them** sin ellos/sin ellas, **she's older than them** es mayor que ellos, **it's them!** ¡son ellos!/¡son ellas!

theme park NOUN **parque** *(MASC)* **temático**

themselves PRONOUN ❶ *(as a reflexive)* se; **they've helped themselves** se sirvieron ❷ *(for emphasis)* ellos mismos/ellas mismas; **the boys can do it themselves** los chicos pueden hacerlo ellos mismos, **the girls will tell you themselves** las chicas te lo dirán ellas mismas ❸ **by themselves** ellos solos/ellas solas

then ADVERB ❶ *(next)* luego; **have a shower and then make your bed** dúchate y luego haz la cama, **I went to the post office and then the bank** fui a Correos y luego al banco ❷ *(at that time)* entonces; **we were living in York then** entonces vivíamos en York ❸ *(in that case)* entonces; **then why worry?** entonces ¿para qué preocuparse?, **that's all right then** entonces vale ❹ **by then** para entonces, **by then it was too late** para entonces era demasiado tarde

theory NOUN **teoría** *FEM*; **in theory** en teoría

there ADVERB ❶ ahí, *(further away)* allí; **put it there** ponlo ahí, *(further away)* ponlo allí, **stand there** ponte ahí, **they're in there** están ahí dentro, **look up there!** ¡mira ahí arriba! ❷ **over there** ahí, *(further away)* allí, **she's over there talking to Mark** está ahí hablando con Mark, *(further away)* está allí hablando con Mark ❸ **down there** ahí abajo, *(further away)* allí abajo, **up there** ahí arriba, *(further away)* allí arriba ❹ *(when there stands for something already mentioned, it is usually not translated)* **I've seen photos of Oxford but I've never been there** he visto fotos de Oxford, pero nunca he estado, **yes, I'm going there on Tuesday** sí, voy a ir el martes ❺ **there is/there are** hay, **there's a cat in the garden** hay un gato en el jardín, **there was no bread** no había pan, **yes, there's enough** sí, hay suficiente, **there are plenty of seats** hay muchos asientos ❻ **there they are!** ¡ahí están!, **there she is!** ¡ahí está!, **there's the bus coming!** ¡ahí viene el autobús!

thermometer NOUN **termómetro** *MASC*

these DETERMINER ❶ (with a masculine noun) **estos**; **these envelopes** estos sobres ❷ (with a feminine noun) **estas**; **these postcards** estas postales

they PRONOUN ❶ (like other subject pronouns 'they' is generally not translated; in Spanish the form of the verb tells you whether the subject of the verb is 'we, you, they', etc., so 'they' is only translated for emphasis) **'where are the knives?'** – **'they're in the drawer'** '¿dónde están los cuchillos?' - 'están en el cajón', **I bought some apples but they're not very nice** compré unas manzanas pero no están muy buenas ❷ (for emphasis) **ellos/ellas**; **they did it** lo hicieron ellos

thick ADJECTIVE ❶ **grueso/gruesa**; **a thick layer of butter** una capa gruesa de mantequilla ❷ **denso/densa** (fog, fumes)

thickness NOUN ❶ (of wall, paper) **espesor** MASC ❷ (of fog) **densidad** FEM

thief NOUN **ladrón** MASC, **ladrona** FEM

thigh NOUN **muslo** MASC

thin ADJECTIVE ❶ **delgado/delgada** (a person); **to get thin** adelgazar [22] ❷ **fino/fina** (a slice) ❸ (too thin, skinny) **flaco/flaca**; **she's very thin** está muy flaca

thing NOUN ❶ (an object) **cosa** FEM; **shops full of pretty things** tiendas llenas de cosas preciosas, **she told me some surprising things** me dijo algunas cosas sorprendentes ❷ (a whatsit) **chisme** MASC (informal); **you can use that thing to open it** puedes usar ese chisme para abrirlo ❸ **things** (belongings) **cosas** FEM

PLURAL, **you can put your things in my room** puedes poner tus cosas en mi habitación ❹ **the best thing to do is ...** lo mejor es ..., **the thing is, I've lost her address** la cuestión es que he perdido sus señas ❺ **how are things with you?** ¿qué tal te van las cosas?

think VERB ❶ **pensar** [29]; **I'm thinking about you** estoy pensando en ti, **Tony thinks it's silly** Tony piensa que es una tontería, **what do you think of my new jacket?** ¿qué piensas de mi chaqueta nueva?, **what do you think of that?** ¿qué piensas de eso?, **he thought for a moment** pensó un momento, **she's thinking of studying medicine** está pensando estudiar medicina ❷ (believe) **creer** [37]; **do you think they'll come?** ¿crees que vendrán?, **no, I don't think so** no, creo que no, **I think he's already left** creo que ya se ha ido ❸ (imagine) **imaginar** [17]; **I never thought it would be like this!** ¡nunca imaginé que sería así!, **just think! we'll soon be in Spain!** ¡imagínate! ¡pronto estaremos en España!

third NOUN ❶ (fraction) **a third** un tercio ❷ **the third of March** el tres de marzo

third ADJECTIVE **tercero/tercera**; **on the third floor** en la tercera planta

thirdly ADVERB **en tercer lugar**

Third World NOUN **the Third World** el Tercer Mundo

thirst NOUN **sed** FEM

thirsty ADJECTIVE **to be thirsty** tener [9] sed, **I'm thirsty** tengo sed, **we were all thirsty** todos teníamos sed

thirteen NUMBER **trece** MASC; Ahmed's thirteen Ahmed tiene trece años

thirty NUMBER **treinta** MASC; she's thirty tiene treinta años, thirty-five treinta y cinco

this DETERMINER ❶ **este** (before a masculine noun), **esta** (before a feminine noun); this paintbrush este pincel, this tree este árbol, this cup esta taza, this morning esta mañana ❷ this one (referring to a masculine noun) **este**, (referring to a feminine noun) **esta**, if you need a pen you can use this one si necesitas un boli puedes usar este, if you want a lamp you can borrow this one si quieres una lámpara puedes coger esta

this PRONOUN ❶ (referring to a masculine noun) **este**; this is my car este es mi coche ❷ (referring to a feminine noun) **esta**; this is the best photo esta es la mejor foto ❸ **esto**; can you hold this for a moment? ¿puedes sostener esto un momento?, what's this? ¿qué es esto? ❹ this is Tracy speaking (on the phone) soy Tracy ❺ (in introductions) this is my sister Carla te presento a mi hermana Carla

thistle NOUN **cardo** MASC

thorough ADJECTIVE ❶ (search) a fondo ❷ (person) **concienzudo/concienzuda**

those ADJECTIVE (before a masculine noun) **esos**, (before a feminine noun) **esas**; those books esos libros, those cups esas tazas

those PRONOUN (referring to a masculine noun) **esos**, (referring to a feminine noun) **esas**; if you want some knives you can take those si

quieres cuchillos puedes coger esos, if you want some cups you can take those si quieres tazas puedes coger esas

though CONJUNCTION ❶ **aunque**; though it's cold aunque hace calor, though he's older than she is aunque es mayor que ella ❷ it was a good idea, though aun así era una buena idea

thought NOUN **pensamiento** MASC

thoughtful ADJECTIVE ❶ (considerate) amable; it was really thoughtful of you fue muy amable de tu parte ❷ (deep in thought) **pensativo/pensativa**

thoughtless ADJECTIVE **desconsiderado/desconsiderada**

thousand NUMBER ❶ **mil** MASC; a thousand mil, a thousand euros mil euros, three thousand tres mil ❷ thousands of miles de, there were thousands of tourists in Barcelona había miles de turistas en Barcelona

thread NOUN **hilo** MASC

thread VERB **enhebrar** [17] (a needle)

threat NOUN **amenaza** FEM

threaten VERB **amenazar** [22]; to threaten to do amenazar con hacer

three NUMBER **tres** MASC; Lily's three Lily tiene tres años

three-quarters NOUN **tres cuartos** MASC PLURAL

thrilled ADJECTIVE **encantado/encantada**; I was thrilled to hear from you me encantó tener noticias tuyas

thriller NOUN ❶ (book) novela (FEM) de suspense ❷ (film) película (FEM) de suspense

thrilling ADJECTIVE emocionante

throat NOUN garganta FEM; **to have a sore throat** tener [9] dolor de garganta

through PREPOSITION ❶ (across) a través de; **a path through the forest** un camino a través del bosque, **to go through something** atravesar [29] algo, **we went through the park** atravesamos el parque ❷ (by way of) por; **the train went through Leeds** el tren fue por Leeds, **through the window** por la ventana ❸ **to go through customs** pasar [17] la aduana

through ADJECTIVE directo/directa (a train or flight)

throughout PREPOSITION **throughout the match** durante todo el partido, **throughout the world** por todo mundo

throw VERB tirar [17]; **I threw the letter into the bin** tiré la carta a la basura, **he threw the book on the floor** tiró el libro al suelo, **throw me the ball!** ¡tírame la pelota!, **we were throwing snowballs** estábamos tirando bolas de nieve
- **to throw something away** tirar [17] algo; **I've thrown away the old newspapers** he tirado los periódicos viejos
- **to throw somebody out** echar [17] a alguien
- **to throw something out** tirar [17] algo (rubbish)
- **to throw up** devolver [45]

thumb NOUN pulgar MASC

thunder NOUN truenos MASC PLURAL; **a peal of thunder** un trueno

thunderstorm NOUN tormenta (FEM) eléctrica

Thursday NOUN jueves MASC; **on Thursday** el jueves, **I'm going out on Thursday** voy a salir el jueves, **see you on Thursday!** ¡hasta el jueves!, **on Thursdays** los jueves, **the museum is closed on Thursdays** el museo cierra los jueves, **every Thursday** todos los jueves, **last Thursday** el jueves pasado, **next Thursday** el próximo jueves

tick VERB ❶ (clocks) hacer [7] tictac ❷ (on paper) marcar [31]

ticket NOUN ❶ entrada FEM (for an exhibition, a theatre or cinema) **two tickets for the concert** dos entradas para el concierto ❷ (for a plane, a train, a bus or the underground) billete MASC; **a bus ticket** un billete de autobús ❸ (for left luggage) ticket MASC ❹ **a parking ticket** una multa

ticket inspector NOUN revisor MASC, revisora FEM

ticket office NOUN ❶ (at a station) mostrador (MASC) de venta de billetes ❷ (at a cinema) taquilla FEM

tickle VERB hacer [7] cosquillas

tide NOUN marea FEM; **at high tide** cuando la marea está alta, **the tide is out** la marea está baja

tidy ADJECTIVE ❶ ordenado/ordenada (a room) ❷ bien escrito/bien escrita (homework) ❸ bien arreglado/bien arreglada (a person)

tidy VERB ordenar [17]

tie NOUN ❶ **corbata** FEM; a red tie una corbata roja ❷ *(in a match)* **empate** MASC

tie VERB ❶ **atar** [17]; to tie your shoelaces atarse los zapatos ❷ to tie a knot in something hacer [7] un nudo a algo ❸ *(in a match)* we tied two all empatamos a dos

tiger NOUN **tigre** MASC

tight ADJECTIVE ❶ to be tight apretar [29], the skirt's a bit tight la falda aprieta un poco, these shoes are too tight estos zapatos aprietan mucho ❷ *(close-fitting)* **ceñido/ceñida**; she was wearing a tight dress llevaba un vestido ceñido

tighten VERB **apretar** [29]

tightly ADVERB **fuerte**; hold it tightly agárralo fuerte

tights PLURAL NOUN **medias** FEM PLURAL; a pair of purple tights un par de medias moradas

tile NOUN ❶ *(on a floor or wall)* **azulejo** MASC ❷ *(on a roof)* **teja** FEM

till¹ PREPOSITION **hasta**; they're here till Sunday están aquí hasta el domingo, till then hasta entonces, till now hasta ahora, she won't be back till ten no volverá hasta las diez

till² NOUN **caja** FEM; pay at the till pase a pagar por caja

time NOUN ❶ *(on the clock)* **hora** FEM; what time is it? ¿qué hora es?, it's time for lunch es hora de comer, ten o'clock Spanish time las diez hora española, on time a la hora ❷ *(an amount of time)* **tiempo** MASC; we've got lots of time tenemos mucho tiempo, there's not much time left no queda mucho tiempo, he talked for a long time habló durante mucho tiempo, she hasn't called me for a long time hace mucho que no me llama ❸ *(moment)* **momento** MASC; is this a good time to phone? ¿es buen momento para llamar?, at any time en cualquier momento ❹ from time to time de vez en cuando, at times a veces, for the time being por ahora ❺ *(in a series)* **vez** FEM *(PLURAL* **veces***)*; six times seis veces, the first time la primera vez, the first time I saw you la primera vez que te vi, three times a year tres veces al año ❻ *(multiplying)* three times two is six tres por dos son seis ❼ to have a good time pasárselo [17] bien, we had a really good time nos lo pasamos muy bien, have a good time! ¡pásatelo bien!

time off NOUN ❶ *(free time)* **tiempo** *(MASC)* **libre** ❷ *(leave)* **días** *(MASC PLURAL)* **libres**

timetable NOUN **horario** MASC; the bus timetable el horario de los autobuses

tin NOUN **lata** FEM; a tin of tomatoes una lata de tomates

tin foil NOUN **papel** *(MASC)* **aluminio**

tinned ADJECTIVE **en lata**; tinned peas guisantes en lata

tin opener NOUN **abrelatas** MASC *(does not change in the plural)*

tiny ADJECTIVE **diminuto/diminuta**

tip NOUN ❶ *(the end)* **punta** FEM; the tip of my finger la punta de mi dedo ❷ *(money)* **propina** FEM ❸ *(a useful hint)* **consejo** MASC

a
b
c
d
e
f
g
h
i
j
k
l
m
n
o
p
q
r
s
t
u
v
w
x
y
z

tip VERB ❶ (to give money to) **darle [4] una propina a**; we tipped the waiter **le dimos una propina al camarero** ❷ **tirar [17]** (liquid)

tiptoe NOUN on tiptoe **de puntillas**

tired ADJECTIVE ❶ **cansado/cansada**; I'm tired **estoy cansado**, you look tired **pareces cansado** ❷ to be tired of **estar [2] harto de/harta de**, he's tired of London **está harto de Londres**, she says she's tired of watching TV **dice que está harta de ver la tele**

tiring ADJECTIVE **cansado/cansada**

tissue NOUN (a paper hanky) **pañuelo** (MASC) **de papel**; do you have a tissue? **¿tienes un pañuelo de papel?**

title NOUN **título** MASC

to PREPOSITION ❶ (to a place) **a**; to London **a Londres**, to Spain **a España**, she's gone to the office **se ha ido a la oficina**, to Paul's house **a casa de Paul**, from Monday to Friday **de lunes a viernes**, (when 'el' follows 'a' they join to become 'al') I'm going to school **voy al colegio**, I'm going to the dentist's tomorrow **voy al dentista mañana** ❷ (to a person) **a**; give the book to Leila **dale el libro a Leila**, who did you give it to? **¿a quién se lo diste?**, to talk to somebody **hablar [17] con alguien**, he didn't talk to me **no habló conmigo**, I was nice to them **fui amable con ellos** ❸ we're ready to go **estamos listos para irnos**, it's easy to do **es fácil de hacer**, I have nothing to do **no tengo nada que hacer**, I have a lot of homework to do **tengo muchos deberes que hacer** ❹ (talking about the time) it's ten to nine **son las nueve menos diez**, it's

twenty to **son menos veinte** ❺ (in order to) **para**; he gave me some money to buy a sandwich **me dio dinero para comprar un sandwich**

toast NOUN ❶ **pan** (MASC) **tostado**; a piece of toast **una tostada**, two slices of toast **dos tostadas** ❷ (to your health) **brindis** MASC; to drink a toast to the future **brindar [17] por el futuro**

toaster NOUN **tostador** MASC

tobacco NOUN **tabaco** MASC

tobacconist's NOUN **estanco** MASC

today ADVERB, NOUN **hoy**; today's her birthday **hoy es su cumpleaños**

toe NOUN **dedo** (MASC) **del pie**; my big toe **mi dedo gordo del pie**

toenail NOUN **uña** (FEM) **de un dedo del pie**

toffee NOUN **toffee** MASC

together ADVERB **juntos/juntas**; Kate and Lindy arrived together **Kate y Lindy llegaron juntas**, they all left together **se fueron todos juntos**

toilet NOUN ❶ (in a house) **baño** MASC; she's gone to the toilet **ha ido al baño** ❷ (in a public place) **servicio** MASC; where's the toilet? **¿dónde está el servicio?** ❸ toilets (in a public place) **servicios** MASC PLURAL; where are the toilets? **¿dónde están los servicios**

toilet paper NOUN **papel** (MASC) **higiénico**

toilet roll NOUN **rollo** (MASC) **de papel higiénico**

token NOUN ❶ (for a machine or game) **ficha** FEM ❷ (as a present) **cheque**

(MASC) **regalo**; **a record token** un cheque regalo para un disco

toll NOUN ❶ *(on motorway)* **peaje** MASC ❷ *(number)* **número** MASC; **the death toll is 25** el número de víctimas mortales asciende a 25

tomato NOUN **tomate** MASC; **a tomato salad** una ensalada de tomate, **tomato sauce** salsa *(FEM)* de tomate

tomorrow ADVERB **mañana**; **I'll do it tomorrow** lo haré mañana, **tomorrow afternoon** mañana por la tarde, **tomorrow morning** mañana por la mañana, **tomorrow night** mañana por la noche, **the day after tomorrow** pasado mañana

ton NOUN **tonelada** FEM; **she gets tons of letters** recibe montones de cartas

tongue NOUN **lengua** FEM; **to stick your tongue out** sacar [31] la lengua
• **it's on the tip of my tongue** lo tengo en la punta de la lengua

tonic NOUN **tónica** FEM; **a gin and tonic** un gin tonic

tonight ADVERB **esta noche**; **I'm going out with my mates tonight** esta noche voy a salir con mis amigos

tonsillitis NOUN **anginas** FEM PLURAL

too ADVERB ❶ **demasiado**; **it's too expensive** es demasiado caro, **the tickets are too expensive** los billetes son demasiado caros, **too often** demasiado a menudo ❷ **too much** *(before a masculine noun)* demasiado, *(before a feminine noun)* demasiada, **it takes too much time** lleva demasiado tiempo, **I watch too much TV** veo demasiada televisión ❸ **too much** *(before verb)*

demasiado, **he eats too much** come demasiado ❹ **too many** *(before a masculine noun)* demasiados, *(before a feminine noun)* demasiadas, **there are too many accidents** hay demasiados accidentes ❺ *(as well)* **también**; **Karen's coming too** Karen también viene, **me too!** ¡yo también! ❻ *(very)* **muy**; **I'm not too convinced** no estoy muy convencida

tool NOUN **herramienta** FEM

tool kit NOUN **juego** *(MASC)* **de herramientas**

tooth NOUN ❶ **diente** MASC; **to brush your teeth** cepillarse [17] los dientes ❷ *(back tooth)* **muela** FEM

toothache NOUN **dolor** *(MASC)* **de muelas**; **to have toothache** tener [9] dolor de muelas

toothbrush NOUN **cepillo** *(MASC)* **de dientes**

toothpaste NOUN **pasta** *(FEM)* **de dientes**

top NOUN ❶ **alto** MASC *(of a ladder, or stairs)*; **at the top of the stairs** en lo alto de las escaleras ❷ *(of a page, container or box)* **parte** *(FEM)* **superior**; **the top of the box is red** la parte superior de la caja es roja ❸ **on top of** *(a table, wardrobe, etc)* **encima de**, **it's on top of the chest-of-drawers** está encima de la cómoda ❹ *(of a mountain)* **cima** FEM ❺ *(a lid, cap)* *(of a bottle)* **tapón** MASC *(of a pan or jar)* **tapa** FEM, *(of a pen)* **capuchón** MASC ❻ **to be at the top of the list** encabezar [22] una lista

top ADJECTIVE ❶ *(a step or floor)* **último/última**; **it's on the top floor** está en el último piso ❷ **de arriba** *(a bunk, drawer or shelf)* ❸ **in the**

top left-hand corner en la esquina superior izquierda
• **and on top of all that** y para colmo
• **it was a bit over the top** fue un poco excesivo

topic NOUN **tema** MASC

topping NOUN **guarnición** FEM; **which topping do you want?** ¿qué guarnición quieres?

torch NOUN **linterna** FEM

torn ADJECTIVE **roto/rota**

tornado NOUN **tornado** MASC

tortoise NOUN **tortuga** FEM

torture NOUN **tortura** FEM

torture VERB **torturar** [17]

Tory NOUN **conservador** MASC, **conservadora** FEM

total NOUN **total** MASC

total ADJECTIVE **total**

totally ADVERB **totalmente**

touch NOUN ❶ (contact) **to get in touch with somebody** contactar [17] con alguien, **to stay in touch with somebody** mantenerse [9] en contacto con alguien, **we've lost touch** hemos perdido el contacto ❷ (a little bit) **poco** MASC; **a touch of vanilla** un poco de vainilla, **it was a touch embarrassing** fue un poco embarazoso

touch VERB ❶ **tocar** [31] ❷ (emotionally) **conmover** [38]

tough ADJECTIVE ❶ **duro/dura**; **the meat's a bit tough** la carne está un poco dura, **a tough guy** un tipo duro, **you need to be tough to survive** tienes que ser duro para

sobrevivir ❷ (severe) **severo/severa** ❸ (fabric) **resistente** ❹ (question, problem or job) **difícil**; **things are a bit tough at the moment** las cosas están un poco difíciles en este momento ❺ **tough luck!** ¡mala suerte!

tour NOUN ❶ **visita** FEM; **we did the tour of the castle** hicimos la visita al castillo, **a tour of the city** una visita a la ciudad ❷ **a package tour** un viaje organizado ❸ (by a band or theatre group) **gira** FEM; **to go on tour** ir [8] de gira

tourism NOUN **turismo** MASC

tourist NOUN **turista** MASC & FEM

tourist information office NOUN **oficina** (FEM) **de información y turismo**

towards ADVERB **hacia**; **she went off towards the lake** se fue hacia el lago

towel NOUN **toalla** FEM

tower NOUN **torre** FEM; **the Eiffel Tower** la torre Eiffel

tower block NOUN **bloque** (MASC) **de apartamentos**

town NOUN **ciudad** FEM; **to go into town** ir [8] a la ciudad, (to the centre) ir [8] al centro

town centre NOUN **centro** (MASC) **de la ciudad**

town hall NOUN **ayuntamiento** MASC

toxic ADJECTIVE **tóxico/tóxica**

toy NOUN **juguete** MASC

trace NOUN **rastro** MASC; **there is no trace of it** no hay rastro de ello

trace VERB ❶ *(on paper)* **calcar** [31] ❷ *(a missing person)* **localizar** [22]

tracing paper NOUN **papel** *(MASC)* **de calco**

track NOUN ❶ *(for sport)* **pista** *FEM*; **a track event** una prueba de atletismo, **a racing track** *(for cars)* un circuito ❷ *(a path)* **sendero** *MASC* ❸ *(song)* **tema** *MASC*; **this is my favourite track** es mi tema favorito

track suit NOUN **chandal** *MASC*

tractor NOUN **tractor** *MASC*

trade NOUN *(a profession)* **oficio** *MASC*

trademark NOUN **marca** *(FEM)* **comercial**; **a registered trademark** una marca registrada

trade union NOUN **sindicato** *MASC*

tradition NOUN **tradición** *FEM*

traditional ADJECTIVE **tradicional**

traffic NOUN **tráfico** *MASC*

traffic jam NOUN **embotellamiento** *MASC*

traffic lights PLURAL NOUN **semáforo** *MASC*

traffic warden NOUN **guardia** *(MASC & FEM)* **municipal**

tragedy NOUN **tragedia** *FEM*

tragic ADJECTIVE **trágico/trágica**

trail NOUN *(a path)* **sendero** *MASC*; **a nature trail** un sendero ecológico

trailer NOUN **remolque** *MASC*

train NOUN **tren** *MASC*; **he's coming by train** viene en tren, **I met her off the train** fui a recogerla en la estación, **the train for York** el tren para York

train VERB ❶ **estudiar** [17] *(a student)* ❷ **to train to be something** estudiar para algo, **he's training to be a nurse** está estudiando para ser enfermero ❸ *(in sport)* **entrenar** [17]; **the team trains on Saturdays** el equipo entrena los sábados

trainer NOUN ❶ *(of an athlete or a horse)* **entrenador** *MASC*, **entrenadora** *FEM* ❷ *(shoe)* **zapatilla** *(FEM)* **de deporte**; **my new trainers** mis zapatillas de deporte nuevas

training NOUN ❶ *(for a career)* **formación** *FEM* ❷ *(for sport)* **entrenamiento** *MASC*

train ticket NOUN **billete** *(MASC)* **de tren**

train timetable NOUN **horario** *(MASC)* **de trenes**

tram NOUN **tranvía** *MASC*

trampoline NOUN **cama** *(FEM)* **elástica**

transfer NOUN ❶ *(of money)* **transferencia** *FEM* ❷ *(to new post)* **traslado** *MASC* ❸ *(sticker)* **calcomanía** *FEM*

translate VERB **traducir** [60]; **to translate something into Spanish** traducir algo al español

translation NOUN **traducción** *FEM*

translator NOUN **traductor** *MASC*, **traductora** *FEM*; **I'd like to be a translator** me gustaría ser traductora

transparent ADJECTIVE **transparente**

transplant NOUN **trasplante** *MASC*

transport NOUN transporte MASC; **air transport** transporte aéreo, **public transport** transporte público

trap NOUN trampa FEM

travel NOUN viajes MASC PLURAL; **foreign travel** viajes al extranjero, **a travel brochure** un folleto de viajes

travel VERB viajar [17]

travel agency NOUN agencia (FEM) de viajes

travel agent NOUN agente (MASC) de viajes

traveller NOUN ❶ viajero MASC, viajera FEM ❷ (gypsy) gitano MASC, gitana FEM

travelling NOUN **I like travelling** me gusta viajar

travel-sick NOUN **to be/get travel-sick** marearse [17] en los viajes

tray NOUN bandeja FEM

tread VERB **to tread on something** pisar [17] algo

treasure NOUN tesoro MASC

treat NOUN ❶ capricho MASC; **to give yourself a treat** darse [4] un capricho, **it's a little treat** es un caprichito ❷ **I took them to the circus as a treat** les llevé al circo como algo especial

treat VERB ❶ tratar [17]; **he treats his dog well** trata bien a su perro, **the doctor who treated you** el médico que te trató ❷ **to treat somebody to something** invitar [17] a alguien a algo, **I'll treat you to a drink** te invito a una copa ❸ **I treated myself to a new dress** me compré un vestido para darme un capricho

treatment NOUN tratamiento MASC (medical)

treaty NOUN tratado MASC

tree NOUN árbol MASC

tree trunk NOUN tronco MASC

tremendous ADJECTIVE tremendo/tremenda; **a tremendous victory/defeat** una tremenda victoria/derrota

trend NOUN ❶ (a fashion) moda FEM ❷ (a tendency) tendencia FEM

trendy ADJECTIVE de moda

trial NOUN juicio MASC (legal)

triangle NOUN triángulo MASC

tribe NOUN tribu FEM

tribute NOUN homenaje MASC

trick NOUN ❶ (card or conjuring trick, knack) truco MASC; **a card trick** un truco con las cartas, **it doesn't work, there must be a trick to it** no funciona, debe tener truco ❷ (a joke) broma FEM; **to play a trick on somebody** gastarle [17] una broma a alguien

trick VERB engañar [17]; **he tricked me!** me engañó!

tricky ADJECTIVE delicado/delicada; **it's a tricky situation** es una situación delicada

tricycle NOUN triciclo MASC

Trinidad NOUN Trinidad FEM

Trinidadian NOUN trinitense MASC & FEM

Trinidadian ADJECTIVE trinitense

trip NOUN **viaje** MASC; **a trip to Florida** un viaje a Florida, **he's on a business trip** está en viaje de negocios, **a day trip to France** un viaje de un día a Francia

trip VERB *(to stumble)* **tropezar** [25]; **Nicky tripped over a stone** Nicky tropezó con una piedra

triple VERB **triplicar** [31]; **the price has tripled** el precio se ha triplicado

trolley NOUN **carro** MASC

trombone NOUN **trombón** MASC; **to play the trombone** tocar [31] el trombón

trophy NOUN **trofeo** MASC

trouble NOUN ❶ **problemas** MASC PLURAL; **we had trouble with the car** tuvimos problemas con el coche, **Steve's in trouble** Steve tiene problemas, **to get into trouble** meterse [18] en problemas ❷ **what's the trouble?** ¿cuál es el problema? ❸ *(difficulty)* **I had trouble finding a seat** me costó encontrar un sitio, **it's not worth the trouble** no vale la pena, **the trouble is, I've forgotten the number** el problema es que he olvidado el número, **it's no trouble!** ¡no es ningún problema!

trousers PLURAL NOUN **pantalones** MASC PLURAL; **a new pair of trousers** unos pantalones nuevos, un nuevo par de pantalones

trout NOUN **trucha** FEM

truant NOUN **estudiante** *(MASC & FEM)* **que falta a clase sin autorización**; **she's playing truant** está haciendo novillos

truck NOUN **camión** MASC

true ADJECTIVE **a true story** una historia verídica, **to be true** ser [1] verdad, **is that true?** ¿es eso verdad?, **it's true she's absent-minded** es verdad que es despistada

truly ADVERB **de veras**

trump NOUN **triunfo** MASC; **spades are trumps** las picas son triunfo

trumpet NOUN **trompeta** FEM; **to play the trumpet** tocar [31] la trompeta

trunk NOUN ❶ *(of a tree)* **tronco** MASC ❷ *(of an elephant)* **trompa** FEM ❸ *(a suitcase)* **baúl** MASC

trunks PLURAL NOUN **swimming trunks** bañador MASC

trust NOUN **confianza** FEM

trust VERB **confiar** [32]; **I trust her** confío en ella

truth NOUN **verdad** FEM; **to tell the truth, I'd completely forgottten** si quieres que te diga la verdad, me he olvidado completamente

try NOUN **intento** MASC; **it's my first try** es mi primer intento, **to have a try** intentar [17], **you should give it a try** deberías intentarlo

try VERB ❶ **intentar** [17]; **to try to do** intentar hacer, **I'm trying to open the door** estoy intentando abrir la puerta ❷ *(taste)* **probar** [24]; **try this sauce** prueba esta salsa, **to try hard to do** esforzarse [26] por hacer
• **to try something on** probarse [26] algo *(a garment)*

T-shirt NOUN **camiseta** FEM

a
b
c
d
e
f
g
h
i
j
k
l
m
n
o
p
q
r
s
t
u
v
w
x
y
z

tub NOUN ❶ (food container) **tarrina** FEM ❷ (bath) **bañera** FEM

tube NOUN ❶ **tubo** MASC ❷ **the tube** (London underground) (informal) el **metro**

tuberculosis NOUN **tuberculosis** FEM

Tuesday NOUN **martes** MASC; on Tuesday el martes, I'm going out on Tuesday voy a salir el martes, see you on Tuesday! ¡hasta el martes!, on Tuesdays los martes, the museum is closed on Tuesdays el museo cierra los martes, every Tuesday todos los martes, last Tuesday el martes pasado, next Tuesday el próximo martes

tuition NOUN **clases** FEM PLURAL; piano tuition clases de piano, private tuition clases particulares

tulip NOUN **tulipán** MASC

tumble-drier NOUN **secadora** FEM

tummy NOUN **barriga** FEM

tuna NOUN **atún** MASC

tune NOUN **melodía** FEM

tunnel NOUN **túnel** MASC; the Channel Tunnel el Eurotúnel

turban NOUN **turbante** MASC

turkey NOUN **pavo** MASC

Turkey NOUN **Turquía** FEM

Turkish NOUN **turco** MASC (language)

Turkish ADJECTIVE **turco/turca**

turn NOUN ❶ (in a game) **turno** MASC; it's your turn es tu turno, whose turn is it? ¿a quién le toca?, it's Jane's turn to play es el turno de Jane, to take turns driving turnarse

[17] para conducir ❷ (in a road) **curva** FEM

turn VERB ❶ **girar** [17]; turn your chair round gira la silla, turn left at the next set of lights gira a la izquierda en el próximo semáforo ❷ **dar** [4] **la vuelta a** (a page or mattress) ❸ (become) **ponerse** [11]; she turned red se puso roja
• to turn back volverse [45]; we turned back nos volvimos
• to turn off ❶ (from a road) girar [17] ❷ (switch off) apagar [28] (a light, an oven, a TV, or radio), cerrar [29] (gas, electricity or a tap)
• to turn on encender [36] (a light, an oven, a TV, or radio), abrir [46] (a tap)
• to turn out ❶ to turn out well/ badly salir [63] bien/mal, it all turned out well in the end todo salió bien al final, the holiday turned out badly las vacaciones salieron mal ❷ it turned out that I was wrong resultó que estaba equivocado
• to turn over ❶ (roll over) darse [4] la vuelta ❷ dar [4] la vuelta a (a page)
• to turn up ❶ (to arrive) presentarse [17]; they turned up an hour late se presentaron con una hora de retraso ❷ abrir [46] más (the gas) ❸ subir [19] (the heating or volume); can you turn up the volume? ¿puedes subir el volumen?

turning NOUN **bocacalle** FEM; take the first turning on the right/ left toma la primera bocacalle a la derecha/izquierda

turnip NOUN **nabo** MASC

turquoise ADJECTIVE **turquesa**

turtle NOUN **tortuga** FEM

TV *NOUN* **tele** *FEM*; **I saw her on TV** la vi en la tele

tweezers *NOUN* **pinzas** *FEM PLURAL*

twelfth *NOUN* **the twelfth of May** el doce de mayo

twelfth *ADJECTIVE* **doceavo/doceava**; **on the twelfth floor** en la planta duodécima

twelve *NUMBER* **doce** *MASC*; **Tara's twelve** Tara tiene doce años, **it's twelve o'clock** *(midday)* son las doce de la mañana, *(midnight)* son las doce de la noche

twenty *NUMBER* **veinte**; **Marie's twenty** Marie tiene veinte años, **twenty-one** veintiuno, **twenty-five** veinticinco

twice *ADVERB* ❶ **dos veces**; **I've asked him twice** le he preguntado dos veces ❷ **twice as much** el doble

twig *NOUN* **ramita** *FEM*

twilight *NOUN* **anochecer** *MASC*

twin *NOUN* **gemelo** *MASC*, **gemela** *FEM*; **Helen and Tim are twins** Helen y Tim son gemelos, **her twin sister** su hermana gemela

twin *VERB* **Oxford is twinned with León** Oxford está hermanado con León

twist *VERB* **girar** [17] *(knob or cap of bottle)*

two *NUMBER* **dos** *MASC*; **Ben's two** Ben tiene dos años, **two by two** dos por dos

type *NOUN* **tipo** *MASC*; **what type of computer is it?** ¿qué tipo de ordenador es?

type *VERB* **escribir** [52]; **I'm learning to type** estoy aprendiendo a escribir a máquina, **I was busy typing some letters** estaba ocupada escribiendo unas cartas a máquina

typical *ADJECTIVE* **típico/típica**

typing *NOUN* **mecanografía** *FEM*; **her typing is awful** escribe muy mal a máquina

tyre *NOUN* **neumático** *MASC*

a
b
c
d
e
f
g
h
i
j
k
l
m
n
o
p
q
r
s
t
u
v
w
x
y
z

Uu

UFO NOUN ovni MASC

ugly ADJECTIVE feo/fea

UK NOUN Reino (MASC) Unido

ulcer NOUN úlcera FEM

umbrella NOUN paraguas MASC (does not change in the plural)

umpire NOUN árbitro MASC, árbitra FEM

UN NOUN ONU FEM (short for 'Organización de las Naciones Unidas')

unable ADJECTIVE to be unable to do no poder [10] hacer, he's unable to come no puede venir

unavoidable ADJECTIVE inevitable

unbearable ADJECTIVE insoportable

unbelievable ADJECTIVE increíble

uncertain ADJECTIVE incierto/incierta no seguro/no segura; I'm uncertain whether they are coming no estoy seguro/segura si vienen o no

uncle NOUN tío MASC; my Uncle Tom mi tío Tom

uncomfortable ADJECTIVE incómodo/incómoda

unconscious ADJECTIVE (out cold) sin sentido; Tessa's still unconscious Tessa está todavía sin sentido

under PREPOSITION ❶ (underneath) debajo de; under the bed debajo de la cama, perhaps it's under there quizás está ahí debajo, to go under something pasar por debajo de algo ❷ (less than) menos de; under £20 menos de veinte libras ❸ children under five niños menores de cinco años

underground NOUN (a railway) metro MASC; shall we go by underground? ¿vamos en metro?

underground ADJECTIVE subterráneo/subterránea; an underground carpark un parking subterráneo

underline VERB subrayar [17]

underneath PREPOSITION debajo de; it's underneath these papers está debajo de esos papeles

underneath ADVERB debajo; look underneath mira debajo

underpants PLURAL NOUN calzoncillos MASC PLURAL; my underpants mis calzoncillos, a pair of underpants unos calzoncillos

underpass NOUN ❶ (pedestrian) paso (MASC) subterráneo ❷ (for traffic) paso (MASC) inferior

understand VERB entender [36]; I don't understand no entiendo, I couldn't understand what he was saying no entendí lo que estaba diciendo

understandable ADJECTIVE comprensible; that's understandable eso es comprensible

underwear NOUN ropa (FEM) interior

undo VERB ❶ desabrochar [17] *(a button or a garment)* ❷ desatar [17] *(shoelaces)* ❸ deshacer [7] *(a parcel or knot)*

undone ADJECTIVE to come undone desabrocharse [17] *(a button)* desatarse [17] *(shoelaces)*

undress VERB to get undressed desvestirse [57], I got undressed me desvestí

unemployed ADJECTIVE parado/parada; she's unemployed está parada

unemployment NOUN paro MASC

uneven ADJECTIVE irregular

unexpected ADJECTIVE inesperado/inesperada

unexpectedly ADVERB *(to happen, arrive)* de improviso

unfair ADJECTIVE injusto/injusta; it's unfair to young people es injusto para la gente joven

unfasten VERB desabrochar [17]

unfold VERB desdoblar [17]

unforgettable ADJECTIVE inolvidable

unfortunate ADJECTIVE desgraciado/desgraciada

unfortunately ADVERB desgraciadamente

unfriendly ADJECTIVE antipático/antipática

ungrateful ADJECTIVE desagradecido/desagradecida

unhappy ADJECTIVE ❶ infeliz; an unhappy childhood una infancia infeliz ❷ *(discontented)* to be unhappy no estar [2] contento/contenta

unhurt ADJECTIVE ileso/ilesa

uniform NOUN uniforme MASC; in school uniform con el uniforme del colegio

uninhabited ADJECTIVE desierto/desierta

union NOUN *(a trade union)* sindicato MASC

unique ADJECTIVE único/única

unit NOUN ❶ *(for measuring, for example)* unidad FEM ❷ *(in a kitchen)* módulo MASC ❸ *(a hospital department)* servicio MASC

United Kingdom NOUN Reino (MASC) Unido

United Nations NOUN Naciones (FEM PLURAL) Unidas

United States (of America) PLURAL NOUN Estados (MASC PLURAL) Unidos (de América)

universe NOUN universo MASC

university NOUN universidad FEM; to go to university ir [8] a la universidad

unjust ADJECTIVE injusto/injusta

unkind ADJECTIVE poco amable

unknown ADJECTIVE desconocido/desconocida

unleaded petrol NOUN gasolina (FEM) sin plomo

unless _CONJUNCTION_ **a no ser que** _(followed by subjunctive)_; **unless he does it** a no ser que él lo haga, **unless you tell her** a no ser que tú se lo digas

unlikely _ADJECTIVE_ **poco probable**; **it's unlikely** es poco probable

unload _VERB_ **descargar** [28]

unlock _VERB_ **to unlock a door** abrir [46] una puerta, **the car's unlocked** el coche está abierto, **the door was unlocked** la puerta no estaba cerrada con llave

unlucky _ADJECTIVE_ ❶ _(a person)_ **to be unlucky** no tener [9] suerte, **I was unlucky, it was shut** no tuve suerte, estaba cerrado ❷ **thirteen is an unlucky number** el trece trae mala suerte

unmarried _ADJECTIVE_ **soltero/soltera**

unnatural _ADJECTIVE_ **poco natural**

unnecessary _ADJECTIVE_ **no necesario**; **it's unnecessary to book** no es necesario reservar

unpack _VERB_ **I unpacked my rucksack** saqué las cosas de mi mochila, **I'll just unpack and then come down** voy a deshacer las maletas y bajo

unpaid _ADJECTIVE_ ❶ **sin pagar** _(a bill)_ ❷ **no remunerado** _(work)_

unpleasant _ADJECTIVE_ **desagradable**

unpopular _ADJECTIVE_ **poco popular**

unrealistic _ADJECTIVE_ **poco realista**

unreasonable _ADJECTIVE_ **poco razonable**; **he's being really unreasonable** no está siendo nada razonable

unreliable _ADJECTIVE_ ❶ **poco fidedigno** _(information)_ ❷ **this computer is unreliable** no te puedes fiar de este ordenador ❸ **informal** _(person)_; **he's unreliable** es informal

unroll _VERB_ **desenrollar** [17]

unsafe _ADJECTIVE_ **peligroso/peligrosa** _(wiring, for instance)_

unscrew _VERB_ **destornillar** [17]

unsuccessful _ADJECTIVE_ **to be unsuccessful** fracasar [17], **I tried, but I was unsuccessful** lo intenté pero fracasé, **an unsuccessful attempt** un intento fallido

untidy _ADJECTIVE_ **desordenado/desordenada**; **the house is always untidy** la casa siempre está desordenada

untie _VERB_ **desatar** [17]

until _PREPOSITION_ ❶ **hasta**; **until Monday** hasta el lunes, **until the tenth** hasta el diez, **until now** hasta ahora, **until then** hasta entonces ❷ **not until** no hasta, **not until September** no hasta septiembre, **it won't be finished until Friday** no estará terminado hasta el viernes

unusual _ADJECTIVE_ **poco corriente**; **an unusual beetle** un escarabajo poco corriente, **storms are unusual in June** las tormentas son poco corrientes en junio

unwilling _ADJECTIVE_ **to be unwilling to do** no estar [2] dispuesto a hacer, **he's unwilling to wait** no está dispuesto a esperar

unwrap _VERB_ **desenvolver** [45]

up _PREPOSITION, ADVERB_ ❶ _(higher up)_ **arriba**; **hands up!** ¡manos arriba!, **up here** aquí arriba, **up there** ahí arriba, **it's just up the road** está en

594

esta calle un poco más arriba, **up on the roof** en el tejado, **up in Glasgow** en Glasgow ❷ **to go up** subir [19] *(stairs or road)*, **we went up the street** subimos la calle, **I ran up the street** subí la calle corriendo, **I'll go up to Glasgow this weekend** iré a Glasgow este fin de semana ❸ *(out of bed)* **to be up** estar [2] levantado, **Liz isn't up yet** Liz aún no está levantada, **to get up** levantarse [17], **we got up at six** nos levantamos a las seis, **I was up late last night** me acosté tarde anoche, **she was up all night** no se acostó en toda la noche ❹ *(wrong)* **what's up?** ¿qué pasa?, **what's up with him?** ¿qué le pasa? ❺ **up to** hasta, **up to here** hasta aquí, **up to fifty people** hasta cincuenta personas, **she came up to me** se acercó a mí ❻ **what's she up to?** ¿qué está haciendo?, **it's up to you (to decide)** tú tienes que decidir
• **time's up!** ¡se acabó el tiempo!

uphill *ADVERB* **cuesta arriba**

upright *ADJECTIVE* **derecho/derecha**; **put it upright** ponlo derecho, **to stand upright** estar [2] derecho

upset *NOUN* **a stomach upset** un dolor de estómago

upset *ADJECTIVE* **disgustado/ disgustada**; **he's upset** está disgustado

upset *VERB* **to upset somebody** disgustar [17] a alguien

upside down *ADJECTIVE* **boca abajo**

upstairs *ADVERB* **arriba**; **Mum's upstairs** mamá está arriba, **to go upstairs** subir [19]

up-to-date *ADJECTIVE* ❶ *(in fashion)* **moderno/moderna**

❷ *(information)* **actualizado/ actualizada**

urgent *ADJECTIVE* **urgente**

urgently *ADVERB* **urgentemente**; **she wants to see you urgently** quiere verte urgentemente

us *PRONOUN* ❶ **nos**; **she knows us** nos conoce, **they saw us** nos vieron, **he gave us a cheque** nos dio un cheque *(when there are two pronouns, 'nos' comes first)*, **they lent it to us** nos lo dejaron ❷ *(with an infinitive or when telling someone to do something, 'nos' joins onto the verb)* **can you help us, please?** ¿puedes ayudarnos por favor?, ¿nos puedes ayudar, por favor?, **listen to us!** ¡escúchanos!, **wait for us!** ¡espéranos!, *(but when telling someone NOT to do something, 'nos' comes before the verb)* **don't push us!** ¡no nos empujes! ❸ *(after a preposition, in comparisons, or after the verb 'to be')* **nosotros/nosotras**; **behind us** detrás de nosotros/nosotras, **they left without us** se fueron sin nosotros/nosotras, **with us** con nosotros/nosotras, **she's older than us** es mayor que nosotros/nosotras, **it's us!** ¡somos nosotros/nosotras!

US, USA *NOUN* **EE.UU** *MASC (short for Estados Unidos)*

use *NOUN* ❶ **uso** *MASC*; **instructions for use** instrucciones de uso ❷ **it's no use** no sirve de nada, **it's no use phoning** no sirve de nada llamar

use *VERB* **usar** [17]; **we use the dictionary** usamos el diccionario, **to use something to do** usar [17] algo para hacer, **I used a knife to open the parcel** usé un cuchillo para abrir el paquete

used   **valley**

- **to use up ❶** consumir [19] todo *(food)* **❷** gastar [17] todo *(money or petrol)*

used *ADJECTIVE* **❶ to be used to something** estar [2] acostumbrado/ acostumbrada a algo, **I'm not used to cats** no estoy acostumbrado a los gatos, **I'm not used to it** no estoy acostumbrado, **I'm not used to eating in restaurants** no estoy acostumbrado a comer en restaurantes **❷ to get used to** acostumbrarse [17] a, **I've got used to living here** me he acostumbrado a vivir aquí, **you'll get used to it!** ¡ya te acostumbrarás!

used *VERB* **they used to live in the country** vivían en el campo, **she used to smoke** antes fumarba

useful *ADJECTIVE* útil

useless *ADJECTIVE* **❶** inútil *(person)*; **you're completely useless!** ¡eres un completo inútil! **❷ this knife is useless** este cuchillo no sirve para nada

user *NOUN* usuario *MASC*, usuaria *FEM*

user-friendly *ADJECTIVE* fácil de usar

usual *ADJECTIVE, ADVERB* **❶** *(time, place, problem)* de siempre; **it's the usual problem** es el problema de siempre **❷** *(method)* habitual **❸ as usual** como siempre **❹ it's colder than usual** hace más frío de lo normal

usually *ADVERB* normalmente; **I usually leave at eight** normalmente salgo a las ocho

utensil *NOUN* utensillo *MASC*

Vv

vacancy *NOUN* **❶** *(in a hotel)* 'vacancies' 'habitaciones libres', 'no vacancies' 'completo' **❷ a job vacancy** una oferta de trabajo

vacant *ADJECTIVE* libre *(room or seat)*

vaccinate *VERB* vacunar [17]

vaccination *NOUN* vacuna *FEM*

vacuum *NOUN* vacío *MASC*

vacuum *VERB* pasar [17] la aspiradora; **I'm going to vacuum my room** voy a pasar la aspiradora por mi habitación

vacuum cleaner *NOUN* aspiradora *FEM*

vagina *NOUN* vagina *FEM*

vague *ADJECTIVE* poco preciso/poco precisa

vaguely *ADVERB* vagamente

vain *ADJECTIVE* vano/vana *(attempt)*; **in vain** en vano

valentine card *NOUN* tarjeta *(FEM)* que se envía el día de los enamorados

Valentine's Day *NOUN* día *(MASC)* de San Valentín

valid *ADJECTIVE* válido/válida

valley *NOUN* valle *MASC*

valuable ADJECTIVE **valioso/valiosa**; **to be valuable** ser [1] valioso/ valiosa, **that watch is very valuable** este reloj es muy valioso, **he gave us some valuable information** nos dio información muy valiosa

value NOUN **valor** MASC

value VERB **valorar** [17] *(somebody's help, opinion, or friendship)*

van NOUN **furgoneta** FEM

vandal NOUN **gamberro** MASC, **gamberra** FEM

vandalism NOUN **gamberrismo** MASC

vandalize VERB **destrozar** [22]

vanilla NOUN **vainilla** FEM; **a vanilla ice cream** un helado de vainilla

vanish VERB **desaparecer** [35]

variety NOUN **variedad** FEM

various ADJECTIVE **varios/varias** *(always goes before the noun)*; **there are various ways of doing it** hay varias formas de hacerlo

vary VERB **variar** [32]; **it varies a lot** varía mucho

vase NOUN **jarrón** MASC

VAT NOUN **IVA** MASC

VCR NOUN **cámara** *(FEM)* **de vídeo**

VDU NOUN **monitor** MASC

veal NOUN **ternera** FEM

vegetable NOUN **verdura** FEM

vegetarian NOUN **vegetariano** MASC, **vegetariana** FEM

vegetarian ADJECTIVE **vegetariano/ vegetariana**; **he's vegetarian** es vegetariano

vehicle NOUN **vehículo** MASC

vein NOUN **vena** FEM

velvet NOUN **terciopelo** MASC

vending machine NOUN **máquina** *(FEM)* **expendedora**

ventilation NOUN **ventilación** FEM

verb NOUN **verbo** MASC

verdict NOUN **veredicto** MASC

verge NOUN ❶ *(the roadside)* **arcén** MASC ❷ **to be on the verge of doing** estar [2] a punto de hacer, **I was on the verge of leaving** estaba a punto de irme

version NOUN **versión** FEM

versus PREPOSITION **contra**; **Arsenal versus Chelsea** Arsenal contra Chelsea

vertical ADJECTIVE **vertical**

vertigo NOUN **vértigo** MASC

very ADVERB ❶ **muy**; **it's very difficult** es muy difícil, **very well** muy bien ❷ **very much** mucho, **I like it very much** me gusta mucho

very ADJECTIVE ❶ **the very person I need!** ¡justo la persona que necesito!, **the very thing he was looking for** justo lo que estaba buscando ❷ **in the very middle** justo en medio, **at the very end** justo al final, **at the very front** justo delante

vest NOUN **camiseta** FEM

vet NOUN **veterinario** MASC, **veterinaria** FEM; **she's a vet** es veterinaria

via PREPOSITION to go via ir [8] por, we're going via Dover vamos por Dover, we'll go via the bank pasaremos por el banco

vicar NOUN párroco MASC

vicious ADJECTIVE ❶ fiero/fiera (a dog) ❷ feroz (an attack)

victim NOUN víctima FEM

victory NOUN victoria FEM

video NOUN ❶ (film) vídeo MASC; to watch a video ver [16] un vídeo, I've got it on video lo tengo en vídeo ❷ (cassette) cinta (FEM) de vídeo

video VERB grabar [17]; I'll video it for you yo te lo grabo

video game NOUN videojuego MASC

view NOUN ❶ vista FEM; a room with a view of the lake una habitación con vista al lago ❷ (opinion) opinión FEM; in my view en mi opinión, a point of view una opinión

viewer NOUN (of TV) televidente MASC & FEM

viewpoint NOUN punto (MASC) de vista

vile ADJECTIVE horrible

villa NOUN chalet MASC

village NOUN pueblo MASC

villager NOUN habitante (MASC & FEM) de un pueblo

vine NOUN vid FEM

vinegar NOUN vinagre MASC

vineyard NOUN viñedo MASC

violence NOUN violencia FEM

violent ADJECTIVE violento/violenta

violin NOUN violín MASC; to play the violin tocar [31] el violín

violinist NOUN violinista MASC & FEM

Virgo NOUN Virgo MASC; Robert's Virgo Robert es virgo

virtual reality NOUN realidad (FEM) virtual

virus NOUN virus MASC; anti-virus software software anti virus

visa NOUN visado MASC

visible ADJECTIVE visible

visit NOUN visita FEM

visit VERB visitar [17]; we visited Auntie Pat at Christmas visitamos a la tía Pat en Navidad

visitor NOUN ❶ visita FEM; we've got visitors tonight hoy tenemos visita ❷ (a tourist) visitante MASC & FEM

visual ADJECTIVE visual

vital ADJECTIVE muy importante; it's vital to book es muy importante reservar

vitamin NOUN vitamina FEM

vivid ADJECTIVE ❶ (colour or imagination) vivo/viva; to have a vivid imagination tener una imaginación muy viva ❷ (memory or dream) vívido/vívida

vocabulary NOUN vocabulario MASC

vocational ADJECTIVE vocacional

vodka NOUN vodka MASC

voice NOUN voz FEM

volcano NOUN volcán MASC

volleyball NOUN **vóleibol** MASC; **to play volleyball** jugar [27] al vóleibol

volume NOUN **volumen** MASC; **could you turn down the volume?** ¿puedes bajar el volumen?

voluntary ADJECTIVE ❶ *(not compulsory)* **voluntario/voluntaria** ❷ **to do voluntary work** trabajar [17] de voluntario

volunteer NOUN **voluntario** MASC, **voluntaria** FEM

vomit VERB **vomitar** [17]

vote NOUN **voto** MASC

vote VERB **votar** [17]; **she always votes for the Greens** siempre vota a los verdes

voucher NOUN **vale** MASC

vowel NOUN **vocal** FEM

voyage NOUN **viaje** MASC

vulgar ADJECTIVE **grosero/grosera** *(person or speech)*

waffle NOUN *(to eat)* **gofre** MASC

wage(s) *(PLURAL)* NOUN **sueldo** MASC

wagon NOUN **vagón** MASC

waist NOUN **cintura** FEM

waistcoat NOUN **chaleco** MASC

waist measurement NOUN **medida** *(FEM)* **de cintura**

wait NOUN **espera** FEM; **an hour's wait** una espera de una hora

wait VERB ❶ **esperar** [17]; **they're waiting in the car** están esperando en el coche, **she kept me waiting** me tuvo esperando ❷ **to wait for** esperar algo, **wait for me!** ¡espérame!, **wait for the signal** espera la señal ❸ **I can't wait to open it!** ¡estoy deseando abrirlo!

waiter NOUN **camarero** MASC

waiting list NOUN **lista** *(FEM)* **de espera**

waiting room NOUN **sala** *(FEM)* **de espera**

waitress NOUN **camarera** FEM

wake VERB ❶ **despertar** [29] *(somebody else)*; **Jess woke me at six** Jess me despertó a las seis ❷ **despertarse** [29]; **I woke (up) at six** me desperté a las seis, **wake up!** ¡despiértate!

Wales NOUN País (MASC) de Gales

walk NOUN paseo MASC; **to go for a walk** ir [8] a dar un paseo, **we went for a walk in the woods** fuimos a dar un paseo por el bosque, **we'll go for a little walk round the village** daremos un paseo por el pueblo, **to take the dog for a walk** sacar [31] a pasear al perro, **it's about five minutes' walk from here** está a unos cinco minutos de aquí a pie

walk VERB ❶ andar [21]; **I like walking on sand** me gusta andar sobre la arena ❷ (on foot rather than by car or bus) ir [8] andando; **it's not far, we can walk** no está lejos, podemos ir andado
• **to walk around** dar [4] una vuelta por; **we walked around the old town** dimos una vuelta por la parte vieja de la ciudad
• **to walk with somebody** acompañar a alguien; **I'll walk to the bus stop with you** te acompaño hasta la parada del autobús

walking NOUN (hiking) hacer [7] senderismo; **we're going walking in Scotland** vamos a hacer senderismo en Escocia

walking distance NOUN **it's within walking distance of the sea** se puede ir andando hasta la playa

walking stick NOUN bastón MASC

wall NOUN ❶ (of a house) pared FEM ❷ (of a city) muralla FEM; **the Great Wall of China** la Gran Muralla de China

wallet NOUN cartera FEM

wallpaper NOUN papel (MASC) pintado

walnut NOUN nuez FEM

wander VERB **to wander around town** pasear [17] por la ciudad, **to wander off** alejarse [17]

want NOUN **all our wants** todo lo que necesitamos

want VERB querer [12]; **do you want some coffee?** ¿quieres café?, **what do you want to do?** ¿qué quieres hacer?, **I don't want to bother him** no quiero molestarlo, **I want them to help me** quiero que me ayuden (note that 'querer que' is followed by the subjunctive)

war NOUN guerra FEM

ward NOUN sala FEM (in a hospital)

wardrobe NOUN ❶ (piece of furniture) armario MASC ❷ (clothes) vestuario MASC

warehouse NOUN almacén MASC

warm ADJECTIVE ❶ (water) templado/templada (not very hot) ❷ (breeze) cálido/cálida ❸ (hot) caliente; **a warm drink** una bebida caliente, **I'll keep your dinner warm** te tendré la comida caliente, **a warm bath** un baño caliente ❹ **it's warm today** hoy hace calorcito, **I'm warm** tengo calor, **are you warm enough?** ¿tienes frío? ❺ (friendly) caluroso/calurosa; **a warm welcome** una bienvenida calurosa, **a warm person** una persona cariñosa

warm VERB calentar [29]; **to warm the plates** calentar los platos
• **to warm up** ❶ (the weather) **it's warming up** está empezando a hacer más calor ❷ (an athlete) entrar [17] en calor ❸ (to heat up) calentar [29] (food); **I'll warm up some soup for you** te calentaré un poco de sopa

warmth NOUN **calor** MASC

warn VERB **advertir** [14]; **I warn you, it's expensive** te lo advierto, es caro, **to warn somebody to do** advertir a alguien que haga *(note that 'que' is followed by the subjunctive)*, **he warned me to lock the car** me advirtió que cerrase el coche

warning NOUN **advertencia** FEM

wart NOUN **verruga** FEM

wash NOUN **to give something a wash** lavar [17] algo, **to have a wash** lavarse

wash VERB **lavar** [17]; **I've washed your jeans** he lavado tus vaqueros, **to wash your hands** lavarse las manos, **I washed my hands** me he lavado las manos, **to wash your hair** lavarse la cabeza, **I have to wash my hair** tengo que lavarme la cabeza, **to get washed** lavarse, **to wash the dishes** lavar los platos
• **to wash up** lavar los platos

washbasin NOUN **lavabo** MASC

washing NOUN ❶ *(dirty)* **ropa** *(FEM)* **sucia** ❷ *(clean)* **ropa** *(FEM)* **limpia**

washing machine NOUN **lavadora** FEM

washing powder NOUN **detergente** MASC

washing-up NOUN **platos** *(FEM)* **sucios**; **to do the washing-up** lavar [17] los platos

washing-up liquid NOUN **lavavajillas** MASC *(does not change in the plural)*

wasp NOUN **avispa** FEM

waste NOUN ❶ *(of food, money, paper)* **desperdicio** MASC ❷ *(of time)* **it's a waste of time** es una pérdida de tiempo

waste VERB ❶ **desperdiciar** [17] *(food, money, paper)* ❷ **perder** [36] *(time)*; **you're wasting your time** estás perdiendo el tiempo

waste-bin NOUN **papelera** FEM

wastepaper-basket NOUN **papelera** FEM

watch NOUN **reloj** MASC; **my watch is fast** mi reloj está adelantado, **my watch is slow** mi reloj está atrasado

watch VERB ❶ *(to look at)* **mirar** [17]; **I was watching TV** estaba viendo la televisión ❷ **to watch a film** ver [16] una película ❸ *(keep a check on)* **watch the time** estate atento al reloj, **could you watch the baby for a while?** ¿puedes cuidar al niño un rato? ❹ *(suspect)* **vigilar** [17] ❺ *(to be careful)* **watch you don't spill it** ten cuidado de no tirarlo, **watch out for nettles** cuidado con las ortigas, **watch out!** ¡cuidado!

water NOUN **agua** FEM *(even though 'agua' is feminine, it takes 'el' in the singular)*

water VERB **regar** [30]; **to water the plants** regar las plantas

watercolours PLURAL NOUN **acuarelas** FEM PLURAL

waterfall NOUN **cascada** FEM

watering can NOUN **regadera** FEM

water melon NOUN **sandía** FEM

waterproof ADJECTIVE **impermeable**

water-skiing NOUN **esquí** (MASC) **acuático**; to go water-skiing **hacer** [7] **esquí acuático**

water sports PLURAL NOUN **deportes** (MASC) **náuticos**

wave NOUN ❶ (in the sea) **ola** FEM ❷ (with your hand) (to say hello) **saludo** MASC (to say goodbye) **adiós** MASC; she gave him a wave from the bus **le saludó con la mano desde el autobús**, (to say goodbye) **le dijo adiós con la mano desde el autobús**

wave VERB ❶ (with your hand) (to say hello) **saludar** [17], (to say goodbye) **decir** [5] **adiós** ❷ (flap) **agitar** [17] (your ticket or the newspaper, for example)

wax NOUN **cera** FEM

way NOUN ❶ (a route or road) **camino** MASC; the way to town **el camino a la ciudad**, we asked the way to the station **preguntamos el camino a la estación**, on the way back **en el camino de vuelta**, on the way **en camino**, 'way in' **'entrada'**, 'way out' **'salida'** ❷ (direction) **dirección** FEM; which way did he go? **¿en qué dirección se fue?**, come this way **ven por aquí**, to be in the way **estorbar** [17] ❸ put it the right way up **ponlo bien**, the wrong way up **boca abajo**, your jumper is the wrong way round **tu jersey está al revés** ❹ (distance) it's a long way **está muy lejos**, Terry went all the way to York **Terry fue hasta York** ❺ (manner) **manera** FEM; a way of talking **una manera de hablar**, he does it his way **lo hace a su manera**, I did it the wrong way **lo hice mal**, that's not the way to do it **no se hace así**, either way, she's wrong **sea como sea, está equivocada**, do it this way **hazlo de esta manera** ❻ no way! **¡ni hablar!** ❼ by the way **por cierto**

way in NOUN **entrada** FEM

way out NOUN **salida** FEM

we PRONOUN ❶ ('we' like other subject pronouns is generally not translated; in Spanish the form of the verb tells you whether the subject of the verb is 'we', you, they', etc., so 'we' is only translated for emphasis) we live in Carlisle **vivimos en Carlisle**, we're going to the cinema tonight **vamos a ir al cine esta noche** ❷ (for emphasis) **nosotros/nosotras** we did it **lo hicimos nosotros**

weak ADJECTIVE ❶ (feeble) **débil**; her voice was weak **su voz era débil** ❷ **poco cargado/poco cargada** (coffee or tea)

wealth NOUN **riqueza** FEM

wealthy ADJECTIVE **rico/rica**

weapon NOUN **arma** FEM

wear NOUN **children's wear ropa** (FEM) **de niños**, sports wear **ropa de deporte**

wear VERB **llevar** [17]; Tamsin's wearing her trainers **Tamsin lleva sus zapatillas de deporte**, he was wearing black trousers **llevaba pantalones negros**, she often wears red **a menudo viste de rojo**, to wear make-up **llevar maquillaje**

weather NOUN **tiempo** MASC; what's the weather like? **¿qué tiempo hace?**, in fine weather **cuando hace buen tiempo**, the weather was cold **hacía frío**, the weather here is terrible **aquí hace un tiempo horrible**

weather forecast NOUN pronóstico (MASC) del tiempo; the weather forecast says it will rain el pronóstico del tiempo dice que va a llover

web NOUN ❶ (spider's) telaraña FEM ❷ (Internet) the Web la Web

web site NOUN sitio (MASC) web

wedding NOUN boda FEM

Wednesday NOUN miércoles MASC (does not change in the plural); on Wednesday el miércoles, I'm going out on Wednesday voy a salir el miércoles, see you on Wednesday! ¡hasta el miércoles!, on Wednesdays los miércoles, the museum is closed on Wednesdays el museo cierra los miércoles, every Wednesday cada miércoles, last Wednesday el miércoles pasado, next Wednesday el próximo miércoles

weed NOUN mala hierba FEM

week NOUN semana FEM; last week la semana pasada, next week la próxima semana, this week esta semana, for weeks durante semanas, a week today una semana a partir de hoy

weekday NOUN on weekdays entre semana

weekend NOUN fin (MASC) de semana; last weekend el fin de semana pasado, next weekend el próximo fin de semana, they're coming for the weekend vienen a pasar el fin de semana, I'll do it at the weekend lo haré durante el fin de semana, have a nice weekend! ¡que pases un buen fin de semana!

weekly ADVERB semanalmente, cada semana; I see her weekly la veo cada semana

weekly ADJECTIVE semanal; a weekly magazine una revista semanal

weigh VERB pesar [17]; to weigh something pesar algo, how much do you weigh? ¿cuánto pesas?, I weigh 50 kilos peso cincuenta kilos, to weigh yourself pesarse [17]

weight NOUN peso MASC; to put on weight engordar [17], to lose weight adelgazar [22]

weird ADJECTIVE extraño/extraña

welcome NOUN bienvenida FEM; they gave us a warm welcome nos dieron una calurosa bienvenida

welcome ADJECTIVE ❶ bienvenido/ bienvenida; you're welcome any time siempre eres bienvenido, welcome to Oxford! ¡bienvenido a Oxford! ❷ 'thank you!' – 'you're welcome!' 'gracias' – 'de nada'

welcome VERB dar [4] la bienvenida a

well¹ NOUN (for water) pozo MASC

well² ADVERB ❶ bien; to feel well sentirse [14] bien, I'm very well, thank you estoy muy bien, gracias ❷ bien; Terry played well Terry jugó bien, the operation went well la operación salió bien, well done! ¡bien hecho! ❸ as well también, Kevin's coming as well Kevin también viene ❹ as well as además de ❺ well then, what's the problem? entonces, ¿cuál es el problema? ❻ very well then, you can go muy bien, entonces ya puedes irte

well-behaved ADJECTIVE a well behaved child un niño que se porta bien, **be well-behaved** pórtate bien

well-done ADJECTIVE muy hecho/muy hecha (a steak)

wellington (boot) NOUN catiusca FEM

well-known ADJECTIVE conocido/bien conocida

well-off ADJECTIVE acomodado/acomodada

Welsh NOUN **①** the Welsh (people) los galeses **②** (language) galés MASC

Welsh ADJECTIVE galés/galesa

Welshman NOUN galés MASC

Welshwoman NOUN galesa FEM

west NOUN oeste MASC; **in the west** al oeste

west ADJECTIVE, ADVERB (does not change) **the west side** la parte oeste, **a west wind** un viento del oeste, **west of Paris** al oeste de París

western NOUN (a film) película (FEM) de vaqueros

West Indian NOUN afroantillano MASC, afroantillana FEM

West Indian ADJECTIVE afroantillano/afroantillana

West Indies PLURAL NOUN Antillas FEM; **in the West Indies** en las Antillas

wet ADJECTIVE **①** (damp) húmedo/húmeda; **the grass is wet** la hierba está húmeda, **to get wet** mojarse [17], **we got wet** nos mojamos **②** a **wet day** un día lluvioso

whale NOUN ballena FEM

what PRONOUN, DETERMINER **①** qué (in questions); **what did you say?** ¿qué has dicho?, **what's she doing?** ¿qué está haciendo?, **what did you buy?** ¿qué has comprado?, **what is it?** ¿qué es?, **what's the matter?** ¿qué pasa?, **what's happening?** ¿qué está pasando? **②** **what's your address?** ¿cuál es su dirección?, **what country is it in?** ¿en qué país está?, **what colour is it?** ¿de qué color es?, **what make is it?** ¿de qué marca es? **③** **what's her name?** ¿cómo se llama?, **what?** ¿cómo?, **what's it like?** ¿cómo es? **④** **what for?** ¿para qué?, **what's it for?** ¿para qué sirve?, **what did you buy it for?** ¿para qué lo has comprado? **⑤** lo que; **tell me what you bought** dime lo que has comprado, **she told me what had happened** me dijo lo que había pasado, **what I want is a car** lo que quiero es un coche

wheat NOUN trigo MASC

wheel NOUN rueda FEM; **the spare wheel** la rueda de repuesto, **the steering wheel** el volante

wheelbarrow NOUN carretilla FEM

wheelchair NOUN silla (FEM) de ruedas

when ADVERB cuándo; **when's she arriving?** ¿cuándo llega?, **when's your birthday?** ¿cuándo es tu cumpleaños?, **ask when the next train is leaving** pregunta cuándo sale el próximo tren

when CONJUNCTION cuando; **it was raining when I went out** estaba lloviendo cuando salí

whenever ADVERB ❶ (any time) cuando; come whenever you like ven cuando quieras ❷ (each time) siempre que; whenever we go out, we lock the door siempre que salimos, cerramos la puerta con llave

where ADVERB dónde; where are the plates? ¿dónde están los platos?, where do you live? ¿dónde vives?, where are you going? ¿dónde vas?, I don't know where they live no sé donde viven

where PRONOUN donde; the place where I live el lugar dónde vivo

where CONJUNCTION donde; this is where I left it ahí es donde lo dejé

whether CONJUNCTION si; I don't know whether he's back or not no sé si ha vuelto o no

which DETERMINER qué; which CD did you buy? ¿qué compacto compraste?, which drawer did you put it in? ¿en qué cajón lo metiste?, which one cuál, 'I saw your brother' – 'which one?' 'ví a tu hermano' – '¿a cuál?'

which PRONOUN ❶ (in questions) which of these jackets is yours? ¿cuál de estas chaquetas es la tuya? ❷ (relative pronoun) que; the lamp which is on the table la lámpara que está en la mesa, the book which you chose el libro que escogiste, the film which I told you about el libro del que te hablé

while NOUN for a while (long time) durante un tiempo, (short time) durante un rato, she worked here for a while trabajó allí durante un tiempo, I read for a while leí durante un rato, after a while (long time) después de un tiempo, (short time) después de un rato

while CONJUNCTION mientras; you can make some tea while I'm finishing my homework puedes hacer un té mientras termino los deberes

whip NOUN (for a horse) látigo MASC

whip VERB montar [17] (cream); whipped cream nata (FEM) montada

whirlpool NOUN remolino MASC

whiskers PLURAL NOUN bigotes MASC PLURAL

whisky NOUN whisky MASC

whisper NOUN susurro MASC; to speak in a whisper hablar [17] en susurros

whisper VERB susurrar [17]

whistle NOUN ❶ (sound) silbido MASC ❷ (instrument) silbato MASC

whistle VERB silbar [17]

white NOUN ❶ (colour) blanco MASC ❷ an egg white una clara de huevo

white ADJECTIVE blanco/blanca; a white shirt una camisa blanca

white coffee NOUN café (MASC) con leche

who PRONOUN ❶ (in questions) quién; who wants some sweets? ¿quién quiere caramelos? ❷ (relative pronoun as subject of the verb) que; my friend who lives in Madrid el amigo mío que vive en Madrid ❸ (as object of the verb: referring to one person) el que/la que; the girl who I gave it to la chica a la que se lo di ❹ (as object of the verb: referring to more than one person) los que/las que; the friends who we invited los amigos a los que hemos invitado

whole NOUN **the whole of the class** toda la clase, **on the whole** en general

whole ADJECTIVE **todo/toda; the whole family** toda la familia, **the whole morning** toda la mañana, **the whole time** todo el tiempo, **the whole world** todo el mundo

wholemeal ADJECTIVE **integral; wholemeal bread** pan integral

whom PRONOUN ❶ (in questions) **quién; whom did you see?** ¿a quién viste? ❷ (as relative pronoun) **que; the person whom I saw** la persona que vi ❸ (after a preposition: referring to one person) **el que/la que; the person to whom I wrote** la persona a la que escribí ❹ (after a preposition: referring to more than one person) **los que/las que; the people to whom I wrote** las personas a las que escribí

whose PRONOUN, DETERMINER ❶ **de quién; whose is this jacket?** ¿de quién es esta chaqueta?, **whose shoes are these?** ¿de quién son estos zapatos?, **whose is it?** ¿de quién es?, **I know whose it is** sé de quién es ❷ (as relative: before a singular noun) **cuyo/cuya** (agree with the noun that follows); **the man whose car has been stolen** el hombre cuyo coche había sido robado ❸ (as relative; before a plural noun) **cuyos/cuyas** (agree with the noun that follows); **the people whose names are on the list** las personas cuyos nombres están en la lista, **a friend whose children I give lessons to** un amigo a cuyos hijos doy clase

why ADVERB **por qué; why did she phone?** ¿por qué llamó?, **nobody knows why he did it** nadie sabe por qué lo hizo

wicked ADJECTIVE ❶ (bad) **malvado/ malvada** ❷ (brilliant) **genial**

wide ADJECTIVE ❶ **ancho/ancha; the Thames is very wide here** el Támesis es muy ancho por aquí, **a piece of paper 20 cm wide** un trozo de papel de veinte centímetros de ancho, **how wide is it?** ¿cuánto mide de ancho? ❷ **a wide range** una amplia gama

wide ADVERB **the door was wide open** la puerta estaba abierta de par en par

wide awake ADJECTIVE **completamente despierto/ despierta**

widen VERB **ensanchar** [17]

widow NOUN **viuda** FEM

widower NOUN **viudo** MASC

width NOUN **ancho** MASC

wife NOUN **mujer** FEM

wig NOUN **peluca** FEM

wild ADJECTIVE ❶ (an animal) **salvaje**, (plant) **silvestre** ❷ (idea) **disparatado/disparatada** ❸ (party) **desenfrenado/ desenfrenada** ❹ (person) **loco/ loca** ❺ **to be wild about something** estar [2] loco por algo

wildlife NOUN **a programme on wildlife in Africa** un programa sobre la flora y la fauna de África

wildlife park NOUN **reserva** (FEM) **natural**

will VERB ❶ (if you are unsure of the future tense of a Spanish verb, you *can check it in the dictionary's verb tables)* **I will/I'll see you soon** te veré pronto, **he'll be pleased to see you** estará contento de verte, **it won't rain** no lloverá, **there won't be a problem** no habrá problemas ❷ *(a hacer (can be used for the immediate future))*; **I'll phone them at once** voy a llamarlos ahora mismo ❸ *(in questions and requests)* **'will you write to me?' – 'of course I will!'** ¿me escribirás? – 'claro que sí', **will you have a drink?** ¿quieres beber algo?, **will you help me?** ¿me ayudas? ❹ **he won't open the door** no quiere abrir la puerta, **the car won't start** el coche no arranca, **the drawer won't open** el cajón no abre

willing ADJECTIVE **to be willing to do** estar [2] dispuesto/dispuesta a hacer, **I'm willing to pay half** estoy dispuesto a pagar la mitad

willingly ADVERB **con gusto**

willow NOUN **sauce** MASC; **a weeping willow** un sauce llorón

win NOUN **victoria** FEM; **our win over Everton** nuestra victoria sobre Everton

win VERB **ganar** [17]; **we won!** ¡hemos ganado!, **Rovers won by two goals** Rovers ganó por dos goles

wind[1] NOUN **viento** MASC; **the North wind** el viento del norte

wind[2] VERB ❶ **enrollar** [17] *(a wire or a rope, for example)* ❷ **dar** [4] **cuerda a** *(a clock)*

wind farm NOUN **parque** *(MASC)* **aeólico**

wind instrument NOUN **instrumento** *(MASC)* **de viento**

window NOUN ❶ *(in a building)* **ventana** FEM; **to look out of the window** mirar [17] por la ventana ❷ *(in a car, bus, train)* **ventanilla** FEM

windscreen NOUN **parabrisas** MASC *(doesn't change in the plural)*

windscreen wipers PLURAL NOUN **limpiaparabrisas** MASC PLURAL *(doesn't change in the plural)*

windsurfing NOUN **windsurf** MASC; **to go windsurfing** hacer [7] windsurf

windy ADJECTIVE ❶ **con mucho viento** *(a place)* ❷ **de viento** *(a day)* ❸ **it's windy today** hoy hace viento

wine NOUN **vino** MASC; **a glass of white wine** una copa de vino blanco

wing NOUN ❶ **ala** FEM, *(even though 'ala' is feminine, it takes 'el' and 'un' in the singular)*; **the wing** el ala ❷ *(in sport)* **alero** MASC & FEM

wink VERB **to wink at somebody** guiñar [17] el ojo a alguien

winner NOUN **ganador** MASC, **ganadora** FEM

winning ADJECTIVE **ganador** *(team for example)*

winnings PLURAL NOUN **ganancias** FEM PLURAL

winter NOUN **invierno** MASC; **in winter** en invierno

wipe VERB **limpiar** [17]; **I'll just wipe the table** voy a limpiar la mesa, **to wipe your nose** limpiarse [17] la nariz
• **to wipe up** *(dishes)* secar [17]

wire NOUN **alambre** MASC; **an electric wire** un cable

wire netting NOUN red (FEM) de alambre

wise ADJECTIVE sabio/sabia

wish NOUN ❶ deseo MASC; **make a wish!** ¡piensa un deseo! ❷ **best wishes on your birthday** nuestros mejores deseos en tu cumpleaños, **'best wishes, Ann'** 'saludos de: Ann' (in letters)

wish VERB ❶ **I wish he were here** ojalá estuviese aquí (note that 'ojalá' is followed by the subjunctive) ❷ **I wished him happy birthday** le deseé un feliz cumpleaños

wit NOUN ingenio MASC

witch NOUN bruja FEM

with PREPOSITION ❶ con; **with James** con James, **with me** conmigo, **with them** con ellos, **with pleasure** con gusto, **beat the eggs with a fork** bate los huevos con un tenedor, **he took his umbrella with him** se llevó el paraguas ❷ (at the house of) **we're staying the night with Frank** nos quedamos a dormir en casa de Frank ❸ (in descriptions) **a man with blue eyes** un hombre de ojos azules, **the boy with the broken arm** el chico con el brazo roto ❹ de; **filled with water** lleno de agua, **covered with mud** cubierto de barro, **red with rage** rojo de ira

without PREPOSITION sin; **without you** sin ti, **without sugar** sin azúcar, **without a sweater** sin un jersey, **without looking** sin mirar

witness NOUN testigo MASC & FEM

witty ADJECTIVE ingenioso/ingeniosa

wizard NOUN brujo MASC

wolf NOUN lobo MASC

woman NOUN mujer FEM; **a woman friend** una amiga

wonder NOUN ❶ maravilla FEM ❷ **it's no wonder you're tired** no es extraño que estés cansado

wonder VERB preguntarse [17]; **I wonder why** me pregunto por qué, **I wonder where Jack is** me pregunto dónde está Jack

wonderful ADJECTIVE maravilloso/ maravillosa

wood NOUN madera FEM; **the lamp is made of wood** la lámpara está hecha de madera

wooden ADJECTIVE de madera

woodwork NOUN carpintería FEM

wool NOUN lana FEM

woollen ADJECTIVE de lana

word NOUN ❶ palabra FEM; **a long word** una palabra larga, **what's the French word for 'window'?** ¿cómo se dice 'ventana' en francés?, **in other words** en otras palabras, **to have a word with somebody** hablar [17] con alguien ❷ (promise) **to give somebody your word** prometer [18] algo a alguien, **he broke his word** rompió su promesa ❸ **the words of a song** la letra de una canción

word processing NOUN tratamiento (MASC) de textos

word processor NOUN procesador (MASC) de textos

work NOUN ❶ trabajo MASC; **Mum's at work** mamá está en el trabajo, **I've got some work to do** tengo trabajo que hacer, **he's out of work**

está sin trabajo, **Ben's off work** *(sick)* Ben no ha ido a trabajar porque está enfermo ❷ **to be hard work** ser [1] difícil, **it's hard work to understand it** es difícil entenderlo

work *VERB* ❶ trabajar [17]; **she works in an office** trabaja en una oficina, **Dad works at home** papá trabaja en la casa, **Ruth works in advertising** Ruth trabaja en publicidad, **he works nights** trabaja por las noches ❷ *(to operate)* hacer [7] funcionar; **can you work the video?** ¿sabes hacer funcionar el vídeo? ❸ *(function)* funcionar [17]; **the dishwasher's not working** el lavavajillas no funciona, **that worked really well!** ¡eso ha funcionado muy bien!

• **to work out** ❶ *(understand)* entender [36]; **I can't work out why** no entiendo por qué ❷ *(exercise)* hacer [7] ejercicio ❸ *(to go well) (a plan)* salir [63] bien ❹ *(calculate)* calcular [17]; **I'll work out how much it would cost** calcularé cuánto puede costar

worked up *ADJECTIVE* **to get worked up** ponerse [11] nervioso/nerviosa

worker *NOUN* ❶ *(in a factory)* trabajador *MASC*, trabajadora *FEM* ❷ *(in an office or bank)* empleado *MASC*, empleada *FEM*

work experience *NOUN* prácticas *(FEM PLURAL)* de trabajo; **to do work experience** hacer [7] prácticas, **to be on work experience** estar [2] haciendo prácticas

working-class *ADJECTIVE* clase *(FEM)* obrera; **a working-class background** un ambiente de clase obrera

work of art *NOUN* obra *(FEM)* de arte

workshop *NOUN* taller *MASC*

workstation *NOUN (computer)* terminal *(FEM)* de trabajo

world *NOUN* mundo *MASC*; **the best in the world** lo mejor del mundo, **the Western world** el mundo occidental

World Cup *NOUN* **the World Cup** el Mundial

world war *NOUN* guerra *(FEM)* mundial; **the Second World War** la segunda Guerra Mundial

worm *NOUN* gusano *MASC*

worn out *ADJECTIVE* ❶ *(a person)* agotado/agotada ❷ *(clothes or shoes)* muy gastado/muy gastada

worried *ADJECTIVE* preocupado/preocupada; **they're worried** están preocupados, **to be worried about** estar [2] preocupado/preocupada por, **we're worried about Susan** estamos preocupados por Susan

worry *NOUN* preocupación *FEM*

worry *VERB* preocuparse [17]; **don't worry!** ¡no te preocupes!, **there's nothing to worry about** no hay razón para preocuparse

worrying *ADJECTIVE* preocupante

worse *ADJECTIVE* peor; **it was even worse than the last time** fue aún peor que la última vez, **to get worse** empeorar [17], **the weather's getting worse** el tiempo está empeorando, **things are getting worse and worse** las cosas van cada vez peor

worst *ADJECTIVE* **the worst** el peor, **it was the worst day of my life** fue el peor día de mi vida, **if the worst comes to the worst** en el peor de los casos

worth   **wrong**

worth *ADJECTIVE* ❶ to be worth valer [43], how much is it worth? ¿cuánto vale? ❷ to be worth doing merecer [35] la pena hacer, it's worth trying merece la pena intentarlo, it's not worth it no merece la pena

would *VERB* ❶ *(if you are unsure of the conditional tense of a Spanish verb, you can check it in the dictionary's verb tables)* that would be a good idea eso sería una buena idea, if we asked her she would help us si la preguntásemos, nos ayudaría ❷ *(expressing wishes)* I'd like to go to the cinema me gustaría ir al cine, I would like an omelette quisiera una tortilla *(the subjunctive is used when ordering something)* ❸ would you like ...? ¿quieres ...?, would you like something to eat? ¿quieres comer algo? ❹ would you mind ...? ¿te importaría ...?, would you mind closing the window? ¿te importaría cerrar la ventana? ❺ he wouldn't answer no contestaba, the car wouldn't start el coche no arrancaba

wound *NOUN* herida *FEM*

wound *VERB* herir [14]

wrap *VERB* envolver [45]; I'm going to wrap (up) my presents voy a envolver mis regalos, could you wrap it for me please? ¿me lo envuelve, por favor?

wrapping paper *NOUN* papel *(MASC)* de envolver

wreck *NOUN* I feel a wreck! ¡estoy hecho/hecha polvo!

wreck *VERB* ❶ destrozar [22] *(an object, a car)* ❷ arruinar [17] *(plans, occasion)*; it completely wrecked my evening! ¡me arruinó la tarde!

wrestler *NOUN* luchador *MASC*, luchadora *FEM*

wrestling *NOUN* lucha *FEM*

wrinkle *NOUN* arruga *FEM*

wrinkled *ADJECTIVE* arrugado/ arrugada

wrist *NOUN* muñeca *FEM*

write *VERB* ❶ escribir [52] *(a letter or a story)*; I'll write her a letter le escribiré una carta, to write to somebody escribirle a alguien, I wrote to Jean yesterday ayer le escribí a Jean ❷ to write somebody a cheque extenderle [36] un cheque a alguien
• to write down anotar [17]; I wrote down her name anoté su nombre

writer *NOUN* escritor *MASC*, escritora *FEM*

writing *NOUN* escritura *FEM*

wrong *ADJECTIVE* ❶ *(not correct)* equivocado/equivocada; the wrong answer la respuesta equivocada, I've brought the wrong file he traído la carpeta equivocada, it's the wrong address no son las señas correctas ❷ to be wrong *(mistaken)* equivocarse [31], I was wrong me equivoqué, I was wrong when I said it was finished me equivoqué cuando dije que estaba terminado ❸ what's wrong? ¿qué pasa?, what's wrong with her? ¿qué le pasa?, something's wrong pasa algo ❹ *(false)* incorrecto/ incorrecta; the information was wrong la información era incorrecta

xerox *NOUN* fotocopia *FEM*

xerox *VERB* fotocopiar [17]

X-ray *NOUN* radiografía *FEM*; **I saw the X-rays** vi las radiografías

X-ray *VERB* hacer [7] una radiografía de; **they X-rayed her ankle** le hicieron una radiografía del tobillo

yacht *NOUN* ❶ *(sailing boat)* velero *MASC* ❷ *(large luxury boat)* yate *MASC*

yawn *VERB* bostezar [22]

year *NOUN* año *MASC*; **six years ago** hace seis años, **the whole year** todo el año, **they lived in Moscow for years** vivieron en Moscú durante años, **he's seventeen years old** tiene diecisiete años, **a two-year-old child** un niño de dos años

yearly *ADVERB* anualmente, cada año

yearly *ADJECTIVE* anual; **a yearly event** un acontecimiento anual

yell *VERB* gritar [17]

yellow *ADJECTIVE* amarillo/amarilla

yes *ADVERB* ❶ sí; **yes, I know** sí, ya lo sé, **'is Tom in his room?' – 'yes, he is'** '¿está Tom en su habitación?' – 'sí' ❷ *(answering a negative)* que sí; **'you don't want to go, do you?' – 'yes I do!'** 'no quieres ir, ¿verdad?' – 'que sí quiero', **'you haven't finished, have you?' – 'yes, I have'** 'no has terminado, ¿verdad?' – 'que sí'

yesterday *ADVERB* ayer; **I saw her yesterday** la vi ayer, **yesterday afternoon** ayer por la tarde, **yesterday morning** ayer por la mañana, **the day before yesterday** anteayer

a
b
c
d
e
f
g
h
i
j
k
l
m
n
o
p
q
r
s
t
u
v
w
x
y
z

yet | **your**

yet *ADVERB* ❶ *(with a negative)* **aún**; **not yet** aún no, **it's not ready yet** no está listo aún ❷ *(in a question)* **ya**; **have you finished yet?** ¿has terminado ya?

yoga *NOUN* **yoga** *FEM*

yoghurt *NOUN* **yogur** *MASC*; **a banana yoghurt** un yogur de plátano

yolk *NOUN* **yema** *FEM*

you *PRONOUN* ❶ *('you' like other subject pronouns is generally not translated; in Spanish the form of the verb tells you whether the subject of the verb is 'you, we, they', etc., so 'you' is only translated for emphasis)* **do you want to go to the cinema tonight?** *(talking to one person)* ¿quieres ir al cine esta noche?, *(talking to more than one person)* ¿quereis ir al cine esta noche? ❷ *(when emphasizing 'you')* *(talking to one person)* **tú**, *(talking to more than one person)* **vosotros/vosotras**; **you said it!** ¡tú lo dijiste!, **you all saw it!** ¡todos vosotros lo vísteis! ❸ *(although 'tú', 'vosotros', and 'vosotras' are now commonly used in most situations, there are the formal translations of 'you', which you use in a job interview and other formal situations)* *(talking to one person)* **usted**, *(talking to more than one person)* **ustedes**; **are you our new teacher?** ¿es usted nuestro nuevo profesor?, **excuse me, are you Mr and Mrs Lawrence?** perdonen, ¿son ustedes los señores Lawrence? ❹ *(when used as the direct or indirect object of the verb)* *(talking to one person)* **te**, *(talking to more than one person)* **os**; **I'll lend you my bike** te presto mi bici, **I'll write to you both** os escribiré a los dos ❺ *(in formal situations)* *(talking to one person)* **le**,

(talking to more than one person) **les**; **I shall send you the document** le mandaré el documento, **Dear Mr and Mrs Jones, I am sending you the information you requested** Estimados señor y señora Jones, les mando la información que solicitaron, *(when used with another pronoun, 'le' and 'les' become 'se')* **I shall send it to you on Monday** se lo mandaré el lunes ❻ *(in comparisons)* **tú**, *(more than one person)* **vosotros/vosotras**; **he's older than you** es mayor que tú, es mayor que vosotros/vosotras ❼ **for you** para ti *(more than one person)*, para vosotros/vosotras, **I'll go with you** iré contigo ❽ *(in formal situations: after a preposition or in comparisons)* **usted**, *(talking to more than one person)* **ustedes**; **for you** para usted, para ustedes

young *ADJECTIVE* **joven**; **he's younger than me** es más joven que yo, **Tessa's two years younger than me** Tessa tiene dos años menos que yo, **young people** la gente joven

your *ADJECTIVE* ❶ *(talking to one person)* *(with a singular noun)* **tu**, *(with a plural noun)* **tus**; **I like your skirt** me gusta tu falda, **you've forgotten your CDs!** ¡te has olvidado tus compactos! ❷ *(talking to more than one person)* *(with a singular noun)* **vuestro/vuestra**, *(with a plural noun)* **vuestros/ vuestras**; **your Spanish test is on Friday** vuestro examen de español es el viernes, **your rucksacks are in the dining room** vuestras mochilas están en el comedor ❸ *(although 'tu', vuestro', 'vuestra' are now commonly used in most situations, there are formal translations of 'your' which you use in a job* interview or other formal situation) *(with a singular noun)* su, *(with a plural noun)* sus; **thank you for your hospitality** gracias por su hospitalidad ❹ *(with parts of the body or clothing) (with a singular noun)* el/la, *(with a plural noun)* los/las; **do you want to take your coat off?** ¿quieres quitarte el abrigo?, **wash your hands** lávate las manos

yours PRONOUN ❶ *(talking to one person) (referring to a singular noun)* el tuyo/la tuya, *(referring to a plural noun)* los tuyos/las tuyas; **my brother's younger than yours** mi hermano es más joven que el tuyo, **these aren't my glasses – are they yours?** estas gafas no son mías – ¿son tuyas?, **yours are better** los tuyos/las tuyas son mejores, **a friend of yours** un amigo tuyo/una amiga tuya ❷ *(talking to more than one person) (referring to a singular noun)* el vuestro/la vuestra, *(referring to a plural noun)* los vuestros/las vuestras; **our house is smaller than yours** nuestra casa es más pequeña que la vuestra, **our car is smaller than yours** nuestro coche es más pequeño que el vuestro, **our children are older than yours** nuestros hijos son mayores que los vuestros, **a friend of yours** un amigo vuestro/una amiga vuestra ❸ *(as with 'you' and 'your' there are formal translations for formal situations) (referring to a singular noun)* el suyo/la suya, *(referring to a plural noun)* los suyos/las suyas *(note that here the translation is the same whether you are talking to one person or to more than one person)*; **excuse me, is this book yours?** ¿perdone, es suyo este libro?, **excuse me, are these books yours?** ¿perdone, son suyos estos libros?

yourself PRONOUN ❶ te; **you'll hurt yourself** te vas a hacer daño ❷ *(for emphasis)* tú mismo/tú misma; **did you do it yourself?** ¿lo hiciste tú mismo?/¿lo hiciste tú misma?, **by yourself** solo/sola ❸ *(like 'you' and 'your' there are formal translations for 'yourself' for formal situations)* se, *(for emphasis)* usted mismo/usted misma; **as you yourself will understand** como usted mismo comprenderá

yourselves PRONOUN ❶ os; **when you have washed yourselves** cuando os hayáis lavado *(when used with a verb in the infinitive or in commands, 'os' is joined to the verb)* **help yourselves** servidos, **by yourselves** solos/solas ❷ *(for emphasis)* vosotros mismos/vosotras mismas; **did you do it yourselves?** ¿lo hicisteis vosotros mismos?/¿lo hicisteis vosotras mismas? ❸ *(like 'you' and 'your' there are formal translations for 'yourself' for formal situations)* se *(when used with a verb in the infinitive or in commands, 'se' is joined to the verb)* **please, help yourselves** sírvanse, por favor, *(for emphasis)* ustedes mismos/ustedes mismas, **did you do it yourselves?** ¿lo hicieron ustedes mismos?/¿lo hicieron ustedes mismas?

youth NOUN ❶ *(stage of life)* juventud FEM ❷ *(young people)* juventud FEM; **today's youth** la juventud de hoy, los jóvenes de hoy ❸ *(young male)* joven MASC

youth hostel NOUN albergue *(MASC)* juvenil

Yugoslavia NOUN Yugoslavia FEM

a
b
c
d
e
f
g
h
i
j
k
l
m
n
o
p
q
r
s
t
u
v
w
x
y
z

English—Spanish

Zz

A
B
C
D
E
F
G
H
I
J
K
L
M
N
O
P
Q
R
S
T
U
V
W
X
Y
Z

zany *ADJECTIVE* **chiflado/chiflada**
(*informal*)

zebra *NOUN* **cebra** *FEM*

zebra crossing *NOUN* **paso** (*MASC*)
de cebra

zero *NOUN* **cero** *MASC*

zigzag *VERB* **zigzaguear** [17]

zip *NOUN* **cremallera** *FEM*

zodiac *NOUN* **zodiaco** *MASC*; **the signs
of the zodiac los signos del zodiaco**

zone *NOUN* **zona** *FEM*

zoo *NOUN* **zoo** *MASC*

zoom lens *NOUN* **lente** (*FEM*) **de
zoom**

LIFE AND CULTURE

At school

Voy al colegio a pie.	I walk to school.
Estoy en primero de ESO.	I'm in year 8.
Hay 25 alumnos en mi curso.	There are 25 pupils in my class.
Los lunes, a las nueve, tengo matemáticas.	On Mondays, at 9 o'clock, I have maths.
Hago inglés y español.	I do English and Spanish.
Se me da(n) bien/Voy bien en ...	I'm good at ...
Se me da(n) mal ...	I'm not very good at ...
Estoy estudiando para el examen de ...	I'm studying for the ... exam.
Tenemos muchos deberes.	We have a lot of homework.
Al mediodía, como en el comedor.	At midday, I have lunch in the canteen.

¡Pasa!/¡Entra!	Come in! *(to one pupil)*
¡Pasad!/¡Entrad!	Come in! *(to two or more pupils)*
Sacad vuestros cuadernos.	Take out your exercise books.
Abrid vuestro libros en la página 23.	Open your books at page 23.
En silencio por favor.	Quietly, please.
Escuchad bien.	Listen carefully.
Escuchad y repetid.	Listen and repeat.
Trabaja con un compañero/ una compañera.	Work with a partner.
Leed el primer párrafo.	Read the first paragraph.
Escribid una descripción de ...	Write a description of ...
Buscad las palabras en un diccionario.	Look up the words in a dictionary.

> Necesito ...
> I need ...

un libro de texto.	a textbook.	una regla.	a ruler.
		una goma.	a rubber.
un cuaderno.	an exercise book.	un sacapuntas.	a pencil sharpener.
un lápiz.	a pencil.	unas tijeras.	scissors.
un bolígrafo.	a ballpoint pen.	una calculadora.	a calculator.
un rotulador.	a felt-tip pen.		

Mi asignatura preferida es ...
My favourite subject is ...

el alemán.	German.	la geografía.	geography.
la biología.	biology.	la historia.	history.
las ciencias.	science.	la informática.	ICT.
el diseño.	art.	el inglés.	English.
el español.	Spanish.	las mática.	maths.
la educación		la música.	music.
física.	PE.	la química.	chemistry.
la física.	physics.	la tecnología.	technology.
el francés.	French.		

Más adelante, quisiera ...
Later on I'd like to ...

ir a la universidad.	go to university.	hacer un aprendizaje.	do an apprenticeship.
estudiar.	study.	encontrar un empleo.	find a job.
hacer un diploma.	do a diploma.	viajar al extranjero.	go abroad.

Did you know ...?

* that Spanish compulsory secondary school (ESO) is for young people between 12 and 16, while 16 to 18 year olds study for the Baccalaureate (Bachillerato).
* that pupils in state schools in Spain do not wear uniforms, but in many countries in Latin America pupils have to wear a uniform.
* that in Spain and most Latin American countries, parents have to pay for their children's school books and other learning materials.
* that the main school holidays in most Latin American countries are from Christmas to February?

At home

En mi familia somos cinco.	There are five of us in my family.
Tengo un hermano/una hermana.	I have a brother/a sister.
un hermanastro/una hermanastra	a half-brother/a half-sister
un mellizo/una melliza	a twin brother/a twin sister
Soy hijo único.	I'm an only child *(boy speaking)*.
Soy hija única.	I'm an only child *(girl speaking)*.

Vivo en ...
I live in ...

una casa.	a house.	en la planta baja.	on the ground floor.
un apartamento.	a flat.		
en la segunda/cuarta planta.	on the second/fourth floor.		

Hay ...
There is ...

una cocina.	a kitchen.	un aseo.	a toilet.
una sala de estar.	a living room.	un estudio.	a study/an office.
un comedor.	a dining room.	un garaje.	a garage.
un dormitorio.	a bedroom.	un jardín.	a garden.
un cuarto de baño.	a bathroom.		

Mi pasatiempo preferido es ...
My favourite pastime is ...

salir con amigos.	going out with friends.
ir al centro (de la ciudad).	going into town.
ir de compras.	going shopping.
ir a conciertos.	going to concerts.
la lectura.	reading.
escuchar música.	listening to music.
ver la tele.	watching TV.
jugar a la consola.	playing on a games console.
ir de fiestas/ir de discotecas.	going to parties/discos.
ir a montar en bici.	going cycling.

¿Qué programas hay en la tele?
What's on the telly?

Mi programa preferido/serie preferida es ...
My favourite programme/series is ...

un programa de deporte.	a sports programme.	un concurso.	a game show.
un culebrón.	a soap.	las noticias/ el noticiero.	the news.

Tengo ...
I've got ...

un televisor (pantalla grande).	a (wide screen) TV.
una consola de juegos.	a games console.
una cámara digital.	a digital camera.
un iPod®.	an iPod®.
un (teléfono) móvil.	a mobile phone.

On the computer

el ordenador	computer
el sitio web, la página web	website
el blog, la bitácora	blog
la webcam, la cámara web	webcam

Con el ordenador ...
On my computer I ...

navego en Internet.	surf the Web.	busco algo en Internet.	look something up on the Internet.
mando correos a mis amigos.	email friends.	tuiteo.	tweet.
descargo música.	download music.	entro en redes sociales.	go on social network sites.
veo DVD.	watch DVDs.		
hago los deberes.	do homework.	visito chats.	visit chatrooms.

Email

un correo electrónico, un email	an email
una dirección de correo electrónico	an email address
enviar un correo electrónico, un email	to send an email
recibir un correo electrónico, un email	to get an email
borrar un mensaje	to delete a message
correo basura	spam
responder	to reply
reenviar	to forward
hacer click (en)	to click (on)
copiar y pegar	to cut and paste
un archivo	a file

On the phone

¡Diga!	Hello!
¿Puedo hablar con?	Can I speak to ...?
¿Quién llama?	Who's calling?
No cuelgues.	Hold on.
¿Puedo dejar un mensaje?	Can I leave a message?
Volveré a llamar más tarde.	I'll call back later.
un mensaje de texto, un SMS	a text
mandar un mensaje de texto	to send a text
mandar un mensaje de texto a alguien	to text someone

Did you know ...?

- that in email addresses, @ is called **arroba** and dot is **punto**.

Food and eating out

¿Qué desea?
What would you like?

Me gustaría tomar ...
I'd like ...

un zumo de naranja. | an orange juice.

¿Tiene usted helado de vainilla? | Have you got vanilla ice cream?

Para comenzar/como entrada deme ...
For a starter I'll have ...

una sopa de cebolla. | onion soup.
la crema de champiñones. | mushroom soup.

Como plato fuerte/principal deme ...
For my main course I'll have ...

el pollo asado | roast chicken
una hamburguesa | a burger

con ...
with ...

patatas fritas. | chips.
una ensalada de tomate. | tomato salad.
una ensalada mixta. | mixed salad.

De postre me gustaría
For dessert I'd like ...

el mousse de chocolate. | chocolate mousse.
la tarta de pera. | pear tart.
helado de fresa. | strawberry ice cream.

Para beber ...
To drink I'll have ...

agua mineral. | mineral water.
una Coca-Cola. | a Coke.
un zumo de fruta. | a fruit juice.

Tengo hambre.	I'm hungry.
Tengo sed.	I'm thirsty.
Tengo alergia.	I have an allergy.

Did you know ...?
- that shops in Spain and some Latin American countries are often closed (cerrado) from about 2 p.m. to 4.30 p.m., but are open (abierto) late into the evening?
- that lunch in Spain (la comida) is usually taken after 2 p.m. and dinner (la cena) from about 10 p.m.?

Meals

el desayuno	breakfast
el almuerzo/la comida	lunch
la cena	dinner

Food and drink

agua If you order bottled water in a restaurant in Spain, you will be asked if you want **agua con gas** (sparkling), or **agua sin gas** (still). A **gaseosa** is like bottled lemonade, whereas **limonada**, more common in Latin America, is made with fresh lemons and is not fizzy.

antojitos In Mexico, **antojitos** (little snacks) are often served before a meal. This might be **guacamole** with **nachos** (tortilla chips), or it might be a variety of delicious small appetizers typical of the region.

bocadillo This is the word in Spain for a sandwich made from French bread. In Mexico it is usually called a **torta**, and in other countries in Latin America a **sándwich**. In Spain a **sándwich** is always made from sliced bread (**pan de molde**).

café Latin America produces some of the best quality coffee in the world, and it is drunk everywhere. In Colombia, a **tinto** is a small black coffee, and in Mexico **café de olla** is prepared on the stove, with spices and sugar. In Spain, **café con leche** is white coffee, usually half milk; **café cortado** is a black coffee with a dash of milk; and **café solo** is black coffee.

chorizo A cured salami-shaped sausage, often eaten in Spain in **bocadillos**, as **tapas**, etc. They are always made with paprika, and may also contain chilli.

churrasco	This is steak and Argentina is famous for its beef. It is usually chargrilled, and often served with **chimichurri**, a hot sauce made with chilli, garlic, and vinegar.
dulce de coco or cocada	A popular sweet all over the Spanish Caribbean, made by boiling grated coconut with brown sugar and water.
empanadas	These small pies are a popular snack in most Spanish Caribbean countries. They are usually filled with meat, but other fillings such as shrimp or chicken can also be used.
enchiladas	These are wheat **tortillas** filled with meat or cheese and often served in Mexico in a spicy tomato sauce. **Tacos** are thinner **tortillas** made of maize and served with a variety of fillings.
frijoles or frijoles	These are beans, which are an essential part of most meals in many Spanish Caribbean and Latin American countries. Often served with rice.
guacamole	A salad made of mashed avocados, seasoned with diced onions, chilli, and sometimes tomatoes. In Mexico it is often eaten as a snack with **nachos**, or tortilla chips.
helados	Ice cream, flavours include **chocolate** (chocolate), **fresa** (strawberry), **pistacho** (pistachio), **vainilla** (vanilla), and many others.
horchata (de chufa)	A thick, creamy, chilled drink made in Spain, particularly around Valencia, from tiger nuts. Often sold in summer in open-air cafes.
jugos or zumos (de fruta)	The word **jugo** is more common in Latin America, and **zumo** in Spain. In Latin America many juices (**jugos**) are made from tropical fruits like mango, **guayaba** (guava), **papaya**, and **piña** (pineapple).
maíz	Maize, or corn, is very important in most Latin American countries, as it forms the basis of the diet. In Mexico and Central America it is usually eaten in the form of **tortillas**, but in other countries it is prepared in different ways.
pan	**Pan** is used to mean both 'bread' and 'loaf'. The most common kind is **una barra**. The narrower variety is called a **baguette** and rolls are **panecillos**. A British-style loaf is **un pan de molde**. A **panadería** (baker's) also sells **croissants**, **bollos** (buns), and **rosquilla** (a kind of doughnut).

patatas or papas	These are potatoes. The word **patatas** is used in Spain, except in the Canary Islands, and **papas** everywhere in Latin America. Chips or French fries are **patatas/papas fritas**.
tamales	A popular Latin American dish found in many countries between Mexico and Peru, made from a corn-based dough stuffed with a spicy filling made of meat, together with carrots, onions, olives, or other ingredients. It is then cut into squares, wrapped in banana leaves, and boiled.
tapas	Small snacks served in bars and cafes in Spain; the selection can be very varied.
tortilla	In Spain a **tortilla** is an omelette: a plain omelette is a **tortilla francesa**, and a potato omelette is a **tortilla española**. In Mexico and Central America, a **tortilla** is made of maize or wheat and is wrapped around fillings of various kinds.

Healthy living

Para mantenerse en forma, hay que ...	To keep healthy, you have to ...
levantarse temprano	get up early
acostarse temprano	go to bed early
hacer deporte	take exercise
ir a pie/caminar	walk
Es saludable/sano.	It's healthy.
No es saludable/sano.	It's unhealthy.
Hay que evitar ...	You must avoid ...
beber	drinking
fumar	smoking
todo los días	every day
una vez a la/por semana	once a week
de vez en cuando	now and then
nunca	never
siempre	always

Soy/Es ...   I am/He/She is ...
deportisa.   sporty.
Estoy/Está ...   I am/He/She is ...
lesionado/lesionada.   injured.
bien.   well.

Me gusta ...   No me gusta ...
I like ...   I don't like ...
              Me gustan ...   No me gustan ...
              I like ... *(+plural)*   I don't like ... *(+plural)*

los refrescos.   fizzy drinks.   los dulces/   sweets.
el zumo de fruta.   fruit juice.   caramelos.
el café.   coffee.   la verdura.   vegetables.
la leche.   milk.   la carne.   meat.
la fruta.   fruit.   el pescado.   fish.

Shopping

hacer la compra ...
to go shopping (for food) ...

en la pastelería   at the cake shop   en el mercado   at the market
en la panadería   at the baker's   en el   at the supermarket
en la carnicería   at the butcher's   supermercado
en la charcutería   at the delicatessen

Querí ...
I'd like ...

un pan de molde.   a loaf of bread   un kilo de   a kilo of
quatro   four rolls.   manzanas.   apples.
panecillos.

¿Cuanto cuesta?
How much is it?

625

On holiday

| El verano pasado fui a España. | Last summer, I went to Spain. |
| El próximo verano voy a ir a Francia. | Next summer, I'm going to France. |

Fuimos ...
We travelled ...

en avión.	by plane.	en barco.	by ship.
en coche.	by car.	en autocar.	by coach.
en tren.	by train.	en bici.	by bike.

Did you know ...?
- that in Spain you can buy stamps in a tobacconist's shop (un estanco)?

Did you know ...?
- that football is the most popular sport throughout Latin America, except in some Caribbean countries like Cuba, the Dominican Republic, and Venezuela, where baseball is preferred?
- that basketball is very popular in Spain, second only to football?
- that FC Barcelona (nicknamed Barça) is one of Europe's biggest football clubs? Barça's home is the huge Camp Nou stadium.
- that Real Madrid is one of Europe's biggest football clubs and that they play at the huge Santiago Bernabéu stadium?
- that Spain's most important road cycle race is called the Vuelta Ciclista a España, and that cycling is very popular in Spain?

Places of interest in Spain

Alhambra   The famous fortified Moorish palace which dominates Granada.

Asturias   Northern Spain. A beautiful mountainous area where it is traditional to drink cider rather than wine, and where some people play the bagpipes.

Baleares or las Islas Baleares   Mediterranean islands of Mallorca, Menorca, Ibiza, and Formentera, popular holiday resorts.

Canarias or las Islas Canarias   A group of islands off the coast of West Africa including Tenerife, Gran Canaria, Lanzarote, and La Palma. They are popular holiday resorts.

Catalunya   The Catalan name for Catalonia, or **Cataluña** in Spanish. Barcelona is its capital and the majority of people speak Catalan as their first language.

Costa   The Spanish for 'coast'. Some of the famous tourist areas are **la Costa Brava** in the northeast, **la Costa Blanca** in the southeast, and **la Costa del Sol** on the southern coast.

Cuevas de Altamira   These caves in northern Spain are famous for their prehistoric paintings (18,000 BC), discovered in 1869.

Euzkadi or Euskadi   The Basque name for the Basque country, or **el País Vasco** in Spanish. A green, rainy area with the industrial city of Bilbao, famous for the Guggenheim Museum of modern art, and the city of San Sebastián, known for the most elaborate **tapas** in Spain.

Galicia   The north-western part of Spain, famous for its wet climate, beautiful coast, excellent seafood, and Celtic culture. The language is **gallego**.

Museo del Prado   This museum in Madrid is one of the finest art galleries in the world.

Palacio de la Zarzuela   The official residence of the royal family in Madrid.

Puerta del Sol   A square in the old part of Madrid. Road distances from the capital are calculated from here.

las Ramblas   A tree-lined avenue in Barcelona famous for the variety of street stalls, entertainers, cafes, and strollers.

Sagrada Familia   This church in Barcelona is the unfinished masterpiece of the Catalan Art Nouveau architect, Gaudí.

Did you know ...?

* that Spain's highest mountain is Teide (3710 m), on the island of Tenerife, and that the highest mainland mountain is Mulhacén (3482 m), in the Sierra Nevada south of Granada?
* that there are about 400 million speakers of Spanish, which makes it the third most spoken language in the world?
* that as well as Spanish, Galician, Catalan, and Basque are important languages in Spain?

Places of interest in Latin America

el Amazonas	**The Amazon.** This great river passes through Peru and Colombia before entering Brazil, forming by far the largest area of tropical rainforest left in the world. Many groups of Indian peoples still live a traditional lifestyle.
las cataratas del Iguazú	**Iguazú falls.** These are spectacular and world-famous series of waterfalls on the Iguazú river, on the border between Argentina, Brazil, and Paraguay, set in a unique tropical forest full of birds and butterflies.
las Islas Galápagos	**The Galapagos Islands.** These are small islands off the coast of Ecuador famous for their unique animals, including giant tortoises, iguanas, and many species of birds. Charles Darwin visited in the 19th century, and his study of the wildlife helped him to develop his theory of evolution.
Macchu Picchu	These ruins in the mountains of Peru, rediscovered in 1911, are one of the most beautiful and mysterious ancient sites in the world. The Inca people built the city near the top of a mountain in the early fifteenth century, and it contained palaces, baths, temples, and about 150 houses. There are many other Inca remains in Peru, and also in Ecuador and Bolivia.
los mayas	**Mayan culture.** In the south of Mexico (especially the Yucatán peninsula) and Guatemala, there are many relics of the Mayan civilization which existed before the Spanish conquest. These include palaces and great pyramids, often very well-preserved, like the ones at Chichén Itza and Tikal.
Salto del Ángel	**Angel Falls.** The highest waterfall in the world at 970m, the Salto del Angel is in the far south of Venezuela, close to the Amazon basin, and falls from a huge flat-topped mountain onto the plains far below.

Did you know ...?
- that the highest mountain in South America, Aconcagua, is the highest in the world outside the Himalayas?
- that Quechua, the language of the Incas, is still spoken by 13 million people, and is an official language in Peru?
- that Mexico City has a population of over 20 million people and is the second largest city in the world?
- that the Amazon river system contains over 20% of all the world's fresh water?
- that the three countries in the world with the greatest biodiversity are all in Latin America—Brazil, Colombia, and Mexico?
- that most of the population of Paraguay speak guaraní, an Indian language, as well as Spanish?

Festivals and celebrations

Año Nuevo	**31 December, New Year's Day.** A public holiday throughout Spain and Latin America.
Carnaval	Carnival is celebrated the week before Lent. People often dress up in elaborate costumes, and there are usually processions.
Día de los Inocentes	**28 December,** the equivalent of April Fool's Day. People play tricks on each other called **inocentadas**, while saying the words **mariposa inocente**.
Día de los Muertos	**1 November, Day of the Dead.** Known as **Día de Todos los Santos** outside Mexico, this is celebrated throughout Spain and Latin America, but is particularly important in Mexico, most famously in the city of Oaxaca.
Día del Trabajo	**1 May, Labour Day** is a public holiday in Spain and many countries in Latin America.
Inti Raymi or Fiesta del Sol	**24 June, the Festival of the Sun,** the most important feast of the Incas, is still celebrated in Peru.
fiestas locales	**Local holidays.** Many cities and towns in Spain and Latin America celebrate local holidays, for example, 15 May in Madrid, and 24 September in Barcelona. These are usually associated with the patron saint of the city or town.

Navidades	**25 December, Christmas Day** is a holiday in Spain and Latin America, but is not as important as it is in Britain or the USA. In Spain the word **Navidades** is used to refer to the period around Christmas when people are on holiday.
Nochebuena	**24 December, Christmas Eve,** and many people go to Midnight Mass, the **misa del gallo**. In most Spanish-speaking countries, this is also the night of a big family meal.
Nochevieja	**31 December, New Year's Eve** when people see the New Year in with parties, and in Spain twelve grapes are eaten (one for each bell toll) at midnight. In Ecuador in South America, it is traditional to make figures, making fun of people who have been in the news in the previous year. These are then burnt.
Reyes (Fiesta de los Reyes Magos)	**6 January, Feast of the Three Kings.** Traditionally Spaniards and Latin Americans exchange gifts on this day. Nowadays many people also give each other presents on Christmas Day.
Semana Santa	**Holy Week,** which precedes Easter, is a very important holiday in Spain and Latin America. Many cities and towns stage religious processions during **Semana Santa**, the most famous being in Seville in Spain.

Dates

el primero/uno de enero	the 1st of January	**duodécimo**	12th
segundo (2°)	2nd	**decimotercero**	13th
tercero (3°)	3rd	**decimocuarto**	14th
cuarto (4°)	4th	**decimoquinto**	15th
quinto	5th	**dicimosexto**	16th
sexto	6th	**decimoséptimo**	17th
séptimo	7th	**decimoctavo**	18th
octavo	8th	**dicimonoveno**	19th
noveno	9th	**vigésimo**	20th
décimo	10th	**vigésimo primero**	21st
undécimo	11th	**trigésimo**	30th

Mi cumpleaños es en febrero.	My birthday is in February.
Se fue en marzo.	She left in March.
Llegamos el 11 de noviembre.	We're arriving on 11th November.
Ricardo nació el 2 de agosto.	Richard was born on 2nd August.
en el año 2006 (dos mil seis)	in 2006

Days

lunes	Monday	viernes	Friday
martes	Tuesday	sábado	Saturday
miércoles	Wednesday	domingo	Sunday
jueves	Thursday		

Months

enero	January	julio	July
febrero	Febuary	agosto	August
marzo	March	septiembre	September
abril	April	octubre	October
mayo	May	noviembre	November
junio	June	diciembre	December

Seasons

la primavera	spring	el otoño	autumn
el verano	summer	el invierno	winter

Time

¿Qué hora es?
What time is it?

Es la una.	It's one o'clock.
Son las cuatro y media.	It's half past four.
Son las seis y cuarto.	It's quarter past six.
Son las seis menos cuarto.	It's quarter to six.
Son las nueve y diez.	It's ten past nine.
Son las nueve menos diez.	It's ten to nine.
Es mediodía.	It's midday.
Es media noche.	It's midnight.
Son las diecinueve horas.	It's 7 pm (19.00).
Son las trece horas y quince minutos.	It's 1.15 pm (13.15).

Numbers

cero	0		cuarenta	40
uno	1		cincuenta	50
dos	2		sesenta	60
tres	3		setenta	70
cuatro	4		ochenta	80
cinco	5		noventa	90
seis	6		cien	100
siete	7			
ocho	8		mil	1000
nueve	9		un millón	1 000 000

cero	0
uno	1
dos	2
tres	3
cuatro	4
cinco	5
seis	6
siete	7
ocho	8
nueve	9
diez	10
once	11
doce	12
trece	13
catorce	14
quince	15
dieciséis	16
diecisiete	17
dieciocho	18
diecinueve	19
veinte	20
veintiuno	21
veintidós	22
veintitrés	23
veinticuatro	24
veinticinco	25
veintiséis	26
veintisiete	27
veintiocho	28
veintinueve	29
treinta	30